The Governors of New Jersey

Rivergate Regionals

Rivergate Regionals is a collection of books published by Rutgers University Press focusing on New Jersey and the surrounding area. Since its founding in 1936, Rutgers University Press has been devoted to serving the people of New Jersey and this collection solidifies that tradition. The books in the Rivergate Regionals Collection explore history, politics, nature and the environment, recreation, sports, health and medicine, and the arts. By incorporating the collection within the larger Rutgers University Press editorial program, the Rivergate Regionals Collection enhances our commitment to publishing the best books about our great state and the surrounding region.

The Governors of New Jersey

Biographical Essays

Edited by

Michael J. Birkner, Donald Linky, and Peter Mickulas

Rutgers University Press

New Brunswick, New Jersey, and London

Library of Congress Cataloging-in-Publication Data
The governors of New Jersey : biographical essays / edited by Michael J.
Birkner, Donald Linky, and Peter Mickulas. — Second edition.
pages   cm. — (Rivergate regionals)
Revised edition of: The governors of New Jersey, 1664–1974 :
biographical essays / edited by Paul A. Stellhorn, Michael J. Birkner.
Trenton : New Jersey Historical Commission, 1982.
Includes bibliographical references and index.
ISBN 978-0-8135-6244-5 (hardcover : alk. paper) —
ISBN 978-0-8135-6245-2 (e-book)
1. Governors—New Jersey—Biography. 2. New Jersey—Politics and
government.   I. Birkner, Michael J., 1950– II. Linky, Donald. III. Mickulas,
Peter, 1968–
F133.G68 2014
974.9'00922—dc23   2013013409
[B]

A British Cataloging-in-Publication record for this book is available from the
British Library.

Visit our website: http://rutgerspress.rutgers.edu

Manufactured in the United States of America

Dedicated to the memory of Paul A. Stellhorn and Alan Rosenthal and to the citizens of New Jersey

Contents

The Constitution of 1844

The Constitution of 1947

Alphabetical List of Governors

Illustrations

Preface

In a version of "rich man, poor man, beggar man, thief," the governor's office in New Jersey has been inhabited since its inception in 1664 by a wide range of characters who for good or ill stamped their influence on the state's polity. In this New Jersey has probably differed more in degree than substance from its neighbors, indeed, from any other state. What makes New Jersey distinctive are the different constitutional arrangements that helped or hindered its governors' attempts to influence policymaking and to leave a positive legacy for the future. Writing for the tercentenary celebration of New Jersey's history, Duane Lockard reminded readers in his *The New Jersey Governor: A Study of Political Power* that even under weak constitutions a strong leader could exert influence; and even under a strong governor constitution (New Jersey has one of the strongest of all the states), a weakling can fail.

Eighteen years after Lockard produced what is still the best single-volume treatment of the governorship, Paul Stellhorn and Michael Birkner published a set of essays treating each governor who served between the colony's founding in 1664 and the close of William P. Cahill's one-term governorship in 1973. The essays in that volume collectively reinforced Lockard's central argument, while adding a great measure of amplifying detail. New Jersey has a strong governor system, but governors who have served since 1964 have demonstrated varying degrees of political vision and sagacity.

There are two major premises behind the decision to publish this revised and expanded edition of *The Governors of New Jersey*. First, and perhaps foremost, we wanted to introduce New Jerseyans to the governors and acting governors who have served the state since the 1974. They are a mixed lot. Each governor made decisions that have had consequences beyond his or her term of office, yet there has been relatively little analysis of the administrations of these governors. Second, a new edition offers the opportunity to bring the governorship of New Jersey to a new audience. While most of the original essays have been only modestly revised to bring the scholarly literature on a particular governor up to date, in at least one instance a fundamental rewriting of an essay was called for, due to a recent revisionist interpretation of one of the state's most controversial governors, Lord Cornbury. Discerning readers of this edition will notice that we continue to run the original illustration that was widely viewed as Cornbury in women's clothing, but this time with the cautionary note that the illustration is much disputed.

No essay or portrait is as much contested as Cornbury's, but the essays herein will provide ample material for ongoing research on and evaluation of the individuals herein depicted. History is an argument without end. To have a good argument you need good material to work with. We hope this volume provides just that for the next generation of governor watchers.

MICHAEL J. BIRKNER
DONALD LINKY
PETER MICKULAS

Acknowledgments

The editors of the new edition would like to thank, at the New Jersey Historical Commission, Sara Cureton, Marc Mappen, Skylar Harris, and Niquole Primiani; at the New Jersey State Archives, Joanne Nestor, Veronica Calder, and Joseph Klett; and at the New Jersey State Library, Deborah Mercer. We are grateful, too, to the authors of the new essays for contributing their expertise on the state's most recent governors. We thank also those authors from the original edition who offered suggestions for updating their essays and provided new biographical information. Thanks, too, go to the staff at Rutgers University Press, especially Marlie Wasserman, Marilyn Campbell, Allyson Fields, Andrew Katz, Anne Hegeman, and Bryce Schimanski. Special appreciation to Joy Stoffers for her intrepid research on images.

MICHAEL J. BIRKNER
DONALD LINKY
PETER MICKULAS

The Governors of New Jersey

Introduction

The role of the governor of New Jersey has shrunk, then grown as the men (and, to date, one woman) of successive eras have applied new ideas about what good government is and how to provide it. Under different systems men with different abilities and motives have been chosen for the office, and different kinds of leadership have been expected of them. In the long run, however, the variations are relatively unimportant. The history of the office divides into four periods. In colonial times the governor was the agent of autocratic, external power. Under the constitution of 1776 he was meant to be a figurehead with little official responsibility. His scope increased under the constitution of 1844, but the legislative branch remained stronger than the executive. Under the constitution of 1947 the governor gained new tools and opportunities for the exercise of vigorous leadership.

From the beginning, however, the governors have performed fairly consistently whether their legal boundaries were narrow or wide. Most of them lacked force and significance; many were controlled by interests outside the government. But in each period a few influenced their own times and the future as well. The careers of New Jersey's governors show that both good government and the executive's importance depend less on the structural relations among the branches of government than on the qualities of the men elected governor.

In 1664 the English took control of the Dutch colony of New Netherland, which comprised the middle Atlantic region of the eastern seaboard. James, Duke of York, gained title to the tract and divided it into colonies, defining New Jersey for the first time. He granted New Jersey to two aristocrats, John, Lord Berkeley, and Sir George Carteret—the original proprietors. Except for several hundred Dutchmen in the northeast and a small enclave of Swedes in the south, no Europeans had moved into the region. To promote immigration Berkeley and Carteret promised a good measure of economic opportunity, political participation, and religious freedom. For the next century settlers of diverse ethnic and religious groups came in growing numbers from other colonies, the British Isles, and even the continent.

There were two New Jerseys until 1702. West Jersey was established when Berkeley sold his interest to a group of Quaker proprietors. East Jersey remained under Carteret's authority until his death in 1681, when his interest

was sold to twenty-four proprietors. The Jerseys differed in social composition—for example, East Jersey had a large Scottish population and many
New England Puritans, whereas West Jersey had a predominance of Quakers
—but they were politically similar. In both, local and county jurisdictions
exerted significant influence. Both were relatively open and in some respects
democratic—especially West Jersey, where the remarkably liberal "Concessions and Agreements of the Proprietors, Freeholders and Inhabitants of the
Province of West Jersey in America" were made the basis of government in
1677. Both were weakened by factional disputation, political opportunism,
and shifting arrangements of power.

During this early period the governors were appointed by the proprietors.
Those who held the office, whether competent and conscientious or not,
had trouble governing effectively for several reasons. Most of the proprietors
remained in England, and the instructions they sent, aimed mainly at foster-
ing their own interests from afar, gave too little thought to the good of the
colony and its inhabitants. In addition, certain questions about land titles
were never clarified. For example, Edmund Andros, a governor appointed
by James, made two attempts to rule the Jerseys in spite of the proprietors.
Meantime the East Jersey proprietors persisted in claiming certain quitrent
rights that the inhabitants disputed.

More important, the governors had to deal with a large number of factions
that grouped and regrouped ceaselessly to aggrandize themselves, thwart
each other, and sometimes flout the proprietary authority. Furthermore,
provincial government was never very important during the period; local
and county power was so strong that many conflicts were beyond the governor's control. In the 1690s discord reached the point where no one, including the governor, was effectively in charge of either of the Jerseys; the major
accomplishment of government was to survive. Even so tactful a governor as
Andrew Hamilton, who served both colonies for much of the decade, could
not stabilize affairs. By 1701 most proprietors were willing to transfer their
governmental authority to the king provided they could ensure their own
economic and political standing. In 1702 Edward Hyde, Lord Cornbury, was
appointed by the crown to be New Jersey's first royal governor.

Although the colony grew and prospered under royal government, it
remained politically unstable for many years. The governorship was usually
given to court favorites or men the king was obliged to, who had little or no
experience as executives and cared more about making money than governing well. Until 1738 New Jersey had to share its royal governors with New
York, which, being larger, received more attention. Furthermore, the old economic, social, and religious divisions continued to afflict the colony. Groups
the governor failed to satisfy often worked with allied interests in New York
or appealed to English patrons to have the crown intervene. Moreover, the
governmental system itself hampered all but the most adroit. Officially the
crown-appointed governor was a figure of nearly final authority. He had the

power to convene and adjourn the legislature at his pleasure, to veto legislation, and to prorogue or dissolve recalcitrant assemblies. He controlled the appointment and dismissal of most unelected public officials. He also had the authority to call elections, though the political advantage of this was small. In spite of this official power, however, his real authority depended heavily on political skill.

Even though all the citizens from the meanest farmer to the richest proprietor were loyal to the English system of mixed government, it did not work as well in the colonies as it did at home. The executive in England had the means to make it work, but the royal governor did not. He lacked the leverage engendered by broad patronage. He was forced to adhere to crown instructions that often restricted the flexibility necessary where various institutions shared power. He could not easily compromise or play loose with instructions to mollify one or another interest group. And he could be dismissed at any time, either for disregarding royal instructions or for displeasing some faction that had influence at court.

The royal governor also faced increasing pressure from the assembly, which initiated all legislation and controlled the government's purse strings. The governor could argue, threaten, cajole, or even veto, but he could not spend public money or even establish his own pay without the consent of the people's representatives. To get that he often had to give special privileges. The assemblymen never formed permanent coalitions because their interests were too local, but frequent single-issue confrontations with the governor gradually increased their ability to resist royal policies. The rising power of democratically elected assemblies was an important condition for a revolution in the 1770s.

The lot of the royal governors, then, was unenviable. To serve the crown's interests and the colony's at the same time required special abilities that few governors had. Some, like Lord Cornbury, were virtually helpless in the face of deep-seated and persistent local antagonisms. Men like John Lovelace, John Montgomerie, and William Cosby, who gained the office without previous executive experience and saw it primarily as a personal financial resource, were outright failures. More able men, like Robert Hunter, Jonathan Belcher, and William Franklin, achieved modest success in overseeing a growing rural economy, stabilizing finances, and exercising crown authority throughout the colony so long as no local issues exploded or upsetting imperial directives arrived. But even their position was precarious.

Frustrating though the system was for the governors, it worked well enough through the first half of the eighteenth century. Local government took care of most colonial needs and affected individuals more directly than did provincial affairs. But in 1763 the imperial policies changed. In wake of the French and Indian War, Parliament and the agents of George III introduced a new policy of "equity and efficiency" in the colonies. In effect they were seeking to subordinate a population that believed itself virtuous and intelligent enough to handle its own affairs. As colonists resisted new measures like the Stamp Act, the British line grew harsher; not even an able administrator like William Franklin could carry out the governor's ideal dual function. To continue as the crown's representative he had to oppose the people he was charged to govern.

Colonial politics, however open and turbulent, always operated within the context of the needs and ambitions of a distinct elite. The people could express opinions, but policy was always decided by a group of acknowledged leaders. After the Revolution the elite did not disappear, but the populace at large had more influence because political initiative came from their direct representatives in the legislative branch of the government.

Revolutionary leaders throughout the country were convinced by their experience with monarchy that one of the chief threats to liberty was "executive influence." Legislatures, they believed, were the proper institutions of authority. In New Jersey the state constitution adopted in July 1776 stripped the governor of virtually all significant authority and made him thoroughly dependent on the legislature. He was elected annually by the two legislative houses in joint meeting. He had no specific executive responsibilities and few patronage powers. He had no vote, no formal influence in the making of legislation, and no powers of fiscal control.

He did have a few substantive functions: he attended council meetings with the right to cast tie-breaking votes; he commanded the state militia; he served as chancellor of the state and presiding judge of its highest appeals court. But he was not responsible for carrying out the legislature's programs and policies or enforcing its laws. These activities were performed by officials elected by the voters or appointed by the legislature. The office was so unimportant that the framers of the constitution neglected to establish any limits of age, residence, property, or even citizenship as qualifications for it. To perform his judicial duties the governor had to be a lawyer, but even this requirement was not officially stated. New Jerseyans had carried the idea of checks on the executive as far as it could go. Many of the problems of the governorship between 1776 and 1844 resulted from extreme fear of the executive and unrealistic optimism about legislatures.

But the governor was not always the weak reed he was meant to be. A few exercised significant influence from the office. Men like William Livingston, William Paterson, and Joseph Bloomfield were formidable leaders who commanded respect and deference from the legislature. Livingston was particularly influential because of his lineage, his talents, and his stature in the revolutionary movement. Organization and leadership were essential to success in the war, and Livingston offered both. Even so, his influence over the legislature diminished enough during the last years of his tenure to make him doubt at times whether he would be reelected. Other governors under the constitution of 1776 enhanced the office by working actively as party leaders. Aaron Ogden, a Federalist, Peter D. Vroom, a Jacksonian Democrat, and the younger William Pennington, a Whig, exercised influence by distributing patronage, espousing party platforms, and informally helping to shape legislative programs.

By and large the office was sought without enthusiasm and held without tenacity. Mahlon Dickerson and Samuel L. Southard quickly abandoned it for the United States Senate, and one prominent politician, Garret D. Wall, actually declined to serve after his party elected him governor in 1829. Wall wanted the more lucrative position of federal attorney for the District of New Jersey, to which President Andrew Jackson soon appointed him. The governorship from 1776 to 1844 was in its worst times an insignificant position held by second-rate men such as Richard Howell, a Federalist, and Elias P. Seeley, a Whig. At other times it was held by men of personal ability but little political skill. Isaac Williamson, a prominent Essex County attorney who served twelve notably uneventful terms (1817–29), took the most literal view of his job. He delivered no annual State of the State messages, kept out of legislative policymaking, and generally stood aloof from the factions of the nearly formless polity of the day. In the late 1820s, when new political alignments began to cohere, Williamson sided with the adherents of President John Quincy Adams. This new activism proved his undoing. When the Jacksonians gained control of the legislature in 1829, they replaced him with Peter D. Vroom.

Vroom's record may give the best example of the opportunities and limitations of the office. Next to Livingston, Vroom was probably the strongest governor during the period. He certainly was one of the most vigorous and admirable. During his terms (1829–32, 1833–36) Vroom brought the office new repute and influence by supporting such projects as a new state prison and the Delaware and Raritan Canal and leading in struggles over such issues as paper money. He was an effective and respected party leader and a skillful and prudent chancellor. He had no illusions that as governor he wielded much power. Indeed, he criticized the constitutional definition of the office on several grounds. It made the governor too dependent, denied him adequate executive authority, and ignored the evolving doctrine of the separation of powers. Convinced that the governor had no business participating in purely legislative activities, Vroom declined to preside over the legislative council. He also suggested that the judicial responsibilities of the office unfairly restricted it to lawyers, disqualifying the mass of the population. These convictions led him to call for an overhaul of the constitution of 1776. In the late 1830s politicians from both major parties who shared his attitude formed a revision movement that reached fruition in the bipartisan constitutional convention of 1844.

The constitution of 1844 strengthened but did not radically transform the executive role of New Jersey's governor. It abolished the legislature's authority to grant divorces, establish lotteries, or enact bills of attainder or ex post facto laws and strongly limited its ability to lend or borrow or to enact bank-charter laws. It removed the governor's judicial duties and augmented his administrative responsibilities and authority. It increased his term of office from one year to three (though it prohibited consecutive terms) and provided for his election by direct popular vote rather than by the legislature. It gave him a limited veto, which could be overridden by simple majorities in both houses. In addition, it empowered him to make many appointments that the legislature had formerly controlled.

These provisions were meant to redistribute the unbalanced powers of the system. In reality the new constitution restricted the legislature very little and undercut some of the new powers it gave the governor. The majority-override provision limited what little leverage he had. The prohibition of a second term made him a lame duck from the moment he was sworn in. Officers largely independent of him had most of the responsibility for spending public funds. And because the governorship and the legislature could now be controlled by opposite parties, his chances of contributing to the legislative process were often no better than under the old constitution, when the office belonged to the majority party but lacked all formal authority.

The governor's new patronage power was weak as well. All his appointments were subject to the senate's approval, and he lacked the authority to create new agencies as new needs arose. As the government grew during the century of rapid change after 1844, the legislature set up more and more boards and commissions outside his supervision, drastically shrinking his share of administrative responsibility. In the main it was still true that the importance of the office depended on the man who occupied it. Only in extraordinary circumstances did gubernatorial leadership prove decisive under the new system. In time, to be sure, the governorship acquired increasing influence because government action was growing more important in the lives of the citizens. The state spent $31,000 in 1804, $89,000 in 1838, and $114,000 in 1854. As the state's population increased and the economy diversified, the government took increasing responsibility for education, criminal justice, corporate aid and regulation, mental health, internal improvement, and other affairs.

Governors joined in controversies over these issues and often took the lead. Even a relatively bland executive like William A. Newell, who "considered the executive function of government secondary to the legislative," promoted a raft of legislative proposals. Newell and his successors, Joel Parker, Charles S. Olden, and Marcus L. Ward, strongly identified themselves with controversial positions on important national issues—notably, North-South relations, slavery in the territories, the conduct of the Civil War, and, after 1865, the reconstruction of the South.

Now that the executive was something more than a ceremonial figure he was an attractive target for influence seekers. And new interests were arising quickly. Not only was the expanding industrial economy putting new demands on the state, but the business community was acquiring substantial—some would say enormous—political power. Early in the century certain corporations that had grown out of the new technology, including the Joint Companies, a transportation monopoly, had begun to advance their ambitions through lobbying and outright cash gifts to key players in Trenton. During the second half of the century all forms of business sought to increase their influence. After the Civil War businessmen dominated high elective offices. Several interests, such as the public utilities, held much power in local and state governmental affairs. The strongest of all were the railroads.

From the inauguration of Theodore F. Randolph in 1868 to the retirement of Robert S. Green in 1890 every chief executive had strong, direct ties with the railroad industry at some point in his career. Randolph and George B. McClellan served railroad companies as officers, Green and George C. Ludlow as lawyers, before becoming governor. Joseph D. Bedle became counsel to a railroad after his term ended. Even Leon Abbett, who made his reputation by breaking the industry's influence in Trenton, began his political career as a spokesman for the Camden and Amboy. Between 1868 and 1895 the Democrats won eight consecutive gubernatorial contests. But the political power of the railroad industry did not depend on the fortunes of one party. More often than not the Republican opposition was as partial to railroad interests as the Democrats in power were. For example, Frederic A. Potts, the Republican whom Ludlow defeated for governor in 1880, was a major stockholder in the Jersey Central. Although control of the legislature shifted back and forth between the parties, nothing threatened the political hegemony of the railroads. Support for them had become virtually institutionalized in the Democratic Party by 1870. A group of Democratic legislators and officeholders known as the State House Ring protected the privileged position of the railroads and received substantial support from them in return. The Democratic governors of this era were caught in a dilemma. On one hand they wanted to hold taxes down and limit public expenditures to maintain what they believed was the best climate for business. On the other hand the government needed more revenues so that it could increase its activities in response to the needs created by industrialization. Taxing the railroads and public utilities as much as other property would have provided fiscal relief, but the governors of the period generally lacked the courage or inclination to try it.

Leon Abbett (1884–87, 1890–93) was the outstanding exception. Abbett, who had no binding ties to the state's business interests, is most noted for destroying the tax-exempt status of the railroads and enabling future administrations to tax them—and the public utilities—more fairly. In taking on important business interests, Abbett overcame the constitutional weaknesses of his office. A master politician, he understood the full potential of the office and used its existing powers more fully than any of his predecessors had. He also added to its power in another way. He perceived himself as a statewide leader whose election gave him the right to interpret the needs of the people and to work for the policies he believed were important. Opportunistic and a bit demagogic, he aroused much stronger feelings of love and hate than most governors do. He was more than the state's chief executive; he also assumed political leadership. Abbett added immeasurably to the importance of the office. But he was succeeded by men who saw the role less boldly. The state did not have such a forceful governor again until Woodrow Wilson.

Abbett's accomplishments in office were substantial, but they were not the only measure of his significance. His rise signaled the initial political stirrings of the state's urban working class. He was the first governor to come from that class. He was also the first New Jersey politician to use ethnic politics successfully and the first to earn the name of "machine boss." His gubernatorial career opened a period that lasted far into the twentieth century. After 1890 business leaders had to make room for two new political forces: reformism and machines.

The reform impulse in New Jersey is often dated 1900–1913, but to confine it so narrowly to the "Progressive Era" is to overlook its origins and precursors. After the Civil War the predominantly agrarian state became a beehive for industry. Urban areas grew quickly; immigrants poured in, especially from Catholic and non-English-speaking countries; the labor movement gathered strength. Economic depression, rapid advancements in technology, radically new business practices, widespread government corruption, and controversies sparked by such issues as taxation, gambling, and drinking stressed and undermined traditional customs and legal norms. Calls for reform came from many segments of society.

Governor Abbett responded to the desire of his urban constituents for significant reform of the labor laws, working especially to protect children and convicts and to improve working conditions for thousands of factory hands. Reform activities were not exclusive to his Democratic Party, however. Indeed, Democratic machines generally ignored calls for reform and neglected progressive politicians, driving young crusaders such as George L. Record to the Republicans. The upswing in the reform impulse coincided with the Democrats' fall from power during the term of George T. Werts (1893–96). Antagonized by the corruption, mismanagement, and partisanship of the Democratic administration and frustrated by the deep depression that began with the Panic of 1893, the voters elected a Republican legislature in 1894 and the first of five consecutive Republican governors in 1895. The first organized reform gathering took place in Newark in the same year. Progressivism grew into a significant political force in New Jersey during the fifteen years of Republican domination that followed.

The Republican governors, conservatives whose ties to the business world were even stronger than those of their Democratic predecessors, neither supported nor sanctioned the reform movement. But in a sense they assisted its growth. They freed the state GOP from the South Jersey machine of General William J. Sewell and made it a statewide organization. Giving new vitality to Republican groups throughout the state, particularly in the northeast, the party began to spawn reform politicians. To all appearances the Republican Party was more business-oriented than ever. Franklin Murphy, elected governor in 1901, was a manufacturer—the first nonlawyer in the office since General McClellan a quarter of a century before. But a reform element known as the "New Idea" movement challenged the party's conservative leadership, pressing for an extensive list of reforms that ranged from local taxation of utilities to primary elections for United States senators. The New Idea faction was most active and had most of its modest success during the terms of the conservative Murphy and his successor, Edward C. Stokes, a bank president.

Meanwhile a new machine in Essex County, run by former United States senator James Smith Jr., unified the Democratic Party and backed the president of Princeton University, Woodrow Wilson, for governor in 1910. To Smith's dismay Wilson gave his campaign a strong progressive tone. The Democrats, winning the office for the first time in fifteen years, assumed the progressive mantle. Like Abbett, Wilson exploited the office to the fullest. He vigorously played the roles of chief executive, legislative leader, and politician. Quickly breaking with Smith, he undertook the most ambitious and successful reform program in the state's history. When Wilson resigned in 1913 to become president of the United States, he left the state's progressive movement in the far less capable hands of James F. Fielder, who had progressive credentials and inclinations but lacked Wilson's capacity to lead. The progressive movement faltered during his administration.

The influence of machine politics began to grow after World War I. Machines of both parties had operated in various localities since the 1880s, and the larger of these, such as Smith's Essex County Democratic organization, had made their strength felt widely. But until Mayor Frank Hague of Jersey City built his Hudson County machine none of them truly dominated a state party. Under Hague, Hudson County was known as the "Gibraltar of the Democracy." The machine provided the votes to keep Hague in control of the party for thirty years and the party in the governor's office for six of the eight terms between 1920 and 1943. No other political figure in the state's history wielded so much power for so long. Besides controlling the selection of Democratic gubernatorial candidates, Hague often influenced the Republican choices as well.

Hague established his power in the 1919 gubernatorial primary. He promoted Edward I. Edwards for the Democratic nomination in a clear challenge to James R. Nugent, Smith's successor as state party leader. By providing Edwards a huge plurality in Hudson County, Hague destroyed Nugent's political standing. He solidified his control of the state party when Edwards went on to become governor.

Edward I. Edwards was more than just the first of Hague's governors. A master of ethnic politics, he realigned the parties in the state. His opponent in the 1919 election was Newton A. K. Bugbee, a Prohibitionist. Edwards appealed to the urban ethnic voters, who saw Prohibitionism as an assault on their way of life, by promising to make New Jersey as "wet as the Atlantic Ocean." He also opposed the blue laws and took other stands that gathered the urban ethnics into a powerful new constituency. The Republicans —despite warnings from many of their own leaders—refused to relax their conservative stance on these issues. They nominated another Prohibitionist for the governorship in 1922 and lost again.

For the next two decades Hague dominated gubernatorial selection by providing enormous Hudson County pluralities and strongly supporting the interests of the ethnic communities. With his partisans serving as governor, Hague controlled a broad range of patronage. He made judicious use of it to increase the influence of his machine throughout the state. His focus on deal making rather than ideology enabled him to work comfortably with the two Republican governors elected during the 1920s and 1930s, Morgan F. Larson and Harold G. Hoffman. Hague did not control the governors or dictate state policies. He expected the governors to cooperate with him whenever his interests were involved. Their dependence on Hague and the hostility of Republican legislatures made them largely ineffectual. Even during the Great Depression the Hague governors rarely tried to buck him. It was easier for them to work with him, for mutual benefit.

The only countervailing force to Hague during the 1920s and 1930s was a remnant of Republican progressivism. It was less dramatic than Hagueism and slower to develop power but far more lasting in its legacy. A group led by a young progressive lawyer, Arthur T. Vanderbilt, kept the New Idea spirit alive in Essex County. This group dominated the government of the county through the 1920s, but regular Republicans in Newark kept them at bay until the spring of 1934. Then Vanderbilt formed the Essex County Clean Government Movement, a tight organization with a nonpartisan appearance. The movement identified itself with the liberalism of President Franklin D. Roosevelt by expressing partial support for the New Deal. Since the state's Democratic organization was only lukewarm for the policies of the enormously popular president, even a superficial connection was enough to advance the cause. Vanderbilt solidified his influence in Essex County and went on to cooperate with like-minded Republicans statewide.

Soon the Clean Government group was dominant in the Republican-controlled legislature. Vanderbilt was building one of the most powerful liberal Republican organizations in the country. In 1937 he challenged the Hague Democrats. The Republicans nominated the Clean Government candidate, Lester H. Clee, to run for governor against A. Harry Moore, a popular Hague man. Although Moore won, Clee ran a strong campaign against him. Further, allegations of voting fraud gave the Republicans ammunition for several damaging investigations of the Hague machine. In 1940 the Republicans ran another Clean Government candidate. He also lost, but the Democrat who beat him, former secretary of the navy Charles Edison, broke with Hague. Hague's era was ending, for more reasons than Vanderbilt's opposition and Edison's rebellion. Social and economic changes were weakening machines throughout the country.

After 1940 the Clean Government Movement and other groups from both parties worked persistently for constitutional revision. Although Hague frustrated their efforts during Edison's term and voters turned down a new constitution submitted in 1944 by a Republican governor, Walter E. Edge, the revision movement continued to grow. In 1946 the Clean Government Republicans won a clear-cut victory. Their candidate, Alfred E. Driscoll, easily defeated Hague's favorites in the Republican primary, triumphed in the general election, and then generated support for a bipartisan constitutional convention. In a brilliant display of leadership Driscoll guided the convention through several serious disputes, producing a new blueprint for state government. In November 1947 a large majority of the electorate approved the new constitution.

In addition to accomplishing the Vanderbilt group's main goal of restructuring the judiciary, the 1947 constitution also further strengthened the role of the governor. Importantly, it increased the length of the governor's term to four from three years and allowed two consecutive terms, which under the 1844 constitution's single three-year term made each incoming governor an immediate lame duck, barred from running in the next election.

The new charter also made clear that the governor was truly the chief executive in administering the state government. He now exercised direct appointment and management control over the state agencies and bureaucracy, thereby consolidating the previously fragmented, overlapping units into a hierarchical structure reporting to the single executive. With the governor now the central source of patronage in appointing all heads of executive departments, judges, and prosecutors, the executive gained further political leverage as legislators and local politicians were forced to secure gubernatorial approval of those they favored to fill the positions. As the state government grew over time to become the largest single employer in New Jersey, the governor's control of the bureaucracy emerged as an important base of the executive's enhanced political stature.

Leverage over the legislature was bolstered further by broadening the veto power. Two-thirds of the legislature was now needed to vote to override a veto, rather than the simple majority allowed by the 1844 constitution. Apart from the stronger absolute veto, the new constitution accorded the governor more flexible tools to influence and shape legislative action through the conditional veto. The governor could now return bills passed by the legislature with proposed amendments before signing the legislation. Through the line-item veto selective reductions or elimination of specific appropriations in the annual budget legislation or in individual bills making appropriations could be effected. By providing the executive with the ability to delete or revise individual items added by legislators, such as pet programs or projects inserted to please key supporters, the governor had new tools to shape legislation and implement executive priorities—collective powers granted only to a minority of governors in other states.

The net effect of the changes under the 1947 constitution, in the view of most analysts, made the formal powers of the New Jersey governor among the strongest of any state. Still, even with governors' extensive formal powers, on occasion they would seek to test the limits of their authority. Governor Brendan Byrne's executive order shutting down most development in the Pinelands until legislation was enacted, for example, sparked constitutional challenges which remained unresolved by the state supreme court when Byrne succeeded in pushing his bill to legislative approval and enactment.

The restructuring of the judiciary under the 1947 constitution also had significant impacts on the role of the governor through the creation of a strong supreme court with broad powers. The state constitution could be and often was expansively interpreted by its chief justices in administering the lower courts and the legal profession and in prodding policy action on such issues as school finance and restrictive zoning. For the most part the court aligned itself as an ally of executive authority and initiatives; indeed, its justices were often appointed from within the inside circle of the governor's chief legal or policy advisers. In the case of Chief Justice Richard J. Hughes, a former governor himself, the political connection could not have been more apparent, albeit in this instance a Republican governor appointed a Democrat as chief justice. Through these appointments governors at least could be assured that justices would have experience with—and likely sympathy for —the executive's authority and responsibilities.

Formal powers were only one aspect of the 1947 constitution's significance for the governor's office. In addition to the express powers embedded in the 1947 constitution, the governor's ability to set the state's policy agenda was also advanced in more informal ways. As government grew larger and more complex, the governor's control of the bureaucracy gave the executive access to staff, information, and money for the development and implementation of policy. New Jersey's commuter legislature, with each legislator through the 1960s usually limited to a single part-time staff person and with a tradition of rotating its leadership, generally lacked the capability to compete with the executive to develop its own initiatives. Gradually, as the legislature expanded its staff resources and its leadership strengthened through longer tenure and expanded political fundraising, the respective power of the executive and legislative branches were brought somewhat more in balance. But on most important issues the governor continued as the primary initiator of public policy.

Nonetheless, neither the new authority granted by the 1947 constitution nor the informal trends strengthening the post-1947 governor changed the reality that the individuals who assumed the office would bring widely varying goals, interests, and skills to their job. Some, such as Driscoll and his successor, Democrat Robert Meyner, employed the new fiscal and management tools they were given to consolidate the state bureaucracy; later governors would push an often reluctant legislature to take action on issues or areas previously thought beyond the scope of statewide concern and intervention. Some of the initiatives undertaken by these governors reflected their personal ideas or experience and indeed were not likely to have been addressed without their special interest in them. Just a few examples include the preservation of the Pinelands by Brendan Byrne (sparked by his attempt to show that his friend, the author John McPhee, was wrong in his prediction that the region would be lost to development); education reform by Thomas Kean (a former teacher who wished to allow those like himself who had not attended teaching programs to have an alternative route to be licensed); and mental-health advocacy by Richard Codey (whose wife had disclosed a long battle with depression). Inevitably differing from one another in temperament and priorities, the contemporary governors helped to define (as their predecessors had) what the state government should do, where the line should be drawn between the scope of authority of state and local government, and how public services at both state and local levels should be paid for.

Through the 1950s governors and legislatures were able, with some difficulty, to defer calls to expand the role of the state government and the taxes supporting its operations. Perhaps they were aware of the ill-fated advocacy in the 1930s by Harold Hoffman of an income and sales tax that ended his political career. As New Jersey's sister states restructured their fiscal structure to cope with statewide needs, it continued as one of the few states without a statewide sales or income tax. State revenues remained heavily dependent on a patchwork of excise levies and special business taxes; local spending continued to be primarily tied to revenue from taxing real estate, a tax structure that led to sharp divisions in wealth and public resources, which became particularly striking as New Jersey's growing suburbs gained political influence at the expense of its deteriorating older cities.

It was becoming increasingly apparent that the state's fiscal needs were outpacing its traditional sources of revenue, at times forcing governors to devise clever ways to find more revenues without resorting to new taxes. Thus, Driscoll built the New Jersey Turnpike with its construction and operation financed by tolls on its users, setting a precedent for subsequent projects, including the Garden State Parkway and the Atlantic City Expressway. Indeed, by shifting substantial portions of the costs of these major projects to out-of-staters the state followed a tradition set by governors and legislatures in the nineteenth century with canals and railroads to export as much as possible of the fiscal burden of state infrastructure to outsiders.

Creative financing devices, however, could not stem demands for a larger state-government role in investing in new public needs beyond the capacity of local governments increasingly stressed by their reliance on the property tax to finance their own services. Suburban development brought pressure for state construction of new highways, water and sewage facilities, and other infrastructure; Robert Meyner, despite his fiscal caution, was the first governor to channel gasoline-tax revenues to help subsidize the faltering commuter railroads. Without new revenue streams higher-education opportunities for the majority of high school graduates would be limited. By the 1950s the percentage of high school graduates leaving the state for college was among the highest of all states. There were only a handful of state-sponsored colleges, most of them former normal schools established to educate prospective teachers. It was not until 1956 that Rutgers University was officially established as the state university. As the baby-boom generation began graduating from high school in the 1960s, demand grew for development of a more comprehensive statewide network of state and community colleges.

The adequacy of the state's tax structure generated sharp debates during the administrations of Governors Hughes and Cahill. Both advocated more state investment in infrastructure, education, health and social services, and aid to local governments. In the summer of 1967, during Hughes's second term, the decline of New Jersey's older cities became strikingly visible through the destruction resulting from riots and civil disorders, most notably in Newark, Camden, and Plainfield. These episodes provoked calls for the state to undertake new initiatives to address urban decay. Neither the genial Hughes nor the combative Cahill, so different in their personal styles of governing, persuaded the legislature and the key leaders in their own parties to support an income tax. Hughes was forced to settle for a three-cent sales tax in 1966—the state's first uniform statewide tax. After the majority of Cahill's fellow Republicans in the legislature rejected his own income tax proposal, he reluctantly signed off on boosting the sales tax by two cents in 1970. The political wounds he suffered contributed to his defeat in the 1973 Republican primary when he sought nomination for a second term. Before he left office, however, Cahill named his predecessor, Richard Hughes, as the new chief justice of the state supreme court, after his initial appointee, Pierre Garvin, died early in his tenure. From the bench Hughes changed the game on the issue of income tax.

Just weeks before Cahill's primary election loss the April 1973 landmark decision of the New Jersey Supreme Court in the *Robinson v. Cahill* litigation again highlighted the conflicts over taxes as the court held that the state government had failed to meet its responsibility under the state constitution to provide a "thorough and efficient" education for public school students in poorer urban districts. The decision, the last major opinion written for the court by Chief Justice Joseph Weintraub prior to his retirement in the following fall, affected the public policy agenda for New Jersey governors into the next century.

Like predecessors Cahill and Hughes, Democrat Brendan Byrne, after his inauguration in January 1974, proposed enactment of an income tax, arguing that it was the most equitable approach to increasing state school aid to comply with the *Robinson* decision. Despite strong Democratic legislative majorities, he was defeated in his first attempts, with his early popularity soon vanishing as critics derided him as "one-term Byrne."

Legislative passage of the eventual tax-reform package—which importantly was to be revised to include politically attractive benefits for property-tax relief, lower taxes for out-of-state commuters, and caps on increases in government and school spending—only came in the summer of 1976 after the state supreme court, now led by Hughes as its chief justice, ordered the closing of all public schools. Byrne's victory in the tax fight should have resulted in his political demise; indeed, his survival in the 1977 primary election was due only to his perceived vulnerability, as his several opponents divided the anti-Byrne vote. In the general election campaign against state senator Raymond Bateman, a respected veteran legislator, Byrne's come-from-behind general election victory settled, at least for a brief time, the divisive battle over tax policy. To the surprise of many observers voters embraced the broad-based income tax to replace the congeries of revenue measures which had so long financed New Jersey's public spending. Byrne's mandate allowed the legislature, after so much time devoted to tax reform, to turn to other issues.

The clash over taxes and the financing of public schools was but one aspect of the continuing debate over the respective roles of the state and local government. Governors from Hughes forward enjoyed more success influencing land-use planning and development, which were traditionally viewed as the exclusive province of local communities. Hughes set a precedent by asserting state interest and authority when he established the Hackensack Meadowlands Commission for regional planning and development. This measure included the first property-tax revenue-sharing system among municipalities. Later governors secured legislation to exercise state oversight or regulatory authority in such regions as the coastal zone (Cahill), the Pinelands (Byrne), Atlantic City (Byrne), freshwater wetlands (Kean), and the Highlands (McGreevey). These initiatives, complemented by court decisions and legislation limiting the traditional local power over zoning on such issues as low-income housing and coastal access, by no means supplanted home rule, but they demonstrated that statewide and regional goals would be considered and at times would override the power of local governments in making decisions about land development.

Even with the income tax, which had its revenues constitutionally dedicated solely to support schools and property-tax relief, governors continued to struggle with financing the state government's other programs and services. Soon after Republican Thomas Kean's 1,797-vote victory over Congressman James Florio was confirmed by a recount completed weeks after the 1981 election, Kean failed to win a tax increase to patch a budget deficit. He subsequently reluctantly endorsed a Democratic package including higher income-tax rates on upper-income taxpayers. The added revenue, boosted by the national economic recovery of the mideighties, enabled Kean to deliver tax relief and fund popular new programs. Combined with his winning persona and good times, Kean won a landslide reelection victory in 1985 over Essex County Executive Peter Shapiro.

New taxes still could boomerang on a governor. In 1990, after James Florio was inaugurated to succeed Kean, the new governor's tax policies sparked a bitter public response. Facing a budget shortfall in the face of a national recession, Florio joined with the Democratic legislature to raise income-tax and sales-tax rates. He extended the sales tax to many previously exempt products, including toilet paper. Voter backlash in the 1991 legislative election gave the Republicans veto-proof majority control of both houses. Resentment of "Florio's taxes" contributed to his narrow loss for reelection in 1993 to Republican Christine Todd Whitman, who shortly before the election proposed sharp cuts in state income-tax rates. Whitman followed through on her tax-cutting pledge after she took office. Her tax cuts were popular but in the longer term problematic. Combined with a controversial decision to issue bonds to pay for state employee pension liabilities (based on wildly optimistic projections about state pension investment returns), the tax cuts proved a formula for structural deficits and increases in the state debt burden. Fiscal issues also undermined Jon Corzine, who was elected by a decided majority and enjoyed early popularity. Corzine's political standing was weakened by his controversial plan to lease the state's toll roads, a plan that failed to gain public or legislative support, and the shutdown of government operations after he failed to negotiate agreement with the legislature on his budget.

New Jersey governors have often been creative and sometimes foolish, but they have all been products of the political and social environment in which they operated. This environment evolved over time, in some instances toward greater democracy, in some respects in the other direction. The election of Thomas Kean in 1981, for example—the direct descendant of William Livingston, the state's first governor, elected in 1776—suggests that the state's longtime political, business, and social establishment, while perhaps not as dominant as in earlier centuries, nonetheless still survives into modern times. But there have been other signs of change. Christine Todd Whitman became the first woman to serve as governor.

County political leaders continued to exercise significant influence in the selection of potential governors, but over time their power diminished. As late as 1961 Democratic bosses were able to anoint a little-known former judge (Richard Hughes) as the Democratic nominee. By 1966, however, amendments to the state constitution were approved that had been compelled by federal court "one man, one vote" decisions. The courts forced reapportionment and redistricting to end the traditional allocation of one senator to represent each county, eroding a significant base of the county party machine by creating districts based on population whose lines might cover parts of different counties. Later developments, including passage of a measure providing public financing of gubernatorial campaigns during the Byrne administration, allowed some gubernatorial candidates to launch campaigns without the support of county bosses. Yet county political organizations and their leaders, while perhaps not as powerful as in the past, remained important political players. Camden's Democratic leader George Norcross, for example, influenced statewide politics during the Florio, McGreevey, Codey, and Corzine administrations. He continues to be a force during the governorship of Republican Christopher Christie.

Television provided governors and candidates a new forum to communicate. Governors Meyner and Hughes first exploited the new medium, at times hosting or appearing in programs on local stations. In 1977 Governor Byrne's come-from-behind reelection victory made effective use of televised commercials. In them he conceded he had made a mistake saying in his 1973 campaign that the state did not need an income tax but concluded by making the argument that New Jersey could not advance without one. As television-focused campaigns became increasingly expensive, wealthy candidates who could spend their own funds and avoid the limits and restrictions of the public-funding campaign subsidy emerged. These candidates could use their wealth to avoid the traditional political path to the governorship, such as in the rise of Jon Corzine to the United States Senate and the governorship aided by his contributions to charities, interest groups, and local political organizations. In the 2005 general election campaign Corzine spent some $40 million of his own money, while his Republican opponent, Douglas Forrester, also a millionaire, spent nearly $20 million, mostly from his own funds. Both candidates declined to accept public financing, and its accompanying spending restrictions, in seeking the office.

Another new path to the governorship may have been created through the new office of lieutenant governor. This position, long established in most states, finally made its appearance in New Jersey as a consequence of two gubernatorial resignations in short order. In 2001 Governor Whitman resigned her post to become administrator of the Environmental Protection Agency in the administration of President George W. Bush. Three years later Governor McGreevey resigned when he disclosed a homosexual affair with a staff member and faced an investigation for misuse of state funds. In accordance with the 1947 constitution, following the resignations, Senate president Richard Codey completed the remainder of McGreevey's term. Donald DiFrancesco served following Whitman's departure. Both individuals served the state concurrently in office as president of the Senate and as acting governor. A constitutional amendment in 2009 provided for a lieutenant governor to be selected by and run on a ticket with the gubernatorial candidate. The new position may give the lieutenant governor increased visibility for future consideration for the top position.

Another continuing theme of the post-1947 governors was their concern for bolstering the state's image, along with their recognition that their position as chief executive allowed them to become New Jersey's leading advocate and spokesperson. During a period when the state was subject to jokes about organized crime, political corruption, and environmental pollution, governors consciously tried to brighten the state's reputation. Efforts to reclaim the Meadowlands and build the Sports Complex under Hughes, Cahill, and Byrne were not only intended to revitalize a polluted marshland but also to develop a modern retail and commercial complex including sports and entertainment facilities that would display a new "major league" New Jersey to outsiders. Similarly, the authorization of casino gambling in Atlantic City under Brendan Byrne drew national attention to the top-flight entertainment, sports, and other events hosted in the state. The construction of the New Jersey Performing Arts Center in Newark, along with the "New Jersey and You: Perfect Together" tourism and economic-development promotional campaign, represented Thomas Kean's contribution to the several programs that governors launched to boost state pride and highlight its attractions.

This book profiles the governors who served prior to Christopher S. Christie, the state's current governor, who has not completed his first term as we go to print. Yet Governor Christie's aggressive use of the tools of his office —both the formal powers to seek legislative and management reforms and the more informal ability to mobilize public opinion through the bully pulpit —has generated national attention for him and the state. While his ultimate success or failure remains to be determined, he has demonstrated, like his most noted predecessors, that New Jersey governors can put their stamp on the state's public policy agenda.

In 1964 Princeton University political scientist Duane Lockard published a study of the individuals who have served as governor and the evolution of their responsibilities over time. While Lockard was writing a generation before the election of a female governor, his précis of those who held the office continues to resonate today: "Some were rogues and thieves; some were the mere agents of powerful outsiders (like business moguls and political bosses); some were amiable nonentities, adept at platitude and evasion, who served their terms and passed into deserved oblivion. But there were others. Some were men of firmness, ability and principle who would compare well with any group of chiefs of state drawn from a comparable society that developed in three centuries from a collection of a few hundred hardy settlers to a metropolitan state of six million people."*

MICHAEL J. BIRKNER
DONALD LINKY
PETER MICKULAS

* Duane Lockard, *The New Jersey Governor: A Study in Political Power* (Princeton, N.J.: D. Van Nostrand, 1964), 1–2.

The Colony

Philip Carteret (1639–83), a native of the Isle of Jersey and a distant cousin of the proprietor Sir George Carteret, was appointed New Jersey's first governor in August 1665, at the age of twenty-five. His father was attorney general of the island. Until then Richard Nicolls, under the proprietor James, Duke of York, had governed New Jersey as a part of New York. In June 1665 the duke presented New Jersey to two Stuart followers, Sir George Carteret and John, Lord Berkeley. Having no interest in colonization, in March 1674 Berkeley sold his portion to two Quakers, John Fenwick and Edward Byllynge.

Sir George, however, sent Philip out at the head of an expedition of thirty colonists from the Isle of Jersey who spoke English and French. In August 1665 they arrived at Elizabethtown, in the northeast corner of New Jersey, where several hundred Puritans from Long Island and New England had settled at the invitation of Governor Nicolls. From 1664 to 1669 they founded six towns, the largest of which were Elizabethtown and Newark. The Dutch town of Bergen, incorporated in 1661, antedated all of them. In addition to incorporating several of these settlements, Governor Carteret granted large patents to a half dozen wealthy men, several of them Quaker exiles from Barbados.

Hoping to attract additional settlers from New England, in February 1665 the proprietor, Sir George, issued the Concessions and Agreement, which set forth a frame of government and a land system. Its terms were liberal. All taking the oath of allegiance would be freemen, and the guarantee of religious liberty was so generous that no New England Puritan could take offense. The Concessions provided for an elected lower house with lawmaking powers and a council appointed by the governor. The assembly would constitute the courts, incorporate towns, impose taxes except on unimproved proprietary lands, and provide for the collection of quitrents due the proprietors. The stipulated quitrent was 1/2 d. per acre for individuals and a fixed sum, usually £15 per annum, on public township lands. Under the prevailing headright system, the Concessions also provided for grants of land to families and their indentured servants. Quitrents were not due until March 25, 1670. Since the settlers resented paying them, collecting them turned out to be a bane for Governor Carteret and his successors. By 1673 about 470 males had taken the oath of allegiance, indicating a population of twenty-five hundred.

The migration from New England and Long Island gradually diminished, while few settlers emigrated from Great Britain.

Carteret's troubles began at Elizabethtown in May 1668. The first assembly met but broke up when the governor refused to permit the council to sit with the representatives. By creating additional associates through skillful repurchase, Carteret took over the control of hostile Elizabethtown. The associates were first purchasers, who alone voted in town meetings. When Carteret insisted on the payment of quitrents there, the unrest spread to other towns. Middletown and Shrewsbury had actually refused to send deputies to the assembly, fearing that they would jeopardize their rights under their Nicolls patents. They insisted that participation in the assembly would constitute the recognition of absolute authority in the proprietor. Newark adopted the specious argument that it would not pay quitrents because it had purchased its lands from the Indians.

In the summer of 1671 the chance arrival of Captain James Carteret, son of the proprietor, afforded the settlers an opportunity to stage a rebellion. A "rump" assembly proceeded to elect this naive young man "president of the country" in May 1672. Governor Carteret, alarmed, left for England to consult Sir George. The "Rebellion of 1672" was crushed. Several "Declarations" supported by the crown repudiated the settlers' claims under the old Nicolls patents and required all settlers to take out proprietary patents and pay up their quitrents. The "Declarations" also stripped the assembly of its principal powers: land distribution, charter incorporation, and appointive powers. It gave the governor and council veto power and ordered the assembly to finance the cost of government. When Carteret returned from England in March 1674, he reigned supreme in East New Jersey. For years the lower house strove bitterly for the restoration of its powers, and despite a period of tranquility from 1674 to 1679 old wounds festered. Alienation from proprietary government was complete.

During Carteret's absence several external events changed the complexion of the province. In July 1673 the Dutch reconquered New York and New Jersey, and they remained until Britain regained the two colonies in November 1674. With the sale of Lord Berkeley's interest to Fenwick and Byllynge, in March 1674 Sir George agreed to a partition of the province into East and West New Jersey. The diagonal boundary gave Sir George all the inhabited lands. The two "divisions" remained separate until 1702, when New Jersey became a royal province.

From 1668 to 1681 the East Jersey assembly held seven meetings. Indian trade and relations became stable. The Concessions gave the inhabitants certain guarantees: no freeholder could be arrested for debt; no man could be deprived of the benefits of the common law, and no one could interfere with the course of justice. But the proprietor's prohibitions of 1672 remained. The governor's power to appoint justices, a violation of the Concessions, flawed the judicial system. The "prerogative courts," appointed by the governor and dominated by a clique of rich landholders, were hated by the people.

In July 1674 the Duke of York commissioned Edmund Andros governor of New York. Andros assumed that he had jurisdiction over the Jerseys; however, disturbed by the opposition there, he returned to England in 1678 for clarifying instructions. He returned with the duke's mandate to impose his authority on both divisions. When he insisted that all vessels bound for East Jersey put in at New York to pay the duke's customs, Governor Carteret rejected his claim. Andros then ordered all in East Jersey "to desist distinct governance" within the duke's jurisdictions "to their utmost peril." In March 1679 Carteret wrote to Andros that "it was by His Majesty's command that this government was established" and that he would not surrender East Jersey. Carteret was taken into custody in spring 1680 and tried by a special court of assize. He argued courageously that "his imprisoner and accuser" was also his judge, and in May the jury, to Andros's chagrin, brought in a verdict of not guilty. The court, however, under pressure from Andros, ruled that should Carteret return to East Jersey, he could not assume any jurisdiction. Andros journeyed to Elizabethtown and guaranteed the inhabitants their rights as "free-born Englishmen." The assembly demanded that he recognize the privileges granted them under their Concessions, but Andros, then and later, rejected their claims.

Unfortunately for Governor Carteret, Sir George, the influential and "testy" proprietor, died in January 1680. The governor expected little assistance from the Duke of York, whose advisers steadily admonished him about his error in giving away the Jerseys. Indeed, Carteret's appeals were ignored. In August, however, through William Penn's efforts in behalf of Quaker West Jersey, James accepted Sir William Jones's dictum that he had no right to withhold the right of government bestowed on Berkeley and Carteret in 1664. James, at that time an exile in Scotland, had no desire to add the Quakers to his list of enemies on the sensitive succession question. A new indenture, signed in October 1680, recognized young Sir George, a minor, as proprietor. Governor Andros was recalled, and in March 1681 Governor Carteret issued a proclamation that he was resuming his post. He ordered the inhabitants not to heed the authority of any officers appointed by Andros.

Philip Carteret's last days as governor were inconsequential. He had learned little since 1665. In October 1681 the assembly demanded that he recognize the rights of the people under the Concessions and especially repudiate the noxious "Declarations" of 1672. A prolonged wrangle ensued, growing more bitter day by day, with Carteret refusing to yield one iota. Finally, on November 2, Carteret dissolved the assembly, and government came to a standstill. Meanwhile Sir George's widow resolved to sell East Jersey at a figure of £5,000. Since no bidders appeared, she put it up for auction and sold it for £3,400 in February 1682 to a group of twelve men, principally Quakers, headed by William Penn. In August the group added twelve more partners, thus inaugurating the regime of the twenty-four proprietors. Carteret died scarcely a year after quitting his post. His widow was the thrice-married daughter of Richard Smith of Long Island.

New Jersey's first governor held office longer than any of his successors—for more than sixteen years. Though he lacked neither courage nor industry, he had not been able to cope with the all-but-insoluble problems that confronted him. He was caught between an arbitrary proprietor and an equally uncompromising populace. Most of his successors, proprietary and royal governors and their deputies, shared his dilemma.

JOHN E. POMFRET

Latschar, John A. "East New Jersey, 1665–1682: Perils of a Proprietary Government." Ph.D. dissertation, Rutgers University, 1978.

Leaming, Aaron, and Spicer, Jacob, eds. *The Grants, Concessions, and Original Constitutions of the Province of New Jersey*. Philadelphia: William Bradford, 1758.

Pomfret, John E. *The New Jersey Proprietors and Their Lands*. Princeton: D. Van Nostrand, 1964.

———. *The Province of East New Jersey, 1609–1702: The Rebellious Proprietary*. Princeton: Princeton University Press, 1962.

Schwarz, Philip J. *The Jarring Interests: New York's Boundary Makers, 1664–1776*. Albany: State University of New York Press, 1979.

Tanner, Edwin P. *The Province of New Jersey, 1664–1738*. New York: Columbia University Press, 1908.

Edmund Andros
Print Collection, Miriam and Ira D. Wallach Division of Art, Prints and Photographs, The New York Public Library, Astor, Lenox and Tilden Foundations; courtesy New York Public Library

Edmund Andros (December 6, 1637–February 1714) played a central role in implementing England's colonial policy during the last quarter of the seventeenth century. From 1674 to 1681 he managed the Duke of York's proprietary interests in New York. In 1686 James II commissioned him to consolidate and administer the northern colonies as the Dominion of New England. This attempt to tighten imperial control was defeated in 1689. Between 1692 and 1697 Andros reached the summit of his career as governor of Virginia, England's most valuable North American colony.

During his tenure at New York and for his final year as governor of the Dominion, Andros was vested with nominal control over New Jersey's affairs. He exercised his authority actively for ten months in 1680–81 and never extended his rule beyond East Jersey. His impact on the development of New Jersey was short but significant. The policies he was ordered to enforce there and in New England showed that the mother country viewed her colonies as exploitable dependencies rather than as potential equals with rights of their own. When Andros acted on his instructions, he inevitably aroused bitter colonial opposition and earned himself a reputation as an implacable foe of colonial liberties and self-government. To his American antagonists he was a tyrant bent on reducing them to the will of a distant and arbitrary power. But to his employers he was a trusted public servant charged with ensuring proper submission to duly constituted authority. Andros never questioned the right of his masters in England to govern the North American colonies; it was his misfortune to rule people who did.

Edmund Andros was born into a family that had for generations ranked among the wealthiest and most aristocratic inhabitants of the Isle of Guernsey. His ancestors had spelled the name "Andrewes," and, though the French-speaking islanders had corrupted the spelling, the name apparently retained its original pronunciation. Though Andros never said so, it is evident that his family's position on Guernsey influenced his character profoundly. His father, Amias, was a staunch Anglican who strongly supported Charles I's claims to supremacy over Parliament. Unfortunately for Amias and his family, the predominantly Puritan inhabitants of Guernsey favored the parliamentary cause. The sense of religious and political isolation that the young man shared with his father undoubtedly contributed to his reserved, austere demeanor and left him with a cold insensitivity to popular opinions. With no desire for employment in Puritan England, in 1656 Edmund turned to the Continent and a career as a professional soldier. He served for three years under Prince Henry of Nassau and apparently distinguished himself in a campaign against Sweden.

The restoration of Charles II in 1660 retrieved the fortunes of the Andros family and opened the door to preferment for Edmund. The king rewarded his loyalty with a place at court and two years later on June 4, 1662, commissioned him an ensign in the Regiment of Guards. England's bitter trade rivalry with Holland soon afforded Andros the opportunity to serve his king in a more responsible position. Early in 1667 he was appointed major of the Barbados Regiment, and he went with his men to garrison that tiny but fertile Caribbean outpost. After serving two tours of duty on Barbados, from February 1667 to February 1669 and again from September 1672 to May 1674, he came home with a reputation for expertise in the management of a colony far removed from the center of power and authority.

Andros's experience eventually came to the attention of James, Duke of York and brother of Charles II, a man in need or someone with ability in colonial affairs. In 1664 the king had given James a vast tract of land centered around the Dutch settlements on Manhattan Island. In his gift Charles had drawn the boundary of the patent generously, east to the Connecticut River and west to the Delaware River, including half of Connecticut and all of New Jersey. Once the Dutch were conquered, James was free to rule in a manner "not contrary to the laws of England" and to do so without the consent of any representative assembly. But the duke had insufficient resources to develop his entire patent, and he sold the land between the Hudson and the Delaware to Sir George Carteret and John, Lord Berkeley. Since James had no legal right to sell or share the powers of government conferred by his charter, the New Jersey proprietors purchased the right to the profits of the land with no authority to collect taxes, levy customs duties, or establish a separate government. James, however, raised an objection when Berkeley and Carteret proceeded to rule their proprietary as though they possessed a valid royal charter.

The Dutch recapture of Manhattan Island for a few months in 1673–74 voided the duke's original patent. When the king issued him a duplicate in 1674, James did not reconfirm the sale of New Jersey. He regarded his colony as a commercial venture and took this opportunity to introduce a new scheme for raising enough money to pay the costs of government and provide him a profit. New Jersey and Connecticut were the key elements in his plans to impose a customs duty in addition to the rate already levied by the Navigation Acts. He had to bring both under his control to prevent New York merchants from evading the tax simply by moving across the Hudson or into Connecticut.

On July 1, 1674, James commissioned Edmund Andros governor of New York and issued him a set of instructions certain to displease the settlers he had to rule. The Dutch Calvinists on Manhattan Island and in the Hudson Valley, already fearful that an English Anglican governor might alter their forms of worship, disliked paying increased taxes on their trade. The English Puritans on Long Island bitterly resented the ban on representative assemblies and sought to annex themselves to the neighboring, self-governing colony of Connecticut. Connecticut, for its part, had no intention of relinquishing its western half and stood ready to defend its charter rights. Oddly enough, the inhabitants of New Jersey had the least to fear from the new governor. Though New Jersey was vital to the duke's commercial schemes, for the moment friends in high places protected its government. Andros had to step carefully because Sir George Carteret was a favorite of Charles II. For five and a half years Andros soft-pedaled James's claims in the Jerseys and found himself powerless to realize the revenues his master expected.

Despite this failure, Andros showed commendable ability in reconciling the Dutch to English rule and in keeping the Indians of New York at peace while their brothers ravaged New England in King Philip's War (1675–76). Both situations encouraged the aristocratic governor to act with a paternalistic concern for his inferiors, a style of government he found congenial. At the same time he was shrewd enough to realize that a representative assembly with limited powers was a small price to pay for making the English settlers more amenable to the duke's government. Andros communicated this suggestion to James, but nothing came of it during Andros's tenure at New York. Andros was intelligent, though insensitive; nevertheless, at no point in his career did he have any say in formulating the policies he was charged with enforcing.

Andros's principal shortcoming as a colonial governor was his lack of tact and imagination in dealing with people who resented his rule. Ordered to annex half of Connecticut, he pressed the issue to the point of armed confrontation at the very time southern New England was fighting for its life against King Philip. When the death of Sir George Carteret in January 1680 freed Andros to move against East Jersey, he acted with a studied ruthlessness which did him little credit. In March he placed Governor Philip Carteret under arrest and then brought him to trial for infringing on the duke's rights. When the jury persisted in finding Carteret innocent, Andros browbeat the jurors, and though they declined to change the verdict, they encouraged Carteret to retire. Andros consistently ignored the need to work subtly and flexibly to attain his ends and preferred to stick as closely as possible to the letter of his instructions.

Having ousted Carteret, Andros for the first time exercised his authority over East Jersey. But he had little time to enjoy his triumph or to implement the duke's system. He was recalled in January 1681, ostensibly to answer charges of financial corruption laid against his administration but actually because he had become a liability to James. His heavy-handed tactics in East Jersey had antagonized the Carteret family, and the threat of similar treatment had alienated the Quaker proprietors of West Jersey. Since James could not afford to lose the support of either group, he removed the offending governor and finally, after seven years, released his claims to the Jerseys.

Though temporarily unemployed, Andros was not out of favor. Knighted in about 1681, he received a post at court in 1683 and became lieutenant colonel of the princess of Denmark's Regiment of Horse in 1685. During these years Charles II laid plans to combine the colonies from Maine to Connecticut into a single royal province. When the Duke of York came to the throne as James II in February 1685, he knew at first hand the wisdom of his brother's plans. The multiplicity of colonies had thwarted his commercial schemes in New York, and now, with the rise of French power in Canada, James believed that both the prosperity and the survival of England's colonies were at stake. He realized that Andros was his ablest and most conscientious colonial official and, on August 1, 1686, appointed him royal governor of the Dominion of New England.

Immediately on Andros's arrival at Boston on December 20, 1686, he offended the Massachusetts Puritans by demanding a place to conduct Anglican services. The following spring he once more demonstrated his lack of diplomatic skill by raucously celebrating the king's coronation on a Sabbath and by sanctioning the erection of a maypole in Charlestown, Massachusetts. His actions convinced the suspicious Puritans that James II, a covert Roman Catholic, was planning to suppress their forms of worship. The governor's needlessly antagonistic behavior hurt his mission, but he quickly proved himself an able administrator by introducing new taxes to put the government on its feet. Though the land tax distributed a lighter burden more equitably across the society, it provoked the most heated opposition, particularly in Essex County north of Boston. Andros moved rapidly to put down this unrest, acting with the severity of a professional soldier accustomed to seeing authority obeyed. He so rigorously enforced the Navigation Acts that in a short time New England's flourishing commerce was brought to a standstill. He reorganized both the judiciary and the system of land tenure to conform to English practice. He gave the justices of the peace added responsibilities which he had stripped from town control and made them administer justice in the king's name. He regularized ownership by regranting land to its occupants and by instituting quitrents. Ironically, his greatest service did little to win over the New Englanders. He shored up the defenses against French aggression by overseeing the construction of frontier forts, by overhauling the militia, and by dealing fairly with the Indians. But his concern for the Indians annoyed the colonists, who were bent on exterminating them.

Andros had undertaken an impossible task, for James demanded nothing short of a radical restructuring of New England society. Andros managed to impose the maximum degree of centralized government which that recalcitrant region would endure before 1775. Given time, he might even have made the idea of imperial regulation more acceptable. But his time ran out in April 1689. Immediately on receipt of the news that William of Orange had replaced James II, the people of Boston arrested and imprisoned the governor and other Dominion officials. Recalled in disgrace for the second time, Andros appeared to have reached the end of his career. But William III, a good judge of men, recognized Andros as the most experienced colonial servant available and a man who stood ready to serve the King of England rather than the House of Stuart. Andros made his final journey to North America in 1692. He came as governor of Virginia, an honorable and on the whole easy responsibility after the tumult of New York and New England.

In Virginia, Andros's conduct seemed to belie the reputation for tyranny he had earned in New England. He encountered little overt hostility from the House of Burgesses and dealt with it in a spirit of compromise. While pressing for measures he thought he must have, he was ready to relent when the house stubbornly opposed him. The fact that his instructions—to promote the Virginia tobacco economy—harmonized with the interests of the people he governed aided him. But Andros was unhappy in Virginia, and he resigned in 1697 amid a bitter dispute with the Anglican commissary, James Blair. Blair, scheming to increase his power and influence, had unjustly charged the governor with failing to support the Anglican Church and being indifferent to the fate of the College of William and Mary. The commissary was the kind of man Edmund Andros neither understood nor knew how to combat. An aristocrat trying to do the best job he could, Andros would not stoop to refute absurd charges, confident that the people who mattered would assess the situation correctly without his help. Defenseless against this unscrupulous liar, he left office a frustrated man.

Andros became lieutenant governor of Guernsey in 1704. He had inherited the office of bailiff from his father thirty years before, and he now joined in his person the entire civil and military authority of the island. Needless to say, the inhabitants thought that this put too much power in the hands of one man, and they made life difficult for him until 1706, when he resigned both offices. He retired to London, where he died in February 1714.

Andros married three times but had no children. He married Mary Craven in February 1671; she died at Boston on January 22, 1688. He married Elizabeth Cripse in August 1692; she died in August 1703. Andros's third wife was Elizabeth Fitz Herbert, whom he married April 21, 1707; she survived him.

HAROLD E. SELESKY

Andrews, Charles M. *The Colonial Period of American History*. Vol. 3. New Haven: Yale University Press, 1934.

———. *Narratives of the Insurrections, 1675–1690*. New York: Barnes and Noble, 1946.

Barnes, Viola F. *The Dominion of New England: A Study in British Colonial Policy*. New Haven: Yale University Press, 1923.

Bloom, Jeanne Gould. "Sir Edmund Andros." Ph.D. dissertation, Yale University, 1962.

Breen, Timothy. *The Character of the Good Ruler: A Study of Puritan Political Ideas, 1630–1730*. New Haven: Yale University Press, 1970.

Hall, Michael G. *Edward Randolph and the American Colonies, 1676–1703*. Chapel Hill: University of North Carolina Press, 1960.

Edward Byllynge (d. 1687), born of an old small-gentry family of Hengar, was a Cornishman. While serving as a cornet of cavalry with General Christopher Monk in Scotland, he was converted to Quakerism by George Fox. In 1661, after the Civil War had ended, he worked as a brewer in London. As a Foxian Friend he constantly courted trouble with the authorities. On one occasion he was "roughly used by soldiers." On another he refused to remove his hat in court until ordered to do so; he lifted his hat, and a pile of ashes he had concealed under it covered the floor. But more than a radical demonstrator, Byllynge was an idealist seeking relief for the persecuted Friends. He wrote several well-known tracts espousing the political and social liberties that Parliament should guarantee to free-born Englishmen.

By 1675 Byllynge had gone bankrupt and had been charged with making off with Friends' funds and bringing the Society into disrepute. Fearing to involve the Friends, Byllynge apologized publicly for his misdeeds. In later years his reputation became still more tarnished, but Fox and the other Quaker leaders, despite the doubts of William Penn, never lost confidence in him. John, Lord Berkeley, coproprietor with Sir George Carteret of all New Jersey since 1664, lacked interest in the province and suggested that Byllynge might reinstate his shattered fortune by purchasing Berkeley's portion of the property. Berkeley and Byllynge completed the sale in March 1674, and Major John Fenwick, also a Friend, as assignee for the legally bankrupt Byllynge, put up part of the purchase price. Then Fenwick and Byllynge quarreled about the portion to which each was entitled, and they had to call on William Penn, a leading Quaker, to arbitrate the dispute. This was Penn's initial venture in the New World, and during the negotiations he found the stubbornness of both men highly irritating. Finally he persuaded Byllynge to agree to a trusteeship of three Quakers—Penn and two of Byllynge's creditors—to straighten out his finances. The trusteeship continued from February 1675 to September 1683, when Byllynge became solvent, and it divided the province into one hundred shares or proprieties, giving Fenwick ten and Byllynge's creditors twenty-odd. The remaining shares were put up for sale among interested Friends, many of them prospective settlers. Fenwick was dissatisfied with his share and took off on his own to found Salem County in November 1675.

The trustees, with Byllynge's consent, proceeded to found a Quaker colony on the east bank of the Delaware. They effected a division of New Jersey with the proprietor George Carteret; issued the famous Concessions and Agreements of West New Jersey, which spelled out a frame of governance and land purchase for prospective settlers; and undertook negotiations to obtain a recognition of the right of government. The boundary of Byllynge's proprietorship, named West New Jersey, ran from Little Egg Harbor diagonally to 41° 40′ on the upper Delaware. The Concessions and Agreements, prepared in 1676 by Byllynge with the knowledge and assent of William Penn, bore the date March 3, 1677. Finally, through Penn's influence, an acknowledgment of the right of government was obtained from the Duke of York, the original proprietor, in August 1680. Since the duke turned out to have no authority to assign the right of government to a third party, the crown later repudiated it.

The chief proprietor, Byllynge, the trustees, and eventually over one hundred purchasers of shares or fractions of shares, including many prospective settlers, signed the Concessions and Agreements. Burlington, the first of several Quaker settlements, was founded in August 1677. The Concessions provided for an elected assembly of council and lower house, thus promising self-government. The document spelled out other privileges in keeping with the convictions of the Society of Friends: trial by jury, religious liberty, and freedom from imprisonment for debt. The Concessions is famous for its guarantees of individual liberty; however, its system of land ownership and land distribution, with its fractioned shares and sporadic land dividends, proved cumbersome.

During the years 1677–83 four of the projected tenths or districts were settled, mainly by Quakers from England and Ireland. Fenwick, the self-styled lord proprietor of Salem Tenth, at first stood aloof. As chief proprietor and governor Byllynge appointed a recent settler, Samuel Jennings, deputy governor, in violation of the Concessions. Penn, believing Jennings a worthy man, advised the inhabitants to accept him. But in May 1683, when Byllynge intimated that he was coming to West Jersey to serve as governor, the assembly adopted strong resolves: the governor, council, and representatives would meet together as the general assembly; the governor would read and explain his proposed laws; and the assembly would either adopt or reject them. The assembly then elected Jennings—who had agreed to accept the Concessions —governor, thus repudiating Byllynge. On the last day Fenwick and Penn joined in the deliberations. The legislature was unanimously resolved that since the land and government together had been purchased from the trustees, the Concessions alone constituted the fundamentals of government. In a special session of March 1684 the assembly voted to send Jennings and Thomas Budd, a councilor, to England to deal directly with Byllynge.

The emissaries arrived in London in the early summer and first interviewed Byllynge. But when he threatened them with imprisonment for usurpation, they informed him that they would seek a remedy from Whitehall or Westminster (the crown or the courts). At this juncture the Society of Friends, disapproving actions in court, persuaded Jennings to submit the dispute to the arbitration of leading Quakers. The arbitration, with George Fox present, lasted from July 31 to October 11. Though six of the fourteen arbiters refused to sign the award, the complainants lost. The decision went in Byllynge's favor because the Concessions could not grant the right of government, which had not been obtained from the duke until 1680. Byllynge, therefore, could not be divested of it without his own consent. Moreover, the award stated that the government should be vested in one person or one corporation; patently, it could not be divided into one hundred parts or shares. The decision also pointed out that since the assembly had accepted Jennings as deputy governor, it could not legally elect him governor. The award concluded that Byllynge, insofar as possible, should fulfill his commitments to the resident shareholders and settlers and made a strong plea for peace "in the name of Jesus Christ."

By virtue of the award Byllynge was undisputed chief proprietor and governor. Though Jennings and Budd remained in London for ten months appealing to the crown for a remedy, their efforts were ignored. Jennings never recovered from the repudiation, and for the rest of his long life he remained an unyielding foe of arbitrary authority. In November 1685 Byllynge appointed John Skene, a supporter, his deputy. Skene's first act was to clear the court bench of Byllynge's opponents. The assembly met in November

1685 with representatives from the five settled tenths. "Reserving their just rights and privileges," though recognizing Skene, they appointed a committee to examine the new charter and laws proposed by Byllynge. One of these laws would enable the English shareholders to vote by proxy, thus assuring Byllynge of control of the assembly.

In May 1686 the assembly voted to reject Byllynge's charter and his proposed laws on the ground that an absentee governor was incapable of making laws for the province. They also objected that Byllynge's appointments of officials in the government and in the courts violated the Concessions. The session of 1686 was the last during Byllynge's regime. His health had been deteriorating since 1684; consequently he designated his son-in-law, Benjamin Bartlet, as his successor. He died of tuberculosis in January 1687, and in the fall Bartlet and the two Byllynge daughters sold the twenty-odd Byllynge shares, with the right of government, to Dr. Daniel Coxe, one of early America's great land speculators.

JOHN E. POMFRET

Holdsworth, L. V. "The Problem of Edward Byllynge: His Connection with Cornwall." In *The Children of Light*, edited by H. H. Brinton. New York: Macmillan, 1938.

Jennings, Samuel. *Truth Rescued from Forgery and Falsehood*. Philadelphia: Reynier Janson, 1699.

Leaming, Aaron, and Jacob Spicer, eds. *The Grants, Concessions, and Original Constitutions of the Province of New Jersey*. Philadelphia: William Bradford, 1758.

[Leeds, Daniel J]. *The Case Put and Decided*. New York: W. Bradford, 1699.

Nickalls, J. L. "The Problem of Edward Byllynge: His Writings and Their Evidence of His Influence on the First Constitution of West Jersey." In *The Children of Light*, edited by H. H. Brinton. New York: Macmillan, 1938.

Pomfret, John E. "Edward Byllynge's Proposed Gift of Land to Indigent Friends." *Pennsylvania Magazine of History and Biography* 61 (1937): 88–92.

———. "The Problem of the West Jersey Concessions of 1676/77." *William and Mary Quarterly* 5 (1948): 95–105.

———. *The Province of West New Jersey, 1609–1702: A History of the Origins of an American Colony*. Princeton: Princeton University Press, 1956.

———. "Thomas Budd's 'True and Perfect Account' of Byllynge's Proprieties in West New Jersey." *William and Mary Quarterly* 5 (1948): 325–31.

Robert Barclay (December 23, 1648–October 3, 1690), a man of uncommon versatility, was one of the principal leaders of seventeenth-century Quakerism. By the age of thirty he was considered the greatest Quaker apologist of his day, and by the time of his death, eleven years later, he had excelled in four disparate occupations—scholarship, the ministry, court politics, and colonial government. Barclay was born at Gordonstown, Murrayshire, Scotland, on December 23, 1648, the first son of David Barclay (1610–86) and Katharine Gordon. His father was a professional soldier who supported the royalist cause during the Civil War, his mother the daughter of Sir Robert Gordon, second cousin to England's King James I. In 1659 young Barclay was sent to Paris to study with his uncle, rector of the Scot's College, an institution for training missionary priests to reconvert Scotland to Roman Catholicism. He returned to Scotland on his mother's death in 1663 and pursued the study of Greek, Hebrew, and ecclesiastical history. Shortly after, a set of confusing political circumstances led to his father's imprisonment, during which he met the persuasive Quaker John Swinton. Profoundly moved by Swinton's sincerity and enthusiasm, the elder Barclay publicly acknowledged himself a Friend in 1666, and Robert followed suit a year later. Robert's marriage in 1670 to Christian Molleson, daughter of a pioneer Scottish Quaker family, cemented the Barclay commitment. The couple had nine children, seven of whom lived to become vigorous and influential Friends.

During the succeeding decade Barclay devoted his intellect and energy to the propagation of his new faith. Between 1670 and 1678 he published more than a dozen religious treatises, including *An Apology for the True Christian Divinity* (1676), a seventeenth-century religious classic. So great was the impact of these works that D. Elton Trueblood, Barclay's biographer, credits him with saving Quakerism from extinction. Between treatises Barclay spent considerable time traveling, speaking, and corresponding in the Friends' behalf, and these activities assumed even greater importance during the last dozen years of his life.

As his literary production waned, Barclay concentrated his energies on politics. Familial and social connections most profoundly affected his career. Like many Scottish Quakers, he suffered persecution and imprisonment. His relentless efforts to win over the king's brother and heir, James, Duke of York, to a policy of religious toleration—a task for which Barclay was particularly well suited—dominated his later life. James remembered the financial assistance the elder Barclay had given his father, the ill-fated Charles I, and moreover he appreciated the political power of Robert's cousin, the earl of Perth. Furthermore, as a Catholic, the future king tended to sympathize with religious nonconformity. James was so fond of Barclay that in 1680 George Fox, a leading spokesman for the Friends, pleaded with his young colleague to use his influence to obtain the right of self-government for the Quaker colony of West Jersey.

Barclay's association with the English heir set the stage for his final, and perhaps most ambitious, undertaking—the proprietary governorship of East New Jersey. After Sir George Carteret died in 1680, his heirs made several efforts to sell his East Jersey holdings. Early in 1682 the province was put up at auction and purchased by twelve men—all Quakers but one—headed by William Penn. Within a few months the group increased to twenty-four, including twenty Quakers, Barclay among them. In September 1682, when the proprietors elected him governor, Barclay recorded the event in his diary with characteristic modesty: "The proprietors of East Jersey would have me a partner with them and did choose me their governor." Under the terms of the agreement Barclay was given a full proprietary share plus five thousand acres, and he received the right of government for life from King Charles II, without the requirement of residence in the province. To be made an influential partner in the enterprise with no personal investment testifies to Barclay's reputation. The proceedings became official in 1683, when the Duke of York granted a patent to the proprietors, and Barclay was appointed governor on July 17.

The governorship of East Jersey presented Barclay the opportunity to realize a persistent vision—the establishment of a colony for persecuted Scottish Quakers. William Penn had recently begun the great Quaker experiment in Pennsylvania, and for a number of years the province of West Jersey had provided a climate of religious toleration. Now it was Barclay's turn to apply his principles to the reality of colonial administration. No doubt another colony devoted to religious liberty bounding James's province of New York satisfied his concern for the Catholic minority in England. Barclay, therefore, had good reason to expect powerful backing from his royal friend. His association with James and the influence of his powerful cousins the earls of Perth and Melfort had been instrumental in his selection as governor. The relationship between Barclay and the other proprietors was meant to be complementary. While James, Perth, and Melfort provided the solidity of political power, Barclay gave the venture the stamp of moral respectability.

The proprietors, having ensured the initial success of their venture with Barclay's election to the governorship, sent a letter to the inhabitants of East Jersey expressing the hope that they would be pleased with their new governor. In it they pledged to strive for prosperity, adding that success was contingent on the settlers' cooperation: "We are resolved to advance, knowing that your interest is now so bound up with ours, that we cannot suffer if you prosper, nor prosper when you are injured." The proprietors next drew up several articles of government, the Fundamental Constitutions. While the elaborate system of laws was never put into effect, it is interesting as a revelation of what they considered a model form of government. The system's principal drawbacks lay in its undue complexity and its concentration of power in the hands of the absentee proprietors. After a cautious delay the proprietors presented the articles to the resident legislators for approval, only to have them rejected by the assembly, the council, and the deputy governor. The historian John E. Pomfret attributes the rejection to the liberal concessions issued by Sir George Carteret and a workable system of town government, both of which had enjoyed two decades of precedence in East Jersey.

To attract Scottish settlement the proprietors sponsored two promotional tracts during the development years. The first, published by John Reid in 1683, maintained that the time was ripe for Scottish colonization in America. It minimized the advantages of remaining in the old country and expounded at length on the financial and political benefits of emigration. A more ambitious effort, George Scot's *Model of the Government of the Province of East New Jersey in America*, provided an interesting account of the province after twenty years of settlement. To counter the natural Scottish predisposition against colonization it rhapsodized about the climate, soil, fish, game, waterways, forests, and available land and enthusiastically described the successful settlements at Woodbridge, Piscataway, Newark, Elizabethtown, Shrewsbury, and Middletown (Middletown Township, Monmouth County) and the liberal system of government. The tract concluded with a discussion of the terms of settlement in the province and included more than thirty favorable letters from Scottish residents.

But the vision of a Scottish colony, Quaker or otherwise, was never realized. The first ship embarked in August 1683, and two more sailed the following summer. Others followed, but always fewer than Barclay and his associates had hoped. As for Quaker migration the extraordinary success of Pennsylvania meant that few Friends would choose to settle in East Jersey. As this became apparent, the governor gradually altered his vision to include all persecuted Scots. After some initial setbacks he secured permission to bring twenty-four prisoners to America. They sailed aboard the *Henry* and *Francis* in September 1685, with about seventy-five others described by a critical contemporary as a mixture of debtors, paupers, "whoores or prodigal wasters," and some of "phaniticall" principles. But the voyage ended in disaster when an epidemic of malignant fever killed more than two-thirds of the passengers en route. Barclay suffered a more personal loss when his younger brother, David, died aboard a ship that had embarked the previous month. By this time the Duke of York had acceded to the English throne, and as James II he drastically curtailed religious persecution in Scotland, removing a primary motive for emigration.

A steady decline in Scottish settlement marked Barclay's closing years as governor. The general antipathy of the Scots toward emigration, the economic failure of Perth Amboy, the increased religious toleration in Britain after the death of Charles II, and the virtual commercial monopoly of the port of New York all contributed to dissolve Barclay's dream. To aggravate matters the other proprietors were losing interest because of poor land sales. Though Barclay should have realized the experiment had failed, his continuing efforts betrayed no sense of defeat. These efforts, however, were of brief duration. On October 3, 1690, the governor died prematurely at his home estate of Ury, at the age of forty-one.

Though an absentee governor, Barclay appears to have been popular in the province. In 1687 the resident proprietors praised him for his services, which included his appointment of George Keith as surveyor of the colony's western boundary. His disinterested commitment to proprietary duties nearly cost him the friendship of his noted associate William Penn. As the pressure from New York for the annexation of the Jerseys intensified, Penn moved toward some kind of appeasement. He may have felt that a concession in East Jersey would save West Jersey (he held interests in both colonies), but Barclay saw this as a sign of weakness which would fail. Obviously he was unwilling to sacrifice the interests of his other partners for any one of them, even if that one was William Penn. Ultimately, Penn must have respected Barclay's courage, for his tribute was the most eloquent of those following the governor's untimely death.

The governorship of Robert Barclay is generally recognized as a positive influence on the development of New Jersey. In intellect he rivaled his most accomplished contemporaries, and his compassion offset the selfish interests of many of his associates. He left a legacy of altruism conspicuous in the colonial history of New Jersey.

CLARK L. BECK, JR.

Landsman, Ned C. *Scotland and Its First American Colony, 1683–1765.* Princeton: Princeton University Press, 1985.

Lurie, Maxine N. "The Barclay Record Book and Its East Jersey Minutes: An Early Look at Context and Content." *Journal of the Rutgers University Libraries* 63 (2007): 10–22.

Pomfret, John E. The Province of East New Jersey, 1609–1702: The Rebellious Proprietary. Princeton: Princeton University Press, 1962.

Trueblood, D. Elton. *Robert Barclay.* New York: Macmillan, 1968.

Daniel Coxe (ca. 1640–January 19, 1730) evinced little concern for the welfare of the inhabitants of his dominion when he governed West New Jersey in absentia from 1687 to 1692. He became involved in colonial land speculation for profit only, and West Jersey was just part of his empire, which at various times extended from Maine to the Gulf of Mexico. He enjoyed some degree of support from fellow proprietor William Penn, but he emulated little of the latter's pragmatism. He spent most of his governing tenure working against the express wishes of his constituents and was apparently unconcerned that his policies were unadaptable to the political climate of the province. Historians have regarded Coxe's governorship as a negative influence on the development of West New Jersey.

Coxe devoted his early years to the study of science and maintained a chemical laboratory. One of the first men to conduct scientific experiments on the effects of nicotine on animals, he read a paper on that subject before the Royal Society at Gresham College in 1665, the year he was admitted to the society. Five years later he received his doctorate of medicine at Cambridge University. In 1674 he published papers on the crystallization of salt in *Philosophical Transactions*, and in 1680 he was elected an honorary fellow at the College of Physicians. Meanwhile he rose rapidly in the medical profession, serving as court physician to King Charles II and Queen Catherine and later to Queen Anne.

While at court he became interested in the Americas and purchased several properties, including three proprietary shares in West Jersey. In February 1687 he purchased the right of government and five additional shares from the heirs of Edward Byllynge, late chief proprietor. The sale made him the largest proprietor in the province, and he continued to accumulate shares until in 1692 he possessed twenty-two out of one hundred. In a long letter written in September 1687 Coxe informed the resident proprietors of the change in governorship and the reasons for it. He stated that the London proprietors had been alarmed at the proposed sale of Byllynge's interests to an unidentified party whose ownership of the right of government would have caused "great uneasiness" among both absentee and resident shareholders. The absentee proprietors had decided "for the good of our country and our own security" that Coxe, as the largest shareholder among them, should gain control. Coxe accepted the responsibility but stipulated that he would gladly relinquish the right of government for one thousand guineas. His associates, including William Penn, assured him that he was well suited for the governorship and that his authority would be respected. Coxe was unaware that as an Anglican he might be resented in the Quaker-dominated colony, and Penn apparently failed to raise the issue with him.

Coxe immediately alienated the residents by denying that the Concessions of 1677—the colony's liberal articles of government—were binding on him. The West Jersey proprietors had proclaimed them before the Duke of York granted sole governing rights to Byllynge, and Coxe therefore considered them superseded. He did, however, promise to adhere to such fundamental concepts as religious liberty and the right of trial by jury. He swore to invest the assembly with "all powers and priviledges consistent with the ends of good government." He would retain all elected and appointed officials, including resident deputy governor John Skene, a Byllynge appointee recommended by William Penn and greatly respected by the colonists. He did not join the residents, however; he had originally planned to emigrate to the province once his home affairs were settled, but he changed his mind, presumably in response to the wishes of friends and relatives and to the confusion wrought by Edmund Andros's attempt to absorb a number of proprietary colonies into the "Dominion of New England." He was formally announced as absentee governor at the February 1688 meeting of the Burlington court.

As a land speculator Dr. Coxe was vitally concerned with the boundary dispute between East and West Jersey. East Jersey governor Robert Barclay (1682–90) had commissioned George Keith to survey the boundary, and the result favored the eastern province. In the September letter, Coxe instructed the proprietors that for their own protection he had rejected Keith's line. But one year later he surprisingly accepted the line as the legitimate division between the provinces. The resident West Jersey proprietors ratified this action. Though they were quick to note that they had been swindled out of some of their finest land, they issued a proclamation of thanks to Coxe for bringing to an end "those differences and debates" that had "so long disquieted" them. At the same time they urged the governor to secure the disputed area for himself either under his West Jersey or his East Jersey rights (he was an East Jersey proprietor as well). The dispute was to have repercussions for almost another century.

Meanwhile the colony's inhabitants acted to counter what they considered the possibility of encroachment on their land interests by the new governor. In the fall of 1688 the resident proprietors organized themselves as the Council of Proprietors of the Western Division of New Jersey. The council was to record proprietary rights to the soil, supervise the distribution of dividends, issue survey warrants, and administer unappropriated lands. The proprietors understandably wanted to protect themselves against the favoritism an absentee governor was bound to show himself and his associates, especially when he had Coxe's reputation as a speculator. Their fears were intensified when Coxe appointed John Tatham, an unpopular Anglican and suspected Jacobite, as his resident agent.

The attempts of the British imperial administration to include West Jersey in its proposed Dominion of New England spelled further trouble for Coxe. In 1685 the Lords of Trade had convinced the new king, James II, that proprietary governments should no longer exist without a clearer dependence on the crown. Within a year writs of quo warranto (judicial writs demanding proof of governing authority) had been issued against the Jerseys, Delaware, Maryland, Connecticut, and Rhode Island. It was evident that James II, so instrumental in creating some of the proprietary colonies, was now attempting to abolish them. The appointment of Sir Edmund Andros as governor of the Dominion—which included the Jerseys from the spring of 1688 to April 1689—angered virtually all inhabitants from Maine to Maryland and further eroded James's already minimal support in the colonies. When the news of James's overthrow reached Boston in April 1689, Andros and his aides were seized and the Dominion was dissolved.

At that time the Council of Proprietors of the Western Division of New Jersey, apprehensive over the future of the province, temporarily overlooked their differences with Coxe and offered to proclaim him governor if he would furnish irrefutable evidence of his right to govern. As evidence of their good faith they pointed to their judicious conduct during the turbulent Andros interlude, especially to the voluntary restraint exercised in increasing their landholdings. Although the resident proprietors stressed the urgency of the situation, Coxe, uncertain of the status of the province under the new rulers, William and Mary, delayed his answer for several months.

Although the resident proprietors refrained from acquiring additional lands for themselves during the Andros regime, Coxe systematically and covertly increased his own holdings in West Jersey. His ambitious plans for exploiting this empire included whaling, establishing sturgeon fisheries in Delaware Bay, and importing French artisans skilled at panning salt for use in the export of salted fish. Late in 1689, at Town Bank, just above Cape May, he built Coxe's Hall, which he intended as a neofeudal manor. Plans there called for winemaking, shipbuilding, and lumber manufacture. He invested in a pottery at Burlington. He suspected that his holdings to the north contained sizable deposits of lead and copper, and he had even more spectacular expectations for the fur trade. The culmination of his grandiose plans was to control a "circular trade," whereby he could exchange the raw products of the domain for the finished goods of Europe and the sugar, cotton, indigo, and ginger of the West Indies. Such predictions did not seem out of line to someone of Coxe's commercial vision, and some of his ventures took hold. But he tended to exaggerate the value of his possessions, as his "Account of New Jersey," an inventory of his real property in New Jersey drawn up about 1688, demonstrates. Moreover, competition from Pennsylvania for settlers was intense, and prospective emigrants were unlikely to choose what seemed to them a poorer and less dynamic province.

Coxe's tenure as governor came to a close in March 1692, when he sold the bulk of his holdings and the right of government to the West Jersey Society, a large land and trading company consisting of London businessmen whose sole interest lay in speculation. It is not known whether his decision was prompted by continued friction with the resident proprietors, the outbreak of war with France, or the unfriendly attitude of the British government toward proprietary colonies. Unfortunately, Coxe's withdrawal did not arrest the political deterioration in the province. On the contrary, it was hastened by the appointment of Jeremiah Basse, a notorious anti-Quaker, as agent for both Coxe and the society. Basse proceeded to purchase lands from the Indians and to relocate the Indians without consulting the Council of Proprietors. Daniel Coxe's exit did not put an end to the legacy of absentee interference.

Coxe lived another forty years after pulling out of West Jersey. His disappointments in the province did not dampen his spirit, and between 1692 and 1698 he purchased the tract of Carolana, which included most of present-day Georgia, Alabama, Mississippi, Louisiana, Tennessee, Arkansas, and Oklahoma. He remained a land speculator until his death on January 19, 1730, in his ninetieth year. To him West Jersey had been little more than an investment, and not one of his more lucrative ones. He had no higher motive for encouraging colonization; therefore he felt no compunction about withdrawing in the face of an adverse economic and political climate. This disregard for the welfare of the West Jersey inhabitants had been a constant source of conflict between him and his constituents. As a scientist Coxe was brilliant; as a businessman he was shrewd; but as a governor he lacked the compassion necessary to good administration. His governorship must be considered an unfortunate failure.

CLARK L. BECK, JR.

Pomfret, John E. *The New Jersey Proprietors and Their Lands*. Princeton: Van Nostrand, 1964.

———. *The Province of West New Jersey, 1609–1702: A History of the Origins of an American Colony*. Princeton: Princeton University Press, 1956.

Scull, G. D. "Biographical Notice of Doctor Daniel Coxe, of London." *Pennsylvania Magazine of History and Biography* 7 (1883): 317–37.

Andrew Hamilton (d. April 26, 1703) served as deputy governor of East Jersey from March 1687 to August 1688. He held the position of governor of both East and West Jersey from April 1692 to April 1698 and again from December 1699 to April 1703. He also briefly filled the office of deputy governor of Pennsylvania.

A talented and effective administrator, Hamilton ranks as one of the most attractive governors of proprietary New Jersey and the foremost figure in New Jersey politics of the 1690s. His career proved highly uneven, the successful administrations of his middle term contrasting sharply with those of the last years, during which New Jersey's proprietary era came to an inglorious end amidst disorder and chaos.

In the 1680s supervision of East Jersey colonization shifted from English Quakers to Scottish businessmen. Hamilton, an Edinburgh merchant, aided in the recruitment of settlers. He acquired a financial stake in East Jersey, procuring one-twentieth of a proprietary share and investing in ten servants, who came to the province in 1683. The future governor made his move to the colony in the summer of 1686 as a confidential proprietary agent. Immediately a man of influence, he held seats on the governor's council and on the resident Board of Proprietors. He began his long career as chief executive in New Jersey in March 1687 when he was named deputy governor.

Throughout that career Hamilton labored under serious problems. Royal authorities challenged the right of East and West Jersey proprietors to govern and sought to bring all private colonies under the control of the monarch. New York claimed jurisdiction over Raritan Bay and required ships trading at Perth Amboy to clear customs at the port of New York. During the war with France authorities in London regarded the defense of New York as vital and expected New Jersey, itself in no danger, to aid in that defense. New Jersey had internal troubles as well. At best inhabitants tolerated proprietary rule. Governors appointed by the proprietors appeared as the representatives of unpopular absentee landowners whose interests clashed with the people's well-being. Groups in East Jersey contested the proprietors' land title and resisted efforts to collect quitrents.

These problems existed when Hamilton first took office. In 1686 quo warranto proceedings had been instituted calling on the proprietors to show "by what authority" they pretended to govern. New York officials seized vessels at Perth Amboy for failure to pay customs at New York. In addition, the Stuarts' consolidated province, the Dominion of New England, had been organized; initially it consisted only of New England colonies, but both Jerseys were included from the spring of 1688 to April 1689.

This term was brief and only mildly productive. Several governmental activities concerned New York. A council of November 1687 issued proclamations to implement a recent decision of the Lords of Trade that ships bound for Perth Amboy might legally enter that port so long as they paid the same customs as were collected in New York. When war threatened, New York called on East Jersey for military assistance that would require a grant of tax revenues by the legislature. Hamilton convened the general assembly in May 1688, and it passed seven acts, including a tax to raise money for the defense of New York. The lower house showed no enthusiasm for the tax bill, but Hamilton secured its passage and even warded off an attempt to include as taxable the proprietors' unimproved lands. Meantime, in April 1688, the East Jersey proprietors had surrendered their government to the crown in apparent despair of maintaining their authority; and four months later Sir Edmund Andros, the governor of the Dominion of New England, arrived to annex New Jersey, and Hamilton's term as deputy governor ended.

The Glorious Revolution caused the Dominion of New England to collapse and its component provinces to resume their former status. That development paved the way for Hamilton's return, this time as governor of both East and West Jersey. Robert Barclay, the nonresident governor of East Jersey, died in 1690. Subsequently, Dr. Daniel Coxe, governor and largest proprietor of West Jersey, sold his holdings and the right of government to a London company known as the West Jersey Society. In the spring of 1692 the society and the East Jersey proprietors in England chose Hamilton to govern both of their provinces.

Although the Stuart monarchs and Governor Andros had been removed, old problems persisted for the New Jersey proprietors and their governor. In 1692 the Lords of Trade ordered a writ of *scire facias* impeaching the proprietors' right of government. Nothing immediately resulted from this action, but it demonstrated that crown authorities retained their design to transform private colonies into royal provinces. Any wrong moves by Hamilton would further that design. During this administration, from 1692 to 1698, Hamilton avoided providing grounds for serious new complaints by officials. He also muted antiproprietary sentiments within the two provinces and provided both with orderly governments.

Evidence of East Jersey's political harmony can be found in the regular functioning of the courts, the governor's council, and the general assembly. From 1692 to 1696 the assembly met annually and usually had worthwhile sittings. Four tax measures supplied monies for the support of government and for the defense of New York. Although the military taxes were smaller than Hamilton desired, they removed a possible criticism by authorities against the proprietors. At times the assembly proved obstreperous, as in 1695 when it successfully resisted Hamilton's recommendations, which included a plan for the collection of quitrents. (The quitrents issue also came before the courts, where juries, reflecting popular feelings, ruled against the proprietors.) East Jerseymen seemed to appreciate the worth of their governor, but they remained hostile to the proprietors who had appointed him.

West Jersey presented Hamilton with a unique problem. The governor had to secure approval of war taxes, despite the pacifism of the Quaker majority in the lower house. Conflict with Quaker scruples was avoided by omitting mention in tax acts of the specific purposes for which funds were raised. This left expenditures to the discretion of Hamilton and his non-Quaker councilmen, who appropriated money to aid New York in the war. Hamilton accepted the Quaker political hegemony and defended Friends against their critics. The cooperation between Hamilton and the Quakers resulted in annual legislative sessions which passed numerous useful bills. In November 1697, when Hamilton received notice that he would be dismissed as governor, the usually tightfisted assembly voted him £200 as a token of the people's "Gratitude and Affection."

The termination of Hamilton's administrations in both provinces proved unnecessary and unfortunate. The proprietors in London were anxious lest their deeds be grounds to end their political jurisdiction and decided that an act of Parliament of 1696 made Scots ineligible for positions in colonial governments, and in 1697 they named Jeremiah Basse governor; there followed a year of turmoil, confusion, and intense factionalism in both provinces. Responding to that sorry condition, the East Jersey proprietors late in 1698 petitioned the king on behalf of Hamilton's eligibility, and subsequently the crown's attorney general ruled that Scots were not disqualified. In March 1699 Hamilton was reappointed to office in both colonies.

During Hamilton's absence from New Jersey conditions had changed drastically and irreversibly. The turmoil of the Basse interim persisted and, indeed, intensified because of the news that the proprietors were once again negotiating to surrender their right of government. Hamilton's caretaker position was most precarious, since like Basse before him he had not obtained the required royal approval of his appointment. His final years as governor witnessed popular disturbances and factional feuds. Division appeared among the proprietors in England; a majority sought the designation of Hamilton as the first royal governor, and a minority actively opposed it. A deluge of angry petitions and counterpetitions from both sides of the Atlantic persuaded the Board of Trade (which had replaced the Lords of Trade under the Navigation Act of 1696) to recommend as the first royal governor someone unconnected with the bitter factionalism.

During Hamilton's last term in West Jersey, Quakers prevailed in both the council and the assembly. Despite their support, the governor could not maintain an effective administration. The assembly met three times and approved some beneficial legislation, but it became preoccupied with partisan maneuvers. The Hamilton-Quaker regime moved against its enemies on several fronts. The assembly reduced the number of its seats to ensure continued Quaker control. Opponents of a tax act of 1700 were imprisoned. These measures provoked resistance, and in a riot in March 1701 a large number of men descended on the Burlington jail and set free several persons confined by the administration.

In East Jersey a half dozen riots occurred. Most resulted from efforts to disrupt provincial courts on the grounds that the government lacked legitimacy. That charge was also asserted at the only general assembly to meet, and it caused the governor quickly to dissolve the legislature. Hamilton's authority met challenges even within his council, most dramatically when a councilor displayed a commission as governor he had received from anti-Hamilton proprietors in England. Beginning in the summer of 1701, with the courts disrupted, the assembly dissolved, and the council divided, no government prevailed in East Jersey. Only slightly better conditions existed in West Jersey. Not until August 1703 and the arrival of the first royal governor did provincial government again function.

In April 1703, when Hamilton died, he had not yet been officially relieved of his Jersey positions. He was also wearing a third hat, having begun his duties as deputy governor of Pennsylvania in November 1701. His attendance at numerous meetings of the Pennsylvania council during the next year accounts in part for his frequent absences from New Jersey; more significant, however, New Jersey had become hostile territory for its last proprietary governor.

Hamilton married three times. When he died, he was survived by his third wife and by John, the son of his first marriage. His second wife had been the daughter of a former deputy governor of East Jersey, Thomas Rudyard. John Hamilton followed in his father's path, and during the first half of the eighteenth century he held important offices in the provincial government of New Jersey and on the East Jersey Board of Proprietors.

In addition to Andrew Hamilton's political career, he merits attention as the architect of an early postal system in colonial America. In 1691 the English government granted Thomas Neale, a minor courtier, a private monopoly for carrying mail in the colonies. Neale never went to America but authorized Hamilton to establish and operate a postal system. The New Jersey governor persuaded the assemblies of five colonies to enact the necessary legislation, although neither of his own governments joined the system. Commencing operations in 1693, the service consisted of weekly mail deliveries carried over routes between major towns in New England and the Middle Colonies. The system worked as well as could be expected until 1699, when it declined. In 1707 the English government purchased the private monopoly, established a royal post office, and appointed John Hamilton as postmaster general.

FREDERICK R. BLACK

Leaming, Aaron, and Jacob Spicer, eds. *The Grants, Concessions, and Original Constitutions of the Province of New Jersey*. Philadelphia: William Bradford, 1758.

Pomfret, John E. *The Province of East New Jersey, 1609–1702: The Rebellious Proprietary*. Princeton: Princeton University Press, 1962.

———. *The Province of West New Jersey, 1609–1702: A History of the Origins of an American Colony*. Princeton: Princeton University Press, 1956.

Jeremiah Basse (d. 1725) served concurrently as proprietary governor of East New Jersey and West New Jersey from April 1698 (when he presented his commission to the council) to November 1699, filling a hiatus in the gubernatorial career of Andrew Hamilton. Conspicuous because of the rapid descent of both colonies into fierce factionalism and confusion, Basse's administration began the final disintegration of proprietary government in New Jersey that culminated in 1702 in the creation of a new royal province. The difficulties in East and West Jersey were inherent in the proprietary system of government as practiced in the Jerseys. Basse probably merits a more favorable place in New Jersey history than he generally receives: though his conduct as governor added fuel to the fire, he was more victim than perpetrator of the strife and disorder.

In 1696 the newly formed Board of Trade intensified an intermittent campaign to extend royal authority over charter and proprietary colonies. Several conditions made the Jersey proprietorships especially vulnerable to that campaign. The challenge by officials in England to proprietary authority encouraged critics in the provinces, such as the East Jersey townsmen who contested proprietary land titles. The tactful Andrew Hamilton had avoided overt antagonism between proprietors and townsmen, and in West Jersey, where dissatisfaction existed among non-Quakers resentful of the hegemony of the Friends, he had formed an effective partnership with the Quakers so that anti-Quakerism could only mark time. His removal as governor unleashed the dissident elements. The resulting turmoil would have severely tested even a resourceful and seasoned executive; Jeremiah Basse, having limited talents and virtually no experience in public affairs, was particularly ill equipped to deal with the situation.

Little is known of Basse's early life. In 1676 a half brother, Joshua Barkstead, migrated to West Jersey; Basse himself first appears in New Jersey records as a resident of Cohansey in 1686, when he was designated Barkstead's agent to sell land. After that he served as agent or attorney for numerous landowners, including Dr. Daniel Coxe, William Penn, and the West Jersey Society. The society, a company of Londoners claiming extensive proprietary landholdings and the right of government in West Jersey, was organized in 1692, when Basse was in England. Recruited by the company, he returned to New Jersey and during Governor Andrew Hamilton's first term performed various services as agent. A non-Quaker and the spokesman for a company that was both absentee landlord and largest proprietor, Basse aroused the hostility of West Jersey Friends. In spite of his unpopularity and his failure to produce any profits, the West Jersey Society decided to retain him as its agent when he returned to England in 1696.

While in England, Basse—always alert for the main chance—found bigger fish to fry. Both the society and the East Jersey proprietors in London believed, erroneously, that a recent act of Parliament disqualified Andrew Hamilton from service as governor because he was a Scotsman. Basse made the most of the opportunity; he sought to persuade the proprietors, the society, and the colonial authorities to substitute him for Hamilton, which they did in the spring of 1697. A leading West Jersey Quaker labeled the act a "miserable . . . exchange."

Winning the proprietors' appointment proved the easiest step in Basse's bid for office. The Navigation Act of 1696 required royal approval for proprietary governors, and the Board of Trade refused to recommend Basse for approval unless the proprietors posted a bond of £3,000 as security for his performance. The proprietors would not provide that guarantee. In numerous appeals to the board Basse presented himself as a champion of the king's prerogative and implied that unless his commission received royal approval, New Jersey would be beset by pirates, Scottish traders, smugglers, Quakers, and others prejudicial to good order. When his entreaties failed, Basse decided to act as royal governor without approbation. The society acquiesced, and the East Jersey proprietors went so far as to inform Hamilton and his council that Basse had been "presented to the king and is owned by him and approved of."

Basse began his term with several liabilities. As a replacement for the popular Hamilton he had to contend with the enmity of resident proprietors, East Jersey Scotsmen, West Jersey Quakers, and other groups favored by the former governor. They had legitimate grounds for opposing Basse because of his failure to secure royal approval, and his arrival in East Jersey in April 1698 occasioned some protest. However, he succeeded in getting his administration under way. He removed some councilors who might cause trouble, such as Lewis Morris; others voluntarily chose not to attend meetings. A general assembly met from February 21 to March 13, 1699, and passed seven acts. Although provincial courts sat, they functioned mainly to repress opposition.

Basse's most positive endeavor during his term was his defense of the proprietors' claim to a legal port at Perth Amboy. New York regarded East Jersey as a commercial appendage and required vessels trading at Perth Amboy to clear customs at the port of New York. Authorities in England differed about the legality of this practice, but in November 1697 the crown ordered ships bound to and from Perth Amboy to pay customs at New York. Following the instructions of the East Jersey proprietors, Basse proclaimed Perth Amboy a free port. New York's governor, Richard, Lord Bellomont, challenged the proclamation, and Basse engineered a test case involving the *Hester*, a ship he and his brother-in-law owned. While unloading a cargo at Perth Amboy in November 1698, the *Hester* was seized. The episode had its comic aspects, with an allegedly terrified Jeremiah Basse presenting a bottle of brandy to the New York force commander making the seizure. In spite of such idiosyncratic behavior, Basse persevered, and in 1700, though no longer governor, he won a suit against Bellomont in Westminster. Basse's conduct during the *Hester* seizure earned him ridicule in East Jersey, and his efforts to finance prosecution of the suit in England by having the assembly vote a tax of £675 generated protest and contributed to the disruption of the lower house. These were not Basse's only conflicts with the assembly.

During the assembly's first session Basse had hoped to gain the legislature's cooperation by signing bills that appealed to the delegates. One such act defined the "Rights and Privileges" of the inhabitants. Several others contained provisions contrary to the interests of the proprietors; the controversial tax imposed a rate on their unimproved lands, and another act reduced their influence in the lower house. Despite these antiproprietary enactments, opposition to Basse mounted. Young Lewis Morris, who had dramatically denied the governor's claim to authority at a May 1698 meeting of the Court of Common Right, headed that opposition. Several days later at Perth Amboy he organized and led a disorderly demonstration against the government. Under his encouragement the town meetings of Newark and other communities resisted the tax act and complained to England about the governor. Morris was twice fined and imprisoned; in May 1699 a large group of men from Elizabethtown broke into the Woodbridge jail and released him.

The Basse administration also failed to establish itself completely in West Jersey. The council was fully compliant and anti-Quaker; and since council members were ex officio justices, the governor also controlled the courts. However, the Quaker-dominated assembly refused to accept him as legal governor. The rejection of Basse's authority took many forms. The governor's summons of a general assembly went unheeded. The former provincial treasurer refused to provide the new administration with his accounts. Samuel Jennings, speaker of the assembly, concealed the "Book of the Laws" and other important papers. Mobs obstructed courts at Salem and Burlington.

By the summer of 1699 provincial government in both colonies had ceased to function. The news of Hamilton's reappointment contributed to the disarray. As early as December 1698 the East Jersey proprietors, who had come to regret their selection of Basse, had sought to restore the former governor. Furthermore, the possibility of their erecting an acceptable government appeared so hopeless that several months later they agreed to surrender their political pretensions to the crown. The West Jersey Society removed Basse not only as governor but also as agent, and the actual exchange of governors took place at the end of 1699. Basse left the governmental machinery of both provinces in a condition beyond repair, and in 1702 the crown took over the administration of both colonies.

After Basse's return to England, he intervened in the surrender proceedings, opposed the nomination of Hamilton as first royal governor, and sought a place for himself in the new government. Though he failed to secure a seat on the governor's council, he won an appointment as provincial secretary. He returned to New Jersey in 1703, and until his death in 1725 he was a persistent if minor political figure. In 1715 he lost his post as provincial secretary, but afterward he filled other offices, serving for five years as attorney general and for brief terms as representative from Cape May, collector of provincial taxes in Burlington County, and provincial treasurer. His later career shows his effectiveness and occasional distinction in executing lesser political positions. But Jeremiah Basse's tenure in 1698–99 as governor of East and West Jersey magnified the flaws in New Jersey government under the proprietors.

FREDERICK R. BLACK

Leaming, Aaron, and Jacob Spicer, eds. *The Grants, Concessions, and Original Constitutions of the Province of New Jersey*. Philadelphia: William Bradford, 1758.

Pomfret, John E. *The Province of East New Jersey, 1609–1702: The Rebellious Proprietary*. Princeton: Princeton University Press, 1962.

———. *The Province of West New Jersey, 1609–1702: A History of the Origins of an American Colony*. Princeton: Princeton University Press, 1956.

Edward Hyde, Lord Cornbury (attributed)
Courtesy Collection of the New-York Historical
Society, object #1952.80

Edward Hyde, Lord Cornbury (1661–

1723). In the long history of the political entity named New Jersey, no governor has been as controversial as the British aristocrat Lord Cornbury, who served from 1702 to 1708 as the first royal governor of the colony. Questions about whether he was corrupt, incompetent, intolerant, arrogant, and a transvestite have echoed in the halls of academia.

Cornbury, whose real name as opposed to his aristocratic title was Edward Hyde, was born in England in 1661 into a family with a landed estate in Oxfordshire. His grandfather had been rewarded for his work as the lord high chancellor of the realm by being granted the title Earl of Clarenden, and the Lord Cornbury who is the subject of this essay could expect that he would one day inherit the earldom. He was educated in Geneva and went into the English military, appointed lieutenant colonel and later colonel of the Royal Regiment of Dragoons. He saw combat in Vienna fighting Turkish invaders and back home in England battling an insurrection against the king. He also served in the British Parliament. In 1688 he married Katherine O'Brien, the descendant of Irish nobility. In the same year he was one of the first military men to throw his support behind the successful effort to bring William and Mary to the English throne —an event in English history revered as the Glorious Revolution.

All of this may sound romantic and exciting, but it overlooks the fact that the lesser nobility, of which Cornbury was a part, was often plagued by financial problems, leaving men with aristocratic titles struggling to feed their families and pay their debts. This fate befell Cornbury, who fell in and out of favor with King William. In part because of a disagreement over Parliamentary legislation, William deprived Cornbury of his military command, a severe blow. William later relented, providing Cornbury a small stipend. In 1701 the king appointed Cornbury as the governor of the New York colony in America. Before Cornbury left for New York he was arrested for nonpayment of his debts, but William interceded to get him released so that he could proceed on to his assignment in the colonies. Cornbury, with his wife, arrived in New York on May 2, 1702. His duties were subsequently expanded to include governorship of the colony of New Jersey, which he is said to have visited for the first time in 1703. (For the next three and half decades New Jersey continued to share its royal governors with New York.)

Since 1674 New Jersey had been divided into two colonies—East Jersey and West Jersey—each with its own governor chosen by the proprietors. Bringing the two colonies together in 1702 and placing them under Cornbury, a governor appointed by the crown, was a step forward in the organization and administration of England's overseas empire. But Cornbury faced a difficult task. For years there had been a bitter antagonism in the Jerseys between the resident proprietary faction, who claimed title to all of the land, and the other settlers, who strenuously denied the proprietors' assertion. The side that could win the favor of the new governor would gain an advantage. It was fertile soil for corruption, and early on in Cornbury's administration, a representative of the proprietor faction met him and provided him with £200 in bribes. Cornbury reciprocated by supporting the proprietors. Later in Cornbury's administration the antiproprietary faction provided him with a larger bribe to bring him over to their side.

Cornbury also coerced the New Jersey Assembly to raise a tax that would provide him £2,000 a year for two years, most of which went to his salary. A group of the governor's friends, known as the Cornbury Ring, received a share of this money and benefited even more by selling off tracts of the colony's land. There was a religious dimension to the situation in New Jersey as well. Cornbury, a firm Anglican, discriminated against the Quaker population of the colony.

From all of this and more a revulsion against Cornbury grew in New Jersey. In 1707 the assembly drew up a list of grievances against him and also sent a "Humble Petition" to Queen Anne, complaining about the "oppression they groan under by the arbitrary and illegal practices" of Cornbury and calling on her to replace him. Other messages were reaching England as well. Lewis Morris, a wealthy and influential figure in New Jersey and New York, wrote letters critical of Cornbury to authorities in the mother country; in one he referred to Cornbury as a "detestable maggot."

In 1708 Cornbury was recalled by Queen Anne and resumed his life as an English nobleman. With the death of his father he finally assumed the title of Earl of Clarenden and was a member of the Privy Council. But the last years of his life were difficult—he was vexed by debts and by the death of his only son.

Cornbury has been regarded as the quintessential arrogant, corrupt, and incompetent royal governor. But his reputation has been stoutly defended by New York University historian Patricia Bonomi, who argued that that Cornbury was not all that different from other royal governors in the American colonies, who struggled with their popularly elected assemblies and battled to get a salary from antagonistic colonials. Bonomi also sought to refute the contention of some colonists that during Cornbury's years as governor of New York and New Jersey he from time to time appeared wearing women's clothing. Bonomi argued that the negative image of Cornbury was the result of two factors: first, the salacious "Grub Street" style of journalism in that era, which delighted in vicious accusations against public figures, and later the "Whig" school of historians, who sought to work out a narrative of the triumph of liberty-loving American colonists against British tyranny.

So perhaps Cornbury was not as utterly bad as the legend would have it, but enough evidence has survived to rank him among the least successful of New Jersey's governors.

MARC MAPPEN

Bonomi, Patricia. *The Lord Cornbury Scandal: The Politics of Reputation in British America*. Chapel Hill: University of North Carolina Press, 1998.
McCreary, John R. "Ambition, Interest, and Faction: Politics in New Jersey, 1702–1738." Ph.D. dissertation, University of Nebraska, 1971.
Pomfret, John E. *Colonial New Jersey: A History*. New York: Scribner's, 1973.
Purvis, Thomas L. *Proprietors, Patronage, and Paper Money: Legislative Politics in New Jersey, 1703–1776*. New Brunswick: Rutgers University Press, 1986.

John Lovelace, Baron of Hurley (d. May 6, 1709) was a grandson of Francis Lovelace, the governor of New York from 1668 to 1673. Residence in America proved unkind to both. Francis returned to England in disgrace after New York City surrendered to the Dutch in 1673; in 1674 his estate was seized for debt; he was eventually imprisoned, and he died in 1675. John, even more unlucky, died in New York less than five months after his arrival there. Though a member of an aristocratic family and a great-grandson of the first baron of Hurley, John Lovelace spent his youth in relative poverty, while the title and family estate went to his cousin, also named John. When his cousin died in 1693 without a male heir, Lovelace succeeded to the peerage only to find that the previous baron had dissipated the family fortunes through gambling and debauchery. A decree of the high court of chancery ordered the estate sold to pay the accumulated debts, leaving Lovelace with a title and a pile of unpaid bills.

During the following years Lovelace served in a number of military posts, including those of guidon of the horse guards, military attaché to the earl of Westmoreland, and colonel of the New Regiment. In 1702 he married Charlotte Clayton, but neither her dowry nor his military career significantly improved his financial position. Consequently, he must have seen his March 1708 appointment to the governorship of New York and New Jersey as a golden opportunity. In September Lovelace sailed from South Hampton, accompanied by fifty-two families from the Palatinate who had fled their homeland in the face of French armies to seek a better life in America. Queen Anne had allowed them to be transported to England, and they were sailing for New York. Though not the first German immigrants to America, these families were the vanguard of thousands of German refugees who in the next few years would make their way through England and Amsterdam to the New World. When the ship arrived in New York on December 18, 1708, the Germans went north to settle Newburgh, and Lovelace assumed his office as governor of New York and New Jersey.

Lovelace faced a delicate situation, both as a representative of the crown and as a man seeking his fortune. He was replacing Edward Hyde, Lord Cornbury, who had been recalled for gross corruption and maladministration. Lovelace's instructions took this into account. They specifically forbade him to accept any "gift or present"; they instructed him to see that the assemblies specified the disposition of all appropriated funds; they required him to provide for his own living by requesting revenues from the New York and New Jersey assemblies. Since both bodies were keenly aware of his predecessor's corruption—and were highly independent as well—Lovelace faced the difficult task of protecting royal prerogatives while getting money from the groups most likely to ignore the crown's rights. When forced to choose, Lovelace bent prerogative in favor of his pocketbook.

In New Jersey Lovelace began his career on December 20 by calling a meeting of the council in Bergen. Because this group included former members of the "Cornbury Ring," as well as their archenemy Lewis Morris, Lovelace probably received a quick introduction to the factionalism which pervaded New Jersey politics. Since becoming a royal colony in 1702, New Jersey had been bitterly divided between two political groups—the "Scotch faction" and the "Cornbury Ring"—whose members sought to obtain huge tracts of land for themselves without concern for the public good. If the Cornbury supporters harbored any hopes of continuing their maneuvers with the new governor's connivance, they were disappointed when Lovelace summoned the assembly into session in March 1709.

No doubt realizing that his personal fortunes depended on cooperation with the lower house, Lovelace adopted a conciliatory tone. "I persuade myself," he told the assemblymen, "I shall not give you any just cause to be uneasy under my administration. . . . Let past differences, and animosities be buried in oblivion," he continued, "and let us seek the peace and welfare of our country." With these blandishments completed Lovelace got to the heart of the matter and asked for a revenue, but tactfully added, "You know best what the province can conveniently raise for its support, and the easiest methods of raising it."

The assembly responded in terms designed to persuade the governor to follow its lead, promising to "contribute to the support of Her Majesty's government to the utmost of our abilities and most willingly so at a time when we are freed from bondage and arbitrary encroachment." This promise, it turned out, had a few strings attached. The assembly did not simply provide Lovelace with a revenue; it also sought to oversee that revenue, first by demanding to examine the books of receiver general Peter Fauconnier and then by insisting that Lovelace submit his nominee for treasurer, Miles

Forster, for assembly approval. Lovelace complied, and the house had won a new right. Meanwhile, the assembly pressed its attack against the Cornbury faction. It secured indictments against former governor Jeremiah Basse, who had been province secretary under Cornbury, for perjury and against Peter Sonmans, the corrupt East Jersey receiver general and Cornbury lieutenant, for perjury and adultery.

With these successes against the Cornbury Ring and the now evident cooperation of the governor the assembly turned its attention to the question of revenue. In early April it passed a one-year measure that specified the salary of each colonial official. The assembly was so specific, it informed Lovelace, not because it distrusted him but because it lacked confidence "in these gentlemen that are now of her majesties council." Lovelace had no choice but to accept this new method of allocating money.

With one revenue now secure Lovelace quickly returned to New York to meet with its assembly, and a similar situation ensued. He made a conciliatory address that included an unfavorable reference to Cornbury. The assembly responded positively but complained of past injustices. The house then spent a month debating a revenue bill. On May 5 it finally agreed to grant Lovelace £1,600 for one year and specified further how all additional revenue would be spent, establishing a precedent in New York. Lovelace was now financially secure. Unfortunately, he never received the benefits, for he suffered a fatal stroke on May 6, 1709, before he could enjoy his new wealth.

EDWARD J. CODY

McCreary, John R. "Ambition, Interest, and Faction: Politics in New Jersey, 1702–1738." Ph.D. dissertation, University of Nebraska, 1971.

Pomfret, John E. *Colonial New Jersey: A History*. New York: Scribner's, 1973.

Smith, William, Jr. *The History of the Province of New-York*. Vol. 1, *From the First Discovery to the Year 1732*. Edited by Michael Kammen. Cambridge, Mass.: Harvard University Press, Belknap Press, 1972.

Richard Ingoldesby (d. March 1, 1719), British army officer and lieutenant governor of New York and New Jersey, 1702–9, was acting governor of both colonies from May 1709 to about April 1710. Richard Ingoldesby's early life is largely obscure. He was born into "a worthy family" and may have been the son of Thomas Ingoldesby, a captain in a parliamentary army during the English Civil War. Before the Glorious Revolution, Richard served the Prince of Orange as a field officer in Colonel Thomas Tollemache's English regiment of foot. In 1688, borne along by the celebrated "Protestant Wind," Ingoldesby accompanied his regiment back to England in support of William and Mary, and in the Irish campaign the year following he took part in the successful siege of the Jacobite stronghold of Carrickfergus. As a reward for his services to the new monarchs, in September 1690 Ingoldesby was commissioned captain and major of one of the independent companies of English regulars that were being sent to New York with Governor Henry Sloughter to help restore royal authority in the wake of Leisler's Rebellion. The Duke of Bolton, an eccentric Whig nobleman and military officer who sometimes acted as Ingoldesby's patron, also influenced the appointment.

Ingoldesby arrived in New York at the head of two independent companies in January 1691, two months before Sloughter, and promptly set about the task of reestablishing royal authority with a vengeance. He refused to recognize the authority of Jacob Leisler, the rebel leader who had assumed the office of lieutenant governor of New York after the collapse of the Dominion of New England in 1689, and demanded the surrender of a fort in New York City held by Leisler and his adherents. Leisler denied Ingoldesby's authority and refused to hand over the fort. In March 1691 a skirmish resulting in the deaths of two English soldiers brought the conflict between Ingoldesby and Leisler to a head. Sloughter appointed Ingoldesby, among others, to a special commission of oyer and terminer to try Leisler and several of his supporters on charges of murder and treason. The tribunal found Leisler and Jacob Milborne, his chief lieutenant, guilty of treason and sentenced them to be hanged, which was done in May 1691. Ingoldesby's role in the suppression and execution of Leisler earned him the undying hatred of the fallen leader's followers. One of them, hearing a rumor that Ingoldesby might be appointed governor of New York, angrily exclaimed, "No, that Murtherers dogg will never have ye place."

After Sloughter's death in August 1691 the New York Council, dominated by anti-Leislerians, selected Ingoldesby to serve as commander in chief of the colony until the imperial administration chose a successor for Sloughter. Ingoldesby, ever ambitious for preferment, requested the Duke of Bolton to obtain the office of governor of New York for him, but in vain. Benjamin Fletcher received the post instead and superseded Ingoldesby in August 1692. In the meantime Ingoldesby governed in the interests of the anti-Leislerians, although even they eventually tired of his arbitrary ways and complained that he "carried things with a high hand, [and] received Severall Sums of Money without a Concurrance in the Councill."

Under Fletcher's administration Ingoldesby was stationed with his company at Albany and put in charge of military security for New York's northern frontier. Inadequate supplies for his men and irregular pay for himself led him to return to England in 1696 on a one-year furlough. He remained in England for seven years, however, soliciting payment of his accounts and engaging in intrigue for promotion to a higher office. He gained the patronage of the Duke of Ormonde, a Tory peer who commanded a unit of the king's Life Troops, and he formed an acquaintance with William Dockwra, the leader of a faction of East Jersey proprietors living in England. During the negotiations in 1701 leading to the establishment of New Jersey as a royal colony Dockwra, backed by Ormonde, advanced Ingoldesby as a candidate for the post of first royal governor of New Jersey. But the imperial administration, anxious to combine in one man the governorships of New Jersey and New York, passed over Ingoldesby in favor of Edward Hyde, Lord Cornbury, who had already been appointed governor of New York. Ingoldesby's claims were not ignored entirely, however, for in November 1702 he was commissioned lieutenant governor of New Jersey and New York.

Ingoldesby finally returned to America in March 1704 and soon found himself in a peculiarly frustrating situation. Although the imperial administration expected him to administer New Jersey or New York when Cornbury was absent, its expectation was never realized. Cornbury refused to allow Ingoldesby to exercise authority in either colony, reducing him to the status of a cipher. Since Cornbury spent the greater part of his time in New York, the New Jersey Assembly was especially distressed that the lieutenant governor "declined doing any act of government at all" in the province. Ingoldesby brought this anomaly to the attention of the imperial administration, and in April 1706 the Privy Council approved an order revoking his commission as lieutenant governor of New York, continuing his commission as lieutenant governor of New Jersey, and making him a member of the New Jersey Council. The Board of Trade informed Cornbury of this order, but since Queen Anne neglected to sign a warrant putting it into effect, Ingoldesby's status and authority remained uncertain for several more years. Despite his differences with Cornbury, however, Ingoldesby loyally defended the governor when the New Jersey Assembly brought serious charges of misgovernment against him.

On the death of John Lovelace in May 1709 Ingoldesby became acting governor of New Jersey and New York. He assumed office in New Jersey when the reaction against Cornbury's misrule there was in full swing and when the struggle between the proprietary and antiproprietary parties was approaching a climax. Not surprisingly, in view of his previous association with William Dockwra and his defense of Cornbury, Ingoldesby aligned himself with the Anglican wing of the antiproprietary party, which then controlled the New Jersey Council and had support in England from Dockwra's faction of proprietors. Consequently, Ingoldesby temporarily dashed proprietary party hopes of purging certain leading Anglican leaders from the council and bestowed on his supporters a lush bounty of public offices and splendid land grants. Ingoldesby's alliance with the Anglicans elicited a challenge to his authority from Lewis Morris, the foremost proprietary party leader. Morris charged that Ingoldesby's commission was invalid and claimed that by virtue of his own position as New Jersey's senior councilor he himself was entitled to succeed Lovelace. Although Ingoldesby suspended Morris from the council and convinced a majority of assemblymen that his commission was valid, an undercurrent of suspicion about the legitimacy of his authority plagued him throughout his administration.

During Ingoldesby's first meeting with the assembly in May 1709 the most pressing issue facing him was New Jersey's role in the "Glorious Enterprise," a projected land and sea invasion of Canada by a joint expedition of American and British forces. Ingoldesby urged the assembly to raise New Jersey's quota of two hundred men for the expedition, but the assembly, with a large minority of Quaker members, was initially less enthusiastic about the project than he. Eventually the assembly decided not to raise the men but to emit £3,000 in bills of credit to pay and equip two hundred volunteers. The Quaker minority voted against a bill for this purpose on all three readings, serenely confident the non-Quaker majority would pass the measure and spare Friends the embarrassment of thwarting a measure deemed vital to local and imperial interests. But Ingoldesby and his allies decided to use the situation to bring the Quakers into disrepute, and on the third reading of the bill two erstwhile supporters from the antiproprietary party changed their votes and thus defeated it. Ingoldesby thereupon declared an adjournment until the end of July, when it probably would have been too late in the season for New Jersey to fulfill its quota, and joined the council in urging the home authorities to exclude Quakers from all public offices in the province. However, Samuel Vetch and Francis Nicholson, the chief promoters of the expedition, persuaded Ingoldesby to recall the assembly only ten days after its adjournment, and it finally approved an emission of £3,000 in bills of credit for the two hundred volunteers—the first emission of paper money in the colony's history. Unfortunately, the British government, because of untoward military developments in Europe, sent no British regulars to invade Canada, and the "Glorious Enterprise" came to an inglorious end.

Ingoldesby recognized that the imperial administration would not grant his request to be appointed governor of New Jersey, and thus the remainder of his administration was almost anticlimactic. In November 1709 Ingoldesby opened a newly elected assembly with a curt admonition to act with dispatch that he "may be Speedily enabled to Attend her Majestys Service in . . . New Yorke," which was exactly the sort of sentiment that made many New Jerseyans long for a governor of their own. At this time his main concern was to persuade the assembly to alter the support act passed earlier in the year for Lovelace and to divert to himself most of the salary granted to his prematurely deceased predecessor. He secured the passage of a revised support act for this purpose at the cost of allowing the assembly to strengthen its control over the salaries of royal officials, a practice that ran counter to the British government's policy of keeping such officials independent of local representative bodies.

In September and October 1709 the imperial administration revoked Ingoldesby's commission as lieutenant governor of New York and New Jersey.

News of this apparently did not reach America until around the following April, when he ceased to be acting governor in both colonies. Thereafter he returned to New York to command an independent company, and after living for a time in "necessitous circumstances" he died there on March 1, 1719.

A man with ability incommensurate to his ambition, Ingoldesby sought several times in his career to become royal governor of New Jersey or New York, but, as contemporaries noted, he was "a rash hot-headed man" unsuited to the tasks of civil government. His record in New Jersey—where he placed a higher value on discrediting his Quaker adversaries than on securing the colony's participation in an important military venture and where, for personal gain, he acquiesced in a serious encroachment by the assembly on royal authority—fully justifies this assessment.

EUGENE R. SHERIDAN

East Jersey Papers, The New Jersey Historical Society, Newark, N.J.

Livingston-Redmond Papers, Franklin D. Roosevelt Library, Hyde Park, N.Y.

Morris Family Papers, Rutgers University Special Collections, New Brunswick, N.J.

Records of the Society for the Propagation of the Gospel in Foreign Parts, Series A, vols. 3 and 4, Library of Congress microfilm.

Calendar of State Papers, Colonial Series, America and West Indies, 1689–1720; Documents Relative to the Colonial History of the State of New York. Vols. 3–5. London: Mackie, 1905.

Dalton, Charles. *George the First's Army, 1714–1725.* Vol. 1. London: Eyre & Spottiswode, 1910.

Ingalsbe, Frederick W., comp. *Ingoldesby Genealogy.* Grand Rapids, Mich.: Press of U. G. Clarke, 1904.

Kemmerer, Donald L. *Path to Freedom: The Struggle for Self-Government in Colonial New Jersey, 1703–1776.* Princeton: Princeton University Press, 1940.

McCreary, John R. "Ambition, Interest, and Faction: Politics in New Jersey, 1702–1738." Ph.D. dissertation, University of Nebraska, 1971.

Webb, Stephen Saunders. "Officers and Governors: The Role of the British Army in Imperial Politics and the Administration of the American Colonies, 1689–1722." Ph.D. dissertation, University of Wisconsin, 1965.

Robert Hunter (1666–1734), born in Edinburgh, Scotland, was the son of a lawyer and the grandson of the laird of Hunterston. He seems to have been well educated, for his correspondence shows a familiarity with Latin, Spanish, and French as well as an unusual felicity in English. He received his first commission in the army in 1689 and for nearly twenty years pursued a military career, serving under the first Duke of Marlborough in the War of the Spanish Succession (in America called Queen Anne's War). Though he fought at Blenheim and Ramillies and reached the rank of colonel, he had neither a regiment of his own nor the large patronage which that position often gave.

Having quarreled with Marlborough, Hunter successfully moved into the nascent colonial service by wangling the lieutenant governorship of Virginia. His means of access to the source of political appointments is obscure, but it is likely that the initial link was through his literary friends, who often doubled as courtiers and civil servants. Among them were Jonathan Swift, Joseph Addison, Richard Steele, and Dr. John Arbuthnot, the Queen's physician. En route to Virginia in 1707 Hunter was captured by the French, and he spent nearly two years in France in what was reportedly a socially dazzling captivity. Exchanged in 1709 (though not for the bishop of Quebec, as is customarily reported), Hunter was appointed governor of New York and New Jersey. He arrived in New York in June 1710.

Each of the two provinces offered grave dangers to a royal governor. New York, a frontier outpost in the long wars between Great Britain and France, lived in constant dread of Indian attack. (Only twenty years before, the town of Schenectady had been destroyed.) As though that were not enough, a long series of corrupt governors had driven the colonists to the point of refusing to raise taxes unless the elective assembly controlled the returns, which meant, in effect, controlling the local government. New Jersey had internal rather than external problems, but they were much more virulent: the province, only recently taken over by the crown, was disrupted by disputing proprietors.

In 1664 James, Duke of York, had given New Jersey to two cronies, John, Lord Berkeley, and Sir George Carteret. Ten years later Berkeley had sold his interest (the western) to the Quakers John Fenwick and Edward Byllynge, beginning a pattern of fragmentation that after thirty years had left each half with dozens of proprietors—a "muddle of perplexity." At Hunter's arrival there were two sets of contending proprietors. Colonel Daniel Coxe, the son of Governor Daniel Coxe; Jeremiah Basse, who had been governor of the colony between 1697 and 1699; Peter Sonmans; Hugh Huddy; Richard Townley; and William Hall formed one group. They were outspoken in their High Church Anglicanism, though in an age when religion and politics were almost interchangeable, they probably had no religious motives per se but used religion as a stalking horse. They had been protected and rewarded by Lord Cornbury, the first royal governor of New Jersey. The other group was led by Lewis Morris, Thomas Gordon, George Willocks, John Johnstone, Thomas Farmer, and Thomas Gardiner. Some of them, Quakers, owned shares bought from the older Coxe's receivers. The younger Coxe made a claim to the property, which if successful would ruin many of these men, for bankruptcy could easily mean life in prison. To add to the confusion each side had support from proprietors who lived in England: Edward Richier and Paul Doeminique supported the Morris faction (called by Hunter the "country party"), and William Dockwra supported the Coxe group.

When Hunter arrived in New Jersey, he found members of the Coxe party happily ensconced in the provincial council, the upper house of the legislature, where they could refuse to pass laws unfavorable to themselves (for example, a law that would permit Quakers to affirm rather than take oaths to serve on juries) and where they could act as the colony's supreme court. Queen Anne's reign was politically unstable, and when a new faction came into power in London, it displaced its rivals' appointees in the colonial service. Consequently, new governors came prepared to believe the worst about their predecessors and to discover evidence of it to disgrace them and embarrass their political supporters in England. In 1711 Hunter, whether to pursue such a plan or to retaliate for Peter Sonmans's attack on him in an election poll of 1710 or, as he himself said, to stop the obstructionism that plagued the government, began calling for the ouster of the Coxe group from the council. His Whig patrons had fallen from power in London in 1710, however, and their Tory successors were not especially inclined to please him. Not until 1713, after Doeminique and Richier pressured the Board of Trade, did the London administration remove Coxe, Sonmans, and their cohorts from the council and replace them with members of the country party. In the interim Hunter dealt with the Coxe party by moving to eliminate it from local judgeships and by failing to call any meetings of the legislature. When the legislature met in 1713, it passed a spate of bills. Some of these were designed to relieve the Quakers by permitting them to serve on juries and to hold local offices such as tax assessor and collector. Other bills made reforms in the court system, and one established a new county named in honor of the governor: Hunterdon.

Coxe and his men tried to regain power in 1715 and 1716 through the assembly elections; Coxe was named speaker, but Hunter, in no mood to be conciliatory or patient, repeatedly dissolved the assembly and called for new elections until the Quaker or country party had 50 percent of the seats. Coxe and his party boycotted the meeting of the legislature; but Hunter informed the remainder that they had a quorum, and the Quakers gleefully expelled the Coxe faction for nonattendance. Coxe fled to Pennsylvania and then to England, returning after Hunter's departure to play a prominent though less controversial role in the colony.

Hunter did not limit his interests to politics in New Jersey. He owned extensive property: more than one house in Perth Amboy, five hundred acres along the Raritan River and on Burlington Island. He urged the establishment of an Anglican episcopate in America, with the cathedral church at Burlington and his old friend Jonathan Swift as the first bishop. In 1715 he recommended that the home government permit minting of copper coins from local mines to relieve the currency shortage that hurt the small farmers. The crown accepted neither of these suggestions, though both were consistent with Hunter's philosophy: "The true Interests of the People and the Government are the same, I mean A Government of Laws. No other deserves the Name, and are never Separated or Separable but in Imagination by Men of Craft."

Sick and worried about political enemies who were traveling to London to try to replace him, Hunter left New York and New Jersey in 1719. The following year he exchanged positions with William Burnet, the comptroller of the customs. In 1727 he was appointed governor of Jamaica, where he died in 1734.

A tall, vigorous, and personable man who was literary as well as literate, Hunter wrote the first published play in America, an astonishingly ribald political satire on New York entitled *Androboros*.

JAMES EDWARD SCANLON

Logan Family Papers, Historical Society of Pennsylvania, Philadelphia, Pa.

Morris Family Papers, Rutgers University Special Collections, New Brunswick, N.J.

Rutherfurd Collection, New-York Historical Society, New York, N.Y.

Lustig, Mary Lou. *Robert Hunter, 1666–1734: New York's Augustan Statesman*. Syracuse: Syracuse University Press, 1983.

Olson, Alison Gilbert. "Governor Robert Hunter and the Anglican Church in New York." In *Statesmen, Scholars and Merchants: Essays in Eighteenth-Century History Presented to Dame Lucy Sutherland*, edited by Anne Whiteman, J. S. Bromley, and P. G. M. Dickson. Oxford, U.K.: Clarendon, 1973.

Pomfret, John E. *Colonial New Jersey: A History*. New York: Scribner's, 1973.

Purvis, Thomas L. *Proprietors, Patronage, and Paper Money: Legislative Politics in New Jersey, 1703–1776*. New Brunswick: Rutgers University Press, 1986.

Scanlon, James E. "English Intrigue and the Governorship of Robert Hunter." *New-York Historical Society Quarterly* 57 (1973): 199–211.

——. "A Life of Robert Hunter, 1666–1734." Ph.D. dissertation, University of Virginia, 1969.

William Burnet (1687–September 7, 1729), who governed New York and New Jersey from 1720 until 1728, was born in the Netherlands, at the Hague. His father, Gilbert Burnet, who became the bishop of Salisbury, had been a chaplain to Charles II, but he was one of the first English subjects to transfer his allegiance from James II to William and Mary. Gilbert Burnet had gone to the Netherlands to pay court to William and, while there, had married his second wife, Mary Scott, a wealthy Dutchwoman of Scottish extraction. Young William Burnet was named for his godfather, the man who became King of England in 1689. After the Glorious Revolution Gilbert's fortunes waxed and waned with the rise and ebb of the Whigs, but in general the family held a privileged position because of its leading role in the events of 1688–89. William developed into a personable but hotheaded young man.

Though he entered Trinity College, Cambridge, at the age of thirteen, he was expelled for laziness and disobedience. He was, however, privileged in having Sir Isaac Newton tutor him for a time.

As an adult William reportedly continued to be hot tempered, but he also displayed an active intellectual curiosity. His younger brother, Gilbert, concluded that William's curiosity was undisciplined and essentially frivolous. When informed that William was writing a book, Gilbert told him that he feared the book would make him a subject of derision. Nonetheless, William wrote the book, *An Essay on Scripture Prophecy, Wherein It Is Endeavoured to Explain the Three Periods Contain'd in the XII Chapter of the Prophet Daniel with Some Arguments to Make It Probable That the First of the Periods Did Expire in the Year 1715*. It was published anonymously in New York in 1724. One of William's brothers-in-law suggested that he might have done better to spend his time at backgammon.

Burnet obtained the dual governorship of New York and New Jersey in 1720 by trading his post as comptroller of the customs with his friend Robert Hunter, who in 1719 had returned to England. Since Hunter and Burnet both had strong Whig connections, the trade was easy to arrange. Burnet, whose first wife had died in 1717 and left him with a two-year-old son, willingly accepted the inconvenience of living in the colonies because he hoped the governorship would prove more lucrative than his post at the customs. He needed money because his heavy investment in the South Sea Company was rapidly depreciated after 1720. Through most of his term as governor, until the death of George I in 1727, he had few worries about opposition at home. Whatever problems he encountered originated in the colonies.

In both New York and New Jersey Burnet relied heavily on the advice of Lewis Morris and James Alexander, who had been principal advisers to Governor Hunter. In New Jersey both men were closely allied with the main proprietary interests. Throughout Burnet's term he tended to favor legislation designed to protect or enhance proprietary claims. This meant that the landholders who claimed titles which had not originated in patents from proprietors, primarily the so-called Nicolls patentees, were predisposed against Burnet.

These antiproprietary forces dominated Burnet's first assembly in 1721. The assembly had been elected in 1716. On Hunter's advice Burnet continued it. However, Lewis Morris, while he was acting governor after Hunter's departure, alienated many of its members with policies favoring the proprietors. After Burnet's arrival the assemblymen's own reluctance restrained them from engaging in open opposition to the governor. But they criticized Burnet's reliance on Morris, and they tried to use their control of finances, unsuccessfully, to effect a change in Burnet's attitude.

Throughout Burnet's early stay in the colonies he reflected his family's history by branding his opponents as Jacobites and High Churchmen. In 1721 he harried George Willocks, one of his East Jersey critics, out of the province by calling him a Jacobite and fomenter of opposition. By harassing Willocks, shrewdly electioneering among an electorate as lacking in deference as any in America, and using patronage after the election, Burnet contrived in 1722 to have a second assembly that was more amenable to his wishes. This assembly sat in three sessions before new elections were occasioned in 1727 by the death of George I. In 1722 the assembly passed an act for the financial support of the government for the years 1720–25; it also agreed to a stringent anti-Jacobite law. In 1723 it passed its famous Loan Act. In its last session, in 1725, it renewed the 1722 support act through 1730.

The Loan Act was the most significant piece of legislation during Burnet's tenure. In spite of the enthusiasm for copper mines that developed in the 1720s, New Jersey was still almost entirely dependent on agriculture. Its trade was largely in the hands of New York and Philadelphia merchants. Since New Jersey had no medium of exchange, its economy fluctuated with the currencies of New York and Pennsylvania. In 1709 New Jersey had begun to issue bills of credit, but after 1716 it had begun to retire them, producing a deflation that in 1720 caused, or at least aggravated, a depression.

James Alexander, a lawyer, land speculator, and New York merchant, strongly favored a new paper issue. So did most of the assemblymen. They made it clear that they would reward Burnet handsomely for his cooperation. Because Burnet insisted that any new currency had to have proper backing, they created a loan office authorized to lend £40,000. Loans to landowners secured by mortgages on their New Jersey farms put the money into circulation. The act provided a stable medium of exchange. Burnet defended the act against the mounting criticisms of London merchants and officials. He even gathered testimonials to the soundness of New Jersey money from New York City merchants. For his troubles Burnet received sizable "incidental" appropriations in addition to his regular salary from 1723 on.

Burnet governed a rapidly growing New Jersey. At the request of the Board of Trade he took a census in 1726. It indicated that the population, which in 1702 may have totaled 12,500, had more than doubled to 32,442, including 2,581 slaves. The growth brought about increasing problems over land titles as more and more of the disputed areas became populated, but the storm did not break until after Burnet's departure.

Burnet's last Jersey assembly, elected in 1727, was led by a vocal antiprerogative Quaker, John Kinsey, Jr. It proved almost as troublesome as his first. Burnet spent hardly any time in the colony between 1725 and 1727. The assembly that gathered at Perth Amboy in December 1727 knew when it convened that Burnet was due to be replaced. It began by requesting that New Jersey be given a governor of its own. The assembly engaged in a continual struggle with Burnet and his council over a bill that amended the procedures for registering deeds. The council sought to protect proprietors, the assembly to circumvent the council's authority over land. Eventually the assembly gained Burnet's assent for a triennial act which was later disallowed. The assembly also continued a practice of using the interest collected on the loan-office notes to support the government, which met strong disapproval from the Board of Trade. Burnet was more than willing to accede to this practice.

Governor Burnet drew an annual salary of £600 in New Jersey, and he also received fees. In addition, the assembly approved "incidentals," which varied from a first grant of £1,000 in 1723 to the £600 his last assembly voted him early in 1728. In return Burnet presided over a growing colony and approved legislation favorable to its growth, but he spent little time in the colony. Between 1720 and 1728 he was absent twice for more than a year. In 1722 Burnet married Mary Van Home, the oldest daughter of a prominent New York Dutch merchant; together they enjoyed the social life of Manhattan. The elder Van Home, who had been a staunch supporter of Hunter's, continued to support Burnet, and Mary's brother Cornelius was added to the New Jersey council in 1727. Burnet's wife bore him three children in New York, but both she and her last-born died in the autumn of 1727. Soon after, Burnet was notified that John Montgomerie, special favorite of the new monarch, George II, would replace him as governor of New York and New Jersey. Burnet's friends protested the change to no avail. Burnet, however, was not forgotten, and he was transferred to Massachusetts. On April 24, 1728, he turned over the government of New Jersey to Montgomerie and headed for Boston, where he encountered a disagreeable assembly and received no salary. As the result of a carriage accident he died there on September 7, 1729.

JOHN STRASSBURGER

Ellertsen, E. Peter. "Prosperity and Paper Money: The Loan Office Act of 1723." *New Jersey History* 85 (1967): 47–57.

McCreary, John R. "Ambition, Interest, and Faction: Politics in New Jersey, 1702–1738." Ph.D. dissertation, University of Nebraska, 1971.

Nelson, William. "The Administration of William Burnet, 1720–28." In *The Memorial History of the City of New-York, from Its First Settlement to the Year 1892*, vol. 2, edited by James Grant Wilson. New York: New York History, 1892.

———, ed. *Original Documents Relating to the Life and Administrations of William Burnet, Governor of New York and New Jersey, 1720–28*. Paterson, N.J.: Press Printing and Publishing, 1897.

Whitehead, William A. *Contributions to the Early History of Perth Amboy and the Adjoining Country, with Sketches of Men and Events in New Jersey during the Provincial Era*. New York: D. Appleton, 1856.

John Montgomerie (d. July 1, 1731) was born in Dumfriesshire, Scotland, and trained as a soldier. Montgomerie served in Parliament and then turned courtier, becoming groom of the bedchamber to the prince of Wales. In 1716, when the prince quarreled with his father, King George I, Montgomerie chose to give up his office rather than risk his friendship with the heir apparent. This act of loyalty probably led the prince, after his accession as George II, to offer Montgomerie the lucrative governorship of New York and New Jersey.

Historians have described Montgomerie as a man of little natural ability, limited education and intelligence, and no real ambition, who was mainly concerned with leading a life of leisure and material comfort. Reputed also to have considerable wealth, he was noted chiefly, according to historian William Smith, for the number of household possessions he brought to New York. Cadwallader Colden, however, an important New York leader at the time, understood the governor and his situation somewhat differently. Colden insisted that Montgomerie lacked neither intelligence nor natural ability but that he had "given himself up to his pleasures especially to his bottle and had an aversion to business." If he had once been wealthy, according to Colden, he had left England deeply in debt, and he wanted to use his new office to recover his fortune as easily as possible. Colden's observation that Montgomerie was "as diffident of himself" as any man he ever knew may help explain some of his difficulties as governor.

During Montgomerie's brief term as governor (April 15, 1728–July 1, 1731), he faced two issues in New Jersey. Either, if improperly handled, could have deprived him of part of his salary. The first was the Board of Trade's insistence that he persuade the assembly to repeal the act passed under Governor Burnet which empowered it to use the surplus money that had accumulated in the New Jersey Treasury for the support of government. This surplus represented interest paid by New Jersey citizens on money they had borrowed from the government-operated land bank set up in 1723. The original intention had been to put this money into a sinking fund. Both Burnet and Montgomerie strongly supported the assembly's position, knowing that the only alternative was to raise taxes and that the assembly would not do that. Since the governors' salaries depended on this money, they had to side with the assembly.

Burnet and Montgomerie were probably correct in contending that the assembly's position was sound. New Jersey's currency, in relation to that of the neighboring provinces, was rising steadily, and its loans were regularly paid off. Nevertheless, the board adamantly refused to accept the arrangement. The disagreement became a source of uneasiness to Montgomerie; he wanted to please both the board and the assembly but seemed, initially at least, unable to please either. The second issue that jeopardized Montgomerie's position was the assembly's firm decision that New Jersey should have its own governor. Although Governor Burnet, in the last assembly session over which he presided, had persuaded the assembly's leaders to table their request for a separate governor, he had only postponed the issue; in the next session the assemblymen placed it first on the agenda.

As Montgomerie had no real plans of his own to initiate and no particular design to pursue apart from retaining his salaries, his governorship can be most clearly understood in the light of his determination to persuade the assembly to give him adequate financial support and to prevent it from obtaining a separate governor. The desire to exert power over men or to distinguish himself as governor appeared to be totally alien to Montgomerie's nature. Essentially, he wanted to please the people he had to deal with and to offend as few as possible as long as they posed no threat to his pursuit of wealth and security.

On September 3, 1727, while still in England before officially receiving his commission as governor, Montgomerie wrote to the Board of Trade begging it to let the New Jersey Assembly apply the accumulated interest money in New Jersey's Loan Office "to the publick Services of the Government." It would be an "ungrateful proceeding," he insisted, to force him as soon as he arrived in the colony "to propose a new tax and burthen to the Province to bear the necessary Support of the Government when there lyes so much useless mony in their coffers already."

From the beginning, Montgomerie gave little indication that he had enough character or leadership to defend the royal prerogative against the more powerful assembly even if he wanted to. A few days before Montgomerie departed for New York in November 1727, New Jersey's ex-governor Hunter wrote a letter to James Alexander, an influential political figure in both New York and New Jersey, that revealed doubts about the new governor's competence. Hunter said Montgomerie "is a very honest Gentleman but will want good advice." In Barbados, where Montgomerie's ship took refuge during the winter storms, he reportedly said that he was bringing no dependents from England because he was sure he could fill all posts of honor with qualified Jerseymen. The statement reflected his desire to please the New Jersey community rather than to lead it.

The problems facing Montgomerie, however, would not go away. He had to both prevent the assembly from applying for a separate governor and persuade it to vote him an ample salary. His problems were compounded when the Board of Trade demanded that he ask for the repeal of the act providing support of the government from the interest money. In this difficult position Montgomerie decided for the first and only time in his short career to use his influence to retain some power over the ambitious assembly. The most urgent issue was the demand for a separate governor. On November 30, 1728, sensing the assembly's supreme confidence after a series of triumphs in its last session under Governor Burnet, Montgomerie wrote asking the Board of Trade to delay royal consent to two of the assembly's acts. The Triennial Act required elections for a new assembly every three years, and the Quakers' Oath Act excused Friends from taking oaths, a practice that was against their convictions. By asking for postponement of royal approval until the board could judge the behavior of the coming assembly, Montgomerie was trying to gain leverage for the coming dispute about a separate governor.

"To ese the Province of the expense" Montgomerie chose not to call for a new election, and the same assembly that had acquired unequaled power under Burnet met in December 1728. Its main preoccupation, as Montgomerie had expected, was the separate governor, and assemblymen were divided only over the choice of strategy. Nearly half the house, according to James Alexander, wanted to cooperate with the governor, offering him a handsome appropriation in exchange for his consent to their resolutions for a separate governor. The rest, following John Kinsey, the assembly's powerful Quaker leader, wanted to pass the resolutions without consulting Montgomerie.

Since the Kinsey group formed the majority, these resolutions would have carried had not Montgomerie, horrified at the prospect of losing his office, dissolved the assembly. The reason he publicly gave for this hasty action was that the assembly's resolutions ignored the king, showing disrespect to the crown, but his real motivation lay in the fear of being replaced by another governor. Montgomerie believed that with the prospect of another governor on the way "the people would worship the rising sun and slight him."

On April 20, 1729, Montgomerie wrote to the Board of Trade to report the "unadvisable and ungovernable" conduct of the assembly, elated with past favors and "having their heads full with impracticable Schemes calculated to weaken if not quite set aside his Majesties prerogative." Obviously he was referring to the assembly's resolutions in favor of a separate governor. He told the board that although the assembly had offered him five years' support as bait, the resolutions that followed made its dissolution absolutely necessary. Then, probably hoping that the board's opposition would undermine the power of the assembly leaders, he strongly recommended the disallowance of both the Triennial Act and the Quakers' Oath Act, implying that because of the Quakers' insolent request for a separate governor they deserved no special favors. This was Montgomerie's last firm stand, in part because the board failed to support his dissolution of the assembly but largely because he realized that the power to govern New Jersey rested in the assembly, not the crown. His best chance to retain the governorship and his salary, he now knew, lay in establishing good relations with assembly leaders.

Although Montgomerie had promised the board in his letter of April 20, 1729, that he would call on the assembly to repeal the act allocating the interest money to the support of the government, it is unlikely that he planned to follow through. Instead, on August 2 that year, in a long and somewhat agitated letter he tried again to convince the board that this use of the interest money was safe, legitimate, and necessary, warning that if the interest money was not used to support the government, New Jersey would be unsupported after the most recent appropriation ran out in September 1730. He expressed confidence that his arguments would persuade the board to reverse its position. This was an ill-founded hope in view of the board's past record.

When the new assembly convened in May 1730, Montgomerie had not yet received an answer to this letter; eighteenth-century transportation was extremely slow, and Montgomerie's administration suffered from unusually long delays in mail delivery. Since mailing it, he had received only one letter relating to New Jersey affairs, a reply to the letter of April 20, 1729, in which he had denounced the assembly's resolutions for a separate governor and requested the disallowance of the Triennial Act and the Quakers' Oath Act. The reply had destroyed whatever hope Montgomerie may have had for the board's support against the assembly on the issue of a separate governor. It refused not only to censure the assembly's resolutions, calling them quite legitimate, but also to recommend that the crown disallow the Quakers' Oath Act, stating that Quakers had similar privileges in England. In the most critical part of the message the board once more asked to hear as soon as possible that the act allowing the use of interest money for governmental support had been repealed. Otherwise, it warned the crown would disallow the act.

In Montgomerie's May 22, 1730, answer to the board, he professed to feel "very uneasie" at the rebuff and claimed that he would have been glad to transmit the assembly's request for a separate governor had it been phrased dutifully and addressed "to his Majesty." The statement, in view of his strong desire to retain the governorship, seems improbable. His real concern was to prepare the board for a new assembly victory. In conversing with all the members of the house, he wrote, he had received no encouragement whatsoever that they would reverse their position on the use of the interest money. During this session Montgomerie gave in to all the assembly's demands. Not only did he allow its leaders to petition for their own governor in exchange for five years' support, but he also accepted an act defraying that year's incidental charges of government from the interest money, a clear violation of the board's instructions. In a letter of November 20, 1730, he apologized for allowing this defiant action by explaining to the board that he had not received its letter of April 24, which explicitly rejected his arguments for this use of the interest money, until late in September after the assembly had adjourned. Having received no response to his letter, he said, he had flattered himself that the board had altered its opinion.

But even if the board's letter had arrived on time, Montgomerie could not have changed the assembly's policy. According to his letter, all his attempts to convince the assemblymen that the Board of Trade was serious in threatening disallowance had brought only taunts for his inability to convince the board that the assembly's position was sound. If he had asked for a repeal, which he never had, he would, he insisted, have received nothing but "a public, or perhaps a rude refusal."

Montgomerie's cooperation in passing on to the board the assembly leaders' petition for a separate governor in the summer of 1730 resolved that issue. His willingness to give way to all the assembly's wishes may have softened the petition's wording. Its signers disclaimed any dissatisfaction with their present governor and insisted, "wee are very well pleased with his Government and desire it may continue during your Royall pleasure."

In spite of this assurance, Montgomerie continued to worry about the appointment of another New Jersey governor. He had, however, only a short time to fret. On July 1, 1731, after months of poor health, he died of a stroke in New York. According to historians, the people much mourned him, probably because of his good nature, modesty, and eagerness to please. Under Montgomerie's governorship the power of the assembly continued to grow because the colonial authorities in England were ineffective and Montgomerie lacked the will and desire to check it. The crown did not disallow the hotly contested support act as the board had threatened it would. The petition for a separate governor was legitimately delivered to the crown at Montgomerie's own request. His only victory lay in the crown's disallowance of the Triennial Act, a veto he had recommended. Montgomerie must be characterized as one of the weakest of New Jersey's colonial governors.

FRANCES D. PINGEON

Cadwallader Colden Papers, New-York Historical Society, New York, N.Y.

Kemmerer, Donald L. *Path to Freedom: The Struggle for Self-Government in Colonial New Jersey, 1703–1776*. Princeton: Princeton University Press, 1940.

McCreary, John R. "Ambition, Interest, and Faction: Politics in New Jersey, 1702–1738." Ph.D. dissertation, University of Nebraska, 1971.

Pomfret, John E. *Colonial New Jersey: A History*. New York: Scribner's, 1973.

Sheridan, Eugene R. *Lewis Morris, 1671–1746: A Study in Early American Politics*. Syracuse: Syracuse University Press, 1981.

Smith, William, Jr. *The History of the Province of New-York*. Vol. 1, *From the First Discovery to the Year 1732*. Edited by Michael Kammen. Cambridge, Mass.: Harvard University Press, Belknap Press, 1972.

Tanner, Edwin P. *The Province of New Jersey, 1664–1738*. New York: Columbia University Press, 1908.

William Cosby (1690–1736) was surely New Jersey's least active governor and perhaps its most inept. The last of the colonial royal governors to hold the joint governorship of New York and New Jersey, he, like his predecessors, concentrated his efforts north of the Hudson River. He deserves mention, however, if only because he was indirectly responsible for the British government's decision in 1736 to establish a separate governorship for New Jersey. Governor Cosby was the sixth of seven sons in an Anglo-Irish family and the sixth to become a soldier. He entered the army in 1704, served in Flanders and Spain, and achieved a colonelcy of the Eighteenth Royal Irish in 1717. His marriage into the Montague family no doubt was hastened by the promotion. His regiment was transferred to Minorca in 1718, and for the next decade he exercised the additional responsibilities of the civil and military governorship of that little British outpost in the Mediterranean.

Cosby remains an obscure figure in the official records of Minorca, but stories of his misdeeds there became current in New York and New Jersey. The most vicious tale—about Cosby's dealings with a Portuguese merchant, Bonaventura Capedevilla—originated with Cadwallader Colden, an opponent. Cosby condemned as contraband a £9,000 cargo of snuff that Capedevilla had consigned to Minorca in 1718. He cowed the local judiciary into confirming his action while refusing to allow them to investigate many of the relevant documents. He also tried to falsify some records he sent to the Privy Council in 1722 when it investigated the affair. Colden states that the Privy Council found for Capedevilla and forced Cosby to pay £10,000 damages. "The Government of New York by the death of Coll Montgomerie came seasonably in his way to repair his broken fortune."

Colden may well have exaggerated the Capedevilla story, but later Cosby's hunger for land and his apparent ruthless intent to increase his estate were to lead many colonists to believe it. William Smith would accuse him of illicitly acquiring lands on Long Island and in the Mohawk Valley but reflect that public protestations were pointless: "No representation, repugnant to his avarice, had any influence upon Mr. Cosby. The weakness of his understanding rendered him insensible even to fear." Like almost all of the seventeenth-century and eighteenth-century British military and naval officers appointed to govern American colonies, Cosby saw the New World as a place to build a personal fortune. Further, the imperial authorities in London viewed governorships as sinecures for their friends and relatives. William Cosby was singularly well situated to be the recipient of such favoritism; neither his lack of character nor his deficiency of ability forestalled his 1732 appointment as successor to Governor Montgomerie.

The British Empire's principal administrator was the secretary of state for the Southern Department, a position held from 1724 to 1728 by the era's most accomplished manipulator of patronage, Thomas Pelham-Holles, Duke of Newcastle. Colonel Cosby had direct access to Newcastle through his wife, Grace Montague, Newcastle's first cousin and the sister of the first earl of Halifax, and he flaunted his influence in America by boasting the protection of "the great interest of the Dukes of New Castle, Montague and Lord Halifax." So powerful were Cosby's connections that he, like Montgomerie, was given a choice of colonial governorships. When he was about to set sail to take the governorship of the Leeward Islands, he learned of Montgomerie's death and returned to London so that Newcastle could secure him the more lucrative governorship on the mainland. According to one of his enemies, Cosby bluntly asserted his confidence in the strength of his patrons by rejecting an accusation that he had violated the law: "How, gentlemen, do you think I mind that: alas! I have a great interest in England." Even after his death, Newcastle and his brother Henry Pelham continued to provide for Cosby's widow and family.

Little can be said about the Cosby "administration" in New Jersey. The governor spent virtually all of this time in New York, where a combination of clumsiness on his part and emerging political maturity among the colonists created years of dangerous political factionalism. Governor Cosby arrived at Sandy Hook in early August 1732 and held office until he died of tuberculosis in New York in March 1736. He lived in New York City, seldom traveling to New Jersey. His first trip occurred shortly after his arrival in America, when he went to Perth Amboy to request the seals of government from Lewis Morris, who, as senior New Jersey councilor, had been the acting governor since the death of Montgomerie. For some time Morris had been agitating for the establishment of a separate New Jersey governorship, a position he hoped to fill. Perhaps for this reason he delayed meeting with Cosby for an hour or more while (as he claimed) he completed a chancery decree. Cosby, incensed by the delay, subsequently identified the incident as the origin of his conflict with Morris, but in fact Cosby's New Jersey governorship began quite happily.

During Cosby's tenure he met the New Jersey Assembly only once, and he never called an election. In his opening speech in April 1733 he promised to spend at least half of his time in the colony (thus responding to the lively separatism issue), and the representatives responded by voting him a continuation of support until 1738, although the existing support act still had two years to run. This may have been a response to Cosby's acquiescence when the assembly voted to issue an additional £40,000 in paper money contrary to royal policy. The governor also permitted the legislature to ratify his ordinance to fix legal fees in the colony, although, strictly speaking, imperial theory considered such legislative authorization unnecessary. Cosby's only disagreement with the assembly was over an act establishing triennial elections, which the legislators periodically tried to sneak through; Cosby vetoed it.

Despite Cosby's promises, this was more or less the sum of his public record in New Jersey. He met eight times with the council but transacted little business during its sessions because he was occupied with defending his position in New York. The most famous episode of Cosby's governorship was the trial of John Peter Zenger, which in fact was related to Cosby's feud with Lewis Morris and James Alexander. Morris and his allies, who were active in both New York and New Jersey, established a paper in New York City, the *New-York Weekly Journal*, that was hostile to Cosby. Furious over the paper's sniping, Cosby suppressed it and arrested its editor, Zenger, for libel. Zenger was acquitted in what some historians have called a landmark case for freedom of the press; Cosby had failed to stifle criticism of his regime in New York or to remove Morris and Alexander from the council in New Jersey (which they had ceased to attend after the first meeting). Indeed, when Morris traveled to London in 1735–36 to organize a campaign for Cosby's removal, it became apparent that New Jersey had little importance except as a pawn in the politics involving New York. Morris tried to persuade the Privy Council to remove Cosby from the New York government; he failed, but to placate him the council separated the colonies and, two years after Cosby's death, made Morris governor of New Jersey. Lewis Morris thought William Cosby a "weak madman"; Morris was doubtless too vehement, but, alas, little good can be said about Governor Cosby of New Jersey.

STANLEY NIDER KATZ

Rutherfurd Collection, New-York Historical Society, New York, N.Y.

[Colden, Cadwallader]. "Cadwallader Colden's History of Governor William Cosby's Administration and of Lieutenant Governor George Clarke's Administration through 1737." *New-York Historical Society Collections* 68 (1935): 280–355.

Katz, Stanley. *Newcastle's New York: Anglo-American Politics, 1732–1753*. Cambridge, Mass.: Harvard University Press, 1968.

Kemmerer, Donald L. *Path to Freedom: The Struggle for Self Government in Colonial New Jersey, 1703–1776*. Princeton: Princeton University Press, 1940.

McCreary, John R. "Ambition, Interest, and Faction: Politics in New Jersey, 1702–1738." Ph.D. dissertation, University of Nebraska, 1971.

Sheridan, Eugene R. *Lewis Morris, 1671–1746: A Study in Early American Politics*. Syracuse: Syracuse University Press, 1981.

Smith, William, Jr. *The History of the Province of New-York*. Vol. 2, *A Continuation, 1732–1762*. Edited by Michael Kammen. Cambridge, Mass.: Harvard University Press, Belknap Press, 1972.

Lewis Morris (October 15, 1671–May 21, 1746), colonial American political leader and jurist, served as governor of New Jersey, 1738–46. Morris was born in New York City, the only child of Richard and Sarah (Pole) Morris, who had come to the province from Barbados the year before. After the sudden death of his parents in the summer of 1672 Morris was brought up by an elderly Quaker uncle also named Lewis Morris. When his uncle died in 1691, Morris inherited large estates in New Jersey and New York and became a member of the landed aristocracy in both colonies. In that year he also married Isabelle Graham, the daughter of James Graham, a highly influential New York merchant and political leader. They had fifteen children, eleven of whom—three boys and eight girls—reached adulthood. Although Morris received little formal education, he transformed himself into a highly cultured country gentleman who mastered several ancient languages, amassed

Lewis Morris

John Watson (American, 1685–1768), *Governor Lewis Morris*, ca. 1726, oil on linen, 30 1/16 × 25 in. (76.3 × 63.5 cm); Brooklyn Museum, purchased with funds given by John Hill Morgan, Dick S. Ramsay Fund, and Museum Collection Fund, 43.196

a library of three thousand books, wrote poetry, and dabbled in natural science. Yet Morris's main preoccupation was politics, and his long and complex political career in New Jersey and New York was among the more remarkable in colonial American history.

Morris's appointment as the first separate royal governor of New Jersey in January 1738 was the high point of his career. At the same time it seemed a fitting climax to New Jersey's longstanding opposition to the British government's practice of having the same official govern New Jersey and New York. For at the time of his appointment Morris had been deeply involved in New Jersey political, economic, and religious affairs for almost half a century. Morris had played a key role in negotiating the 1702 settlement between the Jersey proprietors and the imperial administration whereby the crown assumed the government of the province in return for the confirmation of proprietary rights to the soil. For the next thirty-five years he continued to be one of New Jersey's most influential political leaders while serving as a provincial councilor (1702–5; 1708–37), assemblyman (1707–8), and acting governor (1719–20; 1731–32; 1736–38, though in this last period his authority was disputed). In addition, from 1703 to 1736 Morris acted as American agent for an organization of British land speculators known as the West Jersey Society, and from 1725 to 1730 he also served as president of the Board of Proprietors of East Jersey. Finally, as the first American member of the Society for the Propagation of the Gospel, an Anglican missionary organization based in London, Morris supported the society's efforts to convert Protestant dissenters in New Jersey to the Church of England. Even between 1710 and 1737, when Morris devoted most of his time to politics in New York —managing the provincial assembly for Governors Robert Hunter and William Burnet, serving as chief justice of the supreme court (1715–33), and leading the opposition to the arbitrary rule of Governor William Cosby—he never lost interest in New Jersey affairs.

In addition to Morris's intimate familiarity with New Jersey, he enjoyed another important advantage as he assumed the governorship—the support he received from some influential British connections. His daughter, Euphemia, was the widow of Matthew Norris, a captain of the Royal Navy. Her father-in-law, Sir John Norris, a British admiral who commanded the Royal Navy and held a seat in Parliament, kept a watchful eye on Morris's interests in Great Britain. A shrewd woman who had elected to remain in England after her husband's death, Euphemia Norris was familiar with some of the leaders of the opposition to the Walpole ministry, and she regularly kept her father abreast of political developments in the home country. But Morris's most important British connection was Sir Charles Wager, another admiral. In addition to being first lord of the admiralty, a privy councilor, and a member of Parliament, Wager was a close political ally of Sir Robert Walpole, then the most powerful statesman in the realm. The combined influence of Wager and Walpole did much to put Morris in the office of governor of New Jersey; and initially, the knowledge that Morris enjoyed the patronage of such highly placed British officials greatly enhanced his influence with the provincial assembly. By the same token, Walpole's fall from power in February 1742, and Wager's removal from office soon thereafter, perceptibly weakened Morris's standing in New Jersey, making it more difficult for him to rally support in the assembly.

Unfortunately, Morris failed to satisfy the expectations his appointment had aroused among the people of New Jersey; instead his administration quickly degenerated into a series of bitter conflicts with the assembly. The disputes largely stemmed from his forthright defense of royal authority in New Jersey. From the outset of his administration Morris maintained that although the assembly was duty bound to provide his government with financial support, he had no reciprocal obligation to consent to the laws it passed unless they stood for the common good without infringing on the royal prerogative. Thus in 1739 he dissolved one assembly after approving only a small number of the popular bills it had passed, and in 1742 he dissolved another after withholding assent from every bill passed except one for the support of government. Even when Morris did not resort to the drastic step of dissolution, he frequently refused to approve assembly bills that the representatives considered sound pieces of legislation but he regarded as ill conceived or unconstitutional. As a result, he was often criticized for keeping the assembly in session to little purpose for inordinately long periods of time.

Morris's adherence to royal instructions also antagonized the assembly. In obedience to such instructions he badgered the assembly into supporting a British expedition against the Spanish West Indies in 1740, an effort which offended New Jersey's politically influential Quaker community. For the same reason in 1744 he carried on a fruitless campaign to persuade the assembly to pass a more stringent militia law to bolster the province's defenses against a possible French attack. In this instance Morris offended large numbers of Quakers and non-Quakers alike, who refused to believe that a French assault on New Jersey was likely. Morris himself shared their skepticism but felt his instructions obliged him to suppress his doubts and push for the passage of an unpopular law. Yet Morris was not always consistent in following his instructions from the crown. Although they clearly stated he was to exercise the power with the advice and consent of the council alone, he allowed the assembly to determine how the money it raised for the support of government should be expended. Still, he remained sufficiently inflexible in his defense of royal authority to alienate the assembly, as the shift in its attitudes about the issue of support indicated. Whereas in 1739 the assembly provided him a three-year grant of funds for the support of government, in 1741 it approved only a one-year grant; and in 1744 it passed a support bill that so reduced Morris's salary and the salaries of other royal officials that the council felt obliged to reject it, leaving the government with no money from the assembly for the rest of the administration.

Morris's defense of parliamentary authority further sapped his popularity in New Jersey. Partly because colonial paper money was then under attack in Parliament and partly to avoid incurring the displeasure of the home authorities by allowing a new emission in New Jersey, he refused throughout his administration to approve a highly popular bill for the emission of £40,000 in bills of credit. And when, in 1744, the assembly denounced as subversive of American liberties a proposal by Parliament to give royal instructions the force of law, Morris admonished it for criticizing Parliament, declaring, "a British Parliament can abolish any Constitution in the Plantations that they deem inconvenient or disadvantageous to the Trade of the Nation, or otherwise." The implications of parliamentary supremacy in the empire could not have been stated more nakedly, nor can one imagine a sentiment less congenial to the people of New Jersey.

As Morris's relations with the assembly deteriorated he attempted to retrieve his position by appealing over its head to the New Jersey electorate. More than any other governor before him, Morris carried his case directly to the freeholders and freemen of the province through printed speeches and pamphlets. These inevitably called forth replies from his opponents and brought about an unprecedented outburst of polemics in New Jersey during his administration. Between 1739 and 1746 at least ten political broadsides and pamphlets appeared in the province—approximately twice the number produced during the entire thirty-six years of the royal period preceding Morris's governorship. Morris himself wrote at least one pamphlet, *Extracts from the Minutes and Votes of the House of Assembly* (1743). He also had several of his speeches to the assembly printed separately, particularly those occasioned by dissolutions of this body. Unfortunately, Morris's pamphlet and speeches suffered from certain shortcomings, not the least of which were their dreary prolixity and dry appeals to precedent. Even if he had written more trenchantly, however, it is unlikely that these works would have affected politically aware New Jerseyans more positively. They generally defended unpopular bills or attacked acts of the assembly that Morris interpreted as encroachments on the royal prerogative but others regarded as legitimate expressions of parliamentary privilege or popular rights. In contrast, Morris's polemical adversaries more effectively assailed his refusal to approve popular legislation, his advocacy of unpopular causes such as militia reform, his propensity for long and often unproductive assembly sessions, his explosive temper, and his support of the royal prerogative.

Morris coupled his appeals to the electorate with equally unsuccessful pleas to the imperial administration for drastic British intervention in the colony's political system. Outraged by Quaker opposition to his efforts to win support in New Jersey for the British expedition against the Spanish West Indies in 1740, Morris suggested that the Board of Trade deprive Friends of their right to sit in the assembly—a suggestion the board wisely ignored. Frustrated by his failure to obtain what he regarded as adequate financial support from the assembly and convinced that its powers had grown too great, Morris advanced proposals to make himself and other royal officials fiscally independent of the assembly. Some of these proposals, when the British implemented them after 1763, helped to bring on the American Revolution. As early as 1739 he advised the Board of Trade to consider the feasibility of an act of Parliament requiring provincial assemblies to pay royal officials fixed salaries. Two years later he returned to this theme, this time urging the board to support a proposal that Parliament issue paper money in America and apply part of it to pay the salaries of the king's officers there. Finally, in 1745, he asked the board to persuade Parliament to authorize the king to determine the expenditure of the funds the provincial assemblies raised for the support of government. The board acted on none of these proposals, which had the potential for revolutionizing the relations between royal governors and colonial assemblies, and took no notice of them in its correspondence with Morris. It is difficult to determine whether this was because New Jersey did not bulk large in the board's scheme of things or because the board was too distracted by the instability resulting from the fall of Walpole's ministry and the problems arising from Great Britain's wars with France and

Spain to consider Morris's proposals for radical imperial reform. In any case, it was well for the peace of the empire that the board ignored Morris's plans.

Unable to win support from the people of New Jersey or to convince the imperial administration of the need for parliamentary intervention, Morris spent the last two years of his administration in a bitter deadlock with the assembly. Between June 1744 and May 1746 he met with four different assemblies. An unvarying pattern marked the first three, with Morris insisting that the assembly provide his government with financial support before he consented to the bills it favored and the assembly refusing to pass a support bill until Morris had approved the bills it wanted passed. During the stalemate the assembly granted the government no money, and Morris withheld assent from every act it passed save one granting supplies for the New England expedition against Louisburg in 1745. Only in Morris's last assembly, which first met in February 1746, did it seem that this deadlock might be broken. Both sides appeared ready to retreat from their extreme positions and to reconcile their differences, but not for long. The assembly learned in the midst of its proceedings that the Board of Trade, acting on Morris's advice, intended to recommend royal disallowance of a Fee Act approved in 1743 by both the governor and the assembly. Enraged at what it interpreted as an act of treachery by Morris, the assembly renewed its demand for his assent to certain popular legislation before passage of a support bill. Morris agreed, but only if the assembly promised to increase the appropriations it was planning to make to the government. This the assembly refused to do. Suddenly the prospect of stalemate once more confronted the province. In the midst of this crisis, however, Morris, who had been ill for several years, died on May 21, 1746. Yet not even death could dispel the bitterness his administration had engendered. Three years later, when his widow petitioned the assembly for payment of his salary arrears, the assembly turned down the request by an overwhelming majority, remarking that hers was "a Subject so universally disliked in this Colony, that there is none, except those who are immediately concerned in point of Interest, or particularly influenced by those who are, will say one Word in its Favour."

EUGENE R. SHERIDAN

Morris Family Papers, Rutgers University Special Collections, New Brunswick, N.J.

Batinski, Michael C. *The New Jersey Assembly, 1738–1775: The Making of a Legislative Community*. Lanham, Md.: University Press of America, 1987.

Cook, Richard. "Lewis Morris—New Jersey's Colonial Poet-Governor." *Journal of the Rutgers University Library* 24 (1961): 100–113.

McConville, Brendan. *These Daring Disturbers of Public Peace: The Struggle for Property and Power in Early New Jersey*. Ithaca, N.Y.: Cornell University Press, 1999.

McGuire, Maureen. "Struggle over the Purse: Gov. Morris v. N.J. Assembly." *Proceedings of the New Jersey Historical Society* 82 (1964): 200–207.

Sheridan, Eugene R. *Lewis Morris, 1671–1746: A Study in Early American Politics*. Syracuse: Syracuse University Press, 1981.

Strassburger, John. "Our Unhappy Purchase: The West Jersey Society, Lewis Morris, and Jersey Lands, 1703–1736." *New Jersey History* 98 (Spring–Summer 1980): 97–115.

Turner, Gordon B. "Lewis Morris and the Colonial Government Problem." *Proceedings of the New Jersey Historical Society* 67 (1949): 260–304.

Whitehead, William A., ed. *The Papers of Lewis Morris*. In *Collections of the New Jersey Historical Society*, vol. 4. New York: G. P. Putnam, 1852.

Jonathan Belcher (January 8, 1681 or 1682–August 31, 1757), Massachusetts merchant and politician, was born in Cambridge, the second son of seven children, to Andrew and Sarah (Gilbert) Belcher. The family was rooted in New England society: Jonathan's grandfather had arrived in the 1630s; his father had steadily accumulated property and become one of Boston's wealthiest merchants and a member of the provincial council. After Jonathan graduated from Harvard in 1699, he entered his father's business. In 1705 he married Mary Partridge, the daughter of New Hampshire's lieutenant governor, and entered Boston's Second Church. On his father's death in 1717 he embarked on a public career.

In a political world rent by constitutional conflict between executive authority and the legislature this moderate and unreflective political practitioner shunned permanent identification with either ideological position: first, as a member of the council, he defended Governor William Shute; then, as agent of the house of representatives in London, he opposed Governor William Burnet; and, finally, he returned in 1730 as governor of Massachusetts and New Hampshire with instructions to defend the principles he had left to contest. His success—eleven years' tenure as governor—rested on a careful cultivation of the Anglo-American patronage system. After four trips to London he had important friends and allies who defended his interest with the Walpole government. For example, in return for supporting toleration for Massachusetts Quakers, his brother-in-law Richard Partridge, a prominent London Quaker, who was New Jersey's agent, recruited the English Friends to exert influence in the governor's behalf. However, although conflict between the representatives and the executive abated during Belcher's administration, the years of politics earned him enemies whose London allies campaigned to unseat him. In 1741 the governor's uncompromising opposition to the popular Land Bank antagonized the legislature and discredited his ability to rule, and with the simultaneous demise of the Walpole government his opponents argued for his replacement by William Shirley.

In August 1741 Belcher retired to his estate at Milton. Alone—his wife, who had borne him five children, had died in 1736—he brooded over life's mishaps. In 1744 inactivity roused him to book passage for London, where he hoped to retrieve his fortune through a pension or another appointment. He found none of his familiar patrons at Whitehall, and he could curry the favor only of Lord Hardwicke. Though officialdom received him kindly, it was unresponsive to his pleas. Humiliated and embittered by months of waiting in the anterooms of power, Belcher withdrew to the congenial community of London's dissenters, the Congregationalists and Quakers. He met Mrs. Louise Teale, a widow with some fortune, and decided to "commit matrimony" on condition that he find a suitable appointment. In 1746 he learned that Lewis Morris, the governor of New Jersey, lay dying; although the office was of little consequence and small reward, he pursued the opportunity. Rival New Jersey factions contested the post: Morris's allies sought to maintain control of the executive, and their agent Ferdinand John Paris nominated the governor's son Robert Hunter Morris; in turn the rival Quaker leaders of Burlington hoped to name their own and, through Partridge, discovered their candidate in Jonathan Belcher. The London Friends persuaded the Duke of Newcastle to appoint Belcher, collected the requisite fees, and prepared for his residence at Burlington. Before his departure they advised him on the situation in New Jersey.

In August 1747 the new governor arrived by way of New York, a self-styled exile to an "obscure corner of the world." On his progress south to Burlington discussions with local politicians and clergymen confirmed his initial prejudices. With its religious and ethnic diversity this "Wilderness of Nova Caesarea" compared poorly with his native Massachusetts. An enthusiastic friend of the Great Awakening, Belcher discovered a few scattered churches to his liking in the north, but none in Burlington. On conference with the local evangelicals he concluded that "vital religion" was a tender plant in the Jerseys. The people were a crude lot: the province needed "a Nursery of religion and Learning." And most pressing, the province was aflame with riot: longstanding litigation between the East Jersey proprietors, principally James Alexander and Lewis Morris, and the farming communities in the Elizabethtown-Newark area had erupted into violence. While Jerseymen welcomed the governor with promises of support, and the Burlington Quakers admitted him to their society, the aging governor felt estranged and disappointed. Taking up residence a mile from Burlington, he put the problems of office from his mind and resolved to devote his declining years to religion. Soon, he summoned his "Queen of Nova Caesarea," and on September 9, 1748, he and Mrs. Teale were married.

Belcher entered an uneasy political calm. During the previous decade the irascible Governor Morris and the council, composed of his friends and relatives (principally James Alexander and Morris's son Robert Hunter Morris), had angered assemblymen from East Jersey by defending proprietary claims. Governor Morris had also offended prominent Quaker legislators from the west by denying them patronage, and the entire legislature by insulting its privileges. Government was at an impasse. The self-styled "ploughmen" legislators demanded regulation of the courts and legal fees and regular elections; the council pressed for strict measures against the rioters. Neither prevailed. If Belcher's appointment gratified the assemblymen, the councilors greeted the news with reservations. Agent Paris and Robert Hunter Morris warned of the governor's alliance with the "ploughmen," but Alexander convinced the majority, weary of contention, to suspend judgment. In turn, Belcher translated his predisposition to avoid the burdens of office into a principle of statesmanlike aloofness; while recognizing his debt to the Quakers, he was unwilling to antagonize the Morris faction.

In the first meeting with the legislature the governor recommended action on the riots while deftly resisting the council's pressures for vigorous action and at the same time avoiding association with the rioters. Soon the two houses, left to themselves, reached a compromise, with the assembly introducing a bill for the "preventing of Riots" and the council an amnesty bill. The tactic seemed successful: Belcher signed nineteen bills, including a treasury supply and regulations of sheriff's appointments and court fees. He also promised to recommend to the crown a bill for issuing paper money in excess of his instructions. In Burlington, surrounded by allies, he heard his praises sung and believed that he had been successful. Yet that comfort proved illusory: the rioters rejected amnesty and continued to harass the sheriffs of Morris and Essex Counties. With Robert Hunter Morris seizing the initiative, the council pressed for vigorous measures. For example, when it presented Belcher with a petition to the crown for aid against the rioters, he declined to give his support. The council was soon convinced by Morris's warnings. Belcher's open and regular consultation with the "ploughmen" and his infrequent correspondence with the Morrisites awakened fears that their interest was in jeopardy.

Finally, Alexander was persuaded to join the opposition. In 1749 Morris joined Paris in London, and Belcher warned Partridge to beware of their activities.

The weakness of the governor's position became apparent. Political lobbying in London severely undermined his authority: Morris outmaneuvered Partridge and persuaded the Board of Trade that the governor was consorting with the rioters. Belcher was reprimanded, and Whitehall rejected his nominations to the council in favor of Robert Morris's recommendations. Even friends proved unreliable allies. At times Belcher scolded and prodded the assembly, but to no avail: no riot or tax legislation was passed. In 1751 he grew desperate. On dissolving the assembly, he appealed to the electorate for better representatives and cajoled friends to stand for the legislature. But the results only underscored his impotence: his candidates were not elected. Though the assembly came to agreement with the council on a tax bill, Belcher's influence was negligible. And the next year he helplessly watched the two houses deadlock over taxes. Frustration drove Belcher to desperate measures. He purged the council of offensive members only to earn further reprimands from the Board of Trade. In such a mood he received a suggestion from the assembly leaders that he could sign a tax bill without the council's assent. Only Alexander's firm correction prevented him from pursuing the tactic.

Essentially, Belcher believed that religious and educational decay had brought in the province's ills. A champion of the New Lights and a friend of Jonathan Edwards and George Whitefield, he made religious awakening an integral part of his public life. He invited Gilbert Tennent to preach before the legislature on the principles of godly government. He listened with enthusiasm to Tennent's program to build a college; as New England's colleges had brought pious leadership and learning for the happiness of the community, this "infant college" could reform this "unpolisht ignorant Part of the World" and instruct the "Rising Generation" according to the standards of "vital religion." The college, Belcher's "little Daughter," captured his imagination. Quickly he lent his support, first by rewriting the charter to include himself on the Board of Trustees and then by seeking funds for its construction. After Quakers and Anglicans effectively prevented the assembly from lending aid, he persuaded the government of Connecticut to sponsor a lottery. He wrote throughout the colonies and Great Britain seeking subscriptions. His will provided that his library be given to the college. In 1748 the trustees of the College of New Jersey (later Princeton University) conferred on him the M.A. degree, and in 1756 they offered to name the first building Belcher Hall, an offer he declined, suggesting instead Nassau Hall.

By 1751 Belcher's government stood at precarious equipoise. While friendly with legislative leaders, Belcher found the assembly oblivious to his recommendations and immune to his influence. It would pass no more riot legislation, and if it passed any treasury supply, Belcher could not take credit. Morris had effectively checked the governor's interest in London, but the Quakers well protected his commission. In the fall Belcher moved his family to Elizabethtown, where he hoped to find a more healthful climate, and within the year he joined the congregation of Elihu Spencer, a friend of Jonathan Edwards. In the following years he progressively withdrew from government. Weary of politics, he called fewer assemblies and corresponded infrequently with the legislative leaders. The style of his administration reminded the "ploughmen" of Lewis Morris: his appointments violated residency requirements, and he called the legislature to locations other than the regular sites of Perth Amboy or Burlington. Yet the governor, isolated and preoccupied with the college, was oblivious to this gradual estrangement. Meanwhile, relations with the council improved. Robert Morris, appointed governor of Pennsylvania in 1754, no longer threatened Belcher. At the same time the border dispute with New York challenged the proprietary interests of Morris and Alexander, and they joined the governor to protect the New Jersey claims. In 1756 Belcher nominated Alexander's son William to the council.

Renewed hostilities with the French forced Belcher to confront distasteful assembly politics. In 1754 Virginia's Governor Robert Dinwiddie requested a contingent of New Jersey troops to join his defense of the western frontier, and the Board of Trade recommended an intercolonial conference to meet with the Six Nations. Sick in bed, Belcher summoned the assembly to Elizabethtown instead of the regular site at Perth Amboy. To his recommendations the "ploughmen" replied with a list of grievances, including the extraordinary place of meeting. The assembly disposed of the military question by declaring the peril less obvious and the province too poor. Belcher scolded, dissolved the assembly, and called new elections, but he learned once more the ineffectiveness of the tactic. His patriotic appeals brought meager contributions to the war effort. News of General Braddock's defeat in the summer of 1755 and rumors of Indians approaching the Jersey borders spurred Belcher to call for the destruction of French Canada. Instead, the assembly pressed for redress of grievances. Only after a personal address by Lord Loudon, commander of the British forces in North America, did it vote five hundred men. Before the campaign concluded, Belcher was stricken with palsy, and he died on August 31, 1757.

Since his death Belcher has fared poorly in the hands of historians. They have dismissed him as a sycophant and narrow-minded Puritan, epitomizing the most distasteful elements of his age. Doubtless he was a commonplace citizen of his times, but with a changing appreciation of the eighteenth century his life requires serious reconsideration. Reevaluation need not exaggerate his importance: his accomplishments in New Jersey, with the exception of the College of New Jersey, were minor. But his career is illuminating, if only because he managed to survive in a political world where the average governor could expect to last a mere five years. In sum, his political life illustrates the dynamics of provincial politics—the limitations on the governor and the importance of both the structure of the imperial patronage system and the homegrown legislative process. His career also reflects religion's importance in politics in colonial America, in terms of alliances and in the definition of public policy.

MICHAEL C. BATINSKI

Jonathan Belcher Letterbooks, Massachusetts Historical Society, Boston, Mass.

Jonathan Belcher Papers, The New Jersey Historical Society, Newark, N.J.

Ferdinand John Paris Papers, The New Jersey Historical Society, Newark, N.J.

Smith Family Papers, Historical Society of Pennsylvania, Philadelphia, Pa.

Batinski, Michael C. *Jonathan Belcher: Colonial Governor*. Lexington: University Press of Kentucky, 1996.

———. *The New Jersey Assembly, 1738–1775: The Making of a Legislative Community*. Lanham, Md.: University Press of America, 1987.

Greiert, Steven G. "The Earl of Halifax and the Land Riots in New Jersey, 1748–1753." *New Jersey History* 99 (Spring–Summer 1981): 13–31.

McConville, Brendan. *These Daring Disturbers of the Public Peace: The Struggle for Property and Power in Early New Jersey.* Ithaca, N.Y.: Cornell University Press, 1999.

Pomfret, John E. *Colonial New Jersey: A History.* New York: Scribner's, 1973.

Purvis, Thomas L. *Proprietors, Patronage, and Paper Money: Legislative Politics in New Jersey, 1703–1776.* New Brunswick: Rutgers University Press, 1986.

Shipton, Clifford K. "Jonathan Belcher." In *Sibley's Harvard Graduates*, vol. 4, edited by Clifford K. Shipton. Cambridge, Mass.: Harvard University Press, 1933.

Francis Bernard (July? 1712–June 16, 1779) was royal governor of New Jersey for two years, actively directing the province's war effort from mid-1758 to mid-1760. The son of the Reverend Francis Bernard and Margery (Winlowe) Bernard, of Brightwell, Oxfordshire, he was baptized on July 12, 1712. He attended St. Peter's College, Westminster, and in 1729 he became a student at Christ Church, Oxford, from which he graduated in 1736 with a master of arts degree. He then turned his energy and scholarship to the practice of law. In 1741 he married Amelia Offley, whose cousin, the second Lord Barrington, became his sponsor. Besides gaining sufficient legal notice to be elected to offices in Lincoln and Boston, he edited the *Latin Odes* of Anthony Alsop, published in 1752.

This capable and ambitious man, approved as royal governor of New Jersey on January 27, 1758, arrived in Perth Amboy with his wife and four of his children on June 14. The *Pennsylvania Gazette* reported that four other children had remained in England and four had died. In the autumn of 1759 another child was born to the Bernards in New Jersey. John Adams later described Bernard as "avaricious to a most infamous degree; needy, at the same time, and having a numerous family to provide for." As the governor himself expressed it to his patron, Lord Barrington, almost a year after he arrived in New Jersey, "'till Nature sets bounds to the Number of my children, (which is not done yet) I know not how to limit my wants or desires." Various reports state that eight or ten children survived him, and it is clear that the large family contributed to his restless wish for a more rewarding position.

In two years of service Francis Bernard proved an efficient, politic, and considerate administrator. Certainly he was put to the test immediately. He arrived to find a colony with its government in semisuspension, under pressures from the royal government and the other colonies to contribute increasingly to the war against the French. The colony also suffered from an atmosphere of crisis that had spread from a rash of Indian raids on the Minisink frontier. The previous governor, Jonathan Belcher, had died at the end of August 1757. With great reluctance John Reading, president of the council, though he was seventy-three years old and somewhat lame, had been persuaded to assume his duties as interim executive. Meanwhile, the royal commanders pressed the colonial governments for substantial contributions of men and money for the next campaign against the French in Canada, and in May and June 1758 Indians raiding the region of the Minisink and upper Delaware Rivers killed two dozen colonists. Shortly before this the patrol force had been reduced from 250 to a mere 50 men, an "untimely piece of frugality" that Bernard believed had encouraged the Indians to make their first major attack on New Jersey soil.

Promptly on Bernard's arrival the forty-five-year-old governor ordered the council to meet him two days later, on Friday, June 16. At that time Justice Peter Decker and another Sussex County man arrived in Perth Amboy with the scalp of an Indian. Francis Bernard reported to the Board of Trade, "the scalp which was brought to me" was much "adorned with beads & other finery." It seems almost certain that Bernard, who is remembered for giving more conscientious attention to Indian affairs than any other colonial New Jersey governor, saw the scalp before he had seen a living New Jersey Indian. The council proposed a plan for increasing the frontier force with detachments of militia drawn on a rotating basis from different counties. Bernard adopted it immediately so that no group would have to serve long during the harvest.

After writing a lengthy report to London, the governor, accompanied by prominent residents, left Perth Amboy on Wednesday, June 21. The following day he was greeted with congratulatory statements in New Brunswick; at the College of New Jersey (later Princeton University), where he extemporaneously replied in kind to a Latin oration that one of the students presented in his honor; and in Trenton, where he inquired further about the frontier situation and sent a message to William Denny, lieutenant governor of Pennsylvania. That evening the procession arrived at Burlington, New Jersey's alternate capital, amid bonfires and bell ringing. Bernard spent Friday, June 23, receiving ceremonious greetings in Burlington. Early the following morning, when he was about to return to Perth Amboy, an urgent response from Denny took him to Philadelphia. He stayed overnight consulting with Denny and General John Forbes about rumors of Delaware Indian depredations; Forbes was preparing his march on Fort Duquesne. On Sunday, June 25, Bernard returned to Bristol and sent messages to the Munsi and Pompton Indians and to Teedyuscung as spokesman of other Delawares, inviting them with proper protocol to a conference in Burlington. On that occasion Bernard would "kindle a Council fire, and bury all the blood, that has stained our ground, deep in the earth, and make a new chain of peace." After spending the night in Trenton, Bernard, complaining about the hot weather, returned to Perth Amboy, where he was met with more rumors of Indian troubles.

The governor maintained an active pace for the rest of the summer of 1758, arranging the first phase of the Indian peace he sought and obtaining from the assembly half the augmentation he had proposed for the frontier defenses. Throughout most of October he was at Easton, attending the general treaty conference, where most Indian and British interests of the central Atlantic region were represented. This, with a purchase of claims from the Munsi and the Pomptons in the north and the establishment of a community for the Unami of central and southern New Jersey in lieu of any outstanding claims, completed his settlement of Indian troubles. Bernard's effort was successful, and peace was established on the frontier. In February 1759 the Board of Trade responded to the news of the governor's "vigorous Measures" during the summer and fall of 1758 with "Approbation" and "the greatest Satisfaction." A month later, on March 14, the general assembly addressed "the thanks of the Public" to Bernard for his settlement of Indian claims: "tho' almost one of the first Acts of your Government, and against very popular prejudices."

Bernard's other major achievement during his first year in New Jersey was to satisfy the imperial requirement for provincial contribution to the war effort without a confrontation with the popular general assembly. This he managed by persuading the Board of Trade to recommend certain alterations in his instructions concerning bills of credit; on February 10, 1759, the Privy Council approved the revisions. During the spring of 1759 Bernard described his house as "a War-office" and boasted of the excellence of the "Jersey blues," a regiment finally dispatched up the Hudson on May 21—earlier than the previous year, better equipped than ever, all volunteer, and "full to a man." The governor complimented himself to Lord Barrington, writing, "I can truly say that I have not lost a day."

Bernard then traveled to inspect the houses being constructed under the Burlington and Easton Treaty agreements for the Lenape of central and south New Jersey. He took great interest in the experimental community and named it "Brotherton." Following up the Indian dealings of 1758 with another meeting at Brotherton, he advanced a proposal (never fulfilled) to establish a provincially controlled trading post in northwest New Jersey, like the post Benjamin Franklin planned for Pennsylvania.

At this time the governor felt he had accomplished as much as the small stage of New Jersey permitted, and he wrote his sponsor about his desire to resolve the conflicts in Pennsylvania or in some other, larger, more remunerative governorship. While he enjoyed the "Health & Beauty" of New Jersey and its inhabitants' "favorable Opinion" of him, he wanted larger problems to solve and larger rewards. As part of a general rearrangement of colonial governors Bernard was transferred to Massachusetts in the autumn of 1759, resolving his boredom and satisfying his desire for promotion. He did not move at once, however. The packet ship was delayed three months, and therefore he did not receive the November 14, 1759, letter informing him of the changes until mid-February 1760; and following that, he awaited his replacement, Thomas Boone. In April he made a trip to New England to assess the prospects of making and saving money as the governor of Massachusetts. Though he assured his patron that he would leave New Jersey "with regret" and praised "the pleasantness" of Perth Amboy, he complained that it was "wholly secluded from refined conversation & the amusements that arise from letters arts & sciences," and so looked forward to Boston.

Comments after Thomas Boone's arrival and proclamation as governor continued to indicate warm feelings toward Francis Bernard. The officials of Middlesex County, while greeting his successor, referred to Bernard as one "whose inclinations as well as Abilities seemed to be studiously employed in promoting every plausible Scheme for the Welfare and Prosperity of the Province," and Boone replied, "I am too well appriz'd of the disadvantageous Light I must appear in, to aim at a Competition with my deservedly esteemed Predecessor in any Thing but Zeal for his Majesty's Service, and Ardour for the Prosperity of his People."

Bernard's commission as governor of Massachusetts arrived at the beginning of July 1760, but he delayed several more weeks, deciding to "tarry at Perth Amboy" until a warship came to take him. He finally arrived in Boston in appropriate style on August 2.

Though Bernard's nine years in Massachusetts began well, they ended on a different note: a mob in New York burned him in effigy in November 1768, and the public in Boston rejoiced when he finally left on August 1, 1769, officially for consultation with the British government. A Massachusetts writer said that Bernard had "a peculiar knack for making mountains out of mole hills, and idle chitchat, treason." It is almost as though the Francis Bernard who governed Massachusetts shortly before the Revolution and the well-liked Bernard who led New Jersey during the French and Indian War were different men. Bernard had arrived in New Jersey at the age of forty-five and had waged vigorous war on the French and made peace with the Delawares. At the age of fifty-seven he returned to England, where he was knighted for his troubles. During the remaining ten years of his life he held some pensions but no positions of authority. He was honored in 1772 with the degree of doctor of civil law from Oxford University, and he seems to have lived mostly in retirement in the country. He died at Aylesbury on June 16, 1779.

In American history Francis Bernard is usually described as the unpopular royal governor of prerevolutionary Massachusetts, but in New Jersey he should be remembered as a skillful, energetic, successful, and well-liked executive who managed the colony's part in prosecuting the war with the French. He also maintained a happy relationship with the legislature despite potential conflict over money issues, and he avoided partisanship and entanglement in local politics. Perhaps most important of all, he was the only governor of New Jersey in nearly three centuries to show much concern for the relationship between native North Americans and Euro-Americans. Bernard took decisive military measures to improve the Minisink defenses, but he understood that the best defense against frontier raids was a peace founded on an informed Indian policy that sought to resolve disputes. Other, larger forces made his program more successful than it might have been in isolation, but it is worth noting that after his departure the Indians of New Jersey were again forgotten.

EDWARD MCM. LARRABEE

Bernard, Francis. *Select Letters on the Trade and Government of America; and the Principles of Law and Polity, Applied to the American Colonies.* London: W. Bowyer and J. Nichols, 1774.

Channing, Edward, and Archibald Cary Coolidge, eds. *The Barrington-Bernard Correspondence and Illustrative Matter, 1760–1770.* Cambridge, Mass.: Harvard University Press, 1912.

Higgins, Sophia. *The Bernards of Abington and Nether Winchendon: A Family History.* London: Longmans, Green, 1903.

Letters to the Right Honourable the Earl of Hillsborough from Governor Bernard, General Gage, and the Honourable His Majesty's Council for the Province of Massachusetts-Bay, The. Boston: Edes and Gill, 1769.

Nicholson, Colin. *The "Infamous Governor": Francis Bernard and the Origins of the American Revolution.* Boston: Northeastern University Press, 2001.

Thomas Boone (ca. 1730–1812) was one of many colonial governors who suddenly burst into the public arena only to fade quickly into historical oblivion. Like most men appointed to governorships solely through patronage, Boone was virtually assured by administrative inexperience and political naiveté of a brief—and stormy—gubernatorial career. He was born to Charles and Elizabeth (Garth) Boone at Lee Place in Kent, England, in either 1730 or 1731 (he graduated from college in March 1746 at age fifteen). His was a prominent family—the Boones of Devonshire—which not only enjoyed great wealth and social position but also exercised considerable political influence. There had almost always been a Boone in Westminster since his great-grandfather Thomas Boone sat as a member of Parliament from 1646 to 1656. His father was the member of Parliament for Ludgershall (1727–34) and a director of both the East India Company and the Bank of England. His half brother Daniel served in Parliament for twenty years (1741–61) and his brother Charles, Jr., for almost forty (1757–96). Other members of the family accumulated fortunes as merchants and shippers.

Boone received a traditional gentleman's education at Eton and at Trinity College, Cambridge. At some undetermined time he inherited from his cousin Margaret Colleton a two-thousand-acre rice and livestock plantation in South Carolina known as Mepshoo. In 1751, soon after his twenty-first birthday, he journeyed to South Carolina to take over another inheritance, "Boone's Barony," a 6,815-acre estate of three rice plantations on the Pon-Pon

River, bequeathed to him and his brother Charles by the widow of their uncle Joseph Boone. He returned to England two years later but in 1758 again sailed for Carolina to establish permanent residence.

Thomas Boone's life as a country gentleman abruptly ended late in 1759. On November 14 the Board of Trade recommended his appointment to succeed Francis Bernard as governor of New Jersey, and George III approved thirteen days later. The announcement surprised politicians on either side of the Atlantic—and perhaps Boone himself—because he had previously neither held any government post nor been active in politics. The appointment undoubtedly stemmed from family connections in British political circles. In addition to having two brothers in Parliament, Boone was closely related to the influential Garth and Colleton clans. His uncle John Garth (member of Parliament for Devizes, 1740–64) and his cousin James Edward Colleton (M.P. for Lostwithiel, 1747–68) were staunch allies of the powerful prime minister, the Duke of Newcastle. (In part because of an obligation to John Garth, Boone in 1762 appointed Garth's son, Charles, to the post of colonial agent for South Carolina.)

Such an unusual elevation of a political novice, coupled with the interests of the parties involved, suggests that the New Jersey assignment was intended as a prelude to advancement to the more prestigious and lucrative South Carolina governorship. Boone had no association with New Jersey but was well placed in Carolina society. His uncle Joseph, who had established the American branch of the family in South Carolina in 1694 at the age of seventeen, had become a wealthy planter and a prominent member of the antiproprietary faction, providing his nephew with important social and political connections. Boone was related through his mother to Sir John Colleton, one of the original founders of the colony, whose numerous descendants were also prominent. With his pedigree, his education, and his ties in London and Charleston, he was an ideal candidate for the position. Although there is no evidence that Boone actively sought the Carolina governorship, his transfer at the first opportunity, after less than a year in New Jersey, was probably both anticipated and welcomed.

Whatever the circumstances of his appointment, Thomas Boone took over the New Jersey government amid frustrating delays, which foreshadowed the course of his administration. Though he received official notification of his appointment in mid-February 1760, he remained in Charleston until the end of March awaiting his instructions (dated January 14) and commission (dated February 13). On arriving in New York City in early April, he learned that his credentials were still in transit, and he did not receive them until early July. He hastened to Perth Amboy and took the oath of the chief executive on July 4, some eight months after his appointment. Then, at the request of some assemblymen, he postponed calling the legislature; he therefore did not meet with the general assembly until October 30, almost a year after being named governor. On April 14, 1761, less than six months after first meeting with the assembly, he was named governor of South Carolina.

New to both government service and the province of New Jersey, Boone made "caution" and "prudence" the watchwords of his administration. He consistently declined to take positions on controversial issues such as the border dispute between New York and New Jersey and the struggle between Robert Hunter Morris and Nathaniel Jones for the chief justiceship. And, while firm in support of royal prerogatives and imperial regulations, he refused to challenge provincial political leaders and interests directly. Consequently, his meetings with the assembly were amicable as well as productive, and no serious partisan contentions troubled New Jersey politics during his tenure. Although his term was generally uneventful, several personal achievements serve as standards with which to evaluate his administration.

His first meeting with the assembly, the twenty-first session of the nineteenth assembly, was especially noteworthy. Between October 29 and December 5—the longest legislative session in nine years—the assembly enacted largely routine legislation. But mainly through Boone's efforts the session produced two long-sought-after laws, one providing for the preservation of public records and one regulating the maintenance of roads and bridges. These were no mean accomplishments for a novice governor, but Boone did more: he secured the first two-year government appropriations bill since 1749 and the allocation of a salary for the chief justice without the traditional prior naming of the recipient, which was being delayed by the Morris-Jones controversy. And at the close of the session Boone agreed to the legislators' request for a general election, the first opportunity for Jerseymen to elect representatives in seven years.

The twentieth assembly, which convened on March 27, 1761, proved more troublesome for Boone. The problem was money. The assembly resisted the governor's request for additional tax revenue; it also balked at filling the quota of 666 soldiers requisitioned by General Jeffrey Amherst, commander in chief of the British army in North America, for the final campaign of the Seven Years' War against the French and Indians. After considerable lobbying, Boone increased the assembly's contribution on both scores—a fact he boastfully reported to the Board of Trade.

Just as Boone was beginning to become settled in the New Jersey government, his superiors in London decided to transfer him. Acting on a March 17 recommendation from the Board of Trade, the king on April 14 named Boone governor of South Carolina and Josiah Hardy his replacement in New Jersey. From April through October Boone served as a lame-duck governor, transacting no major public business, content to preside perfunctorily while awaiting Hardy's arrival. Those long months demonstrated Boone's devotion to duty. Although authorized to return to England to take care of private business before assuming the South Carolina government, he remained in New Jersey: "to deliver this Government to my Successor in its Present State of Harmony." Hardy arrived on October 29; after seeing him properly installed in office, Boone settled his personal affairs and sailed for Charleston on December 3.

Too brief to have a measurable impact on New Jersey political affairs, Boone's tenure was long enough to reveal his essential qualities as governor. As chief magistrate he exhibited a reserved manner and an accommodating style of politics. But he could be forceful if necessary, as when he suspended Edward Antill from the legislative council for nonattendance or insisted that the assembly increase its troop levy. A genuine concern about the public welfare is evident in his legislative proposals, his relinquishing a share of a forfeiture to facilitate the condemnation of a smuggling vessel, and his declining leave to remain at the head of government until the transfer of governors.

Above all he was a dedicated civil servant who placed the strict performance of duty above personal and partisan interest. The farewell address delivered to him by the Corporation of Perth Amboy succinctly explains the wide popularity and esteem he enjoyed among Jerseymen: "No selfish or lucrative schemes have appeared in your conduct, or sullied your administration; on the contrary, all your measures have been dictated by generous and benevolent principles, and your Excellency in public life has maintained that good character you so justly and universally acquired in private." In short, Boone was a popular and relatively successful governor in New Jersey because of his genial disposition and reputation for honesty rather than his political acumen and administrative ability.

Ironically, Boone's unflagging adherence to principle and his political impartiality eventually destroyed his gubernatorial career. Upon taking the New Jersey governorship, he pledged that he would "glory in exercising the utmost Impartiality." Many New Jersey politicos, however, considered "impartiality" naive instead of virtuous. That certainly was the opinion of Charles Read, leader of the council and longtime power behind governors, who was unable to deal with Boone on "intimate and friendly terms." In March 1761 a government officer scrawled in Latin on a wall in Perth Amboy, "Long live & flourish the celebrated Boone, who hath neither Generosity, Liberality nor Equity." Aaron Leaming, veteran assemblyman from Cape May, thought the doggerel gave Boone "a very wrong Character." To Leaming, Boone was "a wise knowing Just Governor who had no prime minister & that was the reason the Jersey Courtiers did not Love him."

Boone's political epitaph had been prophesied by the legislative council of New Jersey when, in welcoming him as governor, it had noted that he was a novice in politics—"a Stranger to the low Views and little Arts." Even had Boone remained in New Jersey, where politics were diffuse and local, his zealousness, inflexibility, and determination to reside as "a governor without a prime minister" would eventually have transformed the political skirmishes that appeared in the spring of 1761 into full-scale partisan conflicts.

That Thomas Boone simply was not a politician was quickly demonstrated by his stormy tenure in South Carolina.

Despite family ties and a salary nearly double what he had received in New Jersey, Boone took the South Carolina governorship with some trepidation. In addition to persistent warfare with the Cherokee on the frontier, there was an increasingly bitter conflict between the popularly elected Commons House of Assembly and the royally appointed council. Partly because of the political climate, Thomas Pownall, who in 1760 had been named to succeed William Henry Lyttleton as governor, had refused to take the office; for two years Lieutenant Governor William Bull II had served as acting governor.

Boone's apprehensions proved correct, for he became embroiled in controversy almost immediately after his arrival in South Carolina on December 22, 1761. He was less a victim of partisan machinations than of his own political ineptness. In sharp contrast to his behavior in New Jersey, Boone quickly asserted his authority in Carolina. Because he was a "clumsy tactician," his zealous defense of crown prerogatives and his inflexibility on major issues compounded routine problems and created unnecessary political strife.

He antagonized many of the interested parties in several matters connected with the French and Indian War, and he became embroiled in a territorial controversy with the governor of Georgia and the Board of Trade. More damaging were his efforts to reduce the authority of the Commons House of Assembly by refusing the house certain traditional prerogatives. Though technically correct, he was flying in the face of established practice, and therefore he appeared to be infringing on the rights and privileges of the assembly. When in September 1762 he voided the election of Assemblyman Christopher Gadsden on a minor technicality, challenging the constitutional right of the assembly to determine the validity of legislative elections, the dispute came to a head. The controversy brought public business to a halt for eighteen months, because the assembly refused to heed the governor's summonses to hold sessions. Boone sailed for England on May 11, 1764, to present the case to the Board of Trade. On July 16 the board announced its verdict: while criticizing the commons house for refusing to conduct business, it condemned Boone for handling the matter "with more Zeal than prudence" and with "a degree of Passion and Resentment inconsistent with good Policy, and unsuitable to the dignity of his Situation"; he was guilty of "Conduct highly deserving his Majestys Royal displeasure."

Realizing that this formal censure would prevent him from serving effectively as governor, Thomas Boone never returned to South Carolina. William Bull once again became acting governor, and in 1766 Lord Charles Greville Montagu was named to replace Boone. Within the brief span of four years a gubernatorial career which had begun with promise in New Jersey ended in ignominy in South Carolina.

Little is known about Thomas Boone after his return to England. He married a wealthy widow, Sarah Ann Tattnall Peronneau, but the date of the marriage is unknown; the evidence suggests that he began courting her shortly after becoming governor of South Carolina, that she accompanied him to England in 1764, and that they were finally married in 1771. He lobbied for repeal of the Stamp Act and successfully petitioned for the payment of £1,250 in salary the commons house had withheld. On December 5, 1769, he again entered government service, this time as a customs commissioner with an annual salary of £1,000. Because of his American ties, he served with William Bull as corepresentative for South Carolina on the Board of Loyalist Agents, which sought compensation for refugees in England after the Revolution. His South Carolina property was confiscated in 1782; he claimed £41,207.4.4 in compensation from the British government but was granted only £22,533.8.0. In September 1805 he retired from the customs service and removed to the seclusion of his ancestral home, Lee Place in Kent. His wife died in April 1812; he died five months later, on September 25, 1812.

LARRY R. GERLACH

Batinski, Michael C. *The New Jersey Assembly, 1738–1775: The Making of a Legislative Community*. Lanham, Md.: University Press of America, 1987.

Namier, Lewis. "Charles Garth and His Connexions." *English Historical Review* 54 (July 1939): 443–70.

Josiah Hardy (1715?–1790) is one of New Jersey's most obscure governors. No information survives about his early life, his education, or his primary means of livelihood. He was born into a distinguished English family, which became even more prominent as Josiah reached adulthood. His father, Sir Charles Hardy (1680?–1744), worked his way through the highest ranks in the royal navy, earning peerage status and eventually becoming a vice admiral as well as a lord commissioner of the admiralty. Sir Charles and his wife, Elizabeth Burchett, had six children, among them Josiah, the eldest son, and Sir Charles (1716?–1780), who for a brief time in the 1750s, during an interlude in a distinguished naval career, served as royal governor of New York.

Family connections may have been a factor in Hardy's appointment to the New Jersey governorship. Whatever the source of influence, the Privy Council approved the Board of Trade's March 1761 recommendation that Hardy "be appointed Captain General and Governor in Chief of His Majesty's Province of New Jersey in the room of Thomas Boone Esq." Crossing the Atlantic Ocean on a ship that also carried William Alexander, better known as the aspirant to the title of earl of Stirling, Hardy and his family arrived in New York during late October 1761. The family then traveled to Perth Amboy, where Hardy published his commission. The New Jersey citizenry, although it had been spun around on a whirligig of changing governors of late, seemed pleased with the Hardys. The governor gained a reputation for promptness, attentiveness, and openness.

Knowing very little about New Jersey, Hardy willingly listened to ideas and suggestions about proper provincial administration. The only problem was that he too willingly took the advice of a small, powerful group of men who were both gubernatorial councilors and East Jersey proprietors. These men, including William Alexander and Robert Hunter Morris, wanted a pliable head of state who would support their personal interests, which involved their high provincial offices and their proprietary land claims (less well-placed citizens were still challenging East Jersey proprietary rights, sometimes through rioting). Indeed, Hardy's Atlantic crossing with Alexander may have been fatal in terms of his governorship.

Throughout Hardy's term he listened attentively to the East Jersey proprietary group, especially when making appointments to important offices. As the new governor stated in July 1762, he could not find "Persons from the Western division" who were "properly qualify'd for so important a trust" as serving on the council. Even though his instructions called for balanced council representation between eastern and western leaders, all of his nominees were men with close ties to the East Jersey group. In listening to the Morris-Alexander coterie, indeed favoring them, the new governor made one unredeemable mistake. In December 1761 he accepted "the unanimous advice of His Majesty's Council" and "renew'd the Chief Justice Robert Hunter Morris and the second and third Judges Commission" with tenure during good behavior. The East Jersey proprietary group controlled attendance at that meeting.

Hardy's instructions specifically forbade any "good-behavior" appointments. Officeholding tenure was to be limited to the "King's pleasure," even though a number of high-level provincial judges in various provinces had been appointed with good-behavior terms in previous years. The latter type of commission had become standard in England after the Glorious Revolution of 1688–89, during which time parliamentary leaders constrained crown prerogatives in general and guaranteed in particular that judges would be independent of willful monarchs. Englishmen considered good-behavior commissions to be one hallmark of the preservation of political rights and liberties because judges dependent on the crown for continuation in office could always be corrupted in judicial decision making. Despite what had become well-established English practice, home government leaders were not content with the de facto extension of the same prerogative to the colonies, particularly because some good-behavior judges had been contentious and obstinate with royal officials in America yet virtually unremovable from office.

In this context Hardy compounded his blunder by reappointing Robert Hunter Morris, who had become an extremely obnoxious figure to Board of Trade officials during a protracted controversy over who was the legitimate

New Jersey chief justice. In violating his written instructions and offering Morris a good-behavior commission, Hardy convinced the Board of Trade that he was too weak to control special provincial interests while upholding crown prerogatives and imperial policies. Equally significant, the perceived willfulness of men like Morris was symptomatic and symbolic to crown officials; home government leaders more and more were becoming persuaded that there must be a new assertion, a tightening, of imperial authority over the American colonies. The Seven Years' War (called the French and Indian War in the provinces) so consumed leaders in England that it delayed the thrust, but it further primed British officials for the clamping-down process. During the Seven Years' War, for instance, home ministers were particularly appalled by the extensive amount of illegal provincial trade being conducted with the French enemy. In late 1761 the war was nearing its end; if there were to be effective steps toward greater imperial control, then men like Hardy (those who would countenance, even succumb to local pressures) had to be taught that crown prerogatives could not be compromised, even if they had been compromised in the past. The decision to remove Hardy was an early indicator of the move toward tighter imperial administration, part of a pattern that would become much clearer after hostilities ended in 1763.

Hardy sent letters to England in January 1762 explaining why he had violated his instructions. He thought a delay in reappointing the judges would "occasion great inconveniences and be attended with consequences that might prove very prejudicial in carrying on his Majesty's Service, and likewise much disturb the publick peace." He asked for further advice. At the same time the Privy Council was sending out a new general instruction reminding all governors that they were "to take particular care in all Commissions . . . granted to the said Chief Judges or other Justices, . . . that the said Commissions are granted during Pleasure only, agreeable to what has been the Ancient Practice and Usage in [the] Colonies."

The Privy Council's rationale was both bold and specious. Rather than just admit that Americans, as subordinate members of the empire, were not to have the same rights and privileges as home citizens, the council justified itself by arguing that there were not enough qualified provincial citizens who could hold high judicial office. The low quality of American judges, they claimed, proved that. Thus, removal at the crown's pleasure would be necessary until more suitable, well-educated citizens became available as the colonies continued to grow and develop. In reality an independent American judiciary was a threat to royal prerogatives; it could seriously hinder programs for bringing provincials more in line with imperial goals.

Governor Hardy could find no way to placate his superiors. As soon as he received the general instruction, he persuaded Morris and the other judges to take "during-pleasure" commissions. But the Board of Trade was already acting; it recommended in March 1762 that Hardy be removed from office for "so premeditated and unprecedented an Act of disobedience" and "as a necessary example to deter others in the same situation from like Acts of Disobedience" to the king's "just Rights and Authority in the Colonies." Following through, the Privy Council, in August 1762, moved to appoint William Franklin in Hardy's stead. A month later a formal letter went to Hardy advising him of his dismissal.

Josiah Hardy was an early victim of what developed into a major new assertion of imperial authority. That assertion eventually would become a primary factor in precipitating the American Revolution. For Hardy in 1762 it meant that he would never have the opportunity to prove his capabilities, although the sources reveal good working relations with the assembly and consistent efforts to deal with such vexing issues as persuading New Jerseyans to fill their manpower quotas during the war. Once he had learned his fate, Hardy wrote futilely that he could not comprehend what the objections to his conduct were: "as I never had the honour to see the Boards representation so could have no opportunity of offering any thing in my own justification; however I humbly submit to His Majesty's Commands, but I can with the greatest truth affirm that every step I have taken in the administration of this Government has been to promote His Majesty's Service and the welfare of the people committed to my care." He graciously turned the government over to William Franklin when the two met in New Brunswick late in February 1763. Accepting official provincial statements of praise for his "just and mild administration," Hardy sailed with his family for England in September 1763. His controlled acquiescence in dismissal no doubt helped him gain another office, that of consul to Cadiz. Beyond that nothing is known about Josiah Hardy, a man caught for a moment in countervailing forces that were setting the stage for the American Revolution.

JAMES KIRBY MARTIN

Batinski, Michael C. *The New Jersey Assembly, 1738–1775: The Making of a Legislative Community*. Lanham, Md.: University Press of America, 1987.

Fisher, Edgar Jacob. *New Jersey as a Royal Province, 1738 to 1776*. New York: Columbia University, 1911.

Kemmerer, Donald L. *Path to Freedom: The Struggle for Self-Government in Colonial New Jersey, 1703–1776*. Princeton: Princeton University Press, 1940.

Nadelhaft, J. R. "Politics and the Judicial Tenure Fight in Colonial New Jersey." *William and Mary Quarterly* 28 (January 1971): 46–63.

William Franklin
Emmet Collection, Miriam and Ira D. Wallach
Division of Art, Prints and Photographs,
The New York Public Library, Astor, Lenox
and Tilden Foundations; courtesy New York
Public Library

William Franklin (1730?–November 16, 1813) was the last royal governor of New Jersey. An able servant of both the colony and the crown during the tumultuous years 1763–76, he ranks as the best of New Jersey's colonial governors and one of the finest chief executives in the history of the state. William was born in Philadelphia in late 1730 or early 1731 to Benjamin Franklin and an unidentified Pennsylvania woman; it is unlikely that Deborah Read Rogers, whom Benjamin took as a common-law wife on September 1, 1730, was his natural mother. The cloud of an illegitimate birth and the shadow of a father who was a living legend threatened to eclipse William throughout his life.

William spent the years of his childhood and youth in considerable pain as well as great joy. He was constantly confronted by his bastard status and the hostility of Deborah Franklin, who openly favored her own children, Francis Folger (1732–36) and Sarah (1742–1808).

But America's largest city held countless fascinations for a young boy and much excitement in the print shop and retail store that occupied the ground floor of the Franklin home. Father and son were especially close. Young "Billy," as he was called by the family, grew up helping Benjamin operate the printing presses and stock and sell merchandise. He also listened to conversations between his father and the parade of callers at the house and assisted Benjamin with a variety of scientific experiments.

William advanced toward adulthood under the careful supervision of "Poor Richard." After a brief stint during King George's War (1740–48) as an ensign in a Pennsylvania company sent to Albany in 1746 to fight the French and a trip to the Ohio country in 1748 as an assistant to the Indian trader Conrad Weiser, he settled down in Philadelphia with no higher interests than parties and women. But the elder Franklin was determined to pass on to his firstborn more than an interest in science and land speculation. Through Benjamin's influence William became clerk of the Pennsylvania assembly (1751), postmaster of Philadelphia (1753), and comptroller of the postal system in the northern colonies (1754). Both men joined the Masonic order and later shared involvement in several unsuccessful land-speculation schemes in western New York and the Ohio country, particularly the Vandalia Company, which claimed over one million acres in "Indiana." In the early stages

of the French and Indian War (1754–63) William assisted Benjamin in out-
fitting General Edward Braddock's abortive campaign against the French
(1755) and organizing the colony's military defenses (1756). He also began to
study law with his father's associate Joseph Galloway. And he accompanied
Benjamin to England in 1757 as representative of the Pennsylvania assembly
in its dispute with the Penn family over the taxation of proprietary lands.

William stayed for six years in England, where he not only participated
in the negotiations with the Penns and the crown but also received further
legal training at the Middle Temple (1757). Admitted to the bar as a practic-
ing attorney in 1758, he also became acquainted with Benjamin's circle of
prominent scientists and politicians, toured Britain and western Europe,
and received an honorary master of arts degree from Oxford (1762). There,
too, occurred three of the most important events in his life. Some time in
1760 he sired an illegitimate son, William Temple, whose mother's identity
is unknown. On September 4, 1762, he married Elizabeth Downes, a London
socialite with important West Indian family connections. Five days later he
was sworn in as the new governor of New Jersey.

The unexpected selection of William Franklin to succeed Josiah Hardy as
the head of the New Jersey government created a stir in both Britain and
America. Some doubted his fitness for the post since he had had no previous executive experience; others were disturbed by his reputation as a play-
boy and by his illegitimacy; and all, including William himself, knew that he
owed the position solely to Benjamin's influence with the ministry in London. On the other hand the appointment was not unreasonable. William had
acquired some legislative experience in Pennsylvania and had witnessed
firsthand the operations of provincial and imperial government. Moreover
he was knowledgeable about military affairs and partisan politics, had influential friends on both sides of the Atlantic, and was familiar with the conditions and problems of the Middle Colonies. On balance he was better qualified for the office than most men named to colonial governorships.

Upon arriving in New Jersey in February 1763, William proved his detractors wrong. From his initial introductory tour of the province until the outbreak of the Revolution in 1775 he was a strong, effective, and enormously
popular chief executive. He moved easily and comfortably in New Jersey
social circles, promoted economic programs designed to increase the prosperity of the province, served as an advocate for provincial interests with
superiors in London, and defended the colony and its legislature against
what he considered to be unwise policies and unwarranted criticisms from
imperial authorities. A determined spokesman for the people of New Jersey,
he was also a dedicated representative of the crown who sought to carry
out the instructions of the king and Parliament as well as the duties of his
office with diligence, dignity, and dispatch. Commanding a nearly universal
respect for his administrative abilities and possessing a keen political sense,
he was able to exercise firm control of the provincial government; he was,

perhaps, the single most influential political figure to emerge in colonial New Jersey. Although at times his arrogance, fiery temper, and stubbornness needlessly complicated relations with the assembly, Franklin enjoyed a degree of popularity and success during his long term matched by few, if any, of the other royal governors in North America.

Like his counterparts in the other seven crown colonies, Franklin faced the difficult task of attempting to reconcile the sometimes conflicting expectations and demands of the mother country and the province. In general he performed to the satisfaction of both constituencies, primarily because of the unstructured nature of New Jersey politics and his adept avoidance of the taint of corruption and partisanship that undermined the credibility of many governors. However, the new administrative programs for America instituted by Parliament after the conclusion of the French and Indian War in 1763 ultimately destroyed the First British Empire as well as the political career of William Franklin.

The Stamp Act crisis of 1765–66 taught Franklin the political lessons that would guide his conduct during the remainder of the prerevolutionary decade. While doubting the wisdom of Britain's attempt to raise American revenue by imposing taxes on a variety of colonial publications and legal documents, he granted Parliament's authority to do so and thus strove to implement the statute. Since Jerseymen had not actively opposed earlier attempts to tighten imperial control, such as the Currency and Sugar Acts of 1764 and various revisions in the customs service, the fury of the protest against the Stamp Act caught Franklin by surprise. Protests by legal and extralegal organizations, economic sanctions, civil disobedience, and threats of popular violence thwarted his efforts to enforce the measure. Realizing the impossibility of the task, he was content to ignore the statute and await its eventual repeal. Never again would the governor underestimate the determination of Jerseymen to oppose what they deemed unconstitutional actions and unwarranted encroachments into provincial affairs by imperial authorities, the impact of events occurring in other colonies (especially New York and Pennsylvania) on events in New Jersey, or the difficulty of upholding unpopular imperial policies without firm support from London or adequate military power in the province.

As Anglo-American relations deteriorated, Franklin's political influence in New Jersey diminished. He remained a firm defender of royal authority but increasingly found himself in sympathy with the colonial position and dubious of the ability of politicians in England to devise effective programs for America. Thus he championed the much-needed currency legislation that the legislature enacted despite its repeated disallowance by the British Privy Council, criticized the enactment of the import taxes known as the Townshend duties, and refrained from taking public steps to counter the popular protest against the Townshend Acts (1767), the Tea Act (1773), or the Coercive Acts (1774). Consequently, some imperial officials began to question his performance as governor, and there were periodic rumors of his dismissal. At the same time he came under increased attack from the New Jersey Assembly, aimed not so much at the man as at his position as chief representative of the crown. From 1766 to 1770 annual battles over appropriations to supply royal troops stationed in the colony, periodic disagreements over the prerogatives of the executive and legislative branches of government, and a bitter dispute over the appointment of the provincial treasurers greatly diminished his once pervasive power.

When Britons and Americans took to the battlefield to resolve their disagreements in the aftermath of Lexington and Concord, William Franklin, like all Americans, faced a crucial decision. Yet the allegiance of the native-born American was never in doubt. His years in the governor's mansion had convinced him that under no circumstances could a civil society tolerate disrespect for government and disregard of laws. By temperament and inclination he found himself committed to the established order and the social elite; to his mind the protest-independence movement was the work of a willful minority of malcontents and radicals who did not enjoy the support of the populace at large. Perhaps, too, he rejected the rebellion in a subconscious attempt to establish personal independence from his father, who dreamed of a sovereign American empire. The relationship between the two men had cooled considerably after Benjamin Franklin left in 1764 for an eleven-year stay in England; the growing rebellion drove them further apart; and after a heated argument in November 1775 they went their separate political ways, not to meet again until after the Revolutionary War. Whatever William Franklin's motivation, he did not betray the trust given him by his king and country.

Whereas other royal governors had gone into exile or had ceased to discharge their duties by the fall of 1775, William Franklin worked actively to stem the tide of revolution. He convened the general assembly in November and, capitalizing on the moderation of New Jersey and his still potent power of persuasion, obtained assembly resolutions disavowing independence and calling for reconciliation with Great Britain. Knowing that the rebels were inspecting the mails, he nonetheless sent a steady stream of intelligence to London concerning the development of the rebellion. On January 8, 1776, after one such dispatch fell into the hands of the rebel colonel William Alexander (Lord Stirling), the governor found his Perth Amboy home surrounded by an armed detachment of militia. On the tenth he was taken into custody, but he was released the same day when cooler heads prevailed. Thereafter he remained in seclusion but maintained correspondence with superiors in England. He boldly issued a call on May 30 for the legislature to convene the following month, and on June 15 the Provincial Congress ordered his arrest. Refusing to accept an offer of parole, he was brought before the rebel conclave on June 21 and, at the direction of the Continental Congress, was sent under guard to Connecticut on June 26.

The former royal governor of New Jersey, now a prisoner of the independent United States, arrived in Lebanon, Connecticut, on July 4. After signing a parole tendered by the rebel governor Jonathan Trumbull, he was sent first to Wallingford, then to East Windsor, and finally in October to Middletown. He was permitted freedom of movement and correspondence so long as he did not leave town or do anything to hamper the American cause. In April he was imprisoned in the Litchfield town jail for issuing pardons to Connecticut and New Jersey Loyalists in violation of his parole. There he chafed at the close confinement and grew bitter as he tallied the price of his loyalty. He became despondent on learning of his wife's death on July 28 and deeply resented the fact that his father (who had been more of a father than grandfather to Temple) had taken his son to France. His depression eased and his health improved measurably when, in December, Governor Trumbull permitted his transfer to a private residence in East Windsor; his spirits soared when, in October 1778, he was exchanged for John McKinly, the former governor of Delaware.

William Franklin entered British-occupied New York City on October 31, bent on seeking revenge. For the next four years he devoted his time and energy to suppressing the rebellion. He enlisted propagandists to write on behalf of the crown; aided Captain John André in the intelligence operations of the Secret Service; organized in December 1778 the "Refugee Club" (which conducted unofficial military raids and intelligence operations in Connecticut and New Jersey); devised a plan for the military defense of the city (1780); was a member of the civilian advisory council created by the military in 1779; and served on the Council to the Commissioners for Restoring Peace, established in 1780. In January 1781, when he was named president of the board of directors of the Associated Loyalists, he became responsible for directing destructive raids against the state of New Jersey. He once again became disconsolate as the war wound to an end after the American victory over Cornwallis at Yorktown in September 1781; on September 18, 1782, twenty years to the month after his appointment as the governor of New Jersey, William Franklin sailed for England.

Franklin spent the remainder of his life in exile. During the first seven years he testified on behalf of numerous Loyalist refugees in their efforts to receive compensation from the British government for losses sustained because of the Revolution; he himself received in March 1788 an annual pension of £800 and a meager award of £1,800 for the £48,245.4.4 he claimed in lost property and income. But he never received a position in government or attained the place in society that he had known before the Revolution.

Although his public career had ended, the personal tragedies that marred his private life continued. He initiated contact with his father in 1784, hoping to heal old wounds, but when the two men met a year later for the last time, Benjamin was interested only in arranging for Temple to acquire William's lands in America for a paltry sum. In 1790, having written William out of his will, Benjamin carried his bitterness toward his son to the grave. William finally got the chance to come to know his own son when Temple came to England in 1792, but relations between them were so strained that Temple left angrily for Paris in 1798. They never saw each other again. Even William's blissful marriage to Mary D'Evelin in 1788 ended in sorrow; she became ill in 1808, was bedridden in 1810, and then lapsed into insanity before her death in 1811. The only lasting bright spot in William's life in exile was Temple's daughter, Ellen Franklin, born out of wedlock in 1798 to Mary's sister-in-law, Ellen. William raised the child as if she were his own daughter, and she in turn loved and cared for him until his death on November 13, 1813.

LARRY R. GERLACH

Batinski, Michael C. *The New Jersey Assembly, 1738–1775: The Making of a Legislative Community*. Lanham, Md.: University Press of America, 1987.

Fennelly, Catherine. "William Franklin of New Jersey." *William and Mary Quarterly* 6 (1949): 361–82.

Gerlach, Larry R. *Prologue to Independence: New Jersey in the Coming of the American Revolution*. New Brunswick: Rutgers University Press, 1975.

———. *William Franklin: New Jersey's Last Royal Governor*. Trenton: New Jersey Historical Commission, 1975.

Mariboe, William H. "The Life of William Franklin, 1730(31)–1813: *Pro Rege et Patria*." Ph.D. dissertation, University of Pennsylvania, 1962.

Skemp, Sheila. *William Franklin: Son of a Patriot, Servant of a King*. New York: Oxford University Press, 1990.

Whitehead, William A. "Biographical Sketch of William Franklin, Governor of New Jersey from 1763 to 1776." *Proceedings of the New Jersey Historical Society* 3 (1848): 137–59.

The Constitution of 1776

William Livingston (November 30, 1723–
July 25, 1790) was a son of Philip Livingston,
second lord of Livingston Manor in the colony of New York, and Catrina Van Brugh. William spent his childhood in Albany. He graduated from Yale College in 1741 and began
to study law under the supervision of James
Alexander and William Smith, Sr. Although
he was a Presbyterian, in 1747 William married Susannah French of New Brunswick at
the Dutch church in Acquackanonk. Their
marriage produced thirteen children, several
of whom died young.

A man of broad intellectual interests, William Livingston not only learned the intri-
cacies of the law but also grounded himself
thoroughly in the arts, philosophy, and American education. As a member of the powerful
Livingston family he was able to use his natural talent and his kinship with New York's
elite to assume a major role in the cultural
and social life of the colony. By 1770 William
Livingston had made an imprint on the poli-

William Livingston
Print Collection, Miriam and Ira D. Wallach
Division of Art, Prints and Photographs,
The New York Public Library, Astor, Lenox
and Tilden Foundations; courtesy New York
Public Library

tics of New York, partly because of his writings in the political and religious
controversy over the role of the Anglican church in America. Livingston was
a polemicist best known for his pungent prose in the *Independent Reflector*
and in such essays as "Primitive Whig" and "Watch Tower." In politics he
usually functioned as a manager; he became titular leader of a trio that also
included John Morin Scott and William Smith, Jr., in protracted battles with
the De Lancey family and its lieutenants. From 1758 to 1768 the "New York
Triumvirate" controlled the New York Assembly.

On April 13, 1772, Livingston severed his ties with the province of New
York and moved to Elizabethtown, New Jersey. His reasons for removing
to New Jersey and withdrawing from the New York political scene are not

fully known, but he had often stated his desire to enjoy a "solitary and philo-
sophic retreat" eventually. The growing competition among New York lawyers and the economic dislocations caused by Anglo-American frictions cut
into Livingston's legal practice. Whatever the reason, he decided to devote
himself to the quiet enjoyment of his family, friends, and books at Elizabethtown. The relocation of the Livingston family proceeded gradually. Formerly
he had spent a good deal of time in Elizabethtown attending court, inspecting his crops, and dealing with local merchants and craftsmen. His home,
Liberty Hall, modeled after the mansions of several of his former New York
City associates, was completed by April 1774.

Livingston's reputation for articulate leadership and his connection with
many powerful and wealthy New Jersey families assured that he would not
fall into obscurity. Livingston may have gained a temporary life of rural
contentment, but he did not retreat from public activity when he moved
to New Jersey. His interest in Presbyterianism was recognized when he was
appointed a trustee of the College of New Jersey in 1768 and when the student
newspaper, the *American Whig*, was named in his honor. The dumping of tea
in Boston harbor and the passage of the Intolerable Acts provided the impe-
tus to launch Livingston into a position of political leadership in New Jersey.
The sympathy for the liberties of American colonials that he had expressed
over the previous decade makes it reasonable to assume that he gave pas-
sive, rather than reluctant, support to American resistance. In June 1774 the
people of Elizabethtown called on Livingston to articulate their grievances
at county and provincial committee meetings. He was selected as a delegate
to the First Continental Congress in Philadelphia, where he was involved
chiefly in committee work. Livingston expressed few personal views in the
debate over the appropriate response to British oppression. However, he
cemented working relationships and political bonds with fellow delegates
and with New Jersey's key revolutionary figures in the Provincial Congress
and the new Continental army. Reelected to the Second Continental Congress, Livingston took his seat in May 1775, but early in June 1776 he left the
Congress to assume his responsibilities as brigadier general of the New Jersey militia—before he could sign the Declaration of Independence.

With his headquarters at Elizabethtown, Livingston commanded all
militia stationed in North Jersey, from Bergen south to Amboy. When ten
thousand British and Hessian soldiers landed on Staten Island on July 2,
confusion and chaos set in. Inadequate field supplies, a shortage of arms
and ammunition, and insufficient cash to meet these needs increased the
problem of New Jersey's defense and sorely tested Livingston's leadership.
Although he professed discomfort in the field and lack of military experience, his unending activity to maintain a degree of military effectiveness
indicated that he was beginning to master his complex responsibilities. He
was also beginning to grasp the need for the kinds of coordination and communication he would use with skill in the future.

Livingston's appointment as governor on August 31 by the joint meeting of the two houses of the legislature opened a new and radically different phase in his career. Accorded little power by the state constitution of July 2, 1776, the governorship might well have deteriorated to the status of a benign figurehead handling routine matters. Despite his efforts to seize the initiative and to achieve limited, attainable goals, such as enabling legislation to improve the militia's pay and provisioning, his pleas were heard only politely and acted on rarely.

In the midst of the military crisis when the state was invaded in the fall of 1776, Livingston first grasped the latent power of his designation as commander in chief of the state militia. He began to move on his own to coordinate the defense of New Jersey. Thus he filled both an executive and military void, but his efforts could not halt the British and Hessian advance through Newark, Elizabethtown, New Brunswick, and Princeton. Confusion, panic, destruction, military atrocities, and anarchy accompanied the assault. Livingston himself disappeared from the scene from mid-December 1776 to mid-January 1777. Despite the military successes at Trenton and Princeton, the civil establishment was so badly disrupted in December 1776 that New Jersey's state and local governments had to be totally reconstructed only months after their initial establishment. When Livingston met with the New Jersey legislature in late January 1777, the most urgent items on the agenda included a revival of the courts and the regeneration of New Jersey Continental and militia forces.

Livingston's efforts to persuade the legislature and citizenry of the urgent issues of civil reconstruction and support for the war effort went beyond legislative messages. For the first time he appealed directly to the people. With "The Impartial Chronicle," written in February 1777, he employed his satiric talent for the Whig cause. Mixing wry and bawdy humor with lofty republican rhetoric and employing vivid characterizations of British atrocities, Livingston attempted to galvanize the people for war and rid the state of every "sculking Neutral." Despite his energy in supporting the militia, Livingston remained within the limits of his statutory and constitutional powers. His unremitting efforts to exercise leadership in correcting the inequities of militia legislation were finally rewarded with the passage of a crucial revised statute in March 1777. Although the act was no more than a qualified response to Livingston's pleas for increased executive powers to call out the militia and enact harsher penalties for military delinquents, it became the first instance in which the legislative branch delegated powers to the executive, a transfer of authority based on clear military necessity.

Livingston pressed the legislature on March 11, 1777, for an act creating a mixed executive body empowered to contend with military or civil emergencies, a breakdown in local justice, and threats from the Loyalists. The legislature responded with uncharacteristic dispatch. On March 15 it created the New Jersey Council of Safety. With Livingston as its president the council moved quickly to fill the void of civil order produced by local justices who had been unwilling to take or administer oaths of allegiance. The Council of Safety thus began the interminable process of issuing arrest orders, interrogating witnesses on the activities of suspected Loyalists, and, in general, using the situation to demonstrate that the state government was functioning once again. Livingston grasped the opportunity that widespread disaffection provided to reassert his executive power as head of the council.

Loyalism remained Livingston's biggest problem, and he continued to confront it successfully when, in June 1777, he encouraged legislation that offered clemency to Loyalists who took oaths of allegiance but threatened the confiscation of the personal property of those who did not. Armed with a legislative act to capture Loyalists in order to compel the British to release American political prisoners, Livingston directed the raid of Bergen County that resulted in the capture of numerous Tories. With the establishment of the *New-Jersey Gazette* in December 1777, Livingston initiated a yearlong effort to provide a valuable patriotic commentary on the events of the day. Through numerous pseudonymous essays under such names as "Cato," "De Lisle," "Hortentius," and others, Livingston supported the American army's efforts to fight effectively and addressed the need for responsible legislators. He poked fun at the blustering British generals who could capture cities but could not suppress the rebellion and defeat the American army permanently. The people of New Jersey and the Continental army in Pennsylvania came to rely on the wit, moralizing, and patriotism of the poetry and prose of the governor of New Jersey in his various disguises.

The British reaction to Livingston's barbs was a tribute to their success. His severe treatment of the Loyalists and the barrage of pro-American propaganda he launched in the *New-Jersey Gazette* helped make him infamous among the British generals and the Loyalists. As early as 1778 plots to kidnap or assassinate him were undertaken, but all failed. In the fall of 1779, when the British raided New Brunswick, he barely escaped capture. These numerous plots and more frequent rumors of British retaliation compelled Livingston to continue his peregrinations through the state. He was rarely able to visit his wife and family, and his letters are filled with a yearning for a return of peace and security. Lack of clothing, constant travel, and the necessity of scattering his official papers to ensure their safety were only some of the challenges he faced as an executive on horseback.

By 1780 the unremitting demands for men to serve in the Continental army and militia units, the taxes to pay the state debts to fight the war, the lack of normal trade with the city of New York, the flight of both debtors and creditors to enemy lines, and the depreciation of currency were all major problems. Livingston attempted to stem the flow of illicit trade to New York and halt the communication and traffic of suspected Loyalists to and from the New Jersey coastline and New York City. He examined the petitions of numerous widows or wives of Tories, anxious creditors, and British citizens seeking to return to their homeland. He granted few passes, exhibiting singular adherence to principle and law above sympathy, expediency, and privilege. Several times he denied passports to his sisters and other relatives lest he seem to honor kinship over merit.

The fatigue of seven years of warfare finally ended in March 1783 with the news of the signing of a preliminary peace treaty on January 20, 1783. Livingston issued a proclamation on April 16 and read it before a large gathering in Trenton. On April 23, before he set out for his farm at Elizabethtown, the committee for the inhabitants of Trenton formally thanked the governor for his service to the state. They remarked, "We recollect, with pleasure and veneration, that when the helm of state was committed to your hands, at an early period of the revolution, you accepted, with firmness, the perilous station; and when the storm encreased and raged with the greatest violence, we have seen you persevering in the face of every danger and discouragement, till we happily arrived at the haven of Peace, Liberty, and Independence."

The return to his farm was, at most, a part-time respite from the ongoing business of state. Livingston's personal estate had been depleted by the war. He still had two unmarried daughters who would require support. The farm had fallen into disuse, and the gardens and fields needed work. In 1785 Livingston was recognized for his long relationship with the United Provinces (the Netherlands) when the New Jersey delegation at the Continental Congress pressed for his nomination as ambassador to that country. On March 21 Livingston unofficially declined the post, citing old age. He formally declined the appointment on June 25, 1785. Although he accepted a position as a New Jersey delegate to the Constitutional Convention of 1787, age and ill health severely circumscribed his contributions.

The last two years of Livingston's life were difficult. The first federal election that he supervised resulted in a dispute over the closing of the polls. The rise of factions and parties in the state embroiled him in controversy, and in 1789 he had to testify before a congressional committee. That year his wife died, and his letters reflect his depression over the loss of a partner of over forty years. A fall from a carriage rendered him inactive for months, and in May 1790 his daughter reported him failing. On July 25, 1790, in his fourteenth term as governor of the state of New Jersey, he died in Elizabethtown. He had been the chief executive through war and peace. His standards of personal conduct and his ability to realize the power of his office have since been rarely matched.

DENNIS P. RYAN

Bernstein, David A. "William Livingston: The Role of the Executive in New Jersey's Revolutionary War." In *New Jersey in the American Revolution II*, edited by William C. Wright. Trenton: New Jersey Historical Commission, 1973.

Erdman, Charles R., Jr., *The New Jersey Constitution of 1776*. Princeton: Princeton University Press, 1929.

Klein, Milton M. "The American Whig: William Livingston of New York." Ph.D. dissertation, Columbia University, 1954.

Prince, Carl E. *William Livingston: New Jersey's First Governor.* Trenton: New Jersey Historical Commission, 1975.

Prince, Carl E., and Dennis P. Ryan, eds. *The Papers of William Livingston.* 5 vols. Trenton and New Brunswick: New Jersey Historical Commission (vols. 1–2) and Rutgers University Press (vols. 3–5), 1979–88.

Sedgwick, Theodore, Jr. *A Memoir of the Life of William Livingston.* New York: Harper, 1833.

William Paterson

Print Collection, Miriam and Ira D. Wallach Division of Art, Prints and Photographs, The New York Public Library, Astor, Lenox and Tilden Foundations; courtesy New York Public Library

William Paterson (December 24, 1745– September 9, 1806) was born in Ireland. His family emigrated to America in 1747 and soon settled in Princeton. William, his two younger brothers, and a sister spent their childhood doing chores around their father's store, across from the College of New Jersey (later Princeton University). Because the family's business and real-estate investments were profitable, William could attend the college and, after his graduation in 1763, study law under Richard Stockton. He was admitted to the bar in 1769, and he spent the next years trying to establish a practice in Hunterdon and Somerset Counties.

In his college studies and the influential friends he made as founder of the Cliosophic Society at Princeton, Paterson saw possible avenues to higher social status. But he enjoyed his first real recognition in 1775, when he was chosen to represent Somerset County in the first Provincial Congress. He was reelected to the second Provincial Congress, and he attended all but one session of this revolutionary legislature, serving as its official secretary. During the Revolution he was a member of the legislative council (1776–77) and the Council of Safety (1777–78). He served as attorney general (1776–83), prosecuting the Loyalists and maintaining law and order during a time of political and social chaos. By the time he retired to private life at the end of the war, Paterson had established a secure niche in the leadership elite, and his estate overlooking the Raritan River— the confiscated property of Loyalist attorney Bernardus La Grange, bought from the state—reflected his new social status. Cornelia Bell, whom he married in 1779, bore him three children, but in 1783 she and a daughter died. Two years later Paterson married Euphemia White, a close friend of Cornelia's, who helped him raise his son, William Bell Paterson, and his daughter, Cornelia, later the wife of New York Congressman Stephen Van Rennselaer.

Paterson moved his family from the Raritan farm to New Brunswick and for the next few years lived comfortably on his legal business. In 1787 he was chosen to lead New Jersey's delegation to the Constitutional Convention. Paterson played a significant role at the convention, where he is best remembered for the New Jersey Plan, which he proposed as an alternative to the Virginia Plan favored by the larger states. Because of his unshakable arguments in defense of equal representation for all the states and his adroit procedural strategy as the debate over the Great Compromise reached its climax, Paterson deserves the title "Father of the Senate." Appropriately, New Jersey chose him as its representative to the first meeting of the United States Senate in New York, where he took part in framing the Judiciary Act of 1789 and supported the funding and assumption phases of Alexander Hamilton's financial plan. When William Livingston's death in August 1790 ended fourteen years of stability in the governor's office, many New Jersey leaders immediately turned to Paterson.

Paterson held many of the same conservative political and social ideas as Livingston, and his extensive experience was obvious; however, his really indispensable assets were a widespread reputation for public service and a practically universal popularity. The mild counterrevolution in New Jersey politics that followed the adoption of the Constitution had begun to waver. For example, some of the popular debtor-relief measures, instituted in the Confederation period only to be repealed in 1787 and 1788, were already being reintroduced. Unless a candidate could be found whose bipartisan popularity would guarantee his election, the choice of a new governor might easily become a distressing contest among the state's various factions. This is why New Jersey's conservative leaders prevailed so strenuously on Paterson. Since college days, he had believed it to be the responsibility of the educated and capable to serve the society in offices of public trust. Now his friends—including John Chetwood, Nicholas Bayard, and Jonathan Dayton —played on these feelings to persuade Paterson to accept the post. At least one observer, in a newspaper piece signed "Captain Triumph," disapproved of the tone of condescension that he detected in Paterson's eventual decision to accept the nomination, but, true to the predictions of his supporters, when the legislators met, the vote was unanimous.

During Paterson's tenure as governor, Trenton was chosen as the regular site for meetings of the legislature, and the building of the first statehouse there was begun. Paterson was active in advising New Jersey's representatives in Congress on questions relating to the federal assumption of state debts and to the reapportionment of seats in the House of Representatives. But Governor Paterson made his most significant accomplishments in the areas of economic development and legal reform.

Paterson had come to know Alexander Hamilton and some of the other leading economic thinkers of the day while he was sitting in the Senate. Tench Coxe had written to him early in 1790, explaining that because New Jersey's fertile agricultural land was filling up while its population continued to grow, some sort of commercial development would be necessary to provide jobs for future generations. A year later Coxe, Hamilton, and others, who were framing the prospectus of the Society for Establishing Useful Manufactures (S.U.M.) with a maximum capitalization of $4 million, planned their application for a charter from the New Jersey Assembly. Controversy was anticipated with the company's requests for some extraordinary privileges: to dig canals wherever it saw fit, to run lotteries for its own profit, and to be specially exempt from taxes. But in the judgment of at least one observer, Paterson's attendance at a planning meeting the promoters held in August 1791 was a sure sign that the legislature would grant the desired favors. To dramatize Paterson's approval, the company announced that it would name the industrial town it planned to build in his honor. When the legislature met in November, it quickly approved the charter.

Whether Paterson lobbied actively for the passage of the charter is unclear, but his support of it as a step toward New Jersey's economic independence from neighboring New York and Pennsylvania is certain. Although the governor purchased no stock, John Bayard, his brother-in-law and one of the local promoters, bought $1,000 worth of shares in the name of Paterson's wife. Actually, the legislators probably needed little convincing. Once it became known that Paterson supported the project and that he had allowed his name to be so prominently associated with it, his reputation did the rest. The lawmakers' subsequent decision to invest $10,000 of the state's money amounted to a personal testimonial to their favorite son. The S.U.M. had a disappointing history. The company's leadership was placed in the hands of William Duer and a group of his friends from New York. Within a few months they had become embroiled in a speculative scheme that backfired, forcing three S.U.M. directors into bankruptcy and Duer into debtors' prison. The realization that speculators threatened the entire project appalled Paterson, and he wrote in defense of those who, unlike financial schemers, were "plodding along in the common road of industry." But neither his encouragement nor Hamilton's managerial skill sufficed to repair the damage. Public opinion about the S.U.M. became tangled with the other elements of the Federalists' financial plan, and the manufacturing enterprise never got off the ground. It would take a half century for the future city of Paterson to begin to fulfill the dreams for industrial greatness its founders shared in the 1790s.

Although William Paterson's *Laws of New Jersey* was not published until 1800, it deserves discussion in connection with his governorship. In 1792 the assembly passed the legislation authorizing Paterson to digest and revise the laws so that outmoded colonial statutes could be updated and British laws, retained in force temporarily in 1776, could be finally set aside. The following year, at Paterson's suggestion, the authorization was widened to include a complete reform of the British criminal code, which still applied in New Jersey. As the governor put it, the prevailing system was "written in blood and cannot be read without horror." Because of his revision the first state prison was built, at Trenton. Besides humanizing the penal system, Paterson saw the revision as the opportunity for political, social, and moral reform. But the most enduring changes related to the practice of law and the courts. According to one legal scholar, "Paterson's Practice" did away with many of the "complications and technicalities with which the courts in England were embarrassed for several years to come."

As Paterson prepared to resign his office in March 1793 to accept President Washington's appointment to the federal bench, he expressed some of his thoughts about the governorship in an essay published under the pseudonym "Aurelius" in *The Guardian; or, New-Brunswick Advertiser*. According to Governor Paterson, who had been there in 1776 when the state constitution was written, the framers had considered the document "a temporary thing resulting from the exigency of the moment." To illustrate he pointed to the combination of the chancellorship with the governor's office, a peculiarity carried over from the colonial experience. Though this had not presented much of a problem in colonial days, the business of the chancery court had "wondrously increased" since the end of the war. Now, he argued, the constitution should be "thoroughly revised," and the office of chancellor should be separated from that of governor, which had more political responsibilities.

For the last thirteen years of his life Paterson served as an associate justice of the United States Supreme Court. The job was strenuous, requiring him to attend regular sessions of federal circuit courts as far away as Savannah, Georgia. While he sat on the court, Paterson took part in decisions on several significant cases that helped to define the federal government's authority over the states and provided precedents for the later establishment of judicial review over federal as well as state legislation. Paterson never completely succeeded in divorcing his political point of view from his judicial decisions, as became obvious in cases involving Matthew Lyon and others accused of breaking the 1798 Sedition Act. Although he was considered for appointments as secretary of state and as chief justice, in each case he was passed over, and he remained on the court until his death in 1806.

JOHN E. O'CONNOR

William Paterson Papers, William Paterson College Special Collections, Wayne, N.J.

O'Connor, John E. "Legal Reform in the Early Republic: The New Jersey Experience." *American Journal of Legal History* 22 (April 1978): 95–117.

———. *William Paterson: Lawyer and Statesman, 1745–1806*. New Brunswick: Rutgers University Press, 1979.

Richard Howell (October 25, 1754–April 28, 1802), revolutionary officer, lawyer, and third governor of the state of New Jersey, was born in Newark, Delaware. He was a twin and one of the eleven children of Ebenezer Howell, a farmer, and Sarah (Bond) Howell, Quakers who had emigrated from Wales to Delaware in about 1724. Educated at an academy and then privately, Howell became an Episcopalian during the American Revolution. He married Keziah, the daughter of Joseph Burr, who owned extensive property in Burlington County. The Howells had nine children.

Between the ages of twenty and thirty-nine, from the time he moved with his family to Shiloh, in Cumberland County, New Jersey, to his inauguration as governor, Howell played an active part in the movement for American independence. He participated in the Greenwich Tea Party and, months before the Declaration of Independence, wrote newspaper essays for the *Plain Dealer* calling for armed resistance to the British. During the Revolutionary War, Howell rose to the rank of brigade major and participated in the Canadian campaign and the battles of Brandywine, Germantown, and Monmouth. He spent the winter of 1777–78 at Valley Forge with Washington, for whom he resigned his commission to perform intelligence work.

Howell first practiced law near his home, then in Trenton. While traveling to the first inauguration in New York, he participated in Trenton's reception for President Washington. After being appointed clerk of the New Jersey Supreme Court, he joined the nucleus of the New Jersey Federalist Party, which was made up of members closely connected to Washington and Alexander Hamilton. Howell became the third governor of New Jersey in 1793 and served until 1801. During most of this period he was the only candidate nominated. In 1798 the Republicans nominated several candidates, but Howell was elected by a very large majority. His victory margin was considerably smaller in 1799, when Republicans supported moderate Federalist Andrew Kirkpatrick as their alternative to Howell's reelection.

While governor, Howell carried out the varied and exacting judicial duties that constituted the major functions of the office. He performed the duties of surrogate general, of chancellor—hearing appeals from cases tried in equity—and of presiding judge of the state's Court of Errors and Appeals, the highest appellate court in New Jersey. He also was president of the council, where he possessed a tie-breaking vote. By virtue of the New Jersey constitution he also had the executive power of captain-general and commander of the militia. In September 1794, to comply with President Washington's orders, Howell led the New Jersey militia into Pennsylvania to help crush the Whiskey Rebellion. President Washington met the troops in Pennsylvania and named Howell commander of the right wing of the army. After cowing the insurgents, the president dismissed the troops, and Howell and his men returned to New Jersey in mid-November.

In August 1798, Howell was involved in the sedition charges brought against the most ardent Republican organ in New Jersey, the *Newark Centinel of Freedom*. In May, Republican militia officers had refused to add their names to the state militia's expression of support for the Federalist president, John Adams. As head of the militia, Howell lashed out at them publicly for this. In reply, the Republicans forwarded an address to Howell, charging that the president was at fault, not they. Adams had violated the constitution, they said, and therefore they had no confidence in the government. Governor Howell then attacked his addressers as "the shreds of a French faction [that operated as a] dagger in the hands of . . . [a French] assassin." In the *Centinel*, the Republicans now called him "the Prince of Blackguards." This epithet formed the basis for the governor's charges of seditious libel against the newspaper. Considering his background, it is not surprising that when a Federalist Party split occurred in the late 1790s, the militant Howell sided with war and the army. Under orders from Major General Alexander Hamilton, Howell gladly raised an infantry regiment in case of a French invasion.

Finally, in February 1799, when Fries's Rebellion broke out in Pennsylvania protesting the taxes levied to support the provisional army and other elements of the Federalist defense program, Howell responded with alacrity to President Adams's order to ready two thousand New Jersey militiamen to march. His prompt, decisive action brought one Philadelphia militant Federalist newspaper's praise: "What a charming thing it would be if every state had such a governor as New Jersey! . . . It will be long, very long indeed, 'ere Poor Pennsylvania will see a Howell in her chair of state."

Howell's last term in office ended in October 1801, when the Federalists lost the state legislative elections. Disgrace and death followed in quick succession. As soon as the Republicans had taken office, the legislature accused Howell of failing to account for all monies spent on military preparedness and ordered him to give the state treasurer the unexpended monies and a statement of expenditures. The investigation was incomplete in April 1802, when Howell died with a clouded reputation—at least in Republican minds. In his obituary, the Republican press stated that he was possibly guilty of embezzling funds. The Federalists answered that Howell's failing health had prevented him from maintaining proper accounts. At the end of Howell's long tenure as governor, six months before his death, the Federalists acknowledged publicly that he had not been a statesman of the first magnitude. His popularity with his electors, the members of the Federalist-dominated New Jersey legislature, surpassed his effectiveness as governor.

RUDOLPH J. PASLER

New Jersey Letters, Rutgers University Special Collections, New Brunswick, N.J.
Timothy Pickering Papers, Massachusetts Historical Society, Boston, Mass.

Anthony Walton White Papers, Rutgers University Special Collections, New Brunswick, N.J.

[Agnew, Daniel]. *Major Richard Howell of New Jersey*. [Philadelphia]: n.p., 1876. Rutgers University Special Collections, New Brunswick, N.J.

Pasler, Rudolph J., and Margaret C. Pasler. *The New Jersey Federalists*. Rutherford, N.J.: Fairleigh Dickinson University Press, 1975.

Joseph Bloomfield (October 18, 1753–October 3, 1823) was the fourth governor of the state (1801–2; 1803–12) and the first Jeffersonian-Republican to hold the office. He was first elected in 1801, then successively each year from 1803 to 1812. Described by a contemporary as "rich," and taking great pride in his occasional military service (he preferred to be called "General" rather than "Excellency"), Bloomfield managed to combine the roles of governor and party leader during his long tenure in office. This accomplishment was all the more pronounced because the governor's office possessed but few constitutional and appointive powers and no popular mandate: the post was filled by the joint meeting of the New Jersey legislature and not by popular election until after 1844. Despite the office's inherent weakness in an era of legislative domination, Bloomfield remained a powerful figure in New Jersey for nearly a quarter century.

Bloomfield was born in Woodbridge into a notable family of English origin. His father, Moses Bloomfield, a well-to-do physician and a political figure, served in both the colonial New Jersey Assembly and the Provincial Congress that replaced it at the beginning of the American Revolution. Joseph was educated at an academy in South Jersey, and he had almost finished reading law when the Revolution began. He dropped his studies to accept a captain's commission in the new Continental army, where he served with distinction in the New Jersey Brigade and other units, resigning in 1778 with the rank of major. In that year he married Mary McIlvaine, settled in Burlington, and was admitted to the bar. The Bloomfields had no children but adopted their nephew Joseph McIlvaine and raised him.

Bloomfield's elite background, revolutionary service, inherited wealth, and urbanity all propelled him toward political leadership at a time when many of his class had chosen to side with the Loyalists. After a period of indecision, Joseph Bloomfield emerged as one of the few genuine landed "aristocrats" in New Jersey to join the Jeffersonian cause instead of the more mainline Federalist Party in the decade following the ratification of the federal Constitution in 1788. At first, there was little to indicate that Bloomfield was anything but a good Federalist supporter of Washington's. He was a presidential elector for Washington in 1792, and as the general commanding the New Jersey militia he accepted the president's call to lead the state's troops in helping to suppress the Whiskey Rebellion. Jay's Treaty with Great

Britain in 1795 and, a year later, Washington's announcement that he would retire and support John Adams to replace him, however, gave the prominent militia general cause to ponder his future allegiances. In 1796, as politics in New Jersey became heated for the first time since ratification, rumors of his defection to the Anti-Federalists (budding Jeffersonian-Republicans) began to circulate. He protested, "I am a friend of the President and Government, [as] I have already evinced . . . in 1792 and . . . 1794." In July 1797, moreover, Bloomfield wrote to his friend and New Jersey compatriot Jonathan Dayton, Federalist Speaker of the House of Representatives, recommending an office seeker "as a good federalist."

Bloomfield finally surfaced as a Jeffersonian later that year, but his Federalist ties haunted him throughout his political career. When he appointed a Federalist to office in 1801, for example, one Republican congressman commented that it was "just like him." A year later another congressman commented that Bloomfield was still susceptible to "Federal Flattery and Deception." As late as 1811, after Bloomfield had spent a successful decade as the Jeffersonian-Republican governor of New Jersey, still another party manager wrote cynically, "I did not suppose that any one expected [sic] Bloomfield of belonging to the Republican party from principle." Despite such lingering suspicions, Bloomfield had been a key figure in cementing the Jeffersonian party organization in the state in the years 1796–1800. He continued to identify with Republican Party issues, opposing both the foreign policies of John Adams and the Alien and Sedition Laws of 1798. Parvenu New Jersey Jeffersonian politicians—they were often "new men" brought forward politically by the Revolution—were flattered by invitations to caucus at the Bloomfield family residence in Burlington, with its "fine library and many curiosities." In 1800, after Bloomfield was named chairman of the first statewide Republican nominating convention, a party device introduced to cultivate unity for the pending congressional and presidential elections, he emerged as the titular leader of the party. The New Jersey Jeffersonian Party's efforts in these elections marked its coming of age, and in 1801, for the first time, it captured control of the state. Bloomfield's leadership was instrumental in achieving the victory, and the Jeffersonian legislative majority elected him governor for the constitutionally prescribed one-year term. A legislative deadlock prevented the election of a governor in 1802, but in 1803 and successively through 1811 Bloomfield was reelected with awesome regularity.

Although Bloomfield had almost no constitutional authority, he used his position as party leader with surgical precision to strengthen the governor's office. The state legislature, dominated by a Jeffersonian-Republican majority, introduced the institution of the caucus to encourage party regularity; as a state institution, the caucus has survived the hazards of almost two centuries, down to the present. Bloomfield came to be a fixture in the caucus, which, while he remained governor, was not limited to legislators but included other representative party leaders. He combined this personal authority with the prestige he commanded in Washington, D.C., as an important spokesman for the state party to the Jeffersonian administration. As a result, his was a strong voice in dispensing patronage in the state. He wrote to President Jefferson outlining New Jersey's appointive priorities under the new national administration, and Jefferson chided him for his long shopping list: "It is the case of one loaf and ten men wanting bread." But Bloomfield delivered the federal offices in 1801 and thereafter, and Jefferson seldom afterward treated him lightly.

As governor, Bloomfield used his moral and political leadership to initiate the gradual emancipation of slavery in New Jersey. His father before him had staunchly opposed bondage, freeing fourteen slaves at the time of the Revolution. Joseph himself was a longtime leader of the New Jersey Society for the Abolition of Slavery. A potent lobbyist, he was instrumental in promoting a considerable measure of Republican unity against slavery. Although he was accused of turning his back on his elite ties and background, he also favored controversial legislative reform measures to tax dividends from private bank stock and the creation of state-chartered banks to thwart monopolistic private banking interests in New Jersey.

During Bloomfield's last years in office, from 1808 to 1812, he—like Republican officeholders everywhere—was caught up in defending unpopular foreign policy measures emanating from Washington. In an effort to protect American sovereignty while keeping the nation out of war with England, the Jefferson and Madison administrations had introduced successive measures embargoing trade with England, inevitably interrupting commerce with all of Europe. The consequent economic recession and the popular emotional reactions to continuing impressment of American sailors on the high seas placed New Jersey's Republicans on the defensive and caused a division in party ranks. Bloomfield contended expertly with these political difficulties, defending his party against allegations that it was "the party of war." In the five years before the War of 1812, Jeffersonian-Republicans were hopelessly divided by foreign policy questions and Federalists were revitalized by them, but even so Bloomfield managed to gain reelection in the joint meeting of the legislature each October. When war was finally declared in June 1812, Bloomfield promptly resigned as governor in midterm to accept President Madison's nomination as brigadier general in the rapidly expanding United States Army.

Evidence of Bloomfield's personal popularity and of the unifying strength of his party leadership became all too clear in the succeeding legislative election for governor in October 1812; for the first time in more than a decade, a Federalist was named to fill the chair vacated by "the General." Although his military service was much more prosaic than colorful slogans would suggest (he spent his three years in the military organizing and supervising training and defense establishments in New York and Pennsylvania), he must have been touched by the thoughts of those Republican celebrants who toasted him at a party gathering on the Fourth of July, 1812: "When in the camp, on the march, or under the walls of Quebec, may he never want the genuine character of a Jersey Blue."

When the war ended in 1815, General Bloomfield retired to his mansion in Burlington. His ease was short-lived; his personal popularity and ability to unite warring factions of the party resulted in his election to two terms in the House of Representatives, in 1816 and 1818. Only in 1820, in his sixty-seventh year, was he allowed to decline renomination and retire again to his estate in South Jersey. There he died in 1823, overshadowed in history by the founding fathers, to whom he was contemporary, but bound to them by his able service to the causes that had rendered them immortal.

CARL E. PRINCE

Joseph Bloomfield Letters, Rutgers University Special Collections, New Brunswick, N.J.

Emmet Collection, New York Public Library, New York, N.Y.

Gratz Collection, Historical Society of Pennsylvania, Philadelphia, Pa.

Thomas Jefferson Papers, Library of Congress, Manuscript Division, Washington, D.C.

New Jersey Broadsides Collection, The New Jersey Historical Society, Newark, N.J.

Samuel L. Southard Papers, Princeton University Special Collections, Princeton, N.J.

John W. Taylor Papers, New-York Historical Society, New York, N.Y.

Oliver Wolcott Papers, Connecticut Historical Society, Hartford, Conn.

Fee, Walter R. *The Transition from Aristocracy to Democracy in New Jersey, 1789–1829.* Somerville, N.J.: Somerset Press, 1933.

Lender, Mark E., and James Kirby Martin, eds. *Citizen Soldier: The Revolutionary War Journal of Joseph Bloomfield.* Newark: New Jersey Historical Society, 1982.

Prince, Carl E. *New Jersey's Jeffersonian Republicans, 1789–1817.* Chapel Hill: University of North Carolina Press, 1967.

Aaron Ogden (December 3, 1756–April 19, 1839), a man of impressive physique and a craggy and truculent countenance, had a character to match. To a distinguished family name he added a lustrous military service during the Revolution and a solid reputation among New Jersey lawyers. The family had deep roots in New Jersey. John Ogden, who built a house in Elizabethtown in 1664, was one of the original settlers of that community. He moved there from Long Island, to which he had emigrated in 1640 from Hampshire, England. Aaron's father, Robert Ogden, had been speaker of the New Jersey lower house on the eve of the American Revolution. Aaron graduated from the College of New Jersey (later Princeton University) in 1773. There he met many of the state's future leaders, with whom he worked and fought in the

Revolution and later in the state's courts and in the political arena. In 1787 he married Elizabeth Chitwood, daughter of another prominent family, who bore him two daughters and five sons.

Ogden capitalized on his assets to become one of New Jersey's leading Federalists and to build a long and impressive political career. During the early national period, however, political success in New Jersey depended on party victory, not individual ability. Federalist Aaron Ogden could never overcome the Jeffersonian-Republican Party's control of state politics to achieve sustained political success. He served two years (1801–3) in the United States Senate, completing the term of James Schureman, who had resigned. From 1803 to 1812 he was elected annually to the state's general assembly, where he was the leader and the workhorse of the ineffectual Federalist minority. During these years Ogden's Federalist colleagues nominated him for the governorship whenever they wanted to challenge the Republican majority, but this was only a token action. The governor was elected by the legislature, and the Republican majority elected Joseph Bloomfield every year from 1803 to 1812.

In 1812 New Jersey Federalists shared in the nationwide Federalist revival brought about by the opposition to the national administration's maritime policy and the declaration of war against England. They won a majority in the legislature and elected Ogden governor. In 1813 the Federalists lost their majority and with it the governorship, beginning their slow decline to dissolution. Ogden dropped out of active politics to pursue a career in banking and steamboating. His permanent claim to fame, in fact, rests on his efforts to promote steam navigation, not on his political career. He is the Ogden in the landmark Supreme Court decision *Gibbons v. Ogden*, which ended private monopolies in interstate commerce. In his year as governor Ogden led the Federalist majority without being its captive. He showed an ability, integrity, and independence which the state could have put to good use had partisanship not so dominated its elections. The most immediate issues Ogden faced during his term involved defense against possible British attack, coastal defense in cooperation with the governors of nearby states, and relations with the national government.

On January 21, 1813, Ogden informed the legislature that though the state militia was willing and anxious to take the field in defense of the state, its arms and munitions were deficient for active service. The legislature appropriated a sizable but insufficient sum to remedy this defect. The national government also provided inadequate and deficient arms, having more immediate use for the little equipment it had. Ogden devoted enormous energy to solving this problem, to no avail. The Federalist legislature, which had passed some vitriolic resolutions condemning the war and its "wasteful and disastrous" conduct, refused Ogden's request for adequate appropriations. Diehard Federalists, hoping to drive Ogden to a position totally against the war, condemned the national government for not supplying the New Jersey militia or adequately providing for the state's defense, but he refused to be driven.

Ogden's general orders of November 16 and December 1, 1812, placed portions of the state militia in federal service under federal officers. In a speech at Newark he pledged the state's cooperation with the government's war efforts. He worked out a plan with Governor Daniel D. Tompkins of New York for the joint defense of New York harbor, and with the governors of nearby states on plans for coastal defense. Even though Federalists complained that his exertions were contrary to the party policy of opposing the war effort, Ogden won high praise from moderate Federalists and from his Republican opponents. Under the headline "Honor Where Honor Is Due" the *Trenton True American*, the state's leading Republican newspaper, complimented Ogden on the "patriotic stand he has taken in defense of his country." His conduct, the paper said, was distinctly different from "the anti-American conduct of the friends of peace." The article concluded that Ogden "knows the value of liberty too well to sacrifice it on the altar of faction." The Madison administration appreciated his cooperation so much that Secretary of War John Armstrong offered him command of the New York–New Jersey military district. Ogden refused because Armstrong insisted that to accept the post he would have to resign as governor. When Republican Governor Tompkins of New York took that command without relinquishing the governorship, New Jersey Federalists concluded that the original offer had been a Republican stratagem to remove a Federalist governor. Ogden refused to accept this conclusion and rejected all suggestions that he adopt a more intransigent attitude. Throughout his term he consistently supported the war effort and the national government's conduct of the war.

Other than controversies concerning the war, two issues dominated New Jersey politics during Ogden's term. The Federalists recognized that their victory in 1812 was the result of a peculiar set of circumstances and passed two bills through which they hoped to retain power. They changed the method of choosing presidential electors from popular to legislative election, and they passed a complicated redistricting law, hoping to gerrymander the state in their favor. The governor supported both measures and lost much of the reputation for nonpartisanship won by his attitude toward the war.

Equally partisan, but less divisive, was the issue of state banking. Federalists, with Ogden in the lead, had long advocated the expansion of the state banking system but before 1812 had made no headway against the Republican majorities. Once they had won control of the legislature, they chartered six new banks capitalized at over $2 million. Each bank was to raise its own capital by selling shares par-valued at $50 each. Half of the stock of each bank was reserved for the state, and so was the power to make some appointments to the board of directors. Ogden worked hard behind the scenes to assure the passage of this bill and even harder to assure that the banks created by the law actually came into being. But he refused to cooperate with the Federalist majority when it tried to politicize the banking system.

The Republican legislature of 1811 had passed an act authorizing the governor to sell state-owned shares in the bank of New Jersey to the highest bidder so long as the bid was not below the state's original purchase price. A resolution by the Federalist legislature of 1812 authorized the sale of state-owned bank stock at the best price it would bring on the market. Ogden informed the legislature that the law and the resolution were in conflict. In a rare display of executive independence, he refused "to execute the commission assigned" to him until the conflict was resolved. For this action he once more won high praise in the Republican press. However, his personal popularity could not be converted into another Federalist victory. In the elections of 1813 the Republicans argued that opposition to the war would encourage the enemy and prolong the conflict. They blamed the Federalists for the defenseless condition of the state and condemned them for the change in the election law, some polemicists arguing that the Federalists were more concerned with their own reelection than with the country's defense against attack. The Republican press did not vilify Governor Ogden. If mentioned at all, he was compared favorably to the unpatriotic New England governors and the less-than-patriotic Federalist majority in the state legislature. On this platform the Republicans gained a ten-vote majority in the legislature and by that margin elected William S. Pennington over Ogden to the governorship.

After the war's end in 1815 Ogden shifted his energies from law and politics to steamboats. His ships, the *Sea Horse* and the *Atlanta*, carried freight and passengers from Elizabethtown Point to New York City, earning substantial profits for Ogden and his partner, Thomas Gibbons. A series of personal and commercial differences forced the dissolution of the partnership and began the long and complex litigation which culminated in the landmark Supreme Court decision *Gibbons v. Ogden* in 1824. The expense of the litigation and the loss of the steamboat franchise depleted the fortune Ogden had accumulated. In 1829 Congress created the post of collector of customs for Jersey City especially for Ogden. Though lucrative, the position did not pay enough to enable him to liquidate his obligations, and he was imprisoned for debt in New York. Fortunately, his boyhood friend and Princeton classmate Aaron Burr pushed a bill through the New York legislature prohibiting imprisonment of Revolutionary War veterans for debt. Thus reprieved, Ogden comfortably lived out his life with his sinecure in Jersey City. He died there on April 19, 1839.

VICTOR A. SAPIO

Birkner, Michael J. "Samuel L. Southard and the Origins of *Gibbons v. Ogden.*" *Princeton University Library Chronicle* 40 (Winter 1979): 171–82.

Dangerfield, George. "The Steamboat Case." In *Quarrels That Have Shaped the Constitution*, edited by John Garraty. New York: Harper & Row, 1964.

Fee, Walter R. *The Transition from Aristocracy to Democracy in New Jersey, 1789–1829*. Somerville, N.J.: Somerset Press, 1933.

Lane, Wheaton J. *From Indian Trail to Iron Horse: Travel and Transportation in New Jersey, 1620–1860*. Princeton: Princeton University Press, 1939.

Ogden, Aaron. "Autobiography of Col. Aaron Ogden of Elizabethtown." *Proceedings of the New Jersey Historical Society* 12 (1892–93): 15–31.

Pasler, Rudolph J., and Margaret C. Pasler. *The New Jersey Federalists*. Rutherford, N.J.: Fairleigh Dickinson University Press, 1975.

Strum, Harvey. "New Jersey Politics & the War of 1812." *New Jersey History* 105 (Fall–Winter 1987): 37–70.

William Sandford Pennington (1757–September 17, 1826), the state's sixth governor, was one of those who benefited most dramatically from the social mobility stimulated by the Revolutionary War. He was perhaps the first governor of either the colony or the state who did not derive from hereditary, propertied gentry; in large measure this fact affected his outlook and his place in history.

Pennington was born into a Newark family of limited means. He was orphaned at an early age, and his formal education ended with apprenticeship to a local hatmaker. He joined the Continental army as an enlisted man when the Revolution began. Though his service record is confused by unsubstantiated claims to heroism, it at least partly shows his value to the American cause: he was made sergeant in an artillery unit in 1777, commissioned second lieutenant in the field in 1780, and, having served through the entire war, mustered out as a brevet captain. He returned to Newark to work as a hatter. By the early 1790s he was in business for himself as a retail merchant in his native town.

He typified the new, self-made man attracted to the Jeffersonian-Republican cause in the 1790s. Following a pattern of political involvement not uncommon in other states in the formative years of America's first party system, Pennington and his brother Aaron helped found the Essex County Democratic Society; this was part of a Jeffersonian-Republican movement emerging from popular American support for the French Revolution and encouraged particularly by the organizational efforts of Edmond Genet, French minister to the United States in 1792 and 1793. The Pennington brothers rose to leadership of the society and in 1796 used the organization as a springboard to found the first Jeffersonian newspaper in the state, the *Newark Centinel of Freedom*. This political commitment left the now successful and outspoken Anti-Federalist Revolutionary veteran only a short leap from entry into active politics.

Newark provided fertile ground for men and women with Jeffersonian leanings: it was the home of several families like the Penningtons made prominent by the Revolution. A natural rivalry developed between that growing community and Elizabethtown, the seat of a more traditional, Federalist-oriented aristocracy that included the Ogden, Dayton, Williamson, and Boudinot families. By the 1790s Newark had achieved political domination of Essex County, and this along with rapid increases in its population and its growing economic centricity gave its leaders an advantage in the quest for power. The county in turn formed the vital center of Jeffersonian strength in New Jersey, its political accomplishments enhanced by the remarkable fact that from 1796 through 1807 women were permitted to vote in Essex—and they did so in significant numbers. For two decades, from 1795 through 1815, William Pennington remained a political kingpin in Essex County.

He was elected to the assembly annually between 1797 and 1799 and to the council each year from 1800 to 1804. He became a major figure in the legislature and a powerful voice in the Jeffersonian cause. As a candidate on the "Farmer's [Jeffersonian-Republican] Ticket" at the end of 1796 he was accused by one Federalist of "shouting loudly of the necessity of changing men in order to change measures." In 1798 Pennington's visibility and political stock rose enormously as a result of his moderate and successful leadership in the legislative debate over New Jersey's response to the Alien and Sedition Acts. During this period of deep involvement in politics he continued to operate his store and also plugged away at the study of law. In 1802, at age forty-five, his admission to the bar testified to his perseverance and ability. A year later he was appointed county clerk of Essex; at the beginning of 1804 he resigned from the legislature to accept an appointment to the New Jersey Supreme Court. In 1806 he was named court reporter as well as justice, and he published *A Treatise on the Courts for the Trial of Small Causes* (1806), virtually a layman's guide to the complexities of New Jersey civil law. It was good enough to warrant republication nearly a generation later.

Pennington's service on the bench clearly did not disqualify him from quietly carrying on his political leadership. The Republican mixed caucus of Jeffersonian legislators and other party managers came close to nominating him for governor in both 1810 and 1811, but eventually it renominated Joseph Bloomfield instead. In the meantime, however, Pennington strengthened his ties to Republicans outside Essex County. In 1811, for example, the Woodbridge Jeffersonian organization resolved that as Pennington "is worthy of, so may he soon be called to the highest office of this state."

That call finally came in 1813, when a Republican legislative majority named him to a one-year term. Entering office at the low point of the War of 1812, Pennington conceived it his duty to restore unity to the state by attempting to mute the rivalry and hostility that for a score of years had separated Jeffersonians and Federalists. At first he was relatively successful at this, and he was reelected in 1814; but in order to succeed he had eroded his position in both Essex County and the state by opening himself to charges of "amalgamation"—a contemporary term similar to "appeasement."

When the governor endorsed the Essex County legislative candidacy of Jonathan Dayton, a former Federalist Speaker of the United States House of Representatives, in the autumn of 1814, he drew the fire of Shepard Kollock, a longtime Essex County Republican rival who was the editor of the influential *Elizabethtown New Jersey Journal.* At the same time the governor strongly supported Mahlon Dickerson's losing bid for a seat in the United States Senate against James J. Wilson, a powerful Republican who edited another influential newspaper, the *Trenton True American.* Not only did Pennington incur Wilson's wrath; he also undermined his own support in the Republican caucus. Worst of all, he was widely quoted as having intemperately referred to Wilson's Republican supporters as a bunch of "Clod Hoppers" who boasted "not a man of Talents or of understanding among them." This proved unforgivable in a self-made man who owed his political success to the support of New Jersey's farmers—who, after all, constituted the vast majority of voters in an agrarian state.

After the end of the war in 1815 ideological divisions in New Jersey, which had most recently been exacerbated by foreign policy issues, began to diminish. At the same time Governor Pennington, who had done much to close the rifts caused by party confrontations, found his popularity among rank-and-file Republicans decreasing, his hold on Essex County undermined, and his support in the caucus threatened. In short, Pennington was almost certain to lose the next election. The party found a way out: President Madison nominated Pennington a judge in the United States District Court for the District of New Jersey, and the governor accepted. By gracefully arranging this "elevation," New Jersey's Jeffersonian Republicans avoided a messy public struggle and allowed an old party wheelhorse to save face.

As for the retiring governor, he found himself in a berth that was "almost a sinecure." There were four court terms during the year, but as the historian John Whitehead has noted, "they rarely lasted more than a day. No grand jury was ever sworn in [Pennington's] court, nor were any indictments found." He held the office until his death in 1826. Perhaps there was some justice in his enjoying a tranquil position for the last decade of life after having paid so dearly for his successful efforts to bridge the enmities of a generation of party combat during the era of the first party system. A kind of vindication occurred posthumously when his son was elected governor in 1837.

CARL E. PRINCE

Samuel L. Southard Papers, Princeton University Special Collections, Princeton, N.J.

Fee, Walter R. *The Transition from Aristocracy to Democracy in New Jersey, 1789–1829.* Somerville, N.J.: Somerset Press, 1933.

Link, Eugene P. *Democratic-Republican Societies, 1790–1800*. New York: Columbia University Press, 1942.

Prince, Carl E. *New Jersey's Jeffersonian Republicans, 1789–1817*. Chapel Hill: University of North Carolina Press, 1967.

Schoenbachler, Matthew. "Republicanism in the Age of Democratic Revolution: The Democratic-Republican Societies of the 1790s." *Journal of the Early Republic* 18 (Spring 1998): 237–61.

Strum, Harvey. "New Jersey Politics & the War of 1812." *New Jersey History* 105 (Fall–Winter 1987): 37–70.

Whitehead, John. *The Judicial and Civil History of New Jersey*. [Boston]: Boston Historical Company, 1897.

Wilentz, Sean. *The Rise of American Democracy: Jefferson to Lincoln*. New York: Norton, 2005.

Mahlon Dickerson

A. S. Conrad (after J. Vanderlyn), *Mahlon Dickerson*, 10th Secretary of the Navy, 1 July 1834–30 June 1838; courtesy The Naval Historical Foundation, property of curator for Department of the Navy, accession 43-49-A

Mahlon Dickerson (April 17, 1770–October 5, 1853), was born in Hanover Neck, Morris County, the first child of Jonathan and Mary (Coe) Dickerson. During his life, he demonstrated a diversity and longevity in political leadership and achievement that no other native son appears to have equaled.

Dickerson received his only institutional education as one of the twenty members of the class of 1789 of the College of New Jersey (later Princeton University), where the Reverend John Witherspoon, a signer of the Declaration of Independence, was president. Before attending college, he had been tutored by educated citizens in and around Morristown. His teachers included Caleb Russell, who in 1797 established the *Morris County Gazette* (Morristown). In 1776, another tutor, Dr. Jacob Green, had argued forcibly against slavery in America. Dr. Green served at one time as acting president of the College of New Jersey, and he was the father of the college's longtime president, Ashbel Green.

After Dickerson earned his undergraduate degree from Princeton, he read law in Morristown with his former tutor Caleb Russell, and in 1793 he was admitted to the New Jersey bar. The following year, during the Whiskey Rebellion, he rode as a volunteer cavalryman in the New Jersey militia. The militia saw little military action during the expedition over the mountains to

Pittsburgh, but its quick response reinforced Dickerson's lifelong advocacy of citizen militias rather than standing armies.

From 1797 to 1810, Dickerson practiced law and gained political experience in Philadelphia, then the largest and most cosmopolitan of American cities. While there, he developed a close personal friendship with Meriwether Lewis, wrote extensively for William Duane's Jeffersonian newspapers, and was admitted to the American Philosophical Society. He was also elected to the Philadelphia Common Council, and Governor Thomas McKean appointed him recorder of the city and adjutant general of the state of Pennsylvania.

In 1810, Dickerson moved back to New Jersey, where he established himself in the mining industry and in state politics. He took over his late father's iron mine and turned it into one of the most productive in the nation. In the first quarter of the nineteenth century, Dickerson's mine provided ore for an estimated hundred forges from High Bridge to Hamburg. On a hilltop near Succasunna, he built an estate, with a mansion that he named "Ferromonte" (Mountain of Iron), doubtless emulating Thomas Jefferson, who had named his Virginia estate "Monticello."

In New Jersey politics, Dickerson rose rapidly. In 1811, he was named orphans' court judge in Morris County. Like his father, Jonathan, and his brother, Silas, he was elected three times successively—from 1811 to 1813—to the assembly from Morris. In that last year, the legislature appointed him a justice of the state supreme court, a post he filled for two years. During that time, his major activity, according to his diary, was holding court at Trenton and riding circuit, mainly to the northern county seats. Unfortunately, no official record exists of his activities as a justice because, on constitutional grounds, he declined a concurrent appointment as court recorder. When he was elected governor on October 26, 1815, he resigned his post as justice. Samuel L. Southard succeeded him on the bench.

Among the political issues in New Jersey during Dickerson's governorship were governmental action to combat the economic dislocations of the postwar period; the state's role in banking and internal improvements; and public education. Dickerson responded to the first by urging the passage of national tariffs to protect infant American industries. He saw them as necessary because after the Treaty of Ghent in 1815 had ended the War of 1812, the British had exacerbated the inevitable postwar economic downturn by "dumping" their low-priced industrial products on the American market. At the time, Dickerson was deeply involved, both as a private citizen and as governor, in the state's growing iron industry. The American iron industry, which was relatively inefficient, was particularly hard hit by the British dumping tactics. It was not surprising that the legislature responded to Dickerson's message with a strongly worded resolution to Congress, urging passage of protective tariffs for the iron industry. The recommendations to this end in Dickerson's first substantial gubernatorial address were his first official expressions on the topic, and they became his hallmark. Dickerson was one of the leading pro-tariff spokesmen on the national scene for over a quarter of a century.

In the area of internal improvements, Dickerson proposed immediate attention to improving the state's roads. New Jersey's reputation for having the worst roads along the Atlantic seaboard gave his proposal a certain urgency. Instead of asking the state to build or improve roads, the new governor suggested that it encourage the further formation of private turnpike companies, which had proved successful in Pennsylvania, New Jersey, and other states since the 1790s. Dickerson also pointed out the need for a canal across the state between the Raritan and Delaware Rivers. Though the legislature responded by forming a public stock company, the public failed to purchase subscriptions. The canal was finally built after a private company was chartered in 1830.

As governor, Dickerson played an important role in establishing New Jersey's public school system. In the early nineteenth century, the citizens of New Jersey had demonstrated a growing sentiment for the establishment of a state-financed system of public education. The first successful action toward such a school system—the passage in 1817 of a bill creating a fund for the support of free schools—took place during Dickerson's administration. An act passed in 1829 finally established the first common schools, which were partially supported by an annual appropriation of $20,000 from the income of the 1817 fund. The most traumatic developments during Dickerson's gubernatorial years resulted from a natural catastrophe: in 1816, droughts and killing frosts led to a great shortage of grass and grain. Even during July and August, ice formed in the Hudson River and in waters throughout the state. Because of the unique weather and the resulting widespread distress, 1816 was known well into the twentieth century as "the year without a summer." As a Jeffersonian dedicated to minimal governmental activity, Dickerson would not contemplate official action to relieve the public distress. In a message to the legislature, he noted the shortages but looked for a positive element: he piously hoped that the rising prices would discourage distillers from making "poison" out of what was "intended by the bounty of Heaven to man for his nourishment." In 1817, the weather returned to normal.

Dickerson left the governorship for the United States Senate in 1817. Twice reelected unanimously, he served sixteen years. In Washington, he made his presence felt mainly by his stands on the tariff. At that time, Americans saw the tariff issue as equal in importance to the increasingly troubling issue of slavery. Toward resolving the latter issue, Dickerson could contribute little. As the 1832 presidential election approached, he was seriously considered as President Andrew Jackson's replacement for the out-of-favor vice president, John C. Calhoun. Instead, the politically adroit Martin Van Buren was selected as Jackson's second vice president and, subsequently, as the eighth president of the United States.

Dickerson was not left in the cold. Jackson rewarded Dickerson for faithful service to him and to the Democratic Party by offering him the cabinet post of secretary of the navy. He accepted and served for four years, remaining in office during a portion of the Van Buren administration. His labors as a cabinet member clearly reflected his personal charm and his ability to work with people individually. Again, as during his years in the Senate, he demonstrated his dedication to public service by seldom being absent from his duties. Ironically, he may have performed most notably in calming Baltimore and Washington in the early 1830s when antiblack riots disrupted daily life in the two cities. Because he was on the scene while the secretary of war and President Jackson were absent, Dickerson took charge as acting secretary of war. His years in the cabinet were marked by his success in maintaining law and order during the racial disturbances and his righting of administrative routines which had fallen into near chaos.

Dickerson was sixty-eight years old when he retired as secretary of the navy. Through the last fifteen years of his life, he remained interested and active in politics. His iron-mining business was affected by the economic depression of the late 1830s and early 1840s, but it prospered even in those years, mainly through his personal efforts and attention. After he returned from Washington, he continued to be a leading spokesman for protective tariffs. He was elected president of the protectionist American Institute in 1846, and he gave speeches, wrote articles, and published newspaper propaganda for the cause of higher tariffs. Dickerson never married. The name most commonly linked to his is that of Philemon, his younger brother, who served as Democratic governor in 1836 and 1837. The elder Dickerson served as judge of the United States District Court for the District of New Jersey from August 1840 to February 1841, and when he resigned, his friend President Van Buren appointed Philemon to the vacant seat.

Mahlon Dickerson performed his last public service in 1844 as a member of the state constitutional convention in Trenton. He was elected vice president of the convention and appointed chairman of the committee on the governor's powers of appointment and tenure of office. He died October 5, 1853, and is buried in the Presbyterian churchyard in Succasunna, New Jersey.

ROBERT R. BECKWITH

Mahlon Dickerson Diary, The New Jersey Historical Society, Newark, N.J.

Mahlon Dickerson Diary, Rutgers University Special Collections, New Brunswick, N.J.

Mahlon Dickerson Papers, The New Jersey Historical Society, Newark, N.J.

Beckwith, Robert R. "Mahlon Dickerson of New Jersey, 1770–1853." Ph.D. dissertation, Columbia University, 1964.

Birkner, Michael. *Samuel L. Southard: Jeffersonian Whig*. Rutherford, N.J.: Fairleigh Dickinson University Press, 1984.

Birkner, Michael J., and Herbert Ershkowitz. "'Men and Measures': The Creation of

the Second Party System in New Jersey." *New Jersey History* 107 (Fall–Winter 1989): 41–59.

Ershkowitz, Herbert. *The Origin of the Whig and Democratic Parties: New Jersey Politics, 1820–1837.* Washington, D.C.: University Press of America, 1982.

Pumpelly, Josiah C. "Mahlon Dickerson, Industrial Pioneer and Old Time Patriot." *Proceedings of the New Jersey Historical Society* 11 (1891): 131–56.

Isaac Halsted Williamson (September 27, 1767–July 10, 1844), governor of New Jersey from 1817 to 1829, was born in Elizabethtown, the youngest son of Matthias and Susannah (Halsted) Williamson. In 1808 he married Anne Crossdale Jouet, and they had two sons, Benjamin and Isaac Halsted. Although he received only a common school education, he studied law as an apprentice to his brother Matthias, a well-known lawyer in the state. After his admission to the bar in 1791 he began a practice in Essex County that flourished and soon extended to Morris County, growing with his reputation for a thorough understanding of the law.

Initially a Federalist, Williamson broke with the party over its formal opposition to the War of 1812. When elected in 1815 as a Democratic-Republican to the general assembly, he proved himself to be an able legislator. Legislative leaders indicated their respect for his legal acumen by choosing him to serve on committees that dealt with complex legal questions, including proposals concerning laws for indebtedness and the status of free blacks. During his term in the assembly Williamson also made recommendations on divorce, which was handled by the legislature at that time. He served in the assembly for part of the 1816–17 term, but when Mahlon Dickerson's resignation created a vacancy in the governorship, the legislature chose Williamson as his successor. The support which other representatives from eastern New Jersey gave Williamson was a crucial factor in his selection over his main competitor, Joseph McIlvaine, a Burlington County lawyer who was West New Jersey's candidate in the election.

The constitution of 1776 provided for a strong legislature and a weak governor. Elected annually by a vote of the legislature, the governor lacked the power of veto, and Williamson did little to strengthen the feeble powers the constitution accorded him. He dropped the traditional practice of giving an annual message to the legislature and thereby inadvertently weakened his influence. As governor, Williamson actively supported the construction of canals in the state and closely observed New York's achievement in opening the Erie Canal. After the 1820 failure of a private attempt to build the proposed Delaware and Raritan Canal, Williamson recommended that the state build it; but the weakness of his office hampered him, and he could not influence the assembly to act. By 1826 the issue had become divisive within the Republican Party. Finally, at the end of his last term as governor in 1829, the legislature authorized Williamson to initiate a study of the benefits the canal might provide. He commissioned John Simpson to ascertain the amount of shipping between the ports of Philadelphia and New York and seized on Simpson's estimates to persuade the legislature to act. Williamson felt that "such a canal cannot fail to be of immense advantage." Its benefits would "not be confined to its immediate neighbourhood, but would be felt in every part of the state, and greatly increase her importance in the Union." The legislature chartered the canal in 1830, and by 1834 it was completed.

Under the constitution of 1776 the governor served in a dual capacity as chancellor and governor. Perhaps because of the limitations of the governor's role, Williamson put much of his energy into his work as chancellor. He reordered the rules of the court and drafted new procedures for collection when debts were secured by mortgages. As a result many of the cases considered by Chancellor Williamson dealt with liens on mortgages. He refused to grant an injunction to the Paterson Society for Useful Manufactures against the Morris Canal Company for its proposed use of water from the Rockaway River. In his opinion the society had no legal basis for a complaint since water had not yet been diverted to the canal; therefore the society sustained no damage. Ironically, during this important case he was able to do more for the canal movement as chancellor than as governor.

Contemporaries regarded Williamson as a poor speaker and only a fair writer. However, they rarely questioned his judgment in legal cases. In the realm of ethics Williamson, like many others, could separate his public views from his private life. For example, as governor he apparently supported the state legislature's position against the spread of slavery when the Missouri Question was being debated. However, a bill of sale dated April 13, 1826, lists Williamson as the purchaser of two slaves and their children.

Although Williamson rarely used the governor's office as a forum for political speeches, he supported John Quincy Adams in the elections of 1824 and 1828. Andrew Jackson carried the popular vote in New Jersey in 1824, but the legislature remained anti-Jacksonian. Jackson's forces grew steadily in number during the 1824–28 period, and the decisive national defeat of Adams in 1828 weakened the morale of New Jersey Republicans. This led directly to Williamson's defeat one year later by the Jacksonian candidate, Garret D. Wall, with a 37–15 vote in joint meeting. Wall declined the office, and a Jacksonian successor, Peter D. Vroom, Jr., was chosen in his stead.

From 1830 to 1833 Williamson served as mayor of Elizabeth, and in 1831–32 he represented Essex County in council. In 1832 he declined an appointment to be chief justice of the state supreme court in order to continue his increasingly lucrative law practice.

In the years from 1833 to 1844 Williamson, by 1833 a Whig, kept himself embroiled in most of the state's noteworthy legal battles. In a remarkable reversal he became the legal counsel of the Camden and Amboy Railroad, which he had criticized while governor. In an 1834 legal battle he skillfully attacked the Delaware and Raritan Canal Company's claims that its charter permitted it to construct a railway line along the canal. A year later he argued similarly for the Camden and Amboy against the Trenton and New Brunswick Turnpike Company. In 1844 Williamson was chosen to be a member of the convention which met to design a new constitution. Unanimously elected convention president, he fought hard to replace the constitution that had limited him as governor with one creating a more balanced government by increasing the power of the governor and diminishing the authority of the legislature. The governor would serve a term of three years instead of one, he would be elected by the people, and he would have veto power over legislative acts.

Illness forced Williamson to resign just before the close of the convention to "prevent any delay occasioned by [his] absence." He expressed "great confidence" in the new constitution, which would supersede the "radically defective" 1776 document. On July 10, 1844, only a few weeks after his resignation from the convention, he died at the age of seventy-seven in Elizabethtown. His son Benjamin, who continued his successful legal practice, was himself appointed chancellor of New Jersey in 1852 under the revised system of government.

FRANK J. ESPOSITO

Mahlon Dickerson Papers, The New Jersey Historical Society, Newark, N.J.

Peter D. Vroom Papers, Rutgers University Special Collections, New Brunswick, N.J.

Isaac Williamson Papers, The New Jersey Historical Society, Newark, N.J.

Isaac Williamson Papers, New Jersey State Library, Bureau of Archives and History, Trenton, N.J.

Isaac Williamson Papers, Rutgers University Special Collections, New Brunswick, N.J.

Birkner, Michael. *Samuel L. Southard: Jeffersonian Whig*. Rutherford, N.J.: Fairleigh Dickinson University Press, 1984.

Ershkowitz, Herbert. *The Origin of the Whig and Democratic Parties: New Jersey Politics, 1820–1837*. Washington, D.C.: University Press of America, 1982.

Halsted, Oliver S. *Address upon the Character of the Late, the Honorable Isaac H. Williamson, Delivered before the Bar by Oliver S. Halsted*. Newark: A. Guest, 1844.

McCormick, Richard P. "Party Formation in the Jacksonian Era." *Proceedings of the New Jersey Historical Society* 83 (July 1965): 161–73.

Williamson, Isaac H., and Garret D. Wall. *Opinion of Isaac H. Williamson, Esq., and Garret D. Wall, Esq., in Relation to the Corporate Powers of "The Trenton and New Brunswick Turnpike Company."* Trenton: Joseph Justice, 1835.

Peter Dumont Vroom (December 12, 1791–November 18, 1873), governor of New Jersey from 1829 to 1832 and from 1833 to 1836, was born in Hillsboro Township, Somerset County, New Jersey, the son of Colonel Peter Dumont Vroom and Elsie (Bogert) Vroom. Colonel Vroom (1745–1831), of Dutch and French-Huguenot descent, moved to New Jersey from New York. During the Revolutionary War, he served in the Second Battalion of the Somerset County militia. Subsequently, he occupied almost all the offices in the county, including those of sheriff, justice of the peace, member of the general assembly (1790–98; 1813–17), and member of the legislative council (1798–1804).

The colonel's son received his education at Somerville Academy, and in 1808 he graduated from Columbia College, New York. After reading law in Somerville, he was admitted to the bar in 1813. He practiced in Sussex and Hunterdon Counties and gained some eminence as a lawyer before moving back to Somerville, where Attorney General Theodore Frelinghuysen appointed him prosecutor of the pleas. Vroom married twice: on May 21, 1817, Ann V. D. Dumont; and after her death, Senator Garret D. Wall's daughter Maria Matilda, on March 4, 1840.

Like his father, Peter D. Vroom began as a Federalist. During Vroom's early adulthood, however, Jeffersonian-Republican domination of the state left him little chance of achieving anything more than a local office in Somerset County. But the election of 1824, which fractured the Republican Party, changed that. Like a number of other Federalists in the state, including ex-governor Aaron Ogden, James Parker, and Garret D. Wall, Vroom supported Andrew Jackson. As a Jackson partisan and the advocate of state construction of a canal from the Delaware River to the Raritan, Vroom was elected to the general assembly from Somerset County in 1826 and 1827. Following Jackson's victory in the election of 1828, his supporters (called Democrats after 1834) in New Jersey dominated the state politically through 1837. When, in 1829, they gained control of the legislature, Garret D. Wall was elected governor. He declined the position, and subsequently Peter Vroom was elected, ending the thirteen-year tenure of Isaac Williamson.

An able governor, Vroom achieved considerable popularity during his six years in office (1829–32; 1833–36). He believed in increasing the powers of the executive branch to make it coordinate in power with the legislature. To accomplish this goal and stay within the limitations of the 1776 constitution, Vroom reintroduced the practice of regularly sending a message to the legislature and meeting with his party's legislative caucus to influence its decisions on legislation and patronage. His efforts contributed to an impressive list of accomplishments, especially in the areas of prison and militia reform, education, and internal improvements.

Upon becoming governor, Vroom worked to improve New Jersey's penal system. Responding in his first message to reform groups who criticized the

New Jersey prison at Lamberton, Vroom proposed building a new institution modeled after the Eastern Penitentiary in Pennsylvania. Although the legislature withheld its approval until Samuel Southard's term in office, the prison was completed during Vroom's second tenure as governor. Vroom also proposed the abolition of imprisonment for debt, another concern of reformers. The legislature enacted a partial repeal during his first term, though it did not enact total repeal until 1842. Governor Vroom also urged the legislature to reform the militia system, under which every able-bodied man between eighteen and forty-five had to train regularly with a unit. The training meetings, which accomplished little, ended in 1834 at Vroom's urging. Vroom also pushed the legislature toward school reform. During his first term, the legislature distributed part of the money in the school fund to local townships to support public education. Although the law was inadequate and Governor Vroom consistently sought to reorganize and secure greater public financing for public education, the 1829 act was a milestone in the development of public education in New Jersey and the first step in the creation of a state-supported school system.

During Vroom's administration, nothing generated more controversy than the construction of a canal and a railroad through central New Jersey. At the beginning of the 1829 session of the legislature, Vroom proposed chartering a private company to build the Camden and Amboy Railroad and left the method of building the canal to the legislature. Consequently, the Delaware and Raritan Canal Company was chartered at the same time as the Camden and Amboy Railroad Company. One year later, to secure financing for the canal, Vroom supported merging the railroad and the canal into the so-called Joint Companies. The charter guaranteed the companies a monopoly over all canal and rail transportation between New York City and Philadelphia; but even this measure failed to secure capital for the canal, and Vroom proposed taking the necessary money from the school fund and lending it to the canal company.

After 1834, the growing concern among political leaders about the power the Joint Companies exercised in the state led Vroom, during his last term in office, to suggest that the state purchase them to eliminate them as a partisan issue. However, the companies' president, Robert F. Stockton, made an offer that Vroom and most legislators found unacceptable. The sale went unconsummated, and periodically thereafter controversy ensued. But despite the political problems that the Joint Companies created, the canal and the railroad, both operating by Vroom's last term in office, contributed greatly to the state's economic development. A transit duty the Joint Companies paid the state also substantially reduced state taxes and defrayed the construction costs of the Trenton Prison.

Despite Vroom's support of the Delaware and Raritan Canal Company, he generally acted with the anticorporation wing of his party. As governor, he urged the legislature to desist from issuing new bank charters in the state and from granting other corporate charters that did not contain strong safeguards. Until his last term in office, Vroom generally succeeded in persuading the legislature to restrict the other uses of the corporate form. Nonetheless, during his last year in office, a combination of Whigs and pro-corporation Democrats succeeded in creating a number of banks. As governor, Vroom also served as chancellor of the court of chancery. Because the opinions of the earlier chancellors were unpublished, Vroom's decisions set important precedents for future courts. His decisions on corporations, which were playing an increasing role in New Jersey's economic activities during his administration, were especially significant.

In *Suydam v. Receivers of the Bank of New Brunswick*, Vroom ruled that legislative acts regulating banking corporations could be applied to previously chartered institutions without being considered ex post facto. In several cases, Vroom ruled that the state legislature, to perform public services, had broad powers to delegate its rights of eminent domain to private companies. (See *Scudder v. Trenton Delaware Falls Company* and *Society for Establishing Useful Manufactures v. Morris Canal Company*.) But Vroom's most controversial case, *Joseph Hendrickson v. Thomas L. Shotwell*, grew out of a schism between Hicksites and Orthodox Quakers. In an opinion that had political as well as legal ramifications, Vroom upheld the decision of Chief Justice Charles Ewing and Justice George K. Drake of the supreme court, awarding the school property of the Chesterfield Meeting to the Orthodox Quakers as the sect having the greater theological link to the original Friends who founded the Chesterfield Meeting. Hicksite resentment over the decision led the branch to seek redress from the legislature. Finding their greatest support in Vroom's party, the Hicksites secured the passage of a law dividing church property equally in the case of a schism. In 1836, after Vroom's party had won control of the joint meeting, he declined to stand for reelection on account of ill health. Fellow Democrat Philemon Dickerson replaced him.

Vroom continued to alternate between private legal practice and governmental service. In 1837, President Martin Van Buren sent him to Mississippi as a commissioner to adjust land claims arising from the removal of the Choctaw Indians from the state. In 1838, as one of the five Democratic candidates for Congress, he became involved in the famous "Broad Seal War." Conflict over the accuracy of Monmouth County's returns caused the House of Representatives to challenge Governor William Pennington's certification of a Whig victory. The House of Representatives, with a small Democratic majority, seated Vroom and the rest of the Democratic ticket. This allowed them to choose a Speaker and to control committee appointments.

After Vroom's defeat for reelection in 1840, he remained an active Democrat. He assumed the role of an elder statesman in the party, generally supporting a moderate view against the threats to the Union from abolitionists on one side and secessionists on the other. In his elder-statesman role, Vroom ran as an elector for Pierce in 1852 and for Breckenridge in 1860.

During the Civil War, Vroom urged moderation and played a large role in preventing disturbances in New Jersey over the draft law, an act which he regarded as unconstitutional. In 1863, his son fought for the Union at the Battle of Gettysburg and in other engagements. All the same, Vroom strongly supported the candidacy of General George Brinton McClellan against President Abraham Lincoln in 1864.

After 1840, Vroom continued to be active in public service. He served, for example, in the New Jersey Constitutional Convention of 1844. Relying on his experiences in office, he urged the convention to increase the power of the executive, especially by providing for the governor's direct election, increasing his patronage powers, and giving him a limited power of veto over legislation. At this convention, Vroom also stated again the anticorporation and antibanking sentiments he had expressed as governor. In 1846, Vroom, with Chief Justice Henry W. Green, Stacy G. Potts, and William L. Dayton, revised the statutes of the state to bring them into compliance with the new constitution. In 1853, President Franklin Pierce appointed him ambassador to Prussia, where he remained until 1857. Serving in Prussia during the Crimean War, Vroom dealt with a number of issues arising from the conflict, but his major problem as an American minister developed out of the large German emigration to the United States during this period. Vroom served early in 1861 as a commissioner to the peace conference called by Virginia to try to avert a civil war. In 1865, he replaced his son, John P. Vroom, who had died several months earlier, as a law reporter of the New Jersey Supreme Court and served in this capacity until his death in 1873.

In sum, Peter Dumont Vroom left an important mark on the politics of New Jersey. He helped restore the governorship to a position of prominence; he helped to codify the laws in the state; he was one of the founders of the New Jersey Democratic Party; and he helped rewrite the state constitution.

HERBERT ERSHKOWITZ

Charles A. Philhower Collection, Rutgers University Special Collections, New Brunswick, N.J.

Ferdinand S. Schenck Papers, Rutgers University Special Collections, New Brunswick, N.J.

Samuel L. Southard Papers, Princeton University Special Collections, Princeton, N.J.

Peter D. Vroom Papers, Columbia University Library, New York, N.Y.

Peter D. Vroom Papers, The New Jersey Historical Society, Newark, N.J.

Peter D. Vroom Papers, Rutgers University Special Collections, New Brunswick, N.J.

Garret D. Wall Papers, Princeton University Special Collections, Princeton, N. J.

Birkner, Michael J. "Peter Vroom and the Politics of Democracy." In *Jacksonian New Jersey*, edited by Paul A. Stellhorn. Trenton: New Jersey Historical Commission, 1979.

Birkner, Michael J., and Herbert Ershkowitz. "'Men and Measures': The Creation of

the Second Party System in New Jersey." *New Jersey History* 107 (Fall–Winter 1989): 41–59.

Ershkowitz, Herbert. *The Origin of the Whig and Democratic Parties: New Jersey Politics, 1820–1837*. Washington, D.C.: University Press of America, 1982.

Levine, Peter D. *The Behavior of State Legislative Parties in the Jacksonian Era: New Jersey, 1829–1844*. Rutherford, N.J.: Fairleigh Dickinson University Press, 1977.

McCormick, Richard P. "Party Formation in the Jacksonian Era." *Proceedings of the New Jersey Historical Society* 83 (July 1965): 161–73.

Proceedings of the New Jersey Constitutional Convention of 1844. With an introduction by John E. Bebout. Trenton: Federal Writers' Project, 1942.

Samuel Lewis Southard (June 9, 1787– June 26, 1842) was governor of New Jersey for barely four months. His service was a brief though eventful interlude in a lengthy, varied, and distinguished political career. He was born in Basking Ridge, Somerset County, to Henry Southard, one of the founders of the Jeffersonian-Republican Party in New Jersey, and Sarah (Lewis) Southard. Educated in a classical school run by the Reverend Robert Finley in Basking Ridge, he entered the College of New Jersey (later Princeton University) in 1802. Following his graduation in 1804, Southard taught school in Mendham, Morris County. Less than two years later, a Virginia congressional colleague of his father's, John Taliaferro, offered Samuel a position as tutor to his sons and nephews. He accepted and for five years lived at the Taliaferro plantation, "Hagley," in King George County. There he studied law with the eminent Fredericksburg jurist Francis T. Brooke. In 1809 South-

Samuel L. Southard

A. S. Conrad, *Samuel Southard*, Secretary of the Navy, 16 September 1823–3 March 1829; courtesy The Naval Historical Foundation, property of curator for Department of the Navy, accession 43-48-A

ard was admitted to the Virginia bar and practiced law but in 1811 chose to return to his native state, where he anticipated better opportunities for career advancement. Shortly after his return to New Jersey Southard married Rebecca Harrow, the daughter of a deceased Episcopal clergyman from the Northern Neck of Virginia.

In 1812 the Southards established a residence in Flemington, the seat of Hunterdon County. They moved to Trenton in 1817. From the outset of Samuel Southard's adult life in New Jersey he was deeply involved in politics. As a young lawyer he wrote anonymous newspaper articles for the *New*

Brunswick Fredonian and other leading Jeffersonian papers. During the War of 1812 Southard began his lifelong role as a party organizer and spokesman. His evident talents, in combination with his name, enabled him to exert considerable influence in state politics during the period between the collapse of the first party system and the emergence of a new system organized according to loyalty or opposition to Andrew Jackson. This influence he used not merely in patronage dispensation or as a force in making nominations for elected offices but also to secure lucrative and influential public positions for himself. Before reaching the age of thirty-seven, Southard served as assemblyman, justice of the state supreme court, United States senator, and, beginning in 1823, secretary of the navy under James Monroe—the first Jerseyman ever appointed to the cabinet. Invariably, he no sooner took one post than he began to consider advancement to others.

Officeholding was not his only concern. Adhering to an evolving and progressive Jeffersonian philosophy of government, Southard supported the Republican Party and such causes as internal improvements, public education, the colonization of free blacks, prison reform, and fair treatment of Native Americans. The presidential campaign of 1824 forced him to choose among five major Republican candidates with disparate understandings of the Jeffersonian creed. Southard's support for the policies of President James Monroe, as well as his cordial personal relations with his cabinet colleague John C. Calhoun, led him to support the young Carolinian (then in his "nationalist" phase) for president. Southard effectively organized Calhoun's campaign in New Jersey, and by late 1823 it was widely believed that Calhoun would run well in the state as a "Southern man with Northern principles."

The collapse of the Calhoun movement in March 1824 left Southard adrift. Treasury Secretary William H. Crawford's views were unpalatable, Andrew Jackson was in his view unqualified, Henry Clay's following in New Jersey was insubstantial, and the men running John Quincy Adams's campaign were not his political friends. Hence Southard professed neutrality, though privately he had little difficulty supporting Adams as the man most qualified and congenial to his own political notions and most likely to keep him in the cabinet if elected.

Jackson won a plurality in the general election, but Adams triumphed in the House of Representatives and retained Southard as secretary of the navy. Southard devoted himself to strengthening the department, as he would continue to do in the Senate in the 1830s. The leading student of national public administration Leonard D. White has called Southard "a vigorous and effective secretary," "perhaps the ablest" of any who served during the Jeffersonian era (1801–29). As navy secretary Southard maintained close communication with administration supporters in New Jersey and deepened his commitment to the progressive Jeffersonianism he believed Adams represented. He served as the chief conduit for both patronage and intelligence between state and national capitals.

Southard played a major role in New Jersey in the presidential campaign of 1828, in which Adams carried the state. Jackson, however, won a convincing national triumph, and Southard was out of a job. Because Adams's supporters controlled the state legislature, Southard had expectations of a return to the United States Senate. However, a schism within anti-Jackson ranks in joint meeting resulted in a setback even more mortifying because it was his old political rival Mahlon Dickerson who defeated him.

As his consolation prize Southard was able in 1829 to win election as state attorney general. In this post he assumed leadership of the National Republican Party in New Jersey; from it he rose to the governor's chair in 1832, when his party regained control of the state after three years of Jacksonian dominance. His election was a case of the office seeking the man rather than the man the office. The governorship conferred prestige and a measure of control over patronage (no inconsiderable factor in the party battles of this era), but the opportunity for leadership and national reputation lay in the United States Senate. Southard's National Republican Party, lacking a candidate of stature for the governor's office, entreated him to accept it, and he reluctantly acquiesced.

Southard served as governor for only four months. During this period he presided over a wholesale purge of Jacksonians from state, county, and local posts, demonstrating that in New Jersey at least anti-Jacksonians were as adept as their partisan counterparts in distribution of political patronage. On state issues, however, the parties had few differences at the time. Perhaps the most significant issue was whether the state should erect a new prison (and remove the state arsenal from the capitol building to the old prison) at a cost of $150,000. A bipartisan committee of the legislature agreed with the governor that "long experience has shown, that our present building, and the system of discipline necessarily connected with it, can neither be reconciled with the principles of a just economy, nor with the great purposes of human punishment." The legislature voted the funds for the project, and the new prison was erected during Peter D. Vroom's second tenure as governor.

Southard's other policy recommendations had less impact. No doubt impressed as governor by the weakness of his office, Southard urged that the constitution be amended to permit popular election. He also sought to divest the office of its judicial duties, believing that they inhibited the election of any but lawyers and imposed intolerable political pressures in legal proceedings. In his message of January 11, 1833, Southard also supported curbs on the influx of "colored persons" into the state, though he made no specific recommendations, and favored altering the poorly functioning militia system by making service voluntary; those who did not wish to serve would pay a tax which could be used for public education or some similar purpose. A voluntary system was enacted, but not during Southard's tenure.

In his annual message to the legislature Southard, speaking less as a state administrator than a party leader, injected his credo on national issues. He supported "a tariff which shall protect the industry of the country"; a "sound currency"; "internal improvements"; and "the independence of the judicial power, which was intended to possess and to exercise jurisdiction on constitutional questions and controversies between states." He alluded to the failures of the Jackson administration in each of these areas, with special emphasis on the Jacksonians' war against the Bank of the United States —a war that Southard believed would mean the ascendancy of state and local banks "similar to those which once scattered ruin and distress over the country and affected even the national Treasury."

As governor, of course, Southard could have little influence on the resolution of these highly charged national issues. But on the most emotional question of the moment, the nullification crisis, he was able to present his views at some length. Responding to the Tariff of 1832, South Carolina called a convention and, on November 24, passed an Ordinance of Nullification. South Carolina's challenge to the administration (and implicitly to the North) on this issue provoked a firestorm of controversy. President Jackson, himself a slaveholder and strict-constructionist Jeffersonian, astounded his erstwhile enemies in his December 10 proclamation to the people of South Carolina by coming down firmly against nullification and threatening, if necessary, to coerce that state into submission to federal authority. Northern state legislatures expressed support for the president's forceful message and sent documents calling on New Jersey to join this coalition. Southard conveyed these documents to the legislature on January 11, 1833, with his most noteworthy state paper as governor, a scholarly yet impassioned disquisition on nullification's genesis, sophistries, and potential ramifications.

Several themes surfaced in the eighteen-page analysis. First, the supremacy of law and the need to adjudicate constitutional disputes through normal channels—that is, the court system. Nullification, Southard stressed, was an illegitimate effort to circumvent the system established by the framers. "The provisions which have been received in the South Carolina Ordinance of Nullification," he wrote, "are utterly repugnant to the spirit and existence of all our institutions, and to the rights and privileges under them, of the minority of the people of that state. Their enforcement would, of itself, sever the Union—break the bonds of connection between the states—and render them separate powers. That which was proposed as a peaceful remedy leads, inevitably, in the end, to war."

Second, secession was both unjustified and intolerable. It was "revolution and disunion" entirely unsanctioned by the Constitution and unacceptable to the other states. Observing that Jackson's determination to uphold the laws of the land was "the language of duty, of office, and of the constitution of the United States," Southard made it clear that New Jersey would contribute whatever might be asked of it in a clash between federal authority and South Carolina.

Partly out of longstanding personal dislike of Jackson and public opposition to Jackson's politics Southard felt a need to qualify his words of support for the president. He expressed regret that Jackson's language should be so violent as to encourage defiance by the Carolinians. Moreover, as he would explain in another message to the legislature (January 28, 1833), he disagreed with Jackson's constitutional interpretation in a key particular. Although he reiterated his rejection of nullification, he insisted that the Constitution did not sanction coercion of a state; it provided that the federal government should act directly only on individuals. "Both the coercion and the right of resistance spoken of, are opposed to the theory of our institutions"—a theory on which he elaborated at some length.

The language was constitutional, but the purport was in large measure political. Southard was only too happy to join an assault on nullification. But he did not wish to be locked in embrace with his enemy of long standing—hence his stress on constitutional differences even as he upheld the substance of Jackson's position. The apparent awkwardness of this stance (though in fact the constitutional argument was quite orthodox) led to some political jibes from the Jackson press. The *Newark New-Jersey Eagle* claimed that in staking out a position distinct from President Jackson's, Southard had joined forces with John C. Calhoun, for whom (recalling his friendship with Calhoun during the 1820s) he "has not yet lost his partiality." Should the two men ever again meet in the Senate, the *Eagle*'s editor suggested, "both advocating the doctrine of state supremacy, over the powers of the General Government, who will venture to foretell the consequences? Let the people of New Jersey look to it." To this polemic the National Republican press replied at length and with vigor. Soon after, however, the controversy died; Congress passed a compromise tariff, and South Carolina, realizing its isolation on the issue, relaxed its defiant posture. Southard viewed the denouncement of the crisis not from Trenton but from Washington. The joint meeting of the legislature elected him to the Senate on February 23, and he resigned on February 27 to join his fellow Whigs in Washington to debate the tariff, bank, Indian removal, and land issues. He was succeeded as governor by Elias P. Seeley.

Southard remained in the Senate for the rest of his life. He won a measure of acclaim for his attacks on Jacksonian economic and social policy and respect for his chairmanship of the Senate Committee on Naval Affairs. He was elected president pro tem of the Senate in March 1841, and he became the permanent presiding officer of that body less than a month later when President William Henry Harrison died and Vice President John Tyler succeeded him. When not engaged in politics, Southard was an active member of the New Jersey bar and occasionally argued before the United States Supreme Court. During the 1830s he was counsel for the Joint Transportation Companies in their legal battles with rival railroads. He served other corporations as well. One of them, the Morris Canal and Banking Company, named him president in 1837, compelling Southard and his family to move from Trenton to Jersey City. He served as president of the company for little more than a year and resigned in 1839 when his Senate responsibilities and other business interests prevented his giving full attention to the corporation. He remained, however, on retainer to the Morris Canal and Banking Company until his death.

As a lawyer Southard participated in a number of significant cases, including the hearing before the New Jersey legislature in January 1815 about the monopoly of Aaron Ogden's steamboat line. Another was the "Hicksite" case over the division of properties between contending factions of West Jersey Quakers. A stocky but impressive-looking man, Southard suffered increasingly from ill health. His final illness made him, according to one contemporary, "a mass of gouty afflictions" and forced him to resign from the presidency of the Senate on May 31, 1842. He died in Fredericksburg, Virginia, on June 26, 1842, aged fifty-five, survived by his wife and three of their seven children.

MICHAEL J. BIRKNER

Samuel L. Southard Manuscripts, Library of Congress, Manuscript Division, Washington, D.C.

Samuel L. Southard Papers, Princeton University Special Collections, Princeton, N.J.

Birkner, Michael. *Samuel L. Southard: Jeffersonian Whig*. Rutherford, N.J.: Fairleigh Dickinson University Press, 1984.

Birkner, Michael J., and Herbert Ershkowitz. "'Men and Measures': The Creation of the Second Party System in New Jersey." *New Jersey History* 107 (Fall–Winter 1989): 41–59.

Ershkowitz, Herbert. *The Origin of the Whig and Democratic Parties: New Jersey Politics, 1820–1837*. Washington, D.C.: University Press of America, 1982.

———. "Samuel L. Southard: A Case Study of Whig Leadership in the Age of Jackson." *New Jersey History* 88 (Spring 1970): 5–24.

Fallaw, W. Robert. "The Rise of the Whig Party in New Jersey." Ph.D. dissertation, Princeton University, 1967.

Elias Petit Seeley (November 10, 1791–August 23, 1846), governor of New Jersey for seven months in 1833, was born in Deerfield Township (later Bridgeton), the son of Ebenezer and Mary (Clark) Seeley. His father, a merchant and a lifelong Cumberland County resident, served for many years as a Jeffersonian-Republican legislator.

Elias Seeley was educated informally. After studying with a local attorney, Daniel Elmer, he was licensed as a lawyer in 1815. According to Lucius Q. C. Elmer, a contemporary from Cumberland County, the younger Seeley "never attained much celebrity as an advocate, but had a good local practice as an attorney and Conveyancer." On March 6, 1816, Seeley married Jane E. Champneys. The couple had two children, Elias P., Jr., and Rebecca.

Until the late 1820s, when Seeley ran successfully as an anti-Jacksonian for the legislative council from Cumberland County, he was not active in politics. Reelected three times, he was named vice president of the council late in 1832, when the National Republicans gained power. When his party's governor, Samuel L. Southard, left office for the United States Senate, in February 1833, the legislature designated Seeley to succeed him. Along with Seeley's name, the National Republicans' lack of certified state leaders, especially from West Jersey, dictated the selection. No one could claim that Seeley had the political stature of his gubernatorial predecessor. Introducing him to the public, the National Republican *Newark Daily Advertiser* called Seeley "an amiable man," a characterization the Jacksonian press exploited in the weeks subsequent to the appointment. The *Trenton Emporium & True American* expressed satiric delight that the new governor was "amiable" and proceeded to inquire whether this "amiable" man was capable of performing his duties on the court of appeals, of negotiating the loan of $30,000 the legislature had authorized for a new prison, or of serving effectively as a trustee of the College of New Jersey (later Princeton University). The *Newark New-Jersey Eagle* was more pointed; it cited his "total unfitness" for the office. For this, *Emporium & True American* editor Stacy G. Potts offered, "the party is condemned, not Mr. Seeley," since Seeley had achieved the governorship "not through his own ambition but by the force of circumstances."

As governor, Seeley was more a political target than an active public administrator. Since he was not elected until the close of the legislative session, he was limited as chief executive to making certain appointments (for example, negotiators in a boundary dispute with New York State and compilers of civil and criminal laws in New Jersey), serving on the final appeals board of the state, and preparing an address to the legislature after the October elections. Seeley participated in one important case as presiding officer on the court of appeals (composed of the legislative councilors and the governor): the Hicksite case, a dispute between competing factions of the Society of Friends. For several years New Jersey Quakers had been at odds over matters of doctrine and discipline, and by the late 1820s the contending forces had reached a point of no return. Quaker liberals, or "Hicksites" (a derivation from Elias Hicks, a notable Quaker liberal), broke away from the orthodox establishment. This involved a financial settlement and led to the case decided in 1833 by Seeley and the court of appeals.

Although the wrangling in court and out was prolonged, the facts of the case are relatively simple to abstract. The Hicksites in Crosswicks demanded the remittance of their share of the contributions to a school trust fund administered by the Society of Friends. The orthodox, maintaining that they needed to make no concessions to schismatics, refused—hence the court test. The case was first argued before Chief Justice Charles Ewing and Associate Justice George K. Drake of the state supreme court, sitting as masters in chancery. George Wood, perhaps the state's leading attorney, and former governor Isaac H. Williamson argued for the orthodox, while Garret D. Wall, a leading Jacksonian attorney and politician, and Samuel L. Southard, New Jersey's preeminent anti-Jacksonian politician, argued the Hicksite cause. After lengthy proceedings in a packed courthouse (the "Quaker Case," as it was called, was followed widely in New Jersey and Pennsylvania), the justices decided in favor of the orthodox. They concluded that since the Hicksites were in fact "seceders," they were entitled neither to be considered Quakers nor to regain their school-fund contributions.

Matters did not rest there. The decision was appealed to the court of last resort in New Jersey, the court of appeals, with Governor Seeley presiding. In the arguments before this body Theodore Frelinghuysen replaced Williamson as advocate for the orthodox. The other attorneys and the end result were the same. With a 7–4 vote (across party lines), the court affirmed the decision of Justices Ewing and Drake. In a statement issued with the decision, Seeley, who had voted with the majority against the Hicksites, expressed regret that such "religious controversies" should be brought into the court and urged both parties to seek some accommodation on their own.

The decision had important political ramifications. The New Jersey Quakers, with a clear majority of liberals, had been staunchly anti-Jacksonian since 1824 and thus were a bulwark of the National Republican organization in the state. Having taken their case to a body controlled by their longtime allies, the Hicksites were grievously disappointed at the outcome. It broke their allegiance to the National Republicans, especially when Jacksonian politicians in West Jersey, where Quakers were most numerous, embraced the Hicksite cause. This strategy, with excellent organization, paid off for the Jacksonians in the 1833 legislative elections. They won an overwhelming, statewide triumph, including victories in Burlington, Monmouth, Salem, and Gloucester Counties—all National Republican strongholds. Seeley's failure to "inspire confidence" among East Jersey Whigs, according to one historian, also helped reduce the turnout of traditionally anti-Jacksonian voters and therefore figured in the Jacksonian victory in New Jersey.

Once in control of the joint meeting, the Jacksonians replaced Seeley as governor with Peter D. Vroom, Jr. Seeley ended his term with a message on the state of the state. In it, he commented ably on the results of the operations of the state prison, the increase of the school fund, the treasury accounts, and the progress of the construction of the new penitentiary. He promoted public education, suggested legislation would be needed to relieve problems resulting from the influx of "coloured persons" in the state, and, like his two most recent predecessors, urged that the current militia system be replaced by a volunteer system with inducements. Seeley's strongest words opposed public executions. "The oftener a person frequents these public exhibitions," he observed, "the less impression they make on the mind; and they can witness the melancholy spectacle with less dread and horror, and in a little time can follow their fellow men to the gallows and witness the death scene with perfect composure. It would be better for many other reasons that might be named, that public executions should be dispensed with, and the law be so amended or modified; that in the future they shall take place within the walls of the prison yard, in the presence of the sheriff and the Officers of the Court."

The newspapers of both parties endorsed Seeley's words on public executions, and the National Republican press widely hailed his message. The *Hunterdon Gazette* called the address a "plain sensible document," while the editor of the *Trenton New-Jersey State Gazette* observed, "The manner in which this respectable man was treated by some of the low party papers, during the time he served as Governor of the State, cannot but recur to the minds of many of our fellow citizens, at this time, with regret. The duties which devolved upon him by the constitution and the laws, he certainly discharged with ability and success. His conduct throughout that period was modest, dignified and impartial, and has left a very favorable impression upon the minds of many of his fellow citizens."

It is perhaps ironic that in performing his one notable act as governor —casting a nondecisive vote consistent with his concern for the public welfare in the so-called Quaker case—Seeley greatly damaged his party's chances of maintaining control of the state in 1833. No one, however, seems to have blamed him. With the change in political control in Trenton, Seeley returned to the private practice of law, and he later served several terms in the legislature with no particular distinction. He died of cancer in 1846 at the age of fifty-five. At the outset and the end of his brief period in the political limelight, he was a decent man who was less a shaper than a creature of circumstances.

MICHAEL J. BIRKNER

Birkner, Michael. *Samuel L. Southard: Jeffersonian Whig.* Rutherford, N.J.: Fairleigh Dickinson University Press, 1984.

Ershkowitz, Herbert. *The Origin of the Whig and Democratic Parties: New Jersey Politics, 1820–1837.* Washington, D.C.: University Press of America, 1982.

Fallaw, W. Robert. "The Rise of the Whig Party in New Jersey." Ph.D. dissertation, Princeton University, 1967.

Levine, Peter D. *The Behavior of State Legislative Parties in the Jacksonian Era: New Jersey, 1829–1844.* Rutherford, N.J.: Fairleigh Dickinson University Press, 1977.

Philemon Dickerson (June 26, 1788–December 10, 1862), the twelfth governor under the constitution of 1776, served only one year in the office, from the fall of 1836 to the fall of 1837. Although he was involved in state politics for many years, he spent his entire political career in the shadow of his older brother Mahlon (who served as governor, United States senator, and secretary of the navy) and the two leaders at the center of real power in the

New Jersey Jacksonian party, Garret D. Wall and Peter D. Vroom, Jr. Philemon Dickerson, in fact, attained the governorship only when Vroom, in poor
health, declined election by the Democratic legislative majority to a seventh
one-year term.

Philemon and Mahlon Dickerson were among those attracted to the Jacksonian cause from the ranks of Jeffersonian Republicans. They were somewhat exceptional, since most New Jersey Jacksonian leaders had been notable Federalists. The Dickerson brothers entered the Jacksonian movement
during the presidential campaigns of 1824 and 1828 primarily out of personal
hostility to John Quincy Adams and Henry Clay. They were to be influential in
the Jacksonian party until the late 1830s; the decline of their influence would
coincide with the beginning of a long period of Whig dominance in the state.

Philemon Dickerson was born at Succasunna, in Morris County, a descen-
dant of the Philemon Dickerson who had been part of the great Puritan
migration to Massachusetts Bay in 1638. The earlier Philemon left Salem,
Massachusetts, for Southold, Long Island, in 1672. The founder of the New
Jersey branch of the family, Jonathan Dickerson, moved from Long Island to
New Jersey in about 1745.

Philemon Dickerson received a classical education at the University of
Pennsylvania and studied law in Philadelphia at the instigation of Mahlon,
eighteen years his elder. In 1813 he received his license to practice law in
New Jersey, established a law practice in Paterson, and married Sidney
Stotesbury, daughter of Colonel John Stotesbury of New York. He became a
counselor-at-law in 1817 and a sergeant-at-law in 1834. He served in the state
assembly, 1821–22.

Dickerson saw the Jackson party in New Jersey in the 1830s as a true
embodiment of Jeffersonian principles, particularly in the causes of limited
government and a balanced program favoring both industrial and agricultural development. Yet, like most New Jersey politicians, he considered a protective tariff and internal improvements, such as the Camden and Amboy
Railroad and the Morris Canal, necessary and beneficial.

The Dickerson family's interest in iron mines near Succasunna and its
close identification with the commercial life of northeast New Jersey created
some antagonism among Jacksonian "agrarians" in the southern and western parts of the state who were not so firmly protectionist. Despite these
differences and the ambiguity of President Jackson himself on the tariff and
internal improvements, Philemon Dickerson remained loyal to the general
and to his successor, Martin Van Buren. He distrusted the "unprincipled"
leadership of the opposition Whigs, claiming they promoted no program at
all. Elected to two terms in the United States House of Representatives in
the mid-1830s, he supported the Jacksonian program straight down the line.

When Vroom declined the governorship in the fall of 1836, the Jacksonian majority in the legislature, seeking to replace him quickly with a man
of proven loyalty, turned to Dickerson, and he resigned his seat in Congress

to accept the position. His term as governor was filled with acrimony and party warfare. Growing economic troubles, culminating in the Panic of 1837, combined with President Van Buren's personal unpopularity to depress the party spirit of New Jersey Democrats and stimulate a new Whig challenge for dominance in the state.

Under the 1776 constitution many appointments to local and state office were made by a joint meeting of the council and assembly, with each member having one vote. The Whigs, who had the majority in the council, were determined to prevent the Democratic majority in the assembly from controlling the appointments, but they realized that public opinion might be unfavorable if they blocked the joint meeting. They initially seemed to hope that they could make some kind of deal in advance of the joint meeting to share the offices with the Democrats, and soon after Dickerson's accession as governor they advanced the unprecedented claim that the council's voice in the joint meeting should equal the assembly's because the legislature consisted of two equal bodies. The two sides reached no agreement, and the Whigs on the council prevented a joint meeting. State and local officeholders whose terms were to end during this legislative sitting hesitated to act since their authority was so questionable. The new counties of Atlantic and Passaic, created in February, were without either administrative or judicial officers. Neither side would give in; on March 16, 1837, the legislature adjourned without having held a joint meeting.

Governor Dickerson called a special extra sitting on May 22, ostensibly to deal with the "existing 'public exigency' and devise measures for relief." But the only accomplishment of this sitting was a joint resolution authorizing the state treasurer to borrow up to $15,000 for state debts incurred during the expansionist period of easy money; other relief bills were victims of the impasse over the joint meeting. The Whigs, who had controlled the council eight to six during the earlier sittings, lacked a council majority because one of their councilors was ill and another was "held up." Since Governor Dickerson could break the six-to-six deadlock in the Democrats' favor, the Whig councilors had only one remaining weapon: they would have to walk out and leave the Democrats without a quorum. These circumstances led to an unvarying daily routine. The Whigs would propose relief measures, and the Democrats would vote them down. The Democrats would then raise the assembly's joint meeting request; the Whigs would move to table it, lose, and stalk from the chamber. The Democrats had tied the two issues together: they refused to consider relief measures until the Whigs allowed a joint meeting without any deals. The parties accused each other of disgraceful conduct and blamed each other for the lack of relief measures. Governor Dickerson's administration and the Democrats suffered most, though; they took the brunt of public blame, and when the fall election of 1837 put the Whigs firmly in control of the state legislature, Philemon Dickerson was turned out of office.

Dickerson's short and inconclusive term as governor was but a prelude to other political troubles. Along with four other Democrats and one Whig he was elected to the United States House of Representatives for the session of 1839–41, but the "Broad Seal War" delayed his taking office for a year and a half. The strength of the parties in the House was so even that control depended on the makeup of the New Jersey delegation. The Whigs made charges of illegal voting, and Whig Governor William Pennington rejected returns from two townships and certified the Whigs' entire slate with the great seal of the state. The House overruled this action on July 16, 1840, after a bitter partisan battle, and seated the original winners. But Dickerson's second congressional career was not noted for important activity.

Beset by continued Whig attacks on the Democrats' economic policies, Dickerson was defeated for reelection to Congress in 1840. He had seen a chance to leave the unhappy atmosphere of the House even earlier, when the United States judge for the District of New Jersey, William Rossell, died. He pressed President Van Buren for the appointment. But the president, anxious to preserve the slim Democratic House majority in the climax of his fight for the independent treasury, would agree to the appointment only when Mahlon arranged to come out of semiretirement and hold the judgeship for Philemon until after the election. In March 1841 Mahlon yielded the judgeship to his brother.

Philemon had a rewarding career on the federal bench from 1841 to his death. He approached the work with enthusiasm, dignity, and self-conscious impartiality. The volume of work was small until the Civil War, when a large number of constitutional questions piled a heavy load on the court. Dickerson's health broke under the strain, but he remained on the bench. He died at Paterson on December 10, 1862. Dickerson was involved in no precedent-setting decisions on the court but was popular with the bar and with other judicial officials. He remained a leader in state Democratic Party councils until the growing sectionalism of the 1850s pushed his sympathies toward the Republicans. He took a great interest in the affairs of Paterson; he was instrumental in procuring its city charter in 1851 and wrote *A Lecture on the City of Paterson, Its Past, Present, and Future* (1856). His second son, Edward Nicoll Dickerson, became a prominent member of the New Jersey bar, a scientist, and an inventor.

For two decades Philemon Dickerson was an important figure in the politics of New Jersey. He was not a kingmaker at the center of political power, and much of his career was adjunctive to that of his more influential brother; still, he helped build the party system in an era of transition.

W. ROBERT FALLAW

Philemon Dickerson Papers, The New Jersey Historical Society, Newark, N.J.
Birkner, Michael J., and Herbert Ershkowitz. "'Men and Measures': The Creation of

the Second Party System in New Jersey." *New Jersey History* 107 (Fall–Winter 1989): 41–59.

Ershkowitz, Herbert. *The Origin of the Whig and Democratic Parties: New Jersey Politics, 1820–1837*. Washington, D.C.: University Press of America, 1982.

Fallaw, W. Robert. "The Rise of the Whig Party in New Jersey." Ph.D. dissertation, Princeton University, 1967.

Pitney, Henry C., Jr., ed. *A History of Morris County, New Jersey, Embracing Upwards of Two Centuries, 1710–1913*. 2 vols. New York: Lewis Historical Publishing, 1914.

William Pennington (May 4, 1796–February 16, 1862) was born in Newark, the son of Phoebe (Wheeler) and William Sandford Pennington. After attending Newark schools, he earned a degree from the College of New Jersey (later Princeton University) in 1813 and then studied law with Theodore Frelinghuysen. In 1817 he was admitted to the bar, and he began to practice in his native city. Pennington became a licensed counselor in 1820 and a sergeant-at-law in 1834. Between 1817 and 1826, during the judgeship of his father, he served as clerk of the federal district and circuit courts in New Jersey.

William descended from a long distinguished line. His father was the grandson of Judah Pennington and the great-grandson of Ephraim Pennington. Ephraim, originally of New Haven, Connecticut, had moved to New Jersey as one of the founding fathers of the town of Newark. William's wife, Caroline, was a member of another important and distinguished family. Her grandfather Dr. William Burnet was a member of the Continental Congress eminent for his services in the Revolutionary War, and her father, the younger Dr. William Burnet, was surgeon general of the Continental army.

As founders and leaders, the Penningtons were inevitably and consistently involved with the political and economic growth of the new town and its surrounding area.

By 1800 William's father and uncles had achieved political prominence as organizers and leaders of the new Jefferson-Republican Party in Newark and in Essex County. Before President Madison appointed the elder William a judge of the New Jersey district court, he had served as a state assemblyman, council member, and governor. In 1824 the Pennington family supported John Quincy Adams for president, largely out of anger at Secretary of the Navy Samuel L. Southard, the leading New Jersey supporter of John C. Calhoun. Southard had used his influence with President Monroe to secure the district attorneyship of New Jersey for Lucius Q. C. Elmer of Cumberland County. The younger William Pennington, who had wanted the post, never forgave Southard. In 1828 Pennington was chosen to represent Essex County in the state assembly, and he became a leader of the National Republicans in the state. When the National Republicans and other anti-Jackson politicians coalesced to form the Whig Party in 1834, Pennington emerged as their leader in Newark.

The victory of the Whigs over the Democrats in the congressional and state elections of 1836 opened the way for Pennington's rise to the governorship in 1837. He proved a popular governor, and until 1843 he was reelected annually to the post. In his views and acts Pennington embodied a thoroughly Whig philosophy of government. He believed that the government's chief duty was "to protect the rights of property and the tranquility of society; to secure and support the feeble against the strong, the peaceful against craft and oppression." It seemed obvious to him that the good of any society rested in a harmony of social interests, with mutual dependence and cooperation among the groups and classes. He believed that the legislative power belonged exclusively to the representative body of the government, that the executive branch should have no veto power, and that states' rights should be guarded jealously from federal encroachments. These principles underlay his hostility toward such national Jacksonian measures as the Independent Treasury Act, the Militia Act, and the Bankruptcy Act, which he saw as undue extensions of presidential power at the expense of the states. They also explain his insistence that the proceeds from the sale of public lands should revert to the states.

As governor Pennington fulfilled his dual role as chief executive and chancellor of the state with remarkable skill. His judicial decisions usually pleased the courts and the petitioners; the court of appeals overruled only one of his decrees, and in that instance legal opinion was divided. He was no less distinctive as chief executive. He contradicted the traditional image of the New Jersey governor as a weak executive. The office had limited authority, for it lacked the powers of veto or appointment and its occupant's annual election by a joint meeting of the houses depended on his party's continued dominance in the legislature; the governor's duties lay mainly in signing bills into law and apprising the legislature of general conditions in the state. Pennington's character and personal influence, however, enabled him to overcome the inherent weakness of his office and to exercise an effective, positive leadership. His annual messages, like those of his predecessors, pointed out which conditions needed attention and indicated the priorities for immediate legislative action, but he often adroitly used them as vehicles to propose his own solutions to specific problems as possibilities to be explored. In this way he encouraged and even directed much of the legislation passed in his administration.

Pennington's accession to office came in the wake of the disastrous Panic of 1837. The preceding legislature had seemed unable or unwilling to cope with the economic distress. Even a special session called by Governor Philemon Dickerson had failed to produce a program of relief, largely because of a deadlock between the parties in the legislature. This situation changed with a convincing Whig triumph in the state elections of 1837 and the elevation of Pennington to the governorship. As governor Pennington worked with the predominantly Whig legislature to restore public confidence in the economy. He also expressed strong moral and humanitarian concerns. He brought about a major reform of the judiciary to improve the administration of justice. Orphan courts were established to protect children from exploitation and from being deprived of their inheritances. Under him the state initiated action to establish institutions for the care of deaf-mutes and blind children and an asylum for the insane. It inaugurated prison reform, improving health and work conditions, increasing medical care for the prisoners, and providing more humane treatment for their rehabilitation and moral guidance. Pennington's administration abolished imprisonment for debt and reduced the number of crimes specified for capital punishment.

Governor Pennington refocused attention on the common school question. Joining his predecessors, he repeatedly urged legislation to provide an effective and efficient school system, for he viewed education as "a branch of public service." He urged the establishment of a state normal school to train well-qualified teachers and the appointment of a state superintendent. Although legislation passed in 1838 establishing public schools fell short of these objectives, Pennington continued to press for them and for the creation of free public libraries in every school district as well. Public apathy and the political influence of private interests delayed the reforms for another decade, but Pennington's sustained support quickened their momentum.

Pennington staunchly championed and defended states' rights and conservative economic interests. Early in his term he figured prominently in a political incident which assumed congressional import. A routine executive act erupted into a full-scale political fracas known as the "Broad Seal War." In the close congressional elections of 1838 the governor threw out the returns from two Democratic townships on the grounds that they were questionable. Since the governor had no power to take measures for correcting questionable returns, he argued, he had no choice but to disregard them. Doing so turned the election in favor of the Whigs, and Pennington commissioned all six Whig candidates to represent New Jersey in the House of Representatives. Five Democratic candidates, among them two former governors, Philemon Dickerson and Peter D. Vroom, Jr., contested the decision. When Congress assembled in December, two delegations from New Jersey presented themselves—one with the usual credentials under the broad seal of the state, bearing the governor's signature, the other with a certificate of election signed by the Democratic secretary of state. Because the House was almost equally balanced between Democrats and Whigs, the New Jersey delegation was crucial to its organization and to the determination of the majority party. Ignoring the sealed commissions, the House refused to seat the delegation sanctioned by Governor Pennington. After days of disorder and stormy debate Congress organized itself without five of the six New Jersey representatives. More than a year of intense debate and investigation followed, and finally the House admitted the Democratic claimants by a strictly partisan vote. Pennington, though he admitted Congress's right to investigate the credentials of its members, excoriated it for violating the great seal and for trampling on states' rights by arbitrarily admitting the protesting delegation without ascertaining the legality of the votes in the two questionable townships. The governor himself was highly criticized by his political opponents for granting the Whig commissions, but the supreme court later upheld him. The case made the need for a new election law obvious, and in 1839 the legislature passed a comprehensive act to regulate elections that remedied the defects of the old law and decreased the possibility of a recurrence of the incident.

Pennington was the first governor to bring effective action against the Joint Companies, the Camden and Amboy transportation monopoly. By virtue of special privileges granted them by the legislature in 1831 they had become so powerful that they practically dominated the state's political and economic life. In 1839, when a dispute arose in the legislature over transit duties owed to the state, the governor used his personal and official influence against the companies, which were dominated by Democrats. When the state referred the case to the supreme court, the companies paid the duties. The companies' setback, however, increased their political activity and eventually helped to restore the Democrats to power, in 1843, unseating Pennington after six years in office.

In spite of Pennington's progressive views in some limited areas, he did not favor much-needed constitutional reform. The only reform he advocated and endorsed fully was the separation of the judicial and executive functions of the governor. Ironically, his proposal in 1840 that this basic flaw in the original constitution be removed by legislative action renewed agitation for constitutional revision. Failing to exercise vigorous leadership in the reform movement proved a tactical blunder that lost the Whigs the initiative and contributed heavily to their defeat in 1843. When the new governor, Daniel Haines, a confirmed revisionist, called for a constitutional convention in 1844, leading members of both political parties were elected delegates to the convention, but Pennington was not among them.

Pennington's active political career came to a temporary end with his defeat in 1844, brought on not only by his conservative position on constitutional reform but also by the machinations of politically ambitious Whigs who harbored personal resentments against the "Pennington clique" and entered into collusion with the Camden and Amboy monopolists. Pennington returned to private law practice and never again held an important state office. His hope of becoming chancellor under the new constitution did not materialize; nor did his hope of becoming a minister to Europe. President Fillmore offered him the posts of governor of Minnesota and claims judge under the Mexican treaty, but he declined both.

Persuaded to run for Congress in 1858, Pennington made a brief but spectacular political comeback. He was elected as a Republican. The political ferment and confusion building toward the Civil War made the peaceful organization of the House difficult. After a bitterly hostile contest lasting two months Pennington was chosen speaker. It was conceded that despite his ignorance of the technicalities and complicated rules of the House, Pennington presided in this period of high emotional and political stress with fairness, impartiality, and wise conciliation. In 1860 he ran again as a moderate Republican but lost, in good measure because he declined to campaign. He died two years later, survived by his wife and by four children, William S., Henrietta, Mary, and Edward R. Pennington.

SISTER SERAFINA D'ALESSIO

Birkner, Michael. *Samuel L. Southard: Jeffersonian Whig*. Rutherford, N.J.: Fairleigh Dickinson University Press, 1984.

Gillette, William. *Jersey Blue: Civil War Politics in New Jersey, 1854–1865*. New Brunswick: Rutgers University Press, 1995.

Lane, Wheaton J. *From Indian Trail to Iron Horse: Travel and Transportation in New Jersey, 1620–1860*. Princeton: Princeton University Press, 1939.

Levine, Peter D. *The Behavior of State Legislative Parties in the Jacksonian Era: New Jersey, 1829–1844*. Rutherford, N.J.: Fairleigh Dickinson University Press, 1977.

Nixon, John T. "The Circumstances Attending the Election of William Pennington, of New Jersey, as Speaker of the Thirty-Sixth Congress." *Proceedings of the New Jersey Historical Society* 2 (1872): 207–20.

Weart, Jacob. "Speaker William Pennington." *New Jersey Law Journal* 20 (July–August 1897): 230–39.

Daniel Haines (January 6, 1801–January 26, 1877), the last governor elected by the legislature, was born in New York City. His ancestors had left England in 1637 to settle in Salem, Massachusetts. Later they moved to Southold, Long Island, then left this homestead to join the first settlers of Elizabethtown. While living there, Haines's grandfather Stephen Haines played a distinguished role in the American Revolution. One of his sons, Elias, was the future governor's father. Elias Haines was a well-known and successful New York City merchant. He married Mary Ogden, who was the daughter of Robert Ogden III and the niece of Governor Aaron Ogden. The couple had four daughters and three sons. Their first child became New Jersey's chief executive.

The young Haines's early education took place at a private school in New York under the celebrated instructor Edmund D. Barry. After completing his preparatory education at the academy in Elizabethtown, he graduated from the College of New Jersey (later Princeton University) in 1820. Haines then entered the law office of his uncle Thomas C. Ryerson in Newton, Sussex

County. In 1823, after three years of study, he was admitted to the bar, and he began to practice law in Hamburg, Sussex County. During the election of 1824, Sussex County was strongly pro-Jackson. A Federalist who became an ardent supporter of Andrew Jackson, Haines began his political life by securing Jackson all the votes cast in the small township of Vernon, in which he resided. For the rest of his political career, he continued to work within the Democratic Party.

After fifteen years of private law practice, Haines was elected to the legislative council in 1839 by a large majority. He immediately became involved in the political controversy known as the "Broad Seal War." A dispute over the results of the 1838 congressional election had triggered this intensely bitter, partisan contest. In the legislative session of 1839–40, the Whigs introduced a series of resolutions to denounce the action of the House of Representatives, which had failed to support their candidates. Amzi Armstrong of Essex County and Jacob W. Miller of Morris County were the principal Whig advocates of these motions in the council. In the debates that followed, Haines led the opposition, which questioned the legislature's right and fitness to pass the Whig resolutions. Though he failed to prevent their passage, Haines debated with an ability and tact that contributed to his emergence as a political leader and, ultimately, to his election as the state's chief executive.

The Democratic caucus nominated Haines for governor on October 27, 1843, and since the Democrats had just regained control of the joint meeting after six years in the minority, Haines's election was assured. His major achievement during the first of his two terms in office was the adoption of a new state constitution in 1844. Besides being instrumental in bringing about the convention called to frame it, Haines convinced his contemporaries that the state's original fundamental law had "provisions which are at least inexpedient if not wholly incompatible with the spirit of the present age." The anachronistic unity of the offices of governor and chancellor and the chief executive's election by the legislature instead of the people became two of his chief concerns. Moreover, Haines pleaded successfully for a bipartisan convention, believing the constitution to be "a measure which is too momentous to be made the subject of party difference."

Educational reform and the creation of an efficient militia system received Haines's attention also. He told the legislature that the revision of the common school law was "one of [its] most important duties." Under the permissive sections of the 1838 law, local authorities could easily avoid both the responsibility of reporting on the condition of their schools and the obligation to visit and examine them. To ensure that local government supervise educational matters properly, Haines suggested that the council and assembly "inquire into the expediency of appointing a general superintendent" of schools. Only a year later, Theodore F. King became the first state superintendent of schools.

The militia system was another area of concern for Haines, and in his second annual message he announced that it "seems to have fallen in great disrepute." Insufficient reports from the brigade officers prevented the state from furnishing the national government the militia statistics it needed before it could issue arms and equipment. Consequently, the state sustained an annual loss of military supplies. In addition, Haines complained that the state's troops were poorly disciplined and that "the ordinary militia musters . . . are generally admitted to retard rather than to promote improvement; and to be a tax upon the time and service of the citizen without any corresponding benefit."

Under a special provision of the new constitution, Haines continued in office until the inauguration of his successor, Charles C. Stratton, on January 21, 1845. The last governor under the old constitution, Haines might have been the first under the new had he not peremptorily declined the nomination. However, only a few years later, on September 22, 1847, the Democratic State Convention nominated him for governor on the first ballot. In November, he defeated his Whig opponent, William Wright, a former mayor of Newark and a congressman. The Whigs' triumph in the legislative race made his victory all the more impressive.

On January 18, 1848, Haines became New Jersey's chief executive a second time. His term under the new constitution was three years instead of one. During this tenure, he continued his crusade for educational reform, telling the legislature that the cause of education should be its major priority since "not many more than one half of the children in the state receive instruction in the schools [and] a very large proportion must be growing up in ignorance." To improve the quality of instruction in New Jersey, Haines suggested that the state create a normal school to furnish competent teachers, introduce free public education, and increase the money raised to support schools at the state and local levels.

Besides being committed to education, Haines was deeply interested in the welfare of prisoners, and he became an active agent to improve their condition. He was particularly concerned about the "want of suitable arrangements" in county prisons. Because of the lack of means to separate the prisoners, "the hardened villain and the juvenile delinquent" often occupied the same cell. The prisons also lacked any facilities that would allow the inmates to spend time usefully engaged in labor. Such conditions, Haines believed, made the county prisons "schools for vice, whose youngest pupils may become the ripest scholars and most finished rogues." To correct the situation, he urged the establishment of workshops in the county prisons, the creation of separate cells for the older and younger prisoners, and even the construction of a state reform school for juvenile offenders.

At the end of his term, on January 21, 1851, Haines resumed his law practice in Hamburg and worked on a number of important cases. In one involving the Goodyear Rubber Company's right to vulcanize India rubber, he worked with Daniel Webster. In 1852, Governor George F. Fort, his successor, nominated Haines associate justice of the state supreme court, and he took his seat on the bench in November after the senate's confirmation. He was reappointed in 1859, and in 1866, when David A. Depue replaced him after his second seven-year term, he retired. Commenting on Haines's years as the associate justice responsible for the difficult Newark circuit, his friend Lucius Q. C. Elmer said, "few judges were ever freer from the influence of passion or prejudice."

In 1860, Haines supported the candidacy of Stephen A. Douglas because he feared "that the election of Lincoln as a sectional candidate might precipitate war." After Lincoln's election, he continued to oppose every measure that might produce hostilities, but once Fort Sumter had been attacked, he actively supported the Union cause. During the war, he assisted by helping to raise troops for the Northern army. Still, in 1864, he voted for George B. McClellan instead of Lincoln because he felt that "the measures of the administration tend to protract the war." Four years later, he supported Horatio Seymour rather than Ulysses S. Grant because he was "steadily opposed to most of the measures of reconstruction adopted by the Republican party."

The former governor's involvement in public life was quite extensive. He was a trustee of many public institutions. In the Presbyterian Church, he was a ruling elder, a president of the Sussex County Bible Society, and a member of the committee that brought about the reunion of the church after the Civil War. His special interest in prison reform led the legislature to appoint him in 1868 to study prison systems in New Jersey and other states. In 1870, Governor Theodore F. Randolph named him delegate to the National Congress on Penitentiary and Reformatory Discipline at Cincinnati. The congress named him to a committee to organize a national reform association and to prepare for the International Convention of Prison Discipline and Reform that met in London in 1872. He was a delegate to that meeting, and he served during the same year as the vice president of the National Prison Association of the United States.

Ann Maria Austin of Warwick, New York, was the first of Haines's two wives. They were married on June 28, 1827, and had three daughters and two sons. One of the sons, Thomas Ryerson Haines, died at the battle of Harrisonburg in Virginia during the Civil War. Ann Maria died on December 8, 1844, and Haines married Mary Townsend of Newark on July 6, 1865. On January 26, 1877, he died at his home in Hamburg.

FREDERICK M. HERRMANN

Alumni Biographical Collection, Seeley G. Mudd Library, Princeton University, Princeton. N.J.

Herrmann, Frederick M. "Stress and Structure: Political Change in Antebellum New Jersey." Ph.D. dissertation, Rutgers University, 1976.

Snell, James P. *History of Sussex and Warren Counties, New Jersey*. Philadelphia: Everts and Peck, 1881.

The Constitution of 1844

Charles Creighton Stratton (March 6, 1796–March 30, 1859), the first popularly elected governor and the only working farmer to serve as chief executive, was born in Swedesboro, Gloucester County. His family had emigrated from England to New England in the seventeenth century, moved to East Hampton, Long Island, in 1648, and arrived in New Jersey about fifty years later.

Stratton's father, James, a judge and physician, served at the battle of Princeton as an assistant surgeon. His mother, Mary Creighton of Haddonfield, participated as a nurse in the Revolution. The couple had seven children, of whom six survived. Charles was the second.

Stratton received a common school education, attending the academy that was the forerunner of the Swedesboro public school. He and his elder brother, Samuel, attended Queens College (later Rutgers University) and graduated in 1814; Samuel became an Episcopal minister, and Charles spent the next seven years farming.

Charles Stratton served in the general assembly in 1821 and 1823 and from 1828 to 1829. Between 1829 and 1836, he was a chosen freeholder from Woolwich Township in Gloucester County, and, in 1835, he also served as a county trustee of the poor. He was elected as a Whig to Congress in 1836. Two years later, he gained notoriety as one of the five members of his party that the House of Representatives declined to seat in the Twenty-Sixth Congress during the "Broad Seal War." He was reelected and seated in 1841. On March 18, 1844, the inhabitants of Gloucester County named Stratton one of their two delegates to the constitutional convention. He became an active member of the important committee on the legislative department and demonstrated his strong faith in democracy by opposing the suggestion that paupers be excluded from voting. He was aghast that some of his colleagues believed that "a pauper has not only lost his property, but he has lost his liberty."

He protested government ownership of internal improvements with equal ardor. Fearing the potential for corruption, he supported private control of public works projects. To prevent the state government from becoming too deeply involved in such projects, he supported reducing the proposed thirty-five-year period of state loans for internal improvements to ten years. Many delegates opposed this plan, saying it relinquished forever New Jersey's right to purchase such works regardless of the advantages. Stratton's proposal lost, forty-five to five.

On September 10, 1844, the Whig state convention nominated Stratton to run for governor in the first popular gubernatorial election. His opponent was Democrat John R. Thomson, the secretary of the Joint Companies and a leading lobbyist for them. Stratton's supporters labeled Thomson "the monopoly candidate." The election, the Whigs claimed, would decide whether the people "will govern themselves for three years to come, or be governed by a domineering company of monopolizing aristocrats, with a capital of millions in their hands." One zealous Whig from Cape May summarized his party's position by arguing that the crucial question to be decided at the polls was "whether we shall have Charles C. Stratton, the Jersey farmer to rule over us, or John Railroad Thomson." In October, after a dynamic Whig campaign, Stratton defeated Thomson by 1,358 of the 74,540 votes balloted.

The new governor took office on January 21, 1845, and immediately assumed the responsibility for guiding the state's transition to the new constitution, reminding the legislature, "the circumstances under which we are assembled, mark the commencement of a new era in the political history of the State." The fundamental law of 1844, Stratton continued, required the senate and assembly to enact laws carrying out its principles and to modify existing statutes that conflicted with its provisions. He suggested, therefore, that the time to condense the laws of the state had arrived. The governor noted that the last revision had taken place twenty-five years earlier, in 1820, and that the state's laws were to be found in that year's revised statutes and in annual pamphlets from the various following legislatures. "To the gentlemen of the Bar," he exclaimed, "this may not be a serious inconvenience, but to others less conversant with the legislation of the State, it is a source of constant embarrassment." During the legislative session of the next year, an ad hoc commission reported about 120 revised laws. The state published them in 1847.

Stratton was also influential in aiding the establishment of the first state mental hospital. Under an act of March 26, 1845, he appointed three commissioners to contract for the erection of a hospital and to superintend its construction. When the design proved much more expensive than originally estimated, Stratton helped persuade the legislature to appropriate an additional $50,000. This would build a structure large enough to separate the manageable patients from the unmanageable ones, a division "indispensable to their proper treatment and cure."

The Mexican War created additional challenges for New Jersey's chief executive. On May 22, 1846, Stratton received a requisition from President James K. Polk for one regiment of volunteers. He issued an immediate proclamation "calling on the organized uniform companies and other citizens of the state to enroll themselves," and the companies promptly responded to the request. However, to the governor's chagrin, "not one of them had the number of rank and file required by the memorandum accompanying the requisition; and consequently could not be accepted."

Stratton ascribed this failure to "the defective and prostrate condition of the militia system of the state," admitting, "had the circumstances been different; had the call been to suppress insurrection or repel invasion, we should have been found alike unprepared." The governor appealed to the legislature to extend "encouragement in some way to the volunteer companies" and to adopt "some simple mode of ascertaining the number of the militia of the state" so that New Jersey could receive its proper share of the issue of arms and equipment from the national government. Nevertheless, in 1847, when the War Department called on the state to raise a battalion, New Jersey could provide only four of the five required companies and took over five months to do so.

On January 18, 1848, Stratton left office to devote the last years of his life to agricultural pursuits on his farm in Swedesboro. He married Sarah Taggart of Philadelphia on February 1, 1854. Although he had no children, two of his nephews achieved fame. Thomas Preston Carpenter was an associate justice of the state supreme court, while Benjamin Franklin Howey served in the Forty-Eighth Congress. Because of ill health, Stratton lived in Europe in 1857 and 1858. He died in Swedesboro on March 30, 1859.

FREDERICK M. HERRMANN

Biographical Collection, Rutgers University Special Collections, New Brunswick, N.J.
Herrmann, Frederick M. "The Constitution of 1844 and Political Change in Antebellum New Jersey." *New Jersey History* 101 (Spring–Summer 1983): 29–51.
——. "Stress and Structure: Political Change in Antebellum New Jersey." Ph.D. dissertation, Rutgers University, 1976.
Proceedings of the New Jersey State Constitutional Convention of *1844*. With an Introduction by John E. Bebout. Trenton: Federal Writers' Project, 1942.

George Franklin Fort (1809–April 23, 1872), physician, politician, and judge, who was the uncle of Governor John F. Fort (1908–10), was born near Pemberton, New Jersey. The eldest son of Andrew Fort, a wealthy farmer of New Hanover Township in Burlington County, Fort was educated in the common schools at Pemberton and at the University of Pennsylvania Medical College. After graduation in 1828, he entered the office of Dr. Jacob Eghert of Pemberton. Later that year, he moved to Dr. Charles Patterson's office in New Egypt, located then in Monmouth County. In 1830, Fort opened his own practice at Imlaystown, where he married Anna Marie Wright, the daughter of Samuel G. Wright, an iron manufacturer and future Whig congressman.

A year later, he returned to New Egypt and extended his practice to southern Monmouth and western Burlington Counties, as well as the area which in 1850 became Ocean County.

George F. Fort's public career began when he was elected to the 1844 New Jersey constitutional convention as a Democrat from Monmouth County. His election was made possible by the county Democratic Party organization's refusal to agree to the bipartisan ticket advanced in all other counties. This resulted in a thoroughly Democratic Monmouth delegation and gave the Democrats a voting majority at the convention. During the proceedings, Fort supported universal suffrage, open eligibility for office, abolition of the freehold qualification for public office, and the popular election of all state and county officials.

In the state elections of 1844, Fort was elected to the general assembly, well ahead of his ticket, with a majority of five hundred votes. After a term in the assembly, where he served on the judiciary committee, he was elected to the state senate and once more appointed to the judiciary committee. He also served on the committee for education and the Plainfield Bank Investigating Committee and acted as one of three commissioners for ascertaining the value of state lands under water at Jersey City. Fort's reputation as a reformer originated when he sponsored a bill to ensure township support for public education and created the Manufacturing Incorporation Law, which eliminated private incorporation acts for specific industries.

In 1850, George Fort was widely endorsed for the Democratic gubernatorial nomination, with the moderately influential *Monmouth County Democrat* advancing his name two months before the Democratic state convention. He was nominated on the fifth ballot over John Summerhill of Salem County, John Cassedy of Hudson County, and Henry A. Ford of Morris County. The Whigs nominated John Runk, a former congressman from Hunterdon County.

The state campaign focused on the power and influence of the Joint Companies, on the Democratic Party of New Jersey, and, through that party, on the state. In the first popular gubernatorial election in 1844, the Democratic candidate had been John R. Thomson, secretary of the companies. Thomson was the brother-in-law of Robert F. Stockton, the majority stockholder and president of the Camden and Amboy Railroad. Stockton supported Fort for governor in 1850 and was elected to the United States Senate in 1851. Thomson, the initial Democratic caucus nominee for the Senate in 1851, was elected to the seat when Stockton left it in 1853.

Fort was strongly associated with the monopoly interests. When the Camden and Amboy Railroad was incorporated, his father-in-law was named as a commissioner to sell stock in the company. Fort suggested during his administration that the state government relinquish its right to purchase the works of the Joint Companies in return for a larger guarantee of revenue, arguing that an attempt to annul the exclusive privileges of the companies would constitute a violation of the state constitution. Seven weeks later, on February 28, 1854, Fort was named one of nine incorporators in an act incorporating the Camden and Pemberton Agricultural Railroad Company, a trunk line of the Camden and Amboy. The Whigs attempted to label Fort and other Democrats puppets to the interests of the Joint Companies. Their charges, in substance, accused the companies of subsidizing Democratic candidates for governor in return for the appointment of friendly judges to the state judiciary. Indeed, during Fort's administration, the antimonopoly banner was constantly unfurled in elective battles with the Democratic Party. During the 1850 campaign, as evidence of his antimonopoly sentiments, Fort and his supporters emphasized his sponsorship of incorporation laws.

The monopoly issue never proved effective in defeating the state's Democratic Party. More important in the 1850 elections for governor and Congress was dissension within Whig ranks over the compromise measures of 1850. Leading Whig newspapers condemned the Fugitive Slave Law as "infidelity to the fundamental principles of the Constitution and Liberty, . . . an exhibition of faithlessness by Northern Representatives to the cause of Northern Rights." They portrayed the Democrats as allied with slave power, favorable to the unlimited expansion of slavery, and devoid of principle—demagogues "stimulating here a base and wicked Popular Prejudice against one portion of our inhabitants [blacks], refusing to consider them as entitled to the privileges of man."

The Democratic press countered, charging Whig leaders with "seeking to make the State of New Jersey an Abolition State." Democrats were not proslavery, Fort argued, adding that it was the duty of "every citizen to sustain and carry out" the Compromise of 1850. Fort maintained that the Fugitive Slave Act was binding on northern states because it was "in accordance with the evident intentment of the constitutional compact." Peace, stability, and union depended on its enforcement in Fort's view, and if New Jersey was to remain loyal to the Union, its officials were compelled to enforce the provisions for the rendition of "fugitives from labor."

Procompromise Whigs found themselves closer to Democrats on the slavery extension issue than to fellow Whigs willing to take the stand in defense of the "Liberty" the *State Gazette* (Trenton) and the *Newark Daily Mercury* demanded. Some, like William Wright, the 1846 Whig gubernatorial candidate and a Democratic United States senator from 1853 to 1858, simply switched parties. Their disaffection with the Whig Party began in 1850 when Whig senators William L. Dayton and Jacob W. Miller voted against the compromise, and they began the process of defection to the Democratic Party by exhibiting apathy during the 1850 campaign.

Other procompromise Whigs attempted to develop a campaign theme that ignored the controversy over the expansion of slavery. The *Morristown Jerseyman*, for example, tried to convert the tired tariff issue into a nativist platform, arguing that the Democrats' tariff of 1846 was decidedly pro-European. "It is important," the editor wrote, "that we become independent of foreign nations," through a resurrection of protective features in the tariff of 1842 and the passage of stiffer naturalization laws. The schism between nativist sentiments and anti-slavery-extension forces that would plague political opposition to the Democrats until 1860 had begun to work for the Democratic Party even though no open conflict took place until 1854 with the passage of the Kansas-Nebraska Act.

The Whig Party's failure to unify the themes of its gubernatorial campaign in 1850 led to a stunning Democratic victory. Fort garnered 53.9 percent of the popular vote, the largest percentage any statewide Democratic candidate amassed before the Civil War. More important, Democrats triumphed in Camden, Mercer, Morris, Passaic, and Salem Counties for the first time since the 1843 congressional elections, marking a major voter shift. The change secured statewide dominance for the Democratic Party, which did not lose a state election until the 1856 victory of the "Opposition" party candidate for governor. In the state senate, Democrats gained one member, in the assembly five, achieving a majority in the lower house for the first time in seven years. By 1854, the number of Whig legislators dwindled to twenty-one, while Democrats held fifty-three seats.

During the Fort administration, expenditures for common school education increased substantially, drawn from the income of dividends paid on state-owned Joint Companies stock. Major reform legislation created the ten-hour workday and protected child labor. A homestead exemption act was passed, exempting a family homestead from sale for debts totaling less than $1,000. Administration bills for the regulation of banks were secured, consistent with the "hard money" position of the Democratic platform. The system of representation in the general assembly was altered to provide for a district system to replace the old countywide general elections. General incorporation acts applying to banks, insurance companies, and plank roads were secured, but the old system of private acts to incorporate railroads was retained. The influence of the Joint Companies continued unchecked as two United States senators were elected at their behest, and the conflict over monopoly in a democratic, free-trade economy remained unresolved.

At the expiration of Fort's gubernatorial term, his Democratic successor, Rodman M. Price, appointed him a judge of the Court of Errors and Appeals. After a term on the bench, Fort retired from public life and resumed the practice of medicine in New Egypt. He continued to serve on the board of trustees at Bordentown Female College, and he was a trustee of the Zoar Methodist Episcopal Church in New Egypt. He spent his last years writing a laudatory history of Freemasonry in the United States, published three years after his death on April 23, 1872.

PHILIP C. DAVIS

Lane, Wheaton J. *From Indian Trail to Iron Horse: Travel and Transportation in New Jersey, 1620–1860*. Princeton: Princeton University Press, 1939.

Renda, Lex. "The Dysfunctional Party: Collapse of the New Jersey Whigs, 1849–1853." *New Jersey History* 116 (Spring–Summer 1998): 3–57.

Rodman McCamley Price (May 5, 1816–June 7, 1894), naval officer and politician, the son of Francis and Ann (McCamley) Price, was born in Frankford Township, Sussex County. His forebears, migrating from Connecticut to the Sussex foothills in the 1740s, became established leaders in the county squirearchy. The governor's grandfather and great-uncle quartermastered for the Continental army and later marketed cattle, timber, and distilled whiskey to the port of New York. Rodman Price shared the privileges of his class and attended the Presbyterian academy at Lawrenceville and may have entered the College of New Jersey (later Princeton University), remaining there until illness forced him to drop his studies. He read some law but never practiced, choosing instead to enter the commission business in New York City. In 1840, he used family connections with the expiring Van Buren administration to secure an appointment as a purser in the United States Navy. Price would always find preferment easier with national Democrats than with party patrons at home.

Price married Matilda Decatur Trenchard, the daughter and the sister of navy men, and settled in Brooklyn Heights, comfortably berthed in the peacetime navy. After routine coastal cruises on the sidewheeler U.S.S. *Fulton*, he sailed with the ten-gun frigate U.S.S. *Missouri*, one of the first warships to cross the Atlantic under steam, in July 1843. While recoaling off Gibraltar, an accident gutted the *Missouri*, and its officers spent some time as guests of the British consul. Price struck an acquaintance with the American ambassador to Madrid, Washington Irving; toured Iberia, using his smattering of Spanish to collect documents for Irving's biography of Columbus; and later jaunted to Paris. Back on duty, he joined the sloop of war *Cyane*, part of Commodore John Drake Sloat's Pacific Squadron. He spent his time mainly with payrolls, occasionally going ashore at Monterey, Matamoros, or Lima to provision and bargain with local merchants. On July 7, 1846, at the onset of the Mexican War, the *Cyane* ferried a detachment of marines which had seized Monterey, California. That day, Sloat named Price prefect and *alcalde* (magistrate) at Monterey, where for a month he helped administer an occupied zone.

California proved a giddy experience that dogged Price's reputation the rest of his life. With other magistrates whose duties included recording land titles, Price joined the hunt for choice rancheros, becoming Sloat's investment agent and partner in Monterey and other townsites around San

Francisco Bay. In late 1848, back in New York, "buisey [*sic*] president making," he engineered an appointment as purser for the Pacific Squadron from the Polk administration. With headquarters moved to his own waterfront property in bustling San Francisco, Price became provisioner and payroller for ships and depots from Monterey to Honolulu, a frustrating, highly speculative operation. While gold strikes inflated commodity prices and merchants warily discounted United States bills of exchange, the navy expected Price to supply the "California Station" and establish the hegemony of American credit that would prevent the drain of gold bullion to London. He emerged a real-estate "tycoon," a booster of the city's pioneer "Long Wharf," a Democratic delegate to the territory's constitutional convention, and a member of San Francisco's first common council. But he also made unauthorized drafts on specie in the United States Customs House and neglected quarterly returns on expenses. For this, in August 1849, he was "detached" from the squadron and ordered to Washington to render account. On his return, his steamer, the *Orleans St. John*, burned on the Alabama River, destroying, he claimed, his payroll vouchers. The disaster muddled his ledgers but provided years of litigation when the navy sued for $88,000 in unaccounted funds.

Back East, Price bought a mansion and grounds in Hoboken, entered a Wall Street banking partnership that speculated in the California trade, and looked after his absentee holdings. In 1850, the Hudson County Democratic organization, influenced by Price's father, "Judge" Francis Price, a Weehawken resident and speculator, and by Commodore Robert Field Stockton, the Jerseyman who had been military governor of California while Price was there, sought Price out for his California luster. Safely removed from debates on the issues, Price received the congressional nomination, in the words of one Democrat, J. R. Riggs, "without the least expectation of his success" but with every confidence that he could pay his own way. But Whig factionalism in Essex handed him a narrow victory.

His mind distracted by California deals, Price served an uneventful term in the Thirty-Seventh Congress. He proffered the usual private bills from home voters, like Methodist appeals to end liquor imports and proposals from Jersey City Irish Catholics for subsidized mail packets to Galway, Ireland. He was a responsive if not particularly eloquent agent for Newark harbor masters, Paterson manufacturers, the Stevens shipyards in Hoboken, and the Pacific mail steamships, all anxious for federal protection. He scarcely participated in House debate, save once as "the most immediate and direct representative the Navy has ever had upon this floor" to urge recodification of martial law aboard ship. Price's faith that traditional flogging made a "well-ordered, well-disciplined ship" was balanced by a proper Jacksonian demand that summary courts-martial supersede the captain's powers to punish at sea. Such contributions ended abruptly when he lost reelection in October 1852 and retired to his New York firm to nurse his California property and his claims on the navy.

In 1853, as the party wrangled to tailor a gubernatorial candidate for its antimonopoly stance, many Democrats remembered Price. They reached for the ex-congressman, a figure inconspicuously tied to the privileged Joint Companies, the Camden and Amboy Railroad and Delaware and Raritan Canal. While Whigs taunted the free-spending "California" candidate as the puppet of the Camden and Amboy and argued that western residence disqualified him under the state constitution's five-year requirement, Democrats campaigned as the antimonopoly party, promising "reform" all around. According to Charles Parker, "Many [Democrats] remained at home & others went to the poles feeling little interests in the result, and but for the money used Mr. Price could not have been elected." Although Price's majority was less than his immediate Democratic predecessor's, the party rolled up a two-to-one victory margin in the new legislature.

A Hoboken interloper, vaguely suspect as a tool for New York commerce, the new governor enjoyed little real influence against the state's great oligarchs and entrenched county machines. Except for indulging a few private visions quite beyond his gubernatorial reach, Price hewed to the safe conservatism of the Democratic Party, which had to meet growing unrest in the urbanizing northeastern counties. He rooted his politics in tried-and-true Jacksonian attacks against unbridled corporate power. His annual messages effused orthodox hard-money homilies and denounced "unsettling" competition for special corporate charters. Price vowed to retire all paper bank notes under $25 denominations gradually. His 1855 veto of the Newark Plank Road and Bridge bill, which aided Passaic River commerce and pleased Newark boosters, used classic antimonopoly rhetoric reminiscent of the Taney Court's Charles River Bridge decision.

When the 1853 "reform" pledges fell due, the governor maneuvered to placate antiestablishment voters. The inefficient state court system had long angered the people, and Democrats responded with a Law Reform Commission to reorganize the judiciary. Agreement for more judgeships, however, foundered over the appointment of Whigs to the bench. Persuaded by Democratic leaders that moderation "might save a judge," Price parceled out nominations to the deserving of both parties. He faced a far more difficult chore in cutting the umbilical cord that tied the Democrats to the Joint Companies—a patronage empire that affronted antimonopoly Democrats and proved a liability in Hudson and Essex Counties, where Whigs harangued against "the monster." Democrats in the 1853 legislature considered a state sinking fund to buy the transportation system when its exclusive charter expired in 1864. But the Camden and Amboy president, Robert F. Stockton, bargained for an extension of the Joint Companies' exclusive privileges in exchange for eventual state takeover. In the end, Governor Price, with most of his party, remained a supporter of "Jersey enterprise" and the $200,000 which the monopoly paid annually into the state treasury. He signed a compromise bill which fixed the maximum freight tariffs. But it also extended the corporation's privileges, essentially untouched, until January 1869, with the option of state takeover in twenty years.

As a patron of education, the governor rode the crest of two decades of agitation for public schools. In 1846, the legislature established matching state school-district funds for education, and Governors George F. Fort and Daniel Haines committed the Democratic Party to a system of public education that included the idea of normal schools. By 1853, school reformers had made the "teachers institutes" a part of the educational establishment. Half lyceum and half itinerant camp meeting, the institutes brought the latest pedagogy to the county level, turning an emerging teacher professionalism into a powerful statewide lobby. Price participated in the 1854 Sussex Institute and urged state support to extend the institutes' work to all counties. In January 1855, he called for the establishment of a state training school, and that autumn he and School Superintendent John H. Phillips drafted the bill that established Trenton Normal School.

A cultivated cosmopolite with a taste for European grandeur, Price was also active in the realm of commerce. Jersey shippers, alarmed by booster claims of the New York City Chamber of Commerce and the rapid expansion of Manhattan's wharves into the Hudson River, appealed to Trenton for redress. Price and New York Governor Myron Clark appointed a harbor commission to investigate whether pier construction obstructed river flow and to recommend official bulkhead lines—the first such venture in bistate port regulation. Price also appointed New Jersey's first pilots' board, which protected the Newark and Jersey City tug operators struggling to stave off New York's encroachment of the Liverpool trade. From tidewater, the governor looked landward and created a state geological survey, urged first by agricultural societies in search of cheap phosphates, then by industrialists anxious to exploit the zinc, franklinite, and other ores locked away in the northern counties. To head the corps of surveyors, Price chose William Kitchell, the Newark geologist committed to the city's exploration of its mineral hinterland. Price took "personal interest" in the survey as it began in Sussex, pleased that the sales of engraved maps to European collectors might help defray expenses. His rationalist bent surfaced in continued proposals to scrap the patchwork of town highway commissioners with one road administrator per county—mere grandiloquence, however, when road building was the patronage staple of local politics.

As state commander in chief, the governor tried to invigorate a militia that had decayed into ragged disorder, swollen by Irish and German companies whose foreign ways appalled nativists in the officer cadre. With the governor's hearty support, Adjutant General Thomas Cadwalader held more division parades and used county brigade boards to discipline local formations. He requested, but failed to receive from the legislature, a fifteen-cent tax on all able-bodied males to subsidize the growing number of elite "uniform" companies. In 1856, the governor sent Cadwalader on a fact-finding tour of European arsenals, a frivolous assignment given the state's primitive readiness. Apart from cosmetic improvements, Price presided over a subtle revolution in the ranks and signed, despite protests from nativists, the commissions of numerous ethnic officers.

Governor Price kept the Jersey Democratic Party steered on a "middling" course during the agitation over various issues in the 1850s. Sidestepping demands by Protestant nativists to limit Irish Catholic votes, Price suggested that the legislature enact a limited moratorium on the naturalization of foreigners before elections. Amidst fierce debate on the Maine Prohibition law, he left the saloon issue to the legislature, provided the lawmakers uphold "constitutional rights." A conservative Democrat, unmoved by the antislavery revolt in party ranks—and to some degree a Californian, in any event—Price preferred the southern-oriented, "territorial" solution to the slavery crisis. At the 1856 state party convention, he wielded patronage and money to keep the state platform resolutely favorable to local control of slavery in Kansas. Later, in the presidential canvass, Price stumped the state for James Buchanan, then crossed to New York City for yeoman service with Fernando Wood's "Administration" machine.

Since the New Jersey constitution barred a second term, in spring 1857 Price unsuccessfully sought the ambassadorship to Mexico. Then he plunged into business ventures that had blossomed under his gubernatorial patronage, As early as 1855, he had joined Horace P. Russ in quarrying stone from "Judge" Price's property along the Hackensack River. With contracts for Russ pavement in New York, Brooklyn, and Philadelphia, the partners began a flourishing barge commerce on the inland waterways of Greater New York. While still in office, the governor joined his father in a ferry business to Forty-Second Street in Manhattan. By January 1859, the Weehawken Ferry Company, with its flagship *Rodman M. Price*, was providing regular service across the Hudson River. The two also speculated on lots on Bull's Head Road, expecting the ferry to enhance the suburban appeal of the South Bergen hills.

The retired governor, comfortably settled on his father's property in Ramapo, stood aloof during the Civil War. During the secession winter, he was one of the nine-man New Jersey delegation to the Washington "Peace Conference" which futilely debated John J. Crittenden's resolutions to avert war. In the *Newark Evening Journal*, April 4, 1861, he exhorted Jerseymen not to take up arms against the South; this appeal was congenial to many local merchants worried about their southern markets. Otherwise, Price stuck to business; with his father as security, he temporarily climbed out of debt.

After the war, as a Bergen gentleman farmer, Price lapsed into a political oblivion, stirred occasionally by humiliating appearances in bankruptcy court. Dubious financing forced the Weehawken Ferry into receivership in 1866. After his father's death, he so mismanaged the family estate that in 1873 the court of chancery removed him as executor. Badly in need of money, he again pursued his claims with the navy and later with the United States Court of Claims. In what appears an act of charity, in 1890 the United States Congress approved a relief bill, providing a windfall settlement. He never enjoyed the money, for chancery immediately attached it to settle another bad debt arising out of a San Francisco property sold four decades before. A broken man, Price eluded process servers on both sides of the Hudson and spent time in the Hackensack jail before his health finally gave out. He died a curious relic of "Young America," faintly remembered by a state busy building for the new century.

JOEL SCHWARTZ

Rodman M. Price Papers, Huntington Library, San Marino, Calif.

Rodman M. Price Papers, Rutgers University Special Collections, New Brunswick, N.J.

Rodman M. Price Papers, University of California, Berkeley, Special Collections, Berkeley, Calif.

Gillette, William. *Jersey Blue: Civil War Politics in New Jersey, 1854–1865.* New Brunswick: Rutgers University Press, 1995.

Knapp, Charles M. *New Jersey Politics during the Period of the Civil War and Reconstruction.* Geneva, N.Y.: W. F. Humphrey, 1924.

Lane, Wheaton J. *From Indian Trail to Iron Horse: Travel and Transportation in New Jersey, 1620–1860.* Princeton: Princeton University Press, 1939.

Snell, James P. *History of Sussex and Warren Counties, New Jersey.* Philadelphia: Everts and Peck, 1881.

William Augustus Newell (September 5, 1817–August 8, 1901) was born in Franklin, Ohio. His parents, James H. and Eliza (Hankinson) Newell, both of old Monmouth County families, had moved to Ohio shortly before his birth; they returned to New Jersey in 1819 when he was two years old. Settling in New Brunswick, James Newell worked as a civil engineer and mapmaker. William Newell attended the district public schools, graduated from Rutgers College in 1836, and studied medicine locally. He married Johanna Van Deursen, the daughter of his mentor. They had three children. After completing medical studies at the University of Pennsylvania in 1839, Newell entered practice, first with an uncle at Manahawkin and then alone at Imlaystown. In 1844 he moved to Allentown, which was to be his New Jersey residence for the rest of his life.

Two years later Newell combined politics with medicine when the Whigs of the Second Congressional District nominated him for Congress. He was elected by a narrow margin and reelected in 1848, but in 1850 he refused a third nomination. During his first term in Congress he accomplished what he always considered his most important and lasting achievement: the founding of the United States Life Saving Service. In 1848 he steered through

Congress a measure appropriating $10,000 to found a series of lighthouse stations between Sandy Hook and Little Egg Harbor, a treacherous stretch of coast that had been the scene of many wrecks. Each station had a cannon to shoot a line to stranded ships so that a small car could be pulled from shore to ship and back again, removing passengers. The service soon extended from Long Island to Cape May, and after 1850, when the apparatus saved two hundred passengers and crew members of the Scottish brig *Ayrshire*, it spread over the entire Atlantic coast.

Although the founding of the service enhanced Newell's reputation, it did not lead immediately to higher office. During the 1850s, after the Whig Party foundered, Newell allied with the new American, or Know-Nothing, Party, which sought to limit the immigrant role in American politics. In 1856 the Americans and the Republicans attempted to cooperate at the state level and agreed to run a common gubernatorial candidate to defeat the dominant Democrats. Calling themselves the "Opposition," the Americans and the Republicans nominated Newell at a joint convention in Trenton. As a Know-Nothing who opposed the extension of slavery in the territories, he was acceptable to the majority in both parties, although German Republicans in Newark and Jersey City who opposed the Know-Nothing movement tried to nominate a Republican not associated with nativism.

The American and Republican Parties jointly supported Newell for governor, but each supported its own presidential candidate. The Americans adhered to Millard Fillmore and the Republicans to John C. Frémont. By taking care not to antagonize either faction, Newell defeated William C. Alexander, the Democratic candidate, by less than three thousand votes. The Democrats, however, won control of both houses of the legislature.

In Newell's inaugural address in January 1857 he set the tone of his administration. He believed a governor should follow rather than lead the legislature and should use the veto sparingly. He urged strict economy and an end to state indebtedness. He promoted improvements in the school system and limitations on the sale of liquor and on the use of corporate influence. He opposed a New York plan to move its quarantine station to Sandy Hook and called for improvements in the coastal life-saving system. He also advocated stricter naturalization procedures, restrictions on the suffrage of naturalized citizens, and voter registration laws for the electorate of incorporated cities.

In subsequent annual addresses Newell returned to each of these themes, stressing the need for economy in particular and the desirability of restricting immigration and curtailing the influence of immigrants. One issue that was not a state matter intruded in each message. Newell could not avoid the increasingly important slavery controversy. While he opposed the extension of slave territory, he saw abolitionism as an equal threat to the Union. By 1860 Newell was devoting more space in his annual message to this essentially national issue than to any other subject, urging that a course be found to save the Union from northern and southern extremists.

As the slavery issue forced political realignments, Newell worked to unite the American and Republican wings of the New Jersey Opposition into one harmonious party to work with the Republicans nationally. He divided the patronage and encouraged fusion at the local level. Not always successful, he saw some of his early appointments—such as that of Charles D. Deshler to clerk of the supreme court—defeated by continued factionalism among Opposition legislators.

While no bills of great importance became law during Newell's administration, there were many enactments related to New Jersey's rapid evolution into an urban, industrial state. The legislature carved Union County out of Essex County and granted city charters to Elizabeth, Rahway, and Egg Harbor. It authorized Hoboken and Trenton to improve their water systems and granted Jersey City permission to build a workhouse. Newark, Jersey City, and Hoboken received charters for horse-car street railway companies, and the Erie Railroad consolidated its New Jersey tracks. Granting corporate charters continued to constitute a major portion of the legislative workload.

Since Newell considered the executive function of government secondary to the legislative, he made no attempt to provide strong leadership. However, he vigorously defended the prerogatives of the office when he perceived them to be under legislative attack. When Chancellor Benjamin Williamson's term expired in 1859, Newell nominated Abraham O. Zabriskie from the Republican wing of the Opposition. The Democratic senate denied confirmation and demanded that he reappoint Williamson. Refusing to bow to legislative dictates in the matter of appointments, Newell sent eight more names to the senate, each of which was rejected. Rather than reappoint Williamson, Newell allowed the office to remain vacant; it was not filled until 1860, when Governor Charles S. Olden appointed Chief Justice Henry W. Green.

As governor Newell presided over the court of pardons, and in late 1857 a case came before that body that greatly affected his post–Civil War political career. James P. Donnelly, a medical student from a New York City Irish family, was convicted of murdering Albert S. Moses over a gambling debt at the Sea View House in Navesink and was sentenced to death by a Monmouth County Court. Donnelly unsuccessfully appealed the decision through the state courts and finally sought a commutation to life imprisonment from the Court of Pardons. To the Irish Catholics of New Jersey, Donnelly had been convicted by a Protestant jury before Protestant judges on doubtful evidence. A question of law quickly became a socially and politically significant issue, and petitions in Donnelly's favor circulated in the Irish communities of many northeastern cities. The Court of Pardons voted six to two against commutation, with Newell among the majority. In a two-hour address to the crowd before Donnelly's public hanging, however, he claimed that the court had been evenly divided and that Newell, acting on nativistic prejudice, had cast the tie-breaking vote which would cost Donnelly his life. In Newell's subsequent campaigns the Irish remembered Donnelly's accusation.

When Newell left office in January 1860, the Opposition was more unified at all levels, although the Americans and Republicans continued separate organizations in several areas of the state. Newell moved firmly into the Republican ranks, attending the party's national nominating conventions in 1860 and 1864. Soon after President Abraham Lincoln took office in 1861, he appointed Newell superintendent of the Life Saving Service for New Jersey. Newell held this office until returning to Congress in 1865, regularly inspecting all life-saving stations and urging their improvement.

In 1864 Newell received the Republican nomination for Congress from his district and won election on a platform supporting the administration and its war policy. As a congressman he voted for radical reconstruction of the South, although he was not in the vanguard of the reconstruction movement and did not favor extreme measures any more than he had as governor.

Newell was not reelected in 1866. Out of favor with state party leaders, he was renominated but unenthusiastically supported. Furthermore, remarks unfriendly to immigrants from his gubernatorial messages were circulated in German, and a distorted version of his role in the Donnelly case was spread among the Irish. Newell blamed his defeat in part on the "base and ungenerous appeal to the passions and prejudices of a large class of voters, by misrepresenting [his] motives and action in the discharge of solemn and painful executive duty."

Newell returned to the practice of medicine. In 1868 he once more sought the congressional nomination but without success, and in 1870 he received the nomination but lost the election. He ran for governor again in 1877, opposing George B. McClellan, the popular Civil War general nominated by the Democrats. Newell ran an inept campaign, alienating many regular Republicans, and he lost with 46 percent of the vote. Once again his role in the Donnelly case became an issue, with the Irish-oriented *Jersey City Argus* declaring that "Newell's action toward poor Donnelly" had been "prompted by his intense hatred of foreigners."

Newell continued to practice medicine in Allentown until 1880, when President Rutherford B. Hayes appointed him territorial governor of Washington. Supporting measures similar to those he had sponsored as governor of New Jersey, he urged strict economy, lower taxes, laws to prevent intemperance and desecration of the Sabbath, the forced acculturation of the territory's Indian population, and an improved life-saving service on the Pacific coast.

Newell served as territorial governor until 1884. He then served as a United States Indian inspector in the Northwest for one year. He resumed the practice of medicine in Olympia in 1885 and remained in Washington for fourteen more years, returning to New Jersey only after his wife's death.

In 1899, at the age of eighty-two, Newell returned to Allentown. He practiced medicine and took an active role in the Monmouth County Historical Association, delivering two papers, one dealing with the founding of the United States Life Saving Service. He died at the age of eighty-four and was buried in the Allentown Presbyterian cemetery.

DOUGLAS V. SHAW

Applegate, Lloyd Rogers. *A Life of Service: William Augustus Newell.* Toms River, N.J.: Ocean County Historical Society, 1994.

Gillette, William. *Jersey Blue: Civil War Politics in New Jersey, 1854–1865.* New Brunswick: Rutgers University Press, 1995.

Platt, Hermann K., ed. *Charles Perrin Smith: New Jersey Political Reminiscences, 1828–1882.* New Brunswick: Rutgers University Press, 1965.

Renda, Lex. "The Dysfunctional Party: Collapse of the New Jersey Whigs, 1849–1853." *New Jersey History* 116 (Spring–Summer 1998): 3–57.

Charles Smith Olden (February 19, 1799–April 7, 1876) was born of Quaker ancestry in Stony Brook, near Princeton. He was the son of Hart and Temperance (Smith) Olden. He went to Lawrenceville School. Upon graduation he worked for a while in his father's store and then for the mercantile firm of Matthew Newkirk and Company, first in Philadelphia and later, from 1826 to 1832, in New Orleans. He returned to Princeton after inheriting a large estate from his uncle and built the house now called Drumthwacket. Olden lived the life of a gentleman farmer and became a director of the Trenton Banking Company in 1842. He married Phoebe Ann Smith of Trenton; though they had no children of their own, they adopted a daughter.

Olden was elected to the state senate as a Whig in 1844 and reelected in 1847; he served in the senate until 1851. Little is known about his senatorial career, except that he took an interest in the State Lunatic Asylum and was chairman of the Committee on Education. In 1856 Olden supported Millard Fillmore, the American Party candidate for the presidency of the United States. In 1859 the "Opposition" Party nominated him as its gubernatorial candidate to oppose the Democrat, Edwin R. V. Wright. The Opposition Party, which had been created in 1856 to oppose the Democratic Party, was made up of former Whigs, Know-Nothings, and incipient Republicans. They maintained this name through the election of 1860 and later became the Union Party; they took the name Republican during Reconstruction. Olden was also nominated by the American Party. Olden had not taken part in the heated political debate over the extension of slavery during the 1850s. A conservative, he opposed the extension of slavery and supported the enforcement of the Fugitive Slave Act. His views reflected those of the citizens of the state of New Jersey, who would never have supported an abolitionist. Olden defeated Wright by a mere 1,601 votes, but the Democrats won slim majorities in the general assembly and the senate.

In Governor Olden's inaugural address on January 17, 1860, he said that each state had the "exclusive independent control of its domestic policy" and that slavery was "exclusively and eminently a matter of domestic policy, to be . . . controlled by each State for itself." In the presidential election of 1860, the Opposition Party supported Abraham Lincoln and opposed both Stephen A. Douglas and the fusion ticket. Olden's views were more conservative than the Republicans', but he nevertheless supported Lincoln. New Jersey cast three electoral votes for Douglas and four for Lincoln.

With the election of Lincoln, South Carolina seceded from the Union, and other southern states soon followed. During this period of crisis, Olden attempted to seek a compromise between the North and the South. In his annual message in January 1861, he reaffirmed his support for the Fugitive Slave Act and called for its enforcement by all of the states. However, he did not support the right of secession, which he considered anarchy. He viewed the crisis as having been caused "by a few persons of extreme views both North and South." At this time he felt that the people of New Jersey would "stand as a unit in favor of the Union." But he also said that they would "make all reasonable and proper concessions to insure its perpetuity." At first he placed his hopes for a compromise in the United States Congress; however, fearing that the Congress would find no means to alleviate the crisis, he urged the legislature of New Jersey to adopt a resolution appointing delegates to a convention of state delegates, which would "meet and endeavor to agree upon terms by which our Union may be saved."

When Congress failed to arrive at a compromise, Virginia called on the state to send delegates to Washington, to the Washington Peace Conference, which was attended by most of the states that had not seceded. The New Jersey legislature adopted a series of resolutions known as the "Joint Resolution in Relation to the State of the Union." It supported efforts at compromise, including the so-called Crittenden Compromise and the repeal of the personal liberty laws, and it appointed delegates to attend the Washington Peace Conference. Olden signed this resolution on January 29, 1861.

Olden, elected as a delegate to the conference, was the only governor to attend. While he did not speak at the conference, he supported the resolutions for compromise, including one favoring the extension of slavery into the territories, similar to the Crittenden Compromise; one providing compensation for runaway slaves; and one prohibiting Congress from abolishing slavery in the states. At this time most Republicans were opposing any attempt at a compromise that would extend slavery into the territories.

While Governor Olden was considered conciliatory by most Republicans, his principal fear was that an armed conflict would split the citizens of New Jersey, for there was a growing sentiment for some form of secession or at least for the view that the southern states should be permitted to secede in peace. These fears disappeared when South Carolina and the southern Confederacy attacked Fort Sumter. This act of war by the South brought forth in New Jersey an overwhelming response in favor of the Union, and many who had earlier supported compromise now favored war on the southern states. Olden was one such person; though a month after the firing on Sumter he still feared for the fate of New Jersey, he wrote to President Lincoln that "New Jersey is a border state, & it is of great importance that she stand steadfast in the great conflict."

Olden's first major problem as the war governor was to secure places in the army for the New Jersey regiments, since many more were being offered than the federal government could accommodate. Never again would there be such enthusiasm for the war in New Jersey or elsewhere in the North; before the war was over, the state would have to resort to a draft to fill the military quotas.

As soon as the war began, Olden called a special session of the legislature. In his opening remarks, he expressed his fear of invasion and called for the creation of four regiments to be armed, trained, and stationed in southern New Jersey: "to make provision for the defense of the State, and especially to provide for the protection of our sea coast, the coast of the Delaware, and our frontier." He later abandoned this idea in favor of federal defense of the coast. This special session, which was marked by a lack of political partisanship, borrowed $2 million from New Jersey banks, raised more troops than Washington could accept, passed appropriations for ten thousand stands of arms, and secured a tax to raise monies for soldier's families.

Charles Perrin Smith, the clerk of the New Jersey Supreme Court, wrote in his *Reminiscences* that "had he [Olden] failed to be elected, there can be but very little doubt that New Jersey would have been forced to cast her lot with the South in the Great Rebellion which so soon followed." While this is an obvious exaggeration, Olden assumed a primary role in mobilizing the state during the first two years of the Civil War. According to John Y. Foster, "for a period of twenty-one months, he was only absent from the State capital two days and nights, and during much of this time he worked at his desk not only during the day but far into the nights, making it a rule to complete each day the duties which that day brought." Some nights he even slept in his office at the statehouse.

He did leave the state to attend the conference of governors in Altoona, Pennsylvania, in September 1862. Governor Andrew G. Curtin of Pennsylvania called this conference originally to urge the Lincoln administration to follow a more aggressive campaign in the war and to replace General George B. McClellan. Two events subverted its purpose: Lincoln issued the Emancipation Proclamation the day before the conference convened, and at the battle of Antietam the Union army stopped the Confederate army's advance into the North. The governors adopted a set of resolutions that Olden, with the governors of Delaware, Maryland, Kentucky, and Missouri, refused to sign because they dissented from the section that approved the Emancipation Proclamation.

Olden was a diligent worker who wrote all "letters of importance" himself and "kept everything at all times under his personal supervision." The result was that New Jersey's regiments serving outside the state were relatively well equipped and, unlike many regiments from other states, were not officered by political appointees.

Little is known about the man, for he published only the messages that he delivered to the legislature, and very few of his personal letters exist. His messages to the legislature say little of a personal nature, dealing almost exclusively with routine governmental concerns. His last message, in January 1863, urged the legislature not to abandon the men fighting the war "by lending our influence in favor of vain and fruitless efforts to interpose ill-timed pacific offices between the majestic arm of a nation's law and a wicked rebellion that will be satisfied with nothing but the accomplishment of its object." This was his only reference to the growing peace movement that would reach its zenith in 1863.

John Y. Foster, in one of the only accounts describing Governor Olden, wrote that he was a man of "incorruptible integrity, of inflexible loyalty and of indomitable will; one of those rare men who conceal under a complacent demeanor, vast inherent strength and self-reliance, which, upon emergency, produce in them prodigies of performance."

Charles Perrin Smith, who worked with Governor Olden, recorded his impressions. Smith wrote in his *Reminiscences*, "Governor Olden's financial experience and business training, united with [an] unusual degree of sagacity and untiring industry, alone enabled him to command success; while his strict probity, and unostentatious manners gained for him the entire confidence of the people. . . . Personally cognizant of his zeal and labor, and aware of the vast responsibility with which he was burdened, I could not regard his evidently failing health with[out] great solicitude, but he steadily declined to seek relaxation."

Prevented by the New Jersey constitution from serving a second consecutive term, Olden left the governorship in January 1863. He was succeeded by Joel Parker, a Democrat. After leaving office, he continued to support the war. At a mass meeting in Trenton on April 16, 1863, Olden was elected president of the Loyal National League of New Jersey, which, like similar organizations in other states, attempted to unite those who supported the war regardless of political party, forming a new organization that avoided the existing political nomenclature. Its purpose was to establish a league in each county and town. This had the effect of reviving the Union-Republican Party in the election campaigns of 1863 and 1864.

Following the war, Olden served as a judge of the Court of Errors and Appeals from 1868 to 1873. He was also a member of the Riparian Commission from 1869 to 1875 and a commissioner of the State Sinking Fund. In 1872 he headed the presidential electors from New Jersey for Ulysses S. Grant. He also continued his interest in the College of New Jersey (later Princeton University); having served as its treasurer from 1845 to 1869, in 1863 he was elected to the board of trustees, where he served until 1875. Olden died on April 7, 1876, in his house at Princeton.

WILLIAM C. WRIGHT

Charles Smith Olden Papers, Historical Society of Princeton, Princeton, N.J.

Foster, John Y. *New Jersey and the Rebellion.* Newark: M. R. Dennis, 1868.

Gillette, William. *Jersey Blue: Civil War Politics in New Jersey, 1854–1865.* New Brunswick: Rutgers University Press, 1995.

Jackson, William J. *New Jerseyans in the Civil War: For Union and Liberty.* New Brunswick: Rutgers University Press, 2000.

Knapp, Charles M. *New Jersey Politics during the Period of the Civil War and Reconstruction.* Geneva, N.Y.: W. F. Humphrey, 1924.

Smith, Charles Perrin. *New Jersey Political Reminiscences, 1828–1882.* Edited by Hermann K. Platt. New Brunswick: Rutgers University Press, 1965.

Wright, William C. *The Secession Movement in the Middle Atlantic States.* Rutherford, N.J.: Fairleigh Dickinson University Press, 1973.

Joel Parker

Emmet Collection, Miriam and Ira D. Wallach Division of Art, Prints and Photographs, The New York Public Library, Astor, Lenox and Tilden Foundations; courtesy New York Public Library

Joel Parker (November 24, 1816–January 2, 1888) was born near Freehold, Monmouth County, the son of Charles and Sarah (Coward) Parker. After his father's appointment as state treasurer, the family moved to Trenton. In 1833, his father became the cashier of the Mechanics' and Manufacturers' Bank of Trenton and sent him to Monmouth for two or three years to work his recently purchased farm. Parker then attended the College of New Jersey (later Princeton University), where he graduated in 1839. After graduation, he entered the law office of Henry W. Green, who later became chief justice and chancellor. Parker was admitted to the bar in 1842, and he began to practice law in Freehold.

Active in Democratic politics, Parker campaigned for Martin Van Buren in 1840 and James K. Polk in 1844 in their bids for the presidency. In 1847, he was elected as a Democrat to the assembly, where he took an active interest in tax reform, offering a bill that equalized taxation by taxing personal as well as real property. Although the Whigs held a majority in the legislature, Parker secured the passage of this bill in 1850.

In 1851, Parker declined to run for reelection, and in the same year he was appointed prosecutor of the pleas for Monmouth County; he served in this office for five years. He was also elected brigadier general, commanding the Monmouth and Ocean Brigade of the New Jersey militia in 1857, which he proceeded to reorganize. In 1860, he served as a Democratic elector and voted for Stephen A. Douglas. When the Civil War began, Governor Charles S. Olden appointed him a major general.

The Democratic Party nominated Parker for governor at its convention on September 4, 1862. He defeated Moses Bigelow, the mayor of Newark, for the nomination. Parker was considered a "War Democrat" (as opposed to a "Copperhead," a Democrat who opposed the war and sought peace with the South). In the election, Parker defeated the Republican candidate, Marcus L. Ward, by 14,394 votes, the largest majority in a gubernatorial election to that time. The Democrats also won majorities in both houses of the legislature.

In Parker's inaugural address on January 20, 1863, he outlined his attitude toward the war. Affirming his opposition to secession as a "political heresy," he upheld the principle of states' rights, stating that the states have "sovereignty over all subjects not expressly delegated to the General Government." To Parker, it was "the duty of the States, as well as the duty of the United States, to assert and maintain, in a legal and constitutional manner, their several and appropriate sovereignty." Further, he argued that while "a minority of fanatical and ultra men in each section" had brought about the war, Congress had declared that it was "not for the purpose of conquest or subjugation, overthrowing or interfering with the rights of established institutions of the States—but to defend and maintain the supremacy of the Constitution, and to preserve the Union, with the equality and rights of the several States unimpaired." He insisted that the people who supported this principle "had a right to expect that their own constitutional privileges would be respected. They did not expect that in order to suppress rebellion, the inalienable liberties of loyal citizens must be sacrificed." He condemned the use by the federal government of arbitrary arrests "without due process of law"; imprisonment of New Jersey citizens beyond the state; the suspension of the writ of habeas corpus; the Emancipation Proclamation; and other "war powers" of the Lincoln administration. Parker not only opposed emancipation but felt that if it came about, it should be dealt with by "the people of the States where the institution of slavery exists" and not the federal government. He favored the restoration of peace through the use of military force or through conciliation but held that it should not result in "a union of States where part are held in subjugation as conquered provinces." He challenged the Lincoln administration when he said, "Whatever legal and constitutional powers are vested in the Executive of New Jersey, for the protection of the lawful rights of the citizens of the State, will be exercised during my administration." Parker saw his duties as governor through this philosophy.

In 1863, the Copperheads reached their highest degree of support and power in New Jersey, especially in the legislature, which passed the "Peace Resolutions" that condemned the actions of the Lincoln administration in terms similar to those Parker had outlined in his inaugural address. But the peace resolutions went beyond Parker's view and called on the federal government to appoint commissioners to meet with the southern commissioners to find a way to end the war. Parker signed the joint resolutions on March 24, 1863. Since the resolutions would ultimately permit the South to leave the Union peacefully, the Republicans throughout the country condemned them as nothing less than advocating secession.

While on the one hand Parker supported these "Peace Resolutions," on the other he still supported the war; when the Confederate army commanded by General Robert E. Lee invaded Pennsylvania and was met in battle at Gettysburg, Parker was among the first to raise troops to assist in the defense of that state. He induced several regiments whose enlistments were ready to expire to reenlist and raised additional thirty-day troops for this emergency. His actions won him the thanks of both Governor Andrew G. Curtin of Pennsylvania and President Lincoln. He also became involved in the welfare of the troops on the battlefield and in the hospitals, as well as those that had returned home. He was a principal supporter of the Soldiers' Home. Through providing bounties, he prevented the use of conscription to fill military quotas in 1863; but in 1864 he was unsuccessful, for the draft went into effect that year.

Of all the nation's governors, Joel Parker was one of the Lincoln administration's most outspoken critics. However, while he attacked the administration's handling of political issues and its use of "war powers," he could not bring himself to call for a halt in the fighting. While the North continued to fight, he hoped for some form of conciliation with the South. Even though he had signed the "Peace Resolutions" the previous year, he felt that any halt in fighting would permit the South to leave the Union. In his first annual address, delivered on January 13, 1864, he continued to attack the Emancipation Proclamation and the other Lincoln administration measures he considered unconstitutional. Yet he agreed with the president that it was "the duty of the State authorities to furnish the men necessary to destroy the armed power of the rebellion, and it is equally the duty of the general government to accompany the exercise of the power entrusted to it with proper terms of conciliation."

In 1864, the federal government attempted to establish a railroad route from New York to Philadelphia other than the Camden and Amboy Railroad, which had been given a monopoly for transportation between the two cities. The legislature adopted a joint resolution signed by Parker that condemned the Congress's actions. Parker reacted in accordance with his strong states' rights position, declaring that "the General Government has no right to build a foot of railroad or to charter a corporation to construct the same, in any of the States, for the purpose of carrying passengers or freight for compensation. . . . No power can make the creator superior to or independent of its creator." Though the United States House of Representatives approved the bill, the Senate never voted on it.

In Governor Parker's strongest speech against the Lincoln administration, delivered in Freehold in August 1864, he called for a peaceful settlement to the war and stated that the "majority of the people, without respect to party, wanted peace, and desired compromise, but the Republican leaders would not consent to fair terms, and refused to submit the momentous issue to the people." He condemned conscription, confiscation, and the federal government's abolition of slavery. Again, while he criticized the administration, he continued to support the war by supplying troops to serve for thirty days in July 1864 when the Confederate army invaded Maryland. At this same time, in his second annual address in January 1865, Governor Parker opposed the passage of the Thirteenth Amendment, which abolished slavery, and he expressed himself in favor of gradual emancipation by the states. He also condemned as illegal the establishment of the Reconstruction governments in the southern states.

In Parker's final annual address in January 1866, he opposed black suffrage and called for the "speedy resumption of the relations of all the States with the federal government." He also proudly proclaimed, "Not a single right of the State of New Jersey has been yielded, and not one of her citizens, during my administration, has been deprived of his liberty without due process of law." At the end of his term, he left a surplus in the treasury, a phenomenon that had not occurred for many years.

When Parker left the office of governor in 1866, he returned to his law practice. In 1868, 1876, and 1884 he was the favorite-son presidential candidate of the New Jersey delegates at the National Democratic Convention.

In 1871, Parker was once again elected governor, this time by a majority of six thousand votes, thus becoming the first person to be elected twice to the governorship by the people. During his second term in office, he continued to voice his earlier positions by calling for an end to Reconstruction and by expressing himself in favor of states' rights. He also continually spoke out against corruption in government. The legislature enacted more laws during his second term than in any previous three years. Among them was the General Railroad Law. Parker also used the veto on fourteen occasions. As governor, he entered into the dispute with the state of Delaware over its boundary. He also ardently supported the Centennial Exhibition to be held in Philadelphia in 1876 as a part of the commemoration of the centennial of the American Revolution.

During Parker's second term, he was instrumental in securing the first group of amendments to be made to the New Jersey constitution of 1844.

They included salary adjustments and an oath for legislators, guarantees of a free education, prohibition of the passage of certain special or local laws, and line-item veto in appropriation bills.

After leaving the governorship for the second time, Parker served as attorney general in 1875, as a presidential elector in 1876, and as a justice of the New Jersey Supreme Court from 1880 until his death. He was also a leading figure in the construction of the Battle of Monmouth monument in Freehold.

Parker married Maria M. Gummere of Trenton in 1843, and they had two sons and one daughter. He died in Philadelphia on January 2, 1888.

WILLIAM C. WRIGHT

Gillette, William. *Jersey Blue: Civil War Politics in New Jersey, 1854–1865*. New Brunswick: Rutgers University Press, 1995.

Jackson, William J. *New Jerseyans in the Civil War: For Union and Liberty*. New Brunswick: Rutgers University Press, 2000.

Knapp, Charles M. *New Jersey Politics during the Period of the Civil War and Reconstruction*. Geneva, N.Y.: W. F. Humphrey, 1924.

Personal and Political Sketch of Hon. Joel Parker. Freehold, N.J.: Monmouth Democrat, 1871.

Presidency, The: Sketch of the Democratic Candidate, Joel Parker. N.p., [1876].

Yard, James S. "Joel Parker, 'The War Governor of New Jersey': A Biographical Sketch." *Proceedings of the New Jersey Historical Society* 10 (1888–89): 57–92.

Marcus Lawrence Ward (November 9, 1812–April 25, 1884), governor of New Jersey from January 1866 to January 1869, was a descendant of John Ward, one of the founders of Newark in 1666. His father, Moses, was a prosperous candle manufacturer in Newark. His mother was the former Fanny Brown. Marcus Ward eventually became a partner in the family business, where he put together a considerable fortune. By the 1840s he was devoting his interests to Newark civic affairs and charities and serving as director of the National State Bank and chairman of the executive committee of The New Jersey Historical Society. He was also a founder of the Newark Library Association and the New Jersey Art Union. Thus, as a young man, he gained a reputation as a successful businessman and philanthropist.

Ward did not enter politics until 1856, at the relatively late age of forty-four. It is difficult to determine the precise reason for the start of his political career. Most biographical accounts mention his strong antislavery convictions, which produced enthusiasm for the Republican Party. In view of his interest in social and moral improvement this seems a logical explanation. Though he was concerned enough about slavery to go to Kansas in 1858 to support the free-state cause, he soon returned to Newark and business affairs. The political climate of New Jersey in the late 1850s was not conducive to strong antislavery stands, and it is hard to believe that Ward would have entered politics solely on that issue. Obviously, other state politicians did not consider him a maverick since they chose him as a delegate to the national Republican convention of 1860 in Chicago.

During the Civil War Ward's expanded philanthropic activities gained him a statewide reputation as "the soldiers' friend," a nickname that would serve him well politically. The welfare of the New Jersey soldiers in the field became his major interest. With his own funds he set up an office in Newark. Presided over by several clerks, it handled an elaborate scheme either to forward soldiers' pay to their families or to place it in special savings accounts. If a soldier was killed, Ward's office made sure his pension was paid regularly to his survivors. Ward was also interested in the soldiers' medical needs; he made frequent visits to battlefields to oversee hospital service and, again with his own money, established the Soldiers' Home in Newark as a hospital for wounded veterans. In later years these activities provided grist for political party controversy. Democrats spread the story that Ward made great personal profit through overseeing the soldiers' pay, and Republicans made hearty denials. No solid evidence ever supported the Democratic claims.

However honest the motives may have been, no one can deny that Ward's projects were politically sound, and they provided the springboard for his entry into gubernatorial politics. In a state where the two political parties were extremely evenly balanced and where there was also much resistance to the nationalizing policies of the Lincoln administration (particularly emancipation), Republicans saw Marcus L. Ward as someone whose appeal would transcend partisanship. Nominated first in 1862, he lost to Democrat Joel Parker. Antiemancipation sentiment in New Jersey was too strong. Since there was no provision that year allowing soldiers to vote in the field, he lost what would have been his greatest source of support.

By 1865, however, the atmosphere was ripe for a Republican victory, even in New Jersey. The war had been won, the Union preserved, and the slaves freed. A sense of thanksgiving abounded, with the general recognition that it was the Republican Party that had brought about these good things. The question was not so much whether a Republican would win the governorship as which person would receive the nomination.

Two major aspirants were in the field: Ward, representing Newark and East Jersey interests as well as those of the soldiers, and Alexander G. Cattell of Camden, a wealthy grain merchant who had lived outside the state for many years. The nominating convention in Trenton appeared to deadlock. A move on behalf of the war hero General Hugh Judson Kilpatrick was one effort to break the impasse, but Kilpatrick gave his backers no support. Largely through the endeavors of the numerous veterans who were convention delegates, Ward was nominated on the fourth ballot. The Cattell forces, led by George M. Robeson, made the choice unanimous, and all appeared to be harmonious. Although any Republican probably could have been elected in 1865, the soldier vote, which has generally been considered the decisive factor in Ward's victory, greatly enhanced his large majority. In addition, the Republicans won both houses of the legislature.

As governor Ward was perhaps best known for his role in bringing New Jersey into the forefront of the Reconstruction process. For example, the previous legislature, under Democratic control, had done nothing toward ratifying the Thirteenth Amendment, and the amendment, as a result, became law without New Jersey's approval. Ward devoted a considerable portion of his inaugural address to the problem, recommending that even though it would be only a symbolic gesture, the state should "redeem" itself by approving the amendment. Upon its delayed ratification Republicans facetiously welcomed New Jersey back into the ranks of the Union. A short time later Ward and the legislature again worked in tandem to secure the ratification of the Fourteenth Amendment.

Ward's views on state affairs were probably of greater long-term influence in New Jersey. In this respect he was a typical nineteenth-century Republican, convinced that an active, energetic government could produce wise social and economic policies. His administration concentrated on making the operation of the state prison nonpolitical, establishing a state reform school, providing for compulsory public education, and instituting a statewide uniform code of health. He also called for state action in the matter of riparian rights, asking that owners of underwater land compensate the state for the right to build improvements.

Party division over gubernatorial appointments hindered the effectiveness of Republican leadership during Ward's governorship. Charles Perrin Smith, whose reminiscences supply the only "inside" account of New Jersey politics in this period, places Ward, sought after and flattered by all sides, at the center of factional strife. According to Smith, the basic problem was the challenge the insurgency of Alexander G. Cattell and George M. Robeson posed to the regulars. Ward apparently tried to steer a middle course, appointing Robeson attorney general and reappointing Smith clerk of the supreme court. On the other hand, some party leaders felt Ward gave too many favors to his Newark friends, especially after he appointed Frederick T. Frelinghuysen to the United States Senate.

By the late 1860s few doubted that practical politics was Ward's overriding interest and that, as far as he was concerned, the Republican Party was the instrument of political good. Witness his remarks of November 23, 1866, to the editor of the *Chicago Tribune*: "Our State has done well and I hope and believe that we are now firmly fixed among the Republican states. The change seems great within a period of fifteen months. Two United States senators, three members of the House of Representatives, both Houses of the Legislature, all the officers of the state department Republican, are the tangible proofs that we are entirely reconstructed—the life, the energy, the spirit of an orginazation [*sic*] is fully aroused and we shall be armed and equipped for the next great battle." In the same year he was appointed chairman of the Republican National Committee, and in 1872 he was elected to a term in Congress.

Yet to dismiss Ward as a hack party politician would be unjust. It would be more accurate to describe him—like many who joined the Republican Party prior to the Civil War—as one who saw politics as a means to material and moral progress. It appears that Ward felt a certain moral obligation to look out for the welfare of others. For example, since he felt that the soldiers would spend their money irresponsibly if left to their own devices, his overseeing their pay contained an element of paternalism.

In private life Ward was married to the former Susan Morris, and the couple had eight children. After his public life ended in 1874 with his defeat for reelection to Congress, he devoted the rest of his life to his family and personal affairs. In the spring of 1884 he contracted malaria on a trip he and his wife took to Florida. He was brought back to Newark, where he died on April 25, 1884.

Shortly after his death Ward's son, Marcus L. Ward, Jr., used his estate to found a house in Maplewood for men and women over sixty-five who had been prominent in business and social affairs. Thus the theme of philanthropy in Ward's life reasserted itself.

HERMANN K. PLATT

Marcus L. Ward Papers, The New Jersey Historical Society, Newark, N.J.

Marcus L. Ward Papers, Rutgers University Special Collections, New Brunswick, N.J.

Jackson, William J. *New Jerseyans in the Civil War: For Union and Liberty*. New Brunswick: Rutgers University Press, 2000.

Knapp, Charles M. *New Jersey Politics during the Period of the Civil War and Reconstruction*. Geneva, N.Y.: W. F. Humphrey, 1924.

Shaw, William H. *History of Essex and Hudson Counties, New Jersey*. Philadelphia: Everts and Peck, 1884.

Smith, Charles Perrin. *New Jersey Political Reminiscences, 1828–1882*. Edited by Hermann K. Platt. New Brunswick: Rutgers University Press, 1965.

Theodore Fitz Randolph (June 24, 1826–November 7, 1883), governor of New Jersey and United States senator, was descended from a family that had migrated from England to Massachusetts in the first half of the seventeenth century. Born in New Brunswick, he was the son of Sarah Kent Carman and James Fitz Randolph, a member of Congress from New Jersey and publisher of the *New Brunswick Fredonian*. The younger Randolph attended Rutgers Grammar School and worked as a writer and proofreader for his father's newspaper. At age sixteen he entered a mercantile career, and he spent the next ten years as a clerk, accountant, and principal in business, primarily in the South. At twenty he went to Vicksburg, Mississippi, but in 1850 he returned to New Jersey to enter his father's extensive coal and iron business. He established his residence at Jersey City and lived there until 1862, when he purchased a ninety-acre stock farm in Morristown.

Admitted to the bar in 1848, Theodore F. Randolph became, like his father, a Whig, a states' rights advocate, and a consistent opponent of the abolitionists. With the decline of the Whigs after the elections of 1852 he moved into the Democratic Party. In 1860 an alliance of Democrats and Know-Nothings elected the wealthy businessman-lawyer to the general assembly from the first district of Jersey City. Appointed to the Special Joint Committee on National Affairs, he helped lead the effort to avert civil war. That effort culminated in the passage of resolutions appointing delegates to the Washington Peace Conference of February 1861.

In November 1861 Randolph was elected to fill a vacancy in the state senate, and in 1862 he was reelected for a full, three-year term. As Governor Joel Parker's chief ally in the senate he voiced opposition to many of the war policies of the Lincoln administration but refused to endorse the extreme demands of the Copperheads. More specifically, he succeeded in thwarting Copperhead plans to limit war appropriations and helped defeat resolutions calling for an armistice in 1862. The senator's approach to racial issues reflected humanity and pragmatism. In 1865 he introduced a relief bill, which was passed, extending equal benefits and enlistment bounties to black soldiers. Whites, he explained, should not do injustice to an "inferior" race. In the same year he opposed the adoption of the Thirteenth Amendment on the grounds that slavery was already doomed and that the measure would effectively close the door to peace negotiations. In state affairs he concentrated on monetary and fiscal policy. As chairman of the Senate Finance Committee the conservative Democrat began to advocate a more equitable system of corporate taxation. He successfully urged the creation of a state comptroller's office and led the opposition to a plan under which the state would assume responsibility for paying local bounties to army volunteers.

In the summer of 1865 Randolph sought the Democratic nomination for governor, but he finished second in the balloting to Theodore Runyon, a member of the party's peace faction who had just completed a term as mayor of Newark. Two years later Randolph accepted an appointment as president of the Morris and Essex Railroad. He held that post until he was elected governor in 1868.

Indicating dissatisfaction with Republican Reconstruction policies, New Jersey voters elected Randolph governor over John Insley Blair by more than forty-five hundred ballots. Taking office on January 19, 1869, Randolph advocated prompt readmission of the former Confederate states and outlined a program that would revise election laws, develop a more equitable system of taxation for individuals, impose new taxes on corporations, and create a riparian commission. Less than a month after his inaugural address the governor began to implement this program by urging the legislature to abandon the system of "transit duties" that certain corporations paid the state in lieu of any other "tax or impost" and to adopt a uniform tax law. Aimed especially at the monopolies of the Delaware and Raritan Canal Company and the Camden and Amboy Railroad and Transportation Company, these measures were designed both to regulate business and to increase state revenues. The legislature, still under Democratic control after the elections of 1868, repealed the parts of charters that provided for transit duties, but no uniform railroad tax was passed until 1873.

The legislature of 1869 acted more expeditiously on the governor's advice to end the exemption of certain corporations from New Jersey's general tax law. In effect, privileged companies were being assessed as if they were individual persons—namely on the value of their real and personal property rather than of their capital stock and accumulated surplus. Acting on specific suggestions from Governor Randolph, the legislature levied a tax of 2 percent on the annual earnings of corporations chartered by the state or doing business in it. The governor repeatedly tried to defend this principle of taxing corporations more heavily than individuals; but the law proved unenforceable, and it was repealed in 1872.

In justifying his tax policies, Governor Randolph emphasized that an expansion of state functions was primarily responsible for the increased cost of government. During his term expansion continued: the governor and legislature took steps to improve state facilities for correction, mental care, and education. Randolph had financial as well as humanitarian motives for ameliorating the prison system. By improving the management of penal institutions and by increasing the productivity of convict labor, the governor hoped to make the state prison system self-supporting. Acting on recommendations of a special commission on prison administration, Randolph urged the legislature of 1869 to expand the Trenton State Prison and create a "House of Correction" that would employ short-term convicts at healthful and productive work in an atmosphere free from the negative influence of hardened criminals. Though the legislature made no provision for a house of correction, it approved bills to enlarge the state prison and to erect new workshops on the prison grounds. In Governor Randolph's final annual message he reported that the prison legislation of 1869 had saved the state nearly $200,000. State involvement was less pronounced in education and mental care. The free public school system was made statewide with modest financial aid in 1871, and between 1869 and 1872 the groundwork was laid for a new "lunatic asylum" at Morris Plains to supplement the overcrowded facility at Trenton. The Morris Plains asylum, however, did not open until 1876.

Although most of Governor Randolph's proposals received prompt attention from the legislature, he could not secure action on his plan for election reform until March 1871. Incorporating the governor's recommendation that both corporations and individuals he punished for buying votes, the legislature passed a stringent law that disfranchised both the giver and the receiver of an election bribe and put guilty corporations in jeopardy of losing their charters. The law had little effect, however, and soon there were more complaints about election bribery than ever.

With Republicans controlling both houses in 1871, relations between the legislature and Randolph became more partisan and less cooperative. The governor vetoed more major bills in 1871 than in the previous two years combined, even though he professed to use this executive prerogative "only in such cases as were clearly unconstitutional, where unintentional mistakes had been made, or where the ends of Justice were clearly to be violated by Legislative contrivances remote from if not beyond legislative inquiry." Early in his term, Randolph used the veto to thwart bills that in his view promoted railroad expansion at the expense of individual taxpayers and property owners. Later he directed his efforts against bills that would reorganize municipal governments for partisan purposes. Although Randolph and the Democratic lawmakers had set the precedent for this type of partisan legislation in 1870, the governor unhesitatingly vetoed Republican-sponsored reorganization measures. The most important of these vetoes was of a bill allowing the Republican legislature to restructure the powerful government of Jersey City, then controlled by the Democrats. The bill was passed over his veto, however, and for the next sixteen years Jersey City was ruled by a government appointed by the state and dominated by Republicans.

Randolph's pocket veto of "An Act to Incorporate the German Valley Railway Company" precipitated a constitutional dispute with the state court of chancery. Randolph was subpoenaed to testify in a suit charging that he had received the bill prior to the five closing days of the legislative session, but he answered that only the legislature had constitutional authority to "obtain answer" from the governor for his action or inaction. He further asserted that the governor was the sole judge of what constituted his official duties. Wishing to avoid a constitutional crisis, however, Randolph deposited the engrossed copy of the disputed bill with the state librarian.

Two other potential crises faced the governor in 1870 and 1871. The first resulted from a railroad dispute known as "The Bergen Riot." Randolph used National Guard troops to quell the riot, and the feuding railway companies settled their differences in court. In July 1871 the governor averted a threatened riot in Jersey City when he took action to prevent Irish Americans from disrupting a parade planned by Orangemen on the anniversary of the battle of the Boyne. Although he criticized the Orangemen for reviving an "unnecessary" religious and political feud, the governor issued a proclamation declaring his intention to guarantee the right of peaceful assembly to all citizens. He followed the proclamation with an order to use up to three thousand state troops if needed. These measures proved more than ample, and civil authorities managed to cope with the situation without military assistance.

The governor's handling of the Orangemen affair prompted state and national journals to list him as a leading contender for the Democratic presidential nomination. Randolph directed his efforts toward attaining a more realistic goal—a seat in the United States Senate. In his last message to the legislature he addressed national as well as state issues, and after leaving office he played an active role in the presidential campaign of 1872. Initially a participant in the bipartisan movement to find an alternative to Ulysses S. Grant and Horace Greeley, the ex-governor ultimately campaigned for Greeley amid charges of a deal involving appointment to a cabinet post.

In January 1875 the Democratic majority in the legislature elected ex-governor Randolph to the United States Senate seat previously held by John P. Stockton. Randolph served in the Senate until 1881; he was a member of the Committees on Commerce, Military Affairs, Education, Civil Service Reform, and the Centennial Exhibition. He also served on the special Senate committee to examine South Carolina's returns in the disputed presidential election of 1876, and for two years he was chairman of the Committee on Military Affairs. In his infrequent speeches he criticized President Grant's use of federal troops to uphold Republican governments in the South, opposed government aid to parochial schools, argued against the remonetization of silver, and advocated an early redemption of paper currency.

In addition to his political and governmental activities, Randolph served as a trustee of Rutgers College, founded and was a president of the Washington Association of New Jersey, invented a ditching machine and a steam typewriter, and practiced philanthropy. In 1852 he married Fannie Coleman, daughter of Congressman Nicholas D. Coleman of Kentucky. He died on November 7, 1883, at his home in Morristown.

ROBERT C. MORRIS

Brief Sketch of the Life and Public Services of Theodore F. Randolph, Democratic Nominee for Governor of New Jersey, A. N.p.: Democratic Committee, 1868.

Cadman, John W. *The Corporation in New Jersey.* Cambridge, Mass.: Harvard University Press, 1949.

History of Morris County, New Jersey. New York: Munsell, 1882.

Knapp, Charles M. *New Jersey Politics during the Period of the Civil War and Reconstruction.* Geneva, N.Y.: W. F. Humphrey, 1924.

Leiby, James R. *Charity and Correction in New Jersey: A History of State Welfare Institutions.* New Brunswick: Rutgers University Press, 1967.

Peterson, Kent A. "New Jersey Politics and National Policymaking, 1865–1868." Ph.D. dissertation, Princeton University, 1970.

Randolph, Theodore F. *Address of Governor Theodore F. Randolph of Morris to the Democratic State Convention, Assembled at Trenton, June 26, 1872.* Morristown, N.J.: Louis C. Vogt, 1872.

———. *Letter of Governor Randolph of New Jersey, to Hon. Cortlandt Parker, Relating to Executive Prerogatives and Judicial Authority.* Trenton: Wm. T. Nicholson, 1871.

Joseph Dorsett Bedle (January 5, 1831–October 21, 1894), as a contemporary account put it, was "an instance of a man who, at a comparatively early age, achieves the highest honors of his state, apparently without having passed through any of the highways and byways of the politician."

Certainly, having an established, influential family on both sides did not harm his career. Bedle's paternal grandparents were natives of New Jersey. His parents were Thomas and Hannah (Dorsett) Bedle. His father was a merchant, a justice of the peace for more than twenty-five years, and a judge of the Court of Common Pleas for Monmouth County. Through his mother's family, which had immigrated from Bermuda more than a century and a half earlier, the future governor was related to Garret Dorsett Wall, a Democratic Party leader in New Jersey in the Jacksonian era, who had declined to serve as governor after the legislature elected him in 1829.

Born in Middletown Point (now Matawan) on January 5, 1831, Bedle was educated at the academy there. His apparently delicate health and his father's desire to have a son engaged in commerce made him forgo the college course to work two years in a general country store. But a strong desire to study law led him to become a student for about three and one-half years in the Trenton law office of William L. Dayton, who had been a United States senator and would be the vice presidential candidate of the newly formed Republican Party in 1856 and minister to France in 1861. Bedle spent one winter at the law school in Baliston Spa, New York, and after another winter in the Poughkeepsie office of Thompson and Weeks—on his twenty-first birthday—he was admitted in New York State as an attorney and counselor. He did additional study with Matawan lawyer Henry S. Little, who was to become a member of the "State House Ring," and was admitted to the New Jersey bar the following year, 1853. For the next two years he practiced law in Middletown Point, moving to Freehold in 1855 and advancing to counselor in 1856. There, in 1861, he married Althea F. Randolph, the eldest daughter of Bennington F. Randolph, a local lawyer with an extensive practice. She was the niece of Democratic Governor Theodore F. Randolph (1869–72).

In 1865, when Bedle was thirty-four, he became the second-youngest justice in the state supreme court's history. Democratic Governor Joel Parker, also a Freehold lawyer, appointed him to the largest circuit, Hudson-Passaic-Bergen. Soon afterward Bedle moved his residence to Jersey City, next door to Leon Abbett, who was to serve two terms as governor. In 1871, just before the close of Bedle's term as justice, the Democratic "State House Ring" planned to nominate Bedle for governor. The judge "himself took no steps to secure the nomination, rather discouraging the movement in his favor," reported a Newark daily newspaper; and his new neighbor and rival, Abbett, persuaded Parker to run—successfully—for a second nonconsecutive term. Bedle was reappointed to the bench in 1872.

Unanimously, the 1874 Democratic convention selected Bedle as its nominee for governor. The Republicans had chosen a former congressman from Newark, George A. Halsey, who opposed the system of state legislative commissions under which Jersey City was being misgoverned. In the Hudson County Court of Oyer and Terminer, Bedle's fervent charges to the grand jury had led to the indictment for fraud and conspiracy of the Republican ring that had seized control of Jersey City; he had later tried and sentenced the ring members. Refusing to resign his judgeship or to campaign for office, Bedle nevertheless was elected by 13,233 votes, the second-greatest majority in the state until then. "The country was then very much depressed, and the times were hard, and there was a tendency in the minds of the people to select an Executive who had been out of the arena of politics," according to one explanation. By Bedle's own admission, his information on the actual condition of state affairs was "only cursory."

Pleas for economy, home rule, and general legislation marked Bedle's inaugural address in 1875. He would try "to check all tendency to extravagance," but "the great cause of complaint is not in the State appropriations," the legislature was told, but "in the taxes of municipal bodies including assessment for local improvements." The most effective remedy would to be give direct responsibility to elected officials: "To my mind the best municipal government for our people, and the only one consistent with the spirit of our institutions is that in which they govern themselves. . . . The simpler the machinery of a local government the better." Bedle hoped to see the day "when every city in this State, of a certain population, will be governed by one general law," but he acknowledged that making this practicable would probably require a constitutional change. In an attack on special legislation, he held, "corporate privileges in many matters of legitimate trade and enterprise should be open alike to all, and readily obtainable on compliance with general laws wherever the demands of business require it." Consequently his first veto killed a bill to incorporate a Newark manufacturing and trading company on the ground that the measure was special. During his first year he vetoed at least five similar bills for manufacturing companies and two measures for incorporating fraternal lodges.

A state constitutional amendment ratified in November 1875 restricted special legislation. Bedle's next two years in office therefore differed significantly from the experience of earlier governors. In 1873 his immediate predecessor, Joel Parker, had complained, "the general public laws passed at the last session are contained in about one hundred pages of the printed volume, while the special and private laws occupy over twelve hundred and fifty pages of the same book." During Parker's administration the legislature had passed 603 laws the first year, 724 the second, and 537 the third, only one-sixth of which were general. During Bedle's first year the number had descended to 454; it declined to 213 in the second year and 156 in the third, with 85 percent in the general legislation category. Not until 1961 would fewer statutes—145—be enacted during a single session.

The exact interpretation of the amendment was in doubt. Bedle saw that the prohibition of special legislation did not necessarily apply to laws affecting the state's municipalities. In 1876 he declared in his first annual message that "as to cities and all other municipalities, except towns and counties, the Legislature may yet pass local and special laws, save only for 'appointing local officers or commissions' and wherever on particular subjects enumerated in the amendments it is prevented." That spring Bedle vetoed a bill because it concerned local elections; it applied to any city "*now* wholly or partly governed by local boards or commissions, whose members are chosen by the Legislature in joint meeting" (italics added). Jersey City alone answered that description; and, besides, the public notice now required for passage of local and special bills had not been given. But only because proper notice had not been given did governor veto two other local bills that would apply only to Newark.

Much publicity followed Bedle's 1876 veto of "An act to provide for the maintenance and education of the deaf and dumb, feeble-minded and blind persons in this State," which proposed to establish three institutions to care for these unfortunate persons without any charge, whether or not they or their parents could afford to bear any part of the expense. This bill was "intended to adopt a new policy," and this was "not the time for such a change," Bedle argued. He objected further that the bill was "not in fair compliance with that provision of the Constitution limiting bills to one object." The senate overrode the veto, but the assembly failed to override in a close vote in which eight Republicans crossed party lines to support Bedle.

But in 1876 a strict party vote in both houses repassed "An act for the government and regulation of the State Prison" over gubernatorial disapproval. Bedle had argued that that measure would give a board of inspectors —statutory officers whom the legislature chose in joint meeting—powers paramount to those of the keeper, whom the governor appointed with the senate's advice and consent as required by an 1875 amendment to the state constitution. The Republican *Newark Daily Advertiser*, endorsing the reasoning of its own party, insisted that it was "partisanship which led his Excellency to veto the bill." It made no mention that the legislative joint meeting of eighty-one members included only thirty-three Democrats.

At the close of the 1877 legislative session Bedle refused to be directed by his own party's caucus. He had just approved a reform bill to establish one district court judge in each of six cities and two judges each in Newark and Jersey City to assume the civil jurisdiction of justices of the peace. The senate confirmed the nomination of Bedle's father-in-law, Bennington F. Randolph, for one of the Jersey City judgeships but rejected the governor's nomination of a Republican—an effort at bipartisanship—for the other judgeship, creating "no end of commotion." The submission of another Republican name received like treatment. In response Bedle sent a lengthy gubernatorial message announcing "no further reason for the detention of the Senate" and made the original GOP appointment *ad interim*. (The message received not even the courtesy of being printed in the senate's journal.)

Attention to the railroads marked Bedle's administration. In January 1876 he declared, "The revenue received by the State from Railroad Companies is not near as large as it should be." Although pertinent changes in legislation were proposed then, he made no similar plea in the next two annual messages. But during the great railroad strike of 1877 Bedle called up all companies of the state's National Guard to protect the trains and the new crews of two railroads. "Failure in the use of military to suppress riots only aggravates, and futile effort is reprehensible, if possible to guard against it," he declared. For such action he "earned no end of commendation from all parts of the country," according to a leading New Jersey journalist.

At the expiration of Bedle's term he resumed his law practice, serving as legal counsel for the Delaware, Lackawanna and Western Railroad and becoming a director of many prominent corporations. Three times he refused judgeships, and he declined presidential nominations as minister to Russia and to Austria. During the last year of his life he served on the state's Constitutional Commission of 1894. His death followed an operation for the removal of bladder stones.

HARRIS I. EFFROSS

Applegate, John Stillwell. *Early Courts and Lawyers of Monmouth County, Beginning at Its First Settlement, and Down to the Last Half Century*. Freehold, N.J.: [Monmouth County Bar Association], 1911.

Ellis, Franklin. *History of Monmouth County, New Jersey*. Philadelphia: R. T. Peck, 1885.

Sackett, William Edgar. *Modern Battles of Trenton*. Vol. 1, *Being a History of New Jersey's Politics and Legislation from the Year 1868 to the Year 1894*. Trenton: John L. Murphy, 1895.

George B. McClellan
New Jersey State Archives; Department of State

George Brinton McClellan (December 3, 1826–October 29, 1885) was the son of George McClellan, a prominent Philadelphia physician. Choosing a military career, he went to West Point, from which he graduated in the top 5 percent of his class. He participated in the Mexican War and served as a military observer in the Crimean War. In 1857, for financial reasons, he resigned his commission and became chief engineer of the Illinois Central Railroad; in 1860 he became president of the eastern division of the Ohio and Mississippi Railroad. That same year he married Ellen Mary Marcy. The couple had a son and a daughter.

When the Civil War broke out, McClellan rejoined the army. He quickly became one of the most prominent Union generals and received command of the Army of the Potomac, but he failed to prosecute the war to President Lincoln's satisfaction and was removed in 1862. This ended his military activities. In 1864 he ran for president as a Democrat but lost to Lincoln by a wide margin, winning only the electoral votes of New Jersey and two border states. Between 1864 and 1877 he traveled through Europe, served as a consultant on a variety of engineering projects, held the position of chief engineer of the New York City Department of Docks, and participated actively in the affairs of the Democratic Party.

Highly popular in New Jersey, where he maintained his residence, he was nominated for governor by the Democratic Party in 1877. His selection, however, largely resulted from the maneuverings of key members within the party who wanted to prevent the frontrunner, Leon Abbett, from gaining the nomination. At a crucial moment an unidentified delegate took the convention by surprise and put McClellan's name up for consideration; in a wild scene of well-planned enthusiasm, all other contenders were forgotten, and the ex-general received the prize by acclamation. During the campaign his Republican opponent, William A. Newell, charged that McClellan was not really a resident of New Jersey, but McClellan, who had a home in Essex County, refuted this accusation with little difficulty and won the election by a large majority. So many people sought to attend the inaugural ceremonies in January 1878 that the proceedings had to be held out of doors in front of the statehouse.

In spite of McClellan's highly successful campaign and widespread personal popularity, the course of events quickly diminished whatever opportunity he might have had to exert strong executive leadership in controversial issues. Largely as a result of the size of McClellan's victory, the Democratic Party controlled both houses of the legislature for the first time since 1870; the governor, however, quarreled with influential members of the senate over appointments and patronage and lost standing with that body. At the assembly's instigation, moreover, the legislature enacted several highly partisan measures designed to ensure that the Democrats would remain in command of the state for years to come. These bills, of which one flagrantly gerrymandered assembly election districts and another disfranchised college students (who tended to vote Republican), so antagonized the voters that they elected Republican majorities to both houses for the remaining two years of McClellan's term. In general, his relations with the legislature were strained.

As governor, McClellan urged the reduction of the people's tax burden. Entering office while New Jersey still suffered the results of the Panic of 1873, he announced in his inaugural address that the most urgent matter before the legislature was "to give the people of this State the greatest possible relief from their burdens during the financial depression, and to do all in our power to hasten the return of a better state of affairs." He advocated caution in expenditures so that the state tax, a revenue measure that helped to pay the ordinary expenses of government, could be cut in half; in 1880 he recommended that the tax be abolished and noted that he saw no reason to impose it as long as appropriations were confined to reasonable levels. At the end of his term there was no direct tax on the people for state purposes.

McClellan devoted special attention to measures he felt would help foster the state's prosperity, and his annual messages to the legislature outlined specific ideas to accomplish this end. The abolition of the state tax constituted an integral part of his overall plan, for, as he pointed out, "it is far better for us to leave the money in the pockets of the people, for by them will it be best employed in increasing the wealth of the State and in the development of its resources." More positively, he urged in 1878 that New Jersey follow the example of Massachusetts and institute a Bureau of Statistics of Labor and Industries to gather information on industrial affairs and to serve as a resource in the preparation of legislation; the agency was established during his first year in office. In 1879 he called for the creation of an agricultural experiment station to provide farmers with examples of the benefits of scientific cultivation, and the legislature followed this recommendation in 1880. McClellan felt that specific industries, such as silk culture and sugar growing, should receive the government's encouragement. Similarly, he directed the state library to purchase books on pottery and glassmaking that New Jersey artisans could use for ideas on design, and he called for the creation of a pottery museum to show the finest specimens from Europe, thereby providing actual examples of craftsmanship.

McClellan also stressed the importance of education in industrial development. The schools should, as far as possible, prepare students for their future work. In farming regions he felt that public schools had an obligation to instruct boys not only in the basic subjects but also in the principles of agriculture; in manufacturing regions teachers should stress the pursuits of manual labor. "It is clearly good political economy," he declared, "in the State which educates its children, to make that education tend, in some measure, at least, to the benefit of the commercial and other industries of the State." The governor realized, however, that the existing school system could not carry out such an important task without assistance. The great need, he noted, was to convert unskilled into skilled labor; the pottery industry of Trenton, for example, could not find enough trained workers to hire. To remedy this problem, which afflicted other areas of the industrial community as well, he called for the creation of technical schools throughout the state; these institutions would help to provide the skilled labor necessary for the growth and prosperity of the New Jersey economy. Although he felt that local associations should begin and operate these schools, McClellan declared that "giving State aid freely, at least in the incipiency of the system, will prove as wise an expenditure as can be made." During his term a law was passed permitting the establishment of these schools, but McClellan's overall vision was not fulfilled.

A number of important developments occurred while McClellan was governor. An old soldier, he took a special interest in the condition of the New Jersey National Guard and helped to improve its discipline and organization; during his administration two companies were equipped with Gatling guns, regular rifle practice was instituted, a new battalion was organized, and provision was made to supply new uniforms to the troops. Under legislative authority McClellan appointed special commissions to study the possibilities of revising the state's jumbled and confusing tax laws and of drafting general laws for governing cities; these commissions reported to the legislature, but no positive action resulted from their deliberations. Finally, McClellan emphasized in his messages his belief in a diligent and alert citizenry as the best defense against government corruption, and in 1879 a Republican member of the senate introduced a law echoing these sentiments; the financial accounts of local officeholders were made subject to examination by experts whenever twenty-five freeholders should request such a step.

However, few concrete measures resulted directly from McClellan's actions as governor. He tended to stress issues on which most people could agree; abolishing the state tax and improving the condition of the National Guard were recommendations that met with wide popular approval. His major contribution involved suggestions for economic prosperity that in a loose sense constituted a program to foster development; few of his predecessors thought in such overall and comprehensive terms. On the other hand, his ideas in this regard, had they become reality, would no doubt have increased the level of state expenditure greatly. Although he seemed to recognize this fact, McClellan did not address himself to the problem of raising additional revenue; indeed at one point he lamented the fact that teachers, who were crucial to his plans for development, received such small compensation for their labors, but he suggested no remedy for their condition. His messages to the legislature mentioned no issue that might arouse controversy; consequently, he did not concern himself with such topics as taxing the railroads and restraining the political power of corporations. He made little effort to exert an active influence on the deliberations of the legislature, and where his suggestions became law, it is highly likely that the measures would have passed without his support; the establishment of a Bureau of Labor and Industries, for example, needed little executive support. At best, his record as governor was mixed.

When his term expired in 1881, McClellan retired to private life. Apparently he found the experience as governor somewhat taxing, for he wrote that he was glad it was over "as it was becoming a nuisance to be obliged to go to Trenton in all matters." He died in 1885 of heart trouble at his home in Essex County.

JEROME C. REDDY

Records of Governor George B. McClellan, New Jersey State Library, Trenton, N.J.
Myers, William Starr. *George Brinton McClellan*. New York: Appleton-Century, 1934.
Sears, Stephen W. *George B. McClellan: The Young Napoleon*. New York: Ticknor & Fields, 1988.

George Craig Ludlow (April 6, 1830–December 18, 1900) was born in Milford, Hunterdon County, New Jersey. In 1835 his family moved to New Brunswick, where he lived for the rest of his life. He graduated from Rutgers College in 1850, and he opened a law practice in 1853. Both his father, Cornelius Ludlow, and his grandfather, Benjamin Ludlow, had been active in the affairs of the Democratic Party, and he followed their example; over the next two decades he held a variety of municipal and county governmental positions. As a prominent local member of the party, he was elected to the New Jersey Senate in 1876 and chosen its president in 1878. He received his party's nomination for the governorship at the convention of 1880. Although he had the background and experience to warrant the nomination in his own right, his actual selection was largely the result of an alliance between Leon Abbett, one of the most important Democratic politicians in the state, and the so-called State House Ring, a group of officeholders in Trenton determined to prevent the convention from selecting a political rival of Abbett's. The closely contested election was heavily influenced by railroad interests. Ludlow, a private counsel for the Pennsylvania Railroad, defeated his Republican opponent, Frederic A. Potts, an influential stockholder in the Jersey Central Railroad, by only 651 of the nearly 250,000 votes cast.

That was the closest gubernatorial contest in New Jersey history, and Ludlow entered office with certain handicaps. First, the Republican Party controlled both the senate and the assembly during his first year as governor, and for the remaining two years of his term it had a majority in the senate. Second, although Ludlow had a widespread reputation for integrity and honesty, many people felt that his connection with the Pennsylvania Railroad might unduly influence his decisions as governor; indeed, immediately following his narrow victory, rumors, probably unfounded, circulated that the railroad had thrown the election to Ludlow by ordering its employees to vote for him. Moreover, he owed his nomination in part to the "State House Ring" and quickly reappointed two of its members to lucrative positions in state government. Finally, since he was in no sense a leader of his party, he had no power base or following in the legislature to rely on in any political struggle that might develop during his term. He had little hope of providing strong executive leadership.

Those who feared that Ludlow might be too subservient to the railroads were proved wrong, for he attempted to frustrate corporate plans by using his veto power on two important occasions. During the 1882 legislative session friends of the Central Railroad of New Jersey pushed through both houses a bill designed to allow the board of directors to increase the corporation's capital stock without obtaining the shareholders' approval; the measure was aimed at removing control of the railroad from the stockholders. When the bill reached Ludlow for his signature, he vetoed it, denouncing it as immoral and unjust. He had insufficient power, however, to make his veto stand against the wishes of the Central Railroad, and both senate and assembly voted to override by very large majorities.

During the same session the Pennsylvania Railroad quietly gained senate approval for a bill that would limit public access to large areas of the Jersey City waterfront. The state had awarded the railroad grants of land lying under water, and the railroad had engaged in extensive filling operations and had constructed terminals and warehouses on the property. Erecting fences around the facilities, the railroad refused Jersey City the right to build roads over its holdings to the waterline. When challenged in court by Jersey City, the company asked the assembly to sustain it by approving the bill. When the newspapers pointed out what the bill would accomplish, a furor resulted, but despite public outcry, the railroad's scheme gained the approval of the assembly. When the bill reached Ludlow's desk, he defied intense pressure from the corporation and refused to sign it. In a stinging veto message he denounced the bill as "an abuse of legislative power and a violation of the principles of fair dealing and justice." Nevertheless, the senate quickly overrode the veto by a comfortable margin. Only bribery charges and a legislative investigation prevented the assembly from taking similar action, for the session ended before a vote could be taken.

More positively, Ludlow had to struggle with the problem of balancing the state budget, and in the process he helped to pave the way for reform. Since he believed that the individual citizen and property owner labored under a tax burden that was too heavy, he called for the curtailment of all unnecessary expenditures; aggravating his problem, his predecessor had ended the state tax, a small revenue measure that had helped to fund the ordinary expenses of the government, and reinstating it would have run counter to Ludlow's beliefs and proven politically hazardous to the Democratic Party. As a result, in his first message to the legislature in 1882, Ludlow advocated a host of measures designed to bring expenditures and anticipated receipts into balance by cutting costs. Unfortunately, the legislature did not adhere totally to his recommendations, and in the following year Ludlow noted that the state had spent $280,778.28 more than it had received in revenue.

In 1883, however, Ludlow placed greater emphasis on increasing the state's receipts than on cutting its expenditures, and he focused on the need to tap new sources of revenue. For years many citizens had complained that corporations in New Jersey, especially the railroads, did not pay a fair share of the cost of municipal, county, and state government. Railroads, moreover, paid taxes directly to the state and were by and large exempt from local taxation; in a sense, therefore, by removing valuable property from the local tax lists they increased the tax rate of the individual citizen. A special assembly committee appointed during the 1882 legislative session to inquire into the problem of railroad taxation issued its report just prior to the opening of the 1883 session.

Recognizing that additional income was needed to balance the state budget, and perhaps sensing a good issue when he saw one, Ludlow gave special attention in his annual messages of 1883 and 1884 to the need for railroad taxation. He noted that railroad property was taxed proportionately far less than the property of private citizens; it would be unjust, he said, to subject the people to a state tax until all other options had received consideration. While some people advocated drastic actions against the railroads, he declared that the problem could be resolved through a few simple measures. First, the law of 1876, which taxed railroads for state purposes at a rate of one-half percent on "true value," needed changing, and Ludlow urged the legislature to define precisely what considerations would determine the true value of a railroad. He called for the creation of a special board totally independent of the railroads to assess this value, establish the tax payments, and keep up-to-date records to avoid the problem of outdated valuations. Second, he asked the legislature to repeal the law that exempted certain railroad systems from the "true value" tax. Ludlow believed that these measures, coupled with prudence in expenditures, would produce enough revenue for the state to carry out its tasks without resorting to a direct tax on the people. During the session of 1883 the legislature considered several plans to tax the railroads, but no law resulted from these deliberations. Ludlow lacked the political power to force the reluctant legislature to deal with his objective of equitable taxation for the railroads.

During his term several other important developments took place. The first governor to devote substantial attention to the problem of keeping the water supply of the populous northeastern section of the state pure and healthy, Ludlow appointed a commission to investigate the matter. He asked the legislature to establish a Council of State Charities and Corrections to oversee the asylums, prisons, jails, and alms houses in New Jersey, and he appointed the council's first members. During his term other important legislation was passed, including a law that grouped municipalities into four classifications.

Overall, Ludlow's administration can be characterized best as honest and diligent but basically unproductive. Prominent but not particularly powerful in New Jersey politics before his nomination, Ludlow had little chance of influencing a legislature divided between the parties and dominated by special interests. Like many of his predecessors, Ludlow tended to devote the bulk of his messages to the legislature to summaries of the lengthy reports of minor government officials. By using his veto power he set a moral tone that many people felt New Jersey needed in the 1880s, but few positive achievements can be directly attributed to him. His most noteworthy deed was giving the sanction of the governor's office to the growing movement for equitable taxation of the railroads; by this he helped set the stage for the passage of a more effective railroad-taxing system under his successor, Leon Abbett.

Although Ludlow's administration accomplished relatively little, his actions, especially his vetoes, earned him the animosity of powerful interests. After he left the governorship he resumed the practice of law, but he lived in relative obscurity. Contemporary opinion laid the blame for his less-than-prosperous condition during this period at the doorstep of the railroads. In 1894 he served on the special twenty-member commission established by the legislature to recommend changes in the New Jersey constitution. In 1895 Governor George T. Werts appointed him a justice of the state supreme court. Five years later he died in his hometown, New Brunswick. He was survived by his wife and two sons.

JEROME C. REDDY

Records of Governor George C. Ludlow, New Jersey State Library, Trenton, N.J.

Sackett, William Edgar. *Modern Battles of Trenton.* Vol. 1, *Being a History of New Jersey's Politics and Legislation from the Year 1868 to the Year 1894.* Trenton: John L. Murphy, 1895.

Leon Abbett (October 8, 1836–December 4, 1894) was a formidable man. He was undoubtedly the most powerful person in New Jersey during the late nineteenth century. Twice elected governor, first in 1883 and again in 1889, he proved to be a very effective leader and accomplished much while in office. An ardent Democrat in the Jacksonian spoils tradition, Abbett voiced the sentiments of the common man beset by the intransigent forces of special privilege. Affectionately known as the "Great Commoner," he was considered a man of the people. He reached out for contact, and indeed for confrontation. An eloquent speaker in the flamboyant style of his time, he charged the political atmosphere and helped produce striking policy changes that had previously been considered impossible. He was a man of action, ambitious for his state as well as for himself.

Abbett combined opportunism with principle to advance his cause. As a machine politician he often combined the admirable with the obnoxious. Not for any altruistic reasons but for practical ones, Abbett much to his credit promoted public participation in politics. True Jacksonian that he was, he rewarded loyal Democrats with the spoils of victory. Coming to power as he did during the heyday of machine politics, he built a strong party organization and used it as a convenient excuse for centralizing power in the governor's office. With this power, he did things that none of his predecessors had ever attempted to do. His performance infuriated his critics and those people with rigorous Victorian moral standards and roused passionate hatred. Loved with equal passion, seeking improvement for the downtrodden, using his charm and wit with a flourish, he was a difficult man to beat. Yet despite the political hegemony that he and his followers established, he failed to achieve his lifelong ambition of advancing to the United States Senate.

In physical appearance, Abbett was short and stocky. Standing only five feet eight inches and weighing about 175 pounds, the governor was an image of energy, combativeness, and courage. He had a round face with a high forehead, broad shoulders, brown wavy hair, bright blue eyes, and large bushy eyebrows. Early in his career, he grew a full beard and a wide moustache to make himself look more mature. As a successful New York City lawyer might be expected to do, he dressed in a manner befitting his professional status. He usually wore a dark double-breasted suit with a vest and bow tie. In cold weather, he donned a fashionable Prince Albert overcoat and a brown derby hat.

Abbett's rise to the governorship is a classic American success story. In a day when recruitment to political office depended much on wealth and high position, he came from an urban working-class background in Philadelphia. His father, Ezekiel, worked as a journeyman hatter by trade, while his mother, whose maiden name was Sarah M. Howell, operated a millinery shop. She originally came from a prominent but not well-to-do family in

Mauricetown, New Jersey. Young Abbett grew up a poor boy in the streets of Philadelphia during the Jacksonian era. He attended Central High School, where he met boys like Henry George and Ignatius Donnelly, both of whom were to become famous public figures. Attendance at college was something which only the most privileged families could afford, and after graduating from Central High, Abbett studied law on his own. He served as a clerk in the firm of John W. Ashmead, who was the United States attorney for the Eastern District of Pennsylvania. Abbett passed his bar examination in 1857, but he found Philadelphia to be a closed shop when it came to attracting clients. A year later, he moved to New York City in search of a more lucrative practice. There he soon formed a law partnership with William J. Fuller, a distinguished patent and admiralty lawyer. With the city's expanding commercial activity, the law firm of Abbett and Fuller became prosperous, and it remained intact until Fuller died in 1889.

Shortly after the outbreak of the Civil War, Abbett returned to Philadelphia to marry Mary Briggs on October 8, 1862. She was the daughter of Amos Briggs, a city judge. The couple initially established their residence in Hoboken, which was just a ferryboat ride from Abbett's law office in Manhattan. In the seventeen years of their marriage, they had two sons and a daughter.

Encouraged by his law partner, Abbett entered politics in his newly adopted hometown in 1864, campaigning for General George B. McClellan in the presidential race against Abraham Lincoln. In the same campaign, he was elected to represent Hoboken in the general assembly. The Civil War overshadowed his early political career. He was an intensely loyal Democrat, aligned with the party's Copperhead wing, which vehemently opposed the war. A staunch states' rights advocate, he vigorously objected to the policies of the Lincoln administration, especially its Emancipation Proclamation. Although philosophically opposed to slavery, he went along with his party and voted against the ratification of both the Thirteenth and Fifteenth Amendments. At the time, there were only eight black people living in Hoboken, and he did not favor their advancement. Opposing the use of federal power during the war, Abbett deplored the expanded role of that power during Reconstruction. He gained statewide recognition by defending United States Senator John P. Stockton, whom the radicals of the Republican Party had expelled from Congress.

Seeking to broaden his political base in Hudson County, Abbett moved to Jersey City in 1867. He was reelected to the general assembly for the next two years, and his fellow state legislators chose him speaker. The speakership was an important leadership position which he used to great advantage. The key to his success lay in his instinctive ability to gauge what would be acceptable to his own party, to the opposition, and to Governor Theodore F. Randolph. During the 1870s, he endorsed a conservative approach to public policy while devoting much of his energy to the task of building the party

organization. No crusader, he was at this time a survivor. Thus he identified himself with the powerful Camden and Amboy Railroad and defended
this monopoly whenever it came under attack by people outside New Jersey.
Like most politicians who move into the front ranks, he discovered that the
political system within which he had to operate was not only shaping his
decisions but also formulating his options.

In the late 1860s, the immigrant Irish Catholics in Jersey City were gaining
political power. Frightened, the militant Know-Nothing nativists subjected
them to discrimination and abuse. Abbett was one of the few Protestant
leaders willing to share power with the Irish. As president of the local board
of education in 1869, he openly courted them by assisting in their fight to
soften the Protestant tone of Bible reading and prayers in the public schools.
New Jersey politicians had played ethnic politics before the 1870s, but with
the advent of mass political parties, Abbett developed the strategy to a high
degree. He managed nominations and distributed patronage jobs to ethnics
with a deliberate intent to woo them at election time.

Many more illustrations of Abbett's cooperation with the Irish could be
cited, but one will suffice. Jersey City Republicans realized that the emergent
Irish were outnumbering them. To put the municipal government beyond
their reach, the Republicans persuaded the state legislature in 1871 to pass
the "thieves' charter," which removed the Irish intruders from city office and
replaced them with commissioners appointed by the legislature. Abbett
spoke out against this ripper legislation, and in 1874 he got himself elected
Hudson County state senator by promising to restore home rule.

During the 1870s, the Democratic Party in New Jersey was rent by factionalism. The Theodore Fitz Randolph faction, otherwise known as the "State
House Ring," abhorred the Irish courtship. Conversely, leaders like Abbett
and John R. McPherson, who were interested in maintaining power, realized
that to win elections the party must temper its nativism and enlist broad
support. Breaking sharply and completely with the State House Ring in 1875,
Abbett challenged Randolph's party leadership by supporting Robert Gil-
christ for the United States Senate. This abortive effort failed, but greater
success followed in 1877, when Abbett backed McPherson for the other Senate seat. Abbett continually clashed with the State House Ring both in personality and politics.

As a state senator, Abbett kept his campaign pledge and obtained the passage of a reform municipal charter restoring home rule to Jersey City. He
played subtly on the religious and ethnic issue when he sponsored his "Liberty of Conscience" bill, which allowed Catholic priests access to the state
penal and mental institutions. Elevated to the senate presidency in 1877,
Abbett won the applause of organized labor by sponsoring a statute that
required employers to pay their workers in cash rather than in paper scrip or
company store merchandise. In a similar vein, he helped the employees of the

bankrupt Jersey Central Railroad try to collect their back wages by drafting a statute that made their salaries a prior lien on the assets of the company.

Abbett first sought the governorship in 1877, but the State House Ring, in an episode fraught with party intrigue, conspired to assure the nomination for George B. McClellan. Though disappointed, Abbett showed his party loyalty by campaigning for McClellan. Personal tragedy then struck. His wife died of cancer in 1879 at the age of forty. He never remarried.

Stricken with grief, Abbett temporarily dropped out of politics. Some of his close friends thought that he had lost interest. But in 1880, when he learned that his arch rival Orestes Cleveland was seeking the governorship, he roared back. As chairman of the State Democratic Convention, Abbett single-handedly steered the nomination to George C. Ludlow, a state senator from Middlesex County, who went on to win the election.

Railroads were of paramount interest in New Jersey during the Gilded Age. Governor Ludlow would have liked to tax them, but he could not break through the stalemate of forces surrounding him. To battle the railroads over state and local taxation was Abbett's calling. It struck at the heart of laissez-faire capitalism and brought him into direct conflict with the established order, which saw railroading as the lifeblood of the state's economy. Concerned because the railroads paid few taxes or none, he actually began his fight against them while serving as corporation counsel for Jersey City from 1877 to 1883.

Finally, in 1883, Abbett was nominated for governor. With railroad taxation as his battle cry, he conducted a vigorous campaign, touring New Jersey from one end to the other. Yet his hometown, Jersey City, remained the center stage of the drama. The Republicans ran state supreme court judge Jonathan Dixon, who also lived there. Abbett did not let the voters forget that Dixon had drafted the infamous "thieves' charter," which deprived the Jersey City Irish of power in 1871. Dixon also had handed down court decisions that were construed as antilabor. Abbett's cultural affinity with urban workers and foreign immigrants accounted in large measure for his popular appeal. When the election returns were tabulated, he had defeated Dixon by 103,856 to 97,047.

Abbett's inauguration in 1884 at age forty-seven was a goal he had worked toward for twenty years. Impatient waiting and striving had whetted his appetite for the leadership opportunities that he saw in the office. Seizing the initiative, he made the rail tax issue the major thrust of his inaugural message, which the railroads interpreted as a declaration of war. During the ensuing battle, Abbett encountered all kinds of obstacles. When pressure against the passage of the tax bill intensified, he threatened to refuse to sign appropriations unless the measure was advanced. By skillfully publicizing the issue, he was able to get the bill passed—a feat that had seemed impossible. As soon as the statute had been signed into law, the railroads challenged its constitutionality in the courts. At one point, the opposition created a political smokescreen by impeaching Patrick H. Laverty, the state prison warden. Undaunted, Abbett persisted in his course of action, and the railroads finally capitulated, completely surrendering their tax-exempt status.

As governor, Abbett was one of the rare major party politicians who advocated the cause of New Jersey's black citizens. In an unusual display of gubernatorial prerogative, he intervened in a local incident of racial injustice. The body of Samuel Bass, an ex-slave, had been denied burial in an all-white cemetery in Hackensack. Abbett called for corrective action, motivated by compassion and social justice but evincing a fair and dispassionate consideration of the issues. He persuaded the legislature to pass the "Negro Burial" bill. But that was not all; he also secured the passage of the first public accommodations law. On top of this, he served as the godfather of a black child in Newark, who was baptized Leon Abbett DeKalb. An interracial baptism was an uncommon event in those days. Coming at a high tide of racism in America, these actions were particularly significant; they represented a dramatic reversal of Abbett's earlier attitudes toward blacks.

Several other reform bills were enacted to cope with the onrush of urban industrialism. The practice of using convict labor for private profit was abolished, while the laws regulating the working conditions of women and children were tightened. Aware of the disorderly and chaotic growth of nineteenth-century American cities, Abbett drafted legislation that enabled the bankrupt municipalities of Elizabeth and Rahway to regain their solvency. His appointments displeased civil service reformers. In Jacksonian fashion, he ousted holdover Republicans from office and replaced them with loyal Democrats whenever possible. In retaliation, a hostile Republican legislature stripped him of control of those appointments, but not without a fight.

Prohibited by the state constitution from succeeding himself, in 1887 Abbett sought to become a United States senator. That goal proved elusive. Retribution came, and its name was railroad power. It should be remembered that before 1913 senators were chosen by the state legislatures, not the voters. Conservative prorailroad Democrats, who identified with the State House Ring, withheld their support from Abbett and elected Rufus Blodgett instead. Brooding, vituperative, bitter, Abbett took this defeat hard. Meanwhile, he managed to stay alive politically. He became legal counsel for the liquor dealers' association, an important source of campaign money and financing.

Counting on his continuing popularity, party leaders prevailed on Abbett to run for a second term in 1889. His instinct opposed seeking reelection, hut he could not resist the insistence of his followers, especially since he had no attractive alternatives. After securing an agreement to raise the governor's salary from $5,000 to $10,000, he accepted the nomination. The Republicans ran Edward B. Grubb, a wealthy iron magnate and a Civil War hero. Abbett had little trouble defeating Grubb, compiling an unprecedented plurality of

14,253 votes. He would have won even without the ballot frauds perpetrated in his behalf in the Irish district of Jersey City, where the number of votes cast exceeded the number of registered voters.

Characteristically, Abbett seized the initiative and turned the election-fraud scandal to his advantage by demanding a ballot-reform law. From a friendly Democratic legislature, he acquired greater control over the bureaucracy and regained the appointive powers that had been previously usurped. Never subordinate to the legislature, he now began to ask it for action on a wider and wider range of issues. He obtained a package of labor laws, free public libraries, scholarships for the agricultural college at Rutgers, highway improvements, money increases for public schools, and a department of banking and insurance. His key appointments were typically paradoxical: for some departments he chose men of high competence and integrity, for others he yielded to the demands of unsavory forces that eventually damaged his reputation. A product of the corrupt Hudson County machine, which was then run by Robert Davis, the governor could not escape being tarnished by its rampant public dishonesty.

Abbett also broke new ground in resolving industrial strife. In December 1890, a serious dispute between labor and management erupted at the Clark Thread Mills in Kearny. As it turned out, it was one of the longest and bitterest strikes in New Jersey history. Pinkerton detectives were hired as strikebreakers. Rather than exacerbate the conflict by calling out the National Guard, as governors in the Gilded Age were prone to do, Abbett cleverly defused the situation by deputizing the Jersey City police, who restored order. He then had the legislature create the first state police force and appointed John Parnell Feeney as its head. He also obtained a law that prohibited the use of private detectives in strikes.

Similarly, in 1891, the governor intervened in a labor dispute at the Oxford Iron and Nail Company in Warren County, where employees were being starved into submission by a lockout in the depth of winter. He translated the episode into the first law of any significance on mine safety. He further demonstrated his alignment with the working class by appointing labor leaders to key positions. He named Joseph P. McDonnell to the state board of arbitration and Robert O'Hara as his commissioner of mines. In truth, he never forgot his common origins or his city upbringing. He was the first urban-oriented governor in the state.

When put to the test, Abbett had the capacity to rise above politics and to do what was best for the public good. The two most controversial pieces of legislation during his second term involved legalized gambling at the horse-racing tracks and the incorporation of the Reading Railroad Coal Combine. When these bills were passed, the attendant pressures were transferred in all their intensity from the legislature to the governor. Worried about the potential adverse consequences of both bills, he vetoed them. Afterwards be successfully appealed for public support to sustain the vetoes.

But bargaining with party bosses like Miles Ross and James Smith proved costly, for they made Abbett pay heavily for his legislative vetoes. In 1893, the special interests he had antagonized once again combined to defeat him for the United States Senate. Dejected by having failed to achieve his cherished goal, Abbett finished his career by serving as a state supreme court judge. He died in his home in Jersey City on December 4, 1894, after an attack of sugar diabetes. He was buried in the family plot in the Greenwood Cemetery in Brooklyn.

By any standard, Abbett was one of the ablest and most intriguing men ever to be governor. The social and economic conditions that existed in 1884 made New Jersey manipulable for someone with Abbett's sources of machine power and leadership ability. Few of his contemporaries were comparably positioned. A lifetime in politics had made him wise and ruthless in political bargaining and compromising. This experience, coupled with his determination to lead rather than follow, made him formidable. With a personality well suited for the intense partisanship of his time, he displayed great zest for party politics and party organization. Furthermore, in many ways he was considerably in advance of the times. In this sense, he was an important forerunner of a type of governor that had not yet appeared on the American political stage.

RICHARD A. HOGARTY

Records of Governor Leon Abbett, New Jersey State Library, Trenton, N.J.

Hogarty, Richard A. *Leon Abbett's New Jersey: The Emergence of the Modern Governor*. Philadelphia: American Philosophical Society, 2001.

———. "The Political Apprenticeship of Leon Abbett." *New Jersey History* 111 (Spring–Summer 1993): 1–42.

Record of Leon Abbett, Democratic Candidate for Governor of New Jersey, as Assemblyman, Senator and Governor, The. Jersey City, N.J.: Heppenheimer, 1889.

Sackett, William Edgar. *Modern Battles of Trenton*. Vol. 1, *Being a History of New Jersey's Politics and Legislation from the Year 1868 to the Year 1894*. Trenton: John L. Murphy, 1895.

Shaw, Douglas V. *The Making of an Immigrant City: Ethnic and Cultural Conflict in Jersey City, New Jersey, 1850–1877*. New York: Arno, 1976.

Steffens, Lincoln. "New Jersey: A Traitor State." *McClure's Magazine* 24 (April 1905): 649–64.

Robert Stockton Green (March 25, 1831–May 7, 1895) brought to the governorship a commanding presence, the status of a colonial elite ancestry, and more than three decades of political experience. His greatest single asset was his family name. However, he failed to exploit these obvious advantages. As chief of state, he was a model of dignity and restraint, a symbol of integrity and social respectability; but he lacked passion for his cause or against his opponents. He was cool and dispassionate, cultured and scholarly, impersonal and logical. The press respected him; the electorate admired him but did not embrace him as it had his predecessor, Leon Abbett. He lacked both Abbett's zest for the strategy and tactics of party politics and his mastery of its subtleties. Although imbued with a strong sense of civic duty, Green nevertheless was a captive of the political system and the business interests that dominated it. As such, he did not assume an activist role in shaping public policy, and he did not distinguish himself in office.

A patrician by birth and disposition, Robert S. Green could lay claim to a sterling Yankee background. He was descended from a long line of Presbyterian ministers and a family that had been politically active in New Jersey since the American Revolution. His great-grandfather, the Reverend Jacob Green, had served as chairman of the committee that drafted the first state constitution at the Provincial Congress in Burlington in 1776. His grandmother, Elizabeth Stockton, was the daughter of Commodore Robert F. Stockton, who had been a naval hero in the War of 1812; she was also a direct descendant of Richard Stockton, who had signed the Declaration of Independence. These family credentials gave Green impeccable native-born, blue-blood status. At a time when family lineage and patriotic loyalty counted heavily in state politics, Green was endowed by birth with a valuable political resource. Over the years, the gentry had held power by tradition, by law, by wealth, and not, usually, through the electoral sanction of universal suffrage.

Green was born in Princeton. Not much is known about his early childhood except that he grew up in a household where religion was important, discipline strict, and the moral distinction between right and wrong clearly defined. His mother, the former Isabella McClulloh, read the Bible to her children, spun the material for their clothing, and tried to inculcate the values of honesty and ambition. Raised close to Nassau Hall, Robert received a fine education. He graduated from the College of New Jersey (later Princeton University) in 1850. The family was closely affiliated with the college. The Reverend Ashbel Green, Robert's grandfather, was a renowned theologian who had served as president of the college from 1812 to 1822. His father, James S. Green, was a member of the law faculty. James Green was a man of considerable influence. In addition to having served as a United States attorney, he had been the Democratic Party's candidate for governor in 1837, losing in the legislative balloting to William S. Pennington, the Whig Party nominee. He was also closely identified with the transportation interests of the state, and he served as a director of the Delaware and Raritan Canal Company as well as treasurer of the Joint Railroad and Canal Companies.

Robert S. Green, determined to follow in his father's footsteps, entered the legal profession. As was the custom in those days, he read the law while clerking in a local firm. Admitted to the New Jersey bar in 1853, Green eventually earned repute as one of the ablest constitutional lawyers in the state. Meanwhile, he showed an early interest in politics. In 1852, he served a brief stint on the Princeton Borough Council. The family had a longstanding traditional association with the Democratic Party, which no doubt helped to launch his political career.

In 1856, Green moved from his hometown to the city of Elizabeth, where he promptly became involved in the political effort to establish Union County. He was also instrumental that year in securing the passage of legislation that designated Elizabeth as the county seat. In 1857, Green married Mary E. Mulligan. In due course, they raised a son and three daughters. Step by step, the young lawyer from Elizabeth climbed the political ladder, from prosecutor of the borough courts to city attorney to city councilman to surrogate of Union County. In 1868, he was named the presiding judge of the Court of Common Pleas. In 1869, Governor Theodore F. Randolph chose him to represent the state at the commercial convention in Louisville, Kentucky.

While still young and ambitious, Green came to accept the concept of litigation as a form of political action. He played a leading role in the struggle to break the Camden and Amboy Railroad monopoly of transportation rights between New York City and Philadelphia. This was no small accomplishment. The railroad had amassed enormous political power since its origin in 1831. One by one, legislators came to owe fealty to the homegrown monopoly, and they often succumbed to the blandishments of its lobbyists or to fears of political reprisal. At the time of the Civil War, when rail transportation was needed for military purposes, senators in Congress derisively referred to New Jersey as the "State of Camden and Amboy." The railroad, unwilling to give up its preferential treatment and its guaranteed freedom from competition, resisted newcomers with understandable passion. In 1872, Green brought suit against the monopoly on behalf of the National Railway Company, which had started building a competing line. Although the suit was denied, it stirred a fierce battle in the state legislature and directly led to the passage of the first general railroad law in 1873. With the enactment of this statute, the monopoly was finally crushed. Only in these bold and daring attacks on the Camden and Amboy Railroad did Green win the status of popular hero.

Recognizing Green's talents, Governor Joel Parker appointed him in 1873 to a blue-ribbon commission instructed to revise the state constitution in the light of the myriad problems created for local governments by the onrush of urbanization and industrialization. Green chaired the important committee on general and special legislation. Among other things, the revised consti-tution forbade the legislature to pass special laws for individual cities and required tax authorities to assess property by uniform rules and according to its true value. The state legislature's unwarranted interference in munici-pal affairs had become a serious abuse. Green, by identifying himself with tax reform and the home-rule movement, continued to improve his politi-cal standing.

For the next two decades, Green led a busy double life as attorney and state and national politician. With "railroad fever" sweeping New Jersey, Green became wealthy as a railroad lawyer. In January 1874, he became a member of the New York bar and joined the prestigious Wall Street law firm of Brown, Hall and Vanderpoel. As a Princeton alumnus, he added to the firm's luster. He was later made a full partner, when the firm changed its name to Vanderpoel, Green and Cuming.

Never far removed from politics, Green served as a member of the Union County Democratic Committee, where his skills as a political organizer and campaign strategist were highly valued. In 1868, he made a bid for Congress, but he lost his party's nomination to John T. Bird of Hunterdon County by the bare margin of two votes. In 1880, he was a delegate to the Democratic National Convention which nominated General Winfield Scott Hancock, who had led Union forces at Gettysburg. In 1884, Green finally obtained his party's nomination for Congress, and he defeated the popular Republican incumbent, John Kean, Jr., by a plurality of 1,848 votes.

Before Green's one term in Congress expired, he decided to enter the gubernatorial race of 1886. However, he encountered considerable intra-party opposition for the nomination, mainly from the powerful "State House Ring," which backed Rufus Blodgett, manager of the New York and Long Branch Railroad. Aligned with the more progressive wing of his party, Green received the crucial support of major Democratic leaders like Leon Abbett and John R. McPherson, and he won the nomination.

The gubernatorial contest proved interesting. The Republicans ran Con-gressman Benjamin F. Howey of Warren County, a manufacturer of slate and roofing materials. The emotionally charged issue of temperance was soon interjected into the campaign. No other question did more to inflame reli-gious and ethnic antagonisms. In the eyes of teetotaling, evangelical Protes-tants, drinking was an alien practice that posed a dangerous threat to public morality. They saw it as the root cause of crime, idleness, and poverty. As the campaign progressed, nativism and anti-Catholicism became intermingled with the temperance issue. Drunkenness was associated with immigrants, and Irish Catholics in particular were unfairly scapegoated. Green, for his part, played for the Irish vote and gently embraced the liquor interests. On November 2, he defeated Howey by a vote of 109,939 to 101,919—a victory widely attributed to the surprise impact of the third-party candidate, Clin-ton B. Fiske, who ran on the Prohibition ticket. Advocating total abstinence as his main platform, Fiske polled 19,808 votes. Since Green only beat Howey by 8,020 votes, it was claimed at the time that Fiske's candidacy cost Howey the election.

Green's long experience as a judge and politician contributed little of direct value to him as governor. Entering the office at age fifty-six, he chose to play his role as chief of state in a subdued manner, sharing initiative and responsibility generously with any who would ease his burdens of accountability. In political circles, he was easygoing, soft-spoken, and low-keyed, allowing his wry, often subtle sense of humor to mask his ambition. He was unable to lead the state legislature on the important social issues of the day. He chose to cooperate with party bosses rather than try to dominate them, and the result was a placid and relatively unproductive term.

In his inaugural message, Green paid lip service to the problem of railroad taxation, but as governor he did not do much about it. At the outset of his term, the state board of assessors revealed that the recalcitrant Morris and Essex Railroad owed the state approximately $1.2 million in back taxes. Rather than insist on payment in full, Green submitted the matter to arbitration. He did not press for a settlement, and the dispute was still unresolved when he left office three years later. He was equally lackadaisical about reorganizing the New Jersey National Guard. In spite of a congressional mandate to do so, he preferred to leave the task to his successor.

Not surprisingly, a protracted controversy over liquor regulation dominated politics during much of Green's administration. Temperance zealots publicized the state's failure to enforce its liquor law—at least in Jersey City, where many saloonkeepers openly defied the law and sold intoxicating beverages on Sunday. The violation outraged the Protestants, not only insulting the Christian Sabbath but also offending that sense of moralistic propriety so characteristic of small-town New Jersey. Evangelical church groups flocked to Trenton to petition the legislature to stop the flow of "pagan rum."

Intense lobbying aroused a Republican legislature to pass a stringent liquor control law in 1888. This statute mandated a system of high license fees and established a policy of local option whereby each county could decide in public referendum whether to prohibit the sale of liquor. Green, brushing aside his Presbyterianism for the moment, wished to preserve his good relationship with the Abbett faction of his party and so vetoed the temperance law, but the Republican-controlled legislature quickly overrode his veto.

Temperance next won easy local-option victories in six counties: Cumberland, Warren, Salem, Gloucester, Cape May, and Hunterdon. Stunned German, Irish, and other liquor dealers from the cities sought to overthrow what they considered a tyrannical puritan blue law. The state supreme court upheld the law, but the dealers demanded its repeal when the Democrats regained control of the 1eislature in 1889. Public opinion, however, remained overwhelming in favor of its retention. Under mounting church pressure, Green stayed out of the picture, leaving other party leaders to negotiate a compromise that retained the high license fees but deleted the local-option provision. His failure to lead did not pass unnoticed.

In many ways, constituents and leader were not closely attuned to each other's calculations. Although Green courted the support of urban factory workers, he did little or nothing to help them. Several bills designed to eliminate the hiring of Pinkerton detectives as strikebreakers and union infiltrators were introduced, but they failed to become laws for want of strong gubernatorial leadership. The same fate befell a ballot-reform bill strongly supported by organized labor.

Similarly, Green spurned the Irish shortly after he took office. He showed his nativism by curtly refusing to attend a mass protest rally against British rule of Ireland and the attendant abuse of human rights. Interpreting his refusal as an ethnic insult, the Irish, who consistently gave the Democrats large numbers of votes, considered him an ingrate. His leadership style contrasted sharply with Abbett's, which attempted to have the party uphold the traditional Protestant hegemony without outraging its Irish voters.

Green cooperated with the dominant business community both openly and covertly. Ideologically, he conformed to the safe, comfortable conservatism that characterized the age of industrial expansion. Under his administration, business interests were prominent and powerful. For example, he signed into law the famous statute of 1889 that legalized the holding company and allowed businesses to incorporate for almost any purpose.

Upon leaving office, Green was appointed by his successor, Leon Abbett, to the New Jersey Court of Chancery. Some observers criticized the appointment as a political payoff, but Green performed well as a judge. His temperament seemed better suited for the judiciary than the executive. He died in Elizabeth on May 7, 1895, while serving on the bench. Interment was in the Greenwood Cemetery in Brooklyn.

All things considered, Green was not an effective governor. His concept of the office lacked sufficient scope, his programs were innocuous, and his leadership was insignificant. The essence of the gubernatorial role escaped him both as party leader and policy leader. He found it a burden rather than an exciting opportunity. The Green administration earned the admiration of the business community, but it did not capture the passion of the times or the imagination of the electorate.

RICHARD A. HOGARTY

Records of Governor Leon Abbett, New Jersey State Library, Trenton, N.J.

Hogarty, Richard A. *Leon Abbett's New Jersey: The Emergence of the Modern Governor.* Philadelphia: American Philosophical Society, 2001.

Record of Leon Abbett, Democratic Candidate for Governor of New Jersey, as Assemblyman, Senator, and Governor, The. Jersey City, N.J.: Heppenheimer, 1889.

Shaw, Douglas V. *The Making of an Immigrant City: Ethnic and Cultural Conflict in Jersey City, New Jersey.* New York: Arno, 1976.

Steffens, Lincoln. "New Jersey: A Traitor State." *McClure's Magazine* 24 (April 1905): 649–64.

George Theodore Werts (March 24, 1846–January 17, 1910), lawyer, state senator, supreme court justice, twenty-eighth governor of New Jersey, was born at Hackettstown, Warren County. He attended the public schools in Bordentown and completed his academic training at the State Model School in Trenton. In 1863 he moved to Morristown to study law with his uncle, the former attorney general Jacob Vanatta. Four years later the twenty-one-year-old law clerk was admitted to the New Jersey bar. He promptly established an office in Morristown.

Over the next sixteen years Werts built a lucrative law practice and gained a reputation for integrity and skill as a trial lawyer. Although he was a Democrat in an overwhelmingly Republican community, he was elected recorder of Morristown in 1883 and mayor in 1886. In the latter year, at the age of forty, he was also elected state senator from Morris County. His political success was due in no small measure to his wife, the former Emma Stelle, whom he had married in 1872. His marriage and the subsequent births of his two daughters helped fill an important social and emotional void in his life.

During his six years in the senate Werts compiled a commendable record, highlighted by his election as senate president in 1889. His name is associated with two pieces of legislation—election reform and local liquor option—but neither statute proved more than a politically motivated and ineffectual expedient. His independent legislative record nonetheless brought him to the attention of Governor Leon Abbett. The governor's term would expire in 1893, and he had his eye on a seat in the United States Senate. Fearing that a promising young legislator with political ambitions might threaten his plans, the governor appointed Werts to the state supreme court in February 1892 to fill a vacancy on the Hudson County circuit.

Abbett had little need for concern. Werts was a party man who had previously demonstrated his loyalty by sponsoring an act that shortly before Abbett's inauguration doubled the governor's salary. In 1892, despite the governor's earlier fears, he supported Werts for the Democratic gubernatorial nomination rather than allowing one of his political enemies to gain the nomination. Although the Democratic caucus had considered both Edward F. C. Young and Justice Job Lippincott, Werts won an easy first-ballot convention victory.

His Republican opponent, John Kean, Jr., campaigned against the Abbett administration by condemning such abuses as ballot-box stuffing, the sale of political offices, and Democratic subservience to the liquor and racetrack interests. Although Werts remained inactive during the campaign and continued to sit on the bench, party chairman Allan L. McDermott ably handled Democratic strategy. He sought to divert attention from the damaging Republican charges of corruption by linking the gubernatorial race with the Democratic presidential campaign of Grover Cleveland. For in spite of the political stalemate of national politics between 1876 and 1892, the Democrats had carried New Jersey in every presidential election since the Civil War save that of 1872 and in all but one gubernatorial contest in the same period. The strategy worked perfectly.

Cleveland's fourteen-thousand-vote plurality proved enough of a cushion to carry Judge Werts into the governor's mansion by a margin of over seventy-six hundred votes.

In his inaugural address Governor Werts proposed expanding the state's prison facilities, creating a reformatory for juvenile delinquents, and passing ballot-reform legislation. He directed the bulk of his remarks at those who criticized New Jersey for not having antitrust laws. Long before the United States Supreme Court's enunciation of the "rule of reason," Werts sought to distinguish justifiable from unjustifiable restraints of trade. "The distinction appears to be," he observed, "that where the restraint of combination is . . . simply the natural consequence and not the intent, the combination is not improper; where the object is to destroy competition and obtain control of . . . production, . . . such combination is unlawful." Following the initiative of earlier Democratic administrations, Werts encouraged the combination of capital through the continuation of the state's liberal incorporation laws.

The 1893 legislature distinguished itself only by its excesses in violating morality and constitutionality. The most flagrant abuse occurred in connection with legalizing gambling at the state's racetracks. For a number of years prominent Democratic officials, including Assembly Speaker Thomas Flynn, had enjoyed a profitable working relationship with tracks in Gloucester, Monmouth, and Guttenberg. The legislature's passage of the bill to legalize gambling in arrogant disregard of public opinion stimulated the emergence of an influential antiracetrack league. Though Governor Werts vetoed the legislation, racetrack critics alleged that his haste to do so prevented effective mobilization against the gambling interests and helped enable the "jockey legislature" to override the veto.

The bitterness the gambling legislation provoked was evident in the off-year election of 1893, which produced a thirty-thousand-vote majority for the Republicans and gave them control of both the assembly and the senate. But gambling was only one of many issues with cultural overtones that made themselves felt at the polls. The antiracetrack crusade proved to be overwhelmingly Protestant in leadership and composition. The enthusiasm the antigambling campaign generated among evangelical Protestants and the apathy it met among Roman Catholics suggest the divergent ethnocultural attitudes that characterized New Jersey politics during the late nineteenth century. It was not coincidental that the Republicans imbued their 1893 campaign with a pietistic fervor that viewed gambling as immoral and received its most vocal support from the predominantly rural counties of South Jersey.

The GOP's success also came at the expense of urban, new-stock Democratic legislators who had supported the gambling legislation and succumbed to its moral repercussions. New Jersey's Catholic hierarchy's ill-timed attempt to obtain public approval for state aid to parochial schools further stimulated this pietistic fervor. Though Governor Werts and the Democratic legislators tried to disassociate themselves from the church, the parochial-education issue intensified ethnocultural divisiveness. This, in addition to the impact of the 1893 depression, may account for Democratic defeats in the urban-industrial counties of Hudson, Essex, and Passaic and for the loss to the Republicans of seven of the state's ten largest cities.

Instead of accepting the results, the Democratic minority in the senate organized a rump session and refused to certify the eligibility of the newly elected GOP members. They advised Governor Werts of their decision and asked him to recognize their body as the senate of the state. Displaying the same notable absence of courage that had characterized his mishandling of the racetrack scandals, Werts acquiesced, following a policy of inactivity and neutrality that allowed the capricious, selfish, and partisan actions of this small group of Democrats to paralyze the state's political process. This tragically ludicrous episode, in which the state had two functioning senates, was resolved in March 1894 when the supreme court ruled the rump session illegal.

The substitution of a Republican majority did not materially alter the quality of New Jersey politics. The 1894 legislative session is memorable only for the GOP's efforts to dislodge Democrats from all key appointive positions. Governor Werts's inability to provide even minimal executive leadership encouraged both parties to operate in a factious vacuum rather than face the problems of mass unemployment and poverty. Trying to avoid all responsibility for the depression, the Democrats sought security in a campaign that identified their opponents with anti-Catholicism, Prohibitionism, and antiurbanism. They denounced the GOP for countenancing the existence of secret Protestant societies and for using the pulpit for propaganda purposes. The Republicans, for their part, supported legislation that would restrict religious training in public schools to the reading of the Lord's Prayer and require all schools to fly the American flag.

Cultural divisions continued to dominate state politics. Discussion of the depression revolved solely around its political repercussions and avoided any mention of possible solutions. Although the Democrats succeeded in regaining some legislative seats in 1894, the Republicans continued to capitalize on the depressed economy to secure majorities in state and congressional contests. Indeed, the precipitous Democratic electoral failures after 1892 can best be attributed to depression-created voter realignments and to the residual effects of the antiracetrack and antigambling crusades. Issues such as aid to parochial schools, naturalization, and gambling evolved into moral questions pitting old-stock Protestant Republicans from South Jersey against the new-stock Catholic urban Democrats from northeastern counties.

In Governor Werts's annual message to the 1895 legislature he simply repeated past proposals for prison expansion and ballot reform, adding a call for water conservation. The legislature enacted none of these measures. Instead, it passed the Storrs Naturalization Act over the governor's veto. This infamous statute, which was clearly aimed at new-stock immigrants and the Democratic Party, prohibited naturalization one month before any election. The legislature also rejected two amendments submitted by a special constitutional commission, one to outlaw gambling and the other to give women the right to vote in local school-board elections. But the most spectacular achievement of the 1895 legislative session centered on an investigation that uncovered corruption, graft, and waste in state government. Former Democratic officials were discovered to have sold pardons and accepted bribes and kickbacks from construction companies. The disclosure of Democratic corruption significantly helped the Republicans to elect John W. Griggs governor and to keep control of the legislature in 1895.

It was George T. Werts's misfortune to preside over the dismantling of the Democratic Party, which had dominated New Jersey politics between 1869 and 1896. Though the governor had scrupulously avoided any personal taint of illegality, his party's corruption contributed to its repudiation by the voters. Democratic supremacy in the post–Civil War period had resulted from efficient machine control at the local level. But the 1893 legislature had shocked even the most jaded citizens with its sordid behavior in legalizing racetrack gambling. The onset of the depression only accelerated a voter realignment toward the GOP that reflected a national trend and culminated in the election of William McKinley in 1896. It is clear that the vaunted Republican majorities of that year in New Jersey had actually been over three years in the making.

The governor's failure to provide leadership and his willingness to let the focus of power rest in the legislature characterized the Werts years. While the public was trying to cope with the most severe industrial depression of this generation, Governor Werts was leaving as his most enduring legacy a budget surplus of almost $1 million. His administration was notably deficient in rebuilding the integrity of state government. Once his term ended Werts retired to private life and his Jersey City law practice. He died on January 17, 1910 — the very day that governor-elect Woodrow Wilson inaugurated a new period of Democratic control.

EUGENE M. TOBIN

Records of Governor George T. Werts, New Jersey State Library, Trenton, N.J.

Brooks, Noah. "George T. Werts." *Harper's Weekly* 38 (March 3, 1894): 198.

Leiby, James R. *Charity and Correction in New Jersey: A History of State Welfare Institu-tions.* New Brunswick: Rutgers University Press, 1967.

Link, Arthur S. *Wilson.* 5 vols. Princeton: Princeton University Press, 1947–65.

Sackett, William Edgar. *Modern Battles of Trenton.* Vol. 1, *Being a History of New Jersey's Politics and Legislation from the Year 1868 to the Year 1894.* Trenton: John L. Murphy, 1895.

John William Griggs (July 10, 1849–November 28, 1927) had many politi-cal admirers in a life that included service as New Jersey's twenty-ninth gov-ernor, United States attorney general, and member of the Permanent Court of Arbitration at The Hague. William E. Sackett saw him as a masterful and overpowering personality, "an intellect in a mold of ice." Walter E. Edge recalled, in *A Jerseyman's Journal,* that Griggs was "an attractive man—of fine appearance, an eloquent orator, a keen thinker . . . [with] a fine sense of humor and every attribute of warmth and understanding."

Griggs was a scion of a farming family that had been settled in New Jersey since about 1733. The youngest son of Daniel and Emeline Johnson Griggs, he was born at the family homestead on Ridge Road near Newton, the county seat of Sussex County. He attended the Collegiate Institute in Newton, then matriculated in 1864 at Lafayette College in Easton, Pennsyl-vania. Although he had participated a year before graduation in an unruly protest against the abolition of student fraternities, he graduated in 1868, and he returned to Newton, where he studied law as Robert Hamilton's clerk until May 1871. To complete the prescribed three-year apprenticeship, he served with Socrates Tuttle in Paterson. He received his license as an attorney in November 1871, and three years later he was admitted as a coun-selor. After two years of independent practice he opened a law office with Tuttle. By 1879 he had established a clientele large and important enough to warrant opening his own office. Robert H. McCarter wrote in his memoirs that as a lawyer Griggs showed a "wonderful power of clearing up difficul-ties that arose in the course of protracted trials." Not surprisingly, Griggs's practice prospered.

Griggs entered state politics in 1875 as the Republican candidate from the first assembly district of Passaic County, and he was elected over the Demo-cratic incumbent with 51.9 percent of the vote. Although at twenty-six he was the youngest member of the assembly, he served on several committees and played a key role in restructuring the election laws under the constitu-tional amendments approved in 1875. He was reelected in 1876 but defeated for a third assembly term in the Democratic year of 1877. During the next five years he cultivated his legal practice and served as counsel of the Passaic

County Board of Chosen Freeholders (1878–79) and city counsel of Paterson (1879–82).

In 1882 Griggs returned to Trenton as a state senator, having defeated the Democratic candidate, Judge James Inglis, Jr., by only 182 votes. He spent six years in the senate serving as chairman of eight regular committees, including Railroads, Canals and Turnpikes, and Revision and Amendment of the Laws. His principal achievement came in 1884, when he was organizer and chairman of a six-member joint committee on corporate taxation. Living up to his reputation for fierce partisanship, Griggs overcame Governor Leon Abbett's "thoroughly equitable bill" for the taxation of railroads and other corporations, framing legislation he considered less punitive. Griggs's taxation bill, which became law and survived judicial review, considerably enriched the state coffers. He made an unsuccessful bid to become president of the senate in 1885 and was elected to the position in 1886.

Griggs began to set his sights on higher distinctions. In 1888 he served as a delegate-at-large to the Republican National Convention, where he nominated New Jersey Congressman William W. Phelps for vice president. In 1889 he hoped in vain that his railroad taxation work might win him the Republican gubernatorial nomination in New Jersey. Early in 1892 President Benjamin Harrison seriously considered naming him to fill the United States Supreme Court vacancy created by Joseph P. Bradley's death. As Griggs's confidential correspondence with William T. Hunt, editor of the *Newark Sunday Call*, reveals, Griggs enlisted the aid of Senate President Garret A. Hobart and others to influence Harrison in his favor. He also tried to curb stories that criticized him in the local Democratic press. Nevertheless, he was not selected, and his political ambitions were temporarily frustrated.

The Republicans in 1895 had their work cut out. Not since Marcus L. Ward's election in 1865 had New Jersey chosen a Republican governor. On the third ballot of the 1895 Republican State Convention, Griggs finally overcame the challenge of John Kean, Jr., and received his party's gubernatorial nomination.

Throughout the subsequent campaign against the Democratic candidate, Alexander T. McGill of Jersey City, Griggs waged a battle "for honesty, for retrenchment, for reform." His campaign rhetoric charged the Democrats with eleven years of prodigal and corrupt administration perpetuated by voting fraud in Hudson County. Specifically, he pointed to the Democrats' attempts to pass the Coal Combine Bill and to their abuses in racetrack gambling; he also accused them of staffing the state prison and the state hospital at Morris Plains with political hacks. On national issues he spoke openly for the gold standard, protectionism, and a cessation of Chinese immigration. But he rarely injected such issues into the New Jersey campaign.

Public disaffection from the incumbent party joined with dissension within the Democratic ranks to pave the way for a solid Republican victory. On November 5, 1895, Griggs was elected with 52.5 percent of the 311,609 ballots cast. He had a plurality of 26,900 votes and carried seventeen counties. Interviewed after his victory, he promised "honest government, honest officials, reduction of expenses, reduction and simplification of legislation." His victory initiated a succession of Republican governors broken only by the election of Woodrow Wilson fifteen years later.

In Griggs's inaugural address at Taylor's Opera House in Trenton on June 21, 1896, he called on the legislators to consider "a restriction in the volume of legislation," especially about the unmanageable mass of statutes dealing with municipal corporations; to pass no law "unless there is some public necessity demanding it"; to enact reforms for "the protection of life, limb and health" against danger from public use of the highways and streams, specifically to prevent civilian injuries from trolley cars and to guard against the pollution of New Jersey rivers by urban sewage; and to keep the state's charitable and penal institutions free from political control.

The new governor directed his first efforts toward removing recalcitrant Democratic state officials. He replaced Secretary of State Henry C. Kelsey, who had held the post for twenty-five years, with George Wurts of Paterson. Other officeholders whose careers were ended by the reform-minded administration included the "lay judges" of the courts of common pleas. On March 19 state senator Foster M. Voorhees introduced a bill to eliminate them and reduce the salaries of county court judges; the legislature approved the bill a week later, vacating forty jobs and saving perhaps $100,000.

Griggs turned his attention to the problem of grade crossings, and an act approved on March 25, 1896, eliminated the public menace of grade crossings in Newark and Jersey City. The legislators departed from the spirit of Griggs's inaugural message and produced a series of bills that made it more difficult for the victims of trolley accidents to sue the North Jersey Traction Company and other operators of surface lines in Essex and Hudson Counties. In line with Griggs's views, in 1897 the legislature prepared a constitutional amendment proscribing all forms of gambling, especially horse-track gambling, though that had received legislative sanction only three years earlier; but the amendment was barely approved at public referendum.

Griggs, an avid hunter and fisherman, felt strongly about conservation, and during his two years in Trenton the legislature passed a series of laws preventing water pollution and protecting fish, shellfish, and wildlife. His most important environmental effort was an act approved on February 26, 1896, to curb the pollution of the Passaic River and establish a general sewage system for the area. The act authorized an expenditure of $10,000. Writing to his friend William T. Hunt on December 19, 1897, Griggs said that the real danger lay "in the indifference of the local communities outside of those that actually get the smells. They are afraid of the expense, and are not spurred by the sense of immediate necessity." The preservation of public health and safety demanded state rather than local pollution controls. Under this act Griggs named Hunt and two physicians to consider the problem, hire consultants, and make recommendations. Fifteen years and four commissions later, however, the effort had accomplished nothing of substance.

On January 11, 1898, in Griggs's last message to the legislature, he surprised both parties by recommending an investigation of criminal law administration and other allegedly corrupt Democratic practices in Hudson County. Before an investigative committee could be set up, however, Griggs resigned the governorship to become the United States attorney general. On January 25 he had signed into law an act determining the order of succession to the office of governor, and therefore there was no constitutional crisis. On February 1, 1898, Foster M. Voorhees, president of the senate, was sworn in as acting governor until the fall elections.

Griggs had been offered the post of attorney general at the recommendation of Vice President Garret A. Hobart, his political mentor from Paterson. He was sworn in on February 1, 1898. He shared President McKinley's political outlook, and as early as April 9, 1896, he had spoken before the McKinley Club of Hartford, Connecticut—the first McKinley club in the nation. He fully supported the McKinley administration's imperialistic policies. In fact, near the close of the Spanish-American War, he accompanied the president, the vice president, and the secretary of war on a visit to Theodore Roosevelt's victorious Rough Riders in Cuba. His most important achievement in the cabinet was arguing the "Insular Cases" before the United States Supreme Court. These cases determined the constitutional status of the conquered lands. In them, as he later wrote to Charles Bradley, Griggs relied heavily on the "broad national views of the Constitution" that Associate Justice Joseph P. Bradley had evinced in the case of the *Mormon Church v. the United States.* Griggs remained in the cabinet until McKinley's assassination in 1901.

Though Griggs continued to make his permanent home in Paterson, he turned to corporate law as a member of Griggs, Dill, and Harding in New York City. Soon he accepted an appointment to the Permanent Court of Arbitration in The Hague, where he served from 1901 to 1908. Yet there was still time for politics. When Senator William J. Sewell died in December 1901, Griggs emerged as a leading candidate to replace him. The Republican state legislators, however, selected John F. Dryden over him. Six years later Griggs was once again passed over for the GOP senatorial nomination from New Jersey. On October 13, 1904, he addressed a Republican campaign meeting in Paterson and exhorted party members to take up a "progressive conservative" ideal. He was hostile to New Jersey progressivism, which in 1906 he satirically termed the "New Idea." Service at The Hague did not dim his political interests, but his brand of conservatism was losing some of its popular appeal.

In 1908 Griggs once again resumed legal practice. He became a senior member in the law firm of Griggs, Baldwin and Baldwin, in New York City. His business interests included directorships of the New York Telephone

Company, the Bethlehem Steel Corporation, the American Locomotive Company, and the Marconi Wireless Company. During the battle in 1908 for a public utility commission in Trenton he testified before a senate commit-tee against the regulation of telephone companies. He devoted the remain-der of his active life to corporate law and business interests in New York City and Paterson, and he died on November 28, 1927, leaving a $1 million estate. He was married to Carolyn Webster Brandt in 1874 and to Laura Elizabeth Price in 1893. He had seven children.

DON C. SKEMER

Manuscript Collections, New Jersey Historical Society, Newark, N.J.

Records of Governor John W. Griggs, New Jersey State Library, Trenton, N.J.

Lott, John L., and James A. Finch, eds. *Official Opinions of the Attorneys-General of the United States.* Vol. 23. Washington, D.C.: Government Printing Office, 1902.

McCarter, Robert H. *Memories of a Half Century at the New Jersey Bar.* Camden: New Jersey State Bar Association, 1937.

Moffat, William D., comp. *Addresses by John William Griggs.* N.p.: privately printed, 1930.

Sackett, William Edgar. *Modern Battles of Trenton.* Vol. 1, *Being a History of New Jersey's Politics and Legislation from the Year 1868 to the Year 1894.* Trenton: John L. Murphy, 1895.

Foster McGowan Voorhees (November 5, 1856–June 14, 1927) served as the state's chief executive from 1898 to 1902. He was the young-est governor in more than four decades.

Although Voorhees's career was always associated with Elizabeth, he spent both his youth and his retirement in Hunterdon County. He was born in Clinton of Dutch-English ancestors who had immigrated from Holland about 1660 and had first settled on Long Island. His father, Nathaniel W. Voor-hees, a nonpracticing member of the New Jer-sey bar, was the cashier of the Clinton Bank and a delegate to the Republican National Convention that nominated Abraham Lin-coln for president in 1860. Foster M. Voorhees was educated in the local public schools and at Rutgers College, from which he graduated

Foster M. Voorhees
New Jersey State Archives; Department of State

in 1876 as second-honor man with prizes in moral philosophy and Greek.

He taught school for a year at the Rutgers Grammar School, then studied law in Elizabeth with William J. Magie, Union County's Republican state senator, and Joseph Cross, who later occupied the same office. In 1880 Voorhees was admitted to the bar. In 1884 he became a counselor-at-law. In the same year he was elected to the board of education of Elizabeth. He represented Union County's second district in the 1888 assembly. During that session he secured passage of the legislation that enabled the recently bankrupt city of Elizabeth to solve its financial difficulty.

Voorhees quickly became a leader in the legislature. In 1889 and again in 1890, when he represented Union's first district in the assembly, he headed the Republican minority. He played a major role in framing the "Werts High License Law," which increased the cost of liquor licenses and added $250,000 annually to the state treasury. He took an active part in the defeat of Democratic Governor Leon Abbett's bill to tax railroads at the same rate as other property. Railroads had been claiming exemption from Republican tax-revision plans on the grounds that they had irrepealable contracts with the state. But the enactment of a joint committee bill greatly increased New Jersey's income from the railroads. Serving on a legislative committee that prepared election bills, Voorhees "perfected" the Werts ballot-reform law, which provided for voting secretly on official ballots. At the end of his third assembly term (1890) he refused to stand for reelection. But in 1893, after the people of Union County formed a citizens league to fight corruption, he ran for the state senate and defeated James E. Martine, later a United States senator.

Voorhees's prominence increased in the upper chamber. He became the Republican leader in the "Rump Senate" in the 1894 split over the credentials of state senator James Bradley of Monmouth; when Democratic Governor George T. Werts nominated him circuit court judge, he declined so that he would not have to leave the senate during the dispute. Afterwards, the state supreme court sustained the GOP. "He saved the day for the Republicans, not only by insuring continuance of the slender majority [eleven to ten], but also by his counsel in the exciting days of that session," a Trenton newspaper said a generation later. As senate majority leader (1895–96) Voorhees successfully sponsored a measure requiring a single annual appropriation bill instead of the customary separate bills, the use of which made it difficult to tell the full amount of the annual appropriation. In 1895 Voorhees chaired the special investigating committee of the senate, which, the *New York Times* reported, "exposed the State House Frauds, arousing a storm that resulted in the election of Governor [John W.] Griggs, the first Republican Governor in New Jersey for twenty-five [twenty-seven] years." Voorhees lost the gubernatorial nomination to Griggs and supported him in the election of 1895. In 1896 he declined the position of clerk in chancery. He was reelected to the senate that year and continued as majority leader through 1897. The following year he was unanimously chosen senate president.

When Griggs was appointed attorney general of the United States, a complication arose. Voorhees was in line to assume the duties of the governorship, but the "office seemed to be without title," for he would be merely the president of the senate with the added responsibility of the governor. Accordingly the legislature passed a law creating the office of acting governor and prescribing the text of his oath. Griggs signed the law on January 25, 1898. He resigned on February 1, and Voorhees became the first officially designated acting governor.

At the state Republican convention in September 1898 Voorhees was nominated for governor by acclamation, an unusual distinction. But because the state constitution prohibited a governor from succeeding himself, he resigned his senate seat on October 18 to vacate his position as acting governor. He was replaced in this role by the assembly speaker. He campaigned strenuously, accusing the Democrats of corruption and promising extensive reforms. His party charged that his opponent, Essex County Prosecutor Elvin W. Crane, was the tool of U.S. Senator James Smith, Jr., New Jersey's Democratic boss. In November he won fifteen of the twenty-one counties (including Essex), polling 164,051 votes to 158,552 for Crane. Though small, this was a larger plurality than Griggs had received in 1895.

Voorhees's "career as Governor by his own right was not considered to be as brilliant as when he was Acting Governor," according to the *Elizabeth Daily Journal* (obituary, 1927). The Spanish-American War, it said, had "offered a fine opportunity for him to display his abilities, and his work was so excellent that it overshadowed his subsequent activities." But the Voorhees administration, the newspaper granted, was "characterized by reforms of great and permanent value." More accurate, probably, was the appraisal of Republican former governor Edward C. Stokes, who wrote in 1928 that Voorhees's "gubernatorial term was Coolidge-like in its simplicity, its modesty and devotion to the Commonwealth, economical, conservatively progressive."

Voorhees was notably successful in improving social conditions for the unfortunate. As acting governor in 1898 he signed a bill establishing a state village at Skillman for the care of epileptics. After a newspaper disclosed deplorable conditions at the Hudson County Poor Farm on Snake Hill, he approved a bill in 1899 establishing the State Board of Children's Guardians. That agency, "the most progressive institution of the period," took children out of filthy, ill-run almshouses and placed them with families. In 1899 Voorhees also got the legislature to fund the completion of the Rahway Reformatory. Construction, which had been "practically for more than a year at a standstill," resumed, and the reformatory opened during his term (August 1, 1901). He urged revision of the 1895 reformatory law, which he called "crudely drawn" and "obscure and conflicting in details," and as a result the law was repealed when a new one was enacted in 1901.

State revenues were increased and carefully preserved during the Voorhees administration. In his inaugural address Voorhees directed "attention to the growing surplus in the treasury" and pointed out the "little likelihood of further demands of extraordinary expenditures in the immediate future, except in one or two instances." He warned the legislature that a surplus far larger than required would "prove a constant inducement to extravagance or unwise expenditure." By 1902 he could note that the senate, which had been remitting taxes on certain portions of its revenues since 1898, was employing its surplus to reduce the burdens of local taxation.

One method of distributing the surplus, Voorhees pointed out, had come into use in 1901 as a result of the General School Law of 1900. During his tenure as acting governor a revision commission had been appointed, and Voorhees, maintaining that "no laws were in greater need of revision than those relating to the public school system of the State," had urged careful consideration of its reports. In 1900 the legislature passed the commission's bill with amendments, and by 1902 Voorhees was claiming that the law had "established for the first time 'a thorough and efficient system of free public schools,' as the Constitution expressly empowered and directed it alone so to do." Even though the Court of Errors and Appeals invalidated the law on several technicalities, many of its provisions were adopted later.

The subject of taxing franchises was "probably the most important that will engage your attention during the present session," Voorhees told the 1900 legislature. Corporations of a "public service" character that occupied municipal streets and highways paid taxes to the municipalities only on personal property and real estate. An act of 1900 imposed a tax of 2 percent on the annual gross earnings of the holders of such franchises; the state board of assessors distributed the funds among the taxing districts in proportion to the assessed valuation of the property along the thoroughfares.

Voorhees was also interested in constitutional change. He first spoke on the subject to the senate and assembly leaders during his ninth week as governor (1899). Three hundred or more bills had been passed, but only seventeen had been presented for his signature. The governor's right to approve bills during an unlimited period after the legislature adjourned had been recognized theoretically at least since 1879, but such authority was dangerous, Voorhees held. Believing it contrary to the spirit if not the letter of the constitutional separation of powers, he advocated eliminating it by amending the state constitution. Indeed, he was not convinced that a governor had the right to sign a bill even one day after the legislature had ceased, and he refused to act on bills except during the sessions in which they were passed.

In the concluding paragraphs of his final official gubernatorial message (1902) Voorhees vigorously advocated amending the federal Constitution to elect United States senators by popular vote instead of by state legislature. In 1911, two years before such an amendment was ratified, New Jersey's legislature would become the first in the East to acquiesce in the choice of a prior primary election—James E. Martine, Voorhees's 1893 state senatorial opponent.

The state's leading Republican newspaper, the *Newark Evening News*, appreciated but did not overly laud Voorhees's administration. At the close of the 1899 lawmaking session the journal expressed approval that "Governor Voorhees has not been in any sense a dominating force over the Legislature" and that he had "not led nor visibly guided its sentiment and action." In 1900 whatever praise the legislature deserved was "not so much for what it did as what it refrained from doing." And in 1901 less than a dozen of the 212 laws enacted were "of a nature that will be of any general benefit or disadvantage to the State at large."

But Voorhees's "backbone" was evident in his refusal "despite extraordinary pressure" to sign state senator Edward C. Stokes's 1901 bill providing that a corporation could extend its charter for up to fifty years, at any time before it expired, simply by filing a certificate with the secretary of state. He also showed his independence in another matter that year. He refused to call an extra session to provide a common sewerage system for municipalities in the Passaic River Valley, subjecting himself, as he told the legislature upon leaving office, to "the bitter criticism of ardent advocates of immediate action." Instead, he made emergency funds available to the State Sewerage Commission to survey the pollution problem in the valley and to obtain the opinion of expert engineers. Legislation of 1902 dealt with the problem.

In 1903 the Bankers' Life Insurance Company of New York City, whose affairs were in bad shape, made Voorhees its president in an attempt to reconcile differences among its officers. In 1906, only months before the New York Insurance Department prohibited the company from doing further business, factional strife and reorganization caused Voorhees to resign and go back to his law practice in Elizabeth. In 1908 a special grand jury indicted him and the company's former secretary for perjury, charging that in 1904 Voorhees had signed a false statement that dividends worth $20,000 were not due certain stockholders. He pleaded not guilty and told the press, "It is simply a case of my signing certified reports without careful inspection." He had "reposed trust in subordinates, as is done every day by hundreds of busy men, and . . . [been] misled into signing padded documents." The indictment was dismissed in 1910.

In 1925 illness forced Voorhees to suspend his business and professional activities and retire to his farm in High Bridge for a few months. During the first six months of 1927 he had several severe heart attacks that made him discontinue daily visits to his Elizabeth law office and eventually confined him to bed. Exactly eighteen years to the day and hour after his father's death Foster M. Voorhees succumbed to chronic myocarditis.

He bequeathed his High Bridge property to the State primarily "for forestry and similar purposes." The land is now Voorhees State Park, Hunterdon County.

HARRIS I. EFFROSS

Records of Governor Foster Voorhees, New Jersey State Library, Trenton, N.J.

Honeyman, A. Van Doren, ed. *History of Union County, New Jersey, 1664–1923*. Vol. 2. New York: Lewis Historical Publishing, 1923.

Ricord, Frederick W., ed. *History of Union County, New Jersey*. Newark: East Jersey History, 1897.

Sackett, William E. *Modern Battles of Trenton*. Vol. 2, *From Werts to Wilson*. New York: Neale, 1914.

Franklin Murphy (January 3, 1846–February 24, 1920), governor of New Jersey from 1902 to 1905, was born in Jersey City, the son of Abby Elizabeth (Hagar) and William Hayes Murphy, a shoe manufacturer. He was a descendant of Robert Murphy, who settled in Connecticut in 1756 and whose son Robert, Franklin's great-grandfather, fought in the Revolution. When Murphy was ten, his parents moved to Newark, where he attended Newark Academy. In 1862, at the age of sixteen, he left the academy to enlist as a private in Company A, 13th Regiment, New Jersey Volunteers. For the next three years he was on active duty, both with the Army of the Potomac and with General William T. Sherman in the West and "from Atlanta to the Sea." He fought in nineteen engagements, including Antietam, Chancellorsville, Gettysburg, Missionary Ridge, and Lookout Mountain, and in June 1865 he was mustered out as a first lieutenant.

With capital his father advanced in 1865, when he was nineteen, Murphy established a small varnish-manufacturing business in Newark. The venture prospered and became the nationally known Murphy & Company, incorporated in 1891 as Murphy Varnish Company. Over the years it established additional plants and outlets in cities from Boston to Chicago. Murphy served as its president until 1915 and as chairman of the board of directors until his death.

Meanwhile Murphy had become active in Republican politics. From 1883 to 1886 he was a member of the Newark Common Council, serving the last year as president. During his years in office the council undertook an extensive program to improve streets and parks and introduced electricity for street lighting. In 1885 Murphy went to the state legislature, where he served one term as assemblyman. In the 1890s he struggled within his party to wrest more power for the populous North Jersey counties from state Republican boss William J. Sewell, who dominated the party from his base in South Jersey. Murphy became chairman of the Republican State Committee in 1892, and, assisted by favorable population and economic trends and scandals in the Democratic regime, he helped transform New Jersey into a solidly Republican state. After being made a member of the Republican National Committee, Murphy joined its executive committee. In 1901 he received the Republican nomination for governor and easily defeated his Democratic opponent, Mayor James M. Seymour of Newark.

On assuming the governorship, Murphy, as a successful businessman, was appalled by the unbusinesslike way in which the state government was conducted. He attacked the widespread absenteeism of state officials, partly through his own example: he moved into a house in Trenton and urged the establishment of a permanent governor's mansion. He found state funds held in favored banks at no interest and secured the passage of a law requiring their deposit in interest-bearing accounts. He ordered regular audits of all departmental finances and worked for the abolition of the fee system in state and county offices.

Murphy also showed his business point of view by his strong defense of New Jersey's corporation laws, under increasing attack as breeders of the trusts, and by his action on the attorney generalship. When Thomas N. McCarter resigned as attorney general to head the giant new Public Service Corporation—a firm almost certain to become involved in litigation with the state—Murphy complacently appointed McCarter's brother Robert H. McCarter in his place.

But Murphy was no simple standpatter: he wanted business and politics conducted in a decent orderly way, and to that end he was willing to support needed reforms. Struck by the rampant corruption accompanying New Jersey's unregulated primary elections, in 1903 he strongly backed the passage of a new primary law. Although it provided direct nominations (with which Murphy had little sympathy) for only very minor offices, it carefully regulated the election of delegates to state and local nominating conventions, and it became the base on which all subsequent primary reform was built. Murphy also secured the gradual introduction of voting machines, but, proving unpopular, they were abandoned during the administration of Woodrow Wilson.

When Murphy learned that New Jersey's weak child-labor laws were virtually ignored, he forced out the incompetent state factory inspector and backed new child-labor legislation that compared favorably with that of most of the other states. He helped secure New Jersey's first tenement-inspection law (although it proved weak in practice), a law establishing a state tuberculosis sanitarium, and an act establishing boards of education with fund-raising powers independent of local politicians. Concerned about the effectiveness of state charitable institutions, he urged the legislature to support them generously, as befitted a wealthy state. Murphy faced up to the perils of the dawning automobile age; and although the legislature did not heed his heroic suggestion to prohibit automobiles geared to run over fifteen miles an hour from the roads of New Jersey, it began the regulation of motor vehicles. But it turned a deaf ear to his proposal to ban billboards from railroad rights-of-way. The governor also tackled two perennial problems—the cleanup of the sewage-laden Passaic River and the abandonment of the Morris Canal—unsolved until long after his term of office.

Murphy's governorship coincided with the rise of progressivism in New

Jersey, a part of the larger progressive movement sweeping the nation. Among its primary objectives was the more equal taxation of railroad property, championed particularly by Mayor Mark M. Fagan of Jersey City and his corporation counsel, George L. Record. Jersey City and other financially hard-pressed Hudson County municipalities found much of their most valuable real estate in the hands of railroads with tax rates severely limited by state law and mainstem property that paid taxes only to the state, not the municipalities. Fagan and Record also sought legislation empowering municipalities to tax public utility franchises at full local rates. Supported by other North Jersey municipal executives, they urged the Republican-dominated 1904 state legislature to pass remedial legislation, but the party leaders would have none of it. Railroad and utility interests were too powerful to challenge, and though the local taxation of mainstem railroad property would benefit municipalities, it would deprive the state of a prime source of revenue. This raised hackles in South Jersey and other areas with little or nothing to gain from the proposal, facing instead the possibility of a state tax to replace lost mainstem railroad revenues. When the legislature adamantly refused to act, Mayor Fagan in exasperation addressed a stinging public letter to Governor Murphy, charging that the railroad and utility interests controlled the Republican legislature and that the party was subservient to corporate greed and injustice. Although Murphy refused to comment, the letter spurred the party to action: a commission to investigate the railroad-tax issue was appointed, and the following year, under Murphy's successor, tax legislation was passed that went far toward meeting progressive demands.

Murphy's influence in the national and state Republican Party did not end with his governorship. He had long held the chairmanship of the Republican State Committee, and from 1900 to 1918 he was a member of the Republican National Committee, except for a brief period in 1912 after the progressives had carried the New Jersey Republican presidential primaries. In 1897 he was offered the post of ambassador to Russia, but for business reasons he declined. He was a delegate to five national conventions (1900–1916) and a contender for the vice presidential nomination in 1908. In 1910 he tried unsuccessfully to win the Republican senatorial preference primary. Six years later, with strong organization support, he made a fight for the United States senatorial nomination but lost in an upset to Joseph S. Frelinghuysen.

Despite certain progressive aspects of Murphy's governorship, throughout his political career he was basically conservative. He once described himself as "an old fashioned republican, the son of an old fashioned whig," who had "marched as a boy with the wide-a-wakes in the Frémont campaign of fifty six." He became an implacable foe of the direct primary, opposed the popular election of United States senators, expressed doubts about the civil service law, and once declared that all officeholders, including judges, should contribute annually to the party that elected them. In the growing split in the national party that culminated in the 1912 Roosevelt revolt, Murphy stood solidly with the regulars.

Murphy's public services were not limited to strictly political office. For over twenty years he was a member of the Essex County Park Commission. He long served as a member of the board of managers of the National Home for Disabled Volunteer Soldiers. He was one of the American commissioners to the Paris Universal Exposition in 1900, and in 1916 he headed the Committee of One Hundred, which planned the 250th anniversary of the founding of Newark. A member of the Methodist Episcopal Church, he was a trustee of Drew Theological Seminary. Particularly interested in patriotic societies, he belonged to a number of them and once served as secretary-general and then president-general of the Sons of the American Revolution. While governor he received the LL.D. degree from both Princeton University and Lafayette College.

In his private pursuits Murphy lived graciously. He was concerned with books, art, and music; late in life he taught himself to play a large pipe organ installed in the music room of his Newark home. His large collection of books on art, architecture, and related subjects was sold some years after his death. In 1868 he married Janet Colwell of Newark, who died in 1904; only two of their eight children survived them. In the winter of 1920, while vacationing in Palm Beach, Murphy suffered an intestinal obstruction. He underwent surgery on February 18 and died six days later.

RANSOM E. NOBLE

Records of Governor Franklin Murphy, New Jersey State Library, Trenton, N.J.

Noble, Ransom E. *New Jersey Progressivism before Wilson*. Princeton: Princeton University Press, 1946.

Sackett, William Edgar. *Modern Battles of Trenton*. Vol. 2, *From Werts to Wilson*. New York: Neale, 1914.

Edward Caspar Stokes (December 22, 1860–November 4, 1942), governor of New Jersey from 1905 to 1908, was born in Philadelphia, the son of Edward H. and Matilda G. (Kemble) Stokes. His parents, both of whose families had lived in New Jersey for generations, soon moved back to the state, settling eventually in Millville. There Stokes attended the public schools; later he went to the Friends School in Providence, Rhode Island. He was second in the graduating class of Brown University in 1883. Returning to his hometown, he took a position in the Millville National Bank, where his father was cashier.

Stokes developed an early interest in public education, serving as superintendent of schools in Millville from 1889 to 1898. He had meanwhile entered politics as a Republican, and he was elected to two terms in the state assembly (1891–92) and three in the state senate (1893–1901). As an assemblyman Stokes introduced and pushed to passage a bill requiring the payment of weekly wages in cash, aimed at industries that still paid in orders on company stores. As a senator he fought against the passage of racetrack-gambling bills and joined the movement that led to antigambling amendments to the state constitution. When the senate Democratic majority, repudiated at the 1893 election, attempted to retain its seats and exclude newly elected Republicans, Stokes was a leader in the successful fight to thwart its efforts. At the 1895 session he served as senate president. In 1901 he was appointed clerk of the court of chancery, where he served until his inauguration as governor.

When Stokes was nominated for governor in 1904, the New Jersey progressive movement, with its animus against railroads, trusts, and old-line political machines, was well under way in the northern part of the state. The problem of equal taxation of railroad property had been a major issue in the 1904 legislature. Stokes had entered politics under the aegis of South Jersey Republican boss William J. Sewell and had, by 1904, become a bank president and railroad director. This seemed to make him vulnerable as a candidate, particularly since his Democratic opponent, Charles C. Black, had something of a reputation as a champion of equal taxation. But the Republican Party showed a willingness to make concessions on the issue and united solidly behind Stokes, who won easily with a plurality of over fifty thousand.

A growing split between the regular Republicans and the progressives within the Republican Party, with the latter faction soon becoming known as the "New Idea," marked Stokes's term of office. The progressives were demanding the taxation of all railroad property at full local rates for the benefit of the localities, laws limiting the terms of utility franchises and taxing them at local rates, the establishment of state public utility and civil service commissions, and legislation extending the direct primary. Stokes's political and economic background placed him in the regulars' camp; nevertheless he tried to steer a middle course, urging compromise and making overtures to the New Idea. A law was passed taxing second-class railroad property (that is, property other than main stem used for railroad purposes) at full local rates, though legislation placing a maximum limit on such rates offset its effect considerably. Mainstem railroad property, formerly taxed at only 0.5 percent and exclusively for the state, was now to be taxed at the average state rate; the additional proceeds—as recommended by the governor—were to be apportioned among the counties for school purposes. A law was passed limiting new utility franchises to a term of twenty years (though a municipality could, by popular vote, grant a franchise of up to forty years); a slight increase was voted in the rate at which franchises were taxed; but efforts to establish a state public utility commission were defeated. Direct primary nominations were extended to county and municipal officials and to state legislators, and a law was passed allowing the voters of each party to indicate their choice for United States senator to the legislature. Despite a strong recommendation from the governor, legislation establishing a civil service commission was voted down.

One of Stokes's outstanding personal contributions as governor was his persistent championing of conservation legislation. By the time he left office a State Board of Forest Park Reservation Commissioners had been established, and the state had bought or contracted for over 10,500 acres of woodland; a State Water-Supply Commission had been given supervision over potable waters and their diversion from the state prohibited; and the purchase of freshwater lakes had been authorized. Stokes State Forest was later named in the governor's honor. Stokes also worked to improve the state's jury system, continued Governor Franklin Murphy's efforts for the regulation of automobiles, and secured a law establishing a Department of Charities and Corrections.

Stokes had chaired a commission under Governor Voorhees to revise the school laws, and as governor he continued to press for educational advance. He was influential in diverting a portion of the increased railroad taxes to school purposes. He urged improved teacher training to staff the growing number of high schools, "these poor man's colleges," as he described them. He lectured the legislators, apparently with little effect, on the need for writing bills in clear English. He noted that one-fifth of the state's population was foreign born and urged that immigrants be taught the obligations and duties of citizenship in their own languages. He called attention to the proportionally more rapid growth of New Jersey's black population, and he recommended increased industrial training.

One cherished ambition Stokes never realized—election to the United States Senate. The first opportunity presented itself in 1901 when United States Senator William J. Sewell died in office. Stokes, who also hailed from South Jersey and was looked upon as a Sewell lieutenant, immediately entered the contest but met formidable opposition from John F. Dryden, president of Newark's Prudential Insurance Company of America. When Republican legislators caucused on the issue, Stokes and Dryden tied with twenty-four votes each, and fifteen went to a third candidate. As the third man's support crumbled, enough votes went to Dryden to ensure his election. In 1910, taking advantage of the new senatorial preference primary law, Stokes entered the Republican primary and eked out a slender victory over Congressman Charles N. Fowler and former governor Franklin Murphy. But the Democrats won control of the legislature at the general election and sent the winner of their own primary to the Senate. Stokes's third and last serious effort came in 1928.

In the meantime, however, Stokes attempted in 1913 to win another term as governor. Though he took the Republican primary easily, he faced a difficult general election, opposed not only by the Democratic candidate, James F. Fielder, but also by the progressive Everett Colby. Fielder, who had become acting governor when Woodrow Wilson became president and had Wilson's express support, won the election, but Stokes made a creditable showing, holding down the progressive vote and making large Republican gains over the party's performance in the state in 1912.

In 1919 Stokes was chosen chairman of the Republican State Committee; during his tenure the Republicans lost three successive campaigns for governor. The Democratic Party appealed to the growing number of urban residents, especially those of more recent immigrant stock; its open opposition to Prohibition was especially attractive. The political implications of the Prohibition issue caused Stokes to revise his own thinking; originally a temperance man from a dry section of the state, he came out against the Volstead Act in the 1920s, although he stopped short of advocating Prohibition repeal.

Stokes resigned his chairmanship late in 1927 after announcing his candidacy for the 1928 United States senatorial nomination. His principal opponents were former National Committeeman Hamilton Kean and former United States senator Joseph S. Frelinghuysen. Because of their great wealth, Stokes made an issue of the inordinate use of money in elections; when his own backers urged him to put up $50,000 for expenses, he refused, declaring he would not make it a "campaign of dollars." Kean won in a bitter campaign that left serious scars; Stokes told a United States Senate committee investigating the use of money in the primary that he had lost because of Kean's wealth and the defection of friends.

By the 1920s Stokes had become an archfoe of the direct primary for senatorial and gubernatorial nominations, claiming that it favored wealthy candidates and encouraged corruption. He continued his assaults on the Volstead Act, attacked the Federal Reserve Board as too restrictive in its credit policies, and urged the reduction of income taxes. In 1932 he served as chairman of the New Jersey Republican campaign committee, and although Franklin D. Roosevelt carried the state (owing, Stokes thought, to Hoover's stand on Prohibition), the Republicans elected a United States senator, ten out of fourteen congressmen, and majorities in both houses of the state legislature. It was his last major political effort.

Along with politics Stokes pursued his career as a banker. As early as 1899 he became president of the Mechanics National Bank of Trenton; when it merged to become the First Mechanics National Bank, he was named chairman of the board and later president as well. He was the first president of the New Jersey State Bankers Association. But Stokes never amassed a large personal fortune, and. following the 1929 crash, he suffered reverses. Learning that he was in financial straits, the New Jersey legislature in 1939 moved to award him an annual $2,500 pension, but he refused to accept it. Later that year the legislature created the position of assistant counsel to the New Jersey Council, the state's publicity agency, and designated Stokes as the first incumbent.

Stokes never married. Once described as "a dapper little man with a ready tongue to exploit a ready wit," he enjoyed a reputation as an orator. Temple University, Rutgers University, and Dickinson College awarded him the LL.D. degree. Sports, especially baseball, were among his principal interests until the end of his life. After a year or more of failing health—not long before his eighty-second birthday—he died of a heart attack in Mercer Hospital in Trenton.

RANSOM E. NOBLE

Records of Governor Edward C. Stokes, New Jersey State Library, Trenton, N.J.

Noble, Ransom E. *New Jersey Progressivism before Wilson*. Princeton: Princeton University Press, 1946.

Reynolds, John F. *Testing Democracy: Electoral Behavior and Progressive Reform in New Jersey, 1880–1920*. Chapel Hill: University of North Carolina Press, 1988.

John Franklin Fort (March 20, 1852–November 17, 1920), lawyer, state supreme court justice, thirty-third governor of New Jersey, was born at Pemberton, Burlington County, the only son and eldest child of Andrew Heisler and Hannah A. (Brown) Fort. With familial roots deep in America's colonial past, John F. Fort grew up in an atmosphere in which public service was a responsibility and elective office was the norm. His father had served in the state assembly and his uncle, George F. Fort, had been the Democratic governor of New Jersey from 1851 to 1854.

After spending his early years attending local private schools in Pemberton and Mount Holly, Fort was graduated from Pennington Seminary in 1869. He completed his formal education at Albany Law School, where he shared a house with Alton B. Parker, the Democratic candidate for president in 1904. Prior to receiving his LL.B. degree in 1872, Fort taught school in rural Ewanville and clerked for a number of prominent attorneys, including Edward M. Paxson, later chief justice of the Pennsylvania Supreme Court (1889–93).

Tall, handsome, and articulate, John Franklin Fort began his law career in Newark after being admitted to the state bar in 1873. As the state's largest city and its unquestioned financial, industrial, and social center, Newark offered an ambitious young attorney the best opportunity for rapid advancement. The fact that Fort's maternal grandfather had once been a powerful force in Essex County Republican circles must also have been a factor in his selecting Newark as the site of his law practice. The Fort name soon provided access to political and financial circles denied young men with equal intelligence but less social standing. In 1874 he served as assistant journal clerk of the state assembly. As his income increased he thought of marriage. Charlotte

Stainsby, a charming, intelligent, and vivacious young woman, daughter of William Stainsby, Essex County Republican leader, met Fort shortly after his arrival in Newark, and they were married on April 20, 1876. The Fort family ultimately consisted of two sons, Franklin and Leslie, and a daughter, Margretta.

Despite the fact that the Democratic Party controlled the statehouse between 1868 and 1889, Fort's Republican ties did not prove a serious handicap. In 1878 Governor George B. McClellan appointed the twenty-six-year-old attorney judge of the First District Court of Newark, a position he continued to hold under the Democratic administrations of George C. Ludlow and Leon S. Abbett. He resigned from the bench in 1886 to return to private practice but later served on a number of judicial commissions, including an 1895 panel investigating the need for a uniform set of laws governing divorce, bankruptcy, and insurance. In 1899 he served as a member of an American committee studying European penology, and on his return he introduced the concept of indeterminate sentencing—an idea he would advocate for the rest of his life.

Fort's link to the Republican Party dated back to his law-school days when he actively campaigned for Ulysses S. Grant in 1872. In 1884 he was selected as a delegate to the Republican National Convention, where he demonstrated his awareness of the importance of party regularity by supporting the organization choice, James G. Blame. His rising stature among New Jersey Republicans became evident in 1895 when he was selected chairman of the state Republican convention. The following year brought Fort back into the public eye when he nominated his state's favorite son, Garret A. Hobart, for the vice presidency at the Republican National Convention in Saint Louis. New Jersey's first Republican governor in twenty-eight years, John W. Griggs, then rewarded Fort by appointing him presiding judge of the Essex County Court of Common Pleas. He appeared to have reached the pinnacle of his career in 1900, when Governor Foster M. Voorhees appointed him to the state supreme court, which was assuming a position of prime importance as an alternative channel of policy combat and public decision making.

Between 1880 and 1910 New Jersey was significantly transformed by intensified urbanization, industrialization, and immigration. By 1880 the state's twenty cities made up more than one-half of the total state population. Its three largest cities, Newark, Jersey City, and Paterson, had populations of foreign or mixed parentage comprising over 70 percent of their total inhabitants. By 1910 New Jersey ranked third among the states in population density. Unfortunately, serious growing pains accompanied the state's demographic and industrial development. Corruption and moral bankruptcy characterized the state's Republican and Democratic organizations. Widespread recognition of the evils of concentrated wealth and calls for the restoration of economic democracy led many citizens to denounce the monopoly of the state's political and industrial sectors by an alliance of bipartisan political bosses and corporate magnates. Chief among the latter were the railroads, for though their real-estate holdings represented over one-quarter of the state's property values, they benefited from preferential tax laws at the expense of individual homeowners.

By 1900 the GOP had managed to emerge as the dominant political force in the state. This was partly the result of the election of 1896 and Republican success in attracting the new-stock ethnics disillusioned by the cultural breakdown within the state Democratic Party over such issues as gambling, liquor, and aid to parochial schools. It was partly due, also, to the fruition of a sociopolitical alliance with representatives of the state's railroad and utility corporations, which represented a blatant disregard of the public interest and prompted a number of progressive Republicans to protest the inherent inequalities in railroad taxation, franchise limitation, and the complete absence of economic and political democracy. This "New Idea" faction led by George L. Record and Mark Fagan of Jersey City, Everett Colby and Frank Sommer of Essex, and James Blauvelt of Passaic County demanded election reform through introduction of the direct primary; the initiative, referendum, and recall; and the extension of the civil service system to include a broader range of government positions.

The Republican schism between "New Idea" progressives and their conservative "Old Guard" opponents approached crisis proportions in 1907 when disclosures of malfeasance within the administration of Governor Edward C. Stokes threatened the party's statewide hegemony. The most immediate consequence of this situation was a wide-open struggle for the Republican gubernatorial nomination. Although both conservatives and progressives offered their support to a number of candidates, only one man seemed capable of uniting the warring factions. John Franklin Fort appeared to possess many of the virtues deemed essential for the coming campaign: he had a reputation for integrity and probity; he was well known among party regulars; he had no connection with the Stokes administration; he was promised the support of influential "New Idea" leaders; and his record on the controversial issues of equal taxation and Sunday saloon-closing laws was acceptable, though equivocal.

Although one segment of the "New Idea" movement supported Essex County Sheriff Frank Sommer, the outcome of the gubernatorial nomination was never in doubt as Fort outdistanced his rivals for an easy first-ballot victory. During the campaign that followed both Fort and his Democratic opponent, Mayor Frank S. Katzenbach of Trenton, favored the creation of a public utility commission, the enactment of civil service reform, and the adoption of direct primaries. If the election turned on one issue, it was the enforcement of the so-called Bishops' Sunday saloon-closing act. Katzenbach remained publicly noncommittal, though Democrats, particularly in the industrial, immigrant, and urban counties of Hudson, Essex, and Passaic, forcefully denounced the law. Judge Fort, who seemed to be speaking as often from the pulpit as from the platform, ultimately came out in favor of enforcement. His advocacy seemed to diminish, however, as he campaigned closer to the state's urban centers. In spite of the burdens of a divided party and charges of Republican corruption, Fort managed to squeeze into office by a slim plurality of eight thousand votes.

In his inaugural address Governor Fort proposed to implement campaign proposals for an effective rate-making utility commission, the extension of civil service reform, the adoption of direct primaries, the enforcement of the antisaloon laws, and the creation of three new departments of motor vehicles, public reports, and accounts. The governor-elect further supported legislation to eliminate the retrogressive county tax boards and institute jury reform, judicial reorganization, redistricting of the state assembly, and expansion of public roads. Unfortunately, the governor would present this ambitious and comprehensive program in each of his annual messages to the legislature only to have it rejected every time.

Indeed, the history of the Fort administration chronicles the failure of reformers as they met defeat on almost every major issue. This was due partly to the obstructive tactics of conservatives within the governor's party and partly to Fort's equivocal leadership. For although conservatives suspected his progressive leanings, reformers had similar doubts about the degree of his commitment to economic and social change. Yet Fort proved a persistent and, at times, courageous leader, sure of his convictions and cognizant of political realities. He appeared most combative and most successful in attacking gambling and liquor violations and less heroic and certainly less effective in dealing with the railroads and utilities. His willingness to accept the token compromises the conservatives offered angered the progressives, who rejected the notion of politically motivated piecemeal reforms.

The Fort administration's most noticeable failure lay in its inability to create a strong public utility commission. Here, however, the governor faced overwhelming resistance from the Public Service Corporation, the state's utility giant, and united opposition from the conservative-controlled state senate. The Public Utility Act, which was ultimately passed by the 1910 legislature, proved to be of a quality so diluted that it required complete revision one year later. A similar lack of success accompanied efforts to abolish the county tax boards, which remained bastions of undervaluation and effectively nullified earlier tax reforms.

Fortunately, there was more progress on issues such as railroad property valuation, child labor, civil service reform, workmen's compensation, factory safety inspection, old-age pensions, and direct primaries. Among Fort's secondary achievements one would have to include opening an inland waterway between Bay Head and Cape May, constructing a highway linking the state's resort areas, conserving New Jersey's water resources, and maintaining a treasury balance of over $1 million. When viewed against the successes of reformers in other states, the achievements of the Fort administration pale. Yet the years from 1908 to 1911 were not a time of inertia but a formative period that awakened public opinion to the need for an expanded economic and political democracy. In that respect John Franklin Fort's greatest contribution as governor may have been to lay the foundation on which Woodrow Wilson would build.

Fort left the governor's office in January 1911. He spent the last nine years of his life engaged in a variety of business, political, and public service activities. During the 1912 presidential campaign he served as chairman of the state Progressive Committee. Though Fort was pledged to Theodore Roosevelt, he had close ties with President Woodrow Wilson that kept him in public life. In 1914 and 1915 he served as a special envoy to Santo Domingo, Haiti, and the Dominican Republic, investigating the financial and political difficulties that troubled those nations. In March 1917 Wilson named him chairman of the Federal Trade Commission, a post he held until ill health forced his resignation in November 1919. After a prolonged illness John Franklin Fort died in his South Orange home at the age of sixty-eight, on November 17, 1920.

He left a legacy of moral rectitude, honesty, and hard work. During a period in New Jersey history when corruption and an arrogant disregard of the commonweal characterized government, John F. Fort gave expression to those citizens demanding meaningful social change. His dilemma was simply that he could not be all things to all people. Late in life he was fond of characterizing his term as governor by telling the story of the little girl who returned from school to ask her mother the difference between hope and expectation. "Well," said the mother, "I hope to meet your father in Heaven, but I do not expect to."

EUGENE M. TOBIN

Records of Governor John F. Fort, New Jersey State Library, Trenton, N.J.

Blum, John Morton. *Joe Tumulty and the Wilson Era*. Boston: Houghton Mifflin, 1951.

"Direct Primary and the New Idea in New Jersey, The." *Outlook* 90 (September 12, 1908): 51–52.

Leiby, James R. *Charity and Correction in New Jersey: A History of State Welfare Institutions*. New Brunswick: Rutgers University Press, 1967.

Link, Arthur S. *Wilson*. Vol. 1, *The Road to the White House*. Princeton: Princeton University Press, 1947.

McSeveney, Samuel T. *The Politics of Depression: Political Behavior in the Northeast, 1893–1896*. New York: Oxford University Press. 1972.

Noble, Ransom E. *New Jersey Progressivism before Wilson*. Princeton: Princeton University Press, 1946.

Reynolds, John F. *Testing Democracy: Electoral Behavior and Progressive Reform in New Jersey, 1880–1920*. Chapel Hill: University of North Carolina Press, 1988.

Sackett, William Edgar. *Modern Battles of Trenton*. Vol. 2, *From Werts to Wilson*. New York: Neale, 1914.

Thomas Woodrow Wilson (December 28, 1856–February 3, 1924), thirty-fourth governor, was born in Staunton, Virginia, the son of the Reverend Joseph Ruggles Wilson, D.D., and Janet Woodrow Wilson. His paternal grandparents were James and Anne (Adams) Wilson, who emigrated from northern Ireland in 1807; his maternal grandparents were the Reverend Thomas and Marion (Williamson) Woodrow, who emigrated from Carlisle, England, in 1836.

Presbyterianism, with its Calvinistic emphasis on the sovereignty of God and its covenanter tradition, was a dominant influence on Woodrow Wilson from his boyhood. His father was a leading southern Presbyterian minister, and the son almost literally grew up in the bosom of the church. His home was also a place where education and matters of the mind were highly valued. From his "incomparable father," as Woodrow called him, the boy received intellectual stimulation, the desire to excel, and his best instruction.

Educated in private schools in Augusta, Georgia, and Columbia. South Carolina, Woodrow Wilson spent his freshman year, 1873–74, at Davidson College. His father's fortunes greatly enhanced by a call to a prosperous church in Wilmington, North Carolina, in 1875, Woodrow enrolled in the College of New Jersey (now Princeton University). The next four years were a time of rapid intellectual growth for the precocious youth. Active in sports and campus affairs, he was elected speaker of the American Whig Society and editor of the student newspaper.

Wilson studied law at the University of Virginia, 1879–80, and practiced in Atlanta, 1882–83. Disillusioned by an excess of damage suits, he entered The Johns Hopkins University in 1883 for graduate work in history and political science. His published dissertation, *Congressional Government* (1885), regarded as one of the seminal works in American political science, brought him professorships at Bryn Mawr College (1885–88), Wesleyan University (1888–90), and Princeton (1890–1902). His reputation as a scholar grew with the publication of *The State* (1889), a textbook in comparative government, and *Division and Reunion* (1893), a study of the period 1829–89 in American history.

Meanwhile, Wilson married Ellen Louise Axson of Rome, Georgia, in 1885. They had three daughters: Margaret Woodrow (b. 1886), Jessie Woodrow (b. 1887), and Eleanor Randolph (b. 1889). Mrs. Wilson died in 1914.

Elected president of Princeton University in 1902, Wilson transformed that ancient college into a modern university by reforming the curriculum, revolutionizing teaching methods, and expanding the graduate program. However, frustration plagued him from 1907 to the end of his administration. He tried to abolish the exclusive eating clubs and democratize undergraduate social life but received a sharp rebuff from wealthy alumni and trustees. He also led a fight against Andrew F. West, dean of the Graduate School, over the location and character of a residential graduate college. With the aid of alumni money, West won the battle in the spring of 1910.

In the long run, the greatest significance of Wilson's struggles at Princeton was their impact on his political thought.

Until 1907, Wilson was a moderate conservative interested mainly in administrative and municipal reform and identified only peripherally with the burgeoning progressive, or reform, movements in New Jersey and the nation at large. The struggles over the clubs and graduate college convinced him that privileged wealth threatened economic opportunity and social democracy; the crucible of turmoil and defeat transformed him into a radical social democrat.

The situation at Princeton also caused Wilson to seize the opportunity to make a new career in politics. George B. M. Harvey, editor of *Harper's Weekly*, and Harvey's friend James Smith, Jr., of Newark, boss of the Essex County Democratic machine, tried throughout the spring of 1910 to persuade Wilson to say that he would accept the Democratic gubernatorial nomination at the next state convention. Harvey, who fancied himself a kingmaker, had been touting Wilson for the presidency since 1906. Smith needed the Princetonian as a respectable front to head off a revolt against his dominance in the state party by such young progressives as Mayor H. Otto Wittpenn of Jersey City, state senator George S. Silzer of New Brunswick, and James Kerney, publisher and editor of the *Trenton Evening Times*. After negotiations during which Wilson was assured that he would be left free "in the matter of measures and of men," he announced on July 15, 1910, that he would accept the nomination.

Antimachine Democrats charged bargain and sale, but Smith won the support of his erstwhile rival Robert Davis, boss of the Hudson County Democracy, and achieved Wilson's nomination on the first ballot at the Democratic state convention in Trenton on September 15, 1910. Wilson electrified the convention and won the warm support of his critics by declaring that the nomination had come to him unsought and without any strings attached and by promising to serve the people of the state "with singleness of purpose" if elected.

New Jersey was in the throes of a popular rebellion against an alliance of old-fashioned machine politicians, the Pennsylvania Railroad, the Public Service Corporation, and other corporations. Wilson moved boldly to seize the leadership of the insurgent elements in both parties. He came out for direct primaries to give the people an opportunity to select their own nominees, a public utilities commission with power to establish rates, and legislation to provide compensation for workers and their families when they were injured or killed. He promised to be the leader and tribune of all the people. In a public letter to George L. Record, progressive Republican of Jersey City, Wilson declared that the Democratic bosses were as reprehensible as their Republican counterparts and that they would not control the state if he was elected. Under this onslaught, the dazed Republican candidate, Vivian M. Lewis, could only reply that he agreed with his opponent. The result was a Democratic tidal wave on election day, November 8, 1910. It carried a Democratic majority into the general assembly and Wilson into the governorship by 49,056 votes. Republican President William Howard Taft had carried New Jersey two years earlier by more than 80,000 votes.

During the next three months, a battle over the election of a United States senator determined Wilson's success as governor, indeed his future in politics. Both parties had held nonbinding senatorial primaries in September, and James E. Martine of Plainfield had won easily in the light vote in the Democratic primary. But legislatures still elected United States senators in 1911; and once it was certain that the Democrats would have a majority in the joint session, Smith decided that he would like to return to the body in which he had served somewhat ignominiously in the 1890s. Wilson was in a quandary. He felt deeply obligated to Smith and wanted his support for his legislative program. On the other hand, he could not countenance the election of this agent of big business, and he knew that the voters would never trust him again if he did not fight the Newark boss. His efforts at persuasion failing, Wilson went to the voters in a speaking campaign and rallied the Democratic legislators-elect behind Martine. Smith's support outside Essex County melted. Martine was elected on January 25, 1911, and Wilson emerged the undisputed leader of his party.

Meanwhile, Wilson had been inaugurated as governor of New Jersey on January 17, 1911, and had begun to plan his legislative program. The first item, the Geran elections bill providing for the direct nomination of all elected officials and a preferential presidential primary, aroused the fierce opposition of the professional politicians. Twice Wilson went into the Democratic assembly caucus to plead for the measure. It was the first time in the history of New Jersey that a governor had asserted personal leadership over his party members in the legislature. The Geran bill passed the assembly on March 21, the senate on April 13.

Then followed the much easier adoption of a stringent corrupt-practices law, a statewide workmen's compensation system, a measure giving the Board of Public Utilities Commissioners sweeping powers over rates and services, a bill permitting cities to adopt the commission form of government, and legislation benefiting schools and labor. It was, altogether, the most productive session since the Civil War; overnight, as it were, an aggressive governor with an aroused public opinion behind him had brought New Jersey abreast of the most progressive states in the Union.

Wilson was also hard at work to change the leadership of the Democratic Party in New Jersey and to secure his own control over it. With the assistance of his secretary, Joseph P. Tumulty of Jersey City, as well as that of Kerney, he used his immense patronage to reward his friends and strengthen anti-machine Democrats in every county. In July 1911, when the Democratic state chairman, James R. Nugent, committed the indiscretion of publicly calling the governor "an ingrate and a liar," the state committee deposed him and elected a Wilson partisan in his stead. An intense struggle over legislative candidates in the Democratic primary followed. Wilson campaigned hard for his friends, particularly in Essex County, where a Wilson Democratic League was challenging the Smith-Nugent machine with a full slate of candidates. Wilson Democrats swept the primary on September 26, 1911, in every other county, but they could not dislodge the entrenched Newark organization. Smith and Nugent had their revenge in the general election of November 7 by not supporting their own ticket, thus assuring the election of a legislature that the GOP would control in both houses.

In Wilson's annual message of January 9, 1912, he called for the reorganization and rationalization of the state's commissions and agencies, tax reform, health and welfare legislation, and the gradual elimination of grade crossings over railroad tracks. In response, the Republicans in the legislature, not eager to add to a Democrat's laurels, chipped away at the major legislation of 1911, passed a grade-crossing bill that Wilson thought put undue hardship on the railroads, and offered nothing by the way of constructive reform. There was much public mutual recrimination when at the end of the session Wilson sent forty-two veto messages to the legislature on one day, April 2, 1912.

Wilson had meanwhile emerged as seemingly the leading contender for the Democratic presidential nomination in 1912. He spoke frequently, and everywhere that he went idealistic, progressive Democrats responded eagerly. A group of friends conducted a publicity bureau in New York, but Wilson would not permit them to make any alliances, much less any deals, with the state organizations. For Wilson, the crisis of the preconvention campaign came with the New Jersey presidential primary on May 28, 1912; repudiation by the Democrats of his own state would have killed all his presidential hopes. Except in Essex County, however, New Jersey Democrats gave their governor a thumping endorsement, and his nomination for the presidency remained at least possible.

Though Wilson supporters constituted only about one-fourth of the delegates in the national Democratic convention that opened in Baltimore on June 25, they were fanatically loyal. They hung on even when Champ Clark of Missouri, Speaker of the House of Representatives, won a majority on the tenth ballot, but not the two-thirds then necessary; gradually wearing away the Speaker's strength, they achieved Wilson's nomination on the forty-sixth ballot. The New Jersey governor conducted a strenuous campaign on a platform demanding, principally, tariff reform and legislation to destroy industrial and financial monopoly—as Wilson put it, a "new freedom" for the American people. Even though he received only 42 percent of the popular vote on November 5, 1912, Wilson won an overwhelming victory in the electoral college because the Republicans were divided between the regulars led by Taft and the progressives led by former president Theodore Roosevelt.

The split in the GOP was also crucial in the election of a large Democratic majority in the House of Representatives and a small Democratic majority in the Senate.

The Democrats also won majorities in both houses of the New Jersey legislature, and Wilson decided to remain in harness as long as possible. From mid-January to mid-February 1913, he pushed through the legislature a series of measures called the Seven Sisters, designed to prevent cutthroat competition and monopoly, as well as a new grade-crossing bill, ratification of the Sixteenth Amendment establishing a federal income tax, and other legislation. The remainder of his time as governor he devoted to an unsuccessful fight to remove the power of constituting grand juries from the hands of sheriffs, often allied with corrupt machines, and to vest it in the governor. He also failed to get a bill for a constitutional convention through the rurally dominated senate. He handed over the reins of the state government to the president of the senate, James F. Fielder, on March 1, 1913, saying that serving the people of New Jersey had been the greatest privilege of his life.

Inaugurated as twenty-eighth president of the United States on March 4, 1913, Wilson proceeded with accustomed vigor to rally public opinion and Democrats in Congress behind legislation to overhaul and strengthen the national political economy. He was what historians and political scientists call a strong president. He kept careful watch over the conduct of foreign relations; indeed, during crises he conducted diplomacy personally and wrote the diplomatic correspondence of the United States on his own typewriter. Reviving the custom, abandoned by Jefferson, of addressing Congress in person, he made it clear that he intended to break down the wall that had so long separated the executive and legislative departments. He worked closely with committee chairmen and others in Congress in drafting legislation and used party discipline, patronage, and public opinion to force recalcitrant Democrats into line. Later, when the nation was fighting in World War I, Congress gave him virtual dictatorial authority. Wilson brought presidential power to its apogee, yet, withal, he ruled with restraint and deep respect for constitutional traditions.

The first item on the Wilson legislative program was tariff reduction and reform. The Underwood-Simmons Tariff Act of 1913 not only greatly reduced duties and enlarged the free list but also levied the first income tax under the Sixteenth Amendment. Wilson's victory paved the way for even more important legislation—the Federal Reserve Act of 1913. One of the most important acts in American history, it created a new currency and a system of central banking through the Federal Reserve System. In 1914 came the Federal Trade Commission Act and the Clayton Antitrust Act. They established a new agency to serve as a watchdog over competition and tightened the laws against potential monopolists. A special provision of the Clayton Act declared, for the first time in federal legislation, that labor unions were not to be construed as conspiracies in restraint of trade.

A lull followed this first surge of reform, but Wilson put through an even more significant program in 1916. It included the first federal child-labor law; an employers' liability measure; a heavy increase in the income tax and the first federal estate tax; the eight-hour day for workers on interstate railroads; and a federal farm-credit system. By orchestrating public opinion and leading his party members in Congress like a prime minister, Wilson in less than four years put through the most comprehensive legislative program in American history to that time. It laid the foundations of the present-day political economy of the United States.

In foreign policy, Wilson pursued a course of idealism tempered by an understanding of practical realities. He repudiated Taft's "dollar diplomacy" (the use of private financial resources to advance national interests) in the Caribbean, yet he felt compelled to occupy Haiti and the Dominican Republic to save them from self-destruction. He was more successful in Mexico. There he contributed significantly to the triumph of a democratic revolutionary movement.

The greatest challenge to Wilson's wisdom came with the outbreak of the First World War in Europe in August 1914. His supreme ambition and the objective of all his policies toward the rival alliances was to end the carnage through American mediation. Thus he endured assaults against American maritime rights by British cruisers and German submarines while winning significant concessions from both sides. And when the Germans began to sink American and other neutral ships in early 1917, he accepted a decision for war mainly because he believed the United States could bring peace more effectively as a belligerent than as a neutral.

From the declaration of war against Germany on April 6, 1917, to the armistice of November 11, 1918, Wilson mobilized a great army and the entire domestic economy in the first total war in American history. He also raised the hopes of liberal and democratic forces everywhere in a series of speeches that called for an end of imperialism, rival balance of power, and heavy armaments and demanded a postwar international organization to promote cooperation and prevent war. The most notable of these speeches was the Fourteen Points Address of January 8, 1918.

Going to Paris in December 1918 as head of the American Peace Commission, Wilson was hailed throughout western Europe as the savior and hope of mankind. During the following months at the Paris Peace Conference, he fought with incredible tenacity for a liberal settlement. The Versailles Treaty with Germany, signed on June 28, 1919, was a bundle of compromises that in important particulars violated Wilson's ideals. However, the treaty included provision for a strong international organization, the League of Nations.

Wilson presented the treaty to the Senate on July 10, 1919. The Republicans in that body objected strongly to Article X of the constitution of the League because it guaranteed the independence and territorial integrity of member nations. Led by Henry Cabot Lodge of Massachusetts, they refused to consent to ratification without a clear avowal that the United States did not consider itself bound to support Article X. Wilson rejected ratification with that reservation, saying that it was tantamount to nullification of the treaty. He tried to break the stalemate by embarking on a long speaking tour to rally public opinion to his side. However, he suffered a severe stroke after his return to Washington in early October. Though unable to give any effective leadership to Democrats in the Senate, he still had influence enough to prevent that body's approval of the amended treaty. Thus the United States remained technically in a state of war with Germany until a separate peace was negotiated in 1921.

Somewhat recovered by the spring of 1920, Wilson remained secluded in the White House while the ship of state drifted without a rudder. The anti-League Republican senator Warren G. Harding won the presidency in November 1920. Wilson retired with his wife, Edith Bolling Wilson, whom he had married in 1915, to a home on S Street in Washington. He lived there quietly in declining health. He died on February 3, 1924, and was buried in the Washington Cathedral.

ARTHUR S. LINK

Woodrow Wilson Collection, Princeton University Special Collections, Princeton, N.J.
Woodrow Wilson Papers, Library of Congress, Manuscript Division, Washington, D.C.
Records of Governor Woodrow Wilson, New Jersey State Library, Trenton, N.J.
Baker, Ray Stannard. *Woodrow Wilson: Life and Letters*. 8 vols. Garden City, N.Y.: Doubleday, Page, 1927–39.
Berg, A. Scott. *Wilson*. New York: Putnam, 2013.
Cooper, John Milton. *Woodrow Wilson: A Biography*. New York: Knopf, 2009.
Hirst, David W. *Woodrow Wilson, Reform Governor: A Documentary Narrative*. Princeton: D. Van Nostrand, 1965.
Kerney, James. *The Political Education of Woodrow Wilson*. New York: Century, 1926.
Link, Arthur S., ed. *The Papers of Woodrow Wilson*. 69 vols. Princeton: Princeton University Press, 1966–93.
———. *Wilson*. 5 vols. Princeton: Princeton University Press, 1947–65.
Maynard, W. Barksdale. *Woodrow Wilson: Princeton to the Presidency*. New Haven: Yale University Press, 2008.

James Fairman Fielder (February 26, 1867–December 2, 1954), governor, jurist, was born in Jersey City, the son of George Bragg and Eleanor A. (Brinkerhoff) Fielder. On his father's side his ancestors were English. On his mother's they were Dutch; among them were some of the earliest settlers of the old Bergen section of Jersey City and some of the founders of the Dutch Reformed Church in the state. His father was a member of the Fifty-Third Congress. Fielder received his early education in the Jersey City public schools and at Selleck's School in Norwalk, Connecticut. In 1887, a year after being awarded his LL.B. from Columbia Law School, he was admitted to the Hudson County bar. He began to practice law in the office of his uncle, former state senator William Brinkerhoff, and eventually became his partner. Fielder married Mabel Choiwell Miller of Norwalk, Connecticut, on June 4, 1895.

Large, powerfully built, and active, Fielder was fond of fishing, hiking, and golf. His associates admired him for his mild and pleasant temperament and also for his firm resolve and unshakable integrity once he had set a course.

Developing an early interest in politics, Fielder served on the Hudson County Democratic Committee. In 1903 and 1904 he was elected to the state assembly; three years later he was elected to the New Jersey Senate, and he was reelected in 1910 by the largest plurality ever given a senator from Hudson County to that date. In the senate he served on a number of important committees that included Banks and Insurance, Judiciary, Riparian Rights, Passed Bills, the School for the Deaf Mutes, and the Soldiers' Home. As a measure of his competence and his popularity, in January 1913 his fellow lawmakers chose him president of the senate, knowing that he would become acting governor when Governor Woodrow Wilson resigned to go to Washington. In Wilson's last message to the legislature, he praised Fielder as "a man of proved character, capacity, fidelity and devotion to the public service, a man of the type to which the people of this State desire their public men to conform."

Fielder had been a loyal supporter of the Wilson administration, and as acting governor he turned immediately to the task of completing the Wilson program. Though not a dynamic executive in the Wilson mold, Fielder gained friends through his willingness to combat representatives of the Smith-Nugent machine in the legislature, as well as the state's powerful corporate interests. He vetoed a special Atlantic City bill that would have opened the way to weakening commission government in other cities; he signed the full-crew bill that the railroads had resisted, which afforded maximum safety for passengers. His approval of a bill providing for widows' pensions led the state into a field previously neglected. In the fight for constitutional reform, however, Fielder's personal leadership proved insufficient to bring about the passage of a bill providing for the election of delegates to a convention scheduled to meet in the fall. The bill passed the assembly with bipartisan support but went down to defeat in the senate at the hands of senators from rural counties who feared the reduction of their power in the legislature.

The struggle for reform of the jury system was more complicated. The drawing of juries, particularly grand juries, was "notoriously subject to political influence and control," as Wilson had charged. Sheriffs, unsupervised by the judiciary or any other agency or official, drew the juries for the county courts. Frequently controlled by local machines, sheriffs could easily fix the personnel of the juries to prevent the indictment of any interest protected by the machine. The reformers intended to prevent such corruption by turning the whole process over to the judiciary. Both parties recognized the need for reform, but the Smith-Nugent machine, the liquor interests, and the sheriffs themselves mounted powerful opposition. Despite Wilson's initial leadership and Fielder's vigorous follow-up, this coalition managed through various tactics to prevent the passage of an effective bill before the end of the session on April 4, 1913. In agreement with Wilson and other party leaders, Fielder issued a call for a special session. Before it convened on May 6, President Wilson returned to the state to help with the struggle, but his ambiguous statements and failure to back a specific plan served only to distress and confuse the reformers. Finally, on the eve of the special session, Fielder and other state leaders in conference with the president worked out a compromise bill that provided for jurors to be selected by county jury commissions composed of the sheriff and one other member appointed by the chancellor or head of the court of chancery. An amendment added in the special session required that the bill be submitted to a public referendum. In the election on November 4, 1913, the people approved the new system.

Fielder's intention to seek the Democratic nomination for governor in the fall primary was evident from the beginning. Within a week of becoming acting governor, he announced his candidacy for a full term and began to organize his campaign. For the first time, the gubernatorial candidate would be selected according to the newly reconstructed primary laws. As incumbent, Fielder enjoyed some advantage, but this edge largely depended on Wilson's publicly blessing his candidacy. Fielder's major rival was H. Otto Wittpenn, longtime progressive Democrat, mayor of Jersey City, temporary head of the party in Hudson County, and strong supporter of Wilson's programs in the state and presidential campaign. Frank S. Katzenbach, former mayor of Trenton and perennial candidate for governor, was also in the race, but his support dwindled as the campaign ran on. Wittpenn was just as eager as Fielder to win Wilson's backing, but the president, reluctant to choose between two loyal friends and backers, delayed his decision until late summer. Finally, on July 23, 1913, he wrote to Wittpenn that he thought a three-cornered fight would be "most unwise." He felt the party should unite behind Fielder, who, Wilson wrote, "backed me so consistently, so intelligently, so frankly and honestly throughout my administration and has followed, on the whole, so consistent a course that I feel I would have no ground whatever upon which to oppose his candidacy." Clearly Wilson also believed, in view of the Essex organization's antagonism to Wittpenn's candidacy, that Fielder had the better chance for victory. Wittpenn's graceful withdrawal resulted in a handy victory for Fielder over Katzenbach in the primary on September 23, 1913, by 45,229 votes. The size of the victory had been due largely to support from the Smith-Nugent machine. Even so,

Fielder, emulating his predecessor, felt it necessary to declare his independence, and a week after the primary he attacked the organization, seeking to read James R. Nugent and his associates out of the party. Wilson immediately expressed admiration for Fielder's stand, but other advisers thought he had seriously weakened his chances of winning over his formidable Republican opponent, Edward C. Stokes.

Fielder campaigned vigorously, speaking throughout the state. He resigned from the senate on October 28, 1913, creating a vacancy in the governorship and evading the constitutional provision against succeeding himself. Despite some pessimism, he defeated Stokes by a solid plurality of 32,850 votes, although he received only a minority of the 354,578 total cast. The Democrats retained a slim majority of three in the senate and fourteen in the assembly.

But Fielder's victory, as he knew only too well, was less than it appeared. Shifting loyalties within the Democratic Party had already destroyed any chance of mustering the solid majorities needed to continue progressive legislation. The Smith-Nugent machine had now recovered fully from the Wilson onslaught. It was forming a new alliance with Frank Hague, a rising young Hudson County political leader gradually emerging as boss of the old Davis organization. Together they formed a major legislative force generally obstructive or openly hostile to Fielder's progressive initiative. Meanwhile, the old-line progressives, the bulk of them originally from the Republican Party, once more separately grouped behind Colby, who had taken more than 41,000 votes from Fielder in the gubernatorial contest. And before the end of Fielder's first year, the White House made it clear that it had lost interest in further promotion of the progressive campaign in New Jersey. Wilson, in fact, soon found it politically expedient to put aside old animosities and cooperate with the state organizations that had earlier drawn so much of his wrath.

In the face of these obstacles, Fielder's successes were moderate. He secured repeal of the Hillery Maximum Tax law, one of the few distinctly progressive measures he had called for in his inaugural. The law had been passed to protect the railroads after equal-taxation laws had brought these corporations on a par with other state taxpayers. Other legislation achieved was hardly controversial. It included the imposition of an inheritance tax, improvement in the conduct of preferential primaries in counties and municipalities, strengthening of the pure-food laws, reforms in the penal system, an increase in funds allotted to agricultural research, a bank-stock tax law, and a major improvement in the drafting of legislative bills by establishing a Legislative Reference Bureau in the State Library and appointing an expert bill-drafting adviser in the office of the attorney general. Three constitutional amendments were also submitted to the people. The first, which Fielder opposed, granted woman suffrage; the second simplified the amendment process; and the third expanded the power of municipalities to condemn land for public improvement. All three were voted down in a referendum in October 1915.

At the end of the first legislative session of Fielder's administration, he summed up his despair in a letter to Joseph P. Tumulty. "I have been up against some difficult legislative situations during my experience at Trenton," he wrote, "but this is the worst that I ever encountered. There are several factions of Democrats and at least two of the Republicans with outside influences constantly at work on each and . . . the Democratic Assemblymen, for the most part, are the most unreliable lot of men we ever had to deal with. One never knows upon whom he can count to assist in legislation."

The situation did not improve, for the Democrats lost control of both houses of the legislature in the 1914 elections. The following year the Republicans increased their lead to continue a domination that endured for more than a decade. The remainder of Fielder's term was frustrating and relatively unproductive, although the legislature enacted some laws he supported. It passed some recommendations of the Economy and Efficiency Commission to reduce the number of boards, departments, and political commissions. It created a central purchasing bureau for the state and its institutions. It required advance announcement of proposed expenditures to enable the public to review them and react. It limited a woman's workday to ten hours and safeguarded factory workers from some industrial hazards and occupational diseases. But the governor had little power beyond the ability to threaten with the veto or to use it. A coalition of Democrats and Republicans had already begun to dismantle the Wilson reforms, particularly those referring to New Jersey's corporation laws.

By the end of Fielder's term, he was thoroughly at odds with both parties in the legislature; he charged them with failure to meet the needs of the state and vowed to have done with politics for life. In 1917 he became State Food Administrator to help the war effort. Two years later he was named vice chancellor of the court of chancery, a post he retained for twenty-nine years. He died in Montclair at the age of eighty-seven.

DAVID W. HIRST

Records of Governor James F. Fielder, New Jersey State Library, Trenton, N.J.

Joseph P. Tumulty Papers, Library of Congress, Manuscript Division, Washington, D.C.

Records of Governor Woodrow Wilson, New Jersey State Library, Bureau of Archives and History, Trenton, N.J.

Kerney, James. *The Political Education of Woodrow Wilson.* New York: Century, 1926.

Link, Arthur S. *Wilson.* Vol. 1, *The Road to the White House*; vol. 2, *The New Freedom.* Princeton: Princeton University Press, 1947, 1956.

Lockard, Duane. *The New Jersey Governor: A Study in Political Power.* Princeton: D. Van Nostrand, 1964.

Walter Evans Edge (November 20, 1873– October 29, 1956) enjoyed the unique distinction of serving as governor during both World War I and World War II. Born in Philadelphia to William and Mary (Evans) Edge, Walter descended from a family resident in the Chester Valley since the eighteenth century. After his widowed father remarried in 1877, the boy moved with his family to Pleasantville, New Jersey, where his father worked for the Pennsylvania Railroad. Edge spent his boyhood in the occupations of late nineteenth-century rural youth—fishing, hunting, limited schooling, and work. His autobiography, *A Jerseyman's Journal* (1948), recalls these years with the urban American's nostalgia for the Arcadian myth. Edge's formal education ended at the age of fourteen, when he completed the equivalent of eighth grade. He began his business career in Atlantic City, as

Walter E. Edge
New Jersey State Archives; Department of State

"printer's devil" on the *Atlantic Review*, and when he was sixteen, he found part-time employment with the Dorland Advertising Agency. Within two years he bought the agency and began a rapid approach to his goal of being independently wealthy.

In the best Horatio Alger tradition, Edge worked hard, and circumstances came to his aid. Most significant among them was Atlantic City's boomtown growth as a resort. He had grasped the potentialities of the development early and made himself and his business a part of the movement. In 1893 he established a social-notes paper, the *Atlantic City Daily Guest*; this proved so profitable that in 1895 it became a full-fledged newspaper, the *Atlantic City Daily Press*. His advertising agency, meanwhile, expanded to include general commercial advertising. By 1910 the Dorland agency, with offices in New York City, London, Berlin, Paris, and other European cities, was grossing some $10 million annually. By the early years of the twentieth century Edge had established a financial independence in business enterprises that continued to support him comfortably over the next fifty years, while he engaged in public affairs.

Walter Edge married twice. By his first wife, Lady Lee Phillips, whom he wed on June 10, 1907, he had one son, Walter E., Jr. The first Mrs. Edge died in July 1915. On December 9, 1922, he married Camilla Loyall Ashe Sewell of Bath, Maine. One son, Loyall, and two daughters, Camilla and Mary Esther, were born to this union. His second wife and his four children survived him.

Even while Edge concentrated on his goal of early financial independence, he had always envisioned a career in politics and public service. In the early 1890s he had become active in the Atlantic City Republican Party, and in January 1897 he had been appointed journal clerk of the senate as a reward for his newspaper's endorsement of the GOP candidates. From this undemanding position he observed the tactics of state politics and met its chief figures. With time out for service in the Spanish-American War, Edge served three years in this post and an additional four as secretary of the state senate. He made an unsuccessful attempt in 1904 to gain the GOP state senate nomination from Atlantic County against the candidate of the local Republican organization. In 1909 he won election to the assembly. In the following year he gained the first of two terms in the senate.

Walter Edge's service in the legislature coincided with the climax of the reform movements of the early twentieth century. But Edge was not a reformer. Perhaps chastened by his unsuccessful opposition to the GOP organization in 1904, he carefully remained with the party leadership throughout the upheavals of the "New Idea" and progressivism, though he cooperated with the reformers when their measures appeared sure to triumph. During the Republican travail of 1912 Edge demonstrated his party regularity when he and his newspapers supported William Howard Taft for the presidency and stood strongly against the insurgent Bull Moose candidacy of Theodore Roosevelt.

Although the "Sand Dune Senator," as Edge was sometimes called, was not a reformer, he was not a reactionary either. He supported some significant social legislation. Appointed in 1910 as an assembly representative on a commission to develop an employer's liability law, he worked diligently through the summer of that year examining American statutes and judicial decisions and going to Europe to study developments in the compensation field. As a freshman senator in 1911 he sponsored the commission's bill in the upper house and won Woodrow Wilson's acceptance of it. The measure became an early example of successful legislation on employer's liability. He pushed also for a ten-hour day for women and a measure to protect factory workers against industrial hazards. Edge developed a reputation for concern with the economy and the efficiency of state operations. As chairman of a joint legislative commission he was instrumental in shaping measures to reduce the number of boards and commissions conducting state business and to provide a rational organization of the whole. He introduced and steered to passage a budget bill to make the governor the responsible fiscal head of the state and a measure to create a central purchasing bureau to economize by bulk purchase.

By 1912 Edge was respected enough to be selected majority leader of the senate. His close connection with the notoriously corrupt Republican machine in Atlantic City does not seem to have been a handicap in his political ascent. As one writer put it, he was "as honest as could be hoped for from the Atlantic City organization."

On January 21, 1916, Edge announced his candidacy for the Republican gubernatorial nomination. Well known because of his prominent legislative service, he counted on his business success to win popular confidence and on his long record of party regularity to gain the endorsement of the state and county GOP leadership. In a three-way primary he defeated—by a mere three thousand votes—Austen Colgate of the Colgate Soap Company and George L. Record, prominent reform spokesman. Had Record not been in contention, Edge might have lost. Since Edge was the most conservative of the three, most of Record's twenty-nine thousand votes would probably have gone to Colgate.

In the last summer before the United States entered World War I the New Jersey Democratic Party chose H. Otto Wittpenn as its gubernatorial candidate. A prominent Wilson supporter and former mayor of Jersey City, Wittpenn, with his close ties to the German American community, would supposedly offset any defections resulting from the international situation. The strategy probably would have worked if the New Jersey Democrats had not been so divided between Wilson and anti-Wilson factions that they failed to develop an effective campaign or issues. The Republicans, on the other hand, had for the first time in four years a truly united party, and Edge developed early a campaign slogan and image: "A Business Man with a Business Plan." The GOP platform promised speedy revision of corporation and election laws and effective and efficient government with the governor as "the business manager, the legislature as the board of directors, and the people as the stockholders." The vigorous campaigning of Edge and the entire GOP organization returned New Jersey to its normal place in the Republican column; Edge's margin over Wittpenn was a convincing 69,647.

In Edge's first message to the legislature, in January 1917, he spelled out his conception of gubernatorial leadership and emphasized the need to consolidate state boards and agencies, to improve civil service by the standardization of duties and compensation, and to find solutions to the administrative and fiscal problems of state institutions—penal, custodial, and rehabilitative. He also proposed a close examination of the impact of the "Seven Sisters"—the Wilson-era corporation reform laws—on state finances, greater home rule for municipalities, an increased franchise tax on public utilities corporations, and a complete reorganization of the state board to provide for comprehensive road development. By an effective combination of cajolery, arm-twisting, and patronage, Edge achieved most of his program.

The legislature of 1917 enacted Edge's franchise tax on public utilities corporations, allowed greater home rule for cities, and authorized consolidation of state boards. It also created special commissions to examine the problems of civil service reform, corporation law reform, and the problems of state institutions; the reports of those commissions led to significant improvements in the state institutions, especially the prisons, and to the emasculation of the Wilsonian corporation laws. The 1917 legislature also granted the governor his desired reorganization of the road department. To direct the new department and to lay the groundwork for a comprehensive system of roads, Edge secured General George W. Goethals of Panama Canal fame as state engineer. As part of the overall plan Edge successfully initiated construction of the Holland Tunnel, connecting Jersey City and New York City, and of the Delaware River Bridge (now the Benjamin Franklin Bridge), spanning the Delaware from Camden to Philadelphia. Although completion of these projects came well after his term, Edge secured the preliminary legislation. He also figured prominently in the bistate negotiations that led to the establishment of the Port of New York Authority. In addition, during his term he won improvements in the workmen's compensation law and in public health education, and he pushed for the creation of a state police force to provide adequate protection to rural and developing suburban areas.

The 1917 state legislature adjourned two weeks before the United States entered World War I, but the ominous shadow of war had led it to delegate emergency authority to the governor in advance. Late in March, after conferences with the war department, Edge set in motion the acquisition of the area which became Camp Dix. The New Jersey Committee of Public Safety, composed of municipal executives, was formed to coordinate action throughout the state in emergencies. National Guard units were recruited to full strength, a state militia was created to replace the National Guard, and a system of recruiting high school youths to work on farms was initiated. In Edge's last annual message to the legislature in 1919 he addressed the problems of the returning veteran. He urged the state to inaugurate a transitional program of public works and road building to take up the employment slack created by the conversion to a peacetime economy, retrain and rehabilitate disabled veterans through a special program in the public schools, and establish a public health program to combat the venereal disease that had become alarmingly evident during the war. Little came of these plans, however, since the governor based them on the assumption that the federal government would be equally provident and would cooperate with the states.

By the time Edge presented his postwar program to the legislature, he had already won election to the United States Senate in the 1918 GOP landslide. He continued as governor until May 1919, when he resigned to attend the special session of Congress dealing with the peace settlement. Though active in the Senate, Edge was not among its leaders. He was, however, deeply involved in factional political maneuvers in his home county, alternately working with and against Atlantic City's notorious boss, Enoch "Nucky" Johnson, who had helped launch his gubernatorial candidacy. Edge was friendly with Senator Warren G. Harding and, by one account, "narrowly missed becoming his vice president" in the 1920 election. In November 1929, with a Senate reelection contest looming, President Herbert C. Hoover appointed Edge to the post of ambassador to France, which he held until March 1933.

For the following decade Edge enjoyed a life of retirement at his homes in New Jersey and abroad and served as an elder statesman of the state GOP. With the outbreak of World War II he was anxious to return to some form of public service. In 1943 the state Republican organization was desperately divided and had long been out of power. Edge agreed to run for governor on condition that nobody oppose him in the primary and that the party maintain strong discipline. Other potential candidates were persuaded to withdraw, and Edge was nominated.

The Democrats ran Vincent J. Murphy, the state leader of the American Federation of Labor and the mayor of Newark. Reminding voters that they must choose between the program of the GOP and the domination of "labor leaders, communists and Hagueism," Edge hammered on the theme of the power of Hudson County boss Frank Hague. On the positive side he proposed streamlining state government and planning early to meet postwar problems, and he strongly supported the referendum Governor Charles Edison had initiated for a new state constitution. The voters chose Edge by 127,000 votes and constitutional revision by over 150,000.

Assuming office early in his seventy-first year, Edge ensured party discipline in the legislature by withholding patronage appointments until the end of the session. In the interim between his election and inauguration he set in motion the drafting of measures to fulfill his program. A liberalized servicemen's voting law supplemented the emergency wartime legislation already in effect. But Edge concentrated on measures to secure the modernization of state government and to ensure successful dealing with anticipated postwar problems. In his mind they were closely linked, for only by improving the structure of government could the state solve the problems.

First Edge attended to constitutional revision. On January 24, 1944, he submitted to the legislature a new document drafted by thirty Republican legislators, and it was approved within six weeks. It extended the governor's term to four years and amplified his powers to make him a "strong" executive, increased legislative terms to four years in the senate and two in the assembly, reorganized the judiciary, and provided for one state budget to deal with all receipts and expenditures.

Although the proposed constitution met the demands of most proponents of revision, it was politically vulnerable. Drafted by Republicans only and passed only because Republicans controlled the legislature, it was not assured of ratification by the voters. It was also involved in the battle against Frank Hague, who stood to lose much patronage if the judiciary was reorganized. During 1944 Hague and Edge engaged in a running battle. First they fought over the allocation of $15 million in railroad taxes, which Hague eventually won for the cities where the taxed property was located. Edge won a round by obtaining legislation that required the use of voting machines in

Hudson County and reduced the chance of electoral flimflam. But Hague took top honors when, a few weeks before the elections, he launched a multipronged attack on the new constitution. Charging that it would limit organized labor's activities, inhibit the opportunity for the advancement of returning veterans, and subject all church property to taxation, he engineered its defeat at the polls by 126,000 votes.

Despite defeat on the constitution in 1944, Edge achieved much of his program. He consolidated a number of state boards and commissions, set up a Taxation and Finance Department to handle all fiscal matters, and obtained some support for civil service reform. He also created an Economic Development Department to deal with postwar planning and began to accumulate a fund—initially $25 million—for state support of efforts to ensure an orderly postwar conversion. He obtained legislation that created a state insurance program to guarantee loans to veterans who wished to establish themselves in business or in the professions, an antecedent to the G.I. Bill. After the defeat of constitutional revision Edge sought to accomplish some of the reorganization through legislation and continued to pressure for a new revision of the constitution. In addition, in 1945 he obtained remedial legislation to improve the living conditions of migrant workers and a series of seven measures to ban racial or religious discrimination in employment, schools, hotels, and elsewhere, and he sought legislation to prevent strikes in public utilities.

During Edge's last year in office problems connected with reconversion to a peacetime economy came to the fore. Demobilization brought housing shortages and unemployment. State planning agencies could give some help. Federal involvement sometimes obstructed progress. For example, although Edge complained bitterly that the federal government was using only small portions of Camp Kilmer and Camp Dix, the government refused to consolidate its activities to make housing space available. In addition to these problems, a wave of strikes led to bitter political battles and occasional street confrontations. Edge effectively used the principal state agency, the State Board of Mediation, to end most of the strikes without lengthy disruptions. But like all his contemporaries he failed to find any effective means to preserve public services in disputes between capital and labor, especially in such instances as the Public Service gasworks strike of 1946.

As Edge's term drew to a close in 1946, he had sufficient control of the state Republican organization to ensure the nomination of Alfred E. Driscoll as his successor. In the election of 1946 the Republicans won easily. After Edge's term he continued actively supporting constitutional reform until the constitution of 1947 was adopted. Remaining thereafter an elder statesman of the party, he took little active part in politics. After his death in 1956 he willed Morven—the Stockton family residence, which he had purchased— to the state as an official residence for the governors.

JOSEPH F. MAHONEY

Walter E. Edge Papers, The New Jersey Historical Society, Newark, N.J.

Records of Governor Walter E. Edge, New Jersey State Library, Trenton, N.J.

Dunn, Voorhees E., Jr. "The Road to the 1947 New Jersey Constitution: Arthur T. Vanderbilt's Influence on Court Reform, 1930–1947." *New Jersey History* 104 (Fall–Winter 1986): 23–41.

Edge, Walter E . *A Jerseyman's Journal.* Princeton: Princeton University Press, 1948.

Johnson, Nelson. *Boardwalk Empire: The Birth, High Times, and Corruption of Atlantic City.* Medford, N.J.: Plexus Books, 2002.

Paulsson, Martin. *The Social Anxieties of Progressive Reform: Atlantic City, 1854–1920.* New York: New York University Press, 1994.

Sly, John F. "Walter Evans Edge, 1873–1956: A Tribute." *Proceedings of the New Jersey Historical Society* 79 (1961): 1–15.

Edward Irving Edwards (December 1, 1863–January 26, 1931), a distinguished public servant, was born in Jersey City, to William W. and Emma J. (Nation) Edwards. He attended the Jersey City public schools, went to New York University from 1880 to 1882, and studied law in the office of his brother, William D. Edwards, former state senator from Hudson County. On November 14, 1888, he married Blanche Smith; during their forty-year marriage the Edwardses had two children, Edward Irving and Elizabeth Jule.

A businessman and bank president, Edwards rose to political prominence in his native Jersey City and soon attracted the attention of the Hudson County Democratic organization. He served as state comptroller from 1911 to 1917 and Hudson County's state senator from 1918 to 1920. During this period he became a friend and close political ally of the Jersey City mayor, Frank Hague. Hague supported him for governor in 1919.

The Democratic primary in 1919 resulted in a confrontation between Hague and Essex County Democratic chairman James R. Nugent, who was a former state party chairman. Edwards, a supporter of the Hudson County political machine, defeated Nugent in the primary by polling 53.6 percent of the vote. He won fifteen counties and polled huge majorities in Hudson County. Hague emerged from this primary confrontation as the undisputed leader of the New Jersey Democratic Party, beginning a domination that lasted until the late 1940s.

The gubernatorial race occurred during an exceedingly turbulent period —a period of red scares, major labor strikes in the coal and steel industries, the Boston police strike, race riots across the nation, a Camden trolley strike, the battle for the League of Nations and the Versailles Treaty, the implementation of Prohibition, and a surge of postwar inflation. The elections of 1919 were marked by the resurgence of the Republican Party throughout the United States, the destruction of the old Wilsonian coalition, and a prelude to "normalcy." The GOP won all elections in the North and the West except for Edwards's victory in New Jersey.

An Elizabeth daily newspaper appropriately labeled Edwards's campaign the "applejack campaign." Although Edwards was personally "dry," he ran as an avowed "wet," opposing Prohibition, defending states' rights, and demanding nullification of the Eighteenth Amendment. Despite being labeled a Bolshevik, an anarchist, a traitor, and a seditionist, Edwards won a narrow victory, polling 51.7 percent of the two-party vote—217,486 votes to 202,976 for Trenton businessman Newton A. K. Bugbee, a margin of 14,510.

Edwards won the "applejack" battle in the cities, where anti-Prohibition sentiment was strong. The wet-or-dry campaign produced an urban political revolution against Prohibition and its concept of Americanization. Edwards, an Episcopalian and a Mason, rolled up impressive margins in the urban, Catholic, ethnic centers across the state, especially in Hague's Hudson County. Most significant, he overcame the turmoil of 1919 and the ethnic dissatisfaction with Wilson and the League of Nations.

The urban coalition of immigrants and people of immigrant background that Edwards organized in 1919 established a new majority on the state and local level. This might be called the "Edwards Revolution." Not only did these voters support Edwards, but, significantly, they remained within the New Jersey Democratic Party after 1919. Although they may have slipped back into their old habits enough to vote for Harding and Coolidge, they helped Edwards defeat incumbent United States Senator Joseph S. Frelinghuysen in 1922, and they cast their ballots for Democratic governors in 1922 and 1925. While other states with similar ethnic composition, such as Massachusetts, were electing Republicans during the early twenties, New Jersey elected Democrats in nonpresidential years. The "applejack campaign" had created a new political alignment. It helped prepare the way for the "Al Smith Revolution" and Franklin D. Roosevelt's New Deal coalition, which has been a mainstay of the state and local Democratic organizations throughout the interwar period and beyond.

During Governor Edwards's three-year term he faced a legislature usually controlled by lopsided Republican majorities. The state senate, dominated by rural and small-town interests, with one seat for each county, was the bastion of GOP strength in the twenties. The GOP controlled the general assembly as well, especially after the Harding landslide of 1920 (fifty-eight Republicans, one Democrat, and one vacancy). The legislature frustrated much of Edwards's program and passed most of its own legislation over his repeated vetoes.

Despite the inherent difficulties in working with a Republican-controlled legislature, Governor Edwards continued to pursue the policies first enunciated in the "applejack campaign"—anti-Prohibitionism, cultural pluralism, and urban ethnicity. Although he frequently lost to the legislature, he kept the support of his coalition.

In early 1920 Governor Edwards carried his anti-Prohibition campaign to the legislature. He succeeded in obtaining passage of a bill permitting the manufacture and sale of 3.5 percent alcoholic beverages, and he signed the legislation on March 2, 1920. He carried his "defense of ancient American liberty" further, challenging the constitutionality of the Eighteenth Amendment by joining Rhode Island's lawsuit; in *Rhode Island v. Palma* the Supreme Court upheld Prohibition, but Edwards's fight won popular approval in New Jersey.

In January 1921 the legislature repealed the 3.5 percent alcoholic beverages law and passed the Van Ness Enforcement Act over the governor's veto. This law denied violators the right of trial by jury, and Edwards criticized it as oppressive and unconstitutional. He also asked Congress to modify the newly passed Volstead Act to allow the sale of light wines and beer. In early 1922 the Court of Errors and Appeals set aside the Van Ness Act. In mid-March the legislature passed the Hobart Prohibition Enforcement Act, which contained provisions for trial by jury, and it became law over Edwards's veto. The Republicans' defense of Prohibition—the Eighteenth Amendment, the Volstead Act, and the Van Ness and Hobart Enforcement Acts—weakened their appeal to the urban, Catholic, ethnic minorities.

Throughout Governor Edwards's administration, he fought the Public Utility Commission and the Public Service Railroad Corporation for reduced trolley fares for the urban masses. He fired the five members of the Public Utility Commission; the courts upheld him, but the GOP legislature established a new three-member commission over his veto. Edwards also waged an intense battle for a five-cent fare, but the legislature and the courts imposed an eight-cent fare and a two-cent transfer.

Governor Edwards urged the legislature in early 1921 to defeat any blue laws that might curb outside recreation on Sunday, the day urban working families had free. He attacked blue laws as un-American legislation of morality that usurped civil liberties. He refused to stop the Dempsey-Carpentier heavyweight fight in 1921 and would have sanctioned a Dempsey-Wills fight if one had been arranged in 1922. Despite continuous attacks from conservative, religious, and rural-oriented groups, Governor Edwards steadfastly maintained his principles and programs.

Among the many bills the legislature passed over Edwards's veto was a 1921 measure creating the Port of New York Authority, which Edwards at first believed would put New Jersey in an unsatisfactory, unhappy, and unprofitable marriage with New York. He later withdrew his opposition and supported efforts to link the two states.

Although Governor Edwards advocated tough anticrime policies, including surveillance over known criminals, licensing to carry weapons, and a crackdown on auto theft, he strongly opposed the legislation which created the state police in 1921. He feared that the law might infringe on home rule by allowing intervention in local law enforcement and that the troopers might be used against labor to break strikes or harass pickets. Neither of these fears materialized; the state police assisted and supplemented local law enforcement in urban and rural communities.

The Republican-controlled legislature so frequently frustrated Governor Edwards's programs and circumvented his veto power that in 1922, when a joint committee asked at the close of the legislative session whether Edwards wanted to make a farewell statement or any further communications, he replied, "What's the use? You haven't read those that I did send." Soon he announced his candidacy for the United States Senate seat held by Republican Joseph S. Frelinghuysen. He carried his work for anti-Prohibitionism, cultural pluralism, and urban ethnicity from the governor's chair into the senatorial campaign.

With Harding and "normalcy" the Garden State Republican Party had emerged as the party of 100 percent Americanism, blue laws, Sunday closing laws, compulsory English lessons for foreign-born adults, immigration restriction, and Prohibition. Edwards launched his senatorial campaign with the slogan "Wine, Women, and Song," demanding the repeal of the Eighteenth Amendment and the legalization of light wines and beer. As before, Edwards, Hague, and the New Jersey Democratic Party courted urban ethnic groups with promises of anti-Prohibitionism, cultural liberalism, and ethnic pluralism.

Edwards defeated Frelinghuysen by 451,832 to 362,699—a margin of 89,133. He won 55.5 percent of the senatorial vote and carried Democratic Judge George S. Silzer to victory in the gubernatorial race. The New Jersey Democratic Party dramatically reversed Harding's landslide victory of two years before among the urban masses; reestablishing and enlarging the "applejack" coalition of 1919, Edwards restored ethnic unity in the party and consolidated Mayor Hague's domination over it.

In 1928 Edwards campaigned for a second term in the Senate. Once again he raised the banner of anti-Prohibitionism, often asserting that he was "as wet as the Atlantic Ocean" and calling once again for light wines and beer. His opponent, Hamilton F. Kean, however, declared for modifying the Volstead Act and, in early October, shocked New Jerseyans by announcing that he was as wet as his opponent. The Anti-Saloon League withdrew its support from Kean, but by launching his own crusade against Prohibitionism, he had neutralized the issue in the senatorial race.

Edwards lost, 841,752 to 608,623—a margin of 233,129. The presidential candidacy of New York Governor Al Smith had stimulated an enormous outpouring of antagonistic rural, old-stock voters that worked against Edwards and the Democrats. Edwards ran ahead of the New York governor in both immigrant and old-stock areas, but he simply could not overcome "Coolidge prosperity," the backlash against Al Smith, and the heavy turnout for the presidential race.

After this loss Edwards's fortunes turned downward. His wife died in 1928, and his relationship with Hague deteriorated. During the 1930 campaign he broke with Hague and threatened to join the reform coalition against him. He desired to return to the governor's chair, but Hague's choice, former governor A. Harry Moore, blocked his path. The Great Depression brought bankruptcy and charges of corruption and fraud. On January 26, 1931, Edwards committed suicide.

Governor Edward I. Edwards's contribution to New Jersey political history lies less in the bills approved or vetoed during his governorship than in his ability to articulate the political and cultural outcry of the new majority coalition of urban ethnics. Working with Hague, Edwards revolutionized the state's politics by starting a political realignment that helped to make the Democratic Party the party of urban America.

WARREN E. STICKLE

Records of Governor Edward I. Edwards, New Jersey State Library, Trenton, N.J.

Stickle, Warren E. "The Applejack Campaign of 1919: As 'Wet as the Atlantic Ocean.'" *New Jersey History* 89 (1971): 5–22.

———. "Edward I. Edwards and the Urban Coalition of 1919." *New Jersey History* 90 (1972): 83–96.

George Sebastian Silzer (April 14, 1870–October 16, 1940), son of Theodore C. and Christina (Zimmerman) Silzer, was born in New Brunswick, where his father owned and operated the Bull's Head Tavern. After he was graduated from the public grammar and high schools of his native city, Silzer read law in the offices of J. Kearny Rice. Admitted to the bar in 1892, he immediately opened an office in New Brunswick and, until 1914, built an increasingly successful practice. Already interested in a political career, Silzer was elected to the New Brunswick Board of Aldermen, where he served from 1892 until 1896, and then for ten years he led the Middlesex County Democratic Party as chairman of the county committee. Aided in part by his opposition to the Bishops' Liquor Law, he was elected to the state senate in 1906 and reelected in 1909. In 1910 he announced his candidacy for the governorship on a progressive, antimachine platform, drawing 210 votes in the state convention, which nominated Woodrow Wilson for governor.

Silzer's years in the senate saw the rise of the "New Idea" movement among Republicans and the comparable surge of reformism in his own party; he was in the forefront of Democratic progressivism. Though the Democrats were a minority in that body throughout his service in the upper house, Silzer participated significantly in the passage of several measures during the Wilson years, particularly the workmen's compensation law. He served as one of Wilson's chief lieutenants in the legislature, and in 1912 Wilson appointed him prosecutor of the pleas in Middlesex County. In 1914 Governor James F. Fielder appointed him a circuit court judge, and he served in that office until the Democrats tapped him in 1922 as their nominee for governor.

Silzer's nomination represented an agreement between leading Democrats: Frank Hague of Hudson County supported Silzer in return for Middlesex County's endorsement of the retiring governor, Edward I. Edwards, for the United States Senate. Despite numerous campaign issues, the question of Prohibition dominated the scene. Silzer's opponent, William N. Runyon, a longtime "dry" and conservative Republican, insisted on full enforcement of the Volstead Act. The Democrats charged, as Silzer phrased it in his inaugural address, that the Volstead Act "goes far beyond the [Eighteenth] amendment, for the latter prohibits 'intoxicating liquor for beverage purposes,' while the enforcement act . . . prohibits the use of beverages which are not intoxicating. To say that anything over one-half of one percent is intoxicating is to enact a falsehood; it would be quite as true to say that a jackass is a camel." The press and the defeated Republicans alike almost universally interpreted the electoral results—Silzer won by a margin of 43,894 votes— as a protest against Prohibition.

The election also represented confirmation of Frank Hague's domination of the Democratic Party in New Jersey. Silzer won only six counties; excluding Hudson's vote, he lost the state by some thirty-six thousand votes, but the eighty thousand plurality the Hague machine returned in its home county put him into the governor's chair. The structure of politics in the state, however, limited the electoral influence of the powerful Hague organization. County election of the legislators meant that throughout Silzer's three years in office he faced overwhelmingly Republican majorities in both the assembly and the senate, a situation that plagued him and remained to hamper Democratic governors for another generation. Unlike some of his successors, however, Silzer kept the Hudson County leader at arm's length and maintained a wary cooperation with him.

The new governor's inaugural message to the legislature in January 1923 revealed him to be still the progressive of the Woodrow Wilson era. Charging that "everywhere Special Privilege shows its ugly head," Silzer promised to "put government back into the hands of the people." To further this purpose, he asked for the stringent regulation of public utilities on the basis of physical valuation and the strict enforcement of the limitations on their charges, the enactment of new protective legislation for labor, and the reenactment of the recently repealed elements of Woodrow Wilson's "Seven Sisters" to prevent price gouging and monopolistic practices in the coal industry. In subsequent special and regular messages to the legislature, Silzer dealt with the reform of the prison system, the expansion of institutional services for public welfare, fairer methods of taxation, the construction of a ship canal across New

Jersey to tie together the ports of New York and Philadelphia, more stringent control of narcotics, measures to control pollution of the state's inland and coastal waters, effective gun control, tighter control of state monies, an effective blue-sky law (a law regulating securities sales), support for a federal antilynching act, and numerous proposals for improved road networks. His views were wide-ranging and, in the 1920s, forward-looking. But in most instances neither the temper of the times nor the majority of the legislature rallied to his support.

Governor Silzer began his administration with a startling action calculated to demonstrate his determination to lead the state and to conserve its interests. Six days after his inaugural he announced to the astounded legislature, "I have this day removed the present state highway commission." This was the opening gun in Silzer's attack on "special privilege." The ousted commission, which Silzer considered both subservient to political interests and incompetent, had let road contracts with specifications which could be met only by a patented material controlled by a few corporations. Despite Silzer's announced opposition in the gubernatorial campaign, a $40 million bond issue for road construction had gained the voters' approval in the 1922 elections, and the new governor feared that the monies would be siphoned off for an unjustifiably expensive road surface, to the private gain of a few men. Silzer nominated a four-man bipartisan highway commission of prominent citizens and engineers—Walter Kidde, Major General Hugh L. Scott, Abraham Jelin, and Percy H. Stewart. For six weeks the Republican senate refused them confirmation while it sought to force Silzer to accept other names. But the governor carried the fight to the citizenry and finally won the acceptance of his nominees.

Silzer's concern for transportation reflected his assessment of the state's potential future development. Lying along waterways dominated by the neighboring ports of New York City and Philadelphia, New Jersey, he anticipated, would increasingly develop both commercial-industrial and residential facilities. The automobile, with its flexibility of route, would stimulate the growth of the state's population and industry. To facilitate this expansion, Silzer supported extensive road building, though he would have preferred a pay-as-you-go plan to the bond issues the lawmakers and the electorate supported. He proposed that the legislature create a Port of Camden Authority to develop the lower Delaware area; that it authorize the construction of a bridge from Fort Lee to Washington Heights in New York City (later the George Washington Bridge) and of bridges between New Jersey and Staten Island; and that it give the state highway commission the authority to lay out the state road net. He initiated the proposal to incorporate the Holland Tunnel, then nearing completion, into the Port of New York facilities. Above all, he wanted rational development. "We must also," he wrote, "have in mind scientific planning which will make such development as attractive as possible. In these enlightened days we cannot drift along and permit ugliness to dominate." To this end he strongly supported zoning laws as a tool of planning, and he advocated a constitutional amendment to ensure their legitimacy when judicial decisions appeared to overthrow them.

Though supported by many New Jerseyans, the governor's proposals won only limited success during Silzer's term. The legislature of 1923 passed over his veto a measure authorizing private interests to build tunnels under the Hudson River and to preempt sites for the purpose; only the New York legislature's refusal to adopt similar legislation preserved the sites for public development. The same legislature, again over Silzer's veto, laid out a network of state roads devised by logrolling rather than by analysis of need.

Early in Silzer's term, during the Newark trolley strike of 1923, he seized a second opportunity to strike down "special privilege." A labor dispute between the Public Service Corporation, New Jersey's public utilities giant, and its employees resulted in a shutdown of the trolley system, with consequent severe hardship to residents and businesses alike. When the company's intransigence threatened to prolong the impasse, Silzer directed the state attorney general to bring suit against Public Service for failure to comply with the terms of its charter; the move would have deprived the transit giant of its rights-of-way in public streets. The governor's action brought a quick resumption of service; later he obtained legislation intended to inhibit similar interruption of service by utilities.

In the first year of his term Silzer also attacked "special privilege" on the labor front. After a long battle with the Republican legislature and by dint of indefatigable appeals to the electorate, he obtained legislation prohibiting the employment of women between 10:00 p.m. and 6:00 a.m. and placing some further restraints on child labor. He also managed to improve the terms of the workmen's compensation act and to improve payments to incapacitated workers.

Throughout his term Silzer used the rhetoric and techniques of the Progressive Era to gain substantially progressive ends, though it is unclear whether he did so consciously. His battles with the Republican-dominated legislature won him the sobriquet "veto governor," but neither publicity nor cajolery convinced the legislature to follow his lead. Silzer's social-welfare concerns and his opposition to special privilege nonetheless influenced many New Jersey urban voters to convert to the Democratic Party.

After his term ended in January 1926 Silzer, constitutionally disqualified from succeeding himself, returned to the practice of law and also became active in banking. In 1935 he defended Arthur (Dutch Schultz) Flegenheimer in a federal income-tax case, and in 1937 he was counsel to Ellis Parker, the Burlington County detective involved in the kidnapping of Paul H. Wendel in connection with the Lindbergh kidnap case. In 1926 his successor, Democrat A. Harry Moore, appointed him to a term as chairman of the Port of New York Authority. Silzer thus presided over the groundbreaking ceremonies for the George Washington Bridge, which he had proposed as governor. In 1933 he published *The Government of a State*, an analysis of the functions and operations of state governments, illustrated by examples from his own experience. Silzer suffered a heart attack and died on a Newark street as he was returning home from his office on October 16, 1940. He was survived by his wife, the former Henrietta T. Waite, and a son, Parker W. Silzer.

JOSEPH F. MAHONEY

Records of Governor George S. Silzer, New Jersey State Library, Trenton, N.J.

Doig, Jameson W. *Empire on the Hudson: Entrepreneurial Vision and Political Power at the Port of New York Authority.* New York: Columbia University Press, 2001.

Schroth, Frank D. *The First Year, Being the Record of Accomplishment of George S. Silzer, Governor of New Jersey.* Trenton: MacCrellish & Quigley, 1924.

Silzer, George S. *The Government of a State.* Newark: Soney & Sage, 1933.

Arthur Harry Moore (July 3, 1877–November 18, 1952), New Jersey's only three-term governor under the state's second constitution, was elected in 1925, 1931, and 1937.

Moore was a Jersey City native, born in the Lafayette section, of working-class parents, Robert White and Martha (McCoomb) Moore, of Irish and Scottish descent. Moore, known as "Red," dropped out of the local public school system at the age of thirteen to take a clerk's job at $3 per week. White-collar oriented, he continued his education in his spare time, taking courses at Cooper Union in Manhattan and developing proficiency in bookkeeping and typing. Moore also became involved in local Democratic politics, gaining from his speaking ability the sobriquet "the boy orator of Lafayette." In 1907 his long-

A. Harry Moore
New Jersey State Archives; Department of State

time friend H. Otto Wittpenn was elected mayor of Jersey City, and Moore entered City Hall as his secretary. In 1911, following the death of the Hudson Democratic leader Robert Davis, Moore assumed Davis's post as city collector. On March 28 that year Moore was married to Jennie Hastings Stevens, a downtown neighbor. He taught the men's Bible class in Lafayette Reformed Church, where his bride taught Sunday school. The couple had no children.

In 1913, after Jersey City adopted the commission form of government, Moore ran successfully for a spot on the five-man governing body. As director of Parks and Public Property, he projected an image of "the kiddies' friend" by promoting recreational facilities and opportunities for the city's youth. Gregarious by nature as well as conviction, Moore became increasingly active in church, charitable, and fraternal affairs, and he made programs for handicapped children his area of special concern.

In 1916 H. Otto Wittpenn ran unsuccessfully for the governorship, losing to Republican Walter E. Edge. Subsequently, Wittpenn virtually retired from the political scene. Moore then reworked his cooperative arrangement with a fellow commissioner, Frank Hague, into a formal alliance. Moore led the Hague slate to a clean sweep in the 1917 city commission elections, beginning Hague's thirty-year stay as mayor of Jersey City. In 1921 and 1925 Moore led the ticket to similar municipal victories. During this period he resumed his formal education, attending evening classes at the New Jersey Law School in Newark. He passed the state bar exam in 1922 and received an LL.B. in 1924.

As early as 1921 local politicians began to boom the popular Moore for the governorship. Hague, now in control of the state Democratic organization, waited until 1925, when he easily secured Moore's nomination in an uncontested primary. Moore ran on a "wringing wet," anti-Prohibition platform against the Morris County state senator, Arthur Whitney, a Republican who had the support of the Anti-Saloon League. The state GOP, in turn, focused its campaign on the alleged menace of "Hagueism" in state government. Although Moore carried only three counties, Hudson's plurality of 103,995 gave its local hero a comfortable victory margin in this off-year election.

Frank Hague saw the governor's office primarily as a source of jobs for his patronage-based party machine. Moore gave the right answer when he told the press after his election, "You can say for me that in patronage matters I am strictly organization." Still, the new governor could not maximize his patronage potential unless he cooperated with the Republican senate, which had a broad advise-and-consent power. A political realist, Moore determined that a bipartisan spirit would mark his administration. His conservative political outlook, summed up in a pet phrase as "the best governed are the least governed," furthered this cooperative spirit. His style was generally accorded a friendly reception in New Jersey's legislative halls, and his confrontations with the legislators, rare indeed, came about when he assumed a more conservative stance than they.

Three items from the year 1927 illustrate the temper of Moore's first administration. The first involved improving the potable water supply for North Jersey, a priority item for both governor and legislature. Moore, a proponent of "home rule," recommended that North Jersey municipalities resolve the problem working alone or via intermunicipal arrangements. The legislature, on the other hand, approved a constitutional amendment authorizing a series of regional water-supply districts organized and controlled by the state. With Moore cool and Hudson County hostile, the voters rejected the idea in a November 1927 referendum.

Land-use control was another major issue. After the United States Supreme Court, in a 1926 case, approved such control in principle, the New Jersey legislature proposed that the state constitution be amended to allow municipalities to exercise zoning powers. Since only local governments were to utilize the new tool, Moore and Hague approved of the amendment, campaigned for it, and saw it accepted by the voters.

A third area of controversy was a Republican plan for a major highway-construction program in New Jersey. Moore was sympathetic, believing a modern road network essential to the state's development. But the governor nonetheless refused to sign a tax bill to help fund the program, asserting that it was an undue burden on the taxpayers. The gasoline tax (which became law), coupled with a $30 million bond issue approved that autumn, set the foundation for New Jersey's first comprehensive highway system, totaling some eighteen hundred miles. Complementing this program was the work being done to tie New Jersey and New York City closer together. In 1927 Moore and Governor Al Smith of New York opened the Holland Tunnel to vehicular traffic and marked the start of construction for the George Washington Bridge. During the following year the two chief executives dedicated a pair of bridges connecting Staten Island to New Jersey—the Goethals Bridge and the Outerbridge Crossing.

In Moore's first administration he also had to cope with the social problems of the "Roaring Twenties," including Prohibition. Highway crime and disorder, especially at so-called road house night clubs, led the governor to ask the legislature to enlarge and strengthen the state police, an agency that had been established in 1921. Little progress, however, was made. A crime of another sort brought Moore national headlines in the autumn of 1926. This was the infamous Hall-Mills murder case, an alleged crime of passion that caused a sensation in the press. Moore appointed Hudson's state senator, Alexander Simpson, to prosecute the state's case against the late Reverend Edward Wheeler Hall's widow. Following a tawdry courtroom drama played to the hilt by the prosecution, the jury failed to convict, much to the embarrassment and chagrin of New Jersey officialdom.

In 1928 the Hague organization could not prevent a Republican landslide in New Jersey; the GOP easily secured the governorship for Morgan F. Larson and retained its hold on both houses of the state legislature. But the Republicans' monopoly of power meant that they could not avoid blame for the economic depression that followed. A. Harry Moore, waiting on the sidelines, worked hard to stay in the public eye. He maintained a rigorous speaking schedule, continued his involvement in fraternal and church activities, and even had a weekly radio program over station WOR on Saturday evenings. At the end of 1930 Moore, the unofficial but obvious Democratic choice for governor, began in earnest the long drive that led to his second term.

In 1931 Moore was a polished and hardy campaigner. He believed in emphasizing patriotic and religious themes—"stick to the broad generalities of the eternal verities"—and added color with a series of amusing and tear-wrenching anecdotes. During the campaign he berated President Herbert C. Hoover and incumbent Republican governor Morgan F. Larson for the misery they had brought to nation and state; in counterthrust the GOP's gubernatorial candidate, Camden County leader David Baird, Jr., could do little but cry "Hagueism." It was no contest. Moore, improving on his 1925 campaign, ran well in every county but Camden, and his plurality of 230,053 votes was the largest recorded under the 1844 constitution. Another 1931 milestone was the dedication of the A. Harry Moore School in Jersey City, an institution designed specifically to meet the educational needs of handicapped children.

Economic problems dominated the governor's second term. Moore's own approach was consistent with his conservative political philosophy: the state must reduce or postpone expenditures to enable local governments and the private sector to regenerate themselves. The 1932 legislature gave him discretionary power to curb state spending—and Moore did just that. He pruned state appropriations drastically, from a total of $34.5 million in 1931 to $28.3, $19.7, and $20.7 in 1932, 1933, and 1934, respectively. He diverted money from state programs, especially from highway construction, to keep municipal governments afloat and provide direct relief to the impoverished. Moore, a machine politician who knew the importance of the personal touch, spent long hours in Trenton listening to the woes of the jobless and trying his best to meet their needs.

The governor believed that the Depression was an opportune time to reorganize state and local government. He proposed, among other things, that New Jersey's cumbersome administrative structures be streamlined and placed under the firm control of the chief executive; that the courts be overhauled; that a "home rule" amendment be added to the constitution; and that a sales or income tax be adopted to give the state a stable revenue base. Moore's only success in these matters, however, came when the legislature provided the statutory base for a modern system of municipal finance. Overall, he could do little to accelerate the movement for constitutional reform in New Jersey.

Moore's second term was marked by more than the Depression. Two items that received worldwide publicity were the Lindbergh kidnapping in 1932 and the burning of the cruise ship *Morro Castle* in 1934. Moore supervised the investigation of the kidnapping, and he personally helped direct rescue operations in the waters off Asbury Park. The repeal of Prohibition also took place during this administration. The state legislature authorized a mix of state and municipal Alcoholic Beverage Control Commissions, and it was Moore's responsibility to implement the new program.

The advent of the New Deal put the governor's states' rights philosophy under some strain. Nevertheless, as FDR's program unfolded, Moore lobbied vigorously to ensure that New Jersey receive its fair share of public works projects and federal relief funds. In addition to these gubernatorial duties, in 1934 Moore conducted a campaign for a seat in the United States Senate, a goal he pursued at Hague's insistence. The quest was successful. Although 1934 was a comeback year for the New Jersey GOP, which obtained the governor's office for Harold G. Hoffman, Moore moved on to the nation's capital.

Moore served only half his term as United States senator, and the years were not overly happy ones. True, Moore brought home a generous supply of federal projects for his city and state. (Jersey City's Medical Center and Roosevelt Stadium are prime examples.) But he was ill at ease on the New Deal team, especially after Roosevelt moved in a welfare-state direction. Moore voted against Social Security (the only Democratic no vote in the Senate), the public utility holding company bill, and the 1935 amendments to the Agricultural Adjustment Administration Act, and he opposed Roosevelt's court-packing plan. He referred to the Senate disparagingly as "a cave of winds" and—perhaps with a sense of relief—accepted Hague's invitation to run again for the governorship in 1937.

By now the Democrats' "copyright candidate," Moore faced the Reverend Lester H. Clee of Essex County. Interestingly, Mrs. Moore's sister was married to the minister's brother. Despite this relationship, the 1937 contest was bitter and hard fought. Often on the defensive, Moore claimed that he was really not a foe of Roosevelt and the New Deal and that New Jersey needed an experienced man at the helm. Hudson pulled him through, its 129,237 plurality offsetting the fact that his opponent carried fifteen counties.

Clee's charge of widespread vote fraud in Hudson hung like a dark cloud over Moore's third term, but various Hague maneuvers stymied state legislative investigations and court suits. Then, when a United States Senate investigating committee attempted to reopen the controversy in 1940, it discovered that the Hudson poll books had been burned. Another source of adverse publicity was the governor's appointment of Hague's son to New Jersey's highest court, the Court of Errors and Appeals, in 1939.

During these years the principal concern of the governor and the legislature was economic recovery. With some reluctance Moore began his third term by diverting more road funds to meet direct relief costs. His own preference was for work-relief, via part federal- and part state-funded highway and water-facility construction projects. Though Moore had some success with the WPA, he failed to move a $60 million highway bond issue through the legislature in 1939. The Republicans, who controlled both houses, opted instead for a bond issue of $21 million to finance direct relief. The voters approved the issue in a November 1939 referendum.

The governor once more promoted tax reform as receipts from railroad taxes (a major revenue source in the state for a century) declined. The principal victim of this decline was state school aid, and Moore, always interested in education, suggested that the state consider a broad-based replacement tax. The legislators, believing that new taxes would weaken New Jersey's ability to attract industry and rebuild its economy, turned thumbs down. Their alternative was to bring in new revenue via horse racing, although gambling was then proscribed by the state constitution. Hence an amendment authorizing pari-mutuel betting was presented, and the electorate approved it in June 1939.

World War II began that September, and defense problems soon assumed a prominent place on the governor's agenda. By executive order Moore set up a Governor's Emergency Committee, the first state civil defense agency in the nation. Reorganized in the autumn of 1940 as the New Jersey Defense Council, it became the coordinating mechanism for state and local civil defense efforts. Moore also had to concern himself with the development and training of the National Guard and, in October 1940, with the nation's first peacetime draft. In January 1941 he handed over his office for the last time—but, for the first time, to a fellow Democrat, the former secretary of the navy Charles Edison.

Since Frank Hague wanted Moore to be a gubernatorial candidate once more in 1943, he held off on a nominee until late that July, hoping that Moore would acquiesce as in the past. But Moore adamantly refused to run, and Hague turned to Mayor Vincent J. Murphy of Newark, who lost in November to Republican Walter E. Edge. The whole affair led to bitter feelings between Moore and the Hague organization for a while. But by summer 1944 matters were smoothed over, and Moore was selected as a delegate to the Democratic National Convention. In 1945 Governor Edge paid tribute to Moore's long commitment to the field of education by appointing him to a vacancy on the State Board of Education.

Although Moore continued to maintain a residence in the Lafayette section of Jersey City, during his late years he spent much time at a summer home in Mount Airy, Hunterdon County. Horseback riding was his favorite avocation. His legal practice, corporate directorships, and a multitude of speaking engagements meant that his schedule remained a busy one. Moore's last major political involvement was as campaign manager for Elmer H. Wene, unsuccessful Democratic gubernatorial candidate in 1949. That year also marked the overthrow of the Hague machine in Jersey City. On November 18, 1952, Moore suffered a cerebral hemorrhage and died while at the wheel of his automobile near his Hunterdon retreat. He was seventy-three.

RICHARD J. CONNORS

Records of Governor A. Harry Moore, New Jersey State Library, Trenton, N.J.

Bloodgood, Fred L. *The Quiet Hour*. Trenton: MacCrellish & Quigley, 1940.

Connors, Richard J. *A Cycle of Power: The Career of Jersey City Mayor Frank Hague*. Metuchen, N.J.: Scarecrow, 1971.

Doig, Jameson. *Empire on the Hudson: Entrepreneurial Vision and Political Power at the Port of New York Authority*. New York: Columbia University Press, 2001.

McKean, Dayton. *The Boss*. Boston: Houghton Mifflin, 1940.

Michels, Edward H., Jr. "New Jersey and the New Deal." Ph.D. dissertation, New York University, 1986.

Morgan Foster Larson (June 15, 1882–March 21, 1961), New Jersey's fortieth governor, was born in Perth Amboy. He was the son of Peter and Regina (Knudson) Larson. His father was a Danish blacksmith who immigrated to the United States at the age of twenty-two.

Larson's rise from obscurity to the state's highest elective office in 1929 is a Horatio Alger story in local politics. Educated in the Perth Amboy public schools, Larson later studied engineering at Cooper Union Institute in New York City. In his determination to succeed, he applied the Protestant virtues of hard work and personal sacrifice as a student. He worked in Perth Amboy during the day and commuted to New York for night

Morgan F. Larson
Courtesy New Jersey State Library

classes; by 1907, when he graduated, he had logged a total of sixty thousand miles. Larson served as Middlesex County engineer in 1907–10 and 1923–24. He also served as city engineer for Perth Amboy and township engineer for Woodbridge. In 1914 he married Jennie Brogger, and that union lasted until her death in 1927.

Perhaps the most revealing incident in Larson's private life took place in 1921, when his brothers Lawrence and George Larson were killed in a grade-crossing accident. Larson softened the impact of that tragedy on his brothers' seven children by taking them into his home and giving each a college education.

In 1921, at thirty-nine, Larson ventured into electoral politics and was elected state senator as a Republican from Democratic Middlesex County. He was reelected in 1924 and 1927. In 1925 he became the senate's majority leader and a year later its president.

More than any other public concern, transportation interested Larson while he served in the senate, and it provided an issue of sufficient public appeal to bolster his prospects for statewide office. The rising popularity of the automobile during the 1920s and the resultant shift of thousands of city residents to suburban communities dramatized the obsolescence of New Jersey's road system. In 1925 the engineer-turned-political-leader joined state senators William B. McKay and Arthur N. Pierson, of Bergen and Union

Counties, to win legislative backing for three ambitious transportation projects: the George Washington Bridge, between Fort Lee, New Jersey, and 178th Street in Manhattan; the Outerbridge Crossing, from Perth Amboy to Tottenville; and the Goethals Bridge, from Elizabethport to Holland Hook. Larson achieved his most notable success in the senate in 1927, when he sponsored legislation for a state highway system. It provided for seventeen hundred miles of improved roads, costing an estimated $162 million, and called for a comprehensive plan for the future construction of highways. Moreover, the highway act helped put an end to the acrimonious debates and pork-barrel highway bills that had traditionally subverted efforts to modernize the state's transportation network.

Larson's advocacy of heavy transportation expenditures and his ability to placate his fellow senators gained him increasing support in the Republican hierarchy. As senate majority leader he reportedly "went along with the majority of the members in anything they proposed," in effect associating himself with the stronger, more broadly based Republican leaders. During the 1920s he carefully built an allegiant constituency in Middlesex County, where, one observer noted in 1928, "everybody likes him." A *Newark Evening News* reporter recalled him as "under middle height, compactly built with thick brown-gray hair and complexion tanned by much outdoor life. He is of nervous, vital temperament, full of pep, youthful in outlook, smiles often and alluringly, popular, a 'regular guy' to use the vernacular." This "regular guy" image ultimately made Larson one of Middlesex County's most successful Republican spokesmen, and his adeptness in remaining essentially unscathed by Republican factionalism set the stage for a gubernatorial bid as the 1920s drew to a close.

Larson's final test as a prospective Republican standard-bearer came in 1927, when he faced what appeared to be a stiff challenge for his senate seat from Democrat Frederic M. P. Pearse. After an unusually vigorous campaign Larson handily beat Pearse with the largest plurality any candidate for office had gained in the history of Middlesex County.

As the gubernatorial election of 1929 approached, Republican leaders viewed Larson's candidacy as a remedy to a potentially serious breach caused by the rivalry between two Essex County stalwarts, J. Henry Harrison and Fred G. Stickley, Jr. Furthermore, Mayor Frank Hague, the Hudson County Democratic boss, eyed the senate president with curious favor. Hague had successfully elected three Democratic governors in a row; in the upcoming election, however, his machine faced outspoken opposition from one gubernatorial candidate, reform Republican Robert Carey of Jersey City. A Carey victory in the general election would undoubtedly weaken Hague in Hudson County and perhaps spell disaster for him in other parts of the state. Hague sought to spoil Carey's bid by assuring a Larson victory in the upcoming Republican primary. With the help of twenty thousand votes cast for Larson by Hudson County Democrats—an unethical though not illegal practice at the time—the senate president beat Carey and two other Republican candidates. Hague's short-term strategy had worked, for Larson appeared to be a weaker opponent than Carey. After the primary, however, the scheme backfired. Larson became a formidable adversary to Hague and to Democratic control of the governorship.

Larson's gubernatorial campaign revealed some of the problems that would trouble him after winning office. His amiable, indulgent political style preserved a fragile alliance with Republican senators and with the powerful party chairman and United States senator, David Baird, Jr., of Camden County, yet it worked against him as the party's standard-bearer. Early in his candidacy Larson made his major issues the conservation of potable water, the development of transportation, and the control of water pollution. These laudable concerns stimulated little interest in the electorate, however. Predictably, confidence in Larson's political astuteness waned through the summer and fall of 1929. Most Republican leaders wisely thought Frank Hague the most provocative issue and urged Larson to strike out against him.

In late September, after weeks of spiritless campaigning, candidate Larson finally took the offensive. He began to lash out at Hague's bold domination of state politics, claiming that the supporters of the Democratic candidate, Judge William L. Dill of Paterson, were voting to continue Hagueism. By late October graft and corruption had become the targets of Larson's speeches. "If I am elected Governor," he told audiences, "I will enter the Capitol at Trenton through the front door and the Hague machine will go out the back door." This shift in campaign rhetoric, although it came after three months of lackluster public appearances, worked remarkably well. Although Dill was unquestionably honest and appeared to be independent of Hague, he could never completely shake the implication that he was in some way indebted to the Hudson County machine. Dill received 671,728 votes to Larson's 824,005.

From the beginning of Governor Morgan Larson's administration he encountered serious division in his party and challenge to his authority. The most evident reason for these difficulties was his inept handling of local patronage during his first year in office, but he faced a more fundamental dilemma. During the 1920s and 1930s the state legislature rarely cooperated with the long-range objectives of the governors. Larson's difficulties with the lawmakers exceeded those of his predecessors, in part because after taking office he became somewhat of a political maverick. He sought, perhaps prematurely, independence from the Republican Party chieftains whose support he had cultivated as president of the senate. In the first confrontation Larson insisted that the attorney generalship be given to state senator William A. Stevens of Monmouth County, though traditionally that office had been filled after consultation with county politicos. Later the governor angered Camden Republican boss Baird by selecting John Drewen for

Hudson County prosecutor; Baird, ever the archenemy of Hagueism, wanted Larson to appoint the avowed antimachine Republican Robert Carey to the position.

Following the storm of controversy over the Drewen appointment, Larson made another serious tactical blunder by nominating Mayor Clyde Potts of Morristown to another term on the state board of health. The Potts nomination dismayed many Republican senators. A senate investigating committee had implicated Potts in a scheme to suppress competition in constructing the Dover-Boonton trunk sewer. The committee alleged that Potts, in violation of state law, had permitted the use of expensive patented materials and had destroyed important records bearing on the project. The evidence against Potts was considerably stronger than the governor's rationale for nominating him: Larson called Potts a close friend and political ally and, after examining the testimony, said that "there didn't seem to be anything that involves his work as a member of the State Board of Health." Not surprisingly, the governor's justification only intensified the opposition. Larson's critics argued that he had created an embarrassing dilemma for the senate and called on him to rescind the nomination. Finally, after receiving considerable pressure, Larson followed the advice of leading Republicans and withdrew the mayor's name.

In another episode that alienated legislators he named state senator Clarence E. Case of Somerset County to the state supreme court. This act throttled Case's senate committee, which was investigating improprieties in state government.

Larson's first year as governor ended unsuccessfully. Although his party held majorities in both legislative houses, he never received support for his policies. He faced a defiant legislature that passed "ripper" bills, which deprived him of the power to appoint officials for state agencies and made efficient administration of the government virtually impossible by causing considerable duplication of effort and waste of public funds.

During Larson's second year in office he turned his attention toward improving the state economy, which had begun to slump as a result of the Great Depression. In September 1930 he directed Attorney General Stevens to initiate an action before the Interstate Commerce Commission to end alleged discriminatory freight costs in New York harbor. The complaint, which the governor outlined in his first and second annual legislative messages, claimed the lighterage rates to be in violation of the Act to Regulate Commerce. The Commission disagreed and turned the case down.

In spite of this setback, however, the major achievements of Larson's second year as governor were in interstate affairs. Drawing on his engineering background and his experience in having drafted the first comprehensive highway act in 1927, Larson reached agreement with Governor Franklin D. Roosevelt of New York in 1930 to construct the Lincoln Tunnel under the Hudson River. Although Larson was viewed as a political liability within his own state, he was a knowledgeable spokesman for New Jersey during the talks with New York officials.

During his second year in office Larson, now forty-nine years old, married Adda Schmidt. A native of Denmark, she had been the secretary and companion of his mother.

Widespread unemployment loomed as the major crisis in the state as the Larson administration drew to a close in 1931. In the governor's third and final annual message to the legislature he gave top priority to joblessness and called on the lawmakers to devise ways "to meet the state's responsibility in the crisis." He supported the creation of the state Emergency Relief Administration, a temporary agency that dispensed $8 million in aid to county and municipal programs, but he soon discovered the need for considerably more help from the national government to alleviate the economic and social misery wrought by the collapse of capitalist markets throughout the world. The Great Depression made Larson's last year in office his most frustrating. Like many Americans he believed that the Protestant work ethic and the free-enterprise system were indisputable pillars of strength in a democratic community; the Depression, however, brought these traditional beliefs into serious question.

During Larson's candidacy for governor political pundits often compared him to Herbert Hoover. Both men, after all, were engineers of humble origin who had achieved success through a rugged application of the work ethic. In retrospect another analogy seems appropriate, for the Hoover and Larson administrations both began with unbridled confidence but ended during the early Depression in failure and frustration.

After leaving the governorship Larson had a mixed career. He had a modicum of success in engineering with the Port of New York Authority, but his many financial holdings in banking institutions, gas and petroleum, and real estate collapsed. In 1945 Governor Walter E. Edge appointed him commissioner of the recently created Department of Conservation, a position he held until March 1949. He remained on the state payroll as a consulting engineer with the Water Policy and Supply Council, yet never again did he enjoy notoriety and influence in public affairs. At the age of seventy-eight Morgan Larson died in Perth Amboy.

CLEMENT ALEXANDER PRICE

Records of Governor Morgan F. Larson, New Jersey State Library, Trenton, N.J.

Doig, Jameson W. *Empire on the Hudson: Entrepreneurial Vision and Political Power at the Port of New York Authority*. New York: Columbia University Press, 2001.

Harold G. Hoffman
New Jersey State Archives; Department of State

Harold Giles Hoffman (February 7, 1896–June 4, 1954), forty-first governor of New Jersey, was born in South Amboy, New Jersey, the descendant of a family which traced its lineage to the Dutch colonial settlement of New Amsterdam.

While still in high school, Hoffman became a reporter for a Perth Amboy newspaper and an occasional stringer for the *New York Times* and the *New Brunswick Daily Home News.* Upon graduation, Hoffman joined the *Perth Amboy Evening News* as a full-time employee and quickly rose to assistant city editor and later sports editor. A dispute with the paper's owner ended Hoffman's newspaper career, and he took a job with the Du Pont Laboratory at Parlin. Shortly after the United States declared war on Germany, Hoffman enlisted with Company H, Third Infantry, New Jersey National Guard (later part of the 114th Infantry of the 29th—Blue and Gray —Division of the American Expeditionary Force). The young enlistee quickly earned the rank of sergeant and was enrolled in officers' training school. Graduating third in his class, Lieutenant Hoffman rejoined his regiment as it was about to embark for France. He saw action in the Meuse-Argonne offensive, and, at twenty-one, he was promoted to captain on the battlefield.

Hoffman returned to South Amboy a war hero and took a position as treasurer of the South Amboy Trust Company. Over the next ten years, he assumed a prominent place in South Amboy's business community. He served as vice president of his bank, president of the Hoffman-Lehrer Real Estate Corporation, president of the Mid-State Title Guaranty & Mortgage Company, treasurer of the National Realty & Investment Corporation, and director of the Investor Building & Loan Association. Hoffman also became well known in New Jersey banking circles. In 1919, Hoffman married Lillie May Moss, daughter of a prominent South Amboy dentist, Dr. William Penn Moss.

Young Hoffman also became active in South Amboy and Middlesex County Republican politics. Beginning his political career with an appointment as treasurer of South Amboy, Hoffman entered electoral politics in 1923 as Middlesex County assemblyman. In 1925, the Republicans nominated him for mayor of South Amboy with a write-in vote, and he handily won the fall election. Hoffman continued his meteoric political career as secretary to senate president Morgan F. Larson, and in November 1926 he defeated Democrat Fred W. De Voe for congressman from the Third District by a wide margin. He won reelection in 1928, easily defeating Democrat John R. Phillips, Jr. Though Congressman Hoffman's career in Washington was undistinguished, his success in the usually Democratic Third District earned him the chairmanship of the Middlesex County Republican Party and a prominent place in the state's Republican hierarchy.

When Morgan F. Larson became governor in 1929, Hoffman was slated for a prominent position in his administration. The young congressman had endeared himself to the state's strong Republican machines, in particular the Camden County organization of David Baird, Jr., and when William L. Dill's term as commissioner of the Department of Motor Vehicles expired in 1930, Hoffman gained the four-year appointment, which paid $10,000 annually. Rightfully uncertain of Republican chances in the special election his resignation from Congress would necessitate in the Third District, Hoffman refused to step down, serving out the remainder of his term and holding the motor vehicles position at the same time.

Hoffman used the motor vehicles post to its fullest advantage, speaking at functions of all kinds throughout the state. He was a brilliant speaker, debater, and campaigner, and as commissioner he had an ideal platform from which to exercise his skills. He was even able to build a rather substantial national reputation as a spokesman for highway safety, a comparatively new concern in 1930.

Hoffman always considered the visibility afforded the commissioner of motor vehicles a stepping stone to higher elected office. He built an efficient and fiercely loyal personal political organization, and his arduous campaigning for Republican functionaries from Newark to Cape May earned him the gratitude of many party workers.

In 1934, Hoffman reportedly considered challenging U.S. Senator Hamilton Fish Kean for the Republican senatorial nomination, hut was persuaded instead to seek the GOP gubernatorial nomination. His primary opponents were controversial Atlantic County state senator Emerson L. Richards, Essex County state senator Joseph G. Wolber, and Robert Carey. Hoffman easily won, drawing more votes than his three opponents combined. William L. Dill, Hoffman's predecessor as commissioner of motor vehicles and now a judge of the Court of Errors and Appeals, received the nomination of the Democratic Party. Dill, a protégé of Mayor Frank Hague of Jersey City, won an impressive primary victory over Monmouth County's maverick assemblyman Theron McCampbell. In a show of backing for Dill, the Hague Hudson County machine turned out more than 110,000 votes, of which 107,000 went to Judge Dill. The Democratic nominee had previously been defeated for the governor's post in the Republican landslide of 1928.

The campaign was unimpressive. Dill, though an inadequate campaigner who avoided the public spotlight, attempted to develop issues, primarily in the area of tax reform. Hoffman, an eager and superb campaigner, remained deliberately aloof from issues. The candidates, traditionally but appropriately, accused each other of being the tools of bossism.

The election was an upset. For the first time in twenty-seven years, the Democrats lost the governorship in a nonpresidential election year. Mayor Frank Hague's inability to put his candidate over would be interpreted years later as a sellout of Judge Dill in order to get the affable Hoffman, later branded a Hague Republican, elected to the governorship. Little evidence exists to substantiate this contention. Actually, the vote illustrated the continued power of the Republican county machines, especially Enoch L. (Nucky) Johnson's Atlantic County organization. It also strongly indicated a far-reaching personal popularity for the thirty-nine-year-old governor-elect. And in a period of dramatically declining Republican fortunes throughout the country, Hoffman was widely championed as a potential contender for national office.

When Harold Hoffman became governor, an estimated 650,000 New Jersey residents were directly dependent on state and local government for public relief. Many thousands more were severely affected by the deepening economic depression. In the face of rapidly declining tax revenues, New Jersey's municipal governments were hard-pressed to deliver essential services. Several cities defaulted, and others verged on financial collapse. With the full effect of the New Deal Depression-fighting programs still in the future, the problems of meeting the Depression crisis fell squarely on the shoulders of state and local government.

As governor, however, Harold Hoffman stood only on the peripheries of many of the important developments in state and local government that took place during his tenure. Although he was deeply embroiled in controversy and constantly in the news, his influence on the direction of state affairs declined continuously during his term as governor.

One of the first problems Hoffman attempted to meet—and, owing to his heavy-handed and conspiratorial manner of handling it, the cause of his first controversy—involved increasing state revenues to meet the increased demands for services from the state. In his inaugural address, Hoffman asked for a state sales tax, an unpopular issue he had skillfully avoided mentioning during the campaign. A sales tax, or some other broadening of the state's taxes, had wide support among the state's big-city politicians. However, numerous powerful business and taxpayers' associations, as well as the majority of the governor's own party, opposed any new taxes. To these people, fiscal responsibility meant reduced expenditures and a balanced budget, not increased spending.

Actively opposed by many Republican legislators, Hoffman made the fateful decision to deal with Hague's Democratic supporters in the legislature. Amidst an uproar from his fellow Republicans, Hoffman used his newfound allies to ram through the sales tax. The Hoffman-Hague "unholy deal," coming after just six months of the new governor's term, destroyed the credibility of his leadership with much of the Republican Party. It had an especially adverse effect on Hoffman's relationship with the increasingly powerful Clean Government Group, a Republican faction headed by Essex County lawyer Arthur T. Vanderbilt.

The Vanderbilt wing of the party gave lip service to liberal and reformist ideals, but though it understood that the Republican Party must change its public image to win elections and influence public policy in the Democratic New Deal era, it was fundamentally conservative. Indeed, the Clean Government Group capitalized on Mayor Hague's failure to give the New Deal more than lukewarm support by implying that the Clean Republicans would be the New Jersey standard-bearers of progressive politics. In reality, however, in the midthirties the Clean Government faction devoted most of its energies to preaching governmental cost cutting and maintenance, if not reduction, of existing tax rates.

High on the new movement's list of pariahs were the last vestiges of the old Republican organization in Essex, Camden, and Atlantic Counties. Hoffman, already suspect for his close ties to the state's Republican bosses (the governor virtually ignored the Clean Government faction in awarding patronage) became the Vanderbilt Republicans' public enemy number one after the Hoffman-Hague sales-tax deal.

The well-organized outcry against the tax measure was deafening. The Clean Government Group, skillfully using the issue to strengthen its position within the party, made significant in-roads throughout the state in the September 1935 Republican primary. Beaten, the governor was obliged to sign a sales-tax repeal the following month. With his usual flair for the dramatic, Hoffman signed the bill in red ink, symbolizing what he foresaw as an "unbalanced budget and maybe hungry people."

Hoffman's first year as governor had not ended before a second major crisis rocked his administration. In late 1935, he embroiled himself in the sensational controversy surrounding the Lindbergh kidnapping case. Bruno Richard Hauptmann, convicted of the kidnap-murder of the Lindbergh baby, was awaiting execution at Trenton State Prison when the governor decided to reopen the case. The governor believed that Hauptmann had not committed the crime alone, and in the interest of justice he made a dramatic visit to Hauptmann's death cell, hoping to induce the convicted kidnapper to name his accomplices. The circumstances surrounding the governor's bizarre behavior suggest that Hoffman was more interested in the case for its potential publicity value than, as he professed, for justice.

Just before Hauptmann's scheduled execution date, the governor granted him a thirty-day reprieve and ordered the state police to reopen their investigation. What followed was a grotesque sequence of events which featured a further kidnapping, an induced confession, manufactured evidence, and assorted other travesties of justice, in all of which Governor Hoffman was deeply implicated. Hoffman's apparent intention to grant a second reprieve was blocked, and Hauptmann was electrocuted. If the governor had hoped to advance his reputation by intervening in the case, he had severely miscalculated. A hostile press pilloried his behavior, and the resultant publicity further damaged his credibility.

Nonetheless, Hoffman still entertained national political ambitions. Going into the 1936 presidential election year, Hoffman's political associates were certain that the governor was maneuvering for either the presidential or vice presidential nomination. However, if Hoffman was to have any chance at the Republican National Convention, it was essential that he emerge from a harmonious state primary in May as the head of his party's delegation to Cleveland. He was not to do so.

First, the strong sympathy in the state party for Governor Alfred M. Landon of Kansas made an unpledged delegation impossible. Second, the Republican state committee chose three at-large delegates who were less than enthusiastic about their governor (Hoffman was designated the fourth at-large delegate). Third, Hoffman faced a strong challenge for his place on the delegation from former congressman Franklin W. Fort, who ran a vigorous campaign managed by the Clean Government faction.

Although the governor was able to beat Fort, he came in a poor fourth, thus destroying any chance he might have had at the Cleveland convention. The hollow victory in the 1936 state primary left Hoffman on the defensive within his own party. He devoted the remainder of his tenure as governor to his future political ambitions. Events, many of which carried far-reaching significance, were little influenced by the governor, who was taking on all the early characteristics of a lame-duck executive.

In 1936, the state Emergency Relief Administration was disbanded, and the responsibility for administering and partially financing the relief burden was shifted back onto the municipal governments. That year, even though the governor had expressed reservations about the propriety of federal welfare, the legislature extended the provisions of the Federal Social Security Act to many New Jersey citizens.

The governor played a peripheral role in another hotly contested issue, the question of state supervision and control of municipal finances; his foes within the Republican Party dominated in the struggle. Backed financially by the state's powerful business interests and politically by Vanderbilt's Clean Government Group, the Princeton Local Government Survey was launched late in 1935. Under the direction of Princeton University president Harold W. Dodds, a group of Princeton professors was commissioned to study and draft legislation which would severely restrict the powers of New Jersey local governments to administer their own fiscal affairs. In a skillfully orchestrated lobbying campaign supported by the Clean Government Republicans, the professors pushed the Princeton-survey bills through the legislature. Although the Princeton bills did not go as far as many of their business supporters had desired, they created a strong Department of Municipal Affairs with substantial control and supervisory powers over municipal finances. The governor did not play an instrumental role in these significant developments.

In fact, Hoffman was increasingly preoccupied with his political future. His final annual message to the legislature was groundwork for a 1940 gubernatorial bid. (Hoffman was constitutionally prohibited from succeeding himself, but his vision of a second term in 1940 was not unreasonable. His predecessor and successor, A. Harry Moore, would serve three terms—a record under the 1844 constitution.) Unfortunately, the governor's candidate for the 1937 Republican gubernatorial nomination, state senator Clifford R. Powell of Burlington County, was soundly defeated by the Reverend Lester H. Clee, Essex County's state senator, a Clean Government stalwart who had made his opposition to Hoffman a central issue in his campaign. Clee lost a close November election to Moore.

Under the circumstances, Hoffman was not sorry to see the Republican defeat. The former governor managed to maneuver his own appointment as executive director of the New Jersey Unemployment Compensation Commission (UCC)—a $12,000-a-year post. From there, he could run a nonstop campaign for the 1940 GOP gubernatorial nomination. In the primary that year, however, he was narrowly defeated by Clean Government Republican Robert C. Hendrickson of Gloucester County, despite the considerable, and this time apparent, assistance of Hoffman's old friend Mayor Frank Hague. But Hoffman's substantial organization within the Republican Party withheld its support from Hendrickson, and Charles Edison, businessman son of the Wizard of Menlo Park, overwhelmingly defeated him.

Undaunted, Hoffman took leave of his post at the UCC in June 1942 to accept a commission in the army transport command. (Reportedly, he had to drop thirty-six pounds in order to pass the army physical.) He left the service in March 1946 with the honorary rank of colonel and returned to his post at the UCC.

When the Division of Employment Security was created in the Labor and Industry Department during Governor Alfred E. Driscoll's administration, Hoffman left his UCC position to become its first director. Aside from his official business, he was much in demand as a paid speaker, under the management of Thomas Brady, Inc., of New York City. He was a frequent toastmaster for the Order of Circus Saints and Sinners, an organization of which he was honorary life president.

On March 18, 1954, Robert B. Meyner, the newly inaugurated Democratic governor, suddenly suspended Hoffman from his post in the Division of Employment Security for alleged irregularities in purchases. For weeks, the charges against Hoffman remained unsubstantiated, leading his loyal followers to charge Meyner with a political witch hunt. Then on June 4, while in the New York City apartment of the Circus Saints and Sinners, Harold Hoffman died of an apparent heart attack. The calls for Meyner to clear the former governor's name became intense.

Several weeks later, the government released its well-documented case against Hoffman. A letter Hoffman had written to his daughter shortly before his death substantiated the sordid tale, which spanned most of his political career. Hoffman had embezzled approximately $300,000 from the South Amboy Trust Company, of which he was an officer, in order to pay off early campaign debts. According to Hoffman's letter, a "certain wealthy elder candidate who is now deceased" had agreed to pay Hoffman's campaign costs. The wealthy benefactor had reneged, and Hoffman had embezzled to cover his debts. From at least 1949 on, he had used state funds from the Division of Employment Security to cover his bank's shortages.

Other charges of malfeasance, misfeasance, and misconduct in office were leveled at the former governor and several close associates. In addition, it turned out that another state official who had learned of the embezzlement had blackmailed Hoffman for $150,000.

"Morality, in its ultimate determination, is a funny thing," Hoffman wrote to his daughter. Indeed, for Harold Hoffman, as for many other public officials over the years, morality was not an easily comprehensible commodity.

PAUL A. STELLHORN

Records of Governor Harold G. Hoffman, New Jersey State Library, Trenton, N.J.
Crystal, George. *This Republican Hoffman: The Life Story of Harold G. Hoffman, a Modern Fighter*. Hoboken, N.J.: Terminal Printing and Publishing, 1934.

Charles Edison
New Jersey State Archives; Department of State

Charles Edison (August 3, 1890–July 31, 1969), New Jersey's forty-second governor, was the elder son of the inventor Thomas A. Edison by his second wife, Mina Miller. His maternal grandfather was Lewis Miller of Akron, Ohio, an inventor, industrialist, and philanthropist and a cofounder of the first Chautauqua Assembly. Charles Edison grew up in the sheltered confines of Llewellyn Park in West Orange, and he attended the Dearborn-Morgan School in Orange, the Carteret Academy in West Orange, and the Hotchkiss School in Connecticut. He matriculated at the Massachusetts Institute of Technology because, as he said later, "Father wanted me to be able to read a blueprint." After three years, although his grades were satisfactory, he left MIT, and on the advice of his father he took a job as a $15-a-week helper at the Boston Electric Light Company to gain general administrative training. One year later he went to work for Thomas A. Edison, Inc.

After Edison's return from Massachusetts he became a familiar figure in the growing bohemian community of Greenwich Village. He became interested in folk dancing and folk music, wrote poetry, published a literary magazine called *Bruno's Weekly*, and helped finance a theater. He remained interested in the arts throughout his life and in 1967 published a volume of his poems, *Flotsam and Jetsam*. His artistic inclinations, however, were secondary to his involvement in Thomas A. Edison, Inc. His father had put him through a strenuous apprenticeship to school him for eventual leadership of the company. Charles exhibited nearly as much flair for management and capacity for hard work as his father, but none of the inventive genius. In 1926 he officially succeeded his aging father as president of the firm and immediately began to revamp its structure, improve its financial position—his success enabled the company to weather the Depression—and modify the paternalistic labor policies his father had instituted.

Edison first served in government during World War I, assisting his father, who was president of the Naval Consulting Board, an agency responsible for developing new naval weapons and manufacturing war materials. He also met and became a friend of Franklin D. Roosevelt, then assistant secretary of the navy. In March 1918 he married Carolyn Hawkins of Cambridge, Massachusetts. They had no children.

Although Edison voted for Woodrow Wilson in 1912 and 1916, he remained a Republican until the 1930s, when he became a strong advocate of the New Deal and the only Democrat in the Edison family. "I believe in the new experiments going on," he stated in response to fellow businessmen's criticisms. "It takes courage to try new things and it takes courage to stop them if they are not successful." His support of the Roosevelt administration and his reputation as an extremely able executive drew him into government work during the 1930s. Between 1933 and 1936 he was vice chairman of the New Jersey State Recovery Board, state director of the National Emergency Council, compliance director for the National Recovery Administration, and a member of the Regional Labor Board and the National Industrial Recovery Board. He was also a consultant during the drafting of the Federal Housing Act, and he served as regional director of the Federal Housing Administration for New Jersey, Pennsylvania, Maryland, and Delaware; some historians have credited him with the original idea that led to the FHA.

Edison fulfilled one of his ambitions on November 17, 1936, when President Roosevelt nominated him for the post of assistant secretary of the navy following the death of Henry Latrobe Roosevelt. He was selected because he had a record as an effective industrialist and government administrator and because he agreed with Roosevelt that the nation should build a navy second to none. Edison assumed his new position on January 18, 1937. His tenure was noteworthy in at least two respects. First, Claude A. Swanson, the secretary of the navy, was in poor health, and Edison was, in fact if not in name, the actual secretary of the navy for the next three years. Second, the president and Congress desired to increase the size of the American navy, and Edison's responsibility was to see that the ships were built on time and in conformity with the most recent advances in naval design and technology. He also supervised the naval neutrality patrols in the Atlantic Ocean. One of his major decisions prevented the sale of a group of obsolescent destroyers for junk. These vessels later made up a substantial part of the ships turned over to Britain in the "destroyer deal."

After Swanson died in July 1939, Edison became acting secretary of the navy, and he was appointed secretary on December 30, 1939. While in the department, he was an innovator. Against the advice of the admirals, he insisted on developing high-pressure steam systems for propulsion, which resulted in higher speeds and greater efficiency for all naval vessels. He was also impressed by the threat the dive-bomber posed to capital ships, and he encouraged the building of small torpedo boats, torpedo bombers, and fast destroyers. His major naval accomplishment was to supervise the most ambitious naval building program in American history during a critical period.

Edison was secretary of the navy for only half a year. On March 30, 1940, he surprised his friends and acquaintances by announcing his candidacy for governor of New Jersey, and on June 24 he resigned from the cabinet. This was Edison's first campaign for elective office. It was undertaken with Roosevelt's encouragement. Roosevelt faced a reelection campaign later in the year, and he believed that with Edison running for governor he could carry New Jersey. In addition, in view of America's deteriorating relations with Germany and Japan, Roosevelt wanted to broaden his administration by including a few Republicans in the cabinet. Edison's successor as secretary of the navy was Frank Knox, a Republican newspaper publisher from Chicago. The immediate reaction of New Jersey Republicans to Edison's announcement was negative; they argued that the naval post was next to the presidency in importance and that the threat of war made it Edison's patriotic duty to remain in Washington.

The Republican candidate for governor, state senator Robert C. Hendrickson of Gloucester County, called Edison a tool of Frank Hague, the notorious mayor of Jersey City and boss of Hudson County. Edison could not have been nominated without Hague's support, but during the campaign he projected an independent image, emphasizing his experience in government and business, which would enable him to bring modern, efficient, and economical management to the operations of the New Jersey government. Edison went out of his way to separate himself from Hague. He attacked the recent burning of the poll books in Hudson County as well as Hague's political use of the courts. In his first campaign speech, delivered in August at Sea Girt, Edison declared in Hague's presence his independence of all bosses. "If you elect me," he told the voters, "you will have elected a governor who has made no promises to any man." Edison's stance did not disturb Hague, who assumed that it was mere campaign rhetoric. Edison won the election by nearly 64,000 votes, but he carried only seven of the state's twenty-one counties, losing even his home county of Essex. Without the 108,000-vote plurality Hague had piled up for him in Hudson County, Edison would have lost.

Edison's term in office was not particularly successful. Effective administration was almost impossible for several reasons. The state constitution was outmoded, and furthermore the governor, lacking political skill, failed to establish good relations with the state's political leaders. His partial deafness further impaired his leadership. In addition, the opposing party solidly controlled the legislature; in 1942, for example, the Republicans had majorities of seventeen to four in the senate and forty-four to sixteen in the assembly. Finally, Edison kept his word about resisting Hague and thereby made an enemy of the state's most powerful political figure.

The struggle with Hague brought Edison national attention. Before becoming governor Edison had published a song entitled "Don't Ask Nothin' of Me." This could have served as the theme song of his administration, at least as far as Frank Hague was concerned. From the beginning Edison showed that he had meant what he said at Sea Girt. In one of his first official acts he ripped out the direct phone line connecting the governor's office with Hague's in the Jersey City city hall. The irrevocable break came on January 21, 1941, less than two weeks after the inauguration. Edison nominated Frederic R. Colie of Milburn to the New Jersey Supreme Court, the second highest court in the state. Colie, a Republican, had led the opposition to the 1939 appointment of Hague's son, Frank, Jr., to the state's highest court, the Court of Errors and Appeals.

Edison then attempted to rid the highway department of its pro-Hague head. It took the state senate a full year to vote on Edison's nominee, and the governor won confirmation only after instituting an investigation of the activities of the department, which was a rich source of patronage for the state's political chieftains. The feud with Hague broke into the open over taxation of railroad property. During the Depression the bankrupt railroads had failed to pay $34 million in taxes. With the return of prosperity Hague argued that the railroads should pay the taxes, with interest. Edison instead worked out a compromise whereby the railroads would pay back the $34 million over a twenty-year period and the state would waive the accumulated interest. Hague accused the governor of showing favoritism to the railroads, and Edison charged Hague with using the issue to retaliate for the Colie appointment.

Roosevelt gave Edison no support in the struggle with Hague. In fact, he continued to funnel state patronage through Hague. He even nominated

Thomas F. Meaney, a Hague crony, to fill a vacancy on the federal district court bench in New Jersey without paying Edison the customary courtesy of consultation beforehand. Roosevelt's lack of support noticeably cooled relations between the two men.

Edison made no secret of the fact that he was out "to separate as many Hague Democrats as possible from the state payroll and to try to keep any new ones from catching on." He also struck at the financial basis of Hague's power in 1942 by ousting the entire five-man Hudson County Tax Board from office and replacing it with a board of his choosing. The original board had taxed businesses in the county heavily, and their revenues had provided much of the money that enabled the Hague machine to function. Hague responded by having some of Edison's supporters arrested and prosecuted and by blocking a number of the governor's appointments.

Edison was determined that the Democrats should nominate an anti-Hague candidate for governor in 1943. In February 1943, in preparation for the primary, he announced the formation of the "United Democracy," a state-wide anti-Hague organization. He also denounced Hague over the radio, calling him corrupt and dictatorial. Despite Edison's strenuous efforts to destroy Hague, however, Hague controlled the convention, and the "United Democracy" quietly expired. The Democratic gubernatorial candidate, Vincent J. Murphy, mayor of Newark, drew closer and closer to Hague during the campaign; by election day, in response, Edison had adopted a stance of virtual neutrality. Murphy lost the election to Walter E. Edge by approximately 130,000 votes.

Edison's most notable activity as governor was his promotion of constitutional revision. New Jersey had been operating under the constitution of 1844, an archaic document that severely circumscribed the governor's powers and made it exceedingly difficult for him to function as a true chief executive. The constitution limited the governor's appointive power, permitted a simple majority of the assembly and senate to override his veto, restricted his term to three years, and prevented him from succeeding himself. It also forced him to share his power with more than eighty boards and commissions, which had overlapping functions. The government was a bureaucratic nightmare. Moreover, the antiquated judicial structure consisted of seventeen different court systems. The need for constitutional revision was recognized throughout the state even before Edison became governor. Both Edison and Hendrickson came out in support of it during the 1940 gubernatorial race, Edison proposing a constitutional convention and Hendrickson claiming that Edison, as a tool of Hague's, could not effect the necessary changes. Edison's inaugural address made constitutional revision the first priority of his administration. Opposition was especially strong among rural Republicans, who viewed revision as a threat to their power, particularly in the state senate. When Edison in his inaugural address coupled revision with a plea for restructuring the state senate to reflect the state's population more equitably, he destroyed the possibility of a constitutional convention during his term. He also alienated Hague from the drive by describing revision as a means of curbing Hague's power.

After leaving office, Edison supported the movement for revision actively. He would witness the movement's triumph when the state adopted a new constitution in 1947. Although his maladroit political approach aborted revision during his governorship, he deserves credit for focusing public attention on the question and whipping up support for revision.

After Edison's term ended on January 18, 1944, he resumed his position as president of Thomas A. Edison, Inc. The company prospered under his direction, and in 1957 it merged with the McGraw Electric Company to form the McGraw-Edison Company. Edison was board chairman of the merged firm until he retired in 1961. Meanwhile, he remained active in politics, supporting John V. Kenny's overthrow of Hague in 1949. He also vigorously promoted the China lobby and Douglas A. MacArthur. Disturbed by the growth of federal power under both Democratic and Republican presidents and opposed to the foreign policies of both major political parties, Edison officially joined the New York Conservative Party in 1963.

Edison's wife died in 1963, and he spent his last years at the Waldorf Towers in New York City. He died on July 31, 1969, leaving an estate of approximately $10 million. The vast bulk of it went to the Charles Edison Fund, which he had established to promote "various charities, scientific, literary, and religious education projects."

EDWARD S. SHAPIRO

Records of Governor Charles Edison, New Jersey State Library, Trenton, N.J.

Alexander, Jack. "The Ungovernable Governor." *Saturday Evening Post*, January 23. 1943, 9.

Burritt, Richard D. "Another Edison Makes Some Discoveries." *New York Times Magazine*, October 12, 1941, 16, 27.

Connors, Richard J. *A Cycle of Power: The Career of Jersey City Mayor Frank Hague*. Metuchen, N.J.: Scarecrow, 1971.

———. *The Process of Constitutional Revision in New Jersey, 1940–1947*. New York: National Municipal League, 1970.

Dorsett, Lyle. "Frank Hague, Franklin Roosevelet and the Politics of the New Deal." *New Jersey History* 94 (1975–76): 21–35.

Van Devander, Charles W. *The Big Bosses*. New York: Howell, Soskin, 1944.

Venable, John D. *Out of the Shadow: The Story of Charles Edison*. East Orange, N.J.: Charles Edison Fund, 1978.

The Constitution of 1947

Alfred Eastlack Driscoll (October 25, 1902–March 9, 1975) was born in Pittsburgh, Pennsylvania, the son of Alfred Robie and Mattie (Eastlack) Driscoll. His ancestry can be traced to revolutionary Haddonfield, New Jersey. In 1906, when Driscoll was four years old, the family moved back to Haddonfield. An only child, Driscoll could attribute his interest in public affairs directly to his parents, who participated actively in the affairs of the community. His mother, a participant in many church, reform, and educational movements, including the founding of the Peddie School for Girls in Hightstown, appears to have influenced her son's development profoundly.

Alfred E. Driscoll
New Jersey State Archives; Department of State

Driscoll displayed enormous energy and drive as a child, and these became his most pronounced characteristics as governor. He graduated from Haddonfield High School as the school's most outstanding student, receiving the Childrey Award for his reputation as a hardworking student, his performance as captain of the debating and track teams, and other achievements. At Williams College, he served as captain of the track team again, continued his commitment to debating, and became one of the college's two four-letter men.

During his college years, Driscoll satisfied a thirst for adventure and a love of the outdoors. Later he reflected, "When I was in college I had a bad case of wanderlust. I went to sea during a couple of summer vacations. I worked as a cook with an expedition to the Canadian Rockies and another time, I cooked for an outfit that went north to the arctic circle. I used to justify myself by saying that I was building windows out of which I could look after I had settled down." Besides opening "windows" for the future governor, these excursions helped mold his sense of independence, which, combined with the security of deep roots in his native state, shaped his political style. That style was already visible when, at twenty-eight, he entered politics.

Fresh from Harvard Law School, Driscoll became associated with the Camden firm of Starr, Sumerhill and Lloyd. Shortly after that, he was asked to run for the Haddonfield Board of Education to prevent the local political machine from "politicizing" a nonpartisan body. When Republican leaders informed him that he could not run because the local party had already selected its ticket, Driscoll retorted, "Until a minute ago, I didn't want to run. Now, I'm going to."

Thus, Driscoll entered politics only to keep "politics" from getting in the way of the matters he deemed important. A young man of intelligence and means, he did not need the party as a vehicle for personal, financial, or political success. It was only natural that Arthur T. Vanderbilt's "Clean Government" movement, which was beginning to enjoy success in the northern counties, looked on him as a "corner." Driscoll's disdain for "petty partisan politics" would help him secure a new constitution for the state, which others had failed to do. The same quality, however, would also eventually weaken his influence over many county leaders in the party he led.

Driscoll remained on the school board for seven years, serving for a time as its president. He resigned in 1937 to run for the Haddonfield Borough Commission. After his election, he became director of revenue and finance, in which office he significantly lowered the municipality's taxes and bonded debt.

At this juncture, the Clean Government faction of the Republican Party approached Driscoll to oppose the entrenched Baird machine in the primary for state senator, and he did so successfully. He went on to win the election. In that year, a Frank Hague favorite, A. Harry Moore, won his third term as governor. Moore defeated the Clean Government candidate, Rev. Lester H. Clee, by forty thousand votes, though he carried only Hudson and Middlesex Counties. Driscoll was among the first to notice irregularities. "Funny things happened in that election," he said, "including the burning of ballots." Retaining his borough commission seat, he entered the senate determined to combat machine politics in both parties at every level in the state.

He managed Robert C. Hendrickson's ill-fated campaign in the 1940 election for governor, which Charles Edison won by sixty thousand votes. The following January, the thinned Republican majority selected Driscoll as senate majority leader. He spent his brief term cautiously walking a tightrope between the Hague Democrats and the patronage-hungry "old guard" Republicans from the rural counties. Analyzing his situation, he observed, "My job was to get as much as I could and to yield as little as I would." Shortly thereafter, the Republican legislature designated him New Jersey's alcoholic-beverage commissioner.

In that post, Driscoll displayed the capacity for hard work and for enduring sixteen-hour days that would mark his seven years as governor. He established the reputation of a strict and impartial watchdog over an industry frequently beset by scandal.

In addition to his official duties, he immersed himself in the movement for constitutional revision and administrative reorganization, which gained momentum during the administrations of governors Edison and Walter E. Edge. Edge named Driscoll to the New Jersey Commission on State Administrative Reorganization, which was chaired by Charles R. Erdman, Jr., and included state senator C. Wesley Armstrong, assemblyman Walter Jones, and public member Charles A. Eaton, Jr. The commission thoroughly investigated the existing one hundred independent spending agencies and fifty independent boards and commissions, then recommended consolidating twenty-four agencies into five principal departments. These recommendations were enacted promptly. The defeat of the 1944 constitution precluded further reorganization, but Driscoll's work on the commission gave him a familiarity with the mechanisms of state government that equipped him for his most memorable feat, engineering the ratification of the new constitution.

Supported by Governor Edge, Driscoll stopped former governor Harold G. Hoffman's attempted comeback in the Republican primary of 1946 and then defeated the Democratic candidate, Hudson County judge Lewis G. Hansen, by a plurality of 221,000 votes. By all accounts, the gubernatorial campaign was a lackluster affair, with the Republicans seeking to capitalize on President Harry S. Truman's unpopularity and on the close relationship between Hansen and Hague. Driscoll stressed his experience and promised strong and efficient state government. He expressed support for constitutional revision only in the most general terms.

Driscoll's inaugural address revealed that in the eleven-week transition period he had studied the Edison and Edge constitutions carefully. To the surprise of most of his listeners, he called for a constitutional convention, a remedy he had not alluded to in his campaign or postvictory press conferences. Acting in the belief that the Edison constitution had been filibustered to death by a suspicious legislature and that the Edge draft had been defeated by the partisan nature of its guidance through the legislature, Driscoll decided that a limited convention would help the cause by removing it from legislative halls and partisan politics. He gave assurance that the convention would be prohibited from entering the thicket of reapportionment, and the legislature, after wrangling about how many delegates each county would send to the convention, complied with his request. To reassure skeptics who doubted that New Jersey was ready for a new constitution, Driscoll described the 1944 referendum as a defeat for the specific proposal rather than a vote of confidence for the 1844 document then in use.

The governor was responsible for a number of measures to guarantee the orderly transaction of business during the convention and to ameliorate antagonisms that could have jeopardized the new constitution at any point between the start of deliberations in New Brunswick on June 12 and the referendum in November. He marshaled the state government's resources to facilitate the deliberations and to publicize the document. As soon as the legislature approved the convention, he commissioned a Committee on Preparatory Research, headed by state archivist Sidney Goldman, to develop material that might assist the delegates, to help prepare a tentative draft of rules for the convention, and to set up a library of important reference tools close to the delegates. He minimized procedural and partisan quibbling by encouraging county leaders to field bipartisan delegations and by procuring agreement on the convention's officers before the first session.

Driscoll kept informed of the proceedings through transcripts of committee and floor deliberations, briefings with delegate George Walton, his representative at the convention, and appearances as a witness. He intervened personally to bring about at least two compromises that helped save the constitution from the kinds of sectional and religious antagonism that had defeated its 1944 predecessor.

He issued a plea to "isolate" the emotional issue of gambling from the issue of constitutional reform: he seemed to favor leaving an open door for a future referendum on charity raffles and bingo and letting the 1939 referendum on pari-mutuel betting stand intact. The second intervention involved the issue of second-class railroad taxation. When it became apparent that this matter could not be resolved either in committee or on the floor, Driscoll negotiated directly with the Jersey City leaders. They wanted the constitution to prohibit the preferential tax rate that the legislature had awarded the railroads in 1941 and to provide for the assessment of local property (terminals, yards, and stations) at "true value" instead. The administration held out for uniform rules with the legislature empowered to handle specific problems as they arose. A compromise was reached that in effect committed the governor to the repeal of the 1941 statute but did not mention second-class real property. The compromise also strengthened the power of the legislature without abandoning the "true value" clause. Students of the subject cite this compromise as the saving of the constitution, for it guaranteed that Hudson County would not sabotage the document at the polls as it had done in 1944 and was threatening to do again. The rapprochement with the Hague machine was a significant retreat for Driscoll, however, and it involved a minor risk. While in the senate, he had been one of the sponsors of the legislation Hague wished to nullify, and in yielding now to the demands of practicality he angered longtime advocates of constitutional revision, such as Arthur T. Vanderbilt and Walter E. Edge.

Driscoll's unwavering support for a strengthened executive and a streamlined judiciary, which had been cited by a series of former governors as the reforms most needed in New Jersey and as the major reasons for adopting a new constitution, balanced whatever concessions he made to Hudson County in this and other instances. Other highlights of the Driscoll-inspired draft included a merit system for state employees and a guarantee of the right of collective bargaining for persons in private employment; in abolishing segregation in the militia and in public schools, the document made New

Jersey the first state to outlaw segregation constitutionally. Although Governor Edge had long advocated these measures, he had refrained from including them in his draft constitution on the grounds that they represented concessions to special interests. These deletions had made it possible for Hague to instill fear in disappointed interest groups and to encourage them to vote against any draft not specifically addressed to them. The reverse was true of the 1947 draft, which was approved by a plurality of 470,464 votes.

In 1948, the Driscoll administration continued the reorganization of state government begun by the New Jersey Commission on State Administrative Reorganization and further mandated by the new constitution. Some seventy departments were reduced to fourteen, saving the state an estimated $2 million in administrative costs. One important consolidation unified all law enforcement agencies under one administrative head; another merged all fiscal functions into one department with a single director. The law enforcement reforms also allowed the attorney general to supersede local county prosecutors, creating an important weapon for combating organized crime. New Jersey was the first state to consolidate law enforcement and financial functions in this manner, and it was a model for the twenty-eight states that followed suit after 1948.

Another constitutional mandate Driscoll was quick to act on was the commitment to civil rights. He turned over the enforcement of the new provision to the Division Against Discrimination in the Department of Education and threw his weight behind the legislation the division recommended. That legislation included a bill making it a misdemeanor to bar any child from the public schools or to discharge a teacher on grounds of race, religion, or national origin. He also integrated the National Guard at once, preempting efforts to have the secretary of the army help it thwart integration by creating all-black divisions. He signed the Freeman Bill, which prohibited discrimination because of race, color, or creed in any place of public accommodation. The bill, which predated the Civil Rights Act of 1964 by sixteen years, had been in trouble in the legislature until the governor made it part of his legislative program.

In Driscoll's first three years in office, he also raised minimum teachers' salaries from $1,200 to $2,200, effected a temporary-disability insurance program to protect workers from accidents and illness incurred off the job, and updated the parole system.

Driscoll was reelected in 1949 by a plurality of 75,860 votes, defeating state senator Elmer H. Wene, a South Jersey chicken farmer. His victory was regarded as a fatal blow to Frank Hague, who wanted to regain at the state level the power he had lost in Jersey City. Insurgent Democrats in Hague's bastion had passed the word that Driscoll's reelection would be useful to their purpose, and as a result the governor had become the first Republican since Warren G. Harding to carry Jersey City. He won there by sixteen thousand votes, and he only lost Hudson County by thirty-four hundred. The

$100 million slum-clearance and rehabilitation bond issue he supported in that election was less fortunate, but he later secured passage of a $41 million bond issue to build low-cost housing for veterans.

During Driscoll's second administration, the New Jersey Turnpike and the Walt Whitman Bridge were opened, and the Garden State Parkway was begun. The 118-mile turnpike was perhaps the most spectacular of these achievements. The Turnpike Authority, created in 1949, issued its first bonds in 1950, and the highway was built in twenty-three months. Two of the reasons frequently cited for this record construction pace are that the authority commissioned a multitude of contractors and that the governor closely supervised the project, making countless on-the-spot inspection tours. The New Jersey Highway Authority was created to build the Parkway in 1952. The 164-mile road opened in 1954.

In Driscoll's last year in office, he supervised the state's purchases of Island Beach State Park and the 110,000-acre Wharton Tract in South Jersey, which he called "a rich source of water resources and reserves for the future." He also planned the development of Sandy Hook State Park, which was considered New Jersey's future answer to Jones Beach.

Like most recent administrators, Driscoll took steps to confront the problems of organized crime, racketeering, and political corruption, which had long plagued New Jersey. With Governor Thomas E. Dewey of New York, he created the bistate Waterfront Commission in 1950 to remove racketeers from the Hudson River docks. During the same year, the state police broke up a nationwide Western Union bookmaking network and moved in on a statewide narcotics syndicate.

Two scandals erupted during the Driscoll years. Neither directly touched the governor or his close advisers or damaged the credibility of his administration, but both tarnished his reputation as a party leader. The first scandal involved the purchase of two privately owned bridges by the Burlington County Board of Freeholders from a company whose major stockholders were Republican County Chairman and National Guard Chief of Staff Clifford R. Powell and his associates. The state planned to acquire the bridges for $4.9 million through condemnation, but the freeholders, most of whom owed their positions to Powell, purchased them for $12.4 million, selling bonds to a syndicate at a New York meeting. The courts ordered the return of the profits and the bridges, and Driscoll moved to block public purchase of the bonds. Later, acting as commander of the National Guard, he removed Powell from his position in that organization.

The second scandal involved another Republican bastion, Bergen County. Learning of a major gambling scandal there, the governor sent Deputy Attorney General Nelson Stamler to supersede prosecutor Walter G. Winne. Stamler secured indictments and jail sentences against three defendants. Winne was also indicted, but he was later acquitted. Stamler had further success, but before he was finished the state attorney general removed him.

Later, legislative investigation revealed that the brother of one of the defendants had asked the Republican state chairman to have the heat from Trenton removed. It was also learned that another defendant had briefly been employed as a clerk in Driscoll's office. Though the scandal never brought the governor's integrity into question, it revealed his failure to keep a close enough watch over the local and county Republican organizations. The very independence he had maintained from his party throughout his career may have contributed to his negligence. It is altogether likely that Driscoll's preoccupation with policymaking led him to ignore or fail to scrutinize the administrative and partisan aspects of the job of governor as closely as he would have liked.

On his retirement in 1953, Driscoll assumed the presidency of the Warner-Hudnut Company (now the Warner-Lambert Pharmaceutical Company). He continued his activity in governmental affairs, presiding over the National Municipal League, speaking for a citizens' committee for the establishment of the Gateway National Recreation Area, and serving on the 1967 riot commission. He supported a number of his successors' programs, including Governor Richard J. Hughes's ill-fated 1963 bond issue and Governor William T. Cahill's 1972 tax-reform package. In 1970, Governor Cahill named him head of the New Jersey Turnpike Authority, and he occupied that post until his death. He was also an active member of the New Jersey Historical Commission.

Throughout his years as governor and concerned private citizen, Driscoll embraced a concept he called "working federalism." He argued that states should have greater initiative and should cooperate with each other more fully, and the federal government should share more functions with the states. A careful reading of his second inaugural address shows that this concept resembles the idea of revenue sharing, an innovation of the 1970s. Driscoll's denunciation of what he saw as the national government's growing detachment from the public suggests that he would have had much in common with the "anti-Washington" politicians of the contemporary era: "In our republic, it has been the traditional task of the states to protect individual freedom. . . . Despite the contention of some who would put their trust in a strong, centralized government in the nation's capital, Big Government sooner or later ceases to be either representative or responsible. It retains the appearance of a union of states and of popular representation, but abandons the substance."

ALVIN S. FELZENBERG

Records of Governor Alfred E. Driscoll, New Jersey State Library, Trenton, N.J.

Bryan, Brantz Mayer. "Alfred Eastlack Driscoll: Governor of New Jersey." Senior thesis, Princeton University, 1952.

Connors, Richard. *The Process of Constitutional Revision in New Jersey: 1940–1947.* New York: National Municipal League, 1970.

Cutler, Robert G. "Charter Reviewed: The New Jersey Constitution, 1947–1957." Ph.D. dissertation, Princeton University, 1958.

Dunn, Voorhees E., Jr. "The Road to the 1947 New Jersey Constitution: Arthur T. Vanderbilt's Influence on Court Reform, 1930–1947." *New Jersey History* 104 (Fall–Winter 1986): 23–41.

Felzenberg, Alvin S. "The Impact of Gubernatorial Style on Policy Outcomes: An In-Depth Study of Three New Jersey Governors." Ph.D. dissertation, Princeton University, 1978.

Morris, Joe Alex. "His Heart Belongs to Jersey." *Saturday Evening Post* 225 (July 5, 1952): 36–37, 54–56.

Wood, Robert C. "The Metropolitan Governor." Ph.D. dissertation, Harvard University, 1950.

Robert B. Meyner

New Jersey State Archives; Department of State

Robert Baumle Meyner (July 3, 1908–May 27, 1990), lawyer, governor of New Jersey, was born in Easton, Pennsylvania, the son of Gustave Herman and Mary Sophie (Baumle) Meyner. His parents, who were of German and Swiss ancestry, came from humble backgrounds: his father worked as a loom fixer and silk worker. When Robert was eight, his family moved to Phillipsburg, New Jersey. Except for a short stay at Paterson, his family remained in Phillipsburg. The need to earn a living occupied his youth, and he worked in various jobs as a newspaper boy, grocery clerk, garage mechanic, and foundry handyman. In 1926 Meyner graduated from Phillipsburg High School and entered Lafayette College in Easton, Pennsylvania, financing his education by working in the silk mills near Easton and Phillipsburg. He developed an early interest in politics in 1928, when he became president of the Young People's Al Smith for President Club at Lafayette.

From 1930 to 1933 he attended Columbia University Law School, and in 1934 he was admitted to the New Jersey bar. Working as a law clerk for the firm J. Emil Walscheid and Milton Rosenkranz in Union City and later in Jersey City, Meyner gained "a lot of experience but little money." Offered an opportunity to take over the practice of a deceased lawyer in Phillipsburg, Meyner returned to his native city in 1936. The next year he became a counselor, and in 1940 he was admitted to practice before the United States Supreme Court. His practice centered on trial work. Early in his career he recognized the need for judicial integrity when he "suffered several traumatic experiences with judges." In Warren County he built a political base through his active role in the local, state, and national bar associations— along with his work in civic and social organizations.

In 1941 Meyner first ran for political office but lost in the primary for the Warren County state senate seat. After the start of World War II he left for the military. On August 3 1943, he enlisted in the navy at the rank of lieutenant (j.g.). He used his legal training to defend sailors in court-martial trials, and later he became the commander of a gun crew on a merchant vessel. Discharged December 1945 as a lieutenant commander, he kept this rank in the naval reserve and returned to law and politics. In 1946 he ran for congressman against the powerful, and later infamous, J. Parnell Thomas, but the election went easily to Thomas. Meyner gained a political victory in 1947 when he defeated Republican Wayne Dumont, Jr., for the state senate seat in Warren County. From 1947 to 1951 Meyner gained political experience through work with legislative and party leaders and exerted his independence by criticizing the Republican administration for failing to clean up the corruption in Bergen County. Another expression of his strong will appeared when he cast the sole dissenting vote against the creation of the New Jersey Turnpike Authority, deprecating all such bodies because "they become grossly irresponsible to the will of the people." During his term as senator Meyner became minority leader in 1950 and permanent chairman of the Democratic state convention. Despite party recognition, he experienced political defeat once again, when he lost his senate seat to Dumont in a close race in 1951.

By 1953 Meyner seemed a has-been candidate. Few people thought that he would emerge as the Democratic choice for governor. Being from a rural county and having failed even to carry his home district, Meyner had an added political liability, his religion—he was an apostate from the Roman Catholic Church. Nevertheless, luck and hard work (two important reasons for his political success) reversed his fortune. Since 1949, New Jersey Democrats had been divided by a vacuum in state leadership. John V. Kenny had defeated the former state boss, Frank Hague, in his native Jersey City. A bloody political battle followed. Hague and his followers tried for the fourth time to regain power by supporting Elmer H. Wene, a flamboyant chicken farmer from South Jersey, in the 1953 Democratic gubernatorial primary. Kenny and other county leaders refused to accept Wene. In desperation they turned to Robert Meyner. Offered a unique opportunity, the Warren County senator accepted and later commented, "I realized I had very little chance to win, but I knew it was the only chance I would ever have. I jumped at it."

Meyner's judgment proved correct. Winning only three out of New Jersey's twenty-one counties, he defeated Wene by only 1,683 votes, thanks in large measure to Hudson County's boss, John V. Kenny, and his 30,000-vote majority in that county. In the general election Meyner faced a strong Republican opponent. The Republicans, who had held the governor's office for ten years, selected Paul L. Troast, a contractor who was chairman of the New Jersey Turnpike Authority. Meyner campaigned for strict law enforcement and again criticized the Republicans for making New Jersey "a mecca for syndicated gambling and a haven for the underworld." Meyner's campaign gained momentum when a prison scandal marred his opponent's reputation. Newspaper stories revealed that in 1951 Troast had written a letter to New York Governor Thomas E. Dewey asking commutation of the prison sentence of a convicted labor racketeer and extortionist, Joseph S. Fay. The famous "Fay Letter" became the turning point in the election. Meyner went on to victory with a 153,653-vote majority.

When elected governor, Meyner presented an imposing figure. Relatively young at forty-five, he was almost six feet tall, and his gray, curly hair and baritone voice made him physically a model governor. His political style was less glamorous. He was cautious, skeptical, and guarded in facing problems. Having boundless energy and an even temperament, he seemed well suited to govern a rapidly growing state. New Jersey was in the midst of a dynamic era, and Meyner's administration reflected this change.

Meyner expressed an intense commitment to open government in his inaugural address of January 19, 1954: "I am a strong advocate of submitting important questions to the people on the ground that it makes for livelier, more responsive, and more responsible democracy." He followed this policy in March 1954, when he began a series of television-radio reports on the activities of the state administration. He courted the press by scheduling two news conferences a week, and he arranged a separate conference for editors of weeklies. In an attempt to gain bipartisan support for his legislative program, the governor held prelegislative conferences with both party leaders.

A major theme throughout Meyner's gubernatorial years was his pledge to staff his administration "with men and women who see government as a great challenge to imagination and enterprise." He often incurred the wrath of party leaders but remained determined to "get people into politics who aren't out to make a buck, who aren't out to take advantage of everything." Republicans and business and labor leaders provided him advice and men to help fill four cabinet posts.

Adhering to his promise to clean house, Meyner in his first year as governor concentrated on exposing corruption in the Division of Employment Security. Harold G. Hoffman, a former governor (1935–38), headed the division. When Meyner discovered irregularities, he sought the assistance of Prudential Insurance officials to accelerate the payment of unemployment insurance. After an initial inspection, Hoffman was suspended for improprieties. He died during the investigation, and Meyner was accused of "killing him." But a letter Hoffman wrote to his daughter just before his death disclosed that he had used $300,000 in state funds to cover an embezzlement from the South Amboy Trust Company, of which he was president.

Meyner's first four years included more than exposing corruption and

making qualified appointments. They saw the legalization of bingo and raffles, substantial increases in state aid to education, and the restructuring
of Rutgers University to be "truly a state university." Teachers' salaries were
also increased, as was aid to children with mental and physical disabilities.
All fourteen state departments were reorganized to provide more efficient
and closer communication with the public. Meyner centralized and mecha-
nized motor vehicle registration and streamlined the budget bureau. Government costs were carefully regulated by vetoes of special-interest bills and
investments of state funds in higher-interest-returning securities. Meyner
presaged the women's liberation movement by appointing the first woman
cabinet member in New Jersey. In appointing judges, he carefully screened
applicants and selected men of high stature. He showed conviction in supporting his appointees, as when he vigorously backed Joseph Weintraub's
supervision of the bistate Waterfront Commission.

On state finances the governor preferred to follow rather than to lead the
public. Faced with a Republican-dominated legislature, he refused to broach
the problem of restructuring the state's tax system with an income or sales
tax. Meyner relied on increases in excise taxes to finance a constantly rising
state budget.

As the leader of his party Meyner helped build the Democratic Party
throughout the state, and he made the party a twenty-one-county organization instead of the one-county, Hudson-dominated machine it had been for
thirty years under Frank Hague. Meyner also spoke forcibly against McCar-
thyism and criticized the Wisconsin senator's activities as "a perversion of
basic American principles." The energetic governor also used his office to
defend court rulings on civil liberties and civil rights. Because of his capable
administration and a nationally publicized romance, Meyner's popularity
grew throughout his first term. In January 1957 he married Helen Day Stevenson, a distant cousin of Adlai Stevenson and the daughter of Eleanor B.
and William E. Stevenson, the president of Oberlin College. Meyner's marriage, his ability as an orator, and his charming style made him the "Glamorous Governor of New Jersey." In 1957 Meyner ran for reelection against state
senator Malcolm S. Forbes. Meyner became the first governor to be reelected
for a four-year term when he defeated Forbes by more than two hundred
thousand votes and led the Democrats to control of the assembly. Respected
by both Democrats and Republicans, Meyner was at the pinnacle of his political career. Throughout his second term he groomed himself for the possibility of national office by traveling widely, commenting on foreign policy, and
criticizing President Dwight D. Eisenhower; however, at home he continued
to be a prudent administrator.

Meyner focused attention on the state's transportation problems. In dealing with rail and road problems, he relied on his highway commissioner,
Dwight R. G. Palmer. Symbolic of the rubber and concrete era, Meyner spent
$93 million a year for road building. However, he did not ignore the rail

services. A Rail Transportation Division was formed in the Highway Department to provide for rail improvements and consolidations. Rail subsidies were provided, and in 1959 a mass-transit plan was proposed. Funds from the New Jersey Turnpike Authority were to be diverted to aid the deteriorating railroads, but opposition from Hudson County and rural areas defeated the proposal. Plans to have the Port of New York Authority take over the bankrupt Hudson and Manhattan Tubes were initiated. At the end of Meyner's administration he advocated the construction of a jetport in Morris County, but he failed to convince the public. He constantly emphasized traffic safety, and New Jersey had one of the best safety records in the country.

Strong on conservation, Meyner started the reclamation of fifteen thousand acres of North Jersey's meadowland through the creation of the Meadowland Regional Development Agency. A "Green Acres" program attempted to regain land for recreational use. Educational expansion continued with increased construction and appropriations for higher education. Notable advances were also made in mental health, treatment of juvenile delinquents, care of the aged, and consumer protection. The state's economy prospered with heavy investments in new industrial plants and the extensive growth of New Jersey's research facilities. Meyner continued to avoid a broad-base tax by using a corporate income tax.

Meyner's success as governor led him to the 1960 National Democratic Convention with the hope of achieving a national office or at least helping to determine the convention's choice. He joined Stuart Symington and Lyndon B. Johnson in an attempt to block the nomination of John F. Kennedy. But his luck and good timing ran out. Refusing to allow the New Jersey delegation to vote for Kennedy on the first ballot, Meyner lost the opportunity to make New Jersey the deciding state. Meyner had failed to emulate his idol, Woodrow Wilson, and his political career began to decline. The Kennedys did not forget his actions in 1960.

Meyner spent his last years as governor in recommending further improvements in transportation and education. When he concluded his term, he returned to law and private industry—accepting lucrative positions with banks and insurance companies and becoming the administrator of the cigarette industry's code on fair advertising. In 1969 he attempted to regain the governorship (having been constitutionally prohibited from running in 1961) and won the Democratic primary. But the charisma and appeal of the 1950s were gone. He lost in a one-sided race to William Cahill.

Meyner's stewardship of New Jersey left a legacy of efficiency and economy in government. Though not a social reformer or experimenter, he was certainly a good administrator. Perhaps he best expressed his philosophy of government and life in his first inaugural address: "Above all, we must ever be conscious that in government, as in life, nothing is ever permanently settled, nothing ever disposed of beyond the need for cautious study and action. It is a timeless process and an endless campaign against smug self-approval."

In later years Meyner pursued an active legal and business career. He also supported his wife Helen's involvement in politics. Helen Meyner was twice elected to Congress (1974 and 1976) but was defeated for reelection in 1978. In declining health after suffering a stroke Meyner died at his home in Captiva, Florida, in 1990.

WILLIAM LEMMEY

Robert B. and Helen Stevenson Meyner Papers, Lafayette College, Easton, Pa.

Records of Governor Robert B. Meyner, New Jersey State Library, Trenton, N.J.

Doig, Jameson W. *Empire on the Hudson: Entrepreneurial Vision and Political Power at the Port of New York Authority.* New York: Columbia University Press, 2001.

Felzenberg, Alvin S. "The Impact of Gubernatorial Style on Policy Outcomes: An In-Depth Study of Three New Jersey Governors." Ph.D. dissertation, Princeton University, 1978.

Richard Joseph Hughes (August 10, 1909 – December 7, 1992), lawyer, two-term governor, chief justice of the state supreme court, was born in Florence, Burlington County, to Richard Paul Hughes and Veronica (Gallagher) Hughes. His father, an ironworker and insurance broker, served as a state civil service commissioner, as principal keeper of Trenton State Prison, and as Burlington County Democratic chairman and was otherwise active in politics and public affairs.

Richard J. Hughes graduated from Cathedral High School in Trenton, after which he studied at St. Charles College in Catonsville, Maryland, and at St. Joseph's College in Philadelphia. At one time he intended to become a Roman Catholic priest, but he turned to the

Richard J. Hughes
New Jersey State Archives; Department of State

study of law, receiving an LL.B. from New Jersey Law School in 1931. Admitted to the bar in 1932, he opened a law office in Trenton.

In 1937, after entering Democratic politics in Mercer County, he was elected statewide president of the Young Democrats and Democratic State Committee member from Mercer County. In 1938 he ran as a "Roosevelt Democrat" for Congress from the Fourth District. Though he lost decisively to Republican D. Lane Powers, he drew attention as a vigorous campaigner.

Appointed assistant United States attorney for New Jersey in December 1939, he prosecuted mail fraud, illegal tax withholding, and wartime subversion by members of the German-American Vocational League and similar groups. His careful preparations—and frequent convictions—enhanced his reputation and earned him a press accolade as "the nemesis of Nazis in New Jersey."

For Hughes the call of politics was irresistible. "I like politics," he said. "I think our politics for the next few years is going to be vitally important if we're going to keep our children out of another war." After he was elected Mercer County Democratic chairman in June 1945, he left his federal post and resumed private practice with Thorn Lord, who had been United States attorney over him. Lord and Hughes collaborated in politics as well as law, and under their leadership the Democrats won control of the Mercer County government in 1948.

On September 1, 1948, Acting Governor John M. Summerill, Jr., nominated Hughes to be judge of the Court of Common Pleas (which shortly thereafter was changed under the court reorganization to Mercer County Court). In February 1952, when William J. Brennan, Jr., was appointed to the state supreme court, Governor Alfred E. Driscoll named Hughes to replace him as superior court judge. Hughes was later designated assignment judge for Union County and eventually promoted to the appellate division of superior court.

Hughes's interest in juvenile problems and his reputation for being tough but fair and hardworking led Chief Justice Arthur T. Vanderbilt to appoint him head of a committee reviewing statutes that affected juvenile and domestic relations and probation services. The supreme court accepted that committee's recommendations, and as a result the state's juvenile and domestic-relations courts were revised.

Several times Governor Robert B. Meyner considered Hughes for appointment to the state supreme court. Rather than rise further in the courts, however, Hughes resigned from the bench in November 1957 and resumed private law to support his family. (His first wife, the former Miriam McGrory, whom he had married in 1934, had died in 1950, leaving three sons and a daughter. In 1954 he had married Elizabeth [Sullivan] Murphy, a widow with three sons. The couple had a daughter and two sons.) In a lucrative private law practice Hughes represented the Association of New Jersey Railroads and the Public Service Electric & Gas Company in legislative hearings and rate cases, and he defended polio vaccine manufacturers against antitrust charges.

With Governor Meyner's second term ending, state Democratic leaders divided over a successor. Hughes, backed by Lord, the Mercer County chairman, became a compromise choice, and the leaders from the other counties accepted him in February 1961. His Republican opponent was James P. Mitchell, who had been secretary of labor under President Dwight D. Eisenhower. Since both candidates were Roman Catholics, New Jersey was assured of its first governor of that faith one year after John F. Kennedy was elected as the country's first Catholic president. Mitchell was better known, but Hughes was a better campaigner. Hughes's heartiness, wit, familiarity with state problems, criticism of Mitchell for refusing to debate, and tactful identification with Meyner's achievements generated considerable momentum. Mitchell, handicapped by a broken leg, waged a lackluster campaign. On November 7, 1961, in a major upset, Hughes defeated Mitchell, 1,084,194 votes to 1,049,274. But the legislature remained divided, the senate under Republican control and the general assembly under the Democrats.

Hughes's basic first-term problem was to expand state operations adequately to serve a rapidly growing population. He was constrained by the narrowness of his electoral mandate, by limited revenue due to lack of a broad-based tax, by county political organizations wary of gubernatorial power, and by a public uneducated to state needs. He stumped ceaselessly to build public support for the expansion of governmental operations and other policies he generally termed "Northern Democratic liberalism." By negotiating realistically, he got Republican senate leaders to cooperate on compromise legislation, even though he was feuding with them over their "advise and consent" role on his nominations and vowing to destroy their "vicious" caucus.

His essential optimism helped him survive the voters' decisive rejection of his $750 million capital construction bond referendum in November 1963, for which he campaigned exhaustively and through which he hoped to defer the tax question and aid the state's economy. In that election the Democrats lost fourteen legislative seats; former governor Meyner virtually declared his willingness to be the next Democratic gubernatorial candidate if Hughes chose not to run again, and the archcritical *Newark Evening News* called for Hughes's resignation. Rebounding, he proposed an income tax on February 3, 1964, to finance his record $590 million budget for 1964–65. His proposal stimulated debate but got nowhere.

In Hughes's first term he provided swift emergency relief to the seashore after a severe storm battered it in March 1962; suspended land sales in the Hackensack Meadows pending resolution of title claims; created the Commission to Study Meadowlands Development in May 1963, appointing Meyner as chairman; brought the Democratic National Convention for the first time to New Jersey (Atlantic City, August 1964); vetoed a bill requiring children in public schools to salute the flag and pledge allegiance in contravention to a United States Supreme Court ruling (June 1964); secured the takeover of the Hudson and Manhattan Railroad by the Port of New York Authority in return for approval of the construction of the World Trade Center; formed a citizens' committee, headed by Princeton University president Robert F. Goheen, to examine public higher education; and supported police behavior during civil disorders in Jersey City and Paterson, meanwhile urging social reforms to eliminate causes of discontent.

The character of the 1965 gubernatorial campaign shaped Hughes's second term. He expected sharp campaign debates on state priorities, based on his record and his charges of "legislative inaction." Instead, his Republican rival, state senator Wayne Dumont, Jr., revived the flag-salute controversy and vigorously belabored Hughes for not forcing Rutgers, the state university, to dismiss history professor Eugene D. Genovese, who had welcomed "the impending Viet Cong victory in Viet Nam" at a teach-in. Hughes upheld United States policy in Vietnam and called Genovese "outrageously wrong" but nevertheless stoutly defended his right to speak. When Dumont refused to drop the issue and implied that Hughes was tolerating treason, Hughes charged him with disregarding the Bill of Rights and instigating a process that would end in "book burning and concentration camps." The emotional dispute galvanized liberals and independents behind Hughes, who already had substantial labor support. He swept to victory on November 2, 1965, with 1,279,589 votes to Dumont's 915,996, a record plurality. Further, both legislative branches came under Democratic control for the first time since 1914.

Hughes now had a clear mandate, but he needed a major new source of revenue, He staked all on an income tax. He expected speedy legislative approval in the belief that many Democrats who owed their seats to his sweeping victory would vote along party lines. Consequently he neglected to court the Republicans energetically or to appeal to the wider public. However, he underestimated the Democratic legislators' fear of voter reprisal and overvalued the key Democratic county chairmen's reluctant commitments of support. With some Democrats defecting and Republicans solidly opposed, his income-tax bill only narrowly passed the general assembly on March 17, 1966, and it never reached the floor of the senate, where it faced certain defeat. A chastened Hughes, "the most regular of Regular Democrats," never again relied solely on his party or its chiefs to back major legislation. Turning to a sales tax, he quickly reasserted leadership, secured bipartisan support, and enlisted a sizable public coalition that induced the legislature on April 26, 1966, to pass New Jersey's first permanent broad-based tax and finance an $875 million state budget.

Encouraged by this success, Hughes's administration released a torrent of bills for legislative action that altered the scope and structure of state government and its relationship to the people. But the Democratic tide ebbed in November 1967, when Republicans captured the legislature in sufficient strength to override gubernatorial vetoes. Hughes, therefore, in his final two years, made more compromises than he might have wished on measures affecting the large cities and increasing governmental services. During his eight years 2,174 laws were enacted, more than under any other governor except A. Harry Moore, who served nine years, and Alfred E. Driscoll, who served seven.

Some of the notable legislative and administrative actions in Hughes's second term involved the functions and organization of state government. The Department of Community Affairs became operative in March 1967, the State Commission of Investigation was created for a five-year period in January 1969, and the Division of Criminal Justice, the Office of State Public

Defender, and the Office of Consumer Protection were set up in the Department of Law and Public Safety. The Department of Transportation replaced the State Highway Department in May 1966; it had an enlarged mission to upgrade rail and bus services. The Hackensack Meadowlands Commission was established in November 1968 to plan orderly development for a vast tract in the northeastern part of the state.

The state's role in education grew when the Department of Higher Education, separate from the existing Department of Education, was created in January 1967 with a chancellor and a state board. The county community college system was established in 1966, and construction was begun on new public medical schools at Newark and Piscataway between 1968 and 1970. Two new state colleges were approved, and fiscal autonomy was granted to the state colleges in 1969.

In finance, the Sales and Use Tax Act, with an initial levy of 3 percent, became effective in July 1966; banks got permission to expand across county lines, and voters approved a state lottery in a referendum in November 1969.

The public service roles of state governmental agencies and public authorities expanded enormously at this time. The Garden State Arts Center was constructed, despite a cost overrun from an estimated $1.6 million to over $6.5 million. Funding for the Public Broadcasting Authority was approved by referendum in November 1968, and the first state funds were allotted the New Jersey Symphony Orchestra in December 1969. In 1968 the Housing Finance Agency was set up within the Department of Community Affairs and a $12.5 million low-income housing-assistance bond referendum was passed, and in May 1969 Hughes signed a bill that would eventually provide $1 million to tear down dilapidated structures in cities. Among Hughes's last measures was to sign into law in January 1970 an act allowing people to challenge alleged exclusionary zoning in communities they did not live in.

Two new bridges across the Delaware River in South Jersey were started in 1966, and a $640 million transportation bond referendum was approved by the voters in November 1968. The New Jersey Historical Commission was established in the Department of Education in 1966, and an Educational Opportunity Fund Act, providing support to college-bound disadvantaged youth, was enacted in 1968. In January 1969 the legislature appropriated $23 million as the state's share of county and municipal welfare costs. The Migrant Labor Act of December 1967 set higher living standards for seasonal farm workers, but an act providing unemployment benefits to striking workers, passed in April 1967, was repealed in February 1968. Purchasers of firearms were required to secure police identification cards (June 1966). These and similar measures that increased the dimensions of governmental authority and operations during Hughes's second term generally paralleled the greatly enlarged role of the federal government under President Lyndon B. Johnson's "Great Society" programs of the mid-1960s.

On July 14, 1967, Newark's Mayor Hugh J. Addonizio asked Hughes to dispatch state police and National Guardsmen to end civil disorders in the black ghetto of the city. Hughes took personal charge of the law enforcement operations. He termed the disorders "plain and simple crime and not a civil rights protest" and asserted that "the line between the jungle and the law might as well be drawn here as any place in America." Hughes soon grasped the deeper socioeconomic causes of Newark's crisis. But his initial stance helped shape public opinion and perhaps encouraged excessively forceful police and National Guard actions that injured and killed innocent persons and prolonged the unrest. When violence erupted in Plainfield on July 16, Hughes allowed the state police to search without warrants for stolen weapons in a black neighborhood.

A commission of ten prominent citizens whom he named to analyze the disorders and recommend steps to prevent recurrence barely mentioned his role and actions in its report, issued in February 1968. Hughes hailed the report as "historic" but delayed implementing its recommendations because he was grappling with personal pessimism over urban problems and with the fear of voter backlash against his party. Members of the commission and of his cabinet increased the pressure for remedial action.

Further disorders followed the murder of Martin Luther King, Jr., on April 4, and he delivered a special legislative message on April 25 calling for a "moral recommitment" to the cities. He requested an initial $126.1 million to aid ghetto schools, improve law enforcement, and relieve local welfare burdens. The legislature appropriated $58.5 million, enough to start an urban aid program, and Hughes, consistent in his urban-oriented liberalism, voiced the conviction that the problems of New Jersey's cities were soluble.

Hughes was known nationally for stalwart support of the foreign policies of presidents John F. Kennedy and Lyndon B. Johnson. He once described the latter as "the master strategist of the century." He served on a presidential advisory committee on civil defense until 1967. He helped arrange Johnson's meeting with Soviet Premier Alexei Kosygin, June 23–25, 1967, at the state college in Glassboro. In August 1967 Johnson appointed Hughes to a panel to observe the South Vietnamese elections, which the governor judged to be open and fair. He did not break publicly with Johnson's policies until October 30, 1968, when he urged a bombing halt and a United States withdrawal from Vietnam. In March 1968 he became chairman of the Democratic Party's Equal Rights Committee.

At the party's Chicago convention in August he headed the eighty-vote New Jersey delegation, which endorsed Senator Hubert H. Humphrey's nomination for the presidency. Hughes served as chairman of the convention's Credentials Committee, which screened over one thousand delegate challenges. His firm handling of the challenges on the basis of nondiscrimination won overwhelming convention approval, but he lost his own rather low-keyed quest for the vice presidential nomination to Senator Edmund Muskie. Hughes was "bitterly disappointed" by what he termed "the hate vote" which Governor George Wallace got in the presidential elections in New Jersey in November 1968, and he felt it facilitated Richard M. Nixon's capture of the state. After the Democratic defeat Hughes urged the party to make internal reforms, press voter registration, and build "a coalition which includes labor and the blacks to correct such problems as urban ills." In Richard Nixon's first year in office Hughes criticized the president for reducing urban assistance programs without seeking comparable cuts in funds for antiballistic missiles and the supersonic transport.

At the end of his governorship Hughes maintained that he had fulfilled his intentions of giving the state a sense of identity and destiny and aiding "the forgotten New Jerseyans." On January 16, 1970, he declared his family's net worth, which was $178,986; this unprecedented step exemplified the public disclosure he advocated for state officials.

He resumed private law practice, joining the Newark firm of Hughes, McElroy, Connell, Foley & Geiser and becoming chairman of the American Bar Association's commission on improving prison facilities and rehabilitation procedures. He was named state Democratic national committeeman on February 27, 1970.

After state supreme court Chief Justice Pierre P. Garven died, Governor William T. Cahill nominated Hughes to replace him. Confirmed by the senate, Hughes was sworn on December 18, 1973, the first person in modern history to have been both governor and chief justice of New Jersey.

As chief justice he directed an increasingly activist court, which handed down pathbreaking decisions on zoning, legislative redistricting, and thorough and efficient education. In 1979, when he reached the mandatory retirement age of seventy, he went back to private legal practice. Hughes died of congestive heart failure in 1992, in Boca Raton, Florida. He was interred in St. Mary's Cemetery in Trenton.

STANLEY B. WINTERS

Records of Governor Richard J. Hughes, New Jersey State Library, Trenton, N.J.

Doig, Jameson W. *Empire on the Hudson: Entrepreneurial Vision and Political Power at the Port of New York Authority*. New York: Columbia University Press, 2001.

Felzenberg, Alvin S. "The Impact of Gubernatorial Style on Policy Outcomes: An In-Depth Study of Three New Jersey Governors." Ph.D. dissertation, Princeton University, 1978.

———. "The Making of a Governor: The Early Political Career of Richard J. Hughes." *New Jersey History* 101 (Spring–Summer 1983): 1–28.

Leone, Richard C. "The Politics of Gubernatorial Leadership: Tax and Education Reform in New Jersey." Ph.D. dissertation, Princeton University, 1969.

Report of the National Advisory Commission on Civil Disorders. Washington, D.C.: U.S. Government Printing Office, 1968.

Wefing, John B. *The Life and Times of Richard J. Hughes: The Politics of Civility*. New Brunswick: Rutgers University Press, 2009.

William T. Cahill
New Jersey State Archives; Department of State

William Thomas Cahill (June 25, 1912–July 1, 1996) was born in Philadelphia. His parents, William and Rose (Golden) Cahill, moved to Camden in 1919. William, their only child, attended St. Mary's Grammar School and Camden Catholic High School. He graduated with a B.A. degree from Philadelphia's St. Joseph's College in 1933. While attending South Jersey (Rutgers) Law School and receiving the LL.B. in 1937, he taught in the Camden public school system. Cahill served briefly as an FBI agent, but after passing the state bar in 1939, he entered the private practice of law in Camden. On February 1, 1941, he was married to a former high school classmate, Elizabeth Myrtetus. The couple would eventually have eight children, six girls and two boys.

At various times Cahill filled public offices typically held by politically oriented lawyers. He was Camden city prosecutor, 1944–45, and assistant county prosecutor, 1948–51. As a special deputy attorney general in 1951 he took part in a state investigation of organized crime and gambling in Bergen County. In 1951 Cahill also made his first try for elective public office, a successful campaign for state assemblyman. He served but one term, choosing a return to full-time law practice after the end of the 1953 legislative session. In 1958 he returned to the political wars, winning a congressional seat in a district drawn from Camden, Gloucester, and Salem Counties. He was reelected from this First District in 1960, 1962, and 1964 and, following reapportionment, from the Sixth District in 1966 and 1968. In the House of Representatives, Cahill was a member of the Judiciary Committee. He took particular interest in anticrime, civil rights, and consumer affairs legislation, but he was also active in such areas as medical education, housing, and immigration. Cahill developed an issue image much like that of United States Senator Clifford P. Case, one of moderate-to-liberal Republicanism. And, like Case, he generally enjoyed the support of organized labor.

Cahill's name was presented to the GOP's screening committee as a possible gubernatorial nominee in 1965, but he eventually withdrew it. He did not contest the nomination of state senator Wayne Dumont, Jr. (Dumont, however, had to overcome a primary challenge by South Jersey Congressman Charles W. Sandman.) In 1969 Cahill, Sandman, and three other GOP hopefuls engaged in a free-swinging primary battle. Cahill was triumphant. He had received strong support from Bergen County party chairman Nelson

Gross, who was riding the crest of his own success as Richard M. Nixon's New Jersey strategist in 1968. During both primary and general election campaigns Cahill projected a political personality as a blunt, forthright individual balanced by a quick smile and the traditional Irish sense of humor. Physically, in 1969 he was of medium build, five feet nine inches and 175 pounds, with gray hair and a ruddy complexion.

Cahill's Democratic opponent in the gubernatorial contest was former governor Robert B. Meyner, who argued that he had the experience and sensitivity to meet the challenges ahead. It was "a matter of record," the Democratic nominee argued, that he had the capacity to manage the state's affairs prudently and effectively. Cahill, for his part, characterized the Meyner administrations of the 1950s as "do-little," and he argued that Meyner himself was a passé politician who lacked the vision necessary to handle the increasing responsibilities of the governorship. Cahill endeavored to project the image of a dynamic, progressive statesman—"the" man to meet the needs of New Jersey.

There was more to the 1969 campaign than image projection; there were gut political questions as well. Could the Republicans sustain their party's momentum after the Nixon landslide? Would the hostility of Hudson County boss John V. Kenny and segments of organized labor deprive Meyner of the big-county vote usually considered essential for a Democratic victory? Did the voters want to give the GOP a chance at the statehouse after sixteen years of Democratic control? Did they accept the Republican cry that it was "Sixteen Years Downhill. Time to Go Cahill"? The answers to these questions were apparently all in the affirmative, for on November 4, 1969, the Republicans achieved a classic landslide victory. Cahill swept twenty of twenty-one counties, and his party won impressive majorities in both houses of the state legislature—thirty-one to nine in the senate, fifty-nine to twenty-one in the general assembly. Thus Cahill was in a position rare for a New Jersey governor—facing a friendly legislature—when he took over as the state's chief executive on January 20, 1970.

In his brief inaugural address Governor Cahill pledged to root out corruption in government and refurbish the state's political image, badly tarnished by recurrent scandals involving organized crime and errant public officials. In setting a functional tone for his administration, Cahill implied that he would continue down the paths mapped out by the regimes of the 1960s. He placed particular emphasis on doing more—and better—in the fields of education, law enforcement, and transportation, but he also promised action in such areas as housing and health care. These programs would require funding, and here the new governor faced his first crisis: a projected $268 million deficit for fiscal 1971. The outgoing Hughes administration had largely developed the budget for the new year, but it was Cahill's responsibility to introduce it and suggest how to achieve the income-outgo balance mandated by the state constitution. Cahill opted for a two-cent increase in the sales tax to bridge the budget gap, and the GOP-controlled legislature passed an authorizing statute on February 9.

The governor believed that this was a stopgap measure—that the state sorely needed tax and administrative reform to meet the needs of the 1970s adequately and efficiently. Accordingly, two study groups were authorized by executive order in the spring of 1970. The first was the Governor's Management Study Commission, headed by Prudential Insurance Company vice president William S. Field. The second, the New Jersey Tax Policy Committee, chaired by state senator Harry L. Sears, included such blue-ribbon names as former governors Driscoll and Hughes. The management committee would report back that November; the tax committee did not issue its report until February 1972.

Meanwhile, the governor took advantage of Republican dominance to move a diversified program through the legislature in 1970–71. In the field of education, for example, Rutgers Medical School was merged with the New Jersey College of Medicine and Dentistry, a program of state aid to private and parochial schools was inaugurated, and in October 1970 the so-called Bateman School Funding Act was passed. This law attempted to provide additional state funds for ratable-poor school districts and those with large numbers of disadvantaged students. Finally, in November 1971, the voters approved a $155 million bond issue for higher-education facilities.

In the area of law enforcement new legislation placed prosecutors in the six most populous counties on a full-time basis and created a Division of Criminal Justice to aid the attorney general in dealing with statewide crime and official corruption. In November 1970 the life of the temporary State Commission of Investigation, set up in 1968 to combat organized crime, was extended for five years. Cahill also promoted an ambitious drug-control program that received statutory foundation in a Controlled Dangerous Substances law, as well as in new measures dealing with drug education and treatment.

The 1970–71 legislators, active in the environmental field, passed a solid-waste-management act promoting regional solutions to New Jersey's refuse problems and a wetlands act giving the state controls over land use and pollution in estuaries and tidal areas. In November 1971 an $80 million "Green Acres" bond issue was approved, enabling New Jersey to continue its program of acquiring land for recreation and conservation. The Republican administration could also claim credit for a consumer-protection law and a new program of financial aid to New Jersey's urban centers.

As indicated, Cahill's administrative study commission issued its report late in 1970. Reflecting a business management perspective, the report contained some seven hundred recommendations covering the state's seventeen principal departments, as well as sundry state and interstate agencies. One of its major aims was to reduce the governor's span of control by consolidating the functions of fifteen departments into four new "super-departments"

—administration, planning and control, public services, and development. A reorganized attorney general's department would remain, but the secretary of state would be reduced to the role of the governor's political adviser, with scant administrative responsibility. A second key goal was to give the governor a centralized bloc of management controls—personnel, budgeting, purchasing, planning—over the state bureaucracy. The Civil Service Commission was to be abolished, and many of its functions would be transferred to the proposed department of administration.

Such drastic executive-branch changes would upset existing agency-clientele relationships, reduce the number of patronage positions available for political favorites, and decimate the civil service system—small wonder, then, that the legislature rejected the commission's two central themes. Nonetheless, the Cahill administration carried out a number of its suggestions via executive order, administrative directive, and, in a few cases, specific statutory authorization.

As William Cahill closed out the first half of his term, he had a generally impressive record. In addition to legislative and administrative accomplishments, it contained other "plus" items. Under his aegis a successful state lottery was begun, the New York football Giants were enticed into the sports complex being constructed in the Hackensack Meadows, and riots in the Rahway prison and Yardville correctional center were dealt with in a firm yet humane manner. On the negative side, New Jersey's cities showed few signs of revival, a chronic housing shortage continued, and the costs of proliferating welfare and education programs put inexorable pressure on the state budget. Two special messages from the governor failed to stimulate legislative action in the housing crisis. Finally, the November 1971 elections curbed Republican legislative power. The GOP majority in the senate was reduced to twenty-four to sixteen, while the new assembly contained forty Democrats, thirty-nine Republicans, and one independent. The votes of four Hudson County Democrats enabled the GOP to secure the assembly speakership for 1972–73, but the party situation in the lower house was perilously close to stalemate.

The watershed year of the Cahill administration was 1972, the year it attempted basic fiscal reform, failed, and never regained its momentum. As the year began events conspired to bring the state's fiscal problems into sharp focus. On January 19 Superior Court Judge Theodore Botter, in the landmark case *Robinson v. Cahill*, declared New Jersey's system of school finance unconstitutional and mandated that the legislature develop a new one. On February 14 Cahill presented the state with its first $2 billion budget, including a projected deficit of $126.8 million. On February 23 New Jersey's Tax Policy Committee submitted its five-volume report and recommendations.

The committee's objective was a "balanced" tax structure for New Jersey, to be achieved by drastically reducing the role of the local property tax in New Jersey finance. The committee proposed that the state assume most of the responsibility for school support, that counties be relieved of such financial burdens as courts and welfare, and that a new, bloc-grant approach to urban aid be adopted. To fund this revolutionary shift in state-local responsibilities, the committee proposed a new statewide property tax of $1 per $100 of assessed valuation, a graduated income tax at rates ranging from 1.5 to 14 percent, and the elimination of various exemptions in the sales tax.

The governor said little about the report for the next few months, waiting to see what the public reaction would be. This showed that New Jersey's traditional hostility towards the concept of an income tax was still very much alive. Cahill finally resolved to take the offensive and on June 1 began a crusade in the press and on the podium to promote the basics of the committee program. Concurrently, GOP assembly leader Richard DeKorte prepared and introduced bills, and a special summer session of the legislature was convened. Despite the governor's salesmanship, the income-tax bill—the centerpiece of his fiscal reform package—was slaughtered in the assembly by a fifty-two-to-twenty-three vote on July 17, 1972.

The governor had other setbacks. During the summer indictments were returned against Cahill's longtime friend and confidant Secretary of State Paul J. Sherwin and GOP fund-raiser William C. Loughran, on bribery and extortion charges arising out of a highway construction contract. The two men were tried and convicted in October, tarnishing the administration's anticorruption image. The press also charged that the attorney general's office had tried to "cover up" the Sherwin affair. (This charge was later investigated and refuted by a special prosecutor.) In the November 1972 general elections the voters rejected a $650 million bond issue designed to update the state's highway and mass-transit systems, as well as a proposed constitutional amendment that would have given the governor power to remove the secretary of state and attorney general at pleasure. (The 1947 constitution had specifically exempted these positions from the chief executive's broad removal power.)

Although the Cahill administration had clearly lost much of its initiative and at least some of its image, Richard M. Nixon's 1972 landslide victory in New Jersey led political seers to assert, as 1973 opened, that Cahill would again be the Republican standard-bearer and that he would be almost impossible to beat in the upcoming gubernatorial contest. The governor himself presented an annual message to the legislature, on January 8, that was hardly a "farewell address" in tone and approach. Rather, Cahill spoke of unfinished business—in such areas as transportation, housing, urban aid, and environmental protection—and of his dream of continuing to strive for "the achievement of greatness" by the state of New Jersey.

Cahill once more pointed to the need for tax reform but handed the legislature the mantle of responsibility in that area. That the lawmakers would, however, bestir themselves in an election year was a dubious proposition, as Cahill himself realized. Hence, his policy recommendations (except for a new, urban-oriented Safe and Clean Streets proposal) generally required little new financing, and he designed his fiscal 1974 budget to use existing revenue sources. Representing a $333.8 million increase from 1973's $2 billion budget, it showed how the costs of education, welfare, and other ongoing programs were continuing to escalate.

To no one's surprise, William Cahill announced on March 22, 1973, that he was a candidate for renomination. (Again to no one's surprise, Congressman Sandman entered the primary lists as well.) Cahill brushed aside the corruption issue: "I have enough confidence in the people of New Jersey that they know Bill Cahill is honest and that they know Bill Cahill has done his best to root out corruption in every area." But the issue did not die. On April 8 the press reported that state and federal agents were probing the activities of key administration and Republican figures. On April 19 indictments were returned against two GOP fund-raisers on bribery-conspiracy charges relating to the deposit of state funds in a politically favored bank. Then, in May there was a veritable parade of indictments involving various alleged irregularities, including aspects of the financing of Cahill's 1969 campaign. Among those indicted were former State Treasurer Joseph McCrane, Harry Sears, and Nelson Gross.

The simultaneous unraveling of the Watergate conspiracy added to the governor's woes. Press accounts embarrassing to incumbent President Nixon stood side by side with articles devastating to the cause of incumbent Governor Cahill. In the showdown vote on June 5 the governor carried only five counties, as Sandman secured the nomination in his third successive try. On the Democratic side former superior court judge Brendan T. Byrne, with strong organization support, easily won his party's nomination.

With politics taking center stage in the fall (all 120 legislative seats were at stake in 1973), Cahill conducted what was largely a holding operation to close out his gubernatorial term. He could, however, look back on another productive two years of policymaking, for the 1972–73 legislature added significant measures to the statute books. A modern optional charter law was passed for New Jersey counties, paralleling the Faulkner Act for municipalities; the Safe and Clean Neighborhoods Act was approved and funded; the state began a program of service grants to private colleges and universities; no-fault automobile insurance was introduced; a health-care facilities act was passed, as was legislation designed to cope with problem juveniles. The Coastal Area Facilities Review Act of 1973 (CAFRA) marked another major assumption of power by state government in the area of land-use control. On the other hand Cahill failed in his efforts to obtain a general overhaul of New Jersey's planning and zoning laws. The legislature also refused to act on tax reform in 1973 despite a state supreme court decision on April 3, 1973, upholding the major thrust of the Botter ruling.

Following the November elections, the governor and his staff devoted most of their energies to budget preparation and to orienting the Byrne team to the responsibilities it would assume in January. William Cahill then returned to private life and the practice of law. He died in Haddonfield on July 1, 1996.

RICHARD J. CONNORS

Records of Governor William T. Cahill, New Jersey State Library, Trenton, N.J.

Felzenberg, Alvin S. "The Impact of Gubernatorial Style on Policy Outcomes: An In-Depth Study of Three New Jersey Governors." Ph.D. dissertation, Princeton University, 1978.

Brendan T. Byrne
New Jersey State Archives; Department of State

Brendan Thomas Byrne (April 1, 1924–), governor from 1974 to 1982, was elected in the state's largest landslide as the "man who couldn't be bought." Derided as "a dilettante, an inept politician and an egotist" during his first term, he engineered New Jersey's most dramatic political comeback. When Byrne left office in January 1982 after a tumultuous eight years, the *Philadelphia Inquirer* oberved, "when history makes its judgment, he just may outrank Woodrow Wilson."

Byrne's laid-back style, his lack of interest in engaging in the banter and backslapping long a staple of the state's politicians, frustrated both friend and foe alike. Yet his stubborn persistence demonstrated how an individual governor wielding the power and tools of the governorship could achieve his personal goals in shaping New Jersey's future.

Brendan Thomas Byrne was born on April 1, 1924, the fourth of five children of Francis A. Byrne and Genevieve (Brennan) Byrne of West Orange. His mother was the daughter of a worker in a local hat factory who also was elected as an alderman in Orange, and his paternal grandfather worked as a liveryman in a stable near the family home. Brendan's mother and father, both of whose grandparents had emigrated from northwestern Ireland, met at church, with their relationship also strengthened by their mutual interest in acting and singing, sometimes performing together in amateur local theater productions as leading man and lady.

Brendan's father had been a successful insurance agent for the Travelers Insurance Company but chose to found his own agency in 1929, shortly before the stock-market crash in October of that year which led to the Depression and the failure of the new business. As he struggled to sell insurance on his own, at times the needs of the family were eased by help from better-off relatives. Later, after the economy and his own business improved, Francis became president of a local savings bank. He also was active in politics for over fifty years, appointed at age twenty-two as West Orange tax assessor and later elected to the West Orange governing body and appointed to the Essex County Tax Board, first by Governor Alfred Driscoll and to subsequent terms by Governors Robert B. Meyner and Richard J. Hughes.

Brendan's older brother attended medical school to become a doctor, a decision which limited the funds available for Brendan's own college education, leading him to take jobs while at West Orange High School in a local shoe store and as a locker boy at the well-known Goldman Hotel in West Orange. His high school graduation in June 1942 came after his election as senior class president—his only elected office other than governor of New Jersey—and some six months after the nation had entered World War II following the attack on Pearl Harbor. Anticipating that his college education would be cut short by military service, he briefly attended Seton Hall College, leaving school in the spring of 1943 when he was drafted before completing his freshman year.

After being sent to Fort Dix to train as a tank driver, he took the test to enter flight-training school, ultimately ordered to Texas to train as a navigator on bombers. Deployed to the 15th Air Force based in Italy, he quickly saw combat—the youngest squadron navigator in his B-17 bomber group —on missions targeting the heavily defended refinery complexes supplying one-third of Nazi Germany's total fuel needs. With one in four airmen shot down or otherwise unable to complete their normal bombing tour of twenty-five missions, by war's end Byrne had completed (with extra credit for some lengthy flights) an extraordinary fifty-one missions. At the time of his discharge from active service in September 1945, he had been promoted to the rank of lieutenant and awarded the Distinguished Flying Cross and four Air Medals.

Returning to New Jersey, Byrne pursued his boyhood goal of attending Harvard Law School to prepare for a career as a trial lawyer. He first attempted, without success, to persuade Harvard that he be admitted without a college degree but—told that additional undergraduate work was required—then enrolled at Princeton, where the G.I. Bill paid his tuition and board. After just two years of study, he was awarded his degree due to the expedited schedule allowed war veterans and was admitted to Harvard Law School. While still a Harvard student, he persuaded Joseph Weintraub, a prominent New Jersey lawyer, to take him on during school breaks as an unpaid law clerk at his Newark law firm, initiating a relationship in which Weintraub, later to become counsel to Governor Meyner and chief justice of the New Jersey Supreme Court, was Byrne's mentor, adviser, and friend.

Following graduation from Harvard in 1950, Byrne returned to New Jersey to enter private law practice. In 1953, he married Jean Featherly, a marriage which produced seven children. Also in that year, Robert Meyner was elected governor, appointing Weintraub to serve as his counsel, the primary legal and legislative position on the governor's staff. Byrne soon followed to Trenton to become a state deputy attorney general, initially assigned to the Passaic County prosecutor's office but later rejoining Weintraub as an assistant counsel to Governor Meyner. In 1956, Meyner appointed Weintraub as a superior court judge and in the next year as an associate justice on the state supreme court, replacing William Brennan after Brennan's nomination to the United States Supreme Court by President Eisenhower. When New Jersey Chief Justice Arthur Vanderbilt died from a heart attack in June 1957, the governor named Weintraub to succeed Vanderbilt as chief justice.

As an assistant counsel, Byrne had developed his own independent relationship with Governor Meyner and was appointed as his executive secretary, a role giving him frequent contact with Meyner and other public officials and political leaders. When a stalemate among key Essex County Democrats delayed appointment of a new county prosecutor, the governor acceded to Byrne's request that he be named, albeit on an interim basis, as the acting prosecutor in February 1959.

Even with his temporary status, Byrne acted quickly to reshape the office, bringing in new lawyers and investigators, several of whom continued as close professional, political, and personal allies in future years. Largely on the basis of positive press coverage of Byrne's efforts, including his targeting of organized crime, Meyner made his interim appointment permanent five months later. Despite opposition from politicians threatened by Byrne's vigorous enforcement efforts, Governor Hughes reappointed him to a second term in 1964. Prosecutor Byrne also oversaw the processing of nearly fifteen hundred people arrested during the Newark riots in July 1967, which left twenty-six people dead and hundreds injured. As was then allowed, Byrne served as prosecutor while also concurrently a partner in a private law firm, chairman of an insurance company, and director of a bank.

In 1968, he resigned as prosecutor to accept appointment by Governor Hughes as president of the Public Utility Commission, a position which made him a member of the Hughes cabinet as head of the agency overseeing the operations and finances of electric, gas, and water utilities.

He continued with the commission into 1970, resigning after his nomination as a superior court judge by Governor William T. Cahill. Byrne largely admired Cahill's record as governor, including his program to develop the Meadowlands and his forthright—albeit unsuccessful—effort to restructure the state's finances through an income tax. But Cahill's moderate record placed him at odds with more conservative Republicans, and a series of scandals implicating key political advisers, including his secretary of state and his state treasurer, had undermined his reelection prospects. Outside

New Jersey, public reaction to the Watergate scandal embroiling the Nixon White House further tainted the Republican Party.

Viewing this political landscape, Democratic leaders asked Judge Byrne to enter the 1973 race, arguing that his profile as a judge and prosecutor would appeal to voters weary of the Republican scandals in Washington and Trenton. Byrne's reputation also had been enhanced over media coverage of transcripts of FBI wiretaps recorded in the 1960s in which Mafia figures boasted of their control of New Jersey officials but mentioned Prosecutor Byrne as one of the few that they could not buy. On the Democratic side, none of the declared gubernatorial candidates had broadened their support beyond narrow geographic bases, and, significantly, powerful Hudson County Democratic leaders remained uncommitted.

As Judge Byrne was mulling his options, his mentor Joseph Weintraub, as the state's chief justice, released on April 3 a unanimous opinion he wrote for the supreme court in the *Robinson v. Cahill* litigation that would have a major impact on Byrne and subsequent governors into the next century. The court found that the heavy reliance on the local property tax for funding public education created wide disparities in spending per student between poorer districts, particularly in older cities, and property-rich suburban districts and held that the funding system accordingly violated the state constitution's guarantee that the state government provide "a thorough and efficient system of free public schools" for all children between the ages of five and eighteen. Out of deference to the separation of powers, the court allowed the funding system to continue until there was sufficient time for legislative action, fixing a deadline of December 31, 1974—the end of the new governor's first year in office—for the legislature to enact and fund a more equalized school-aid formula. *Robinson* was the last major decision of the court headed by Weintraub before he retired at the end of the court's term in summer 1973.

On April 24, just six weeks before the primary election, Byrne traveled to Trenton, delivered his letter of resignation as a judge to Governor Cahill, and then promptly announced his candidacy for governor. The Byrne campaign, which soon gained important backing from Hudson leaders, highlighted his roles as prosecutor and judge, adapting the quote from the Mafia wiretaps to brand Byrne as "the man who couldn't be bought." Byrne won the primary comfortably with 195,000 votes, outpolling his closest opponents, Morris County assemblywoman Ann Klein (115,000 votes) and Essex County state senator Ralph DeRose (96,000 votes).

In the Republican primary, Congressman Charles Sandman, a conservative from Cape May who became one of President Nixon's staunchest defenders in the Watergate proceedings, defeated Governor Cahill, whose struggling campaign had been jolted just days before the primary by federal indictments of his former state treasurer and, separately, of his choice as state Republican chairman.

Byrne's win over Sandman in the general election was the largest plurality in the state's history, with his 1,397,613 votes more than doubling the 676,235 cast for the Republican. Byrne's victory also swept Democrats to strong majorities in the legislature as the party won twenty-nine seats of the forty in the senate and sixty-five of the eighty in the assembly.

Byrne's postelection transition, normally devoted to selecting members of the new administration and planning a legislative program, was interrupted by more immediate developments. On the day after the election, Governor Cahill nominated former governor Richard Hughes to be chief justice of the state supreme court, filling the vacancy created by the unexpected death only weeks following his swearing-in of Pierre Garven, who had served as counsel to Cahill and whom the governor had named to succeed Chief Justice Weintraub upon Weintraub's retirement.

During the transition, Governor Cahill also called on the governor-elect to help salvage his high-priority initiative to develop the Meadowlands and the Sports Complex. The project's keystone, a newly built football stadium for the New York Giants, had become threatened when Wall Street financial institutions, under pressure from New York Governor Nelson Rockefeller and his brother David, chairman of the Chase Manhattan Bank, had declined to support the stadium's financing. As a candidate, Byrne had criticized the original Cahill agreement with the Giants, but after meeting with Giants officials, he renegotiated the contract to secure better terms for the state, including the right to host other events and tenants at the facility, a provision that later enabled the New York Jets to move to the stadium in 1984. Shortly after his swearing-in, Byrne again had to act to keep the project alive when New York underwriters reneged on commitments for additional bonds, forcing the new governor to hastily convene New Jersey–based financial institutions to make up the financing shortfall. As governor, Byrne placed his own stamp on the Meadowlands by building the indoor arena opened in 1981, which bore his name for some fifteen years.

The governor-elect also intervened during the transition to stop an effort by the outgoing governor and Republican legislature to have the New Jersey Turnpike Authority expedite construction of a new link from the Turnpike in Middlesex County to Toms River. Before Byrne's election, the legislature and Governor Cahill had designated the new road to be named "The Alfred E. Driscoll Expressway" in honor of the former Republican governor, who also previously had been named by Cahill as chair of the Authority's board. During the campaign, Byrne had criticized the project as wasteful and facilitating overdevelopment, including cutting through pristine forests in the Pinelands. After his election, Byrne mobilized opponents of the project to block the issuance of the bonds, eventually killing the project after he took office.

On January 14, 1974, Byrne delivered his inaugural address, focusing primarily on the public cynicism that prevailed over the government scandals and the need to respond to the *Robinson* decision, announcing that he would call the legislature into special session in the spring to address the school-funding issue.

While the legislature waited for the Byrne financing plan, the new governor was confronted by a more immediate crisis. Following the Arab embargo on oil exports instituted in October 1973 in retaliation for the U.S. support of Israel in the so-called Yom Kippur War, long lines of motorists waited for hours at the few gas stations with gas to sell, provoking occasional violence as frustrated drivers jockeyed for position. Among other directives, Byrne's first executive order imposed an "odd-even" system requiring motorists to buy gas only on odd or even dates as designated by the last number on their license plates. The system's success in easing waits for gas gained national attention, with other jurisdictions quickly adopting the New Jersey plan.

The new administration also acted to fulfill Byrne's campaign pledge for a more open and accountable "government under glass," creating a department of public advocate to represent the public interest and combat abuses of government power; enacting the nation's first program for the public financing of gubernatorial campaigns; setting strict rules on financial reporting and conflicts of interest for high-level appointees; limiting political contributions and lobbyist spending; mandating public bidding for most state purchases and contracts; and under the so-called Sunshine Act, making most public authority and agency proceedings open to the press and public with advance publication of meeting agendas.

Despite the record compiled on these and other issues, Byrne's first term was dominated by the divisive issue of tax reform. Four months after he was inaugurated and just over a year since Chief Justice Weintraub delivered the *Robinson* opinion, the governor addressed the joint session of the legislature he had called, proposing enactment of a $1.1 billion tax and spending package, including a personal income tax.

On July 15, the Byrne tax program passed the assembly by the bare minimum of forty-one votes, but the legislation stalled in the senate, where its sponsors, recognizing they lacked a majority, did not post it for a formal vote. Subsequent attempts to forge a consensus also foundered as the court's *Robinson* deadline for action by the end of 1974 passed without any resolution. When two separate tax plans also failed to gain sufficient support in January 1975, the governor personally appeared before the court in March (believed to be the only governor to do so in state history), urging the justices to take the extraordinary action to redistribute state school aid from wealthier to poorer communities. But the governor and the tax supporters were disappointed when the court, now led by Chief Justice Hughes, gave the legislature additional time to act, allowing the existing school-aid formula to remain in place for the following school year.

The court, perhaps reacting to the criticism of its ruling extending its deadline, later toughened its stance, finally ordering "that on and after July 1, 1976, every public state and local officer was barred from expending any

funds for public schools under the existing formula." Still, subsequent compromise efforts also failed; when the legislature had not approved legislation
by the July 1 deadline, public schools holding summer sessions were closed
under the court's order. Finally, on July 7, a bill which had been amended in
the senate to add supplemental aid for local governments passed the assembly by a bare majority of forty-one, including two Republicans. The governor
promptly signed the legislation and advised the court of its approval, with
the court then vacating its injunction closing the schools.

The protracted battle over the tax and school reform program and Byrne's
resulting loss of popularity provoked wide speculation that he would choose
not to stand for reelection in 1977, indeed to fulfill his critics' prediction that
he would be "one-term Byrne." At the ceremony marking the opening of
the new Meadowlands Race Track in September 1976, the governor's brief
appearance in a circuit around the track provoked vociferous boos and
curses from the crowd of thirty thousand, forcing his security detail to take
precautions against potential physical attacks.

As the 1977 election campaign got under way, Byrne's prospects still appeared bleak. Polls reported more than 70 percent of New Jerseyans disapproving his performance; *New Jersey Monthly* magazine's April issue featured
a cover article titled "The Tragicomedy of Brendan Byrne."

In at least one part of the state—Atlantic City and its region—Byrne
remained a popular figure. As a prosecutor during the 1960s, he was the only
law enforcement official to testify in favor of authorizing casino gambling,
arguing that casinos overseen by the state would undercut profits of organized crime from illegal wagering. During his first year in office in 1974, a
referendum to authorize casinos statewide was rejected after strong opposition by religious leaders, but in 1976 a revised referendum restricting casinos
to Atlantic City alone was approved with the governor's support. On June 2,
1977, less than a week before the Democratic gubernatorial primary, the governor was cheered by hundreds on the Atlantic City boardwalk as he signed
the Casino Control Act establishing the regulatory program to license the
first casinos, gaining national media coverage for his declaration, "I've said
it before and I will repeat it again to organized crime: Keep your filthy hands
out of Atlantic City. Keep the hell out of our state."

In the early months of 1977, Byrne remained noncommittal about his reelection plans. An internal Democratic Party poll reported that 69 percent
of Democrats surveyed stated they would not vote for Byrne under any circumstances. Ten other candidates—either assuming that he would not run
or, if he did, that he would be soundly defeated—filed to run in the June
1977 Democratic primary election. But the governor's political weakness
proved to be a crucial to his renomination as his opponents fragmented the
anti-Byrne turnout. With some seven in ten voters casting ballots for candidates other than their incumbent governor, Byrne's 30 percent of the vote
nonetheless was enough to win the nomination over his closest competitors

—Congressman Robert Roe (23 percent), former state senator Ralph De Rose (17 percent), and Congressman James Florio (15 percent).

The Republican primary was won by former senate president Raymond Bateman, who defeated former assembly speaker Thomas Kean. Both candidates, seeking to appeal to the party's right wing that dominated primary turnouts, pledged to abolish the new income tax.

In the month after the primary, a poll reported that Bateman held a 17 percent lead over Byrne, with the governor's job performance rated as "poor" or "only fair" by 68 percent of respondents. In September, Bateman unveiled his alternative to the Byrne tax program, developed with the assistance of former Nixon treasury secretary and New Jersey resident William Simon. The Republican plan proposed allowing the income tax to expire; enacting a package of smaller revenue raisers; boosting projections for future tax revenues; and, in the event of any shortfall, increasing the sales tax by one cent. Byrne then responded at a statehouse press conference, which he closed by dryly noting that the Bateman-Simon plan would "always be known by its initials." The Democratic campaign continued to attack the "B-S" plan, succeeding in also persuading most independent analysts that the plan lacked credibility.

Political calculations made by the Byrne team and Democratic legislators in crafting the tax program also helped to shift public opinion. Most famously, the legislation provided for rebates to homeowners. Treasury Secretary Richard Leone, who had resigned to manage the Byrne campaign, had insisted, overriding his own staff, that the rebates be sent to taxpayers in the form of checks rather than credits on tax bills. The two rebate mailings, including a letter signed by Brendan Byrne, with an endorsed check, were sent just before the 1977 primary and general elections. In an interview many years later, Bateman recalled arriving home after a hectic day of campaigning, sitting down, and opening his mail to find his own check with a "Dear Homeowner" letter from Byrne. Recognizing that the check guaranteed his defeat, the highly respected Republican wryly summarized the result, "When all the bullshit is done, that was the election, the homestead rebate."

On election day, Byrne easily defeated Bateman by 54.5 percent to 40.9 percent, a victory the *New York Times* labeled "one of the most dramatic comebacks in New Jersey politics history."

With the new confidence and mandate instilled by Byrne's surprising reelection, he used his second term to pursue a variety of measures that had been deferred by the protracted battle over the income tax.

Preservation of the Pinelands—comprising over a fifth of the state's land area with a million acres of pine forests, streams, farms, and small towns in southern New Jersey—was his highest second-term priority and, in Byrne's view, his most important achievement as governor. The Pinelands preservation program was, as Byrne later put it, "unique in the sense that it would not have been passed if I didn't take an interest in it. The Pinelands was on nobody's particular political agenda. It was on no political party's agenda." Byrne's interest in the region had been sparked by his relationship with John McPhee, the noted author and Princeton faculty member who also was an occasional tennis companion of the governor. McPhee's 1968 book reviewing the special history and ecology of the area, *The Pine Barrens*, had concluded pessimistically "that the Pine Barrens are not very likely to be the subject of dramatic decrees or acts of legislation. They seem to be headed slowly toward extinction."

After Byrne blocked construction of the proposed Driscoll Expressway through the region during his 1973 transition, he had begun to push in his first term for a permanent Pinelands preservation program. In 1975, a state commission created in the Cahill administration and dominated by county appointees released a proposed Pinelands master plan that David Bardin, Byrne's environmental commissioner, denounced with the governor's approval as "a developer's dream." In December 1976, the governor convened a conference at Princeton University at which the region's future development was debated and, less than a week before the June 1977 primary election, issued an executive order appointing his own task force to draft an alternative plan clearly focused on preservation.

The attention Byrne placed on Pinelands preservation also led New Jersey's congressional delegation to introduce contrasting bills for federal action. An eventual compromise created a commission, with its appointees equally divided between the governor and affected counties and the U.S. secretary of the interior naming a single representative, to draft a master plan but without power to regulate development, deferring to the state for any action to enforce compliance with the plan.

The subsequent state legislation introduced with Byrne's support, largely based on his own task force's recommendations, clearly defined preservation as the dominant goal of the master plan. The commission was given unprecedented power to oversee and override municipal planning and zoning decisions, an intrusion into traditional local home-rule prerogatives, particularly strong in the Pinelands region, which provoked stiff opposition from local officials and legislators, including key Democrats who had been elected in previously Republican-dominated districts.

When the legislation stalled, Byrne issued an executive order in February 1979 imposing a building moratorium on fifteen hundred square miles in the Pinelands, justifying the action as needed to allow sufficient time for the planning process to proceed without further degradation of the ecosystem. The order was promptly challenged by lawsuits filed by the state builders' association, affected counties, and others as an unconstitutional exercise of the governor's executive authority. After advising Byrne that the legal attacks would likely succeed, Attorney General John Degnan was surprised at the highly positive reception he received at the oral argument before the state supreme court to defend the action, perhaps signaling the opponents that legislation might be preferable to the court's sanctioning the governor's authority to act by executive order. In any event, after an assembly session continuing into the early morning which required recruiting Republicans to compensate for Democratic defections, the bill was passed and signed by the governor, with the supreme court soon dismissing the lawsuit before it in light of the new law. Twenty years after Byrne left office, his vital role in preserving the Pinelands, which permanently reshaped New Jersey's future land use by removing nearly a fifth of the state's land area from development, was recognized by the state when the Lebanon State Forest was renamed as the Brendan T. Byrne State Forest.

Byrne's second term also focused on pursuing the implementation of the casino-gambling initiative in Atlantic City. On May 26, 1978, he presided over the opening of the first casino-hotel operated by Resorts International, cutting the ribbon that allowed the thousands of people lined up to gamble, with the casino's revenues and profits during its first months far exceeding even the most optimistic predictions.

Yet less than two years after the opening of the first casino, the optimism over Atlantic City's renewal was shaken by the Abscam scandal, which evolved from an FBI undercover "sting" operation in which agents posed as henchmen of a fictitious Arab sheik exploring potential investments in the United States. During the investigation, Camden mayor and state senator Angelo Errichetti told agents that he could help the "sheik" get a gaming license from the Casino Control Commission with the aid of a bribe for its vice chairman, who Errichetti reported "controlled" Chairman Joseph Lordi, a Byrne appointee who had succeeded him as Essex County prosecutor after working on the Byrne staff. Errichetti's allegations were never substantiated, but Abscam resulted in bribery and conspiracy convictions for, among others, Errichetti, U.S. Senator Harrison Williams, and veteran congressman Frank Thompson. In response to Abscam, Byrne restructured the commission, changing it from a part-time to full-time body and mandating that it focus solely on licensing and overseeing casino operations, prohibiting contacts with casino applicants on development and investment issues.

Following the Abscam retrenchment, the Atlantic City casino industry resumed its rapid growth. By the time Byrne left office in January 1982, five other casinos had joined Resorts in Atlantic City; eventually the industry generated over forty thousand jobs and spent over $2 billion annually in purchasing goods and services from New Jersey suppliers. Yet the lack of visible progress in development of nongambling attractions, housing, and other needs became a continuing criticism. After leaving office, Byrne himself said his "biggest mistake" as governor was his failure to condition his support of gambling on the creation of a regional development agency, akin to that in the Meadowlands, giving the state a strong role in planning and development.

At the beginning of his second term, Byrne recruited Louis Gambaccini, a career executive with the Port Authority of New York and New Jersey who ran its PATH rapid-transit commuter line, to take a leave from the Authority to head the state Department of Transportation. Gambaccini set as his major priority the renewal of the deteriorated public transit system, successfully drafting and overseeing passage of legislation, signed into law by the governor as the Public Transportation Act of 1979, creating a state authority, New Jersey Transit, to consolidate the fragmented rail and bus system under state operation. In the year after the new agency's founding, it acquired the state's largest private bus company and in 1983, after Byrne had left office, assumed operation of commuter rail passenger service. New Jersey Transit became the nation's largest statewide public transit system and the third largest in the number of riders on its bus, rail, and light-rail transit network.

Beyond Byrne's highest-profile initiatives, his years in office resulted in several other changes with lasting impact. He initiated the reclamation of the garbage-strewn Hudson waterfront by the development of Liberty State Park; rewrote the state's archaic criminal code; and established the nation's first compensation fund for losses from spills of oil and chemicals, the model for the national Superfund program. He created the Economic Development Authority, the state's primary agency to assist private economic development, as well as the Motion Picture and Television Development Commission, which helped to attract a series of productions to the state. He oversaw the cleanup of polluted waterways and the end of dumping of waste in the ocean, with over $1 billion spent to construct sewage treatment facilities. He established an urban capital finance program providing the initial funding for such facilities as the New Jersey Performing Arts Center and the Camden Aquarium. His health commissioner introduced a pioneering system for fixing hospital charges that later was adopted nationally by the federal Medicare system. Regulations fixing minimum prices for the sale of alcoholic beverages were repealed, leading to major savings for consumers. He completed construction of Interstate 287, allowing traffic to avoid the congested route through New York City. The state's first water-supply master plan was adopted and implemented, leading to the building of reservoirs and pipelines and helping to avoid constructing the controversial Tocks Island Dam blocking the flow of the Delaware River. He restructured the organization of the governor's office through designating a chief of staff and establishing a policy unit; within the bureaucracy, he created the Department of Corrections and revamped emergency response services by centralizing control and management in the state police.

After Byrne left office in January 1982, he returned to private law practice, joining the law firm headed by Charles Carella, who had worked under him in the Essex County prosecutor's office and later during his gubernatorial administration. His marriage to Jean Byrne ended in divorce, followed by his subsequent marriage to Ruthi Zinn, head of her own public relations firm. He also accepted appointments to several boards of corporations and nonprofit causes and became a minority shareholder in the New Jersey Devils National Hockey League franchise, which he had previously helped persuade to relocate from Denver to New Jersey. Byrne divested his interest in the Devils when his successor, Thomas Kean, appointed him to the board of the Sports Authority. He became a popular speaker, known for his wit at events both in and outside the state, and, after Governor Kean left office, exchanged views with Kean in a weekly newspaper column. His son Tom (Brendan Thomas Byrne, Jr.) served as chairman of the state Democratic Committee for three years beginning in 1994.

DONALD LINKY

Brendan T. Byrne Archive, Center on the American Governor, Eagleton Institute of Politics, Rutgers University.

Papers of Brendan T. Byrne, The Monsignor Field Archives and Special Collections Center, Seton Hall University.

Papers of Brendan T. Byrne, Special Collections and University Archives, Rutgers University Libraries.

Records of Governor Brendan T. Byrne, New Jersey State Library, Trenton, N.J.

Thomas Howard Kean (April 21, 1935–), New Jersey's forty-ninth governor, was born in New York City. The fifth of the six children of Robert Winthrop Kean and the former Elizabeth Stuyvesant Howard, Kean claimed kinship with some of the nation's most politically and socially prominent families. The Keans trace their ancestry in the United States to John Kean, first Cashier of the United States. A South Carolinian, John Kean married the daughter of New Jersey's first constitutional governor, William Livingston. Tom Kean's grandfather Hamilton Fish Kean served in the United States Senate from 1929 until 1935. John Kean, Hamilton's older brother, also served in that body, from 1899 until 1911. Thomas Kean is the father of three children with his wife, the former Deborah Bye, whom he married in September 1967: twin sons, Thomas Jr. and Reid (born in 1968), and a daughter, Alexandra (born in 1974).

Thomas H. Kean
New Jersey State Archives; Department of State

When Tom Kean was three years old, his father won election to the House of Representatives; he served from 1939 through 1959. Tom Kean spent much of his childhood commuting back and forth from his family's residences in Washington, D.C., and Livingston, New Jersey. Conflicts between the academic and congressional calendars dictated that he undergo frequent absences from his parents and playmates.

Kean settled into a more routine life after he enrolled in the St. Mark's School in Southborough, Massachusetts, in 1946. There, under the tutelage of his teacher William Gaccon, Kean overcame his boyhood stutter. While at St. Mark's, Kean won distinction as a student journalist and developed a lifelong passion for history and the arts while cultivating an interest in a teaching career. He also took an interest in current affairs. At the time, his father was making headlines from his post on the House Ways and Means Committee for his efforts to expand the reach of the Social Security system.

In 1957, after graduating from Princeton University with a degree in history, Kean reported to Fort Drum, in Watertown, New York, to complete basic training with the National Guard's Fiftieth Armored Division.

Before long, Kean was immersed in his first political campaign. His father had declared for an open seat in the United States Senate, and his family joined the effort. Along with his two brothers, Kean acted as a surrogate speaker for the candidate. He found that he liked campaigning and enjoyed speaking before groups. After winning a vigorously contested Republican primary, the elder Kean lost the general election to former representative Harrison A. Williams by eighty-five thousand votes. In the fall of 1959, Kean accepted St. Mark's invitation to return to the school to fill in for a teacher who had died. Kean proved a popular teacher and a much-sought-after adviser. He taught history and English; coached several sports; advised the student newspaper, student government, and photography magazine; and introduced changes to the school's curriculum. The year he departed to continue his educational training at Columbia's Teachers College, the class of 1962 dedicated its yearbook, *The Lion*, to him.

Qualifying for a master's degree in the teaching of history, Kean completed his Ph.D. entrance examinations in the spring of 1964. Seeking a break from academe before commencing his dissertation, Kean tried his hand at politics again. He volunteered in Pennsylvania Governor William Scranton's belated campaign to wrestle the 1964 Republican presidential nomination away from Arizona Senator Barry Goldwater. Kean became Scranton's national youth coordinator.

In an era when party bosses and handpicked delegates selected presidential nominees, Kean, through a series of carefully orchestrated publicity stunts, sought to persuade the press and state delegations that Scranton commanded more support than he actually did. After Goldwater's defeat in the general election, New Jersey Republican Party Chairman Webster B. Todd retained Kean as his personal liaison to younger voters.

When the New Jersey legislature was expanded in 1967, new open seats provided ample opportunities for well-educated, well-known political aspirants. With Kean's connections and family background, he was a favorite for one of the two assembly nominations in a new, heavily suburban, Essex County district. The party's screening committee selected Philip D. Kaltenbacher, a Yale-educated attorney and businessman from neighboring Short Hills, as his running mate. Kean and Kaltenbacher campaigned especially hard in heavily Democratic Irvington, which comprised 40 percent of their district. In their district, Kean and Kaltenbacher outpolled their opponents by two to one. Statewide, a heavy Democratic legislative majority in both houses gave way to one that was three-to-one Republican. Running again with Kaltenbacher, Kean twice won reelection. Later, in a slightly changed district (in which the more conservative-leaning Wayne had replaced blue-collar Irvington), Kean, running with Jane Burgio, won reelection two additional times. In total, Kean served ten years in the state assembly.

Shortly after the 1967 election, the seven new Republican assemblymen from Essex County designated Kean their leader. He was quick to realize that with suburban legislators composing the largest bloc, they held the balance between both urban and rural interests. Kean first forged an alliance with Bergen County's ten-member delegation. Whenever the members from Monmouth, Morris, Union, and Somerset joined them, representatives of a majority of state residents could control the policy agenda, as advocates of reapportionment had intended. With Kean as their spokesman, they stood to the left of the more rural, conservative-leaning Republicans in the chamber and to the right of the more liberal-leaning, urban Democrats.

In a surprise move, the suburban freshmen, asserting their collective strength, challenged the Republican bosses' choice for assistant majority leader. They succeeded in electing their own candidate, Barry Parker of Burlington County, to the post. The following year, with Parker slated to become majority leader, Kean succeeded Parker as assistant majority leader. He became majority leader the following year and speaker the year after that.

In response to the report of the Kerner Commission (the group President Lyndon B. Johnson named to investigate the cause of the 1967 riots in Newark and Detroit), Governor Richard J. Hughes proposed that the state absorb county and municipal welfare costs and provide direct monetary aid to New Jersey cities. Kean took on the responsibility for passing these measures in the assembly. Hughes's proposals took on increased urgency after the assassination of Martin Luther King, Jr., in April 1968.

To make the governor's proposals more appealing to his colleagues, Assemblyman Kean dropped the state's absorption of welfare costs from 100 percent to 75 percent on two categorical programs (Assistance to Families with Dependent Children and Medicaid) and agreed to have the state absorb 50 percent of a third (disability insurance). When some members of his caucus balked at passing the compromise he had brokered, Kean announced that the Republican legislature could not "count on Essex votes for other types of legislation" if they did not "take an interest in critical urban problems." Kean's enacted bill was the first urban-aid measure ever to become law in New Jersey.

Again joining forces with Hughes, Kean steered to passage additional measures, including direct aid to cities, beefed-up law enforcement, emergency school aid, a school lunch program, and neighborhood education centers. Kean sponsored the bill that established the Educational Opportunity Fund, which enabled disadvantaged youths to attend college. "A-767" (more popularly known as the "Kean Bill") not only allocated funds to cover students' costs of tuition, fees, and books but also provided for compensatory education to equip graduates of poorly performing high schools to do college work and made available to them counseling to help ease their transition to college.

Environmental protection proved another of Kean's principal concerns while in the assembly. His efforts to prevent Sunfish Pond, a forty-four-acre glacial lake in the northwest corner of the state from becoming incorporated into a pumped storage station for a proposed new reservoir resulted in the cancellation of the Tocks Island Dam project. The proposal, which included the creation of a thirty-seven-mile man-made lake at the foot of the Delaware River, had the support of New Jersey power companies, the AFL-CIO, and the governors of New York, New Jersey, Pennsylvania, and Delaware.

Kean sponsored legislation that created the state's Department of Environmental Protection. Governor William T. Cahill signed it into law April 22, 1970, the nation's first Earth Day. Kean was also the moving force behind the Coastal Area Facility Review Act (CAFRA). The measure banned industries that were deemed most likely to pollute from locating near the state's waterways. Foreshadowing an approach Kean was to take as governor, he insisted that economic development and conservation were not incompatible goals.

Once part of the assembly's leadership, Kean invested considerable energies changing how the chamber conducted its business. As assistant majority leader, he produced written rules for his party's caucus. As majority leader, Kean retained the first full-time executive director to the assembly majority and permitted the Democratic minority to do the same. He also established the first full-time majority party communications operation. Kean established an Assembly Conference Committee that could release for floor consideration measures that had been bottled up in other committees. Composed of the heads of every county's delegation, the committee assured that the minority party would have at least some input in assembly proceedings. To enable the legislature to act as a check on the governor, Kean helped establish the Office of Fiscal Affairs. After he became assembly speaker, Kean had committees hold, for the first time, regularly scheduled meetings and take recorded votes. He also had them retain professional partisan staff.

In the election of 1971, voters elected an assembly of forty Democrats, thirty-nine Republicans, and one independent. With neither party able to muster the forty-one votes necessary to organize the chamber, deadlock ensued. The stalemate broke after Hudson County's David H. Friedland, the former Democratic minority leader, and three other Democrats joined with the Republicans and elected Kean speaker. Critics of the arrangement speculated that Kean and Friedland (who was at the time under suspension from the practice of law because he had improperly sought to settle a loan-sharking case) had entered into a "secret deal." Kean responded by making the terms of the agreement public. The Hudson renegade would receive half the speaker's patronage and co-chair the Conference Committee, while his three cohorts would each chair a committee.

Within months, Kean, together with Friedland Democrats, regular Democrats, and Republicans, reached consensus on many issues that had long been on the public agenda. Kean's colleagues unanimously reelected him speaker, making him the first legislative leader in state history to serve more than one year in the post. As speaker, Kean steered CAFRA to final passage. Other hallmarks of his tenure included the creation of the Division of Consumer Affairs, enactment of the state's first rent-stabilization bill, and the final agreement to bring the Giants to play in New Jersey in a newly constructed stadium. Two measures that failed to pass were Governor Cahill's proposed graduated state income tax and Kean's bill to permit class-action suits against polluters.

The Democratic landslide of 1973 reduced Republican strength in the assembly from thirty-nine to fourteen. Now the minority leader, Kean worked to hold the majority party accountable (often through the press), to cast the GOP as the reform party, and to exploit Democratic divisions. He was particularly deft in using his knowledge of parliamentary procedure to extract concessions from the majority. He worked to elect more Republicans in the next election, recruiting candidates, raising money, and insisting that funds be spent on toss-up races rather than directed to incumbents. (In 1975, GOP strength in the assembly climbed from fourteen to thirty-one.)

Kean twice opposed referenda allowing casino gambling in Atlantic City. He broke with Republican conservatives when he voted for an early version of the income tax that Governor Brendan Byrne proposed. He also supported Byrne's proposal to establish a cabinet Department of the Public Advocate.

In 1974, Kean hoped to succeed twenty-year incumbent congressman Peter H. B. Frelinghuysen, who was retiring. Although Kean's legislative district comprised only 5 percent of Frelinghuysen's congressional district, Kean mounted a spirited campaign against late entrant Millicent Fenwick. He lost by eighty-six votes. Two years later, President Gerald Ford, who had served with Kean's father in Congress, tapped Kean to manage his presidential campaign in New Jersey. Although Ford lost the election, he carried New Jersey by 51 percent to Jimmy Carter's 48 percent.

In 1977, the year Tom Kean first sought the Republican nomination for governor, he declined to seek reelection to the assembly. He had served in that body for a decade, completing five two-year terms. (Shortly after declaring for governor, he stepped down as GOP assembly leader but did not resign from that body.) Kean's decision to seek the gubernatorial nomination pitted him against Republican Party favorite Raymond H. Bateman for the gubernatorial nomination. A decade Kean's senior, Bateman had served as state senate president while Kean headed the assembly. After a decade in the assembly, Kean was ready for new challenges. After losing the primary to Bateman 172,911 to 112,561, Kean spent the next four years as a political commentator, professor of public administration at Rutgers University in Newark, chief operating officer of a small family business (the Realty Transfer Company), and a commissioner of the New Jersey Highway Authority, to which Governor Byrne appointed him to assure bipartisan representation. (Byrne, the Democratic nominee, had defeated Bateman in the November 1977 general election.)

The availability for the first time of matching public funds to primary candidates and a low qualifying threshold attracted multiple candidates into the 1981 gubernatorial primaries. Kean competed against six rivals. His major opponents were Lawrence F. "Pat" Kramer, the favorite of most county organizations, and Joseph "Bo" Sullivan, a wealthy businessman who cast himself as a Reaganesque fiscal and social conservative.

With the state and nation in recession and unemployment in New Jersey exceeding 10 percent, Kean proposed to jump-start the state's economy by cutting business taxes by 50 percent, reducing the sales tax by 20 percent, and eliminating the state corporate net-worth tax and estate tax over four years. He also promised to enact "urban enterprise zones," an idea that Buffalo congressman and conservative hero Jack Kemp advanced as a means of attracting business development to inner cities. Kean also pledged to restore the death penalty, improve New Jersey schools, resist statewide zoning, and imprison those who illegally dumped toxic substances.

With a well-organized campaign that reached voters through television, direct mailings, and telephone banks, Kean won an easy victory, receiving 118,692 votes to Kramer's 79,652 and Sullivan's 64,112. On the Democratic side, Camden County Congressman James J. Florio placed first in a field of thirteen, with 164,179 votes.

In the general election, discussions of the economy predominated. Florio blamed the state's difficulties on President Reagan's tax and budget cuts. Kean countered that the Byrne administration and Democratic legislature had driven businesses and high-paying jobs from the state through high taxes and overregulation. He promised to create a more favorable business climate. With the media regarding the New Jersey and Virginia gubernatorial elections as barometers of Reagan's strength and popularity, handicappers gave Florio a slight edge. Kean ended election night holding a slight lead. Several days later, certified county results put him ahead by 1,677 votes. Results of a statewide recount showed that Kean had won by 1,797 votes, the smallest margin in the state's history. In the legislature, Democrats continued to enjoy comfortable majorities in both houses.

Budgetary shortfalls, prison overcrowding, and a deteriorating infrastructure proved the most urgent problems awaiting Kean as he took office. After failing to obtain passage of a gas tax to fund a deficit estimated to hit $700 million by the end of Kean's first year, Kean reluctantly agreed to raise the sales tax one cent, to increase the income tax on people earning over $50,000 per year, and to raise that tax's top rate from 2.5 percent to 3.5 percent.

As the recession of the early 1980s waned, these tax hikes produced a surplus that approached $1 billion by the time Kean sought reelection. Kean used it to fund cuts in some taxes, phase out others, and increase funding for arts and other programs. He also funded fully, for the first time, the state's school-aid formula.

A combination of rising crime, mandatory sentencing, and restrictions on parole had increased the state's inmate population in the years preceding Kean's election. Prosecutors and victims feared that judges would begin releasing offenders before they had served most of their sentences. As a stopgap measure, Kean obtained permission from the Reagan administration to construct a prefabricated five-hundred-bed unit to house nonviolent offenders on land the military owned at Fort Dix, while erecting similar structures elsewhere. Working through a broad-based bipartisan coalition chaired by former governor and chief justice Hughes, Kean persuaded voters to approve two bond issues for construction of new prisons and to refurbish old ones.

To provide a stable source of funds to finance infrastructure repairs, Kean relied on revolving funds. He promoted a plan in which the state would pool into a common fund unspent monies from previously passed bond issues, authorized federal grants, additional state expenditures, user fees, and surplus revenue from the state's three toll roads. The funds would be lent at low or no interest to municipalities. As the loans were repaid, the state would lend to other jurisdictions. The program became known as the Transportation Trust Fund.

Seeking to enhance the state's visibility as a means of attracting would-be vacationers and companies seeking to relocate their operations, Kean pressed for increased funds to market on television and print publications highlighting the state's assets and attractiveness. The "New Jersey and You —Perfect Together" marketing campaign, in which Kean was often featured as principal spokesman, became synonymous with his administration. Kean raised the state's profile by participating in foreign trade missions, personally lobbying companies to locate in the state, and showcasing the state's assets at national forums.

As governor, Kean made education reform his highest priority. He set as one of his goals attracting the "best and the brightest" liberal arts graduates into New Jersey schools, improving the quality of teacher training, bringing into classrooms people who had had successful careers in noneducational pursuits, and improving the quality of urban education. In his efforts to reach them, Kean sought to include in the debate over education policy all that had a stake in the public schools' success, including parents and businesses, as well as professional educators and their representatives.

Under Kean, New Jersey became the first state to provide an alternate route to teacher certification for liberal arts graduates. After passing nationally devised tests in their chosen fields, these "provisional" new teachers underwent additional training after they had been hired by school districts. A decade after Kean stepped down as governor, 40 percent of the state's licensed teachers were entering New Jersey classrooms through this path.

Kean's other educational initiatives included increased pay for new teachers, a deemphasis on methodology in favor of subject matter in teacher training; cash bonuses to outstanding teachers, the establishment of academies for teachers and governor's schools for gifted students, the removal of habitually disruptive students from classrooms, the institution of proficiency standards in English for high school graduates and increased high school graduation requirements, and the elimination of annual monitoring of well-performing schools. Kean pushed through legislation authorizing the state to take over entire school districts with a history of failure, corruption, and incompetence. During his eight years in office, he established a reputation as a national leader in education reform.

Seeking to encourage high-technology companies to remain in or locate to New Jersey, Kean won approval of a high-technology bond issue to upgrade university laboratories and research facilities and to invest public funds in start-up companies. Kean brought into being the Liberty Science Center. He also sponsored a challenge grant through which colleges and universities applied for funding to attain specified goals.

As governor, Kean managed a series of unanticipated environmental challenges. These included feared and actual discoveries of dioxin in cities, radon in suburban basements, asbestos in schools, PCBs in fish caught in New Jersey waters, and medical wastes littering state beaches, as well as hurricanes and floods. In each instance, Kean made an immediate assessment of the problem, sent professionals to the site, made regular announcements to address the situation, and met with residents—often early in the process. Kean promised severe penalties for perpetrators of environmental crimes.

To prod the legislature to enact a bill to protect the state's wetlands, Kean conditionally vetoed what he considered a weak version of what he wanted. As the legislature contemplated his recommended changes, Kean declared an eighteen-month moratorium on development around more than three hundred thousand acres of freshwater wetlands. The bill he eventually signed protected 6 percent of the state's land from haphazard development and set aside buffer zones to protect animal life, threatened species, and secondary wetlands.

In response to the washing up of wastes on New Jersey shores and what had been the chronic problem of ocean dumping, Kean pushed through measures to ban sludge dumping, remove lead and cyanide from material discharged into sewage systems, and prevent municipal trash from flowing out to sea during storms. Through the National Governors Association, he and colleagues persuaded the federal government to ban ocean dumping of sludge. Meanwhile, Kean played a key role in assuring construction of the Hope Creek nuclear plant in Salem.

Kean also sought to raise the prominence of the state's cultural and arts attractions nationally, using the New Jersey Department of State as an advocate for these organizations. His administration also undertook the initial planning for what became the New Jersey Performing Arts Center in Newark. Kean made world headlines when he approved legislation that divested New Jersey's portfolio of investments in companies that did business in South Africa. He helped persuade President Reagan to approve legislation providing redress to Japanese Americans interned during World War II and pressed for teaching of the Holocaust in New Jersey schools. When the Soviet Union shot down a South Korean passenger jet that had wandered off course, killing two hundred civilians, Kean and New York Governor Mario Cuomo had the bistate Port Authority close the region's airports to Soviet aircraft.

Kean won reelection in 1985 by the widest margin in state history up to that time. Running against Essex County Executive Peter Shapiro, Kean received 68 percent of the vote, carrying every municipality in the state save for Audubon Park, Chesilhurst, and Roosevelt. He received a majority of African American votes and ran well among other Democratic constituencies. Elected with Kean was the first Republican-controlled assembly in a decade. Kean's "politics of inclusion" approach caught the attention of the national Republican Party, and Kean's colleagues elected him chairman of the Republican Governors Association. At the invitation of the GOP presidential nominee, Vice President George H. W. Bush, Kean delivered the keynote address at the 1988 Republican National Convention.

Early in his second term, Kean pressed for the reconfirmation of Robert N. Wilentz as chief justice of the state supreme court over the opposition of state senators in his own party, some of whom called attention to the chief justice's residence in New York City while his wife underwent cancer treatment. Others objected to the Wilentz court's activist decisions. Citing the principle of judicial independence, Kean secured the jurist's reconfirmation.

During his second term, Kean won national acclaim for his efforts to reform state welfare programs. Kean obtained federal waivers to launch a pilot program to motivate people off welfare through incentives. Through it, recipients who agreed to accept work and/or undergo training were allowed to retain for a time benefits to cover transportation, day care, and health care.

After leaving the governorship, Kean became president of Drew University. He proved an effective fund-raiser, erecting a new athletic center, a concert hall, a new theater, and other structures on the Madison campus. Under his leadership, the university's endowment also grew considerably. Kean's class on state government became one of the most popular on campus.

On several occasions, Kean considered and declined invitations to run for the United States Senate and to serve in various presidents' cabinets. President George H. W. Bush named Kean to the American delegation to the World Conference on Education for All in Thailand and designated him chairman of the New American Schools Development Corps. Kean also joined the board of the National Endowment for Democracy. President Bill Clinton appointed Kean to the bipartisan commission on entitlement and tax reform, designated him vice chairman of the U.S. delegation to the Fourth United Nations Conference on Women, and appointed Kean to the President's Initiative on Race. Kean served on corporate and nonprofit boards, as chairman of the Carnegie Corporation and the Robert Wood Johnson Foundation and as president of the Campaign to Prevent Teen Pregnancy.

Late in 2002, President George W. Bush named Kean chairman of the ten-member bipartisan National Commission on Terrorist Attacks upon the United States (the "9/11 Commission"). Its charge was to investigate what led to the attacks of September 11, 2001, and recommend policy changes to reduce the likelihood of reoccurrences. Analysts of all persuasions credited Kean and his vice chairman, former Indiana congressman Lee H. Hamilton, for setting a high standard for bipartisanship, transparency, and professionalism. The commission held twelve public hearings and interviewed more than twelve hundred witnesses. In response to its report, Congress enacted and the president signed the most extensive revamping of the nation's intelligence-gathering apparatus since 1947.

ALVIN S. FELZENBERG

Records of Governor Thomas H. Kean, New Jersey State Library, Trenton, N.J.

Felzenberg, Alvin S. *Governor Tom Kean: From the New Jersey Statehouse to the 9-11 Commission.* New Brunswick: Rutgers University Press, 2006.

Kean, Thomas H. *The Politics of Inclusion.* New York: Free Press, 1988.

Kean, Thomas H., and Lee Hamilton. *Without Precedent: The Inside Story of the 9/11 Commission.* New York: Knopf, 2006.

James Joseph Florio (August 29, 1937–)
was born in the Red Hook section of Brooklyn,
New York. Known to everyone as Jim, he left
school in 1955, after his junior year, to join the
navy. During his four years of service, Florio
earned his high school diploma by taking correspondence courses that eventually led him
to pass his GED test. Following his discharge,
he enrolled at Trenton State College (now
The College of New Jersey) and graduated in
1962 magna cum laude with a B.A. in social
studies. He attended Columbia University in
1962–63 on a Woodrow Wilson Fellowship.
Florio received his law degree from Rutgers
University Law School in 1967 and was admitted to the bar later that year. He continued in
the naval reserves until 1975, when he retired
with the rank of lieutenant commander.

James J. Florio
New Jersey State Archives; Department of State

Florio started out early in public service. From 1963 to 1969, he served
as assistant urban renewal director in Glassboro and then as a research
assistant and assistant city attorney in Camden. First elected to the general
assembly in Trenton in 1969, he was reelected twice.

Florio ran for Congress in the First Congressional District in 1972 and lost,
but then ran again in 1974 and won, becoming the first Democrat to represent the district since the 1880s. In Congress, Florio served on the Energy
and Commerce Committee, eventually chairing the Subcommittee on Commerce, Consumer Protection, and Competitiveness. He also served on the
Subcommittee on Housing and Consumer Interests as well as on the House
Select Committee on Aging.

At the time, the perils of toxic-waste sites were becoming increasingly
evident to the nation. In Florio's position on the Energy and Commerce
Committee, he helped draft what is perhaps his most significant national
achievement, the Comprehensive Environmental Response, Compensation,
and Liability Act of 1980 (CERCLA), more commonly known as the "Superfund law." The legislation authorized the federal Environmental Protection
Agency (EPA) to determine responsibility for the polluting of a site and to
require the responsible company or companies to clean it up. Where responsibility could not be determined, a special trust fund was established to pay
for the cleanup. Throughout Florio's career, environmental issues remained
a core part of his agenda.

In 1977, Florio was one of ten Democrats pursuing the party's gubernatorial nomination that was eventually won by incumbent Brendan T. Byrne,

whose popularity had dropped sharply due to his advocacy of an income tax. Despite Florio's fourth-place finish, he began preparing for another statewide run in 1981. His growing base in southern New Jersey as well as his national reputation in environmental affairs made him the favorite. His opponent for the governorship, Thomas H. Kean, the former speaker of the general assembly and scion of a wealthy New Jersey family with deep roots in state politics, embraced the tax-cutting politics of his fellow Republicans in Washington, D.C. Sensing advantage during an economic recession, Florio focused his attacks on the domestic policies of Republican President Ronald Reagan and, according to most polls, seemed poised to win. On Election Day, Kean won by 1,797 votes, or less the one-thousandth of a percent of the total ballots cast. It was the smallest margin of victory since New Jersey began electing its governors by popular vote in 1844.

Florio returned to his career in Congress and bided his time for a third shot at the statehouse. He chose not to run in 1985—when an extremely popular Kean was reelected with 70 percent of the vote—and instead waited for 1989, when Kean would be term-limited and the governor's seat would be open.

In the June 1989 primary, Florio easily defeated Princeton Mayor Barbara Boggs Sigmund and former assembly speaker Alan J. Karcher for the Democratic nomination by garnering 68 percent of the vote and winning in all twenty-one counties.

The 1989 general election pitted Florio against another congressman, James A. Courter, from Warren County. A self-described "Reagan Republican," Courter had made a name for himself on defense issues and as a strong advocate of tax cuts. The campaign has been widely described as one of the most negative in modern memory because of the barrage of personal attacks employed by each side in television advertising.

Florio and Courter each presented very different views regarding the role government should play in the state. Florio argued for a strong, activist government, one that would offset the new challenges arising after several years of strong economic growth, such as overdevelopment and pollution. At the same time, he repeatedly told audiences on the campaign trail that he "saw no need for new taxes." Courter advocated more free-market approaches to address social problems and also stressed his commitment not to raise taxes. The high cost of auto insurance in New Jersey was by far the biggest issue in the mind of the public during the campaign. While Courter presented a plan to lower premiums by allowing greater competition, Florio argued that the government needed to play a more active role in monitoring and restricting insurance companies.

Another major issue for the public was crime. Courter emphasized mandatory prison terms and reinvigorating the death penalty, unused in New Jersey since it was reinstated in 1982. Florio also supported the death penalty and made a pledge to ban assault weapons to make streets safer.

Even through Republican presidential and gubernatorial candidates had won in New Jersey throughout the decade, Florio's lead in public opinion polls was never seriously threatened. On November 7, 1989, the Democrat was elected the forty-ninth governor of New Jersey with 1,379,937 votes as compared to Courter's 838,553, a plurality of more than 540,000 votes. His coattails also brought the Democrats back to power in the general assembly, where they had been in the minority since Tom Kean's 1985 landslide victory. The state senate was not up for election in 1989 and remained in Democratic control.

Several serious problems immediately faced the new governor. A $550 million structural deficit had to be accounted for in the new budget to be passed by July 1, 1990. In addition, during the first part of 1990, the New Jersey Supreme Court was deciding *Abbott v. Burke*, part of the ongoing litigation that challenged the constitutionality of New Jersey's overreliance on property taxes to fund public school education. Though the state income tax had been instituted in 1977 to address this very issue, advocates for urban schoolchildren still charged that New Jersey was not doing enough. Many observers expected the high court to order the state to spend millions of additional dollars on schools in property-poor urban districts.

Florio stated in his inaugural address that he wanted to be "remembered as the governor who brought new ideas to preserve old ideals." His agenda touched on the environment, the urban poor, and education and called for a special session of the legislature to address the high cost of auto insurance.

The Florio auto-insurance plan shut down the Joint Underwriting Association (JUA), the unpopular, government-sponsored, industry-run pool of "bad drivers" which had come to cover almost 40 percent of all drivers in the state and had run up a debt of $3.1 billion. Every New Jersey driver, even those who were not in the pool, was already paying an extra $212 insurance surcharge to keep it afloat. The Florio plan eliminated the driver surcharge and replaced it with assessments spread among anyone who had been involved with the old system, including insurance companies, lawyers, chiropractors, doctors, and auto-repair shops.

The auto-insurance plan was controversial. Over the next four years, the administration waged a public relations and legal battle with the insurance companies, which disputed Florio's attacks on their profits and rate schedules. Auto-insurance rates were to remain a potent issue in future gubernatorial contests well into the next decade.

Florio also quickly fulfilled another campaign promise by naming an "environmental prosecutor," with broad investigative powers, to track down and hold polluters accountable. One of his most notable accomplishments was the subsequent passage of the Clean Water Enforcement Act, which required the state to inspect every permitted facility at least annually to ensure compliance with antipollution regulations. At the time, it was one of the strongest such laws in the nation.

However, it was Florio's controversial first budget that ultimately was to define his tenure as governor. In his March 1990 budget address, the governor balanced his $12.1 billion proposal with what would eventually be $2.8 billion in new and higher taxes, including raising the state's top income-tax rate to 7 percent from 3.5 percent, raising the sales tax to 7 percent from 6 percent and applying it to many new products (including toilet paper), increasing alcohol and tobacco taxes, and imposing a new tax on telephone and cable transmissions.

The breadth of the new taxes, just as New Jerseyans were facing recessionary pressures, dominated the political discussion in Trenton and drowned out the governor's proposed cost-cutting measures, such as reducing spending by all state departments, except Corrections and Human Services, by an average of 15 percent. Florio faced fierce criticism from advocates of programs that received cuts in funding and from Republicans who adamantly opposed tax increases. He defended his plan as "facing reality," declaring that new revenue would help increase property-tax rebate programs and provide additional aid to schools.

Traditionally, each state department head presented his or her section of the budget to the appropriate legislative committees and answered questions on spending choices and policy. Florio chose to have state treasurer Douglas Berman be the only one to speak on behalf of the administration. The decision to use one person in this role fed into mounting criticism that Florio was arrogant, aloof, and dictatorial, all of which had been raised against him by detractors in his previous statewide campaigns.

The public reacted strongly against Florio's proposals, and the new governor who had come to Trenton following a huge electoral victory was quickly and widely out of favor with many of his past supporters. Florio's political standing was both helped and hurt by his commitment to fulfilling another campaign pledge: the ban on a wide range of semiautomatic weapons. Although pro-gun-rights groups led a furious lobbying effort to derail the bill, in May 1990, the Democratic-controlled state legislature passed and then Florio signed one of the nation's strictest bans on these kinds of weapons. While popular with voters, the new legislation helped mobilize a number of gun-rights advocates across the nation who were dedicated to overturning the new law and defeating Florio when he ran for reelection.

Even as the budget proposals began to take shape in the spring of 1990, Florio unveiled a revised school-funding formula, one that anticipated the likely decision in *Abbott v. Burke* and, in effect, shifted hundreds of millions of dollars from suburban towns to the public schools in poorer urban and rural areas. In early June 1990, the New Jersey Supreme Court ruled as expected: the old way of financing public schools was unconstitutional, and New Jersey's poorest municipalities must be given additional aid to spend what the wealthiest districts spend per student. While administration officials breathed a sigh of relief, suburban voters were increasingly disenchanted with the Florio education proposals.

Florio's budget was passed by the slimmest of majorities. Despite the rising opposition to his policies, the governor remained steadfast in his message that the new funds would eventually provide substantial property-tax relief, address issues that had long been ignored by Trenton, and respond to the court's ruling. The public was not convinced. By July 1990, Florio's popularity had dropped to 23 percent, with nearly seven out of ten voters having a negative view of him.

Spurred on by a few aggressive media outlets, such as the *Trentonian* newspaper and a radio station known as New Jersey 101.5, voters began to organize in protest. Two radio-show callers eventually started a group called Hands Across New Jersey, which became the primary vehicle for a statewide tax revolt. One of the key arguments made by the group was that Florio had lied to the public when he said during his campaign that he "saw no need for new taxes." In an August statewide television address, the governor defended himself against this charge and insisted that the outgoing Kean administration had not left him with $250 million surplus, as promised, but with "a $3 billion gap to close."

In 1991, the national economic recession had not yet ended, thereby making the political situation even more difficult for the Florio administration. That year's legislative session did not offer much of a silver lining for Democrats and their governor who had taken politically risky moves in the first year of the administration in the hope that all would be forgotten once the economy turned around.

In fact, revenues came in lower than expected, leaving the budget again out of balance. With the possibility of new tax increases politically untenable, cutting government appeared to be the only way to bring things into alignment. Florio's 1991 State of the State Address remained focused on jobs and efforts to move New Jersey out of the recession by utilizing the Transportation Trust Fund to put people to work with new highway construction. He also highlighted a savings-bond program for parents to help pay for college tuition and a $250 million fund to help middle-income people finance the purchase of a new home. All of these programs used existing funding sources.

While the second year of the Florio administration was more modest in terms of its agenda, the governor's fellow Democrats in the legislature, preparing to face an angry electorate in November, attempted to alter one of the core Florio initiatives. Led by senate president John Lynch, Democrats worked to change the education-funding formula they had helped pass the year before by shifting money back to the suburban districts.

The $14.3 billion budget that Florio proposed for fiscal year 1992 closed the mounting budget deficit by reducing the state workforce and cutting the funding of all departments (with the exception of Corrections and Human Services) by 8 percent. Despite all the cost cutting, the overall budget grew, largely as a result of increases in property-tax relief programs and school aid.

Perhaps the most controversial element of the second Florio budget was a plan to generate $400 million by selling the northernmost portion of the New Jersey Turnpike to the New Jersey Turnpike Authority. It was widely derided as a one-time influx of revenue that moved money from one state agency to the general treasury, while leaving a huge structural deficit for the next year. The debate garnered even more attention because the proposal came in the wake of Florio's approval of significant increases in Turnpike tolls.

While voter anger in 1991 had abated somewhat since the summer of 1990, Florio remained unpopular. Two previous allies, the state worker unions and the teachers union, now joined the ranks of his opponents. State workers protested the administration's demands for salary givebacks and ongoing layoffs. Teachers argued that more than $1 billion promised under the education reforms of the previous year would not actually reach school districts because the state capped spending for those districts and then diverted $360 million for property-tax relief.

The budget that was passed and signed into law at the end of June 1991 totaled $14.7 billion. It included no new taxes and made attempts to address the property-tax burden in the state by increasing aid to school districts, municipalities, counties, and the homestead rebate program by nearly $2 billion. The budget laid off approximately twenty-five hundred state workers, while the sales tax on paper products—a part of the 1990 tax plan that had been mockingly referenced as the "toilet paper tax"—was repealed.

Running in 1991, the Democratic majorities in both houses faced a swelling storm of public discontent. Taxpayer groups such as Hands Across New Jersey and their advocates in the media were whipping up voters to "send a message to Florio." Powerful organized interests such as the teachers union, state worker unions, and the pro-gun-rights advocates were spending money and organizing against Democratic incumbents. Florio called on his fellow partisans to stand up and fight back, arguing that they had made the tough, but right, decisions. Republican legislative candidates generally ignored their opponents and ran against the governor, whose approval ratings, according to public polls, remained in the low to mid-twenties. The results were decisive and stunning.

The November 1991 elections eventually became widely known as "the Florio backlash." Democrats went from having a forty-three-seat majority in the eighty-member assembly to having only twenty-two seats. In the forty-member Senate, the twenty-three-vote Democratic majority was reduced to just thirteen members. Republicans took control with veto-proof majorities in both houses.

Shortly after the new Republican majorities were sworn in, Florio delivered his 1992 State of the State Address. He continued to call for the use of dedicated public funds that could be leveraged with private investment to create new jobs and provide worker training, both of which were still key issues for a state that had not yet left the recession behind. Republicans blasted the governor's view that the state was simply a victim of national economic forces and announced their intention to roll back many Florio initiatives from the previous two years.

Florio's $15.7 budget proposal for fiscal year 1993 was not well received by the new Republican legislative majorities in both houses. In part, this was because Florio assumed a 7 percent sale tax even though Republicans made it clear that they would cut it to 6 percent. In May, when the sales-tax rollback was approved by the legislature, Florio vetoed it. He explained that the Republicans had not explained how the revenue would be replaced or what services would be cut. His veto was overridden.

The legislature then produced its own state budget that cut more than $1 billion from the governor's proposal. In announcing what would be the first veto by a governor of an entire budget, Florio said, "I cannot sign a budget that would force state government to renege on its responsibilities and turn its back on our people." The Republicans again promptly overrode the veto.

Later in the summer of 1992, Republican legislators voted to rescind another signature Florio policy, the ban on semiautomatic assault weapons. Sensing an opportunity after a string of defeats, the governor vetoed the bill and then stumped across the state building public support on behalf of his decision. More than any other issue, the fight over the assault-weapons ban symbolized Florio's perseverance and commitment to an issue. It was an image he would use extensively in his reelection campaign the following year.

Despite the bitterness between the governor and Republican legislative majorities, both sides agreed in 1992 to establish an Economy Recovery Fund to help create jobs and support business development and to overhaul the state's welfare system, including the elimination of additional payments for mothers who have children while already on state assistance. A funding plan to use money from the state's unemployment-insurance fund to cover "charity care" (payments to hospitals to offset their care of the uninsured) eventually received bipartisan support as well. The parties also came together to redesign campaign finance, most notably by placing new limits on contributions and establishing Legislative Leadership Committees, through which the leader of each party's caucus in each house was able to accept much more money than any other member and could disburse unlimited amounts. There was also bipartisan agreement for sweeping anti-car-theft legislation and for establishing "charter schools" that would be funded by the public but run by volunteer parents and teachers.

As Florio entered his reelection year of 1993, he was reasonably well positioned. Public anger over his first-year tax plan had abated somewhat, and his approval ratings began to improve. The contentious issues of auto insurance, education spending, and reimbursing charity care were resolved and off the table. In addition, Florio was an early and strong supporter of fellow Democrat Bill Clinton in his race for the presidency and now had an appreciative friend in the White House.

Relations between the governor and the Republican legislative majorities, while not warm, were generally more cordial than they had been, with both sides wary of the fallout of being seen as too partisan during an election year. Florio's third annual message to the legislature praised the bipartisan progress that had been made, and then, as befitting the times, focused largely on jobs and the economy.

In February, when Florio proposed a $15.6 billion budget for fiscal year 1994, he was able to offset a significant structural deficit by relying on a growing economy that was bringing in more money to state coffers and the willingness of the Clinton administration to reimburse New Jersey for an additional $412 million in contested Medicaid payments. The proposed budget again avoided new taxes and was not seen as particularly controversial.

The brief peace between the parties in Trenton ended shortly after the governor floated the idea of delivering a $100 million tax cut to middle-class New Jerseyans. The soundness of the proposed election-year tax cut was questioned by Christine Todd Whitman, a former head of the Board of Public Utilities, who had secured the Republican nomination for governor in early June. Republican legislators quickly retreated from whatever bipartisan support they might have been considering, thereby dooming the idea. The $15.4 billion budget that Florio signed later than month was slightly smaller than what he originally proposed and did not include what could have been a politically beneficial election-year tax cut.

The most contentious issue of 1993 involved Republican attempts to override the governor's 1992 veto of the repeal of the assault-weapons ban. Facing aggressive, grass-roots lobbying from all sides, the assembly found the votes to override in late February. However, a few weeks later, the senate was unable to follow suit. Florio had what was to become his most popular legislative victory as governor.

Shortly thereafter, the John F. Kennedy Library Foundation gave Florio its nationally recognized "Profile in Courage Award" for his efforts to stand by his policy despite the considerable strength of gun-rights advocates. In his acceptance speech, the governor restated his belief that true leadership meant sometimes doing what was unpopular but right. This became a dominant image promoted by the Florio reelection campaign: a man who stands up for what he believes is the best course for his constituents, regardless of contrary political pressure.

However, the campaign was knocked off course by scandal. In May 1993, Merrill Lynch, one of the nation's largest financial-services companies and a major underwriter of New Jersey bonds, suspended three executives for inappropriate actions involving a bond consulting firm owned by two long-time Florio political allies, Nicholas H. Rudi and Joseph C. Salema; Salema was then serving as Florio's chief of staff. As a federal investigation was launched, Florio moved quickly to limit the political fallout. Salema resigned his position, and the governor issued an executive order that banned the sale of bond-underwriting services without the use of competitive bidding.

Previously, a government entity would simply select an underwriter and then negotiate the fees, a system that critics claimed was ripe for abuse. The process was so widespread across the country that, eventually, the Securities and Exchange Commission approved a ban on investment bankers donating to any state official who was in a position to influence municipal finance business.

The Florio-Whitman race of 1993 was one of the closest in New Jersey history. The Florio campaign attacked the wealthy Whitman, whose only previous elective office was as a freeholder in Somerset County, as being inexperienced and unable to relate to the common New Jerseyan. The governor took full advantage of his incumbency and would often be seen at public events or major public works projects giving speeches, signing bills, and announcing new grants and initiatives.

Florio worked assiduously to secure the Democratic base in urban areas and make amends with old allies such as the state worker and teacher unions. He reached out to more independent voters by emphasizing his stands on welfare reform and the assault-weapons ban. In late September, Whitman, who was trailing in public polls, unveiled her signature economic proposal: a 30 percent tax cut in state income taxes. Florio decried it as more of the Reagan-era fiscal policies that would eventually hurt far more than they helped.

As the race drew tighter in the final weeks, each side focused on its core messages. Whitman reminded audiences that Florio had raised taxes more than any other previous governor and promised that she would cut them. Florio argued that he should be rewarded for making the tough decisions that would now help the state move forward on a stronger footing, and he predicted that Whitman would roll back the assault-weapons ban and provide disproportionate benefits to the wealthiest New Jerseyans.

Despite most public polls showing Florio with a significant lead on the eve of the election, Whitman received 1,236,124 votes to Florio's 1,210,031. The narrow upset win was marred a few days after the election when Edward J. Rollins, Jr., Whitman's campaign manager, told a group of reporters that the campaign had funneled cash to African American ministers in an effort to suppress turnout for Florio among their congregants. The reaction from Democrats and the ministers was both immediate and furious. Whitman angrily denied that it happened, and Rollins retracted his earlier statements. An investigation examining the charges was eventually dismissed. Subsequently, New Jersey's election laws were changed to prohibit the use of campaign cash to pay supporters for their work. All such payments instead had to be made by check.

In Florio's final State of the State Address, shortly before he left the governor's office in January 1994, he gave a spirited defense of his legacy. "If there was a political price to pay," he said, "it was worth it." A week later, at age fifty-five, he was out of government for the first time in three decades.

In private life, Florio built a successful law practice and teaches classes at Rutgers University, where he is a Senior Planning Fellow for Public Policy and Administration at the Edward J. Bloustein Graduate School of Planning and Public Policy. He served as chairman of the Pinelands Commission in New Jersey and on the Board of Directors of the New Jersey Heath Care Quality Institute. He made one more attempt at elected office. In 2000, following the retirement of U.S. Senator Frank R. Lautenberg, Florio entered the Democratic Senate primary against Jon S. Corzine, the former chairman of the investment bank Goldman Sachs. Endorsed by most of the Democratic Party establishment and outspending the former governor by almost twenty to one, Corzine won decisively in all areas outside Florio's southern New Jersey base. Florio returned to his law firm and continues to serve as an elder statesman in the Democratic Party.

In 1988, Florio married the former Lucinda Coleman. Each had been previously married and divorced. He has three children and she has one child from their first marriages.

BENJAMIN DWORKIN

Records of Governor James J. Florio, New Jersey State Library, Trenton, N.J.
Salmore, Barbara G., and Stephen A. Salmore. *New Jersey Government and Politics: The Suburbs Come of Age.* 4th ed. New Brunswick: Rutgers University Press, 2013.

Christine Todd Whitman
New Jersey State Archives; Department of State

Christine Todd Whitman (September 26, 1946–) was born into a distinguished political family, and she developed a predictable, if not foreordained, interest in politics. Undertaking government service on local, state, and national stages—and becoming a leader of the moderate wing of the Republican Party—grew naturally out of values absorbed from her earliest days.

Christine Todd was born on September 26, 1946, in New York City, the youngest of four children of Eleanor Schley Todd and Webster Todd, Sr. She spent most of her childhood at the Todd family home, Pontefract, a two-hundred-acre farm in Hunterdon County. Her parents and grandparents were actively involved in the Republican Party. Her maternal grandfather chaired the state's Republican finance committee; her father was the

Republican State Committee chairman; and both her mother and maternal grandmother served as chairwomen of the New Jersey Federation of Republican Women and Republican National Committeewomen. These strong familial ties to the party had a noticeable impact on the youngest Todd, who went with her family to her first Republican National Convention at the age of nine and four years later went door-to-door collecting signatures for Richard M. Nixon's 1960 presidential bid.

In 1964, Christine Todd enrolled at Wheaton, a women's college in Massachusetts, where she earned a B.A. in government. She remained politically involved throughout college, becoming president of the Young Republicans Club and vice president of her graduating class. While in college, she was vocal in exploring and sharing her political views. She argued in favor of the Vietnam War, though she questioned "the whole premise that got us into the war in the first place." She also participated in a student demonstration for reproductive rights after Bill Baird, an activist for women's rights, was arrested for giving birth-control pills to a group of students at Wellesley College. Finding it "outrageous" that someone was arrested simply for sharing information, she stuck firmly to her belief in reproductive freedom. The summer before her senior year, she interned in the office of New Jersey's senior United States Senator Clifford Case in Washington, D.C. After graduating from Wheaton with honors in 1968, her first paid job was for her work on Nelson Rockefeller's presidential campaign.

Subsequently Whitman took positions working for Donald Rumsfeld in the U.S. Office of Economic Opportunity in Washington, D.C., and for the Republican National Committee. As the Republican base became more conservative, she advocated for diversity, believing that incorporating more points of view would attract more members to the Republican Party. Under the auspices of the RNC, she spent a year in 1969–70 working on a "listening post" project, traveling around the nation talking to people about how the GOP could broaden its appeal to older Americans, minorities, and students. Later she served as deputy director of the New York State Office in Washington, D.C., and worked for President Nixon's 1972 reelection campaign.

Christine Todd invited banker John Whitman, an acquaintance from New York, as her date to Nixon's 1973 inaugural ball; the relationship blossomed, and they married on April 20, 1974. John Whitman was the son of a New York City judge, Charles Whitman, Jr., and the grandson of former New York governor Charles Whitman, Sr. When John's work took the couple to London, Christie took courses at the London School of Economics and became active with the organization for U.S. Republicans in the United Kingdom. They welcomed a daughter, Kate, in April 1977. Their son, Taylor, was born in January 1979, shortly after the family moved back to New Jersey.

In 1982, the Somerset County Republican Party recruited Christie Whitman as a candidate for a county freeholder position. She ran alongside Branchburg Mayor John Kitchen, taking on an entrenched Democratic incumbent and a former Democratic freeholder. Kitchen and Whitman received the most and second-most votes, respectively, and Whitman replaced Doris Dealaman on the Somerset County Board of Freeholders. After serving a three-year term, Whitman ran for reelection, receiving the endorsement of the *Home News*, which described her as "the most active, the most visible and the most effective freeholder Somerset County has seen of late." During her second term, she became freeholder director.

Whitman's tenure as a freeholder was marked by accomplishments as well as controversies. During a period of growth and prosperity, the county greatly increased spending and undertook numerous major projects, including the construction of a long-delayed new courthouse and a jail as well as other county facilities. While revenues, budgets, and payrolls increased, the county tax rate decreased. The freeholders voted a raise for county employees, including themselves, creating an issue that was later cited by Whitman's Democratic opponents. Among the most contentious concerns was trash. Somerset County had been dumping its trash in neighboring Middlesex County, but a new plan was required by the state as local residents fought against building new trash facilities in the county. Whitman drew praise for holding a lengthy public hearing on the issue. Ultimately a local site was selected for an incinerator ash landfill, but it was never built. Later, the freeholders arranged to ship the county's trash to Pennsylvania.

Another issue bedeviling Whitman was the deposit of county funds in the Somerset Trust Company. The county had long kept funds in that bank, but because Christie Whitman's grandparents, her parents, and Christie and John Whitman themselves had a long history of holdings in the bank and still owned a considerable amount of its stock, some people questioned the ethics of Whitman's votes to deposit county funds there. Whitman never cast a deciding vote in favor of such deposits, and votes were taken in open meetings; but the issue fueled criticism from opponents at the time as well as later when she ran for governor.

In 1988, Whitman resigned as freeholder to accept an appointment to Governor Thomas Kean's cabinet as chair of the Board of Public Utilities. Her selection had been greeted with criticism that she lacked expertise in the areas governed by the BPU, but she won senate confirmation and served until 1990, when she resigned to run for the U.S. Senate. During her tenure at the BPU, she implemented a new code of ethics and addressed complex issues related to waste management, rate setting, and utility costs. A controversial land-sale issue clouded her last days at the agency, and the board's decision in that case was later overturned by the courts.

Entering the U.S. Senate race in spring 1990, Whitman challenged popular Democratic incumbent Bill Bradley. His $12 million campaign war chest dwarfed her $1 million budget, and she was viewed as a sacrificial lamb. The Republican Party on both state and national levels did little to support her campaign. President George H. W. Bush, a Todd family friend, never came to

New Jersey to stump for her. The $420,000 contributed by the National Republican Senatorial Committee was $180,000 less than had been promised. The New Jersey GOP invested only $5,000. Even with a $100,000 personal loan from Whitman, the campaign could not afford private tracking polls. While accusing Bradley of wasting taxpayer dollars on overstaffing and frivolous constituent mailings, Whitman also attempted, with a greater degree of success, to link her opponent with Governor Jim Florio's highly unpopular proposals for new taxes on toilet paper, beer, and gasoline, among other products. Calling the tax issue a state matter, Bradley refused to engage, perhaps misreading the strong feelings of the electorate on the issue. The surprisingly close results on Election Day—Bradley prevailed by three points—allowed Whitman to position herself as a legitimate contender for a future race.

That future was soon in view. With an eye on the 1993 New Jersey gubernatorial election, Whitman spent time and money painstakingly building a base of support among local party officials and voters across the state, arguing that Governor Florio could and should be defeated.

Florio had pushed through a $2.8 billion tax increase, inciting a grassroots tax revolt throughout the state. New Jersey lost nearly three hundred thousand jobs during his tenure, and his job approval had sunk as low as 18 percent. Whitman offered herself as the Republican alternative who could best defeat an embattled Democrat. In November 1992, she established People for Whitman '93, her gubernatorial campaign committee.

The Republican primary was tightly contested among Whitman, former New Jersey attorney general and Bergen County assemblyman W. Cary Edwards, and former state senator James Wallwork. Whitman prevailed, becoming the first woman in New Jersey history to represent a major party in a gubernatorial election. In the years since the Senate race, Whitman had laid careful groundwork, marshaling the support of Republican leaders and grass-roots workers around the state. Whitman focused her attacks more on Florio's policies than on her Republican rivals. Opponents attacked Whitman as an inexperienced, unqualified candidate protected by family wealth. She criticized a middle-class tax-cut proposal that had surfaced in the Republican-led state legislature and argued that there was "no point to giving an election-year tax break when you have to come back next year, and the year after, and hit them for two times the cut."

In the general election, the candidates battled most intensely over taxes, the economy, and gun control. Whitman's campaign suffered from organizational problems and mistakes. Six weeks before Election Day, Whitman released a startling plan to cut income taxes by 30 percent over three years for most New Jersey residents. Failure to indicate exactly where she would find money for the program left Whitman exposed to skepticism by the media and sharp attacks by her opponent. The Florio campaign used the issue in advertisements and during debates. Whitman also vowed to deliver a business tax cut to promote job growth in the private sector, citing the steep job losses that occurred during Florio's administration. She believed that she could win if the campaign remained focused on these issues and reminded the public why they disliked Florio. The Florio campaign believed that its path to victory lay in focusing on the semiautomatic-weapons ban passed during his administration. Whitman had proposed removing several weapons from the ban and focusing more attention on people who commit crimes. Florio used these statements, and also video footage of Whitman at a shooting range during the 1990 Senate campaign, to paint her as soft on crime and a friend of the National Rifle Association. Whitman actually favored a ban on assault weapons, with exceptions for hunting weapons and weapons owned by collectors, but the image Florio created hurt her with women voters.

Even though Whitman was the first woman to win her party's nomination in a New Jersey gubernatorial election, women across the state were not especially enthusiastic about her candidacy. The gender gap evident in the final vote tally reflected the standard partisan pattern of women favoring the Democrat; Florio carried the female vote.

Among feminist organizations, the Women's Political Caucus of New Jersey endorsed Whitman. Both Whitman and Florio met the National Organization for Women's criteria on key issues such as reproductive rights, gay/lesbian rights, and the Equal Rights Amendment, but both candidates supported welfare reform, which NOW opposed. However, since Whitman exhibited a degree of flexibility on the issue, she received their "recommendation," still less than a full endorsement.

Whitman was hurt among women voters by Florio's depiction of her as soft on crime, based on her purported support for weakening the semiautomatic-weapons ban. Florio maintained a significant lead with female voters throughout most of the election campaign, depicting Whitman as out of touch. In October, the Whitman campaign fought back, deliberately reaching out to women with a variety of tactics: a bus tour that brought a casually dressed, down-to-earth, and relaxed Whitman to meet voters in supermarkets and diners; television advertisements depicting her as warm and reachable; a radio ad in which her daughter defended her and praised her as a mother; and accusations that Florio supported traditional sex roles for women.

Governor Florio had maintained a lead in the polls throughout most of the campaign. As Election Day dawned, most polls and pundits assumed Florio would be reelected. To near-universal surprise, when the votes were counted, the challenger had edged out the incumbent, winning by a 1 percent margin, or 26,093 votes out of a total of approximately 2.5 million cast. In addition to winning traditionally Republican counties such as Hunterdon and Somerset, Whitman carried typically Democratic areas such as Middlesex, Mercer, and Passaic Counties. In addition to predictable suburban support, she drew blue-collar white voters attracted to her promises to reduce government spending and lower taxes.

Shortly after her victory, governor-elect Whitman confronted a crisis that drew national media attention and distracted her and her team from focusing exclusively on organizing the transition and planning her inauguration. Campaign manager Ed Rollins, in what he later described as a failed attempt to one-up his Democratic rival James Carville, told a group of reporters that the campaign had spent $500,000 to suppress the Florio vote in black communities. Rollins claimed that the campaign had contacted black ministers and campaign workers to dissuade them from promoting Florio's candidacy or making special efforts to encourage voting. From the start, governor-elect Whitman asserted that there was no basis for any allegations of wrongdoing. A few days before Whitman's inauguration, after state and federal investigations found no evidence of the alleged activities, the matter was dropped, as was a lawsuit that had been filed by the New Jersey Democratic Party.

On January 18, 1994, Christine Todd Whitman was inaugurated as New Jersey's fiftieth governor, beginning her first term with a historic victory. Whitman was the first challenger to defeat an incumbent governor of New Jersey since the adoption of the 1947 state constitution. She entered the statehouse as New Jersey's first woman governor, the second Republican woman chief executive in any state, and the thirteenth woman governor in American history. Whitman was one of four women among the fifty governors serving in 1994.

Throughout the almost two terms of Whitman's governorship, while pursuing her substantial policy agenda, she recognized responsibilities as a "first" and role model, demonstrating a consistent interest in supporting broadened opportunity for women and girls. Soon after her election, she named Judy Shaw as the first woman to serve as a New Jersey governor's chief of staff. Subsequent appointees included the state's first woman attorney general, Deborah Poritz, later named by Whitman as the first woman chief justice of the state supreme court, as well as several other cabinet officials. (Whitman later opened her second inaugural address with "Madam Chief Justice . . . ," thereby highlighting that historic appointment.) These two highly visible frontline appointments were accompanied by many others at lower levels where policies are implemented. In an interview, Whitman observed, "That's how it starts to happen. You put women or minorities in positions where they can affect the hiring or appointment process, and they will then begin to open things up." Beyond the statehouse, Whitman regularly accepted invitations to address classrooms and programs where she could encourage young girls and women to think about how they could make a difference and to consider public leadership as an attractive option.

From the start of Whitman's tenure, she identified three central policy themes for her administration. In her first inaugural address, she stated, "Our blueprint to make New Jersey first is an agenda of economic growth, good schools, and safe streets." The same focus reappeared in her State of the State Address in 1998 and again, just days later, in her second inaugural address, when she said, "As I said last week in my State of the State Address, I want to make our state more affordable, our schools stronger, and our communities safer."

Nearing the end of her term in 2001, Whitman claimed that the signature achievement of her administration was "promises made, promises kept." While assessments of the policies encompassed in those promises varied widely, with intense and continuing criticism of her tax-reduction policies and bond financing of state pensions, she had indeed fulfilled her promises. Whitman's economic policies echoed Reagan-era approaches, relying on a mix of tax cuts, deregulation, support for business, and tight reins on spending. Property taxes, a perennial issue in New Jersey, increased no more than during the previous administration, and employment grew, albeit more modestly than she had anticipated.

During Whitman's first term, the key promise she fulfilled was reducing the size and cost of government, implementing a 30 percent income-tax cut over three years and several reductions in business taxes. She downsized the cabinet from nineteen departments to sixteen, eliminating the Department of Higher Education and the Department of the Public Advocate and combining Banking and Insurance into one department. The Department of Health expanded to include Senior Services, and the Department of Environmental Protection was no longer responsible for energy-related policies. The Department of Commerce and Economic Development was reduced to a commission. Whitman also sought to facilitate privatization of some government services.

Whitman's treasurer reported early on that the state had overestimated the size of contributions necessary to sustain state employee pension funds, in part due to a booming stock market that increased the value of the funds. Thus, she developed her budget for fiscal year 1995 assuming the availability of an unexpected $1.3 billion, and her administration began withholding payments from the pension funds. However, Whitman later learned that the actual unfunded liability was closer to $4.7 billion. Her strategy for addressing this gap was the 1997 "Pension Security Plan," which entailed issuing $2.7 billion in bonds. Her administration asserted that the sale of these bonds would generate sufficient income to fund the system and obviate the need for additional contributions to the pension fund for some time; its calculations were based on an overoptimistic estimate of 8.75 percent annual returns. Whitman also signed legislation guaranteeing that current state workers' pensions could not be changed, in contrast to the ability of private-sector employers to alter their pension plans at will. Standard & Poor's warned that the plan could jeopardize the state's strong credit rating, and others pointed out that while the pension funds might be strong at that time, the "excess" would be necessary to support an influx of retirees in coming years. Later, even as subsequent administrations continued the practice of withholding additional pension-fund contributions, critics blamed the Whitman administration's original plan for initiating the practice and therefore contributing to ongoing problems with the pension fund and the state budget. As late as July 30, 2002, in a *New York Times* column, economist Paul Krugman criticized Whitman's policies, accusing her of setting the state on an unhealthy fiscal course. Defenders pointed to upgrades from credit-rating agencies and growth in state government matching that of the state's economy during her time in office as evidence of fiscal responsibility. They also insisted that the pension bonds were not used to fund Whitman's tax cuts, which they claimed paid for themselves via increased economic activity.

Environmental protection and preservation of undeveloped space were high priorities for the Whitman administration. During her second term, in 1998, a signature achievement in this area was approval by voters of a constitutional amendment creating a plan for preserving open space, farmland, and historic sites. To implement that amendment, the legislature adopted Governor Whitman's plan for the Garden State Preservation Trust to approve projects and oversee financing for them. Whitman aimed to acquire three hundred thousand acres out of the one million acres set as a ten-year goal. In addition, the Whitman administration moved on other environmental initiatives, including incentives for businesses to clean up and develop contaminated areas. Environment-friendly transportation policies included stricter auto-emissions testing, implementation of high-occupancy vehicle (HOV) lanes, and completion of railway and light-rail projects already under way.

New Jersey's state constitution had long required that the state's K–12 schools provide a "thorough and efficient education" (T&E), a challenging mandate in view of widely varying distribution of income and wealth. During Whitman's years as governor, the title "Abbott districts" (named for the plaintiffs in the *Abbott v. Burke* case on school-funding formulas) was applied to the twenty-eight districts (later thirty) designated as requiring special support to meet T&E standards. The Whitman plan to meet these requirements focused on a set of Core Curriculum Content Standards and a system of "whole school reform" to apply those standards. Central to the plan was a system of accountability in the form of a Statewide Assessment Program. A court-approved funding formula determined how much state aid the commissioner of education would allocate to ensure that Abbott districts received funding comparable to that in wealthy districts. Acknowledging the importance of early childhood education, the Whitman administration also promoted development of pre-K programs in Abbott districts.

The Whitman administration backed two initiatives to broaden the educational options for K–12 families. In 1996, Governor Whitman signed the Charter School Law, and by 2000 charters had been approved for sixty-seven schools, which were either open or in the planning stages. A five-year pilot School Choice Program offered families opportunities to enroll their children in schools with open seats outside their local districts. Whitman also championed character education, encouraging schools to apply for small grants to develop their own program models within the curriculum. Initiatives aimed at professional development for teachers included a pilot Teacher Quality Mentoring program for new instructors and mandated continuing education for all teachers. With the passage of the 2000 Educational Facilities Construction and Financing Act, the state supported school construction plans throughout the state, with special emphasis on the Abbott districts.

In line with Whitman's campaign promise to streamline government and in response to calls for changing the governance of higher education, she took steps to create a new structure, abolishing the state's Board of Higher Education and replacing it with a decentralized system with three components: a Commission on Higher Education, a Presidents' Council, and boards of trustees at each institution. Supporters liked the autonomy granted to individual institutions, while opponents claimed that there was no longer a powerful voice representing the interests of higher education within state government. During the Whitman years, efforts to make higher education affordable and attractive for New Jersey students included support for the New Jersey Better Education Savings Trust (a 529 college savings plan); a Tuition Aid Grant (TAG) program to provide need-based assistance for college students; the longstanding Educational Opportunity Fund; and, beginning in 1997, a newly established Outstanding Scholar Recruitment Program to entice top students to attend New Jersey institutions.

Whitman, in line with her reputation, stood on the moderate side of a number of social policy issues. While she vetoed a ban on "partial-birth abortion" in 1997, she also signed legislation in 1999 containing language requiring parental notification for teens seeking abortions (which was later ruled unconstitutional by the New Jersey Supreme Court). Aware of the needs of a quickly growing population of senior citizens, the Whitman administration consolidated programs for them under the newly named Department of Health and Senior Services and launched the NJ EASE (Easy Access, Single Entry) toll-free line and website to streamline access to information. Under the ElderCare Initiative, the state sought to expand options for seniors to receive long-term care services, whether at home or in institutions. KidCare and FamilyCare programs aimed to offer health-care coverage to previously uninsured low-income individuals, while the Health Care Quality Act of 1997 defined rights and responsibilities for those served by health-insurance plans and HMOs. She focused attention on an issue she considered top priority by visiting facilities for youthful offenders, creating a Juvenile Justice Advisory Council, and signing legislation to reform the juvenile justice system.

Whitman took particular pride in Work First New Jersey, the welfare-reform plan she helped to craft, which included a work requirement for most recipients and placed a five-year lifetime cap on welfare benefits.

In Whitman's 1997 reelection bid, her general election opponent was Woodbridge mayor and state senator James McGreevey, who had won a three-way primary over Congressman Rob Andrews and former Morris County prosecutor Michael Murphy. A highly disciplined candidate, McGreevey created an effective campaign attack by pounding relentlessly on voter frustration with New Jersey's skyrocketing automobile-insurance rates. Among numerous minor-party candidates, only libertarian Murray Sabrin attracted significant attention and qualified for public funding. Although he ultimately drew votes away from both major-party candidates, Sabrin's appeal to social conservatives offered an alternative to Whitman's moderate Republican profile.

While Whitman had appeared invincible earlier in her term, polls showed a tight race as the election approached. Ultimately, despite McGreevey's attacks, voters generally found Whitman likable and did not find her opponent a sufficiently appealing alternative to turn her out of office. She won reelection, albeit by only 1 percent, or twenty-six thousand votes, almost duplicating her 1993 margin.

Whitman maintained close relationships with Assembly Speaker Chuck Haytaian and Senate President Donald DiFrancesco. These relationships and a willingness to wage public campaigns for legislative initiatives led to successful enactment of her major legislative programs. Still, as a governor who had never served in the statehouse and as a woman in a male-dominated capital, Whitman was often viewed as a Trenton outsider.

From early in her governorship, Whitman attracted recognition well beyond the state's borders, both because of her distinctive status as one of a handful of female governors and because she spoke effectively to policy issues of national significance. She was frequently sought out by the national media and also by her party, notably in 1995 when she gave the Republican response to President Bill Clinton's State of the Union Address.

On January 31, 2001, with less than a year remaining in her second term, Whitman resigned the governorship to accept an appointment by President George W. Bush as administrator of the Environmental Protection Agency. She served the Bush administration in Washington, D.C., until 2003, when she stepped down to return to New Jersey. There she established her own consulting firm specializing in energy and environmental issues, the Whitman Strategy Group, and joined the boards of directors of several corporations including Texas Instruments, United Technologies, and S. C. Johnson.

While the media and pundits frequently mentioned Whitman's name as a vice presidential or even presidential prospect, her opportunities for national office were limited by her reputation as a consistent moderate who took a prochoice stance on abortion. A lifelong Republican committed to her values and her party as she saw it, she joined Senator John Danforth and Lieutenant Governor Michael Steele in establishing the Republican Leadership Council, which advocated a fiscally conservative and socially "tolerant" GOP. Whitman wrote and published a book titled *It's My Party Too* and established a political action committee by the same name. She traveled the country arguing for a more inclusive Republican Party and a more civil tone in American political discourse. In the 2012 election cycle, Whitman was a founding organizer of Americans Elect, a nonpartisan organization that unsuccessfully sought to use the Internet to select a presidential ticket in an open process.

KATHERINE E. KLEEMAN

RUTH B. MANDEL

Records of Governor Christine Todd Whitman, New Jersey State Library, Trenton, N.J.

Beard, Patricia. *Growing Up Republican: Christie Whitman: The Politics of Character.* New York: HarperCollins, 1996.

Belkin, Lisa. "Keeping to the Center Lane." *New York Times Magazine,* May 5, 1996.

Hartman, Mary S., ed. *Talking Leadership: Conversations with Powerful Women.* New Brunswick: Rutgers University Press, 1999.

McClure, Sandy. *Christie Whitman for the People: A Political Biography.* Amherst, N.Y.: Prometheus Books, 1996.

Salmore, Barbara G., and Stephen A. Salmore. *New Jersey Politics and Government: The Suburbs Come of Age.* 4th ed. New Brunswick: Rutgers University Press, 2013.

Donald T. DiFrancesco

New Jersey State Archives; Department of State

Donald Thomas DiFrancesco (November 20, 1944–) was born in Scotch Plains, Union County, New Jersey. DiFrancesco began a long legislative career in Republican Party politics in 1976, when he entered the New Jersey General Assembly. He served in the assembly for three years and was then elected to the state senate, which he entered in 1979. During his legislative career, he supported bills that, at times, placed him outside the mainstream of his party, including the 1990 Family Leave Act and another aimed at securing employment rights for temporarily disabled workers.

The son of Italian immigrant parents, DiFrancesco attended Pennsylvania State University, where he received a B.S. degree in 1966; he graduated from Seton Hall University School of Law in 1969 and was admitted to the New Jersey bar later that year. DiFrancesco began his career as a municipal prosecutor in his native Scotch Plains, serving in that post between 1970 and 1975. At times during the 1980s and 1990s, he served simultaneously as township attorney for the municipalities of both Scotch Plains and Berkeley Heights; these years also coincided with his terms in the New Jersey Senate.

DiFrancesco was elected senate president in 1992, when the Republican-controlled state senate, part of the 205th State Legislature, was seated during the administration of Governor James Florio. Upon assuming this new post in the legislature, DiFrancesco, the first Republican senate president in eighteen years, promised to wield the investigatory powers of the senate to serve as a watchdog for government operations. He also urged his fellow Republican legislators to push for a constitutional amendment allowing for direct citizen lawmaking through initiative and referenda and to pursue new campaign-finance regulations limiting contributions to candidates.

As senate president, DiFrancesco took the gubernatorial oath of office on February 1, 2001, after the resignation of Governor Christine Todd Whitman, who was appointed by President George W. Bush to lead the federal Environmental Protection Agency. Under the provisions of the state constitution, he retained the senate presidency. Upon entering executive office, DiFrancesco had the good political fortune to inherit a major increase in the rebate of state property tax. Once again, DiFrancesco's governing priorities—which, according to a contemporary description in the *New York Times*, included "aid to municipalities; providing prescription-drug coverage for elderly, middle-income residents; promoting water quality; and bolstering hospitals with increased state aid"—appeared to lie outside the mainstream of traditional Republican Party thought.

Upon taking office, DiFrancesco initiated policies aimed at bolstering his chances for election to the governorship in his own right in November 2001. Early in his tenure, the new governor declared his opposition to an increase in highway tolls, promising to veto any plan to raise state revenue in this way. He also faced a new legislative agenda in a proposed family leave act, as well as a health insurer accountability act (a so-called right-to-sue bill). This latter bill, which DiFrancesco supported, was inspired by similar Texas legislation and was supported by the state's leading consumer advocacy group, the New Jersey Public Interest Research Group. With the support of the Republican-controlled legislature, DiFrancesco also raised New Jersey pension benefits 9 percent and lowered the retirement age to fifty-five, adding to a future burden on the state's pension system. With a budget surplus, DiFrancesco appeared enviably poised to win the endorsement of the state's Republican Party for governor.

In fact, the new governor spent his first few months in office in part preparing for electoral challenges from both within and outside his party. Woodbridge Mayor James McGreevey, a Democrat, was the frontrunner for his party's nomination, and Jersey City Mayor Bret Schundler sought the Republican nomination. Though DiFrancesco led Schundler in fund-raising in the late winter, the DiFrancesco candidacy was fatally wounded by the revelation, in early March 2001, that the acting governor and his family had benefited financially from a complicated 1996 land-development deal in his hometown, which his opponents claimed was unethical. By March 2001, negative publicity about this land deal had become a persistent hindrance to

DiFrancesco's campaign, and the *New York Times*'s editorial page had begun questioning his readiness for executive office.

In April, the acting governor drew further criticism—this from the state's environmental groups—for signing a bill at the New Jersey Builders' Association convention that gave developers automatic zoning approval if forced to wait more than ten days for a construction permit. In response, the state's League of Municipalities began urging local governments to deny zoning permits automatically if they were unable to meet this new deadline. Prior to this bill, DiFrancesco had enjoyed substantial support from environmental groups.

By mid-April 2001, as DiFrancesco faced an investigation from the legislature's Joint Legislative Committee on Ethics, his public approval rating —as measured by the Quinnipiac University Polling Institute—stood at 24 percent. Further revelations in the *New York Times* that in 1998 the acting governor had narrowly escaped being removed from his job in Scotch Plains government for ethics violations further tarnished his reputation. As such questions were raised, DiFrancesco's ability to withstand a challenge from Democrat James McGreevey appeared compromised. On April 25, 2001, DiFrancesco withdrew from the race; he was replaced on the Republican primary ballot by former U.S. representative Bob Franks, prompting a lawsuit by Republican Bret Schundler.

No longer preoccupied by a political campaign, DiFrancesco began the remainder of his one-year term by rejecting plans for the creation of an artificial reef off the New Jersey coast composed of New York City subway cars. Citing environmental concerns—the cars contained asbestos that could conceivably be released if the metal deteriorated—the acting governor denied the request of New York City's Transit Authority to dispose of thirteen hundred 1960s-era subway cars off the New Jersey coastline. Subsequent policy debates also ensued over the affordability of automobile insurance in the state, as State Farm, one of the state's largest insurers, announced plans to cease doing business in New Jersey. DiFrancesco followed the lead of his predecessor, Governor Whitman (who had secured 1998 legislation lowering car-insurance premiums), and refused to allow State Farm to increase its rates.

By mid-June 2001, the short-lived DiFrancesco administration faced additional political trouble. Two weeks before the end of the fiscal year, DiFrancesco acknowledged that the state faced a $1 billion budget gap. Though the governor had proposed a budget for fiscal year 2002 of $23.2 billion, his acting treasurer revised projections of state tax revenue by over $940 million.

During the summer of 2001, however, DiFrancesco continued to pursue development of a new $355 million sports arena in Newark in an effort to bring the professional basketball team the Nets, as well as the state's professional hockey team, the New Jersey Devils, to the city, hoping this could prove a durable legacy. DiFrancesco's efforts to develop the Newark sports arena, however, were blocked in early September. A plan to construct the new venue with funds from a state borrowing agency was defeated—at least for the remainder of DiFrancesco's term in office—when a planned vote by the Assembly Appropriations Committee was canceled after Republican assembly members withdrew support for this bill, which had grown in scope to include a minimum of $1 billion in projects around the state in addition to the Newark arena.

DiFrancesco simultaneously sought to reduce the population of the state's psychiatric hospitals by 20 percent in an effort to reduce overcrowding, proposing instead an increase in state funding for community-based, outpatient mental-health treatment centers. In addition, during this busy month, the acting governor had the opportunity to appoint six of fifteen members of the state's Pinelands Commission, in which rested the authority to regulate development in that region of the state. Other policy initiatives the governor pursued during his summer in office included the successful establishment of a fund to help house and treat victims of domestic violence; legislation designed to allow lawsuits against health management companies (HMOs) for harm resulting from denial or delay of care; a law to bring off-track betting facilities to the state; legislation designed to curb Internet stalking; a new "KidsNeeds" program, designed to increase state aid to low-income families with children; and new legislation requiring child car seats for children under eighty pounds or seven years of age.

The September 11, 2001, terrorist attack on Manhattan's World Trade Center, just across the Hudson River from Jersey City, lent a sense of urgency to DiFrancesco's otherwise brief and fairly unremarkable term in office. New Jersey lost more than 660 residents to the attack—nearly one-fourth of the total deaths that day. Given New Jersey's geographic proximity to lower Manhattan, the state provided many of the public emergency and rescue services in the aftermath of the towers' collapse. Warehouses in both Bayonne and Newark served as staging areas for recovery work and hosted FBI operations.

During the autumn of 2001, DiFrancesco ordered the state's National Guard to patrol the state's nuclear facilities in an effort to bolster security at these potential terrorist targets. Such efforts, along with the role played by the emergency services of various New Jersey municipalities and government agencies, strained the state's budget. In an effort to control costs, the state's attorney general, John Farmer, a Whitman appointee, proposed hiring retired police officers to provide security at Newark airport and other high-visibility sites. These retirees would be used in lieu of state police and National Guard soldiers. DiFrancesco, however, did not support Farmer's proposal, which had been made public without the acting governor's knowledge. And the proposal, which required legislation to be enacted, came just before the election in November, when Democrats took control of the assembly as well as the governor's office. DiFrancesco, in his own effort to control the cost to the state of increased security measures and support of New York City's emergency service agencies, sought $29 million in federal antiterrorism aid as well as designation of the state as a disaster area, which would qualify state businesses for federal loans. In late September, in an effort to address costs to local municipal budgets on a short-term basis, the Governor's Advisory Council for Emergency Services recommended an appropriation of $8.9 million to reimburse state departments and agencies for expenditures related to September 11.

The governor's staff projected the cost to the state in dollars of additional security needs in the attack's aftermath to be in excess of $675 million. To address these increased public needs, DiFrancesco and his staff conferred in the fall of 2001 with the state's representatives in Washington. DiFrancesco outlined a three-part "New Jersey Initiative" plan for post–September 11 recovery to U.S. Senator Jon Corzine. DiFrancesco's plan entailed "relief and recovery," "Preparedness," and "Economic Stimulus" phases. On September 17, DiFrancesco created a centralized office under gubernatorial supervision charged with the responsibility to coordinate and administer the state's recovery efforts. This new agency, the Office of Recovery and Victim Assistance, was created by Executive Order 132.

In early October, Governor DiFrancesco also established a New Jersey World Trade Center Victims Memorial Commission by executive order and secured the participation of former governors Florio, Kean, and Byrne as co-chairmen. On November 1, DiFrancesco convened an "emergency summit," where he introduced the ambitious "New Jersey Initiative" plan that he had outlined to Corzine earlier that autumn. DiFrancesco's proposal entailed a "series of . . . programs for public safety, health, transport, and labor, all designed to help New Jersey recover from the September 11 attacks, and to prepare for the possibility of future attacks."

DiFrancesco left office in 2002 and has practiced law in a private firm since the end of his political career.

PETER MICKULAS

Capuzzo, Jill P. "Favorite Son, Unfavorable Light: Scotch Plains Embraces DiFrancesco While in Trenton, There's a Wariness." *New York Times*, April 15, 2001.

Gray, Jerry. "G.O.P. Vows Change in Trenton as It Takes Over the Legislature." *New York Times*, January 15, 1992.

———. "Mr. Bland Goes to Trenton, and Takes Over the Senate." *New York Times*, January 18, 1992.

Halbfinger, David M. "Builder Aided DiFrancesco in Land Deal: Home Builder's Money Helped DiFrancesco Pay Judgment in Land Deal." *New York Times*, March 1, 2001.

Smothers, Ronald. "New Jersey: Tolls Emerge as Issue in the Race for Governor." *New York Times*, January 18, 2001.

James Edward McGreevey (August 6, 1957–), lawyer, Democrat, assemblyman, mayor of Woodbridge, senator, and governor, resigned three years after his election amid scandals, citing an extramarital relationship with the man he had appointed a staff assistant for homeland security issues.

McGreevey was born in Jersey City, the oldest child of John P. McGreevey, a Marine Corps veteran and sales manager for a trucking company, and Veronica Smith McGreevey, a nurse and instructor of nursing. Reared in Carteret, McGreevey attended St. Joseph Grammar School and St. Joseph High School in Metuchen. He displayed an early interest in politics. One of his high school teachers remembered of "a skinny, 14-year-old Jim McGreevey," who confidently said that he

James E. McGreevey
New Jersey State Archives; Department of State

intended to be governor or a U.S. senator someday. As the teacher recalled, "Either he was extremely cocky or he knew exactly where he was going. Probably a little of both."

After graduating from high school, McGreevey enrolled in the Catholic University of America, where he spent three semesters before transferring to Columbia University. He graduated in 1978. He earned his law degree at the Georgetown University Law Center and then enrolled in the Harvard Graduate School of Education for a master's degree.

In 1982, McGreevey joined the Middlesex County prosecutor's office, moved to Woodbridge, and became active in Democratic politics. Party leaders noticed him, and he joined the assembly majority staff. Assigned to a committee studying the state parole board, McGreevey was soon appointed the board's executive director. After Republican Thomas H. Kean was elected governor, McGreevey joined the pharmaceutical company Merck and Company as a manager working on state regulatory issues. His first performance review at the company described him as "transparently ambitious."

As the 1989 elections approached, McGreevey decided to run for the assembly. He secured the support of Joseph A. DeMarino, the Democratic mayor of Woodbridge, the district's most populous town. McGreevey later recalled that he campaigned in fear that the homosexual encounters he had engaged in at parkway rest stops and adult bookstores would become public. They did not. McGreevey, at age thirty-two, won by twenty-four hundred votes in an election in which the Democrats, with James J. Florio at the top of the ticket, swept the state to win control of the assembly and senate.

In the assembly, McGreevey voted for Florio's unpopular tax increases and gained some prominence as an environmental advocate. During the second year in his term, McGreevey met Kari Schutz on a vacation cruise. The young librarian from British Columbia became his wife later that year, and their child, Morag, was born in 1992. Democratic prospects in the 1991 legislative elections were grim because of voter anger over the Florio tax increases. Redrawn district lines would pit McGreevey against two other Democratic incumbents in the primary. Before McGreevey could decide how to proceed, DeMarino made the decision for him, announcing that he would not endorse McGreevey.

Motivated in part by a desire for revenge, McGreevey entered the Democratic primary for mayor against DeMarino, who looked vulnerable—he had been indicted for bribery. DeMarino, denouncing McGreevey as a "traitor," withdrew from the primary to run as an independent. That handed the Democratic nomination to McGreevey. In court, DeMarino was acquitted, but in the election, he lost to McGreevey, who had been supported by other Democratic leaders, including state senator Raymond Lesniak of Union County. One of Mayor McGreevey's first actions was to appoint a partner in Lesniak's law firm as Woodbridge's town counsel, which brought the firm $5 million over the next ten years.

McGreevey had to deal immediately with pressing budget, taxation, administrative, and corruption issues. He found ways to borrow funds to close a budget gap. He became ubiquitous in neighborhood events and houses of worship, and he tried to learn "seven words in every language spoken in Woodbridge." He wanted to be "everything anybody in Woodbridge wanted [him] to be." McGreevey served three terms as mayor and believed no job ever suited him better.

Halfway through his first term as mayor, McGreevey ran for the senate seat in the Nineteenth District. Buoyed by his reputation as an effective mayor and the support of influential Democrats including state senator John Lynch of Middlesex County, McGreevey won the seat, swimming against the tide of Christine Todd Whitman's victory over Governor Florio. He became one of New Jersey's many dual-office-holders.

In the senate, McGreevey voted for Whitman's 5 percent income-tax cut but resisted her move to deregulate utilities. And he explored the idea of running against her for governor in 1997. The duties of mayor, senator, and gubernatorial candidate did not leave much time for family. Kari Schutz McGreevey filed for divorce, alleging that McGreevey was concerned "only in presenting a façade of a united family . . . in order to enhance his political career."

McGreevey declared his intention to run for governor in November 1996. The leading candidate was Representative Robert Andrews. Former Morris County prosecutor Michael Murphy, stepson of former governor Richard J. Hughes, was also in the race. The keys to the nomination were held by

the Democratic county chairs. Nine county chairs from South Jersey supported Andrews. McGreevey had the backing of Democratic leaders in central Jersey. The Essex County chair, Thomas Giblin (who initially favored
Andrews), urged that McGreevey drop out of the race in part because of
rumors that he had been arrested after a homosexual encounter in a grave-
yard. But after Lesniak and Lynch struck a deal to make Giblin the Democratic state chairman, the Essex County leaders endorsed McGreevey. To win
the primary, McGreevey would need to raise more funds than ever before.
A generous donor appeared: Charles Kushner, a real-estate developer who,
with his companies and family, contributed more than $550,000 to the
McGreevey campaign.

McGreevey outspent his primary opponents and beat Andrews by about
ten thousand votes. Whitman, a popular incumbent, loomed as a more
formidable opponent. The general election campaign focused on auto-
insurance, taxes, and education. Most New Jerseyans disapproved of the way
Whitman had handled the rising cost of auto insurance. Conservatives who
did not like Whitman's stand on their issues had another place to turn—
Murray Sabrin, a Ramapo College economics professor, was on the ballot for
the Libertarian Party.

Relentlessly on message, McGreevey was dubbed "Robo-candidate" by
reporters. One article described him this way: "His desk was tidy. His hair
was trimmed. His suits were pressed. He owned more than 100 white dress
shirts." Beneath his buttoned-down appearance, McGreevey campaigned in
fear that rumors about his sex life would bring him down, but he continued to behave recklessly, visiting bars with his young staffers. As he prepared
for the first televised debate, he learned that a prostitute confined in the
Middlesex County jail was claiming that he had regularly paid her for sex.
McGreevey knew her but denied that relationship. His patrons arranged her
bail and, when she signed a disavowal of her story, had her escorted on a
vacation at Disney World for the duration of the campaign.

Late in the campaign, Whitman aired a commercial apologizing for
not doing more to hold down auto-insurance rates and property taxes.
McGreevey's rise in the polls leveled off. But when the value of the state
pension fund fell $2 billion during a stock-market plunge, the focus of the
campaign shifted. To fill a budget gap, Whitman had borrowed $2.75 billion
based on the value of the pension funds. McGreevey called that "irresponsible gambling." Whitman won the election with a margin of fewer than thirty
thousand votes over McGreevey, who became the presumptive Democratic
candidate for 2001.

Separated from Kari, McGreevey met Dina Matos, a hospital public relations executive, during the campaign. She volunteered as the campaign's
Portuguese-language coordinator and was involved romantically with Mc-
Greevey. They married in 2000, and their daughter, Jacqueline, was born the
next year.

McGreevey never stopped running. In 1999, he was handily reelected mayor in Woodbridge. He kept a statewide profile and created a campaign fund. Kushner was a leading contributor to it. As the primary approached, South Jersey county chairs turned against McGreevey when U.S. Senator Robert Torricelli announced he was interested in running for governor. Democratic leaders in several northern counties who had endorsed McGreevey shifted to Torricelli. But a Democratic Party poll found that likely primary voters narrowly preferred McGreevey. News about investigations into Torricelli's finances helped McGreevey to win the backing of Hudson and Essex County leaders. Without those large counties, Torricelli stood little chance in a contested primary. He ended his twelve-day insurgency as abruptly as he had begun it.

The Republicans had their own troubles: what had appeared to be a predictable Republican primary was unraveling. After Whitman's resignation in January 2001, she was succeeded by Senate President Donald DiFrancesco, a Union County Republican. He was the favorite for the nomination. His only announced opponent was Jersey City Mayor Bret Schundler. But DiFrancesco dropped out of the race after news articles raised questions about his personal finances. Republican leaders, who regarded Schundler as too conservative for the general election, looked for another centrist. Moderate, former U.S. representative Robert Franks replaced DiFrancesco on the ballot, with the support of Republican chairs in every county except Hudson. Schundler attacked Franks as too liberal, mobilized the party's conservative base, and defeated him decisively.

In the aftermath of the September 11 attacks, the general election campaign was subdued. Schundler ran on his record as mayor of Jersey City—making government more efficient, boosting the economy, and transforming the waterfront. He proposed tax credits to underwrite private education but failed to attract the swing voters who had given Whitman her victory in 1997.

With higher name recognition and favorability ratings, McGreevey campaigned against "business as usual in Trenton." His positions on wedge issues such as abortion and gun control were aligned more closely to the New Jersey electorate than Schundler's. McGreevey carried fifteen counties and took 56 percent of the vote. His solid victory helped produce a forty-four-seat Democratic majority in the assembly, but the senate was tied twenty to twenty.

Again McGreevey suffered anxious moments in the campaign. He had "lurked in Parkway rest stops," he wrote later, "exchanging false names and intimacies with strangers." One of his furtive partners, seeing his face in a campaign commercial, might take a story to the press. He was tied to campaign contributors who expected a return on their investment. He owed his nomination to party leaders who looked for their reward. Later, he reflected, "The political backrooms where I spent my career were just as benighted as my personal life." Dina wrote that he "spent a great deal of time accruing secrets and arranging his life to conceal them." McGreevey campaigned in fear that those secrets, if revealed, would bring him down.

And he had a new secret: his relationship with Golan Cipel. During a trip to Israel weeks after his engagement to Dina, he had met the young, Israeli public relations man. He invited Cipel to work on his campaign. With a work visa arranged by Kushner, Cipel arrived and was installed in an apartment near McGreevey's. As McGreevey tells it, they were engaged in an affair. Cipel depicts himself as the victim of sex harassment. Whatever their relationship, McGreevey had to keep it hidden.

The election failed to conclude an unsettled period in the state's politics. Four men acted as governor in the week between convening of the new legislature on January 8 and the inauguration on January 15. Before being sworn in, McGreevey threw himself into the deal-making that selected new leadership in the assembly. The process elevated an "obscure and inexperienced" Hudson assemblyman, Albio Sires, to speaker, balanced by a majority leader from South Jersey. McGreevey's role in these backroom dealings prompted some political commentators to conclude that he had broken his pledge to "change the way business was done in Trenton."

"Changing the way Trenton does business," however, remained the theme of McGreevey's inaugural address. He identified the challenges facing the state: keeping New Jersey "safe from further acts of terror and violence," living within its means during a recession, and making public schools work. But the first impression his administration made was one of scandal. McGreevey's appointment of Cipel as his adviser on homeland security drew scrutiny. Cipel, who lacked experience in intelligence, could not be granted a security clearance because he was a foreign national. News articles described him as a "friend" and "traveling companion" of the governor, hinting at one of McGreevey's most sensitive secrets. After weeks of turmoil, McGreevey shuffled Cipel off to a position with a lower profile, where he remained until August, when he resigned to take a private-sector job brokered by McGreevey.

The Cipel affair presaged the continual intertwining of scandal, personnel, policy, and politics that characterized McGreevey's abbreviated term. As McGreevey noted in his book, "it really was remarkable how many people in my administration turned out to have totally crazy meltdowns." The results became public in quick succession.

Press reports on Joseph Santiago, McGreevey's appointee as superintendent of the state police, exposed an arrest record, an assault conviction, and problems with the IRS. He spent $100,000 decorating his office and awarded himself a diploma from the state police academy. Only after months of controversy did McGreevey decide that "the price of keeping [Santiago] was becoming too great."

During the campaign, two of McGreevey's closest aides had created a company that controlled billboards around the state. The pair had closed a lucrative deal to sell their firm for more than $4 million just before disclosure of their ownership would have been required. But a news article reported on their role in gaining approvals for a huge billboard along the Atlantic City Expressway. U.S. Attorney Christopher Christie gained prominence leading the investigation into their activities. The probe concluded that the two had created the perception of using their influence for personal gain. They resigned before the end of the year.

A campaign fund-raiser who held a high-level position at the Department of State came under scrutiny after allegations that he pressured business owners in Woodbridge to contribute to McGreevey by suggesting that otherwise permits and approvals would be hard to get. Damaging headlines and the fund-raiser's resignation soon followed. Even the appointment of a poet laureate sparked a political backlash when Amiri Baraka (the Newark activist formerly known as LeRoi Jones) published a poem that suggested Israel had advance knowledge of the attack on the World Trade Center.

McGreevey also caused trouble for himself. When he led a trade mission to Ireland that cost more than $100,000—and included a McGreevey family reunion—a press-driven furor ensued. A labor union met some of the expenses of a family trip to Puerto Rico, causing another storm of bad press.

Overall, McGreevey's policy proposals were too modest in scope to distract attention from scandal, but they were all New Jersey could afford. The economy had slowed following the attacks of September 11; in 2002, it grew at about one-third of the rate in 2001. Unemployment crept upward, peaking at almost 6 percent in 2003. The politics of the budget were difficult, with an operating deficit of about $3 billion. McGreevey cut departmental spending, closed loopholes to raise an extra $1 billion from the corporate business tax, and borrowed on future payments from the tobacco settlement that had ended litigation against cigarette manufacturers. The savings and new income made it possible to expand preschool and increase spending for homeland security. But New Jersey's underlying fiscal problems were left unresolved.

The next year's budget proved even more challenging, with a deficit projected at $5 billion. McGreevey made ends meet with another series of cuts, small tax increases, and borrowing. In his annual message, he called for controlling sprawl, promised to reform auto insurance, and announced an initiative to boost reading scores in primary schools. To guide development, he produced the Blueprint for Intelligent Growth (BIG) Map, which he soon abandoned in the face of opposition from development interests. But he enjoyed early success dealing with festering auto-insurance problems that made it difficult for many drivers to obtain coverage. He streamlined regulation and increased competition. Drivers found it easier to get a policy. They were also pleased by shorter lines and the customer orientation that McGreevey brought to motor vehicle offices. And he made the E-ZPass system work. He merged the New Jersey Turnpike and Garden State Parkway authorities.

McGreevey's literacy initiative put sixty reading coaches in 158 schools during the course of the year, a small start on a big problem. He took on one big, potentially expensive educational issue: merging Rutgers with the University of Medicine and Dentistry and the New Jersey Institute of Technology. He recruited a former Merck chief executive to lead the exploratory committee, but the governor backed off after encountering opposition from the schools and important political patrons.

Despite the relatively modest scope of most of McGreevey's programs, his reluctance to stand firm on controversial issues, the drumbeat of scandal, and his low poll ratings, the Democrats picked up six seats in the 2003 legislative election, the first time the majority party had gained seats in fifty years. At the midpoint in what was supposed to be McGreevey's four-year term, the state's largest newspaper summed up his performance: "The latest poll shows him struggling, with an approval rating of 34 percent. His friends don't trust him, and his enemies don't fear him. . . . He has made no dramatic mark on the state that could form the basis for a legacy." But McGreevey could point to some real, if not earthshaking, accomplishments. He had reformed the corporate tax, strengthened the protection for freshwater streams, and advocated successfully for bonds to preserve open space. In April 2004, McGreevey took on a big issue: New Jersey's overreliance on property taxes. His new FAIR tax plan included a higher tax rate on those who earned more than $500,000 a year, big property-tax rebates, and caps on school budgets. Teachers and school boards insisted on looser spending caps, but the governor got most of what he wanted. He balanced his budget by securitizing cigarette taxes and surcharges to permit bonding $1.5 billion for current expenses. The state supreme court subsequently declared such borrowing unconstitutional.

McGreevey's proposals for the year included a call to expand his literacy program, enroll more children in preschool, increase state funds for school construction, and consolidate school districts. But the emphasis of his annual message was environmental protection, particularly the preservation of the Highlands. The Highlands Act was McGreevey's most notable accomplishment. This region in the northwest part of the state comprises 1,343 square miles, the source of drinking water for five million New Jerseyans. During the late '90s, twenty-five thousand acres of Highlands forests and farmlands were lost to development. McGreevey appointed a task force to study the area, and its report became the basis for protective legislation. Development interests, land owners, and many local officials opposed it. The region was overwhelmingly Republican; McGreevey stuck by his bill. Prospects for its passage increased when it was linked to a measure to speed state review of construction projects. Environmentalists felt that was too high a price, but the deal got the bill through. The new regional planning regime for the Highlands was approved in August 2004, just days before McGreevey's resignation speech.

McGreevey left an environmental legacy in the Highlands, but in the state's account books he left IOUs. To be sure, he had inherited billions of dollars of debt when he took office, but he bequeathed his successor additional billions in bonded obligations. He had incurred over $5 billion in long-term debt for day-to-day operating expenses—$2 billion in his final year alone.

Defining McGreevey's political philosophy is difficult. In *The Confession*, he describes himself as a Kennedy Democrat, but without specifying which Kennedy. He added, "My friend [and aide] Eric Shuffler says . . . being on the cutting edge of liberalism was the only aspect of me that was totally genuine." In fact, his views varied over the years. He was seen as a "lunch bucket" populist in his campaign against Whitman. In 1985, he favored the more moderate state senator John Russo over liberal Essex County Executive Peter Shapiro in the gubernatorial primary. In the general election, he rooted for the Republican candidate, Tom Kean, although he voted for Shapiro. As mayor, he was a Clintonesque New Democrat, fiscally conservative and socially moderate. In the assembly, McGreevey voted for Florio's $2.8 billion tax increase but as a senator supported Whitman's income-tax cuts. During the 1997 gubernatorial primary, he shared the moderate Democratic positions of his opponent: "pro-choice, pro-environment, pro-death penalty, pro-welfare reform, pro-gay civil rights," and "opposing gay marriage."

With an improving economy, this inconstancy did not seem to bother the electorate. In June, McGreevey's poll numbers were no longer upside down. The Quinnipiac University poll showed him with his first positive ratings in twenty months, a 45 percent approval rating, with 39 percent disapproving. That proved to be his high point.

In July, the U.S. attorney released a transcript of a recording in which McGreevey seemed to be involved in bribery and extortion. The case centered on a land condemnation by Middlesex County. David D'Amiano, a McGreevey associate and fund-raiser, was alleged to have peddled his influence to get better terms for the landowner. That landowner was cooperating with federal investigators and wore a wire to record conversations. One recording caught an individual, described on the transcript only as "State Official 1," using the word "Machiavelli," the code D'Amiano had established with the landowner as confirmation that the official had agreed to make a favorable deal for a payoff. "State Official 1" was McGreevey, as he quickly acknowledged. To explain his mention of "Machiavelli," he said it was coincidence, that he often quoted literary figures. But D'Amiano testified in court that he had prompted McGreevey to use the word. The inconsistency between those explanations remains unresolved.

A week later came another blow. Charles Kushner, McGreevey's largest contributor, was indicted. McGreevey had appointed Kushner as a Port

Authority commissioner and intended to make him chairman. But a former accountant sued Kushner and made charges of illegal campaign contributions. Kushner refused to appear before the Senate Judiciary Committee and resigned from the Port Authority to avoid further public airing of the charges. To stymie the lawsuit, it was alleged Kushner hired prostitutes to solicit the plaintiff and a potential witness, his sister's husband. The encounters were to be videotaped. The plaintiff rejected the prostitute, but the brother-in-law did not. Kushner had the video delivered to his sister, who turned it over to federal prosecutors. Kushner was charged with conspiracy, obstruction of investigation, and promotion of prostitution. He faced twenty-five years in prison.

Then came worse news. A lawyer representing Cipel told the governor's counsel that he was preparing to sue McGreevey for sexual assault and harassment. He offered to settle for $50 million. Negotiations between Cipel's lawyer and McGreevey's private attorney failed to reach agreement, although the price to settle the suit dropped to $5 million. The governor's staff and advisers were called in to help manage the crisis. One adviser saw a way forward. McGreevey reports the advice this way: "Tell the truth. And suddenly the tawdry affair with your political appointee makes sense. You were the man in the closet and now you're free. I think the voters will understand."

In that scenario, the resignation story would not be about a governor driven from office by entanglement with corrupt supporters or charges of sexual harassment. Instead, it would be a narrative of truth triumphing over lies and genuineness over repression. Surveys indicated that New Jerseyans were tolerant enough that being a "Gay American" would not be political poison.

On August 13, McGreevey appeared on television from the statehouse to announce his resignation and proclaimed, "My truth is that I am a gay American." Cipel later told the press that he believed McGreevey resigned not because of his sexual orientation but because he "sexually harassed" Cipel. Perhaps the sharpest insight into the speech was an observation made almost thirty years earlier by a male student at Catholic University whom McGreevey had a crush on. When his friends asked if McGreevey was gay, the student replied, "He's not hetero, he's not homo, he's just McGreevey."

The resignation would not take effect until mid-November. If McGreevey had stepped down more than sixty days before the November 3 election, his successor would have been chosen in a special election. McGreevey had to announce his resignation in August to take away Cipel's leverage for a settlement, but by delaying the effective date, he ensured his successor would be a Democrat, Senate President Richard Codey. McGreevey claimed the issue of the election never occurred to him, that he merely wanted to allow time for a smooth transition.

McGreevey's lame-duck status after the speech liberated him politically. McGreevey had resisted real restrictions on political contributions by donors seeking government contracts, known as pay-to-play. Ethics bills he signed earlier that year left loopholes through which the flow of political contributions could continue. But now he felt free to act. He announced that he found pay-to-play "corrosive and cancerous" and signed an executive order to bar firms with government contracts worth more than $17,500 a year from contributing to state or county campaigns.

McGreevey left the statehouse as governor for the last time on November 15. He joined Lesniak's law firm but resigned quickly when it became known that he had been doing legal work for a company whose project he had approved as governor. His next stop was at a psychiatric acute hospital and treatment center in a program for patients suffering post-traumatic stress disorders. There he was served Dina's divorce papers. For the next four years, newspaper reports about the divorce featuring lurid charges and counter-charges appeared under the standing head "The Battling McGreeveys."

He signed a $500,000 contract with a publisher, and in October 2006, *The Confession* rose to number three on the *New York Times* nonfiction best-seller list. *The Confession* mentions few events or issues not already known from press reports. McGreevey cites his post-traumatic stress as the reason for memory lapses, but the book re-creates verbatim conversations when its serves his purpose.

McGreevey subsequently took courses at the General Theological Seminary of the Episcopal Church, the faith to which he had converted after his resignation. He received his master of divinity degree in May 2010 from that institution and sought to be ordained in the Episcopal priesthood. In 2012, the Newark Diocese denied his bid. As of this writing, McGreevey devotes much of his time in the Hudson County Correctional Center in Kearney, working with women fighting addition. He also teaches a course on "Law and Public Policy" at Kean University, as part of its global MBA program.

McGreevey lives in Plainfield with Mark O'Donnell, the chief investment officer for a company headed by McGreevey's longtime contributor Charles Kushner. In March 2013, McGreevey was the subject of an HBO documentary, *Fall to Grace*, which sympathetically examined his life's journey.

THOMAS M. O'NEILL

Records of Governor James E. McGreevey, New Jersey State Library, Trenton, N.J.

Green, Michelle. "This Side of Redemption." *New York Times*, March 28, 2013.

McGreevey, Dina Matos. *Silent Partner*. New York: Hyperion, 2007.

McGreevey, James E. *The Confession*. New York: HarperCollins, 2006.

"Special Report—The McGreevey Scandal." *Star Ledger*. http://www.nj.com/news/ mcgreevey/.

Richard James Codey (November 27, 1946–) succeeded to the governor's office in 2004 under circumstances without precedent in New Jersey history. His predecessor, James E. McGreevey, resigned after revealing that he had a sexual relationship with a male staff member who served briefly as a homeland security adviser. Codey, as president of the state senate, was next in line to serve out McGreevey's term. The post of lieutenant governor did not exist at the time. Although Codey had been in state politics for more than three decades and had served as acting governor for three days in early 2002, he was relatively unknown outside his district in Essex County. But among political insiders, he was a popular and respected figure, known for his sense of humor, his accommodating nature, and his survival skills as the

Richard Codey
New Jersey State Archives; Department of State

product of Essex County's bare-knuckle politics. Still, he was not without political enemies, and several sought to block his succession by calling on McGreevey to leave office in time to schedule a special election in November 2005. The outgoing governor, however, refused to alter his timetable.

After becoming acting governor, Codey retained the title of president of the state senate but promised to devote his full attention to the governor's office. He deputized state senator Bernard Kenney of Hudson County, the senate's majority leader, to act as de facto president of the senate.

Codey enjoyed an extended political honeymoon, one that eased painful memories of McGreevey's wrenching announcement that he, although married with a child, was gay and had been living a lie even before his election. McGreevey was a bundle of nerves and energy, a kinetic and effective retail politician who craved the public spotlight. Codey seemed much more comfortable in his own skin. He was soft-spoken but quick with a joke. The redheaded son of a funeral director from Orange, he was devoted to his wife and two sons and seemed to enjoy basketball as much as he loved politics. Codey played to his everyman image, announcing that he would not move into the governor's mansion, Drumthwacket, because his wife taught school near their modest home in West Orange, and that was that. He did not hesitate to remind reporters that some of the power brokers who helped elect McGreevey in 2001 were the very people who tried to block his succession. He quickly gained a reputation as a politician who answered to his conscience, the voters, and his party, not to powerful private interests.

Richard Codey was born in Orange in the afterglow of America's victories in World War II, a time of high hopes and prosperity in his family's hometown. He and his four siblings grew up in an apartment above the family's funeral home on High Street, not far from the factories and smokestacks that often rose next to rows of modest single-family homes in working-class Orange. As a teenager, Codey helped his father with the family business, which meant that he sometimes responded to late-night calls to pick up corpses from accidents and other tragedies. Those early encounters with death meant, he later said, that he grew up quickly and developed an appreciation for life's fragility. He also developed a keen sense of humor that might have served him well as a shield against tragedy and misfortune. After he served as acting governor briefly in 2002 before McGreevey was sworn into office, Codey dryly announced, "During my tenure as governor, there were no scandals or tax increases."

Codey attended Oratory Prep, a Catholic high school, in Summit and continued his studies at Fairleigh Dickinson University. He left FDU before graduating, although he later returned to earn a bachelor's degree in education. He obtained a funeral director's license and joined the family business in the mid-1960s.

His work and good-natured personality put him in touch with hundreds of his neighbors, sparking an interest in local politics during the tumultuous late 1960s, when urban riots and antiwar protests transformed New Jersey society. He was elected to the Essex County Democratic Committee when he was twenty-one, and in 1973, he was elected to the state's general assembly after winning the Democratic nomination on a ticket that the party's gubernatorial nominee, Brendan Byrne, opposed. In Trenton, Codey quickly joined forces with the Byrne administration in supporting a controversial but successful effort to allow casinos in Atlantic City. He won a seat in the state senate in 1981, making a name for himself in 1987 when, after his wife, Mary Jo Rolli, suffered from postpartum depression, he took a job in Marlboro Psychiatric Hospital under an assumed name. He exposed Dickensian conditions at the facility and led an effort to reform mental-health facilities around the state.

Through force of personality and shrewd political maneuvering, Codey became a force to be reckoned with in Essex County politics, a locale where no grudge is ever forgotten and no slight ever forgiven. His ability to build effective coalitions led to his election as minority leader in the senate in 1998, when he emerged as a voice of Democratic opposition to Republican Governor Christie Whitman. In January 2002, when the forty-member state senate was split evenly between Republicans and Democrats, Codey and Republican John O. Bennett worked out a compromise allowing the two men to alternate as the senate's presiding officer. In Codey's capacity as senate co-president, he served as acting governor for three days when, due to a quirk in state election law, Governor Donald DiFrancesco's term expired before

James McGreevey, his successor, took the oath of office. Codey actually was one of several acting governors who filled in during a strange interregnum between DiFrancesco's departure and McGreevey's arrival.

Matters became stranger still during McGreevey's stormy tenure. Codey became first in line of succession in early 2004 when Democrats took full control of the state senate and elected Codey as the body's president. On August 12, 2004, McGreevey announced to a surprised state and nation that he was a "gay American" who had had an affair with an Israeli citizen, Golan Cipel, whom McGreevey appointed as an adviser on homeland security issues in the aftermath of the terrorist attacks on the World Trade Center on September 11, 2001. McGreevey announced his intention to resign in mid-November, after the fall's elections. Codey and McGreevey met several times during the ensuing weeks as the outgoing governor ignored calls from Republicans and Codey's Democratic opponents to leave quickly and so allow for a special election, a maneuver which might have prevented Codey from filling the rest of McGreevey's term.

Codey took the oath of office in a modest ceremony in his home on Sunday afternoon, November 15, 2004. In a gesture that did not go unnoticed in Trenton, he personally invited the senate's minority leader, Leonard Lance, to attend, a bipartisan grace note that helped restore a measure of decorum in an age of fierce partisanship in New Jersey and throughout the country. But even as Codey sought to repair relations within the legislature and tried to distance his administration from the McGreevey era, he demonstrated the political acumen that helped him survive for so long in Trenton and Essex County. He pointedly refused to rule out running for a full term in 2005, even after it became clear that the state's junior U.S. senator, Jon Corzine, was interested in moving from Washington to Trenton. Codey understood that if he ruled out a campaign in 2005, he would have little leverage over the legislature as Trenton prepared to deal with a looming budget deficit brought on by recession, borrowing, and the high cost of medical and retirement benefits for state employees.

Codey's first task, however, had little to do with policy and much to do with perception. The short McGreevey era was marred by headlines about scandals and allegations of corruption at both the state and local level. Two of McGreevey's top appointees were implicated in a scheme to profit from the sale of billboards around the state, while one of his mentors, former state senator John Lynch of Middlesex County, would be jailed on corruption charges in 2006. Codey sought to restore the public's shattered faith in state politics by emphasizing his distance from private power brokers and his lack of interest in the trappings of power. He cultivated a strong relationship with members of the press, who responded to the new governor's candor and wit with glowing pieces about the positive changes in Trenton.

In one of Codey's first important official acts, he issued an executive order that barred politically connected brokers from working on behalf of bond underwriters seeking to win state business. Many of the middlemen were large contributors to political campaigns, leaving the perception that they were, in essence, purchasing influence with decision makers. Codey said that his office would no longer deal with brokers and middlemen who represented underwriting firms. While it was hardly a high-profile issue, Codey's leadership inspired another flurry of good publicity and accolades from good-government groups.

Lurking in the background was the formidable shadow of Senator Corzine, a wealthy former chief executive officer of the investment firm Goldman Sachs. Corzine transformed himself from political unknown to U.S. senator in 2000 by financing his own campaign, which spent $62 million. By the end of 2004, Corzine was actively seeking support for a gubernatorial campaign in 2005. With his millions, Corzine quickly snapped up key endorsements, leaving Codey to contemplate the cost, fiscally and emotionally, of challenging his fellow Democrat for the nomination. Weeks of speculation ended on January 2005, when Codey announced that he would not seek a full term, ceding the nomination to Corzine.

The announcement seemed to liberate Codey from politics, allowing him to focus instead on the state's perilous finances and other pressing issues, including mental health, homeland security, and construction of a new football stadium in the Meadowlands Sports Complex. His interest in mental health was of long standing, and his wife, Mary Jo, used her new public profile to speak up about her own episodes of postpartum depression. A radio talk-show host made several cruel remarks about Mrs. Codey, leading the governor to rush to her defense. During a face-to-face confrontation, Codey told the host that he would love to take him outside the studio and teach him a lesson. The episode was reminiscent of President Harry Truman's combative defense of his daughter when her singing career inspired an unfavorable review in a Washington newspaper in 1950. Codey emerged from the unpleasant encounter with his popularity and image intact.

Codey, who continued to coach youth basketball while serving as the state's chief executive, governed as if the clock were about to expire, which, of course, it was. While Corzine and several Republican challengers ramped up their gubernatorial campaigns, Codey devoted himself to several pressing issues, including continued concerns about terrorism, the state's fiscal condition, and a deal to transform the Meadowlands Sports Complex. Early April brought a major political victory for the sports-loving governor when the state Sports and Exposition Authority approved a plan to build a new football stadium in the Meadowlands to replace Giants Stadium. Although the Giants and the Jets agreed to pay for construction costs, which grew to more than $1.5 billion, the plan was not without critics. Chief among them was the president of the Sports and Exposition Authority, George R. Zoffinger, a blunt-spoken real-estate executive from Middlesex County who argued that the state could not afford to pay for infrastructure costs and other expenses related to the new stadium. Codey, however, insisted that the authority put aside its internal debate and come to a satisfactory deal with the Giants. Zoffinger abstained from the final vote and went on to become one of Codey's most persistent critics. In the meantime, work began on the new stadium, and the state followed through with promises to improve access to the complex, including construction of a rail station nearby. (The stadium opened in 2010, and a year later, MetLife purchased naming rights to the stadium for $400 million over twenty years.)

In late winter and early spring of 2005, the Codey administration worked with federal and regional authorities on a massive drill designed to test and rehearse responses to a catastrophic terrorist strike using chemical and biological weapons. In the weeks leading up to the drill, dubbed Operation Topoff (short for Top Officials), Codey introduced legislation calling for creation of a new state medical examiner's office that would coordinate emergency efforts carried out by a hodgepodge of local and county medical offices. He also issued an executive order on February 3 creating a training center to coordinate the state's response to possible chemical, biological, and nuclear attacks. Codey designated the University of Medicine and Dentistry of New Jersey in Newark to develop the center and lead a program of preparedness training for state and local officials. These grim but necessary steps led up to the execution of Operation Topoff in May. Hundreds of staff members from Codey's office, the attorney general's office, the state police, and the state Department of Health worked with officials and staff from federal agencies, including the Environmental Protection Agency, the Centers for Disease Control, and the Department of Transportation, to respond to a mock attack involving the use of biological agents released throughout the Northeast.

Two months later, New Jersey residents were reminded why their governor placed such emphasis on preparedness. Terrorists struck London's mass-transit system on July 7, killing fifty-two people. Within minutes of the attack, Codey signed an emergency executive order increasing state police patrols at mass-transit hubs and on trains and buses. The London bombings reemphasized the state's vulnerabilities and led to a stepped-up law enforcement presence on the state's sprawling public transportation system.

Codey spent the balance of the spring formulating his first budget and using his powers of persuasion to get lawmakers to go along with a plan that sought to limit the growth of state spending after massive increases during the McGreevey years. In McGreevey's budget for fiscal year 2005, he increased state spending by 17 percent and borrowed nearly $2 billion to pay for the state's popular property-tax rebate program. Codey found himself in a politically untenable position since he felt obliged to restrain spending in a gubernatorial election year. While he was not running for a new term, Codey's fellow Democrats desperately hoped to retain the governor's office, adding to pressure to keep the spending spigot flowing.

Instead, Codey proposed a no-growth budget of nearly $28 billion. To the consternation of his party and of members of the general assembly running for reelection, Codey eliminated the property-tax rebate program, which sought to soften the state's high property taxes—which pay for local services such as schools and police protection—by returning an average of $800 per year to homeowners from the state treasury. Codey also proposed a new tax on cable television services.

Weeks of hard negotiation followed. Codey had the upper hand thanks to the state's unusual system of succession. As both governor and president of the state senate, Codey wielded executive and legislative powers that no other governor and no other legislator in the nation possessed, even though he was a lame duck as governor. He put those formidable powers to use in persuading Assembly Majority Leader Joseph Roberts of Camden County to drop his highly public campaign to restore the property-tax rebate program. Instead, Codey agreed to restore the program in full for seniors, but homeowners aged sixty-five and younger saw their rebates cut in half. Codey's budget allowed Democrats to enter the fall campaign with a credible claim to be the party of fiscal responsibility.

As the clock ticked down and the candidates to succeed Codey sought to dominate the news, the governor continued to build a legacy for his short-lived administration. He and his wife launched a campaign for the rights of the mentally ill in a series of well-received public service commercials on local television. To the chagrin of the state's Roman Catholic bishops, Codey, whose sister is a Catholic nun, allocated funds for stem-cell research and called for a massive public commitment to make New Jersey a leader in the field. Many ethicists and religious figures questioned the morality of stem-cell research since the work required the destruction of a human embryo. Codey, however, argued that the research could lead to advances in the treatment of myriad medical conditions, including spinal-cord injuries and Parkinson's disease.

Even as time ran out on Codey's term and Jon Corzine took a commanding lead in the campaign to become the state's new governor, Codey's popularity was astonishing. A *Star-Ledger*/Eagleton poll showed that 76 percent of respondents approved of the job he was doing, the highest approval rating for a New Jersey governor in two decades. The state's economy certainly helped Codey's popularity—even though the state's finances were far from perfect, New Jersey's private economy was prosperous. The unemployment rate was 4.3 percent in the spring of 2005, and U.S. Census figures showed that New Jersey and Connecticut were the wealthiest states in the nation based on median household income. (Connecticut's median income of $56,409 per year was slightly higher than New Jersey's $56,356.) But more than anything else, Codey's image as a regular guy who understood the concerns of his fellow citizens lifted his approval ratings and inspired the public's affection.

In one of Codey's last acts before turning the governor's office over to

Corzine, who defeated Republican Douglas Forrester in the 2005 general election, he signed a bill that removed the phrase "acting governor"—his official title during his term—from his résumé. The bill, signed on January 9, 2006, declared that anyone who served as acting governor for more than 180 days would have the full title of "governor" in state records.

Codey returned to the state senate after Corzine was inaugurated on January 19. However, he was pressed into service again as acting governor when Corzine was injured in a car accident in April 2007. He remained in that capacity for a month while Corzine recuperated.

Codey remained a highly accessible public figure through the Corzine years, but behind the scenes, old enemies were rallying to dislodge him from his source of power, the senate presidency. In the fall of 2009, as Corzine fought a losing battle for reelection against Chris Christie, several of Codey's fellow Democrats launched a quiet campaign to replace Codey as senate president. With the support of South Jersey power broker George Norcross and top Democrats in Codey's home county of Essex, state senator Stephen Sweeney of Gloucester County overthrew Codey from the senate presidency in early 2010. Codey gained a measure of satisfaction, if not revenge, several years later when he published a memoir, *Me, Governor?*, which was highly critical of Norcross and other political operatives who supported Sweeney.

Codey won reelection to a new four-year term in the state senate in 2011 despite a reconfigured district which included parts of Republican-leaning Morris County. He continued to enjoy a visible public presence as an advocate for mental-health issues, his signature cause for most of his political career.

Richard Codey's short stint as governor was memorable, and it very likely was the last of its kind. With the creation of a new office of lieutenant governor in 2010, it is highly unlikely that another senate president will ever again be called on to fill out the unexpired term of a governor.

TERRY GOLWAY

Author's interviews with Governor Richard Codey, July–August 2005.

Records of Governor Richard J. Codey, Governor's Office of Policy, 2001–2005, New Jersey State Library, Trenton, N.J.

Records of Governor James E. McGreevey, Governor's Office of Policy, 2001–2005, New Jersey State Library, Trenton, N.J.

Benson, Josh. "Development: Football? Nah, Hardball." *New York Times*, April 17, 2005.

Codey, Richard J. *Me, Governor? My Life in the Rough-and-Tumble World of New Jersey Politics*. New Brunswick: Rutgers University Press, 2011.

Kocieniewski, David. "In Budget, a Sign of Codey's Tenure." *New York Times*, July 4, 2005.

Mansnerus, Laura. "Man in the News: A Political Veteran Ascendant: Richard James Codey." *New York Times*, November 16, 2004.

Jon Stevens Corzine (January 1, 1947–) served as New Jersey's fifty-fourth governor from 2006 to 2010. Corzine grew up in Wiley Station, Illinois, on a 120-acre family farm. Corzine's grandfather had been an affluent farmer with a two-thousand-acre farm who lost everything during the Great Depression. His father worked the farm and sold insurance, while his mother taught at Memorial Elementary School in Taylorville, Illinois. He was a sports star at Taylorville High School, where he was captain of the basketball team and quarterback of the football team. After graduating in 1965, Corzine attended the University of Illinois at Urbana-Champaign. He graduated Phi Beta Kappa in 1969. Faced with the prospect of being drafted into the armed services during the height of the Vietnam War, that year Corzine enlisted in the U.S. Marine Corps Reserve. At the age of twenty-two, Corzine married his childhood sweetheart, Joanne Dougherty, whom he had known since kindergarten. Together, they had three children, Jennifer, Josh, and Jeffrey. Their marriage lasted thirty-three years until the couple separated in 2002. The Corzines divorced in 2003.

Upon Corzine's completion of his service in the Marine Corps Reserves, he began his career in banking and finance. His first job was as a portfolio analyst at the Continental Illinois National Bank in Chicago. In Chicago, Corzine enrolled in night school at the graduate business school of the University of Chicago, where he earned an M.B.A. in 1973. After earning his graduate degree, Corzine began work at BancOhio National Bank in Columbus. In 1975, he interviewed for a position as a bond trader at Goldman Sachs in New York. He moved his family to New Jersey that year. He has said that one of his first responsibilities at Goldman Sachs was fetching coffee for his boss. Five years later, he was named a partner. During his tenure at Goldman Sachs, Corzine was a protégé of Robert Rubin, who went on to serve as secretary of the treasury during Bill Clinton's presidential administration. In 1994, Corzine became the investment firm's chairman and chief executive officer, earning approximately $20 million annually. Three years after he took over the helm, Goldman Sachs was making $3 billion a year—six times what it was making when Corzine assumed his leadership role. Yet though he succeeded in transforming the investment firm from a private partnership to a publicly held company, Corzine's sour relationship with co-CEO Henry Paulson led to a coup d'état that resulted in Corzine being pushed out of the investment firm in 1999. Nonetheless, the initial public offering that resulted from taking Goldman public meant a personal profit of hundreds of millions of dollars for Corzine and other Goldman Sachs partners. By 1999, Corzine's net worth was estimated to be between $300 to $400 million.

When U.S. Senator Frank Lautenberg announced his retirement in 2000, Corzine, looking both for redemption from his Goldman Sachs demise and for a new challenge, announced his intention to seek the Democratic nomination for the Senate seat. He told a *New York* magazine reporter, "whether I put another zero on my net worth didn't seem nearly as interesting or important" as the challenge of the Senate seat. During the primary, the bearded, spectacled Corzine who favored sweater vests touted his humble roots, his Wall Street experience, and his status as a Washington outsider. He faced a primary challenge from former governor Jim Florio and initially trailed Florio in the polls by a two-to-one margin. But Corzine spent $36 million in the primary, including more than $30 million of his own money. At the peak of the primary race, the Corzine campaign was spending $2 million per week on television ads alone. Corzine also spread contributions to county and municipal Democratic parties and candidates who had endorsed him, including Democratic Party bosses such as Camden County's George E. Norcross III and Newark's Stephen N. Adubato, Sr. Investigative reports also revealed that Corzine, through his foundation, funded numerous nonprofit and community organizations throughout the state, leading critics to assert that he was buying the election. Florio spent a mere $2 million total and was defeated by Corzine 58–42 percent. The cost per vote in the primary was a record-setting $140.

In the general election campaign against Bob Franks, a four-term member of the U.S. House of Representatives, Corzine embraced what some political observers found to be a surprisingly liberal platform given his background on Wall Street. He advocated universal health care, universal gun-registration laws, and universal public preschool. He came out in favor of same-sex marriage and for affirmative-action policies. He advocated more spending for education. His inexperience on the campaign trail (and in New Jersey politics) was evident when he commented to an Italian American man in the construction business, to whom he was introduced, "Oh, you make cement shoes." (A quarter of New Jersey voters characterize themselves as Italian American.) And a firestorm ensued when it was revealed that Corzine, through his foundation, had made a $25,000 contribution to the Black Ministers Council and then was endorsed by the council's leader, Rev. Reginald Jackson, and other influential black ministers in what appeared to be a quid pro quo. But Corzine went on to beat Franks 50–47 percent.

In large part, Corzine's successful Senate campaign could be traced to record-setting campaign expenditures: the $35 million spent in the primary and another $29 million spent against Congressman Franks resulted in the election becoming the most expensive Senate campaign in history. At $64 million, Corzine's self-financed campaign doubled the previous record set in 1994 by Michael Huffington's unsuccessful bid to become a U.S. senator representing California.

Elected to the U.S. Senate in 2000 in a class of ten new senators, Corzine was appointed to the Committee on Banking, Housing, and Urban Affairs; the Budget Committee; the Energy and Natural Resources Committee; and the Senate Intelligence Committee. Corzine's status as the lone Democrat who had served as CEO of a Wall Street company earned him the immediate status as Democratic point man on banking and finance issues. In the wake of a series of scandals in several large U.S. companies including Enron, Corzine coauthored and cosponsored the Sarbanes-Oxley Act, which increased accounting requirements and restructured the regulatory environment of public corporations. As the number of corporate accounting scandals grew and as the number of investors bilked out of their savings increased, Corzine joined with several other liberal Democrats, including Barbara Boxer (D-CA) and the late Senator Edward Kennedy (D-MA) in the U.S. Senate in sponsoring legislation that would have minimized the investment risk for individuals' 401(k) retirement plans. The measure faced significant opposition in Congress and from then-president George W. Bush, who favored the opposite tact and advocated privatizing Social Security.

While in the U.S. Senate, Corzine cosponsored the Darfur Peace and Accountability Act, which affirmed the U.S. government stance that the conflict in the Darfur region of the Sudan constituted genocide and asked that government expand the peacekeeping force in the region, while providing improved logistical support to the force stationed there. The act also called for the federal government to assist the International Criminal Court in prosecuting war criminals from the Darfur region. Passed by the House and Senate, the bill was signed into law by President Bush in 2006.

Corzine also was one of very few (twenty-three) no votes in the U.S. Senate on the Authorization for Use of Military Force Against Iraq Resolution of 2002, the congressional action that authorized the use of force in Iraq. Requested by President Bush after his September 12, 2002, speech before the United Nations General Assembly calling for the Security Council to enforce U.N. resolutions against Iraq, the legislation provided for the U.S. military to use force to compel compliance.

During Corzine's tenure in the Senate, he also developed a reputation as a prodigious fund-raiser for the Democrats and for his colleagues in Congress. Corzine often acted as a go-between for congressional candidates and potential Wall Street donors. Elected chair of the Democratic Senatorial Campaign Committee (DSCC) in 2002, Corzine helped raise $400 million. As chair, he led the Democrats to match the amount raised by their Republican counterparts for the first time in thirty years.

In 2002, Corzine and his wife, Joanne, separated, and Corzine began appearing in public with Carla Katz, who was the president of Communications Workers of America (CWA) Local 1035, a public-employee labor union that represents sixteen thousand state employees. Katz later reported that she had initially met Corzine while he was running for the U.S. Senate seat in the spring of 1999. He reportedly had offered her a job, which she declined. Shortly after the Corzines separated, Katz moved into Corzine's apartment in Hoboken. Joanne Dougherty Corzine later told a reporter that Corzine's extramarital affair with Katz led to the breakup of their marriage.

Katz lived in Corzine's apartment until he ended the relationship in 2004. After Corzine broke up with Katz, his attorneys reached a $6 million financial settlement with her that included a lump-sum payment to be used to purchase a home, a college trust fund for her two children, an automobile, and the forgiving of a $470,000 loan that Corzine had extended to her in 2002, which enabled her to buy out her ex-husband's share of their home in Alexandria Township.

Five years into Corzine's Senate term in 2005, he announced his candidacy for New Jersey governor. At the time, Acting Governor (state senator) Richard Codey, who had assumed the office after the resignation of Governor James McGreevey, enjoyed strong popularity. But Codey decided not to seek the governorship given Corzine's entry into it, along with the presumption that Corzine would back his entry with millions of dollars to win the nomination, if necessary.

In the 2005 general election, Corzine faced former West Windsor mayor and state treasury official Douglas Forrester, who, with 36 percent of the primary vote, had beat out a field of six other candidates (including conservative former Jersey City mayor Bret Schundler, who received 31 percent of the vote), spending $11 million to win the nomination.

During the 2005 campaign, Corzine's platform centered on overhauling the state's property-tax structure, ethics reform, improving the state's economic competitiveness, and its health-care and education programs. Corzine combined advocacy of liberal positions on agenda items with his Wall Street background, which promised a unique brand of compassionate government combined with acute business sense. In the general election, Corzine raised only $400,000 from contributors but spent over $43 million of his own money. Forrester spent $29 million of his own funds, focusing nearly all his expenditures on television advertising. The Forrester-Corzine race was particularly nasty and personal. Corzine consistently outpolled Forrester, despite revelations regarding the loan to Carla Katz and despite criticism levied at him from his ex-wife. In an interview with the *New York Times*, Joanne Dougherty Corzine said of Corzine, "When I saw the campaign ad where Andrea Forrester (Douglas Forrester's wife) said, 'Doug never let his family down and he won't let New Jersey down,' all I could think was that Jon did let his family down, and he'll probably let New Jersey down, too." Forrester's campaign seized on the quote, which was used in television ads, and Republicans seized on the idea that Corzine's relationship with a top union leader in the state presented a conflict of interest. Nonetheless, Corzine consistently outpolled Forrester and handily won the election, 54–43 percent.

In January 2006, Corzine was sworn into office. He declined the $175,000 salary that accompanied the job. The story of his term as governor is the story of promise unfulfilled. Save for his brief honeymoon with voters and a period of compassion associated with an auto accident in 2007, public opinion of Corzine was consistently mediocre to poor. Known to voters as an unabashed liberal, Corzine favored a strong role for government in everything from health care to preschool education. Yet his background in the banking and investment industry along with his own enormous personal wealth promised a business-oriented vision of state government. During his campaign, he promised to overhaul the state's budget process, bring a business-oriented approach to managing the state's asserts, and cut spending. He contended that these changes would ease the property-tax burden and would encourage investment in the state, spawning job creation. Voters thought that a Corzine administration would right the fiscal ship of the state while enabling it to provide high levels of services and programmatic support. By all accounts, Jon Corzine thought that he could accomplish this too.

As governor, Corzine was thwarted in his efforts by a number of different factors. In part, the Corzine administration, like those in so many other states, fell victim to the slowing economy, including decreases in state tax revenues. The types of programs that Corzine sought to support—universal health, universal preschool, increased funding for schools—all cost money. And even before the recession hit, the state of New Jersey was facing a fiscal crisis resulting from years of unfettered borrowing and spending, combined with Band-Aid solutions and one-shot revenue deals by both Democratic and Republican administrations. During Corzine's tenure, he cut the state budget by over $4 billion and restarted payments to the state's pension fund, an obligation sporadically ignored by governors of both political parties who served both before and after Corzine. Initially through retirement and attrition and then through layoffs, the state's workforce shrunk by about five thousand employees. Yet the economy dogged Corzine's administration, and failure to significantly tackle the state's economic woes contributed both to voters' dissatisfaction with him throughout his tenure and their eventual rejection of him at the polls in his bid for reelection.

Jon Corzine was also stymied because of a lack of deep partisan roots among leading Democrats in the state. He had won both his election to the U.S. Senate in 2000 and his gubernatorial election in 2005 by drastically outspending his rivals, but without developing the unmitigated political loyalty that often comes from having colleagues and supporters witness and facilitate one's ascendancy. And so while he initially sought to solve the state's financial crisis, in doing so, he underestimated the willingness of a Democratically controlled state legislature to go head-to-head with the supposed leader of the party in the state, and he underestimated the capability of party leaders in the state to hold a grudge—and to shift their loyalties.

During the 2006 budget process, Corzine's initial budget called for slashing $2 billion of state spending, reducing the total budget to $30.9 billion. To fill a $4.5 billion budget gap, Corzine proposed increased sin taxes on alcohol and tobacco, a luxury tax on expensive cars, and, most controversially, a 1 percent increase in the state sales tax. Corzine stated that he would not accept a budget without an increase in the sales tax, which then stood at 6 percent.

State Senate President Dick Codey supported the sales-tax increase, but it faced significant opposition in the lower house, particularly from Assembly Speaker Joe Roberts. Roberts, an ally of Camden County Democratic leader George E. Norcross III, then got into a battle of wills with Corzine, who used the budget battle as means of asserting his independence from the political bosses who ran the state's Democratic Party. Interpreting the constitution as mandating a shutdown when the governor and the legislature failed to reach a compromise budget by July 1, 2006, many legislators perceived Corzine's threat to shut down state government as a bluff, designed to pressure the state legislature to go along with his proposed one-cent increase in the sales tax. Several budget negotiations had extended beyond the deadline in years past, but Corzine was not bluffing. He issued Executive Order 17, which ordered a shutdown of nonessential state government services at midnight July 1, 2006, the first shutdown of state government in New Jersey's history. More than forty thousand state employees were directed to stay home, and all nonessential state functions ceased. After the July Fourth holiday, public parks, beaches, and racetracks were closed, as were the Meadowlands Sport Complex and Atlantic City's casinos, which are monitored and regulated by the state Casino Control Commission. The shutdown of casinos was estimated to cost the state $1.3 million per day, while $2 million was not realized in lottery proceeds. (In 2008, Corzine signed legislation that would enable casinos and racetracks in the state to remain open in the event of a future government shutdown.) As the budget battle escalated, Corzine issued an executive order calling on the state legislature to meet in special session on July 4. The legislature did meet, listened to Corzine's speech, and adjourned. After two more days of meeting, a compromise budget, which included the 1 percent hike in the sales tax, was included. While blinking on the sales-tax increase, the legislature won a concession that provided that half of the additional revenue generated by the tax hike would go toward property-tax relief. State government services were restored at 8:00 a.m. on July 10, 2006. Immediately following the shutdown, most polls in the state indicated that Corzine had won in the court of public opinion, with many New Jerseyans blaming the legislature for the shutdown. But the shutdown created ill will between Corzine and many Democrats in the legislature, who were unhappy that they had to take the blame for increasing the state sales tax and who resented being blamed for shutting down the state government, when the action had been taken at Corzine's direction. The spat also exacerbated a rift between Corzine and the Democratic Party bosses who perceived Corzine's brinkmanship on the budget as defiance.

Corzine also evoked the ire of machine bosses and politicians when he emphasized components of governmental reform in his policy agenda. Counted among his accomplishments was the eradication of dual-office-holding for new elected officials, a part of his platform for reining in corruption. But many critics argued that the bill he pressed for and signed did not go far enough, as it exempted legislators who were serving when the bill was signed.

Finally, in some ways, Jon Corzine's administration was constrained by one external event—an auto accident that nearly claimed his life—which also significantly interrupted a policy agenda timeline that could have been more effective in achieving some of his goals. On April 12, 2007, Corzine had left the New Jersey Conference of Mayors meeting in Atlantic City and was headed to Drumthwacket, the governor's mansion in Princeton, to meet with radio personality Don Imus and the Rutgers University women's basketball team. Imus's offensive remarks concerning the athletes had created a national controversy, and Corzine had scheduled the meeting to diffuse some of the tension associated with the comments. At Garden State Parkway mile marker 37 in Galloway Township, a pickup truck pulled onto the shoulder to make way for Corzine's motorcade of two cars, which were traveling in excess of ninety miles per hour and had their emergency lights flashing. When the pickup truck pulled back onto the highway, another pickup truck swerved to avoid hitting it. The second pickup truck hit Corzine's SUV, being driven by a New Jersey state trooper, causing the SUV to career into a guardrail. Corzine, who was not wearing a seatbelt, was thrown into the backseat and suffered extensive injuries, including eleven broken ribs, a broken collarbone, a broken sternum, a fractured lower vertebra, a fractured femur, and a gash on his face that necessitated plastic surgery. Corzine was medevacked to the Level I Trauma Center at Cooper University Medical Center in Camden, where he remained in critical condition for eleven days. After undergoing three surgeries for his leg, he was sedated and placed on a ventilator. At the time, doctors were not sure that he would survive his injuries. After being upgraded to stable condition, Corzine was released from the hospital on April 30 and reassumed the duties of office (which had been taken over by Senate President Richard Codey after the accident) on May 7. At his own expense, he installed a videoconferencing system at Drumthwacket to facilitate his communication with legislators during his recuperation. Corzine paid a $46 fine for not wearing a seatbelt. (He also paid all of his medical expenses, choosing not to bill state taxpayers.) Later in his term, he created a public service announcement advocating seatbelt use, proclaiming, "I'm New Jersey Governor Jon Corzine, and I should be dead right now." Though the time away from government was less than a month, the accident came at a crucial time in his administration, and in the power struggle between his administration and the legislature over the budget and other issues, the legislature was able to gain an upper hand in the vacuum that the accident created.

Corzine's tenure was not without legislative successes, however. In 2007, Corzine signed a bill that had been fast-tracked in the legislature's lame-duck session which abolished the death penalty in New Jersey. The bill passed the Democratically controlled legislature largely along party lines, with Democrats voting in favor and Republican opposing. New Jersey was the first state to abolish the death penalty, and Corzine enjoyed international praise for his leadership on the measure.

Among Corzine's top policy priorities was an overhaul to the state's K–12 education funding formula. Governors and state lawmakers were constrained in funding state education expenditures by the 1985 New Jersey State Supreme Court ruling in *Abbott v. Burke* (and subsequent derivative decisions). In the *Abbott* decision, the court found that public elementary and secondary schools in New Jersey's poorest school districts were substandard and unconstitutional. The court sought to remedy the inequality by mandating parity funding in thirty-one of the state's poorest school districts. Corzine sought to change the school-funding formula by including factors other than income in education funding, including increasing funding by billions of dollars in districts that saw large amounts of student mobility and increases in the numbers of poor students, primarily in suburban settings. In securing passage of education funding reform in 2008, the Corzine administration cobbled together an unlikely bipartisan mix of legislators of various racial and ethnic backgrounds whose commonality was that their districts would benefit from the reforms. In 2009, the New Jersey State Supreme Court upheld the new school-funding formula as constitutional, while reiterating that the protections built in to protect the thirty-one *Abbott* districts should remain intact.

One of the more controversial issues of Governor Corzine's administration was his asset-monetization plan, a proposal that would have enabled a newly formed nonprofit corporation to lease the states' toll roads. Corzine's proposal came about because of the need to address the state's ongoing debt crisis (in 2008 it was $32 billion) and the continued underfunding of the state's pension and health-benefits programs for state employees. Under the asset-monetization plan, the nonprofit would operate and maintain the roads by issuing bonds and using toll revenue. The proceeds from the lease would have been used to pay down half the state's debt. But the plan met with significant opposition even before it had been fully outlined by the governor. Portrayed by opponents as a plan to sell off New Jersey's assets, the plan met with widespread opposition from constituents and legislators from both political parties. By September 2007, 58 percent of New Jerseyans polled by Quinnipiac University opposed the plan, and forty-six municipalities throughout the state passed resolutions opposing it. Corzine made the specifics of the asset-monetization plan the centerpiece of his budget address to the state legislature in 2008 and then, accompanied by his chief of staff (and former state treasurer), Bradley Abelow, began a series of twenty-one town-hall meetings held in each county in the state to sell the public on his proposal. But the proposal was dead in the water and dogged Corzine throughout the remainder of his administration and during his reelection campaign. In the aftermath of the asset-monetization plan, an effort began to recall Corzine from office, but organizers failed to acquire the requisite hundred thousand signatures necessary to put the recall on the ballot.

Corzine also antagonized influential leaders of organized labor in the state, who initially believed that the liberal Corzine would prove a consistent ally. But with the state's fiscal situation worsening, Corzine demanded concessions from of the state's public-employee unions, forcing contributions to health-care premiums by workers, invoking mandatory furloughs, and laying off state workers. Other constituencies—including those at state colleges and universities who saw funding slashed, and farmers and employees of the State Department of Agriculture, which Corzine proposed eliminating in 2008—also were frustrated with Corzine's budgetary stance given his liberal rhetoric.

In 2009, Corzine faced reelection and was challenged by Chris Christie, who had served as the state's U.S. attorney. Christie was seen as a tenacious adversary and enjoyed strong popularity from the outset. Christie had developed a reputation as a no-nonsense reformer and had gained name recognition throughout the state by prosecuting numerous high-profile cases involving corrupt politicians. Christie, whose brash outspokenness made him a favorite among the media, conducted a campaign that was vague in terms of specific policy stances but heavily criticized the Corzine administration and conveyed an energy and passion that was missing from the Corzine campaign. Throughout the campaign, Corzine stuck to his unabashedly liberal principles. He argued that despite the bad economic times, New Jersey was better off because of his efforts, and he urged New Jerseyans to give him another term.

Again in 2009, Corzine relied on his personal fortune to fund his campaign, but like most people, his wealth had decreased during the recession. Having already invested more than $100 million in his two previous campaigns, Corzine exerted greater efforts in fund-raising in the 2009 campaign but was impeded by the perception among reluctant potential donors that he could spend unlimited sums. He spent $27 million in his reelection bid, more than $25 million from his own pocket. Estimates had his net worth at the time pegged at $150 million. The less well-heeled Christie opted in to the state's Gubernatorial Public Financing matching-fund program, which provides a two-to-one match for candidates who raise more than $340,000 but mandates a $10.9 million expenditure limit for the general election. Throughout the summer of 2009, Christie led Corzine in the polls. Corzine, whose approval rating had always been mediocre, became a symbolic candidate, with many analysts using Corzine's campaign as an early gauge on the Obama administration. Corzine tried to trade on Obama's popularity in the state and on the enthusiasm his campaign had generated the year before. Though Corzine had been an early supporter of Senator Hillary Rodham Clinton in the 2008 Democratic primary, when Obama won the nomination, Corzine backed him and raised money for the Obama campaign. Obama repaid the favor by visiting the state and trying to mobilize the Democratic base. In October 2009, Corzine managed a last-minute surge in the polls to bring the candidates neck in neck in the days preceding the election. But despite the fact that Corzine outspent Christie by a more than two-to-one margin, Christie won the election 48 to 44 percent. When the election results came in, it became clear that Corzine had failed in part because Christie had maximized turnout in Republican areas of the state but also because several of the state's Democratic Party machines had sat on their hands and did not turn out the traditional Democratic vote, thus paving the way for a Corzine loss.

On November 23, 2010, Corzine wed Sharon M. Elghanayan, a New York psychotherapist, at a ceremony presided over by Judge Edward McBride of the Camden County branch of the New Jersey Superior Court, who had served as the governor's chief of staff, and by New Jersey State Supreme Court Chief Justice Stuart Rabner, who was the state attorney general in the Corzine administration.

But Corzine's postadministration notoriety came as a result of his return to the investment world. In March 2010, Corzine was named chairman and chief executive officer of MF Global Holdings, then a global financial-derivative brokerage firm. Under his leadership, MF Global invested heavily in the European bond market but experienced difficulty maintaining its levels of capital as a result of the European debt crisis. MF Global ultimately filed for bankruptcy protection. On November 4, 2011, Corzine stepped down as CEO of the company, and subsequent investigations probed his management of the company. Congressional probes concluded the firm had not engaged in proper risk-management practices in protecting brokerage funds of its clients from the firm's trading losses.

BRIGID CALLAHAN HARRISON

Records of Governor Jon S. Corzine, New Jersey State Library, Trenton, N.J.

Chen, David W. "Corzine Prevails in a Nasty Governor's Campaign in New Jersey." *New York Times*, November 9, 2005.

Dopp, Terrence. "Corzine to Propose New Jersey Budget That Cuts Jobs." *Bloomberg.com*, February 26, 2008.

Horowitz, Craig. "The Deal He Made." *New York Magazine*, July 10, 2005.

Kocieniewski, David, and Patrick McGeehan. "Corzine's Mix: Bold Ambitions, Rough Edges." *New York Times*, November 2, 2005.

Bibliography

Books and Pamphlets

[Agnew, Daniel]. *Major Richard Howell of New Jersey*. [Philadelphia]: n.p., 1876. Rutgers University Special Collections, New Brunswick, N.J.

Andrews, Charles M. *The Colonial Period of American History*. Vol. 3. New Haven: Yale University Press, 1934.

———. *Narratives of the Insurrections, 1675–1690*. New York: Barnes and Noble, 1946.

Applegate, John Stillwell. *Early Courts and Lawyers of Monmouth County, Beginning at Its First Settlement, and Down to the Last Half Century*. Freehold, N.J.: [Monmouth County Bar Association], 1911.

Applegate, Lloyd Rogers. *A Life of Service: William Augustus Newell*. Toms River, N.J.: Ocean County Historical Society, 1994.

Baker, Ray Stannard. *Woodrow Wilson: Life and Letters*. 8 vols. Garden City, N.Y.: Doubleday, Page, 1927–39.

Barnes, Viola F. *The Dominion of New England: A Study in British Colonial Policy*. New Haven: Yale University Press, 1923.

Batinski, Michael. *Jonathan Belcher, Colonial Governor*. Lexington: University Press of Kentucky, 1996.

———. *The New Jersey Assembly, 1738–1775: The Making of a Legislative Community*. Lanham, Md.: University Press of America, 1987.

Beard, Patricia. *Growing Up Republican: Christie Whitman: The Politics of Character*. New York: HarperCollins, 1996.

Berg, A. Scott. *Wilson*. New York: Putnam, 2013.

Bernard, Francis. *Select Letters on the Trade and Government of America; and the Principles of Law and Polity, Applied to the American Colonies*. London: W. Bowyer and J. Nichols, 1774.

Bigelow, Samuel F., and George J. Hagar, eds. *The Biographical Cyclopedia of New Jersey; Being an Account of the Lives of Individuals Who Have Contributed to the Advancement of the Intellectual, Moral and Material Interests of the Commonwealth*. New York: National Americana Society, 1909.

Biographical Encyclopedia of New Jersey in the Nineteenth Century, The. Philadelphia: Galaxy, 1877.

Birkner, Michael. *Samuel L. Southard: Jeffersonian Whig*. Rutherford, N.J.: Fairleigh Dickinson University Press, 1984.

Bloodgood, Fred L. *The Quiet Hour*. Trenton: MacCrellish & Quigley, 1940.

Blum, John Morton. *Joe Tumulty and the Wilson Era*. Boston: Houghton Mifflin, 1951.

Bonomi, Patricia. *The Lord Cornbury Scandal: The Politics of Reputation in British America*. Chapel Hill: University of North Carolina Press, 1998.

Breen, Timothy. *The Character of the Good Ruler: A Study of Puritan Political Ideas, 1630–1730*. New Haven: Yale University Press, 1970.

Brief Sketch of the Life and Public Services of Theodore F. Randolph, Democratic Nominee for Governor of New Jersey, A. n.p.: Democratic Committee, 1868.

Cadman, John W. *The Corporation in New Jersey*. Cambridge, Mass.: Harvard University Press, 1949.

Calendar of State Papers, Colonial Series, America and West Indies, 1689–1720; Documents Relative to the Colonial History of the State of New York. Vols. 3–5.

Channing, Edward, and Archibald Cary Coolidge, eds. *The Barrington-Bernard Correspondence and Illustrative Matter, 1760–1770*. Cambridge, Mass.: Harvard University Press, 1912.

Codey, Richard J. *Me, Governor? My Life in the Rough-and-Tumble World of New Jersey Politics*. New Brunswick: Rutgers University Press, 2011.

Connors, Richard J. *A Cycle of Power: The Career of Jersey City Mayor Frank Hague*. Metuchen, N.J.: Scarecrow, 1971.

———. *The Process of Constitutional Revision in New Jersey, 1940–1947*. New York: National Municipal League, 1970.

Cooper, John Milton. *Woodrow Wilson: A Biography*. New York: Knopf, 2009.

Crystal, George. *This Republican Hoffman: The Life Story of Harold G. Hoffman, a Modern Fighter*. Hoboken, N.J.: Terminal Printing and Publishing, 1934.

Cunningham, John T. *New Jersey: America's Main Road*. Garden City, N.Y.: Doubleday, 1966.

Cyclopedia of New Jersey Biography: Memorial and Biographical. 6 vols. New York: American Historical Society, 1923.

Dalton, Charles, ed. *English Army Lists and Commission Registers, 1661–1714*. Vol. 2. London: Eyre & Spottiswode, 1894.

———. *George the First's Army, 1714–1725*. Vol. 1. London: Eyre & Spottiswode, 1910.

Doig, Jameson. *Empire on the Hudson: Entrepreneurial Vision and Political Power at the Port of New York Authority*. New York: Columbia University Press, 2001.

Edge, Walter E. *A Jerseyman's Journal*. Princeton: Princeton University Press, 1948.

Ellis, Franklin. *History of Monmouth County, New Jersey*. Philadelphia: R. T. Peck, 1885.

Elmer, Lucius Q. C. *The Constitution and Government of the Province and State of New Jersey, with Biographical Sketches of the Governors from 1776 to 1845 and Reminiscences of the Bench and Bar, during More than Half a Century*. In *Collections of the New Jersey Historical Society*, vol. 7. Newark: Martin R. Dennis, 1872.

Erdman, Charles R., Jr. *The New Jersey Constitution of 1776*. Princeton: Princeton University Press, 1929.

Ershkowitz, Herbert. *The Origin of the Whig and Democratic Parties: New Jersey Politics, 1820–1837*. Washington, D.C.: University Press of America, 1982.

Fee, Walter R. *The Transition from Aristocracy to Democracy in New Jersey, 1789–1829*. Somerville, N.J.: Somerset Press, 1933.

Felzenberg, Alvin S. *Governor Tom Kean: From the New Jersey Statehouse to the 9-11 Commission*. New Brunswick: Rutgers University Press, 2006.

Fisher, Edgar Jacob. *New Jersey as a Royal Province, 1738 to 1776.* New York: Columbia University, 1911.

Foster, John Y. *New Jersey and the Rebellion.* Newark: Martin R. Dennis, 1868.

Gerlach, Larry R. *Prologue to Independence: New Jersey in the Coming of the American Revolution.* New Brunswick: Rutgers University Press, 1975.

———. *William Franklin: New Jersey's Last Royal Governor.* Trenton: New Jersey Historical Commission, 1975.

Gillette, William. *Jersey Blue: Civil War Politics in New Jersey, 1854–1865.* New Brunswick: Rutgers University Press, 1995.

Hall, Michael G. *Edward Randolph and the American Colonies, 1676–1703.* Chapel Hill: University of North Carolina Press, 1960.

Halsted, Oliver S. *Address upon the Character of the Late, the Honorable Isaac H. Williamson, Delivered before the Bar by Oliver S. Halsted.* Newark: A. Guest, 1844.

Hartman, Mary S., ed. *Talking Leadership: Conversations with Powerful Women.* New Brunswick: Rutgers University Press, 1999.

Hawke, David F. *The Colonial Experience.* Indianapolis: Bobbs-Merrill, 1966.

Higgins, Sophia. *The Bernards of Abington and Nether Winchendon: A Family History.* London: Longmans, Green, 1903.

Hirst, David W. *Woodrow Wilson, Reform Governor: A Documentary Narrative.* Princeton: D. Van Nostrand, 1965.

History of Morris County, New Jersey. New York: Munsell, 1882.

Hogarty, Richard A. *Leon Abbett's New Jersey: The Emergence of the Modern Governor.* Philadelphia: American Philosophical Society, 2001.

Honeyman, A. Van Doren, ed. *History of Union County, New Jersey, 1664–1923.* Vols. 2, 3. New York: Lewis Historical Publishing, 1923.

———. *Northwestern New Jersey: A History of Somerset, Morris, Hunterdon, Warren and Sussex Counties.* 4 vols. New York: Lewis Historical Publishing, 1927.

Ingalsbe, Frederick W., comp. *Ingoldesby Genealogy.* Grand Rapids, Mich.: Press of U. G. Clarke, 1904.

Jackson, William J. *New Jerseyans in the Civil War: For Union and Liberty.* New Brunswick: Rutgers University Press, 2000.

Jennings, Samuel. *Truth Rescued from Forgery and Falsehood.* Philadelphia: Reynier Janson, 1699.

Johnson, Nelson. *Boardwalk Empire: The Birth, High Times, and Corruption of Atlantic City.* Medford, N.J.: Plexus Books, 2010.

Katz, Stanley. *Newcastle's New York: Anglo-American Politics, 1732–1753.* Cambridge, Mass.: Harvard University Press, 1968.

Kean, Thomas H. *The Politics of Inclusion.* New York: Free Press, 1988.

Kean, Thomas H., and Lee Hamilton. *Without Precedent: The Inside Story of the 9/11 Commission.* New York: Knopf, 2006.

Kemmerer, Donald L. *Path to Freedom: The Struggle for Self-Government in Colonial New Jersey, 1703–1776.* Princeton: Princeton University Press, 1940.

Kerney, James. *The Political Education of Woodrow Wilson.* New York: Century, 1926.

Knapp, Charles M. *New Jersey Politics during the Period of the Civil War and Reconstruction.* Geneva, N.Y.: W. F. Humphrey, 1924.

Kull, Irving S., ed. *New Jersey: A History; Biographical and Genealogical Records.* Vol. 5. New York: American Historical Society, 1930.

Landsman, Ned C. *Scotland and Its First American Colony, 1683–1765.* Princeton: Princeton University Press, 1985.

Lane, Wheaton J. *From Indian Trail to Iron Horse: Travel and Transportation in New Jersey, 1620–1860.* Princeton: Princeton University Press, 1939.

Leaming, Aaron, and Jacob Spicer, eds. *The Grants, Concessions, and Original Constitutions of the Province of New Jersey.* Philadelphia: William Bradford, 1758.

Lee, Francis Bazley. *Genealogical and Memorial History of the State of New Jersey.* 4 vols. New York: Lewis Historical Publishing, 1910.

———. *History of New Jersey from the Most Remote Period to the Close of the 19th Century.* Newark: Newark Book Publishing and Engraving, 1905.

———, ed. *New Jersey as a Colony and as a State: One of the Original Thirteen.* Vol. 5, *Biographical Volume.* New York: Publishing Society of New Jersey, 1902.

[Leeds, Daniel]. *The Case Put and Decided.* New York: W. Bradford, 1699.

Leiby, James R. *Charity and Correction in New Jersey: A History of State Welfare Institutions.* New Brunswick: Rutgers University Press, 1967.

Lender, Mark E., and James Kirby Martin, eds. *Citizen Soldier: The Revolutionary War Journal of Joseph Bloomfield.* Newark: New Jersey Historical Society, 1982.

Letters to the Right Honourable the Earl of Hillsborough from Governor Bernard, General Gage, and the Honourable His Majesty's Council for the Province of Massachusetts-Bay, The. Boston: Edes and Gill, 1769.

Levine, Peter D. *The Behavior of State Legislative Parties in the Jacksonian Era: New Jersey, 1829–1844.* Rutherford, N.J.: Fairleigh Dickinson University Press, 1977.

Link, Arthur S., ed. *The Papers of Woodrow Wilson.* 69 vols. Princeton: Princeton University Press, 1966–93.

———. *Wilson.* 5 vols. Princeton: Princeton University Press, 1947–65.

Link, Eugene P. *Democratic-Republican Societies, 1790–1800.* New York: Columbia University Press, 1942.

Lockard, Duane. *The New Jersey Governor: A Study in Political Power.* Princeton: D. Van Nostrand, 1964.

Lott, John L., and James A. Finch, eds. *Official Opinions of the Attorneys-General of the United States.* Vol. 23. Washington, D.C.: Government Printing Office, 1902.

Lurie, Maxine N., and Marc Mappen, eds. *Encyclopedia of New Jersey.* New Brunswick: Rutgers University Press, 2004.

Lurie, Maxine N., and Richard Veit, eds. *New Jersey: A History of the Garden State.* New Brunswick: Rutgers University Press, 2012.

Lustig, Mary Lou. *Robert Hunter, 1666–1734: New York's Augustan Statesman.* Syracuse: Syracuse University Press, 1983.

Maynard, W. Barksdale: *Woodrow Wilson: Princeton to the Presidency.* New Haven: Yale University Press, 2008.

McCarter, Robert H. *Memories of a Half Century at the New Jersey Bar*. Camden: New Jersey State Bar Association, 1937.

McClure, Sandy. *Christie Whitman for the People: A Political Biography*. Amherst, N.Y.: Prometheus Books, 1996.

McConville, Brendan. *These Daring Disturbers of the Public Peace: The Struggle for Property and Power in Early New Jersey*. Ithaca, N.Y.: Cornell University Press, 1999.

McCormick, Richard P. *Experiment in Independence: New Jersey in the Critical Period, 1781–1798*. New Brunswick: Rutgers University Press, 1950.

———. *The History of Voting in New Jersey: A Study of the Development of Election Machinery, 1664–1911*. New Brunswick: Rutgers University Press, 1953.

———. *New Jersey from Colony to State, 1609–1789*. Newark: New Jersey Historical Society, 1981.

McGreevey, Dina Matos. *Silent Partner*. New York: Hyperion, 2007.

McGreevey, James E. *The Confession*. New York: HarperCollins, 2006.

McKean, Dayton. *The Boss*. Boston: Houghton Mifflin, 1940.

McSeveney, Samuel T. *The Politics of Depression: Political Behavior in the Northeast, 1893–1896*. New York: Oxford University Press, 1972.

Moffat, William D., comp. *Addresses by John William Griggs*. N.p.: privately printed, 1930.

Municipalities of Essex County, New Jersey, 1666–1924, The. 4 vols. New York: Lewis Historical Publishing, 1925.

Murrin, Mary. *To Save This State from Ruin: New Jersey and the Creation of the United States Constitution, 1776–1789*. Trenton: New Jersey Historical Commission, 1987.

Myers, William Starr. *George Brinton McClellan*. New York: Appleton-Century, 1934.

———, ed. *The Story of New Jersey*. 5 vols. New York: Lewis Historical Publishing, 1945.

Nelson, William, ed. *The New Jersey Coast in Three Centuries*. 2 vols. New York: Lewis, 1902.

———, ed. *Original Documents Relating to the Life and Administrations of William Burnet, Governor of New York and New Jersey, 1720–28*. Paterson, N.J.: Press Printing and Publishing, 1897.

Nelson's Biographical Cyclopedia of New Jersey. 2 vols. New York: Eastern Historical Publishing Society, 1913.

Newcomb, Benjamin H. *Political Partisanship in the American Middle Colonies, 1700–1776*. Baton Rouge: Louisiana State University Press, 1995.

Nicholson, Colin. *The "Infamous Governor": Francis Bernard and the Origins of the American Revolution*. Boston: Northeastern University Press, 2001.

Noble, Ransom E. *New Jersey Progressivism before Wilson*. Princeton: Princeton University Press, 1946.

O'Connor, John E. *William Paterson: Lawyer and Statesman, 1745–1806*. New Brunswick: Rutgers University Press, 1979.

Ogden, Mary Depue, ed. *Memorial Cyclopedia of New Jersey*. 4 vols. Newark: Memorial History, 1915–21.

Pasler, Rudolph J., and Margaret C. Pasler. *The New Jersey Federalists*. Rutherford, N.J.: Fairleigh Dickinson University Press, 1975.

Paulsson, Martin. *The Social Anxieties of Progressive Reform: Atlantic City, 1854–1920*. New York: New York University Press, 1994.

Personal and Political Sketch of Hon. Joel Parker. Freehold, N.J.: Monmouth Democrat, 1871.

Pierce, Frank H., Jr. *The Governors of New Jersey*. Newark: Newark Evening News, [1952].

Pitney, Henry C., Jr., ed. *A History of Morris County, New Jersey, Embracing Upwards of Two Centuries, 1710–1913*. 2 vols. New York: Lewis Historical Publishing, 1914.

Pomfret, John E. *Colonial New Jersey: A History*. New York: Scribner's, 1973.

——. *The New Jersey Proprietors and Their Lands*. Princeton: D. Van Nostrand, 1964.

——. *The Province of East New Jersey, 1609–1702: The Rebellious Proprietary*. Princeton: Princeton University Press, 1962.

——. *The Province of West New Jersey, 1609–1702: A History of the Origins of an American Colony*. Princeton: Princeton University Press, 1956.

Presidency, The: Sketch of the Democratic Candidate, Joel Parker. N.p., [1876].

Prince, Carl E. *New Jersey's Jeffersonian Republicans, 1789–1817*. Chapel Hill: University of North Carolina Press, 1967.

——. *William Livingston: New Jersey's First Governor*. Trenton: New Jersey Historical Commission, 1975.

Prince, Carl E., and Dennis P. Ryan, eds. *The Papers of William Livingston*. 5 vols. Trenton and New Brunswick: New Jersey Historical Commission (vols. 1–2) and Rutgers University Press (vols. 3–5), 1979–88.

Proceedings of the New Jersey Constitutional Convention of 1844. With an introduction by John E. Bebout. Trenton: Federal Writers' Project, 1942.

Purvis, Thomas L. *Proprietors, Patronage, and Paper Money: Legislative Politics in New Jersey, 1703–1776*. New Brunswick: Rutgers University Press, 1986.

Randolph, Theodore F. *Address of Governor Theodore F. Randolph of Morris to the Democratic State Convention, Assembled at Trenton, June 26, 1872*. Morristown, N.J.: Louis C. Vogt, 1872.

——. *Letter of Governor Randolph of New Jersey, to Hon. Cortlandt Parker, Relating to Executive Prerogatives and Judicial Authority*. Trenton: Wm. T. Nicholson, 1871.

Record of Leon Abbett, Democratic Candidate for Governor of New Jersey, as Assemblyman, Senator and Governor, The. Jersey City, N.J.: Heppenheimer, 1889.

Report of the National Advisory Commission on Civil Disorders. Washington, D.C.: U.S. Government Printing Office, 1968.

Reynolds, John F. *Testing Democracy: Electoral Behavior and Progressive Reform in New Jersey, 1880–1920*. Chapel Hill: University of North Carolina Press, 1988.

Ricord, Frederick W. *Biographical Encyclopedia: Successful Men of New Jersey*. Vol. 1. New York: New Jersey Historical Publishing, 1896.

——, ed. *History of Union County, New Jersey*. Newark: East Jersey History, 1897.

Rosenthal, Alan. *The Best Job in Politics: Exploring How Governors Succeed as Policy Leaders*. Thousand Oaks, CA: CQ Press, 2012.

Sackett, William E. *Modern Battles of Trenton*. Vol. 1, *Being a History of New Jersey's*

Politics and Legislation from the Year 1868 to the Year 1894. Trenton: John L. Murphy, 1895.

————. *Modern Battles of Trenton.* Vol. 2, *From Werts to Wilson.* New York: Neale, 1914.

Salmore, Barbara G., and Stephen A. Salmore. *New Jersey Government and Politics: The Suburbs Come of Age.* 4th ed. New Brunswick: Rutgers University Press, 2013.

Scannell's New Jersey's First Citizens. 6 vols. Paterson, N.J.: J. J. Scannell, 1917–27.

Schroth, Frank D. *The First Year, Being the Record of Accomplishment of George S. Silzer, Governor of New Jersey.* Trenton: MacCrellish & Quigley, 1924.

Schwarz, Philip J. *The Jarring Interests: New York's Boundary Makers, 1664–1776.* Albany: State University of New York Press, 1979.

Sears, Stephen W. *George B. McClellan: The Young Napoleon.* New York: Ticknor & Fields, 1988.

Sedgwick, Theodore, Jr. *A Memoir of the Life of William Livingston.* New York: Harper, 1833.

Shaw, Douglas V. *The Making of an Immigrant City: Ethnic and Cultural Conflict in Jersey City, New Jersey, 1850–1877.* New York: Arno, 1976.

Shaw, William H. *History of Essex and Hudson Counties, New Jersey.* Philadelphia: Everts and Peck, 1884.

Sheridan, Eugene R. *Lewis Morris, 1671–1746: A Study in Early American Politics.* Syracuse: Syracuse University Press, 1981.

Silzer, George S. *The Government of a State.* Newark: Soney & Sage, 1933.

Skemp, Sheila. *William Franklin: Son of a Patriot, Servant of a King.* New York: Oxford University Press, 1990.

Smith, Charles Perrin. *New Jersey Political Reminiscences, 1828–1882.* Edited by Hermann K. Platt. New Brunswick: Rutgers University Press, 1965.

Smith, William, Jr. *The History of the Province of New-York.* 2 vols. Edited by Michael Kammen. Cambridge, Mass.: Harvard University Press, Belknap Press, 1972.

Snell, James P. *History of Sussex and Warren Counties, New Jersey.* Philadelphia: Everts and Peck, 1881.

Sobel, Robert, and John Raimo, eds. *Biographical Directory of the Governors of the United States, 1789–1978.* 4 vols. Westport, Conn.: Meckler Books, 1978.

Tanner, Edwin P. *The Province of New Jersey, 1664–1738.* New York: Columbia University Press, 1908.

Taylor, George Rogers. *The Great Tariff Debate, 1820–1830.* Boston: D. C. Heath, 1966.

Trueblood, D. Elton. *Robert Barclay.* New York: Macmillan, 1968.

Vance, Alanson A. *A Political Reminiscence.* Morristown, N.J., [1902].

Van Devander, Charles W. *The Big Bosses.* New York: Howell, Soskin, 1944.

Van Winkle, Daniel, ed. *History of the Municipalities of Hudson County, New Jersey, 1630–1923.* 3 vols. New York: Lewis Historical Publishing, 1924.

Venable, John D. *Out of the Shadow: The Story of Charles Edison.* East Orange, N.J.: Charles Edison Fund, 1978.

Wefing, John B. *The Life and Times of Richard J. Hughes: The Politics of Civility.* New Brunswick: Rutgers University Press, 2009.

Weissman, Art. *Christine Todd Whitman: The Making of a National Political Player*. New York: Birch Lane, 1997.

Westervelt, Frances A. *History of Bergen County, New Jersey, 1630–1923*. 3 vols. New York: Lewis Historical Publishing, 1923.

Whitehead, John. *The Judicial and Civil History of New Jersey*. [Boston]: Boston Historical Company, 1897.

Whitehead, William A. *Contributions to the Early History of Perth Amboy and the Adjoining Country, with Sketches of Men and Events in New Jersey during the Provincial Era*. New York: D. Appleton., 1856.

———, ed. *The Papers of Lewis Morris*. In *Collections of the New Jersey Historical Society*, vol. 4. New York: G. P. Putnam, 1852.

Who's Who in New Jersey 1939. Chicago: A. N. Marquis, 1939.

Wilentz, Sean. *The Rise of American Democracy: Jefferson to Lincoln*. New York: Norton, 2005.

Williamson, Isaac H., and Garret D. Wall. *Opinion of Isaac H. Williamson, Esq., and Garret D. Wall, Esq., in Relation to the Corporate Powers of "The Trenton and New Brunswick Turnpike Company."* Trenton: Joseph Justice, 1835.

Wright, William C. *The Secession Movement in the Middle Atlantic States*. Rutherford, N.J.: Fairleigh Dickinson University Press, 1973.

Articles

Alexander, Jack. "The Ungovernable Governor." *Saturday Evening Post*, January 23, 1943, 9.

Belkin, Lisa. "Keeping to the Center Lane." *New York Times Magazine*, May 5, 1996.

Benson, Josh. "Development: Football? Nah, Hardball." *New York Times*, April 17, 2005.

Bernstein, David A. "William Livingston: The Role of the Executive in New Jersey's Revolutionary War." In *New Jersey in the American Revolution II*, edited by William C. Wright. Trenton: New Jersey Historical Commission, 1973.

Birkner, Michael J. "Journalism and Politics in Jacksonian New Jersey: The Career of Stacy G. Potts." *New Jersey History* 97 (1979): 159–78.

———. "Peter Vroom and the Politics of Democracy." In *Jacksonian New Jersey*, edited by Paul A. Stellhorn. Trenton: New Jersey Historical Commission, 1979.

———. "Samuel L. Southard and the Origins of *Gibbons v. Ogden.*" *Princeton University Library Chronicle* 40 (Winter 1979): 171–82.

Birkner, Michael J., and Herbert Ershkowitz. "'Men and Measures': The Creation of the Second Party System in New Jersey." *New Jersey History* 107 (Fall–Winter 1989): 41–59.

Brooks, Noah. "George T. Werts." *Harper's Weekly* 38 (March 3, 1894): 198.

Burritt, Richard D. "Another Edison Makes Some Discoveries." *New York Times Magazine*, October 12, 1941, 16, 27.

Capuzzo, Jill P. "Favorite Son, Unfavorable Light: Scotch Plains Embraces DiFrancesco While in Trenton, There's a Wariness." *New York Times*, April 15, 2001.

Chen, David W. "Corzine Prevails in a Nasty Governor's Campaign in New Jersey." *New York Times*, November 9, 2005.

Cody, Edward J. "The Growth of Toleration and Church-State Relations in New Jersey, 1689–1763: From Holy Men to Holy War." In *Economic and Social History of Colonial New Jersey*, edited by William C. Wright. Trenton: New Jersey Historical Commission, 1974.

[Colden, Cadwallader]. "Cadwallader Colden's History of Governor William Cosby's Administration and of Lieutenant Governor George Clarke's Administration through 1737." *New-York Historical Society Collections* 68 (1935): 280–355.

Cook, Richard. "Lewis Morris—New Jersey's Colonial Poet-Governor." *Journal of the Rutgers University Library* 24 (1961): 100–113.

Dangerfield, George. "The Steamboat Case." In *Quarrels That Have Shaped the Constitution*, edited by John Garraty. New York: Harper & Row, 1964.

"Direct Primary and the New Idea in New Jersey, The." *Outlook* 90 (September 12, 1908): 51–52.

Dopp, Terrence. "Corzine to Propose New Jersey Budget That Cuts Jobs." *Bloomberg.com*, February 26, 2008.

Dorsett, Lyle. "Frank Hague, Franklin Roosevelet and the Politics of the New Deal." *New Jersey History* 94 (1975–76): 21–35.

Dunn, Voorhees E., Jr. "The Road to the 1947 New Jersey Constitution: Arthur T. Vanderbilt's Influence on Court Reform, 1930–1947." *New Jersey History* 104 (Fall–Winter 1986): 23–41.

Ellertsen, E. Peter. "Prosperity and Paper Money: The Loan Office Act of 1723." *New Jersey History* 85 (1967): 47–57.

Ershkowitz, Herbert. "Samuel L. Southard: A Case Study of Whig Leadership in the Age of Jackson." *New Jersey History* 88 (Spring 1970): 5–24.

Felzenberg, Alvin S. "The Making of a Governor: The Early Political Career of Richard J. Hughes." *New Jersey History* 101 (Spring–Summer 1983): 1–28.

Fennelly, Catherine. "William Franklin of New Jersey." *William and Mary Quarterly* 6 (1949): 361–82.

Florio Perrucci Steinhardt & Fader LLC. "James J. Florio." http://www.florioperrucci.com/attorneys_james.html.

Gray, Jerry. "G.O.P. Vows Change in Trenton as It Takes Over the Legislature." *New York Times*, January 15, 1992.

———. "Mr. Bland Goes to Trenton, and Takes Over the Senate." *New York Times*, January 18, 1992.

Greene, Larry A. "The Emancipation Proclamation in New Jersey and the Paranoid Style." *New Jersey History* 91 (Summer 1973): 108–24.

Greiert, Steven G. "The Earl of Halifax and the Land Riots in New Jersey, 1748–1753." *New Jersey History* 99 (Spring–Summer 1981): 13–31.

Halbfinger, David M. "Builder Aided DiFrancesco in Land Deal: Home Builder's Money Helped DiFrancesco Pay Judgment in Land Deal." *New York Times*, March 1, 2001.

Herrmann, Frederick M. "The Constitution of 1844 and Political Change in Antebellum New Jersey." *New Jersey History* 101 (Spring–Summer 1983): 29–51.

Hogarty, Richard A. "The Political Apprenticeship of Leon Abbett." *New Jersey History* 111 (Spring–Summer 1993): 1–42.

Holdsworth, L. V. "The Problem of Edward Byllynge: His Connection with Cornwall." In *The Children of Light*, edited by H. H. Brinton. New York: Macmillan, 1938.

Horowitz, Craig. "The Deal He Made." *New York*, July 10, 2005.

Horowitz, Gary S. "New Jersey Land Riots, 1745–1755." *In Economic and Social History of Colonial New Jersey*, edited by William C. Wright. Trenton: New Jersey Historical Commission, 1974.

Klinghoffer, Judith Apter, and Lois Elkis. "The 'Petticoat Electors': Women's Suffrage in New Jersey, 1776–1807." *Journal of the Early Republic* 12 (1992): 159–93.

Kocieniewski, David. "In Budget, a Sign of Codey's Tenure." *New York Times*, July 4, 2005.

Kocieniewski, David, and Patrick McGeehan. "Corzine's Mix: Bold Ambitions, Rough Edges." *New York Times*, November 2, 2005.

Lurie, Maxine N. "The Barclay Record Book and Its East Jersey Minutes: An Early Look at Context and Content." *Journal of the Rutgers University Libraries* 63 (2007): 10–22.

———. "New Jersey's Three Constitutions: 1776, 1844, 1947." *Journal of the Rutgers University Libraries* 59 (December 2000): 1–18.

Mansnerus, Laura. "Man in the News: A Political Veteran Ascendant: Richard James Codey." *New York Times*, November 16, 2004.

McCormick, Richard P. "Party Formation in the Jacksonian Era." *Proceedings of the New Jersey Historical Society* 83 (July 1965): 161–73.

McGuire, Maureen. "Struggle over the Purse: Gov. Morris v. N.J. Assembly." *Proceedings of the New Jersey Historical Society* 82 (1964): 200–207.

Morris, Joe Alex. "His Heart Belongs to Jersey." *Saturday Evening Post* 225 (July 5, 1952): 36–37, 54–56.

Nadelhaft, J. R. "Politics and the Judicial Tenure Fight in Colonial New Jersey." *William and Mary Quarterly* 28 (January 1971): 46–63.

Namier, Lewis. "Charles Garth and His Connexions." *English Historical Review* 54 (July 1939): 443–70.

National Governors Association. "New Jersey Governor Donald T. DiFrancesco." http://www.nga.org/cms/FormerGovBios.

Nelson, William. "The Administration of William Burnet, 1720–28." In *The Memorial History of the City of New-York, from Its First Settlement to the Year 1892*, vol. 2, edited by James Grant Wilson. New York: New York History, 1892.

Nickalls, J. L. "The Problem of Edward Byllynge: His Writings and Their Evidence of His Influence on the First Constitution of West Jersey." In *The Children of Light*, edited by H. H. Brinton. New York: Macmillan, 1938.

Nixon, John T. "The Circumstances Attending the Election of William Pennington, of New Jersey, as Speaker of the Thirty-Sixth Congress." *Proceedings of the New Jersey Historical Society* 2 (1872): 207–20.

O'Connor, John E. "Legal Reform in the Early Republic: The New Jersey Experience." *American Journal of Legal History* 22 (April 1978): 95–117.

Ogden, Aaron. "Autobiography of Col. Aaron Ogden of Elizabethtown." *Proceedings of the New Jersey Historical Society* 12 (1892–93): 15–31.

Olson, Alison Gilbert. "Governor Robert Hunter and the Anglican Church in New York." In *Statesmen, Scholars and Merchants: Essays in Eighteenth-Century History Presented to Dame Lucy Sutherland*, edited by Anne Whiteman, J. S. Bromley, and P. G. M. Dickson. Oxford, U.K.: Clarendon, 1973.

Pierce, Arthur D. "A Governor in Skirts." *Proceedings of the New Jersey Historical Society* 83 (1965): 1–9.

Pomfret, John E. "Edward Byllynge's Proposed Gift of Land to Indigent Friends." *Pennsylvania Magazine of History and Biography* 61 (1937): 88–92.

———. "The Problem of the West Jersey Concessions of 1676/77." *William and Mary Quarterly* 5 (1948): 95–105.

———. "Thomas Budd's 'True and Perfect Account' of Byllynge's Proprieties in West New Jersey." *William and Mary Quarterly* 5 (1948): 325–31.

Pumpelly, Josiah C. "Mahlon Dickerson, Industrial Pioneer and Old Time Patriot." *Proceedings of the New Jersey Historical Society* 11 (1891): 131–56.

Renda, Lex. "The Dysfunctional Party: The Collapse of the New Jersey Whigs, 1849–1853." *New Jersey History* 116 (Spring–Summer 1998): 3–57.

Rubincam, Milton. "The Formative Years of Lord Cornbury, the First Royal Governor of New York and New Jersey." *New York Genealogical and Biographical Record* 81 (1904): 106–16.

Scanlon, James E. "English Intrigue and the Governorship of Robert Hunter." *New-York Historical Society Quarterly* 57 (1973): 199–211.

Schoenbachler, Matthew. "Republicanism in the Age of Democratic Revolution: The Democratic-Republican Societies of the 1790s." *Journal of the Early Republic* 18 (Spring 1998): 237–61.

Scull, G. D. "Biographical Notice of Doctor Daniel Coxe, of London." *Pennsylvania Magazine of History and Biography* 7 (1883): 317–37.

Sheridan, Eugene R. "Daniel R. Coxe and the Restoration of Proprietary Government in East Jersey, 1690—A Letter." *New Jersey History* 92 (1974): 103–9.

Shipton, Clifford K. "Jonathan Belcher." In *Sibley's Harvard Graduates*, vol. 4, edited by Clifford K. Shipton. Cambridge, Mass.: Harvard University Press, 1933.

Sly, John F. "Walter Evans Edge, 1873–1956: A Tribute." *Proceedings of the New Jersey Historical Society* 79 (1961): 1–15.

Smothers, Ronald. "New Jersey: Tolls Emerge as Issue in the Race for Governor." *New York Times*, January 18, 2001.

"Special Report—The McGreevey Scandal." *Star Ledger*. http://www.nj.com/news/mcgreevey/.

Spencer, Charles Worthen. "The Cornbury Legend." *New York State Historical Association Proceedings* 13 (1914): 309–20.

Steffens, Lincoln. "New Jersey: A Traitor State." *McClure's Magazine* 24 (April 1905): 649–64.

Stickle, Warren E. "The Applejack Campaign of 1919: As 'Wet as the Atlantic Ocean.'" *New Jersey History* 89 (1971): 5–22.

Stickle, Warren E. "Edward I. Edwards and the Urban Coalition of 1919." *New Jersey History* 90 (1972): 83–96.

Strassburger, John. "Our Unhappy Purchase: The West Jersey Society, Lewis Morris, and Jersey Lands, 1703–1736." *New Jersey History* 98 (Spring–Summer 1980): 97–115.

Strum, Harvey. "New Jersey Politics & the War of 1812." *New Jersey History* 105 (Fall–Winter 1987): 37–70.

Turner, Gordon B. "Lewis Morris and the Colonial Government Problem." *Proceedings of the New Jersey Historical Society* 67 (1949): 260–304.

Weart, Jacob. "Speaker William Pennington." *New Jersey Law Journal* 20 (July–August 1897): 230–39.

Whitehead, William A. "Biographical Sketch of William Franklin, Governor of New Jersey from 1763 to 1776." *Proceedings of the New Jersey Historical Society* 3 (1848): 137–59.

Yard, James S. "Joel Parker, 'The War Governor of New Jersey': A Biographical Sketch." *Proceedings of the New Jersey Historical Society* 10 (1888–89): 57–92.

Unpublished Studies

Beckwith, Robert R. "Mahlon Dickerson of New Jersey, 1770–1853." Ph.D. dissertation, Columbia University, 1964.

Black, Frederick R. "The Last Lords Proprietors of West Jersey: The West Jersey Society, 1692–1702." Ph.D. dissertation, Rutgers University, 1964.

Bloom, Jeanne Gould. "Sir Edmund Andros." Ph.D. dissertation, Yale University, 1962.

Bryan, Brantz Mayer. "Alfred Eastlack Driscoll: Governor of New Jersey." Senior thesis, Princeton University, 1952.

Cutler, Robert G. "Charter Reviewed: The New Jersey Constitution, 1947–1957." Ph.D. dissertation, Princeton University, 1958.

Fallaw, W. Robert. "The Rise of the Whig Party in New Jersey." Ph.D. dissertation, Princeton University, 1967.

Felzenberg, Alvin S. "The Impact of Gubernatorial Style on Policy Outcomes: An In-Depth Study of Three New Jersey Governors." Ph.D. dissertation, Princeton University, 1978.

Herrmann, Frederick M. "Stress and Structure: Political Change in Antebellum New Jersey." Ph.D. dissertation, Rutgers University, 1976.

Klein, Milton M. "The American Whig: William Livingston of New York." Ph.D. dissertation, Columbia University, 1954.

Latschar, John A. "East New Jersey, 1665–1682: Perils of a Proprietary Government." Ph.D. dissertation, Rutgers University, 1978.

Leone, Richard C. "The Politics of Gubernatorial Leadership: Tax and Education Reform in New Jersey." Ph.D. dissertation, Princeton University, 1969.

Mahoney, Joseph F. "New Jersey Politics after Wilson: Progressivism in Decline." Ph.D. dissertation, Columbia University, 1964.

Mariboe, William H. "The Life of William Franklin, 1730(31)–1813: *Pro Rege et Patria*." Ph.D. dissertation, University of Pennsylvania, 1962.

McCreary, John R. "Ambition, Interest, and Faction: Politics in New Jersey, 1702–1738." Ph.D. dissertation, University of Nebraska, 1971.

Michels, Edward H., Jr. "New Jersey and the New Deal." Ph.D. dissertation, New York University, 1986.

Moore, Louis B. "Response to Reconstruction: Change and Continuity in New Jersey Politics, 1866–1874." Ph.D. dissertation, Rutgers University, 1999.

Peterson, Kent A. "New Jersey Politics and National Policymaking, 1865–1868." Ph.D. dissertation, Princeton University, 1970.

Scanlon, James E. "A Life of Robert Hunter, 1666–1734." Ph.D. dissertation, University of Virginia, 1969.

Stellhorn, Paul A. "Depression and Decline: Newark, New Jersey, 1929–1941." Ph.D. dissertation, Rutgers University, 1981.

Stickle, Warren E. "New Jersey Democracy and the Urban Coalition: 1919–1932." Ph.D. dissertation, Georgetown University, 1971.

Strassburger, John R. "The Origins and Establishment of the Morris Family in the Society and Politics of New York and New Jersey, 1630–1746." Ph.D. dissertation, Princeton University, 1976.

Webb, Stephen Saunders. "Officers and Governors: The Role of the British Army in Imperial Politics and the Administration of the American Colonies, 1689–1722." Ph.D. dissertation, University of Wisconsin, 1965.

Wood, Robert. "The Metropolitan Governor." Ph.D. dissertation, Harvard University, 1950.

Manuscript and Records Collections

Records of Governor Leon Abbett, New Jersey State Library, Bureau of Archives and History, Trenton, N.J.

Alumni Biographical Collection, Seeley G. Mudd Library, Princeton University, Princeton, N.J.

Jonathan Belcher Letterbooks, Massachusetts Historical Society, Boston, Mass.

Jonathan Belcher Papers, The New Jersey Historical Society, Newark, N.J.

Biographical Collection, Rutgers University Special Collections, New Brunswick, N.J.

Joseph Bloomfield Letters, Rutgers University Special Collections, New Brunswick, N.J.

Brendan T. Byrne Archive, Center on the American Governor, Eagleton Institute of Politics, Rutgers University.

Papers of Brendan T. Byrne, The Monsignor Field Archives and Special Collections Center, Seton Hall University.

Papers of Brendan T. Byrne, Special Collections and University Archives, Rutgers University Libraries.

Records of Governor William T. Cahill, New Jersey State Library, Trenton, N.J.

Records of Governor Richard J. Codey, Governor's Office of Policy, 2001–2005, New Jersey State Library, Division of Archives and Records Management, Trenton, N.J.

Cadwallader Colden Papers, New-York Historical Society, New York, N.Y.

Mahlon Dickerson Diary, The New Jersey Historical Society, Newark, N.J.

Mahlon Dickerson Diary, Rutgers University Special Collections, New Brunswick, N.J.

Mahlon Dickerson Papers, The New Jersey Historical Society, Newark, N.J.

Philemon Dickerson Papers, The New Jersey Historical Society, Newark, N.J.

Records of Governor Alfred E. Driscoll, New Jersey State Library, Trenton, N.J.

East Jersey Papers, The New Jersey Historical Society, Newark, N.J.

Walter E. Edge Papers, The New Jersey Historical Society, Newark, N.J.

Records of Governor Walter E. Edge, New Jersey State Library, Trenton, N.J.

Records of Governor Charles Edison, New Jersey State Library, Trenton, N.J.

Records of Governor Edward I. Edwards, New Jersey State Library, Trenton, N.J.

Emmet Collection, New York Public Library, New York, N.Y.

Records of Governor James F. Fielder, New Jersey State Library, Trenton, N.J.

Governor James J. Florio Archives, Center on the American Governor, Eagleton Institute of Politics, Rutgers University.

Records of Governor James J. Florio, New Jersey State Archives, Trenton, N.J.

Records of Governor John F. Fort, New Jersey State Library, Trenton, N.J.

Gratz Collection, Historical Society of Pennsylvania, Philadelphia, Pa.

Records of Governor John W. Griggs, New Jersey State Library, Trenton, N.J.

Records of Governor Harold G. Hoffman, New Jersey State Library, Trenton, N.J.

Records of Governor Richard J. Hughes, New Jersey State Library, Trenton, N.J.

Thomas Jefferson Papers, Library of Congress, Manuscript Division, Washington, D.C.

Governor Thomas H. Kean Archive, Center on the American Governor, Eagleton Institute of Politics, Rutgers University.

Records of Governor Morgan F. Larson, New Jersey State Library, Trenton, N.J.

Livingston-Redmond Papers, Franklin D. Roosevelt Library, Hyde Park, N.Y.

Logan Family Papers, Historical Society of Pennsylvania, Philadelphia, Pa.

Records of Governor George C. Ludlow, New Jersey State Library, Trenton, N.J.

Manuscript Collections, New Jersey Historical Society, Newark, N.J.

Records of Governor George B. McClellan, New Jersey State Library, Trenton, N.J.

Records of Governor James E. McGreevey, Governor's Office of Policy, 2001–2005, New Jersey State Library, Trenton, N.J.

Robert B. and Helen Stevenson Meyner Papers, Lafayette College, Easton, Pa.

Records of Governor Robert B. Meyner, New Jersey State Library, Trenton, N.J.

Records of Governor A. Harry Moore, New Jersey State Library, Trenton, N.J.

Morris Family Papers, Rutgers University Special Collections, New Brunswick, N.J.

Records of Governor Franklin Murphy, New Jersey State Library, Trenton, N.J.

New Jersey Broadsides Collection, The New Jersey Historical Society, Newark, N.J.

New Jersey Division of Elections, Election Results Archives, New Jersey Department of State.

New Jersey Letters, Rutgers University Special Collections, New Brunswick, N.J.

New Jersey State Archives, Executive Branch—Office of the Governor Records.

Charles Smith Olden Papers, Historical Society of Princeton, Princeton, N.J.

Ferdinand John Paris Papers, The New Jersey Historical Society, Newark, N.J.

William Paterson Papers, William Paterson College Special Collections, Wayne, N.J.

Charles A. Philhower Collection, Rutgers University Special Collections, New Brunswick, N.J.

Timothy Pickering Papers, Massachusetts Historical Society, Boston, Mass.

Rodman M. Price Papers, Huntington Library, San Marino, Calif.

Rodman M. Price Papers, Rutgers University Special Collections, New Brunswick, N.J.

Rodman M. Price Papers, University of California, Berkeley, Special Collections, Berkeley, Calif.

Rutherfurd Collection, New-York Historical Society, New York, N.Y.

Ferdinand S. Schenck Papers, Rutgers University Special Collections, New Brunswick, N.J.

Records of Governor George S. Silzer, New Jersey State Library, Trenton, N.J.

Smith Family Papers, Historical Society of Pennsylvania, Philadelphia, Pa.

Records of the Society for the Propagation of the Gospel in Foreign Parts, Series A, vols. 3 and 4, Library of Congress microfilm.

Samuel L. Southard Manuscripts, Library of Congress, Manuscript Division, Washington, D.C.

Samuel L. Southard Papers, Princeton University Special Collections, Princeton, N.J.

Records of Governor Edward C. Stokes, New Jersey State Library, Trenton, N.J.

John W. Taylor Papers, New-York Historical Society, New York, N.Y.

Joseph P. Tumulty Papers, Library of Congress, Manuscript Division, Washington, D.C.

Records of Governor Foster Voorhees, New Jersey State Library, Trenton, N.J.

Peter D. Vroom Papers, Columbia University Library, New York, N.Y.

Peter D. Vroom Papers, The New Jersey Historical Society, Newark, N.J.

Peter D. Vroom Papers, Rutgers University Special Collections, New Brunswick, N.J.

Garret D. Wall Papers, Princeton University Special Collections, Princeton, N.J.

Garret D. Wall Papers, Rutgers University Special Collections, New Brunswick, N.J.

Marcus L. Ward Papers, The New Jersey Historical Society, Newark, N.J.

Marcus L. Ward Papers, Rutgers University Special Collections, New Brunswick, N.J.

Records of Governor George T. Werts, New Jersey State Library, Trenton, N.J.

Anthony Walton White Papers, Rutgers University Special Collections, New Brunswick, N.J.

Governor Christine Todd Whitman Archives, Center on the American Governor, Eagleton Institute of Politics, Rutgers University.

Isaac Williamson Papers, The New Jersey Historical Society, Newark, N.J.

Isaac Williamson Papers, New Jersey State Library, Trenton, N.J.

Isaac Williamson Papers, Rutgers University Special Collections, New Brunswick, N.J.

Woodrow Wilson Collection, Princeton University Special Collections, Princeton, N.J.

Woodrow Wilson Papers, Library of Congress, Manuscript Division, Washington, D.C.

Records of Governor Woodrow Wilson, New Jersey State Library, Trenton, N.J.

Oliver Wolcott Papers, Connecticut Historical Society, Hartford, Conn.

Notes on Contributors

Michael C. Batinski, emeritus professor of history at Southern Illinois University, is author of *The New Jersey Assembly from 1728 to 1775: The Making of a Legislative Community* (1987) and *Jonathan Belcher, Colonial Governor* (1996).

Clark L. Beck, Jr., formerly an assistant curator of Special Collections at Rutgers University, was a coauthor of the exhibit catalogue *As We Saw Them: Westerners Interpret Japan, 1853–1912*.

Robert R. Beckwith, formerly professor of history at Montclair State College, is the author of *Mahlon Dickerson, Jacksonian Aristocrat* (1964). He is deceased.

Michael J. Birkner, professor of history and Benjamin Franklin Professor of Liberal Arts at Gettysburg College, is the author or editor of twelve books, including *Samuel L. Southard: Jeffersonian-Whig* (1984), *A Country Place No More: The Transformation of Bergenfield, New Jersey* (1994), and *McCormick of Rutgers: Scholar, Teacher, Public Historian* (2001).

Frederick R. Black, emeritus associate professor of history at the C. W. Post Center of Long Island University, has published articles in American colonial history, including "Provincial Taxation in Colonial New Jersey, 1704–1735," *New Jersey History* (1977); and "The Fate of the Concessions," in *The West Jersey Concessions and Agreements of 1676/77: The Document, Its Background in English History, and Its Influence in the American Colonies* (1979).

Edward J. Cody, emeritus professor of history at Ramapo College, has published articles in religious history, including "The Growth of Toleration and Church-State Relations in New Jersey, 1689–1763: From Holy Men to Holy War," in *Economic and Social History of Colonial New Jersey* (1974); and a pamphlet, *The Religious History of Revolutionary New Jersey* (1975).

Richard J. Connors, emeritus professor of government at Seton Hall University, is the author of *A Cycle of Power: The Career of Jersey City Mayor Frank Hague* (1971) and *The Process of Constitutional Revision in New Jersey, 1940–47* (1970) and coauthor of *The Government of New Jersey: An Introduction* (1984; rev. ed., 1993).

Sister Serafina D'Alessio taught history at the Villa Victoria Academy, Trenton, New Jersey. A student of New Jersey politics in the nineteenth century, she did her graduate work at Catholic University.

Philip C. Davis completed his Ph.D. at Washington University in St. Louis. He is the author of "Political Oligarchy, Egalitarianism and Continuity in New Jersey: 1840–1860," in *Jacksonian New Jersey*, edited by Paul A. Stellhorn (1979), and a coauthor of "Party Competition and Mass Participation: The Case of the Democratizing Party System, 1824–1852," in *The History of American Electoral Behavior: Quantitative Studies* (1978).

Benjamin Dworkin is an adjunct assistant professor of political science at Rider University and serves as the director of the Rebovich Institute for New Jersey Politics. A graduate of both Princeton University and Rutgers University, he has appeared on numerous network and cable news shows and is frequently quoted by state and national publications.

Harris I. Effross, emeritus professor in the Bureau of Government Research at Rutgers University, is the author of *County Governing Bodies in New Jersey: Reorganization and Reform of Boards of Chosen Freeholders, 1798–1974* (1976) and other works on New Jersey local government.

Herbert Ershkowitz, emeritus professor of history at Temple University, is the author of *The Origins of the Whig and Democratic Parties: New Jersey Politics, 1820–1837* (1982).

Frank J. Esposito taught history for many years at Kean University, serving also as founding dean of the Nathan Weiss graduate college, vice president for academic affairs, and interim president of the university. He has lectured and published widely on local history and the Lenni Lenape Indians of New Jersey. His publications include *Travelling New Jersey* (1978); "New Jersey's Identity Crisis," in *The Outlook on New Jersey* (1979); and a two-volume history of Ocean City, New Jersey (1996, 1998).

W. Robert Fallaw, emeritus professor of history at Washington College, received his Ph.D. from Princeton University with a dissertation on the Whig Party in New Jersey. He is a specialist in nineteenth-century intellectual and political history.

Alvin S. Felzenberg received his Ph.D. in politics from Princeton University in 1978 with a dissertation titled "The Impact of Gubernatorial Style on Policy Outcomes," a study of the managerial styles of five New Jersey governors. He is a coauthor of *The Evolution of the Modern Presidency: A Bibliographical Survey* (1977) and author of *Governor Tom Kean: From the New Jersey Statehouse* *to the 9/11 Commission* (2006) and *The Leaders We Deserved* (*and a Few We Didn't*): *Rethinking the Presidential Ratings Game* (2008).

Larry R. Gerlach, emeritus professor of history at the University of Utah, has published widely on colonial and revolutionary New Jersey, including *Prologue to Independence: New Jersey in the American Revolution* (1976) and *New Jersey in the American Revolution, 1763–1783: A Documentary History* (1975). He is also the author of numerous articles on sports history.

Terry Golway is director of the Kean University Center for History, Politics, and Policy. He is a former member of the *New York Times* editorial board.

Brigid Callahan Harrison is professor of political science and law at Montclair State University, where she teaches courses in American government. A frequent commentator in print and electronic media, she is the author of five books on American politics, including *American Democracy Now* and *Power and Society*, and serves as president of the New Jersey Political Science Association. She also writes a weekly column on New Jersey politics, which appears in the Sunday edition of the *Bergen Record*.

Frederick M. Herrmann, formerly executive director of the New Jersey Election Law Enforcement Commission, is the author of "Anti-Masonry in New Jersey," in *New Jersey History* (1973); and "The Political Origins of the New Jersey State Insane Asylum, 1837–1860," in *Jacksonian New Jersey* (1979); as well as a pamphlet study, *Dorothea Dix and the Politics of Institutional Reform* (1981).

David W. Hirst, formerly senior research historian at Princeton University and senior associate editor of *The Papers of Woodrow Wilson* (69 vols.; 1966–93), is the author of *Woodrow Wilson, Reform Governor: A Documentary Narrative* (1965). He is deceased.

Richard A. Hogarty taught political science at the University of Massachusetts in Boston for many years. He was formerly staff director of the Governor's Special Task Force on Migrant Farm Labor in New Jersey. He is the author of *New Jersey Farmers and Migrant Housing Rules* (1966), *The Dilemma of Financial Disclosure in Massachusetts* (1978), and *Leon Abbett's New Jersey: The Emergence of the Modern Governor* (2001), among other books. He is deceased.

Stanley Nider Katz, professor in public and international affairs at Princeton University and emeritus president of the American Council of Learned Societies, has published widely in American history, including *Newcastle's New York: Anglo-American Politics, 1732–1753* (1968); "The Politics of Law in

Colonial America: Controversies over Chancery Courts and Equity Law in the Eighteenth Century," *Perspectives in American History* (1971); and "Thomas Jefferson and the Right to Property in Revolutionary America," *Journal of Law and Economics* (1977).

Katherine E. Kleeman is senior communications officer at the Eagleton Institute of Politics and its Center for American Women and Politics (CAWP). She works on CAWP's education and information services efforts, evaluating new programs, responding to inquiries, and speaking to groups about women's political participation. She writes and/or edits a variety of Eagleton and CAWP materials. Kleeman coauthored *Political Generation Next: America's Young Elected Leaders* with Eagleton Institute director Ruth B. Mandel and coauthored several CAWP monographs including *Legislating by and for Women* and *Term Limits and the Representation of Women*. She earned her A.B. at Radcliffe College and her Ed.M. at Harvard University's Graduate School of Education.

Edward McM. Larrabee earned a Ph.D. in history from Columbia University and taught anthropology at Hunter and John Jay Colleges (CUNY). His publications include "Recurrent Themes and Sequences in North American Culture Contact," *Transactions of the American Philosophical Society* (1976), which discusses the Brotherton experiment. He is deceased.

William Lemmey taught history in Hicksville High School, New York. His publications include "The Last Hurrah Reconsidered," in *Cities of the Garden State*, edited by Joel Schwartz and Daniel Prosser (1977); and "Boss Kenny of Jersey City, 1949–1972," *New Jersey History* (1980).

Arthur S. Link, formerly George Henry Davis '86 Professor of American History at Princeton University, was the director and editor of *The Papers of Woodrow Wilson* (69 vols. 1966–93). Dr. Link is the author of a five-volume biography of Wilson covering his life to 1917 (1947–65) and many other works in twentieth-century American history. He is deceased.

Donald Linky has previously served as visiting professor and senior policy fellow at the Eagleton Institute of Politics at Rutgers University, where he coordinated the development of its program now known as the Center on the American Governor. Linky was counsel and director of policy for Governor Brendan T. Byrne.

Joseph F. Mahoney, formerly a professor of history at Seton Hall University and editor of *New Jersey History*, is the author of many articles on New Jersey in the Gilded Age and the Progressive Era, including "The Impact of Industrialization on the New Jersey Legislature, 1870–1900: Some Preliminary

Views," in *New Jersey since 1860: New Findings and Interpretations* (1972). He is deceased.

Ruth B. Mandel is director of the Eagleton Institute of Politics and Board of Governors Professor of Politics at Rutgers University. In 1971 Professor Mandel cofounded Eagleton's Center for American Women and Politics (CAWP) and spent over two decades developing and directing what has become the nation's premier research and education center for the study of women's changing political roles. Since 1995 Mandel has led Eagleton, the research and education institute at Rutgers that explores state and national politics and government, linking the study of politics with its day-to-day practices. Mandel held a presidential appointment as vice chair of the U.S. Holocaust Memorial Museum from 1991 to 2006. Her board service also includes the Charles H. Revson Foundation and the New Jersey Council on the Humanities. Mandel's B.A. in English is from Brooklyn College, and her M.A. and Ph.D. degrees in American literature are from the University of Connecticut.

Marc Mappen is a lecturer in history at Rutgers–New Brunswick and was the executive director of the New Jersey Historical Commission. He is co-editor of *The Encylopedia of New Jersey* (2004).

James Kirby Martin, the Hugh Roy and Lillie Cranz Cullen University Professor of History at the University of Houston, has published widely in colonial and revolutionary American history. His books include *Men in Rebellion: Higher Governmental Leaders and the Coming of the American Revolution* (1973), *In the Course of Human Events: An Interpretive Exploration of the American Revolution* (1979), and *Benedict Arnold, Revolutionary Hero: An American Warrior Reconsidered* (1997).

Peter Mickulas is an acquisitions editor at Rutgers University Press and the author of *Britton's Botanical Empire: The New York Botanical Garden and American Botany, 1888–1929* (2007). He is a founding editor of the online journal *New Jersey History*.

Robert C. Morris, formerly Special Collections librarian at the New Jersey Historical Society and subsequently head of the manuscripts and rare books collection at the Schomberg Center for Research in Black Culture in New York City, is the author of *Reading, 'Riting, and Reconstruction: The Education of Freedmen in the South, 1861–1870* (1981) and the editor of *Freedmen's Schools and Textbooks: Black Education in the South, 1861–1870* (6 vols., 1980). He is deceased.

Ransom E. Noble, professor of history emeritus at Pratt Institute and formerly dean of the faculty of liberal studies, is the author of *New Jersey*

Progressivism before Wilson (1946) and other publications on America since the Civil War. He is deceased.

John E. O'Connor, formerly professor of history at the New Jersey Institute of Technology, is the author of *William Paterson: Lawyer and Statesman, 1745–1806* (1979). He has also published articles on the colonial and early republican periods, as well as many works on history and film.

Thomas M. O'Neill, a visiting associate at the Eagleton Institute of Politics, is a consultant on public policy issues who lives and works in Pennington, New Jersey. For twenty years he served as president of the Partnership for New Jersey, where he designed and led civic leadership development programs. As executive director of the Center for Analysis of Public Issues in Princeton, he edited *New Jersey Reporter* magazine. A graduate of Wesleyan University, he did graduate work at the Woodrow Wilson School of Princeton University.

Rudolph J. Pasler, emeritus professor of history and political science at Salem Community College, is a coauthor of *The New Jersey Federalists* (1975).

Frances D. Pingeon taught U.S. history at the Kent Place School in Summit, New Jersey. She is the author of the pamphlet *Blacks in the Revolutionary Era* (1975) and several articles on slavery and blacks in New Jersey and coauthor of *At Speedwell in the Nineteenth Century* (1981). Dr. Pingeon is deceased.

Hermann K. Platt is an emeritus professor of history at St. Peter's College. He is the editor of *Charles Perrin Smith: New Jersey Political Reminiscences, 1828–1882* (1965) and the author of several studies in New Jersey urban history, including "Jersey City and the United Railroad Companies, 1868: A Case Study of Municipal Weakness," *New Jersey History* (1973); and "The Jersey City Water-Rights Controversy, 1845–1850," *New Jersey History* (1976). He has published a number of monographs on Edward F. C. Young, a power broker and financier in late nineteenth-century Jersey City.

John E. Pomfret, president of William and Mary College from 1941 to 1951, had a distinguished career as a teacher, scholar, and administrator. He was the author of many books and articles on colonial New Jersey, including *The Province of West New Jersey, 1609–1702: A History of the Origins of an American Colony* (1956) and *The Province of East Jersey, 1609–1702: The Rebellious Proprietary* (1962). He is deceased.

Clement Alexander Price, Board of Governors Distinguished Service Professor of History at Rutgers University, Newark, is the author, among other works, of "The Beleaguered City as Promised Land: Blacks in Newark, 1917–1947," in *Urban New Jersey since 1870* (1975), and the editor of *Freedom Not Far Distant*, a documentary history of blacks in New Jersey (1980).

Carl E. Prince, emeritus professor of history at New York University and editor in chief of *The Papers of William Livingston* (5 vols., 1979–88), is the author of *New Jersey's Jeffersonian-Republicans* (1967) and *The Federalists and the Origins of the U.S. Civil Service* (1977).

Jerome C. Reddy attended graduate school at Duke and Rutgers Universities. He was for many years a senior planner for the city of Plainfield, New Jersey.

Dennis P. Ryan, a coeditor of several volumes of *The Papers of William Livingston* (5 vols., 1979–88), has written extensively on New Jersey in the American Revolution. His publications include "The Revolution in East Jersey: A Whig Profile," *New Jersey in the American Revolution* (1973); "Landholding, Opportunity, and Mobility in Revolutionary New Jersey," *William and Mary Quarterly* (1979); and *A Salute to Courage: The American Revolution as Seen through Wartime Writings of Officers of the Continental Army* (1979).

Victor A. Sapio, emeritus professor of history at Pensacola Junior College, is the author of *Pennsylvania and the War of 1812* (1970).

James Edward Scanlon, professor of history at Randolph-Macon College, is the author of "British Intrigue and the Governorship of Robert Hunter," *New-York Historical Society Quarterly* (1973), as well as a two-volume history of Randolph-Macon College: *Randolph-Macon College: A Southern History, 1825–1967* (1983) and *Randolph-Macon College: Traditions and New Directions, 1967–2005* (2013).

Joel Schwartz taught for many years at Montclair State College, publishing widely in nineteenth-century New Jersey social and urban history. He is the author of "The Education Machine: The Struggle for Public School Systems in New Jersey before the Civil War," in *Jacksonian New Jersey* (1979); a coeditor of *Cities in the Garden State: Essays in the Urban and Suburban History of New Jersey* (1977); and author of *The New York Approach: Robert Moses, Liberals, and the Redevelopment of the Inner City* (1993). He is deceased.

Harold E. Selesky earned a Ph.D. at Yale University and has taught for many years at the University of Alabama. Among other works, he is the author of *A Guide to the Microfilm Edition of the Ezra Stiles Papers at Yale University* (1977) and *War and Society in Colonial Connecticut* (1990).

Edward S. Shapiro, formerly professor of history at Seton Hall University, is the author of several books and over one hundred articles and reviews on American history, including "Jews," in *The New Jersey Ethnic Experience* (1977), *A Time for Healing: American Jewry since World War II* (1992), and *We Are Many: Reflections on American Jewish History and Identity* (2005).

Douglas V. Shaw taught in the Department of Urban Studies at the University of Akron. His scholarship on New Jersey includes *The Making of an Immigrant City: Ethnic and Cultural Conflict in Jersey City, New Jersey, 1850–1870* (1976). He is deceased.

Eugene R. Sheridan served as associate editor of *The Papers of Thomas Jefferson* and editor of *The Papers of Lewis Morris*. His publications include "Daniel Coxe and the Restoration of Proprietary Government in East Jersey, 1690 — a Letter," *New Jersey History* (1974); and *Lewis Morris, 1671–1746: A Study in Early American Politics* (1981). He is deceased.

Don C. Skemer, formerly editor of publications at the New Jersey Historical Society and subsequently curator of manuscripts at Princeton University's Special Collections, is the author of numerous articles in scholarly journals, including "David Alling's Chair Manufactory: Craft Industrialization in Newark, New Jersey, 1801–1854," *Winterthur Portfolio* (1987). He is the principal compiler of *Guide to Manuscript Collections of the New Jersey Historical Society* (1979) and author of *Binding Words: Textual Amulets in the Middle Ages* (2006).

Paul A. Stellhorn, formerly assistant director of the New Jersey Committee for the Humanities and development director for the Newark Public Library, is the author of "Boom, Bust and Boosterism: Attitudes, Residency and the Newark Chamber of Commerce, 1920–1941," in *Urban New Jersey since 1870* (1975); a coeditor of the *Directory of New Jersey Newspapers, 1765–1970* (1976); and the editor of the papers of several New Jersey Historical Commission symposia. Stellhorn coedited the original edition of *The Governors of New Jersey* (1982). He is deceased.

Warren E. Stickle earned a Ph.D. from Georgetown University. He is the author of several books and articles in post–Civil War American history, including "Edward I. Edwards and the Urban Coalition of 1919," *New Jersey History* (1972). He is a coeditor, with A. Blaine Brownell, of *Bosses and Reformers: Urban Politics in America, 1880–1920* (1973). He is deceased.

John Strassburger earned a Ph.D. from Princeton University. He taught at both Hiram College and Knox College and later served for fifteen years as president of Ursinus College. His publications included "'Our Unhappy Purchase': The West Jersey Society, Lewis Morris, and Jersey Lands, 1703–1736," *New Jersey History* (1980); and "Lewis Morris and Colonial Politics," *Reviews in American History* (1983). He is deceased.

Eugene M. Tobin, currently the program officer for higher education and the liberal arts program at the Andrew W. Mellon Foundation, was formerly a professor of history and president at Hamilton College. He has published widely on New Jersey in the Progressive Era, including "Direct Action and Conscience: The 1913 Paterson Strike as Example of the Relationship between Labor Radicals and Liberals," *Labor History* (1979). He is a coeditor of *The Age of Urban Reform: New Perspectives on the Progressive Era* (1977) and the author of *George L. Record and the Progressive Spirit* (1979) and *Organize or Perish: America's Independent Progressives* (1986).

Stanley B. Winters, emeritus professor of history at the New Jersey Institute of Technology, edited *Newark, 1967–77: An Assessment* (1978). He is a coauthor of *From Riot to Recovery: Newark after Ten Years* (1979) and author of "Charter Change and Civil Reform in Newark, 1953–1954," *New Jersey History* (2000).

William C. Wright, formerly head of the Bureau of Archives and History, New Jersey State Library, is the author of *The Secession Movement in the Middle Atlantic States* (1973), a coeditor of the *Directory of New Jersey Newspapers, 1765–1970* (1976), and the editor of the papers of several New Jersey Historical Commission symposia.

Index

167, 295; Kean and, 320–321; in Middlesex County, 264, 268, 269; political corruption of, 230; political domination by, 208, 241, 259, 289–290, 301, 302; state committee of, 220, 222, 226, 235, 272; Whitman's family ties to, 336–337. *See also* Clean Government Group; National Republican Party; New Idea Republicans; Old Guard Republicans

Revolutionary War. *See* American Revolution

Richards, Emerson L., 269

Richier, Edward, 57, 58

Riots, 14, 43, 77–79

Riparian rights, 171, 178, 181, 239

Roads, 124. *See also* Highways

Roberts, Joseph, 366, 373

Robert Wood Johnson Foundation, 326

Robeson, George M., 177–178

Robinson v. Cahill (1973), 14, 303, 309, 311

Rockefeller, David, 310

Rockefeller, Nelson, 310, 337

Rodman M. Price (ferry), 163

Roe, Robert, 313

Rogers, Deborah Read, 94

Rollins, Edward J., Jr., 335, 341

Roman Catholics, 28, 33, 208–209, 289, 293, 294, 366. *See also* Irish Americans

Roosevelt, Franklin D., 10, 226, 250, 261, 266, 275–276, 277–278

Roosevelt, Henry Latrobe, 275

Roosevelt, Theodore, 214, 231, 235, 244

Roosevelt Stadium (Jersey City, N.J.), 261

Ross, Miles, 201

Rossell, William, 144

Rubin, Robert, 368

Rudi, Nicholas H., 334

Rudyard, Thomas, 43

Rumsfeld, Donald, 337

Runk, John, 156

Runyon, Theodore, 180

Runyon, William N., 254

Russ, Horace P., 163

Russell, Caleb, 122

Russo, John, 358

Rutgers College, 164, 183, 191, 200, 215

Rutgers Medical School, 302

Rutgers University, 14, 153, 227, 291, 296, 322, 336, 357; women's basketball team, 374

Ryerson, Thomas C., 149

Sabrin, Murray, 345, 353

Sackett, William E., 211

Safe and Clean Neighborhoods Act (N.J.), 305

Salem, N.J., 30

Salema, Joseph C., 334

Sales and Use Tax Act (N.J., 1966), 297

Same-sex marriage, 369

Sandman, Charles W., 300, 305, 309–310

Sandy Hook, N.J., 165

Sandy Hook State Park, 286

Santiago, Joseph, 355

Sarbanes-Oxley Act (U.S.), 370

School Choice Program, 343

Schundler, Bret, 347, 348, 354, 371

Schureman, James, 116

S. C. Johnson, 345

Scot, George, 35

Scot's College, 33

Scott, Hugh L., 255

Scott, John Morin, 101

Scranton, William, 318

Sears, Harry L., 302, 305

Securities and Exchange Commission, 335

Seeley, Ebenezer, 138

Seeley, Elias Pettit, 5, 137, 138–141

Seeley, Mary Clark, 138

Senate, state, 346–347, 352; Codey and, 361, 367; Corzine and, 369

Senate Intelligence Committee, 369

Senate Judiciary Committee, 359

Senior Services, 342, 344; retirement age and, 347

September 11, 2001, 349–350, 354, 356, 363, 370; 9/11 Commission and, 326

Seven Sisters (corporation reform laws), 236, 245, 254

Sewage. *See* Water pollution

Sewell, William J., 9, 214, 220, 224, 225

Seymour, Horatio, 152

Seymour, James M., 220

Shapiro, Peter, 325, 358

Shaw, Judy, 341

Sheriffs, 239–240

Sherwin, Paul J., 304

Shipping. *See* Commerce; Port of New York Authority

Shirley, William, 76

Shrewsbury, N.J., 22, 35

Shuffler, Eric, 358

Shute, William, 76

Sigmund, Barbara Boggs, 328

Silzer, Christina Zimmerman, 253

Silzer, George Sebastian, 233, 252, 253–257

Silzer, Henrietta T. Waite, 257

Silzer, Parker W., 257

Silzer, Theodore C., 253

Simon, William, 313

Simpson, Alexander, 259

Simpson, John, 127

Sires, Albio, 355

Skene, John, 31–32, 37

Skillman, N.J., 217

Slavery, 136; abolitionism, 114, 131, 157, 165, 168, 175, 180; Emancipation Proclamation, 170, 171, 173, 174, 196; Fugitive Slave Act, 157, 168, 169; governors' opinions of, 6, 114, 122, 127, 163, 165–166, 168–169, 173, 175, 176–177, 180, 196; Whig opinion of, 157–158. *See also* African Americans

Sloat, John Drake, 159

Sloughter, Henry, 53

Smith, Al, 250, 252, 259, 288

Smith, Charles Perrin, 170, 171, 178

Smith, James, 201

Smith, James, Jr., 9, 217, 233–235

Smith, Richard, 24

Smith, William, 63, 68, 101

Smith, William, Jr., 101

Smith-Nugent machine, 235, 239–241

Social Security, 318, 370

Social Security Act (U.S., 1936), 272

Society for Establishing Useful Manufactures (S.U.M.), 108